Theorizing About
Intercultural
Communication

Theorizing About
Intercultural Communication

Editor
William B. Gudykunst
California State University, Fullerton

SAGE Publications
Thousand Oaks ▪ London ▪ New Delhi

For information:

Sage Publications, Inc.
2455 Teller Road
Thousand Oaks, California 91320
E-mail: order@sagepub.com

Sage Publications Ltd.
1 Oliver's Yard
55 City Road
London EC1Y 1SP
United Kingdom

Sage Publications India Pvt. Ltd.
B-42, Panchsheel Enclave
Post Box 4109
New Delhi 110 017 India

Printed in the United States of America

Library of Congress Cataloging-in-Publication data

Theorizing about intercultural communication / edited by William B. Gudykunst.
     p. cm.
Includes bibliographical references and index.
ISBN 0-7619-2748-4 (cloth)—ISBN 0-7619-2749-2 (pbk.)
   1. Intercultural communication. I. Gudykunst, William B.
HM1211.T47 2005
303.48′2—dc22   2004014063

05   06   07   08   09   10   9   8   7   6   5   4   3   2   1

Acquiring Editor:	Todd Armstrong
Editorial Assistant:	Deya Saoud
Production Editor:	Sanford Robinson
Typesetter:	C&M Digitals (P) Ltd.
Copy Editor:	Kristin Bergstad
Indexer:	Julie Grayson
Cover Designer:	Ravi Balasuriya

Contents

Preface   ix

PART I: INTRODUCTION   1

  1. Theorizing About Intercultural Communication: An Introduction   3
      William B. Gudykunst, Carmen M. Lee,
      Tsukasa Nishida, and Naoto Ogawa

PART II: THEORIES OF
COMMUNICATION INCORPORATING CULTURE   33

  2. The Coordinated Management of Meaning (CMM)   35
      W. Barnett Pearce

  3. Speech Codes Theory: Restatement,
      Revisions, and Response to Criticisms   55
      Gerry Philipsen, Lisa M. Coutu, and Patricia Covarrubias

PART III: THEORIES FOCUSING ON
CROSS-CULTURAL VARIABILITY IN COMMUNICATION   69

  4. The Matrix of Face: An Updated Face-Negotiation Theory   71
      Stella Ting-Toomey

  5. Culture-Based Conversational Constraints
      Theory: Individual- and Culture-Level Analyses   93
      Min-Sun Kim

PART IV: THEORIES FOCUSING
ON ADAPTATIONS IN INTERACTIONS   119

  6. Communication Accommodation Theory   121
      Cindy Gallois, Tania Ogay, and Howard Giles

  7. Cross-Cultural and Intercultural Applications of Expectancy
      Violations Theory and Interaction Adaptation Theory   149
      Judee K. Burgoon and Amy S. Ebesu Hubbard

  8. From the Margins to the Center:
      Utilizing Co-Cultural Theory in Diverse Contexts   173
      Mark P. Orbe and Regina E. Spellers

PART V: THEORIES FOCUSING ON IDENTITY 193

9. Identity Management Theory:
    Facework in Intercultural Relationships 195
    Tadasu Todd Imahori and William R. Cupach

10. Identity Negotiation Theory: Crossing Cultural Boundaries 211
    Stella Ting-Toomey

11. Theorizing Cultural Identifications:
    Critical Updates and Continuing Evolution 235
    Mary Jane Collier

12. A Communication Theory of Identity:
    Development, Theoretical Perspective, and Future Directions 257
    *Michael L. Hecht, Jennifer R. Warren,
    Eura Jung, and Janice L. Krieger*

PART VI: THEORIES FOCUSING ON EFFECTIVE COMMUNICATION AND DECISIONS 279

13. An Anxiety/Uncertainty Management (AUM) Theory of
    Effective Communication: Making the Mesh of the Net Finer 281
    William B. Gudykunst

14. Association and Dissociation:
    A Contextual Theory of Interethnic Communication 323
    Young Yun Kim

15. Effective Intercultural Workgroup Communication Theory 351
    John G. Oetzel

PART VII: THEORIES FOCUSING ON ADJUSTMENT AND ACCULTURATION 373

16. Adapting to a New Culture: An Integrative Communication Theory 375
    Young Yun Kim

17. Cultural Schema Theory 401
    Hiroko Nishida

18. An Anxiety/Uncertainty Management (AUM) Theory of Strangers'
    Intercultural Adjustment 419
    William B. Gudykunst

Index 459

About the Editor 475

About the Contributors 476

Preface

Theorizing about communication and culture has made tremendous progress in the last 20 years. When I completed my doctorate, there were no theories of intercultural communication. Initial attempts to theorize about interpersonal communication between people from different cultures were included in the first thematic volume of the *International and Intercultural Communication Annual* published by Sage (Volume 7: Gudykunst, 1983; see Chapter 1 of this volume for references). By the time the second volume of the *Annual* on theory was published (Volume 12: Kim & Gudykunst, 1988), theorizing had increased in sophistication and there were theories supported by lines of research. There was another leap in the quality of theorizing when the most recent volume of the *Annual* on theory was published (Volume 19: Wiseman, 1995).

There has been extensive progress in theorizing since the publication of the last volume of the *Annual* that focused on theorizing, and there was a need for a volume addressing this progress. I, therefore, asked the theorists whose theories are cited most frequently to contribute to this volume (Chapter 1 contains an overview of prior versions of these theories and other theories not included in this volume). I asked the theorists to address a set of common questions:

1. What got you interested in developing your theory?

2. What is the scope of your theory? What is it designed to describe and/or explain?

3. What are the metatheoretical assumptions and theoretical assumptions underlying your theory (including assumptions about communication and culture)?

4. How did you develop your theory (e.g., a historical overview of the development of the theory)?

5. What are the theoretical propositions of the theory?

6. What research has been conducted testing the theory?

7. How can your theory be applied (e.g., to improve the effectiveness of communication)?

Most authors address these questions in some way in their chapters.

There are several approaches to incorporating culture into communication theories. First, culture can be integrated with the communication process in theories of communication (e.g., Applegate and Sypher [1983, 1988] integrate culture into constructivist theory; Cronen, Chen, and Pearce [1988] integrate culture into coordinated management of meaning theory, see Pearce's chapter in this volume; cultural communication, see

Philipsen, Coutu, and Covarrubias' chapter in this volume). In other words, culture is linked to communication within the theory. Second, theories can be designed to describe or explain how communication varies across cultures (e.g., see M. S. Kim's chapter on conversational constraint theory in this volume; see Ting-Toomey's chapter on face-negotiation theory in this volume). Third, theories can be generated to describe or explain communication between people from different cultures. By far, the most theorizing exists in the third category (it is overviewed below).

Many of the theorists who attempt to describe or explain communication between members of different cultures focus on intergroup communication generally rather than intercultural communication specifically. Theorists using an intergroup approach tend to assume that culture is one of the many group memberships influencing communication. These theorists also tend to assume that the processes occurring in intercultural, interethnic, and intergenerational communication, among others, are similar. These theories are divided into five categories that are not mutually exclusive: theories focusing on effective outcomes (e.g., see Gudykunst's anxiety/uncertainty management theory in this volume; see Oetzel's theory of effective small group decisions in this volume), theories focusing on accommodation and adaptation (e.g., see Gallois, Ogay, and Giles' communication accommodation theory in this volume; see Orbe & Spelling's co-cultural theory in

this volume), theories focusing on identity management (e.g., see Imahori and Cupach's identity management theory in this volume; see Collier's cultural identity theory in this volume), theories focusing on communication networks (e.g., Yum's theory comparing intracultural and intercultural networks), and theories focusing on adjustment and adaptation to new cultural environments (e.g., see Y. Y. Kim's communication acculturation theory in this volume). Some theorists focusing on intergroup or intercultural communication also address cross-cultural variability in the processes involved in their theories.

I want to thank the theorists for agreeing to update their theories for this volume. The volume would not exist without their contributions. Taken together, the theories included in this volume provide an excellent overview of the major theories in use today. The various theories also provide the foundation for future research on intercultural communication. Given the state of theorizing today, atheoretical research is simply not warranted.

I also want to thank Margaret Seawell, the Communication editor at Sage, for originally supporting the publication of this volume. Todd Armstrong, the Interpersonal Communication editor at Sage, has overseen the processing of this volume since it was accepted for publication. Their support of my work over the years has been invaluable.

Bill Gudykunst
Laguna Beach, CA

PART I

Introduction

1

Theorizing About Intercultural Communication

An Introduction

WILLIAM B. GUDYKUNST

CARMEN M. LEE

TSUKASA NISHIDA

NAOTO OGAWA

Theorizing about intercultural communication has made tremendous progress in
the last 20 years. When two of the authors
(Gudykunst and Nishida) completed their doc-
torates, there were no theories of intercultural
communication.[1] Initial attempts to theorize
about interpersonal communication between
people from different cultures were included in
the first thematic volume of the *International
and Intercultural Communication Annual*
published by Sage (Gudykunst, 1983).[2] By the
time the second volume of the *Annual* on

theory was published (Kim & Gudykunst,
1988), theorizing had increased in sophistication and there were theories supported by
lines of research. There was another leap in the
quality of theorizing when the most recent
volume of the *Annual* on theory was published
(Wiseman, 1995).[3]

There are several approaches to incorporating culture into communication theories.[4] First,
culture can be integrated with the communication process in theories of communication (e.g.,
Applegate & Sypher, 1983, 1988, integrate

3

culture into constructivist theory[5]; Cronen, Chen, & Pearce, 1988, integrate culture into coordinated management of meaning theory, see Pearce, Chapter 2 in this volume; cultural communication, see Philipsen, Coutu, and Covarrubias, Chapter 3 in this volume). In other words, culture is linked to communication within the theory. Second, theories can be designed to describe or explain how communication varies across cultures.[6] Third, theories can be generated to describe or explain communication between people from different cultures. By far, the most theorizing exists in the third category.

Many of the theorists who attempt to describe or explain communication between members of different cultures focus on intergroup communication generally rather than intercultural communication specifically. Theorists using an intergroup approach tend to assume that culture is one of the many group memberships influencing communication. These theorists also tend to assume that the processes occurring in intercultural, interethnic, and intergenerational communication, among others, are similar. We divide the intergroup and intercultural theories into five categories that are not mutually exclusive: theories focusing on effective outcomes, theories focusing on accommodation and adaptation, theories focusing on identity management, theories focusing on communication networks, and theories focusing on adjustment and adaptation to new cultural environments.

Whatever the approach that is used to develop theories, the theories are based upon a set of metatheoretical assumptions. Gudykunst and Nishida (1989) use Burrell and Morgan's (1979) distinction between objectivist and subjectivist approaches to theory (see Table 1.1) to compare theories in intercultural communication. Objectivists, for example, see a "real world" external to individuals, look for regularities in behavior, and see communication as "determined" by situations and environments. Subjectivists, in contrast, contend that there is

no "real world" external to individuals, try to understand individual communicators' perspectives, and view communication as a function of "free will." Gudykunst and Nishida contend that extreme objectivist or subjectivist perspectives are not defensible. They argue that both approaches are necessary to understand intercultural communication, and that the ideal is eventually to integrate the two perspectives.

The goals of theories in the objectivist and subjectivist perspectives tend to be different. Objectivists, for example, argue that theories should explain and predict the phenomena under study. Subjectivists, however, argue that theories should describe the phenomena under study. Both types of theorists might agree that theories should be heuristic; that is, they should generate future research. When evaluating theories, we must grant the theorists' assumptions and examine the theories for logical consistency and heuristic value. Theories rarely are designed to describe or explain the same thing. Unless they are, they are not directly comparable.

It is important to understand the metatheoretical assumptions that theorists make. The theoretical propositions in theories should be logically consistent with the metatheoretical assumptions on which the theories are based. The methods used to test theories also should be consistent with the metatheoretical assumptions. We can question a theory's metatheoretical assumptions, but when we evaluate the theory we must grant the assumptions and not impose other metatheoretical assumptions in our critiques.

In evaluating theories, we also need to look at logical consistency. Are the metatheoretical assumptions and the theoretical statements logically consistent? Are the theoretical statements logically consistent with each other? We also must pay attention to scope and boundary conditions that theorists specify when we evaluate their theories (see Walker & Cohen, 1985). Do theorists, for example, limit their theories to certain types

Table 1.1   Assumptions About Theory

Subjectivist Approach *(Human Action/Interpretive)*	*Objectivist Approach* *(Causal Process)*
ONTOLOGY	
Nominalism: There is no "real" world external to individual; "names," "concepts," and "labels" are artificial and used to construct reality.	Realism: There is a "real" world external to individual; things exist, even if they are not perceived and labeled.
EPISTEMOLOGY	
Antipositivism: Communication can be understood only from the perspective of the individuals communicating; no search for underlying regularities.	Positivism: Attempts to explain and predict patterns of communication by looking for regularities and/or causal relationships.
HUMAN NATURE	
Voluntarism: Communicators are completely "autonomous" and have "free will."	Determinism: Communication is "determined" by the situation, environment in which it occurs or by individuals' traits.
METHODOLOGY	
Ideographic: To understand communication, "firsthand knowledge" must be obtained; analysis of subjective accounts.	Nomothetic: Research should be based on systematic protocols and "scientific" rigor.

*These are "extreme" statements of the assumptions drawn from Burrell and Morgan (1979, pp. 3–7) by Gudykunst and Nishida (1989).

of situations (e.g., initial interactions between strangers)? If theorists limit their theories to initial interactions, then data in romantic relationships that are inconsistent with the theory do *not* call the theory into question. Theories should not be criticized because they do not explain something beyond the scope theorists specify for their theories. Theorists may limit complete theories to specific conditions or limit certain theoretical claims to only specific conditions. If a theorist claims that a statement holds only for people who feel secure in their identities, then data from respondents who do not feel secure do not test the theoretical claim.

Our purpose in this chapter is to overview the theories in intercultural communication, both theories included in this volume and theories not included. Our goal is to put the theories presented in this volume in context. By understanding the variability in the approaches used to construct theories, readers will be in a good position to understand and question the choices the theorists in this volume make.

We divide the theories into seven categories that are not necessarily mutually exclusive: (1) theories that integrate culture with communication processes, (2) theories explaining cultural variability in communication,[7] (3) intergroup/intercultural theories focusing on effective outcomes,[8] (4) intergroup/intercultural theories focusing on accommodation or adaptation, (5) intergroup or intercultural theories focusing on identity management or negotiation, (6) intergroup/intercultural theories focusing on communication networks, and (7) intercultural theories focusing on acculturation or adjustment. For the theories included in this volume, we focus on the most recent version of the theory prior to this volume. Both objectivistic and subjectivistic theories are included. The majority of the theories that have been developed and those included in this volume, however, are objectivistic. Very few of the theorists attempt to integrate objectivistic and subjectivistic assumptions.[9]

THEORIES IN WHICH CULTURE AND COMMUNICATION ARE INTEGRATED

Several theorists have integrated culture with communication processes. We briefly overview the three major approaches: (1) constructivist theory (Applegate & Sypher, 1983, 1988), (2) coordinated management of meaning (Cronen et al., 1988; see Pearce, Chapter 2 in this volume), and (3) cultural communication (e.g., Philipsen, 1992; see Philipsen, Coutu, and Covarrubias, Chapter 3 in this volume).

Constructivist Theory

Applegate and Sypher (1983, 1988) integrate culture with constructivist theory (e.g., Kelly's, 1955, personal construct theory; see Delia, 1977). They make several assumptions, including that "theory should be interpretive," "dense and detailed accounts of everyday interaction . . . are needed," "the focus of study should be the relationship between culture and communication," "value judgments should be made," and "theory and training should be linked closely" (p. 44, italics omitted here and in other quotes).

Applegate and Sypher (1988) point out that communication occurs when individuals have "a mutually recognized interaction to share, exchange messages" in constructivist

theory (p. 45). This process is goal driven and individuals do what they think will help them accomplish their goals. Applegate and Sypher view complex message behavior (a function of the number of goals and situational factors incorporated in messages) as leading to "person-centered" communication (which involves the degree to which individuals adapt to their interactional partners). Individuals' constructs generate "communication and goal-relevant beliefs" that influence their definition of the situation and guide their "strategic behavior" (p. 48).

Applegate and Sypher (1988) believe that "culture defines the logic of communication" (p. 59) and that different cultures emphasize different goals and ways to achieve these goals. They go on to argue that "cultural communication theories specify how to place and organize events within larger contexts of meaning and elaboration" (p. 59). Hong et al. (2003) argue that construct activation is a major factor influencing cultural differences in social perception (they also review evidence for a dynamic constructivism approach). Applegate and Sypher conclude that intercultural communication training "should focus on developing flexible and integrative strategic means for accomplishing goals" (p. 59).

Coordinated Management of Meaning

Cronen et al. (1988) examine the role of culture in the coordinated management of meaning (CMM; e.g., Pearce & Cronen, 1980; see Pearce, Chapter 2 in this volume). They isolate three goals of CMM: (1) "CMM seeks to understand who we are, what it means to live a life, and how that is related to particular instances of communication" (p. 67), (2) "CMM seeks to render cultures comparable while acknowledging their incommensurability" (p. 67), and (3) "CMM seeks to generate an illuminating critique of cultural practices, including the researcher's own" (p. 68).

Cronen et al. (1988) isolate several propositions regarding CMM. To illustrate, they argue that "all communication is both idiosyncratic and social" (p. 72, italics omitted in all propositions), "human communication is inherently imperfect" (p. 74), "moral orders emerge as aspects of communication" (p. 76), and "diversity is essential to elaboration and transformation through communication" (p. 78).

Cronen et al. (1988) propose three corollaries involving culture: "cultures are patterns of coevolving structures and actions" (p. 78), "cultures are polyphonic" (p. 79), and "research activity is part of social practice" (p. 80). They believe that it is necessary to describe the cultural context if we are going to understand communication within cultures and/or across cultures. It also is necessary to understand the individuals' interpretations of their communication.

CMM tends to be viewed as a "rules" theory (e.g., Cushman & Sanders, 1982) that is based in U.S. pragmatism (e.g., Dewey, 1920). CMM is used to analyze rules that are used as social episodes (e.g., communication that occurs at the dinner table; Cronen et al., 1988). The description of the episodes generates "a critical focus" on the situation being described.

Cultural Communication

Philipsen (1981) lays out the groundwork for the study of cultural communication. Philipsen argues that

> the function of communication in cultural communication is to maintain a healthy balance between the forces of individualism and community, to provide a sense of shared identity which nonetheless preserves individual dignity, freedom, and creativity. This function is performed through maintaining a balance or equilibrium between the two sub-processes of cultural communication, (1) the creation, and (2) the affirmation, of shared identity. (p. 5)

Cultural communication, therefore, involves the negotiation of cultural codes through communal conversations. Communal conversations are communicative processes through which individuals negotiate how they will "conduct their lives together."

Philipsen (1992) proposes speech code theory: a theory of "culturally distinctive codes of communication conduct" (p. 56). Speech code theory posits that communal conversations imply distinctive codes of communication. He suggests that "a speech code refers to a historically enacted, socially constructed system of terms, meanings, premises, and rules pertaining to communicative conduct" (p. 56).

Philipsen (2002) isolates two principles of cultural communication. Principle one states that "every communal conversation bears traces of culturally distinctive means and meanings of communicative conduct" (p. 53). Philipsen believes that the notion that members of groups engage in communal conversations is a universal of human life, but that each communal conversation has culture-specific aspects. The second principle of cultural communication is that "communication is a heuristic and performative resource for performing the cultural function in the lives of individuals and communities" (p. 59). The communal function involves "how individuals are to live as members of a community" (p. 59). Communication is "heuristic" because it is through communication that babies and newcomers to the community learn the specific means and meanings in the community. Communication is "performative" because it allows individuals to participate in the communal conversation.

THEORIES OF CULTURAL VARIABILITY IN COMMUNICATION

A few theorists have attempted to explain cross-cultural differences in communication using cultural-level and/or individual-level dimensions. These theories include: face-negotiation theory (FNT; Ting-Toomey, 1988;

Ting-Toomey & Kurogi, 1998), conversational constraints theory (CCT; Kim, 1993, 1995), and expectancy violations theory (EVT; Burgoon, 1992, 1995). EVT, however, is not a formal theory of cross-cultural communication. Rather, the focus is on cross-cultural variability of a theory designed in the United States. Each of these theories draws on Hofstede's (1980, 1991, 2001) dimensions of cultural variability. We, therefore, provide a brief introduction to these dimensions here.

Hofstede's Dimensions of Cultural Variability

Hofstede (1980, 1991, 2001) isolates four dimensions of cultural variability: individualism-collectivism, low-high uncertainty avoidance, low-high power distance, and masculinity-femininity. Both ends of each dimension exist in all cultures, but one end tends to predominate in a culture. Individual members of cultures learn the predominate tendencies in their cultures to various degrees. It, therefore, is necessary to take both cultural- and individual-level factors into consideration when explaining similarities and differences in communication across cultures.

Individuals' goals are emphasized more than groups' goals in individualistic cultures. Groups' goals, in contrast, take precedence over individuals' goals in collectivistic cultures. In individualistic cultures, "people are supposed to look after themselves and their immediate family only," and in collectivistic cultures, "people belong to ingroups or collectivities which are supposed to look after them in exchange for loyalty" (Hofstede & Bond, 1984, p. 419).

Triandis (1995) argues that the relative importance of ingroups is the major factor that differentiates individualistic and collectivistic cultures. Ingroups are groups that are important to their members and groups for which individuals will make sacrifices. Members of individualistic cultures have many specific ingroups that might influence their behavior in any particular social situation. Since there are many ingroups, specific ingroups exert relatively little influence on individuals' behavior. Members of collectivistic cultures have only a few general ingroups that influence their behavior across situations.

Cultural individualism-collectivism influences communication in a culture through the cultural norms and rules associated with the major cultural tendency (e.g., the U.S. tends to have individualistic norms/rules, Asian cultures tend to have collectivistic norms/rules). Cultural individualism-collectivism also indirectly influences communication through the characteristics individuals learn when they are socialized. There are at least three characteristics of individuals that mediate the influence of cultural individualism-collectivism on communication: their personalities, their individual values, and their self construals (see Gudykunst & Lee, 2002).

Individualism-collectivism provides an explanatory framework for understanding cultural similarities and differences in self-ingroup behavior. Hall's (1976) differentiation between low- and high-context communication can be used to explain cultural differences in communication.[10] High-context communication occurs when "most of the information is either in the physical context or internalized in the person, while very little is in the coded, explicit, transmitted part of the message" (Hall, 1976, p. 79). Low-context communication, in contrast, occurs when "the mass of information is vested in the explicit code" (p. 70). Low- and high-context communication are used in all cultures. One form, however, tends to predominate. Members of individualistic cultures tend to use low-context communication and communicate in a direct fashion. Members of collectivistic cultures, in contrast, tend to use high-context messages when maintaining ingroup harmony is important and communicate in an indirect fashion (Gudykunst & Ting-Toomey, 1988).

High uncertainty avoidance cultures tend to have clear norms and rules to guide behavior for virtually all situations (Hofstede, 1980). Norms and rules in low uncertainty avoidance cultures are not as clear-cut and rigid as those in high uncertainty avoidance cultures. In high uncertainty avoidance cultures, aggressive behavior is acceptable, but individuals prefer to contain aggression by avoiding conflict and competition (Hofstede, 1980). There also is a strong desire for consensus in high uncertainty avoidance cultures, and deviant behavior is not acceptable. Tolerance for ambiguity and uncertainty orientation are two individual-level factors that mediate the influence of cultural uncertainty avoidance on communication (see Gudykunst & Lee, 2002).

Power distance is "the extent to which the less powerful members of institutions and organizations accept that power is distributed unequally" (Hofstede & Bond, 1984, p. 419). Members of high power distance cultures accept power as part of society (e.g., superiors consider their subordinates to be different from themselves and vice versa). Members of high power distance cultures see power as a basic factor in society, and stress coercive or referent power. Members of low power distance cultures, in contrast, believe power should be used only when it is legitimate and prefer expert or legitimate power. Egalitarianism and social dominance orientation are two individual-level factors that mediate the influence of cultural power distance on communication (see Gudykunst & Lee, 2002).

The major differentiation between masculine and feminine cultures is how gender-roles are distributed in a culture.

Masculinity pertains to societies in which social gender roles are clearly distinct (i.e., men are supposed to be assertive, tough, and focused on material success whereas women are supposed to be more modest, tender, and concerned with the quality of life); *femininity* pertains to societies in which social gender roles overlap (i.e., both men and women are supposed to be modest, tender, and concerned with the quality of life). (Hofstede, 1991, pp. 82–83)

Members of cultures high in masculinity value performance, ambition, things, power, and assertiveness (Hofstede, 1980). Members of cultures high in femininity value quality of life, service, caring for others, and being nurturing. Psychological sex-roles are individual-level factors that mediate the influence of cultural masculinity-femininity on communication (see Gudykunst & Lee, 2002).

Face-Negotiation Theory

Cultural norms and values influence and shape how members of cultures manage face and how they manage conflict situations. Originally a theory focusing on conflict (Ting-Toomey, 1985), face-negotiation theory (FNT) has been expanded to integrate cultural-level dimensions and individual-level attributes to explain face concerns, conflict styles, and facework behaviors (e.g. Ting-Toomey, 1988; Ting-Toomey & Kurogi, 1998; see Ting-Toomey, Chapter 4 in this volume).

Ting-Toomey (1985) argues that conflict is a face-negotiation process whereby individuals engaged in conflict have their situated identities or "faces" threatened or questioned (Ting-Toomey, 1988). Face is "a claimed sense of favorable social self-worth that a person wants others to have of her or him" (Ting-Toomey & Kurogi, 1998, p. 187). Although mentioned only briefly in the 1988 version of the theory, the concept of face is an integral part of the most recent version of the theory (Ting-Toomey & Kurogi, 1998).

Ting-Toomey and Kurogi (1998) argue that members of collectivistic cultures use other-oriented face-saving strategies more than members of individualistic cultures. Conversely, members of individualistic cultures use more self-oriented face-saving strategies more than members of collectivistic cultures. Members of low power distance cultures defend and assert their personal rights more than members of high power distance cultures. Members of high power distance cultures, in contrast, perform their ascribed duties responsibly more than members of low power distance cultures. Members of low power distance cultures tend to minimize the respect-deference distance via information-based interactions more than members of high power distance cultures. Members of high power distance cultures are concerned with vertical facework interactions more than members of low power distance cultures.

Ting-Toomey and Kurogi (1998) contend that members of collectivistic cultures use relational, process-oriented conflict strategies more than members of individualistic cultures. Members of individualistic cultures, in contrast, tend to use more substantive, outcome-oriented conflict strategies than members of collectivistic cultures. High-status members of high power distance cultures tend to use verbally indirect facework strategies more than low-status members of high power distance cultures. High-status members of low power distance cultures tend to use verbally direct strategies more than high-status members of high power distance cultures.

Ting-Toomey and Kurogi (1998) also link individual-level mediators of the dimensions of cultural variability to face behaviors and conflict styles. Emphasizing self-face leads to using dominating/competing conflict styles and substantive conflict resolution modes. Emphasizing other-face leads to using avoiding/obliging conflict styles and relational conflict resolution modes. Independent self construal types tend to use dominating/competing conflict styles and substantive conflict resolution modes. Interdependent self construal types tend to use avoiding/obliging conflict styles and relational conflict resolution modes. Biconstrual types (high on both self construals) use substantive and relational conflict resolution modes, and ambivalent types (low on both self construals) tend not to use either.

Conversational Constraints Theory

Conversations are goal-directed and require coordination between communicators in CCT (Kim, 1995; see M.-S. Kim, Chapter 5 in this volume). Kim (1993) isolates two types of conversational constraints: social-relational and task-oriented. Social-relational constraints emphasize concern for others that focuses on avoiding hurting hearers' feelings and minimizing imposition on hearers. The task-oriented constraint emphasizes a concern for clarity (e.g., the degree to which the intentions of messages are communicated explicitly; Kim, 1995).

Kim (1993) explains cross-cultural differences in the selection of communicative strategies. Members of collectivistic cultures view face-supporting behavior (e.g., avoiding hurting the hearers' feelings, minimizing imposition, and avoiding negative evaluation by the hearer) as more important than members of individualistic cultures when pursuing goals. Members of individualistic cultures, in contrast, view clarity as more important than members of collectivistic cultures when pursuing goals.

Kim (1995) argues that individuals who activate interdependent self construals view not hurting hearers' feelings and minimizing impositions on hearers in the pursuit of their goals as more important than individuals who activate independent self construals.[11] Individuals who activate independent self construals view clarity as more important in pursuing goals than individuals who activate interdependent self construals. Individuals who activate both self construals are concerned with relational and clarity constraints. Kim (1995) also argues that the more individuals need approval, the more important they view being concerned with hearers' feelings and minimizing impositions on hearers. The more individuals need to be dominant, the more importance they place on clarity. The more masculine individuals' psychological sex-roles, the more importance they place on clarity. The more feminine individuals' psychological sex-roles, the more importance they place on not hurting hearers' feelings and not imposing on hearers.

Expectancy Violation Theory

Every culture has guidelines for human conduct that provide expectations for how others will behave (Burgoon, 1978). Expectancy violation theory (EVT) frames interpersonal communication within the context of the expectations held by individuals and how individuals respond to violations of those expectations (EVT has been incorporated into interpersonal adaptation theory: Burgoon, Stern, & Dillman, 1995; see Burgoon and Hubbard, Chapter 7 in this volume). Expectancies are based on social norms and rules as well as individual-specific patterns of typical behavior (Burgoon, 1995). Individual deviation in expected behavior causes arousal or alertness in others. Whether or not deviant behavior is interpreted as positive or negative depends on communicators' valences. Communicators' valences refer to characteristics of individuals (e.g., how attractive and familiar they are perceived to be). Burgoon (1995) argues that "the communicator's positive or negative characteristics are posited to moderate how violations are interpreted and evaluated" (p. 201).

Burgoon (1992) contends that the "content" of each culture's expectancies vary along Hofstede's (1980) dimensions of cultural variability.[12] Specifically, members of collectivistic cultures expect greater verbal indirectness, politeness, and non-immediacy than members of individualistic cultures. Uncertainty avoidance is linked to expectancies to the extent that communication behavior is regulated by rules and social norms (Burgoon, 1995). Low uncertainty avoidance cultures have fewer rules and norms regulating behavior than high uncertainty avoidance cultures. Members of high uncertainty avoidance cultures tend to be more intolerant of deviant behavior than members

of low uncertainty avoidance cultures. Power distance influences how violations of high status and low status are interpreted (Burgoon, 1995). A violation (e.g., nonverbal proxemic violation) by a high-status person in a high power distance culture, for example, would be perceived as a violation of ascribed role behavior, and such an action would inevitably produce stress and anxiety, a negative outcome.

THEORIES FOCUSING ON EFFECTIVE OUTCOMES

One goal of theorizing is to explain specific outcomes. One outcome that intercultural theorists have used in developing theories is effective communication and effective group decisions. Four theories fit in this category: (1) cultural convergence theory (e.g., Barnett & Kincaid, 1983), (2) anxiety/uncertainty management theory (e.g., Gudykunst, 1995), (3) effective group decision making theory (e.g., Oetzel, 1995), and (4) Kim's (1997, 2004) integrated theory of interethnic communication.

Cultural Convergence

Cultural convergence theory (Barnett & Kincaid, 1983; Kincaid, 1988) is based upon Kincaid's (1979; also see Rogers & Kincaid, 1981) convergence model of communication.[13] Kincaid (1979) defines communication as "a process in which two or more individuals or groups share information in order to reach a mutual understanding of each other and the world in which they live" (p. 31). He argues that mutual understanding can be approached, but never perfectly achieved. "By means of several iterations of information-exchange, two or more individuals may converge towards a more mutual understanding of each other's meaning" (p. 32).

Barnett and Kincaid (1983) use the convergence model of communication to develop a mathematical theory of the effects of communication on cultural differences. They argue that "the laws of thermodynamics predict that all participants in a closed system will converge over time on the mean collective pattern of thought if communication is allowed to continue indefinitely" (p. 175). Information that is introduced from outside the system can delay convergence or reverse it (i.e., lead to divergence). They present a mathematical model that predicts the convergence of the collective cognitive states of members of two cultures whose members are interacting. Kincaid's (1979) convergence model applies to individual-level communication, and Barnett and Kincaid's mathematical theory applies to group-level (e.g., culture) phenomena.

Kincaid (1987b, 1988) presents the theory in verbal form. Kincaid (1988) summarizes the theory in two theorems and three hypotheses. Theorem 1, for example, states that, "In a relatively closed social system in which communication among members is unrestricted, the system as a whole will tend to *converge* over time toward a state of greater cultural *uniformity*" (p. 289). The system will tend to diverge toward diversity when communication is restricted (theorem 2). The hypotheses apply the theorems to the case of immigrant groups and native/host cultures.

Anxiety/Uncertainty Management

Gudykunst (1985a) extended Berger and Calabrese's (1975) uncertainty reduction theory (URT) to intergroup encounters as the first step in developing anxiety/uncertainty management (AUM) theory (see Gudykunst, Chapters 13 and 18 in this volume). Gudykunst and Hammer (1988) used uncertainty (e.g., the inability to predict or explain others' attitudes, behavior, feelings) and anxiety (e.g., feelings of being uneasy, tense, worried, or apprehensive) to explain intercultural adjustment (see adjustment section below).

Gudykunst (1988) proffered a general theory using uncertainty and anxiety reduction to explain effective interpersonal and intergroup communication (i.e., minimize misunderstandings; this theory was not referred to as AUM). Intercultural communication is one type of intergroup communication in AUM theory. Gudykunst (1988) used Simmel's (1908/1950) notion of "the stranger" (e.g., individuals who are present in a situation, but are not members of the ingroup) as a central organizing concept. Gudykunst (1990) applied the axioms of the 1988 version of the theory to diplomacy, a special case of intergroup communication.

Gudykunst (1993) expanded the theory using a competency framework (Note: the label AUM was first used in this version). Gudykunst specified the metatheoretical assumptions of the theory in this version. The assumptions underlying the theory avoid the extreme objectivist or subjectivist positions (e.g., he assumes that individuals' communication is influenced by their cultures and group memberships, but they also can choose how they communicate when they are mindful). This suggests that under some conditions objectivist assumptions hold and other conditions subjectivist assumptions hold. Further, Gudykunst expanded the number of axioms in the theory to make the theory easier to understand (see Reynolds, 1971) and easier to apply.[14] This version of the theory also incorporates minimum and maximum thresholds for uncertainty and anxiety. Finally, Gudykunst integrated Langer's (1989) notion of mindfulness as a moderating process between AUM and effective communication in this version.

Following Lieberson (1985), Gudykunst (1995) argues that there are "basic" and "superficial" causes of effective communication. He contends that anxiety and uncertainty management (including mindfulness) are the basic causes of effective communication, and the effect of other "superficial" variables (e.g., ability to empathize, attraction to strangers) on effective communication is mediated through anxiety and uncertainty management. The extent to which individuals are mindful of their behavior moderates the influence of their anxiety and uncertainty management on their communication effectiveness. Gudykunst (1995) suggests that dialectical processes are involved in AUM (e.g., the uncertainty dialectic involves novelty and predictability), but these processes have not been elaborated.

Effective Decision Making

Oetzel (1995) proposes a theory of effective decision making in intercultural groups. Oetzel integrates Hirokawa and Rost's (1992) vigilant interaction theory (VIT) and Ting-Toomey's (1988) cross-cultural theory of face negotiation and conflict management.

Hirokawa and Rost (1992) assume that the way members of groups talk about things (e.g., problems) associated with group decisions influences how they think about things associated with the decisions they must make. How group members think about things associated with the decisions they make influences the quality of their decisions. A group's final decision is a result of "a series of interrelated subdecisions" (p. 270). Oetzel (1995) suggests that VIT may be limited to monocultural groups in the United States because different outcomes are emphasized in individualistic and collectivistic cultures. He, therefore, defines decision effectiveness in terms of quality and appropriateness.

Oetzel's (1995) theory contains 14 propositions. The initial set of propositions focuses on homogeneous (e.g., monocultural) and heterogeneous (e.g., intercultural) groups. He contends that when members of homogeneous groups activate independent self construals, they emphasize task outcomes; when they activate interdependent self construals, they emphasize relational outcomes. Members of homogeneous groups who activate independent self construals are less likely to reach consensus and will have more conflict and manage it less cooperatively than members of homogeneous groups who activate interdependent self construals. Member contributions tend to be more equal in homogeneous groups and

members are more committed to the group than members in heterogeneous groups.

Oetzel (1995) contends that when most members activate independent self construals, they tend to use dominating conflict strategies. When most members activate interdependent self construals, in contrast, they tend to use avoiding, compromising, or obliging conflict strategies. Groups that use cooperative styles to manage conflict make more effective decisions than groups that use competing or avoiding styles. Groups in which members activate personal identities make better decisions than groups in which members activate social identities.

Oetzel's (1995) theory suggests that the more equal members' contributions and the more group members are committed to the group and its decision, the more effective the decisions. Consensus decisions are more effective than majority or compromise decisions. Finally, Oetzel believes that the "fundamental requisites" of VIT apply to intercultural groups: Groups that understand the problem, establish "good" criteria, develop many alternatives, and examine the positive/negative consequences of the alternatives make more effective decisions than those that do not.

An Integrated Theory of Interethnic Communication

Kim (1997) lays the groundwork for the integrated theory of interethnic communication she presents in this volume (also see Kim, 2004). She uses general systems theory (open systems) as an organizing framework. Her organizing scheme consists of a set of four circles; a circle with behavior in the center surrounded by three circles representing contexts (from center to outer circles): (1) behavior (encoding/decoding), (2) communicator, (3) situation, and (4) environment.

Kim (1997) organizes various aspects of encoding and decoding using an associative-disassociative behavior continuum. She argues that "behaviors that are closer to the associative end of this continuum facilitate the communication process by increasing the likelihood of mutual understanding, cooperation . . . behaviors at the disassociative end tend to contribute to misunderstanding, competition" (p. 270). To illustrate, associative decoding behaviors include processes like particularization, decategorization, personalization, and mindfulness. Disassociative decoding behaviors include processes like categorization, stereotyping, communicative distance, and making the ultimate attribution error. Associative encoding behaviors include processes like convergence, person-centered messages, and personalized communication. Disassociative encoding behaviors include processes like divergence, prejudiced talk, and the use of ethnophaulisms.

Kim (1997) examines the communicator in terms of "relatively stable psychological attributes" (p. 271). She includes such factors as cognitive structures (e.g., cognitive complexity, category width), identity strength (e.g., ethnic identity, ethnolinguistic identity, ingroup loyalty), group biases (e.g., ingroup favoritism, ethnocentrism), and related concepts (e.g., intercultural identity, moral inclusion).

Kim (1997) views the situation as defined by the physical setting. She isolates interethnic heterogeneity, interethnic salience, and interaction goals (e.g., goals) as critical factors of the situation. The environment includes national and international forces that influence interethnic communication such as institutional equity/inequity (e.g., history of subjugation, ethnic stratification), ethnic group strength (e.g., ethnolinguistic vitality), and interethnic contact (e.g., interaction potential of environment).

Kim (1997) argues that the organizing model provides a framework for integrating research in a variety of disciplines. It also serves as "a framework for pragmatic action. . . . For instance, we can infer from the model that, by changing certain existing conditions in the environment, we can help facilitate associative communicative behaviors" (p. 281).

THEORIES FOCUSING ON ACCOMMODATION OR ADAPTATION

Another goal on which theorists focus is how communicators accommodate or adapt to each other. There are three theories that fit this category: (1) communication accommodation theory (e.g., Gallois, Giles, Jones, Cargile, & Ota, 1995), (2) intercultural adaptation theory (e.g., Ellingsworth, 1988), and (3) co-cultural theory (e.g., Orbe, 1998b).

Communication Accommodation

Communication accommodation theory (CAT) originated in Giles' (1973) work on accent mobility (see Gallois, Ogay, and Giles, Chapter 6 in this volume). CAT began as speech accommodation theory (SAT; e.g., Giles & Smith, 1979). SAT proposed that speakers use linguistic strategies to gain approval or to show distinctiveness in their interactions with others. The main strategies communicators use based on these motivations are speech convergence or divergence. These are "linguistic moves" to decrease or increase communicative distances, respectively.

Giles et al. (1987) expanded SAT in terms of the range of phenomena covered and relabeled it CAT. Coupland et al. (1988) adapted CAT to intergenerational communication and incorporated additional modifications to the theory (e.g., conceptualizing speaker strategies as based on an "addressee focus" and incorporating addressees' attributions about speakers' behavior). Gallois et al. (1988) adapted Coupland et al.'s (1988) model to intercultural communication. This modification integrated predictions from ethnolinguistic identity theory (ELIT; e.g., Giles & Johnson, 1987), and emphasized the influence of situations on intercultural communication. Gallois et al. (1995) updated the 1988 version of the theory incorporating research that had been conducted and cross-cultural variability in accommodative processes.

CAT begins with the "sociohistorical context" of the interaction. This includes the relations between the groups having contact and the social norms regarding contact (intercultural contact is one type of intergroup contact in CAT). This component also includes cultural variability.

The second component of CAT is the communicators' "accommodative orientation"; their tendencies to perceive encounters with outgroup members in interpersonal terms, intergroup terms, or a combination of the two. There are three aspects to accommodative orientations: (1) "intrapersonal factors" (e.g., social and personal identities), (2) "intergroup factors" (e.g., factors that reflect communicators' orientations to outgroups, such as perceived ingroup vitality), and "initial orientations" (e.g., perceived potential for conflict; long-term accommodative motivation toward outgroups).

The perceived relations between groups influences communicators' tendencies to perceive encounters as interpersonal or intergroup. Similarly, members of dominant groups who have insecure social identities and perceive threats from outgroups tend to perceive convergence by members of subordinate groups negatively. Also, individuals who are dependent on their groups and feel solidarity with them tend to see encounters in intergroup terms and tend to emphasize linguistic markers of their groups.

The third component in CAT is the "immediate situation." There are five aspects to the immediate situation: (1) "sociopsychological states" (e.g., communicators' interpersonal or intergroup orientation in the situation), (2) "goals and addressee focus" (e.g., motivations in the encounter, conversational needs, relational needs), (3) "sociolinguistic strategies" (e.g., approximation, discourse management), (4) "behavior and tactics" (e.g., language, accent, topic), and (5) "labeling and attributions." The five aspects of the immediate situation are interrelated.

The final component of CAT is "evaluation and future intentions." The propositions here focus on communicators' perceptions of their interlocutors' behavior in the interaction. Convergent behavior that is perceived to be based on "benevolent intent," for example, tends to be evaluated positively. When interlocutors who are perceived to be typical group members are evaluated positively, individuals are motivated to communicate with the interlocutors and other members of their groups in the future.

Intercultural Adaptation

Ellingsworth (1983) assumes that all communication involves some degree of cultural variability. He, therefore, argues that explaining intercultural communication needs to start from interpersonal communication and cultural factors need to be incorporated.[15] Ellingsworth's (1983) theory is designed to explain how communicators adapt to each other in "purpose-related encounters." He isolates eight "laws" (i.e., "ongoing relationships by which units affect one another," p. 201). Examples of Ellingsworth's laws are "Adaptation of communication style affects invocation of culture-based belief differences" (p. 202) and "The burden of adaptive behavior is affected by the extent to which setting favors one or the other participant" (p. 202).

Ellingsworth (1983) argues that functionally adapting communication and equity in adaptation facilitate task completion. Nonfunctional adaptive communication leads to invocation of cultural differences and slowing task completion. When communicators have to cooperate there is equity in adapting communication. Using persuasive strategies leads to adapting communication. When the situation favors one communicator or one communicator has more power, the other communicator has the burden to adapt. The more adaptive behavior in which communicators engage, the more their cultural beliefs will change. Ellingsworth

(1988) updated the theory by expanding discussion of the laws and propositions in the theory. The theory, however, remains essentially the same.

Co-Cultural Theory

Orbe (1998a, 1998b) uses a phenomenological approach to develop co-cultural theory (see Orbe & Spelling, Chapter 8 in this volume). Co-cultural theory is based in muted group theory (e.g., social hierarchies in society privilege some groups over others; Ardener, 1975; Kramarae, 1981) and standpoint theory (e.g., specific positions in society provide subjective ways that individuals look at the world; Smith, 1987). Co-cultures include, but are not limited to, nonwhites, women, people with disabilities, homosexuals, and those in the lower social classes.

Orbe (1998b) points out that "in its most general form, co-cultural communication refers to interactions among underrepresented and dominant group members" (p. 3). The focus of co-cultural theory is providing a framework "by which co-cultural group members negotiate attempts by others to render their voices muted within dominant societal structures" (p. 4). Two premises guide co-cultural theory: (1) co-cultural group members are marginalized in the dominant societal structures, and (2) co-cultural group members use certain communication styles to achieve success when confronting the "oppressive dominant structures."

Orbe (1998b) argues that co-cultural group members generally have one of three goals for their interactions with dominant group members: (1) assimilation (e.g., become part of the mainstream culture), (2) accommodation (e.g., try to get the dominant group members to accept co-cultural group members), and (3) separation (e.g., rejecting the possibility of common bonds with dominant group members). Other factors that influence

co-cultural group members' communication are "field of experience" (e.g., past experiences), "abilities" (e.g., individuals' abilities to enact different practices), the "situational context" (e.g., where are they communicating with dominant group members?), "perceived costs and rewards" (e.g., the pros and cons of certain practices), and the "communication approach" (i.e., being aggressive, assertive, or nonassertive).

Orbe (1998a, 1998b) isolates practices (e.g., ways members of "marginalized groups negotiate their muted group status," 1998b, p. 8) co-cultural group members use in their interaction with dominant group members. The practices used are a function of the co-cultural group members' goals and communication approaches. The combination of these yield nine communication orientations in which different practices tend to be used: (1) nonassertive separation involves practices of "avoiding" and "maintaining interpersonal barriers"; (2) nonassertive accommodation involves practices of "increasing visibility" and "dispelling stereotypes"; (3) nonassertive assimilation involves practices of "emphasizing commonalities," "developing positive face," "censoring self," and "averting controversy"; (4) assertive separation involves practices of "communicating self," "intragroup networking," "exemplifying strengths," and "embracing stereotypes"; (5) assertive accommodation involves practices of "communicating self," "intragroup networking," "utilizing liaisons," and "educating others"; (6) assertive assimilation involves practices of "extensive preparation," "overcompensating," "manipulating stereotypes," and "bargaining"; (7) aggressive separation involves practices of "attacking" and "sabotaging others"; (8) aggressive accommodation involves practices of "confronting" and "gaining advantage"; and (9) aggressive assimilation involves practices of "dissociating," "mirroring," "strategic distancing," and "ridiculing self."

THEORIES FOCUSING ON IDENTITY NEGOTIATION OR MANAGEMENT

Another goal that theorists use as a focus of their work is negotiating identities in intercultural interactions. These theories address adaptation of identities, not specific communication behaviors (as in the preceding section). Four theories focus on identity: (1) cultural identity theory (Collier & Thomas, 1988), (2) identity management theory (Cupach & Imahori, 1993), (3) identity negotiation theory (Ting-Toomey, 1993), and (4) Hecht's (1993) communication theory of identity.

Cultural Identity

Collier and Thomas (1988) present an "interpretive" theory of how cultural identities are managed in intercultural interactions (also see Collier, 1998; see Collier, Chapter 11 in this volume). Their theory is stated in six assumptions, five axioms, and one theorem. The assumptions are: (1) individuals "negotiate multiple identities in discourse" (p. 107); (2) intercultural communication occurs "by the discursive assumption and avowal of differing cultural identities" (p. 107); (3) intercultural communication competence involves managing meanings coherently, and engaging in rule-following (i.e., appropriate) and outcomes that are positive (i.e., effective); (4) intercultural communication competence involves negotiating "mutual meanings, rules, and positive outcomes" (p. 112); (5) intercultural communication competence involves validating cultural identities (i.e., "identification with and perceived acceptance into a group that has shared systems of symbols and meanings as well as norms/rules for conduct," p. 113); and (6) cultural identities vary as a function of scope (e.g., how general identities are), salience (e.g., how important identities are), and intensity (e.g., how strongly identities are communicated to others). Given the six assumptions, Collier and Thomas (1988) develop five axioms. The first axiom states that "the more that norms and meanings differ in discourse, the more intercultural the contact" (p. 112). The second axiom suggests that the more individuals have intercultural communication competence, the better they are able to develop and maintain intercultural relationships. The third axiom is similar to the first and states that "the more that cultural identities differ in the discourse, the more intercultural the contact" (p. 115).

The fourth axiom in Collier and Thomas' (1988) theory suggests that the more one person's ascribed cultural identity for the other person matches the other person's avowed cultural identity, the more the intercultural competence. The final axiom states that "linguistic references to cultural identity systematically covary with sociocontextual factors such as participants, type of episode, and topic" (p. 116). The theorem claims that the more cultural identities are avowed, the more important they are relative to other identities.

Identity Management

Cupach and Imahori's (1993) identity management theory (IMT) is based in interpersonal communication competence (see Imahori & Cupach, Chapter 9 in this volume).[16] IMT is based on Goffman's (1967) work on self-presentation and facework.

Cupach and Imahori (1993) view identity as providing "an interpretive frame for experience" (p. 113). Identities provide expectations for behavior and motivate individuals' behavior. Individuals have multiple identities, but Cupach and Imahori view cultural (based on Collier & Thomas, 1988) and relational identities (e.g., identities within specific relationships) as central to identity management. Following Collier and Thomas, Cupach and Imahori view identities as varying as a function of scope (e.g., number of individuals who share identity), salience (e.g., importance of identity), and intensity (e.g., strength with which identity is communicated to others). Intercultural communication occurs when interlocutors have different cultural identities and intracultural communication occurs when interlocutors share cultural identities.

Cupach and Imahori (1993) argue that aspects of individuals' identities are revealed through the presentation of face (e.g., situated identities individuals claim). They contend "the maintenance of face is a natural and inevitable *condition* of human interaction" (p. 116). In IMT, "interpersonal communication competence should include the ability of an individual to successfully negotiate mutually acceptable identities in interaction" (p. 118, italics omitted). The ability to maintain face in interactions is one indicator of individuals' interpersonal communication competence. Cupach and Imahori believe this extends to intercultural communication competence as well.

Cupach and Imahori (1993) argue that since individuals often do not know much about others' cultures, they manage face in intercultural encounters using stereotypes. Stereotyping, however, is face-threatening because it is based on externally imposed identities. The result is a dialectic tension regarding three aspects of face: (1) fellowship face versus autonomy face, (2) competence face versus autonomy face, and (3) autonomy face versus fellowship or competence face. Intercultural communication competence involves successfully managing face, which involves managing these three dialectical tensions.

Cupach and Imahori (1993) contend that competence in developing intercultural relationships goes through three phases. The first phase involves "trail-and-error" processes of finding identities on which communicators share some similarities. The second phase involves enmeshment of the identities of the participants into "a mutually acceptable and convergent relational identity, in spite of the fact that their cultural identities are still divergent" (p. 125). The third phase involves renegotiating identities. "Competent intercultural interlocutors use their narrowly defined but emerging relational identity from the second phase as the basis for renegotiating their separate cultural identities" (p. 127). Cupach and Imahori argue that the three phases are "cyclical" and individuals in intercultural relationships may go through the three phases for each aspect of their identities that are relevant to their relationships.

Identity Negotiation

Ting-Toomey (1993) argues that intercultural communication competence is "the effective identity negotiation process between two interactants in a novel communication episode" (p. 73). She makes several assumptions in constructing identity negotiation theory (INT; see Ting-Toomey, Chapter 10 in this volume): cultural variability influences the sense of self, self-identification involves security and vulnerability, identity boundary regulation motivates behavior, identity boundary regulation involves a tension between inclusion and differentiation, managing the inclusion-differentiation dialectic influences the coherent sense of self, and a coherent sense of self influences individuals' communication resourcefulness (i.e., "the knowledge and ability to apply cognitive, affective, and behavioral resources appropriately, effectively, and creatively in diverse interaction situations," p. 74).

Ting-Toomey (1993) argues that the more secure individuals' self-identifications are, the more they are open to interacting with members of other cultures. The more vulnerable individuals feel, the more anxiety they experience in these interactions. Individuals' vulnerability is affected by their need for security. The more individuals need inclusion, the more they value ingroup and relational boundaries. The more individuals need differentiation, the more distance they place between the self and others.

Individuals' resourcefulness in negotiating identities is affected by effectively managing the security-vulnerability and inclusion-differentiation dialectics. The more secure individuals' self-identifications, the greater their identity coherence and global self-esteem. The greater individuals' self-esteem and the greater their membership collective esteem, the more resourceful they are when interacting with strangers.

Individuals' motivation to communicate with strangers influences the degree to which they seek out communication resources. The greater individuals' cognitive, affective, and behavioral resourcefulness, the more effective they are in identity negotiation. The more diverse individuals' communication resources are, the more effective they are in interactive identity confirmation, coordination, and attunement. Finally, the more diverse individuals' communication resources, the more flexible they are in "co-creating interactive goals" and "developing mutual identity meanings and comprehensibility" (Ting-Toomey, 1993, p. 110).

A Communication Theory of Identity

Hecht (1993) lays the foundation for the theory he and his colleagues present in this volume (see Chapter 12).[17] He argues that there are "polarities or contradictions in all social life. . . . elements of these polarities are present in all interactions" (p. 76). Hecht argues that identity is a "communicative process" and must be studied in the context of exchanged messages. He starts from several assumptions:

1. Identities have individual, social, and communal properties;

2. Identities are both enduring and changing;

3. Identities are affective, cognitive, behavioral, and spiritual;

4. Identities have both content and relationship levels of interpretation;

5. Identities involve both subjective and ascribed meanings;

6. Identities are codes that are expressed in conversations and define membership in communities;

7. Identities have semantic properties that are expressed in core symbols, meaning, and labels;

8. Identities prescribe modes of appropriate and effective communication. (p. 79)

Hecht contends that these assumptions are consistent with dialectical theory.

Hecht (1993) argues that there are four identity frames: personal, enacted, relational, and communal. Frames "are means of interpreting reality that provide a perspective for understanding the social world" (p. 81). Identity as a personal frame involves the characteristics of individuals. He makes three assumptions about the personal frame: "Identities are hierarchically ordered meanings," (2) "Identities are meanings ascribed to the self by others," and (3) "Identities are a source of expectation and motivation" (p. 79).

Hecht (1993) argues that identities are enacted in interactions with others. He contends that "not all messages are about identity, but identity is part of all messages" (p. 79). There are three assumptions about identity enactment: "Identities are emergent," "Identities are enacted in social behavior and symbols," and "Identities are hierarchically order[ed] social roles" (p. 79).

Hecht (1993) sees identities as emerging in relationships with others and part of the relationships because they are "jointly negotiated." He isolates three relationship frame assumptions: "Identities emerge in relationship to other people," "Identities are enacted in relationships," and "Relationships develop identities as social entities" (p. 80).

Hecht (1993) also views identities in a communal frame; "something held by a group of people which, in turn, bonds the group together" (p. 80). He isolates one proposition: "Identities emerge out of groups and networks" (p. 80).

THEORIES FOCUSING ON COMMUNICATION NETWORKS

Network theories are based on the assumption that individuals' behavior is influenced by relationships between individuals rather than the characteristics of the individuals. "In network theory, the main focus is on positions and social relationships, rather than beliefs or internalized norms. Also, the focus is on series of interconnecting relationships, rather than static, bounded groups" (Yum, 1988b, p. 240). These theories focus on explaining linkages between people from different cultures.[18] Three theories focus on networks: (1) outgroup communication competence theory (Kim, 1986), (2) intracultural versus intercultural networks theory (Yum, 1988b), and (3) networks and acculturation theory (Smith, 1999).

Networks and Outgroup Communication Competence

Kim (1986) uses a personal network approach to explain outgroup communication competence. Personal networks emphasize the links between individuals. She argues that "one of the most important aspects of a personal network is ego's conscious and unconscious reliance on the network members for perceiving and interpreting various attributes and actions of others (and of self)" (p. 90).

Kim (1986) assumes that having outgroup members in individuals' personal networks and the nature of these outgroup ties influence their outgroup communication competence. Theorem 1 states that "a higher level of heterogeneity of a personal network is associated with a higher level of ego's overall outgroup communication competence" (p. 93). This theorem suggests that having outgroup members in individuals' personal networks facilitates outgroup communication competence.

Theorem 2 in Kim's (1986) theory proposes that "a higher level of centrality of outgroup members in a personal network is associated with a higher level of the ego's outgroup communication competence" (p. 93). This theorem suggests that having outgroup members in central positions in individuals' personal networks facilitates outgroup communication competence.

Theorem 3 contends that "a higher level of an ego's tie strength with outgroup members is associated with a higher level of his/her ego's outgroup communication competence" (p. 94). This theorem suggests that the more frequent the contact and the closer the ties individuals have with outgroup members, the more their outgroup communication competence.

Intracultural Versus Intercultural Networks

Yum's (1988b) theory is designed to explain the differences in individuals' intracultural and intercultural networks. She begins with the assumption that there is more variance in behavior between cultures than within cultures. There are six theorems in Yum's theory.

Yum's (1988b) first theorem posits that intercultural networks tend to be radial (e.g., individuals are linked to others who are not linked to each other) and intracultural networks tend to be interlocking (e.g., individuals are linked to others who are linked to each other). Theorem 2 predicts that intracultural networks are more dense (e.g., the ratio of actual direct links to number of possible links) than intercultural networks.

Yum's (1988b) third theorem proposes that intracultural networks are more multiplex (e.g., multiple messages flow through linkages) than intercultural networks. Theorem 4 states that "intercultural network ties are more likely to be weak ties than strong ties" (p. 250). Strong ties involve frequent and close contact (e.g., friendships). Links between acquaintances and people with whom individuals have intermittent role relationships (e.g., hair dressers) tend to be weak ties.

Theorem 5 in Yum's (1988b) theory states that "the roles of liaison and bridge will be more prevalent and more important for network connectedness in intercultural networks than in intracultural networks" (p. 251). Liaisons are individuals who link cliques (e.g., a group of connected individuals) but are not members of any of the cliques. Bridges are individuals who link cliques and are members of one of the cliques. Both are "intermediaries" and can form indirect linkages between members of different groups.

Yum's (1988b) final theorem suggests that "transivity will play a much smaller role in creating intercultural networks than intracultural networks" (p. 252). Transivity occurs when "my friend's friends are my friends" (p. 252). Since intercultural networks tend to be uniplex and involve weak ties, they do facilitate forming networks with friends of outgroup members in the network.

Networks and Acculturation

Smith's (1999) theory links social networks to immigrant acculturation.[19] The theory consists of seven assumptions about the nature of networks, and seven propositions. The first proposition suggests that immigrants tend to be linked to those individuals who define their identities (e.g., other immigrants from their cultures or host nationals). The second proposition claims that the way immigrants experience their social networks is influenced by their native cultures.

Smith's (1999) third proposition suggests that the more host nationals are in immigrants' social networks, the more likely immigrants are to acculturate. The fourth proposition claims that as immigrants become integrated into host communities, their social networks change. Proposition 5 contends that factors like where immigrants live and their social class influence their abilities to form intercultural networks and acculturate.

Smith's (1999) sixth proposition states that dense networks (e.g., links connected to each other) decrease immigrants' abilities to obtain the resources needed for acculturation. The final proposition contends that "intercultural networks will be less dense, with more radial ties in cultures reflecting a contextual-based relationship norm than those found in cultures reflecting a person-based relationship norm" (p. 650).[20]

THEORIES FOCUSING ON ACCULTURATION AND ADJUSTMENT

The acculturation of immigrants and the adjustment of sojourners has been of interest to scholars for over 50 years. Only in recent years, however, have formal theories focusing on communication been proposed. Five theories are examined in this section: (1) communication acculturation theory (e.g., Kim, 1988, 2001), (2) interactive acculturation model (Bourhis et al., 1997), (3) anxiety/uncertainty management theory of adjustment (e.g., Gudykunst, 1998a), (4) communication in assimilation, deviance, and alienation states theory (McGuire & McDermott, 1988), and (5) a schema theory of adaptation (Nishida, 1999).[21] The first two focus on the acculturation of immigrants and the other three focus on the adjustment of sojourners.

Cross-Cultural Adaptation

Kim has been developing her theory of communication and acculturation for over 20 years. The first version of the theory appeared in a causal model of Korean immigrants' acculturation to Chicago (Kim, 1977). She has refined the theory several times using an open-system perspective (e.g., Kim, 1979, 1988, 1995, 2001; Kim & Ruben, 1988; see Y. Y. Kim, Chapter 16 in this volume). One of the major changes incorporated into the theory is adding the "stress, adaptation, and growth dynamics" that immigrants go through, and focusing on immigrants becoming "intercultural." In addition, the current version of the theory attempts to portray "cross-cultural adaptation as a collaborative effort, in which a stranger and the receiving environment are engaged in a joint effort" (1995, p. 192).

The current version of Kim's (2001) theory contains assumptions based on open-systems theory, axioms, and theorems. The axioms are "law like" statements about relationships between units in the theory. Theorems are derived from the axioms. The first five axioms are broad principles of cross-cultural adaptation: acculturation and deculturation are part of the cross-cultural adaptation process, the stress-adaptation-growth dynamic underlies the adaptation process, intercultural transformations are a function of the stress-adaptation-growth dynamic, the severity of the stress-adaptation-growth dynamic decreases as strangers go through intercultural transformations, and functional fitness and psychological health result from intercultural transformations. The final five axioms deal with the reciprocal relationship between intercultural transformations and host communication competence, host communication activities,[22] ethnic communication activities, environmental conditions, and strangers' predispositions.

The first three theorems posit relationships between host communication competence and host communication activities (+), ethnic communication activities (−), and intercultural transformations (+).[23] Host interpersonal and mass communication activities are related to ethnic communication activities (−), and intercultural transformations (+). Ethnic interpersonal and mass communication activities are related negatively to intercultural transformations.

The next three theorems relate host receptivity and conformity pressure to host communication competence (+), host communication activities (+), and ethnic communication activities (−). Ethnic group strength is related to host communication competence (−), host communication activities (−), and ethnic communication activities (+). Ethnic proximity is related to host communication competence (+), host communication activities (+), and ethnic communication activities (−).

Strangers' preparedness for change is related to host communication competence (+), host communication activities (+), and ethnic communication activities (+). Strangers' adaptive personalities are related to host communication competence (+), host communication activities (+), and ethnic communication activities (−).

Interactive Acculturation Model

Bourhis et al.'s (1997) interactive acculturation model (IAM) suggests that relational outcomes between host nationals and immigrant groups are a function of the "acculturation orientations of both the host majority and immigrant groups as influenced by state integration policies" (p. 369). They begin by adapting Berry's (1980, 1990) model of immigrant acculturation.

Berry's (1980) model is based on immigrants' responses to two issues: (1) do they want to maintain their native cultural identities, and (2) do they want to maintain good relations with members of the host culture. If the answer is "yes" on both issues, they use an "integration" orientation with respect to the host culture. If they answer "yes" to having relations with hosts and "no" to maintaining their cultural identities, immigrants have an "assimilation" orientation toward the host culture. If immigrants answer "yes" to maintaining their native cultural identities and "no" to having good relations with hosts, they have a "separation" orientation toward the host culture. If they answer "no" to both issues, they have a marginal orientation toward the host culture. Bourhis et al. (1997) divide the marginal orientation into "anomie" (e.g., cultural alienation) and "individualism" (e.g., they define themselves and hosts as individuals rather than as members of groups).

Bourhis et al. (1997) develop a similar model for hosts' acculturation orientation. The model is based on responses on two questions: "(1) Do you find it acceptable that immigrants maintain their cultural heritage?

(2) Do you accept that immigrants adapt to the culture of your host culture?" (p. 380, italics omitted). If hosts answer "yes" to both questions, they have an "integration" orientation toward immigrants. If they answer "no" to question 1 and "yes" to question 2, they have an "assimilation" orientation. If hosts answer "yes" to question 1 and "no" to question 2, the "segregation" orientation. If hosts answer "no" to both questions, they have an "exclusion" or "individualism" orientation.

Bourhis et al. (1997) combine the two models to form the IAM.[24] They use the IAM to predict whether there are "consensual," "problematic," or "conflictual" relational outcomes between hosts and immigrants. To illustrate, "the most consensual relational outcomes are predicted in three cells of the model, namely when both host community members and immigrant group members share either the integration, assimilation, or individualism acculturation orientations" (p. 383, italics omitted).

Anxiety/Uncertainty Management

Defining strangers is a figure-ground phenomenon. The effective communication version of AUM theory (e.g., Gudykunst, 1995) is written from the perspective of individuals communicating with strangers (e.g., others approaching individuals' ingroups). The adjustment version of the theory is written from the perspective of strangers (e.g., sojourners) entering new cultures and interacting with host nationals (see Gudykunst's chapters in this volume).

The original version of AUM theory (the label AUM, however, was not used) was a theory of adjustment (Gudykunst & Hammer, 1988).[25] Gudykunst (1998a) includes axioms comparable to the 1995 version of the effective communication version, plus two additional axioms focusing specifically on adjustment (i.e., pluralistic tendencies in host culture decreases and permanence of stay increases strangers' anxiety).

When strangers enter a new culture they have uncertainty about host nationals' attitudes, feelings, beliefs, values, and behaviors (Gudykunst, 1998a). Strangers need to be able to predict which of several alternative behavior patterns hosts will employ. When strangers communicate with hosts, they also experience anxiety. Anxiety is the tension, feelings of being uneasy, tension, or apprehension strangers have about what will happen when they communicate with hosts (Stephan & Stephan, 1985). The anxiety strangers experience when they communicate with hosts is based on negative expectations.

To adjust to other cultures, strangers do not want to try to reduce their anxiety and uncertainty totally (Gudykunst, 1995). At the same time, strangers cannot communicate effectively with hosts if their uncertainty and anxiety are too high.[26] If uncertainty is too high, strangers cannot accurately interpret hosts' messages or make accurate predictions about hosts' behaviors.[27] When anxiety is too high, strangers communicate on automatic pilot and interpret hosts' behaviors using their own cultural frames of reference. Also, when anxiety is too high, the way strangers process information is very simple, thereby limiting their ability to predict hosts' behaviors. When uncertainty is too low, strangers become overconfident that they understand hosts' behaviors and do not question whether their predictions are accurate. When anxiety is too low, strangers are not motivated to communicate with hosts.

If strangers' anxiety is high, they must mindfully manage their anxiety to communicate effectively and adjust to the host cultures. Managing anxiety requires that strangers become mindful (e.g., create new categories, be open to new information, be aware of alternative perspectives; Langer, 1989). When strangers have managed their anxiety, they need to try to develop accurate predictions and explanations for hosts' behaviors. When strangers communicate on automatic pilot, they predict and interpret hosts' behaviors using their own frames of reference. When strangers are mindful, in contrast, they are open to new information and aware of alternative perspectives (e.g., hosts' perspectives; Langer, 1989) and they, therefore, can make accurate predictions.

Lieberson (1985) argues that it is necessary to isolate "basic" and "superficial" causes of the phenomenon being explained. In AUM theory, managing uncertainty and anxiety are the basic causes of strangers' intercultural adjustment. The amount of uncertainty and anxiety strangers experience in their interactions with hosts is a function of many superficial causes (e.g., self-concepts, motivation, reactions to hosts, social categorization, situational processes, connections with hosts). Research supports the theoretical argument that the superficial causes of adjustment (e.g., ability to adapt behavior) are linked to adjustment through uncertainty and anxiety (e.g., Gao & Gudykunst, 1990; Hammer et al., 1998).

Assimilation, Deviance, and Alienation

McGuire and McDermott (1988) argue that assimilation and adaptation are not permanent outcomes of the adaptation process, rather they are temporary outcomes of the communication process.[28] The reason is that everyone, no matter how well integrated into their cultures, deviates from social norms and rules at some point. They contend that "individuals (or groups) have achieved the assimilation state when their perceptions are receiving positive reinforcement from others' communications. . . . the group accomplishes an assimilation state when an individual conforms to expected norms" (p. 93, italics omitted).

McGuire and McDermott (1988) contend that the hosts' response to immigrants' deviation from cultural norms is neglectful communication. Neglectful communication involves negative messages or the absence of messages. When immigrants are not deviant or engage in assimilative communication (e.g., interact with hosts, increase fluency in host languages), host nationals respond with assimilative communication (e.g., praise immigrants' behavior, being available to interact with immigrants).

When immigrants are in a deviance state they experience tension with their new cultures (McGuire & McDermott, 1988). Host nationals tend to respond with neglectful communication (e.g., low level of communication, negative feedback). One possible response to host nationals' neglectful communication is for immigrants to become alienated from the host cultures. Alienation involves feelings of "normlessness and social isolation" (p. 101). Immigrants, therefore, may feel that they cannot accomplish their goals and are being excluded from the host cultures. This does not, however, necessarily "involve hostility, aggression or conflict" (p. 101).

The way host nationals respond to immigrants when immigrants feel alienated influences whether immigrants stay in an alienated state. If host nationals respond in a way to strengthen alienation (e.g., refusing to interact with immigrants, being obscene, ridiculing immigrants), immigrants are likely to withdraw from host cultures, be hostile toward the host cultures, or refuse to use the host languages.

McGuire and McDermott (1988) argue that the way host nationals and immigrants respond to neglectful communication is similar. They conclude that "changes in the amount or kind of deviance or amount or kind of neglectful communication will push an individual toward or into either the alienation or the assimilation state. . . . Alienation or assimilation, therefore, of a group or an individual is an outcome of the relationship between deviant behavior and neglectful communication" (p. 103).

A Schema Theory of Adaptation

Nishida (1999) uses schema theory to develop a theory of sojourner adaptation to new cultural environments (see Nishida,

Chapter 17 in this volume). She defines schemas as "generalized collections of knowledge of past experiences which are organized into related knowledge groups and are used to guide our behaviors in familiar situations" (p. 755). Nishida contends that sojourners' failures to understand host nationals' behavior is due to sojourners' lack of schemas used in the host culture.

When sojourners do not have the schemas used in the host culture, they tend to focus on "data-driven processing which requires effort and attention" (p. 767). Data-driven processing is affected by sojourners' self-schemas. In other words, sojourners pay attention to information that is important to them (as opposed to what is important to host nationals). Nishida argues that sojourners "actively try to reorganize their native-culture schemas or to generate new schemas in order to adapt to the host culture environment" (p. 768).

CONCLUSION

As indicated earlier, theorizing about intercultural communication has improved tremendously in recent years. There are, however, still several issues that need to be addressed in future theorizing on intercultural communication.

First, the vast majority of the theories proposed to date are objectivistic in nature. Only a few of the theorists included here claim to have developed subjectivistic theories. Some objectivistic theories include subjectivistic components (e.g., mindfulness in AUM), but the general trend is for the two types of theorizing not to be integrated. Clearly, there is a need for more subjectivistic theorizing and for integrating subjectivistic and objectivistic theories.

Second, the vast majority of the theorists were born in the United States. Researchers born in other cultures, however, have developed several of the theories discussed (e.g., Todd Imahori, Young Yun Kim, Hiroko Nishida, Stella Ting-Toomey, June Ock Yum). There may be theories of intercultural communication published in languages other than English of which we are not aware. The lack of theories from outside the United States may be a function of the role of theory in scholarship in different cultures (e.g., developing theories is not emphasized in many cultures). There is, nevertheless, a need for indigenous theories developed by scholars outside the United States.

Before theories of intercultural communication can be developed by theorists from outside the United States, indigenous theories of communication must be developed. There is extensive work on indigenous Asian concepts related to communication[29]; for example, *amae* (roughly dependence, Doi, 1973, 2001; Miike, 2003; Tezuka, 1993); *awase* (roughly reciprocal adjustment to the other person, Tezuka, 1992); *chi/ki* (roughly energy flow, Chung et al., 2003); face (e.g., Lim & Choi, 1996); indirectness (e.g., Okabe, 1987; Lim & Choi, 1996); *ishin-denshin* (roughly communicating without talk, Tsujimura, 1987); *sasshi* (roughly guessing what others mean, Nishida, 1977); and *sunao* (roughly being upright and obedient, Tezuka, 1992).

There also are beginning attempts to develop indigenous conceptualizations of topics like Japanese communication competence (e.g., Miyahara, 1995, 1999; Takai, 1994, 1996; Takai & Ota, 1994), and to develop indigenous models of communication (e.g., *enryo-sasshi*, *enryo* is roughly reserve; Ishii, 1984; Miike, 2003), as well as discussions of how Asian philosophy influences communication (e.g., Yum, 1988a) and how Asian conceptualizations of self construals lead to different patterns of communication than Western conceptualizations of self construals (e.g., Kim, 2002). To date, however, none of this work approaches what might be called an indigenous theory of communication.

Dissanayake (1986) called for indigenous Asian approaches to the study of communication. Similarly, Chan (2000) argues that indigenous theories are needed to guide indigenous research. Miike (2002) suggests assumptions for an Asian-centric approach to theorizing about communication in English. It is important to recognize that indigenous theorizing cannot take place when authors write in English. Indigenous theories must be constructed in the theorists' native languages; they cannot be constructed in English.[30] Once constructed in the native language, we hope indigenous theories are "translated" into English so that theorists in the United States can incorporate them in their theories of communication in general and intercultural communication in particular.[31]

Third, the issue of power is not incorporated in very many of the theories constructed to date. Clearly, power plays a role in many, but not all, intercultural and intergroup encounters. Reid and Ng (1999), for example, describe the relationships among language, power, and intergroup relations. Power needs to be incorporated in theories of intercultural communication. Berger (1994) examines power in interpersonal communication, and his analysis provides one starting point for looking at power in intercultural communication.

Fourth, many of the theories proposed to date are compatible with each other. Many of the theories proposed have different scopes and boundary conditions. This allows for the possibility of integration. Gallois et al. (1995), for example, indicate that CAT can incorporate other theoretical positions but do not present specifics (e.g., one possibility is co-cultural theory, which is not inconsistent with CAT). Similarly, Cupach and Imahori's (1993) theory appears to be theoretically compatible with Collier and Thomas' (1988) theory. Gudykunst (1995) suggests that dialectical theory can be integrated with AUM. We believe that integrating theories, especially objectivistic and subjectivistic theories, will increase our ability to understand intercultural communication.

Finally, there is little or no published research supporting some of the theories presented in this chapter. Given the state of

theorizing in intercultural communication, conducting atheoretical research is unwarranted. Research designed to test theories is needed to advance the state of our understanding of intercultural communication, not more atheoretical research.

NOTES

1. Hall (1976) had been published and this could be considered a cross-cultural theory of communication, but not an intercultural theory.

2. This volume was based on an "Action Caucus" Gudykunst organized at the Speech Communication Association convention 2 years earlier. The volume included both cross-cultural and intercultural theorizing. Prior to the publication of the volume there was a theory of communication and intercultural adaptation (Kim, 1977).

3. Another volume of the *Annual* that Wiseman edited on intercultural competence also included theories (Wiseman & Koester, 1993).

4. Theories designed in one culture also can be generalized to other cultures (e.g., Gudykunst & Nishida, 2001), or culture can be treated as a boundary condition for propositions within theories. We do not discuss this approach in this chapter.

5. Applegate and Sypher were invited to write a chapter but declined because insufficient research had been conducted to update their earlier position.

6. These approaches to integrating culture with communication theory are not necessarily incompatible. It is possible, for example, to integrate cultural communication and cross-cultural variability in communication. The integration tends not to occur because the theorists have different objectives.

7. Portions of this section are adapted from Gudykunst and Lee (2002).

8. Some of the material in this section is adapted from Gudykunst (2002).

9. We have not included theoretical discussions that are not developed into full theories (e.g., Martin & Nakayama's (1999) discussion of dialectical processes). We also have not included rhetorical approaches to intercultural communication (e.g., Gonzalez & Tanno, 2000).

10. Some might argue that Hall's low- and high-context communication is a separate dimension of cultural variability. We believe that there is too much overlap with individualism-collectivism for it to be treated as a separate dimension.

11. Kim does not complete the comparison, we do.

12. Burgoon draws on Gudykunst and Ting-Toomey's (1988) discussion of cultural differences in expectation violations. What Burgoon presents is not a cross-cultural theory per se, but rather cultural variability in a theory developed in the U.S.

13. This theory could have been discussed in the acculturation section. It is discussed here because the convergence model of communication focuses on mutual understanding, an effective outcome.

14. The large number of axioms often is viewed as violating the principle of parsimony. This, however, is not the case. The principle of parsimony essentially suggests that if two theories explain the same phenomena, select the simpler explanation.

15. He uses procedures outlined by Dubin (1969) to generate his theory.

16. Cupach and Imahori do not present formal propositions.

17. Hecht (1993) is based, in large part, on his work in Hecht, Collier, and Ribeau (1993).

18. Two theories could have been presented in other sections. Kim's theory could have been included in the section on effective outcomes and Smith's theory could have been included in the acculturation section. Yum's theory, however, does not fit any of the other categories.

19. Given the focus, this theory could have been included in the next section. As indicated earlier, our categories are not mutually exclusive.

20. This proposition is different in kind from the other propositions in that it adds a cross-cultural comparison to the proposition that is not present in the others.

21. We have not included work that is not a complete theory and work that does not focus on communication (e.g., Ady, 1995).

22. Host and ethnic communication activities include interpersonal and mass communication components.

23. The direction of the posited relationship in the theorems is given in parentheses.

24. This model is somewhat similar to Gudykunst's (1985b) model of normative power and conflict potential in stranger-host interactions.

25. Witte (1993) recasts the theory using her fear appeal theory.

26. In the 1995 version of the theory, Gudykunst discusses the idea of minimum and maximum thresholds for uncertainty and anxiety (also see Gudykunst, 1998b; Gudykunst & Kim, 1997). This idea has practical implications in training. To illustrate, trainees can be taught to isolate their maximum thresholds for anxiety (i.e., that point at which if anxiety increases they are more concerned with their anxiety than with what is happening in the situation in which they find themselves). Once trainees know the physical symptoms associated with their maximum thresholds (e.g., the amount of "butterflies" in their stomach), they can isolate a point that is slightly lower and use the physical symptoms associated with this point as an indicator that they should become mindful.

27. We use only behavior here (and below), but the claim also applies to hosts' feelings, attitudes, values, and so on.

28. McGuire and McDermott do not present formal theoretical propositions.

29. We focus on Asia here because writing on communication in Latin America and Africa tends to focus on mediated communication.

30. Kincaid (1987a) contains Asian "perspectives" on communication. None of the contributions to this volume are indigenous theories.

31. There may be a problem with publishing theories of communication in some Asian cultures. There is not, for example, a national communication journal published in Japanese in Japan. Professors tend to publish in research annuals published by their universities that are not widely circulated.

REFERENCES

Ady, J. (1995). A differential demand model of sojourner adjustment. In R. L. Wiseman (Ed.), *Intercultural communication theory* (pp. 92–114). Thousand Oaks, CA: Sage.

Applegate, J., & Sypher, H. (1983). A constructivist outline. In W. B. Gudykunst (Ed.), *Intercultural communication theory* (pp. 63–78). Beverly Hills, CA: Sage.

Applegate, J., & Sypher, H. (1988). A constructivist theory of communication and culture. In Y. Y. Kim & W. B. Gudykunst (Eds.), *Theories of intercultural communication* (pp. 41–65). Newbury Park, CA: Sage.

Ardener, S. (1975). *Perceiving women.* London: Malaby.

Barnett, G. A., & Kincaid, D. L. (1983). Cultural convergence. In W. B. Gudykunst (Ed.), *Intercultural communication theory* (pp. 171–194). Beverly Hills, CA: Sage.

Berger, C. R. (1994). Power, dominance, and social interaction. In M. Knapp & G. Miller (Eds.), *Handbook of interpersonal communication* (2nd ed., pp. 450–507). Thousand Oaks, CA: Sage.

Berger, C. R., & Calabrese, R. (1975). Some explorations in initial interactions and beyond. *Human Communication Research, 1,* 99–112.

Berry, J. W. (1980). Acculturation as varieties of adaptation. In A. Padilla (Ed.), *Acculturation: Theory, models, and findings* (pp. 9–25). Boulder, CO: Westview.

Berry, J. W. (1990). Psychology of acculturation. In J. Berman (Ed.), *Cross-cultural perspectives: Nebraska Symposium on Motivation* (pp. 201–234). Lincoln: University of Nebraska Press.

Bourhis, R., Moise, L., Perreault, S., & Senecal, S. (1997). Towards an interactive acculturation model. *International Journal of Psychology, 32,* 369–386.

Burgoon, J. K. (1978). A communication model of personal space violations. *Human Communication Research, 4,* 129–142.

Burgoon, J. K. (1992). Applying a comparative approach to nonverbal expectancy violation theory. In J. Blumler, K. Rosengren, & J. McLeod (Eds.), *Comparatively speaking* (pp. 53–69). Newbury Park, CA: Sage.

Burgoon, J. K. (1995). Cross-cultural and intercultural applications of expectancy violations theory. In R. L. Wiseman (Ed.), *Intercultural communication theory* (pp. 194–214). Thousand Oaks, CA: Sage.

Burgoon, J. K., Stern, L., & Dillman, D. (1995). *Interpersonal adaptation.* New York: Cambridge University Press.

Burrell, G., & Morgan, G. (1979). *Sociological paradigms and organizational analysis.* London: Heinemann.

Chan, M. (2000). Theory as pivot of indigenous studies and international scholarship. *Communication Research Brief, 2,* 1–3.

Chung, J., Hara, K., Yang, C., & Ryu, J. (2003). Contemporary *chi/ki* research in East Asian countries. *Ibunka Komyunikeshon Kenkyu* [Intercultural Communication Studies], *15,* 41–66 (in English).

Collier, M. J. (1998). Researching cultural identity. In D. Tanno & A. Gonzalez (Eds.), *Communication and identity across cultures* (pp. 122–147). Thousand Oaks, CA: Sage.

Collier, M. J., & Thomas, M. (1988). Cultural identity. In Y. Y. Kim & W. B. Gudykunst (Eds.), *Theories of intercultural communication* (pp. 99–120). Newbury Park, CA: Sage.

Coupland, N., Coupland, J., Giles, H., & Henwood, K. (1988). Accommodating the elderly. *Language in Society, 17,* 1–41.

Cronen, V., Chen, V., & Pearce, W. B. (1988). Coordinated management of meaning. In Y. Y. Kim & W. B. Gudykunst (Eds.), *Theories of intercultural communication* (pp. 66–98). Newbury Park, CA: Sage.

Cupach, W. R., & Imahori, T. (1993). Identity management theory. In R. L. Wiseman & J. Koester (Eds.), *Intercultural communication competence* (pp. 112–131). Newbury Park, CA: Sage.

Cushman, D., & Sanders, R. (1982). Rules theories in human communication processes. In B. Dervin & M. Voigt (Eds.), *Progress in communication sciences* (Vol. 3, pp. 49–83). Norwood, NJ: Ablex.

Delia, J. (1977). Constructivism and the study of human communication. *Quarterly Journal of Speech, 63,* 66–83.

Dewey, J. (1920). *Reconstruction in philosophy.* New York: Holt.

Dissanyake, W. (1986). The need for the study of Asian approaches to communication. *Media Asia, 13,* 6–13.

Doi, T. (1973). *The anatomy of dependence* (J. Bester, Trans.). Tokyo: Kodansha.

Doi, T. (2001). *Zoku amae no kozo* (The structure of *amae* revisited). Tokyo: Kobundo.

Dubin, R. (1969). *Theory-building.* New York: Free Press.

Ellingsworth, H. W. (1983). Adaptive intercultural communication. In W. B. Gudykunst

(Ed.), *Intercultural communication theory* (pp. 195–204). Beverly Hills, CA: Sage.

Ellingsworth, H. W. (1988). A theory of adaptation in intercultural dyads. In Y. Y. Kim & W. B. Gudykunst (Eds.), *Theories of intercultural communication* (pp. 259–279). Newbury Park, CA: Sage.

Gallois, C., Franklyn-Stokes, A., Giles, H., & Coupland, N. (1988). Communication accommodation in intercultural encounters. In Y. Y. Kim & W. B. Gudykunst (Eds.), *Theories of intercultural communication* (pp. 157–185). Newbury Park, CA: Sage.

Gallois, C., Giles, H., Jones, E., Cargile, A., & Ota, H. (1995). Accommodating intercultural encounters. In R. L. Wiseman (Ed.), *Intercultural communication theory* (pp. 115–147). Thousand Oaks, CA: Sage.

Gao, G., & Gudykunst, W. B. (1990). Uncertainty, anxiety, and adaptation. *International Journal of Intercultural Relations, 14,* 301–317.

Giles, H. (1973). Accent mobility: A model and some data. *Anthropological Linguistics, 15,* 87–105.

Giles, H., & Johnson, P. (1987). Ethnolinguistic identity theory. *International Journal of the Sociology of Language, 68,* 66–99.

Giles, H., Mulac, A., Bradac, J., & Johnson, P. (1987). Speech accommodation theory. In M. McLaughlin (Ed.), *Communication yearbook 10* (pp. 13–48). Newbury Park, CA: Sage.

Giles, H., & Smith, P. (1979). Accommodation theory. In H. Giles & R. St. Clair (Eds.), *Language and social psychology* (pp. 45–65). Oxford, UK: Blackwell.

Goffman, E. (1967). *Interaction ritual: Essays on face to face behavior.* Garden City, NY: Anchor.

Gonzalez, A., & Tanno, D. (Eds.). (2000). *Rhetoric in intercultural contexts.* Thousand Oaks, CA: Sage.

Gudykunst, W. B. (Ed.). (1983). *Intercultural communication theory.* Beverly Hills, CA: Sage.

Gudykunst, W. B. (1985a). A model of uncertainty reduction in intergroup encounters. *Journal of Language and Social Psychology, 4,* 79–98.

Gudykunst, W. B. (1985b). Normative power and conflict potential in intergroup relationships. In W. B. Gudykunst, L. P. Stewart, & S. Ting-Toomey (Eds.), *Communication, culture, and organizational processes* (pp. 155–176). Beverly Hills, CA: Sage.

Gudykunst, W. B. (1988). Uncertainty and anxiety. In Y. Y. Kim & W. B. Gudykunst (Eds.), *Theories of intercultural communication* (pp. 123–156). Newbury Park, CA: Sage.

Gudykunst, W. B. (1990). Diplomacy: A special case of intergroup communication. In F. Korzenny & S. Ting-Toomey (Eds.), *Communicating for peace* (pp. 19–39). Newbury Park, CA: Sage.

Gudykunst, W. B. (1993). Toward a theory of effective interpersonal and intergroup communication. In R. L. Wiseman & J. Koester (Eds.), *Intercultural communication competence* (pp. 33–71). Newbury Park, CA: Sage.

Gudykunst, W. B. (1995). Anxiety/uncertainty management (AUM) theory. In R. L. Wiseman (Ed.), *Intercultural communication theory* (pp. 8–58). Thousand Oaks, CA: Sage.

Gudykunst, W. B. (1998a). Applying anxiety/uncertainty management (AUM) theory to intercultural adjustment training. *International Journal of Intercultural Relations, 22,* 227–250.

Gudykunst, W. B. (1998b). *Bridging differences* (3rd ed.). Thousand Oaks, CA: Sage.

Gudykunst, W. B. (2002). Intercultural communication theories. In W. B. Gudykunst & B. Mody (Eds.), *Handbook of international and intercultural communication* (2nd ed., pp. 183–206). Thousand Oaks, CA: Sage.

Gudykunst, W. B., & Hammer, M. R. (1988). Strangers and hosts: An uncertainty reduction based theory of intercultural adaptation. In Y. Y. Kim & W. B. Gudykunst (Eds.), *Cross-cultural adaptation* (pp. 106–139). Newbury Park, CA: Sage.

Gudykunst, W. B., & Kim, Y. Y. (1997). *Communicating with strangers* (3rd ed.). New York: McGraw-Hill.

Gudykunst, W. B., & Lee, C. M. (2002). Cross-cultural communication theories. In W. B. Gudykunst & B. Mody (Eds.), *Handbook of international and intercultural communication* (2nd ed., pp. 25–50). Thousand Oaks, CA: Sage.

Gudykunst, W. B., & Nishida, T. (1989). Theoretical perspectives for studying intercultural communication. In M. K. Asante & W. B. Gudykunst (Eds.), *Handbook of international and intercultural communication* (pp. 17–46). Newbury Park, CA: Sage.

Gudykunst, W. B., & Nishida, T. (2001). Anxiety, uncertainty, and perceived effectiveness of communication across relationships and cultures. *International Journal of Intercultural Relations, 25,* 55–72.

Gudykunst, W. B., & Ting-Toomey, S. (1988). *Culture and inter-personal communication.* Newbury Park, CA: Sage.

Hall, E. T. (1976). *Beyond culture.* Garden City, NY: Doubleday.

Hammer, M. R., Wiseman, R. L., Rasmussen, J., & Bruschke, J. (1998). A test of uncertainty/anxiety reduction theory: The intercultural adaptation context. *Communication Quarterly, 46,* 309–326.

Hecht, M. L. (1993). 2002—A research odyssey toward the development of a communication theory of identity. *Communication Monographs, 60,* 76–82.

Hecht, M. L., Collier, M. J., & Ribeau, S. (1993). *African American communication: Ethnic identity and cultural interpretation.* Newbury Park, CA: Sage.

Hirokawa, R., & Rost, K. (1992). Effective group decision-making in organizations. *Management Communication Quarterly, 5,* 267–288.

Hofstede, G. (1980). *Culture's consequences.* Beverly Hills, CA: Sage.

Hofstede, G. (1991). *Cultures and organizations: Software of the mind.* London: McGraw-Hill.

Hofstede, G. (2001). *Culture's consequences* (2nd ed.). Thousand Oaks, CA: Sage.

Hofstede, G., & Bond, M. (1984). Hofstede's culture dimensions. *Journal of Cross-Cultural Psychology, 15,* 417–433.

Hong, Y. Y., Benet-Martinez, V., Chiu, C. Y., & Morris, M. (2003). Boundaries of cultural influence: Construct activation as a mechanism for cultural differences in perception. *Journal of Cross-Cultural Psychology, 34,* 453–464.

Ishii, S. (1984). *Enryo-sasshi* communication. *Cross Currents, 11,* 49–58.

Kelly, G. A. (1955). *The psychology of personal constructs* (2 vols.). New York: Norton.

Kim, M. S. (1993). Culture-based interactive constraints in explaining intercultural strategic competence. In R. L. Wiseman & J. Koester (Eds.), *Intercultural communication competence* (pp. 132–150). Thousand Oaks, CA: Sage.

Kim, M. S. (1995). Toward a theory of conversational constraints: Focusing on individual-level dimensions of culture. In R. L. Wiseman (Ed.), *Intercultural communication theory* (pp. 148–169). Thousand Oaks, CA: Sage.

Kim, M. S. (2002). *Non-Western perspectives on human communication.* Thousand Oaks, CA: Sage.

Kim, Y. Y. (1977). Communication patterns of foreign immigrants in the process of acculturation. *Human Communication Research, 4,* 66–77.

Kim, Y. Y. (1979). Toward an interactive theory of communication acculturation. In B. Ruben (Ed.), *Communication yearbook 3* (pp. 435–453). New Brunswick, NJ: Transaction Books.

Kim, Y. Y. (1986). Understanding the social structure of intergroup communication. In W. B. Gudykunst (Ed.), *Intergroup communication* (pp. 86–95). London: Edward Arnold.

Kim, Y. Y. (1988). *Communication and cross-cultural adaptation.* Clevendon, UK: Multilingual Matters.

Kim, Y. Y. (1995). Cross-cultural adaptation: An integrative theory. In R. L. Wiseman (Ed.), *Intercultural communication theory* (pp. 170–194). Thousand Oaks, CA: Sage.

Kim, Y. Y. (1997). The behavior-context interface in interethnic communication. In J. Owen (Ed.), *Context and human behavior* (pp. 261–291). Reno, NV: Context Press.

Kim, Y. Y. (2001). *Becoming intercultural: An integrative theory of communication and cross-cultural adaptation.* Thousand Oaks, CA: Sage.

Kim, Y. Y. (2004). *Interethnic communication.* Manuscript in preparation.

Kim, Y. Y., & Gudykunst, W. B. (Eds.). (1988). *Theories of intercultural communication.* Newbury Park, CA: Sage.

Kim, Y. Y., & Ruben, B. (1988). Intercultural transformations. In Y. Y. Kim & W. B. Gudykunst (Eds.), *Theories in intercultural communication* (pp. 299–322). Newbury Park, CA: Sage.

Kincaid, D. L. (1979). *The convergence model of communication.* Honolulu: East-West Communication Institute.

Kincaid, D. L. (1987a). *Communication theory from Eastern and Western perspectives.* New York: Praeger.

Kincaid, D. L. (1987b). The convergence theory of communication, self-organization, and cultural evolution. In D. L. Kincaid (Ed.), *Communication theory from Eastern and Western perspectives* (pp. 209–221). New York: Academic Press.

Kincaid, D. L. (1988). The convergence theory of intercultural communication. In Y. Y. Kim & W. B. Gudykunst (Eds.), *Theories of intercultural communication* (pp. 280–298). Newbury Park, CA: Sage.

Kramarae, C. (1981). *Women and men speaking.* Rowley, MA: Newbury House.

Langer, E. (1989). *Mindfulness.* Reading, MA: Addison-Wesley.

Lieberson, S. (1985). *Making it count: The improvement of social research and theory.* Berkeley: University of California Press.

Lim, T. S., & Choi, S. H. (1996). Interpersonal relationships in Korea. In W. B. Gudykunst, S. Ting-Toomey, & T. Nishida (Eds.), *Communication in personal relationships across cultures* (pp. 122–136). Thousand Oaks, CA: Sage.

Martin, J. N., & Nakayama, T. K. (1999). Thinking dialectically about culture and communication. *Communication Theory, 9,* 1–25.

McGuire, M., & McDermott, S. (1988). Communication in assimilation, deviance, and alienation states. In Y. Y. Kim & W. B. Gudykunst (Eds.), *Cross-cultural adaptation* (pp. 90–105). Newbury Park, CA: Sage.

Miike, Y. (2002). Theorizing culture and communication in the Asian context. *Intercultural Communication Studies, 11*(1), 1–22.

Miike, Y. (2003). Japanese *enryo-sasshi* communication and the psychology of *amae. Keio Communication Review, 25,* 93–115.

Miyahara, A. (1995). Meta-theoretical issues in the conceptualization of Japanese communication competence. *Keio Communication Review, 17,* 63–82.

Miyahara, A. (1999). Explaining cultural boundaries in communication studies: The case of Japanese interpersonal communication competence. *Keio Communication Review, 21,* 23–35.

Nishida, H. (1999). A cognitive approach to intercultural communication based on schema theory. *International Journal of Intercultural Relations, 23,* 753–777.

Nishida, T. (1977). An analysis of a cultural concept affecting Japanese communication. *Communication, 6,* 69–80.

Oetzel, J. G. (1995). Intercultural small groups: An effective decision-making theory. In R. L. Wiseman (Ed.), *Intercultural communication theory* (pp. 247–270). Thousand Oaks, CA: Sage.

Okabe, K. (1987). Indirect speech acts of the Japanese. In D. L. Kincaid (Ed.), *Communication theory from Eastern and Western perspectives* (pp. 126–136). New York: Academic Press.

Orbe, M. P. (1998a). *Constructing co-cultural theory.* Thousand Oaks, CA: Sage.

Orbe, M. P. (1998b). From the standpoint(s) of traditionally muted groups: Explicating a co-cultural communication theoretical model. *Communication Theory, 8,* 1–26.

Pearce, W. B., & Cronen, V. E. (1980). *Communication, action, and meaning: The creation of social realities.* New York: Praeger.

Philipsen, G. (1981). *The prospect for cultural communication.* Paper presented at the Seminar on Communication Theory from Eastern and Western Cultural Perspectives, Honolulu. (A revised version is published in D. L. Kincaid [Ed.], *Communication theory from Eastern and Western perspectives.* New York: Academic Press, 1987)

Philipsen, G. (1992). *Speaking culturally.* Albany: State University of New York Press.

Philipsen, G. (2002). Cultural communication. In W. B. Gudykunst & B. Mody (Eds.), *Handbook of international and intercultural communication* (2nd ed., pp. 51–68). Thousand Oaks, CA: Sage.

Reid, S., & Ng, S. H. (1999). Language, power, and intergroup relations. *Journal of Social Issues, 55*(1), 119–139.

Reynolds, P. (1971). *A primer in theory construction.* Indianapolis, IN: Bobbs-Merrill.

Rogers, E., & Kincaid, D. L. (1981). *Communication networks.* New York: Free Press.

Simmel, G. (1950). The stranger. In K. Wolff (Ed. & Trans.), *The sociology of Georg Simmel* (pp. 402–408). New York: Free Press. (Original work published 1908)

Smith, D. E. (1987). *The everyday world as problematic: A feminist sociology of knowledge.* Boston: Northeastern University Press.

Smith, L. R. (1999). Intercultural network theory. *International Journal of Intercultural Relations, 23*, 629–658.

Stephan, W. G., & Stephan, C. (1985). Intergroup anxiety. *Journal of Social Issues, 41*(3), 157–166.

Takai, J. (1994). *Taijin konpitensu kenkyu to bunkateki youin* [Cultural considerations in interpersonal communication competence research]. *Taijinkoudougeku Kenkyu* [Japanese Journal of Interpersonal Behavior], *12*, 1–10.

Takai, J. (1996). *Nihonjin no taijin conpitensu* [Japanese interpersonal competence]. In M. Osada (Ed.), *Taijin kankei no shakaishinrigaku* [Social psychology of interpersonal relations] (pp. 21–241). Tokyo: Fukumura Press.

Takai, J., & Ota, H. (1994). Assessing Japanese interpersonal competence. *The Japanese Journal of Experimental Social Psychology, 33*, 224–236 (in English).

Tezuka, C. (1992). *Awase* and *sunao* in Japanese communication and their implications for cross-cultural communication. *Keio Communication Review, 14*, 37–50.

Tezuka, C. (1993). *Amae kara mita Nihonjin no komyunikeshon to ibunka seshoku* [Communication among Japanese from the perspective of *amae* and its implications for intercultural encounters]. *Ibunka Komyunikeshon Kenkyu* [Intercultural Communication Studies], *6*, 21–44.

Ting-Toomey, S. (1985). Toward a theory of conflict and culture. In W. B. Gudykunst, L. Stewart, & S. Ting-Toomey (Eds.), *Communication, culture, and organizational processes* (pp. 71–86). Beverly Hills, CA: Sage.

Ting-Toomey, S. (1988). Intercultural conflict styles: A face-negotiation theory. In Y. Y. Kim & W. B. Gudykunst (Eds.), *Theories in intercultural communication* (pp. 213–238). Newbury Park, CA: Sage.

Ting-Toomey, S. (1993). Communicative resourcefulness: An identity negotiation theory. In R. L. Wiseman & J. Koester (Eds.), *Intercultural communication competence* (pp. 72–111). Newbury Park, CA: Sage.

Ting-Toomey, S., & Kurogi, A. (1998). Facework competence in intercultural conflict: An updated face-negotiation theory. *International Journal of Intercultural Relations, 22*, 187–225.

Triandis, H. C. (1995). *Individualism & collectivism*. Boulder, CO: Westview.

Tsujimura, A. (1987). Some characteristics of the Japanese way of communication. In D. L. Kincaid (Ed.), *Communication theory from Eastern and Western perspectives* (pp. 115–125). New York: Academic Press.

Walker, H., & Cohen, B. (1985). Scope statements: Imperatives for evaluating theories. *American Sociological Review, 50*, 288–301.

Wiseman, R. L. (Ed.). (1995). *Intercultural communication theory*. Thousand Oaks, CA: Sage.

Wiseman, R. L., & Koester, J. (Eds.). (1993). *Intercultural communication competence*. Thousand Oaks, CA: Sage.

Witte, K. (1993). A theory of cognition and negative affect: Extending Gudykunst and Hammer's theory of uncertainty and anxiety reduction. *International Journal of Intercultural Relations, 17*, 197–216.

Yum, J. O. (1988a). The impact of Confucianism on interpersonal relationships and communication. *Communication Monographs, 55*, 374–388.

Yum, J. O (1988b). Network theory in intercultural communication. In Y. Y. Kim & W. B. Gudykunst (Eds.), *Theories in intercultural communication* (pp. 239–258). Newbury Park, CA: Sage.

PART II

Theories of Communication Incorporating Culture

2

The Coordinated Management of Meaning (CMM)

W. BARNETT PEARCE

In one way of telling the story, formal study and teaching about communication began in Sicily in the middle of the fifth century B.C.E.[1] The Tyrant (the term had not yet acquired its pejorative connotations) had been overthrown and the victors had to sort out conflicting claims about who owned parcels of land. To their credit, they decided to resolve their differences through talk rather than (continued) violence. As they set up courts to adjudicate the issues, an unintended consequence of some importance occurred: They found that some forms of talk were more persuasive than others and that some people were more skilled than others in these forms of talk. Some skilled persuaders became arguers-for-hire and/or speech coaches; some of these began to study what differentiates good from bad argument; and the art of persuasion became an important thread throughout the development of Western culture.

In the subsequent 2,500 years, social and political changes have often challenged the efficacy or desirability of existing patterns of communication. Sometimes the barbarians have won. Instead of institutionalizing more productive forms of communication (as did the citizens of Sicily), society has fallen back on less sophisticated, more brutal patterns of interaction. At other times, powerful new ways of thinking and acting have been developed, such as persuasion rather than force as a means of governance in ancient Greece and argument based on empirical evidence rather than on authority or analogy in Enlightenment Europe (Toulmin, 1990).

I am far from the only person who believes that the current situation (variously described as globalization, postmodernity, late modernity, or simply post-9/11[2]) challenge the efficacy and desirability of patterns of communication that sufficed when most people could live without confronting the fact that their own culture is one among many and without having to engage in interaction with those whose taken-for-granted truths, values, and ways of doing things are not like ours. Berger (2001) described the challenge facing all of us in this way:

> The process of modernization, which by now has fundamentally affected virtually every society on earth, has as one of its most important consequences the situation commonly called pluralism. The term means quite simply that people with very different beliefs, values, and lifestyles come to live together in close proximity, are forced to interact with each other, and therefore are faced with the alternative of either clashing in conflict or somehow accommodating each other's differences.

. . .

> Put simply, pluralism *relativizes*. What in an earlier time was a belief held with absolute conviction now becomes an opinion or a matter of taste. . . . This relativization is often experienced at first as a great liberation; after a while it may come to be felt as a great burden. There appears then a nostalgia, a yearning for the comforting certainties of the past. Pluralism, the erstwhile liberator, now becomes an enemy, the "great satan" who must be fought in the name of timeless truths. This social-psychological process unleashes a curious dialectic between relativism and fanaticism. . . . Every fanaticism is vulnerable to relativization, just as every relativism may be cut short by this or that "Damascus experience."
>
> While these two positions are psychological and sociological opposites, they share an important cognitive assumption: Both the relativist and the fanatic believe that there can be no reasonable communication between different worldviews, no worthwhile search for mutually acceptable criteria of truth by which the differences could be discussed. Given that assumption, there is no middle ground between challenging nothing that those others are saying and hitting them over the head until they surrender or disappear. (pp. xi-xii)

Just as the citizens of ancient Sicily avoided continued warfare by developing the arts and habits of persuasion and institutionalizing them into their culture, we are challenged to develop and valorize ways of communicating that transcend the apparent dichotomy between ignoring the Others and hitting them over the head until they surrender or disappear. If we fail to meet this challenge, the barbarians will win again, with more sophisticated social techniques for isolating and oppressing the Others or technical techniques for breaking things and people. Despite their prominence in the headlines, the victory of the barbarians is not inevitable. Berger (2001) notes,

> ordinary experience shows that this assumption of non-communication does not hold universally. There have been many cases in which there has been meaningful communication between people with widely differing beliefs and values, as a result of which a middle ground was indeed established so that the several groups could co-exist amicably without either open conflict or giving up everything in their cherished tradition. . . . The success has very rarely been the result of negotiations between theologians or other accredited theorists. The cognitive and moral compromises have rather been hammered out over lunchbreak conversations between fellow-workers, over backyard fences by neighboring housewives, or by parents coming in contact because of shared concerns for their children's schools or recreational activities. (p. xiii)

One of the most exciting aspects of the current, wonderfully chaotic period is the unprecedented attention given by practitioners to finding ways of communicating better. Examples include what some call "track 2" or person-to-person diplomacy, interethnic and interfaith dialogue groups seeking to find ways of living together amicably in support of, or despite, the efforts of their political leaders; the alternative dispute resolution movement that has experimented with and found ways of institutionalizing nonadversarial ways of dealing with conflict; and nations carrying the burdens of civil war who have turned to truth and reconciliation rather than retribution as ways of moving forward together. I think Berger is, with significant exceptions, right about scholars following rather than leading these developments, but, just as the citizens of ancient Sicily discovered, there are important roles to be played by scholarly contemplation; theoretical formulation; and effective teaching of ideas, values, and skills.

"If I had all my druthers" (a phrase from my culture-of-origin), the theory of the coordinated management of meaning (CMM) would be seen as a scholarly response to these unsettled times and a valuable resource for understanding, describing, and facilitating the development of the new forms of communication called for by the challenges of contemporary society.

Vernon Cronen and I were the initial developers of the theory, and we began working on CMM during the middle 1970s. The social and political upheavals in the United States associated with the civil rights movement, the war in Vietnam, and an unprecedented series of assassinations of progressive leaders, were raising questions for all of us about our culture, social institutions, personal freedoms, and the range of ways in which we might legitimately engage in the pursuit of happiness. The decade of the 1970s was also a time of metatheoretical ferment within the discipline increasingly being called "communication." The half-century imbroglio between "rhetoric" and "speech" was being set aside by new developments in "communication" (Pearce, 1985) and the generation of theorists who are now full professors or professors emeritus were young turks, excitedly exploring the implications of laws, rules, and systems as alternative frameworks for their theories (Pearce & Benson, 1977).

CMM began as an interpretive theory primarily focused on interpersonal communication, developed a critical edge in work in a wide range of communication settings, and

has now morphed into a practical theory that collaborates with practitioners to improve the patterns of communication that it describes and critiques (Barge, 2001; Cronen, 2001; Pearce & Pearce, 2000). In this chapter, I'll use these three phases in the development of CMM as a means to describe it and ground the discussion in two communication events that illustrate the challenges Berger described.

A MEETING BETWEEN CENTRAL AND NORTH AMERICANS

Before dawn on November 16, 1989, soldiers in the army of El Salvador crossed the street from their base and entered the campus of the University of Central America (UCA). They broke into the Jesuit residence and murdered six professors and administrators, their housekeeper, and her daughter. The bodies were left lying on the lawn of the campus as a blatant statement of the fate awaiting those who sympathized with rebel forces. In 1991, the officers who ordered the murders (but not the soldiers who carried them out) were found guilty; peace accords between the government and rebels were signed in 1992. With the reduction in violence, Loyola University Chicago (LUC) explored ways in which it might help its sister-Jesuit university recover from 10 years of civil war. I was one of three department chairs sent to El Salvador to participate in the commemoration of the murders—in a midnight mass held on the site where the bodies were found—and to work with our counterparts at UCA.

All of us in the Loyola group appreciated the cultural differences between academics in the United States and in El Salvador and were particularly sensitive to the possibility of reproducing patterns of cultural imperialism. In a planning session before our first meeting, we reminded ourselves that Central Americans have a different sense of time than North Americans. Wanting to respect our hosts' culture, we agreed that the first meeting would have no agenda; we would concentrate on building relationships rather than discussing specific decisions. When we met our colleagues from UCA, we North Americans were relaxed, prepared to enjoy good Salvadoran coffee with our new friends, and to end the meeting without substantive discussions.

To our surprise, the Salvadorans had barely greeted us before they began to discuss the agenda for our meetings and to make specific proposals for collaboration. It took only a couple of minutes for us to realize that the Salvadorans had had a planning session similar to ours in which they took into account the differences between North and Central American cultures and decided to accommodate to the visitors' cultural predispositions. With a lot of laughter and goodwill, each group confessed their strategy to the other. Our meetings were reciprocally respectful and productive, and we were able to bring into our discourse our preferences for the pace of the meetings and the needs of both sides to maintain their agency independent of the other.

TWO MORALITIES OF TERRORISM

On February 26, 1993, a bomb exploded beneath the World Trade Center in New York. Six people were killed and more than 1,000 injured. Five years later, a jury in New York City found Ramzi Ahmed Yousef guilty of the bombing. As customary in American criminal courts, he was asked if he wanted to make a statement before being sentenced. This is an occasion in which the person convicted often expresses remorse for the crimes or explains circumstances that might affect the severity of the sentence. In this case, however, Yousef defiantly explained that in his worldview, he had acted honorably. He said,

> You keep talking also about collective punishment and killing innocent people to force governments to change their policies; you call this terrorism when someone would kill innocent people or civilians in order to force the government to change its policies. Well, you were the first one who invented this terrorism.

> You were the first one who killed innocent people, and you are the first one who introduced this type of terrorism to the history of mankind when you dropped an atomic bomb which killed tens of thousands of women and children in Japan and when you killed over a hundred thousand people, most of them civilians, in Tokyo with fire bombings. You killed them by burning them to death. And you killed civilians in Vietnam with chemicals as with the so-called Orange agent. You killed civilians and innocent people, not soldiers, innocent people every single war you went. You went to wars more than any other country in this century, and then you have the nerve to talk about killing innocent people.

> And now you have invented new ways to kill innocent people. You have so-called economic embargo which kills nobody other than children and elderly people, and which other than Iraq you have been placing the economic embargo on Cuba and other countries for over 35 years. . .

> The government in its summations and opening said that I was a terrorist. Yes, I am a terrorist and I am proud of it. And I support terrorism so long as it was against the United States Government and against Israel, because you are more than terrorists; you are the one who invented terrorism and using it every day. You are butchers, liars and hypocrites. (Wanniski, 2001).

Immediately after this statement, Judge Kevin Duffy sentenced Yousef to 240 years in prison. He went beyond the requirements of his role by recommending that the sentence be served in solitary confinement, imposing a fine of $4.5 million, and ordering Yousef to provide $250 million in restitution. In explaining the recommendation for solitary confinement, Duffy said, "Your treatment is like a person who has a virus that could communicate plague around the world." He explained that he added the fines and demand for restitution because someone might be "perverse enough" to buy the 29-year-old terrorist's story and he didn't want Yousef to profit from it. Duffy then denounced the defendant, quoting from the Koran to accuse Yousef of betraying the humanitarian principles of his own faith. He said,

> You adored not Allah, but the evil you had become. I must say as an apostle of evil, you have been most effective. You had planned to topple one of the twin towers onto the other. If your plan had been successful, you would have killed a quarter of a million people. Your god is not Allah. Your god is death. (*San Francisco Chronicle*, January 9, 1998, p. A2)

SOME REFLECTIONS ON THESE COMMUNICATION EVENTS

In both situations, the people involved acted according to the communication patterns of their culture. Each of us as individuals develops habitual or characteristic patterns of interacting with others; these personal consistencies are a large part of what we call "personality." In addition, those who study family and organizational communication have noted that these systems have their own "cultures." To be a "native" in your family, school, or workplace is to have learned to act with sufficient coordination within these patterns. In addition, there are cultural patterns—Gerry Philipsen (1997) calls them "speech codes"—that constitute talking like a member of a culture.

When my colleagues and I went to El Salvador, both our Salvadoran counterparts and we were aware that our "speech codes" differed and would cause us problems if both they and we simply followed them. Because we all were aware of what was going on, and were all committed to making the meeting work, we made patterns of adjustments to each other that allowed us to communicate successfully.

The conversation between Yousef and Duffy in the New York courthouse was not so successful. Those of us with an ear for such things noted at the time that they talked past each other. More specifically, each made a

virtue of remaining within his cultural values, beliefs, and manners of expression. Neither felt that the other understood him; both felt that they had acted virtuously; and both felt that the other was a terrorist. And, tragically, we know that the issue was not resolved in the courthouse that day. Eight years later, 18 equally dedicated men succeeded in doing to the World Trade Center (and the Pentagon) what Yousef had attempted—and most Americans were surprised and, although Yousef had explained it clearly, did not understand why so many people hated us so much.

CMM AS INTERPRETIVE THEORY

When Vern Cronen and I began working on CMM, we didn't know how the communication theory we were developing could be used to engage the social issues of our times, but we were convinced that it would. We were initially concerned with the questions, "What are people doing when they communicate the way that they do?" and "Why did they do that?" The first question located us squarely in the scholarly tradition of those who look at communication as performative (i.e., what people *do* by what they say) rather than (at least primarily) referential (i.e., what are people *talking about*). More specifically, it located us in the Wittgensteinian version of this tradition (see chap. 3, "Speech Acts," in Pearce, 1994), although we didn't yet know it.

The second question, why did they do that, has most often been answered within the vocabularies of cognitive states or personality traits. However, since we take communication as performative, as something with characteristics in itself rather than just an expression of or reference to other things, we developed a number of concepts tied more closely to the communication event itself.

One such concept is the notion of multiple levels of embedded contexts, or the "hierarchy model of actor's meanings." This model starts with the familiar notion that meaning is dependent on the context in which it occurs, but adds the idea that communication acts are always in multiple contexts. While there may be any number of stories and these may be in any pattern, we almost always find stories of personal identity; of relationships among the people involved in the communication event; of the episode itself; and of the institutions, organizations or cultures involved.

As shown in Table 2.1, I interpret Yousef's actions, both in carrying out the bombing and denouncing the United States in the courtroom, knowing that it would result in a harsher sentence, in the context of four asymmetrically embedded stories. His declaration, "I am a terrorist and I am proud of it," seems to name his story of himself as the highest/most inclusive context, but, in my interpretation, that statement in that place and time is in the context of his "culture" and perception of the "episode." I'm using the term *culture* in a nontechnical way to index his view of the world, of what is right and wrong, of honor and duty, and of appropriate ways of acting out of and into situations. While Yousef's public actions and statements don't describe them very fully, I'm struck by how much his actions are grounded on these untold stories. Most of what he says describes what I call the "episode," the sequence of events that has a beginning, a plot or narrative development, and an end. Yousef insists that his actions are an honorable response to atrocities initiated by the United States. Within these contexts of culture and episode, Yousef's concept of self is, to use a phrase from literary criticism, overly determined. How could he have acted otherwise? In Table 2.1 I've placed the story of relationship with others as the lowest or least inclusive. By "others," I mean the victims of his terrorist acts. Yousef may or may not regret killing and injuring innocent people and have compassion for their families and friends. Either way, it was not enough to change his actions, and that's why I placed it where I did in my interpretation.

My interpretation of Duffy, also shown in Table 2.1, shows an identical structure in the pattern of embedded contexts, although with very different content of the stories that comprise each level. Like Yousef, Duffy acted out of a largely unarticulated matrix of values, assumptions, morals, and sense of appropriate actions. Within this "culture," the "episode" is a highly structured one with rituals, roles, and prescribed behaviors: a criminal trial in a courtroom. I call this the "episode" because the trial had gone through a long series of turns (indictment, prosecution's case, defense case, deliberations, verdict) and now was in the sentencing phase with appeals yet to come. In this episode, Duffy was both highly constrained and empowered by his role. From the text, it is clear that he had contempt for Yousef, but his role as judge dictates that whatever his feelings, they should be subservient to the rule of law. He was not free to lead a lynch mob, for example. But he did skate close to the line: by quoting the Koran (rather than the laws of the state) and lecturing Yousef about Islam, he blurred the nature of his role and of the episode.

Because actions are meaningful in contexts, the interpretive process of describing the embedded contexts helps answer the question, "What did they do?" To address the subsequent question, "Why did they do that?" we used the philosophical concept of "deontic logic." This is a logical system that uses terms of "oughtness" to act rather than the verb "to be." That is, rather than starting with the premise that "all men *are* mortal," deontic reasoning might start with the premise, "I *should not* kill innocent people." As we employ the concept in CMM, it is a way of expressing the extent to which all of us, when interacting with each other, feel that we must/should/may/must not respond in certain ways.

With this as a lens for reading what Yousef and Duffy said, note how prominent the "imperatives"—must/must not—were in their

Table 2.1   My Interpretation of Yousef's and Duffy's Hierarchy of Meanings

Yousef:

Culture:

Largely unarticulated; powerful sense of morality and duty grounded in a story of oppressive international relations

Episode:

The United States is the first and most prominent terrorist and hypocritically accuses others of being terrorists

Self:

"I am a terrorist and proud of it" so long as it is against the oppressors, the United States and Israel

Relationship:

(to victims): untold story
(to the U.S.): opposing "butchers, liars, hypocrites"

Duffy:

Culture:

Largely unarticulated; powerful sense of morality grounded in the rule of law and humanistic ethics

Episode:

The "sentencing phase" of a legally prescribed and carefully followed criminal trial procedure

Self:

I am the judge; an officer of the court; the spokesperson for justice

Relationship:

Perceived Yousef as "evil," carrying a plague-causing virus, betraying his own religious principles

NOTE: Stories positioned lower in the model are said to be embedded in, and derive their meaning from, stories positioned higher in the model.

accounts of their actions. This contrasts sharply with the less categorical "mays" and "shoulds" and "mights" in the meeting between representatives from LUC and UCA. In addition, note that Duffy and Yousef primarily justify their actions by referring to atrocities committed by the other. That is, whatever they are doing—planting a bomb or sentencing a terrorist—it is the other person's fault: "You made me do it!"

In an attempt to distinguish among forms of motivation, CMM has developed some technical language. Both Duffy and Yousef, we would say, are acting because of contextual and prefigurative forces (i.e., what the existing contexts were and what the other person did in those contexts) rather than because of practical or implicative forces (i.e., what contexts they wanted to call into being or what they wanted the other to do—or not do—subsequently). Neither seemed particularly thoughtful about the consequences of their actions. Would destroying the World Trade Center lead to a cessation of economic embargoes on Iraq and Cuba? Would it stop the oppression of Palestinians? Would sentencing Yousef to solitary confinement in prison and muting him by creating an economic barrier to any profits

Table 2.2　My Interpretation of the Hierarchy of Meanings in the Delegations From UCA and LUC

The delegation from Loyola University Chicago

Episode:

Explore ways to assist UCA recovery from the war while avoiding cultural imperialism

Relationship:

Respect, collaboration

Self:

Thoughtful, sensitive, capable of choosing how to act

Culture:

Aware of speech codes of task-oriented behavior in meetings; great emphasis on punctuality and efficiency

The delegation from University of Central America

Episode:

Explore ways in which collaboration with LUC might assist recovery from the war

Relationship:

Initially cautious

Self:

Thoughtful, sensitive, capable of choosing how to act

Culture:

Aware of speech codes of relationally oriented behavior in meetings; little emphasis on punctuality or efficiency

NOTE: Stories positioned lower in the model are said to be embedded in, and derive their meaning from, stories positioned higher in the model.

resulting from telling his story protect the World Trade Center from subsequent attacks or reduce the fervor of militant anti-Westerners around the world? There is nothing in these stories that indicates that these questions had any part in these men's decisions to act as they did.

My interpretation of the meeting between department chairs from UCA and LUC is shown in Table 2.2. In many ways, this communication situation was easier than Yousef's trial, but had either or both sides determinedly stuck to an enactment of their own culturally appropriate ways of acting, it could have turned out badly. As in my analysis of Yousef and Duffy, I think that both groups had

similar patterns in their hierarchies of meanings, but unlike Yousef and Duffy they also had similar stories within each level of context.

The placement of "culture" is the most striking difference between my analyses of the two situations. Here, I've placed culture as the least inclusive or "lowest" level, deriving its meaning from being contextualized by episode, relationships, and self-concept. In fact, awareness of culturally appropriate patterns of interaction was included in the discourse—this is part of what is meant by the term *coordinated management of meaning* that has become the name of this theory.

Another difference from the courtroom confrontation is that the participants explain their behavior by referring to their intentions to call into being something in the future. In CMM's technical language, the strongest aspects of logical force were practical (intending to elicit specific responses from the other) and implicative (intending to create specific contexts, such as the episode) forces. We've found that when these aspects of deontic logical force predominate over prefigurative and contextual, communicators seem freer to respond to each other and to the immediate situation rather than to follow predetermined scripts, and have more success in finding ways of moving forward together with those who are not like them.

CMM'S CRITICAL EDGE

The primary question in CMM-ish criticism is, "What are they making together?" That is, what kind of identities, episodes, relationships, and cultures are being constructed by the patterns of communication put together as people interact with each other?

Start with the plural pronoun *they* and the modifier *together*. CMM envisions communication acts as doing things (i.e., as performatives) and thus as making the events and objects in our social world. However, communicative acts cannot be done alone. Each act is done *to*, *for*, or *against* someone. Further, what is done is usually *after* and *before* what others do. The events and objects of the social world are not only made in communication, the process is one of co-construction, of being made by the conjoint action of multiple persons.

CMM's serpentine model, shown in Figure 2.1, is designed to call attention to the to- and fro-ness of the process of communication, and to the way it unfolds over time. When we use this model, we begin by describing the communicative acts in the sequence in which they occurred; for example, from left to right on a large sheet of paper. The second step is to use the hierarchy model for each act as a way of understanding what is being done as it

is perceived, first, by the person performing the act and, second, by the person who interprets and responds to it. We often put the hierarchy model for one person above and for the other person below the horizontally arranged sequence of communicative acts. A serpentine movement, from which this model gets its name, is produced by moving up and down from the meanings of the person producing the first act to the meanings of the person responding (the second act), and from left to right through the sequence of acts.

This serpentine path displays the interaction between two or more persons. Two things happen as you follow this to-and-fro movement. First, the force of the deontic logic (the sense of what you "ought" to do) shifts from intrapersonal to interpersonal. That is, the reason why a person in, for example, the fifth turn in a conversation says or does what she does is not only a function of her embedded contexts but also what the other person did and how that intermeshes with her own meanings. After doing this analysis a number of times, I've lost my appetite for judging individuals alone for what they've done; instead, I want to know what happened before the act in question (perhaps the immediately previous act or something a long time in the past) and after they did what they did. This is not a moral relativism; it is a move from an individualist ethic that evaluates specific acts to a social, systemic ethic that focuses on taking responsibility within a dynamic pattern. This social, systemic ethic is far from adequately worked out, but it is clear that the LUC/UCA personnel were working within it while Duffy and Yousef were not.

Second, the serpentine model positions the critic to address issues of which the participants may be unaware. If we were to look only at Yousef's story, we would get a picture of heroism; his statement of being proud to be a terrorist might inspire us in the same way as do Nathan Hale's last words—"I only regret that I have but one life to give for my

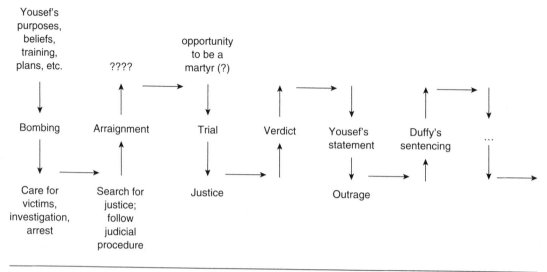

Figure 2.1   An Example of the Serpentine Model, Using the Communication Event Between Yousef and Duffy as an Example

country"—before being hanged for spying and becoming the first martyr for the American revolution. A similar story might be told of Judge Duffy, heroically stemming the tide of foreign terrorism. But the critic using the serpentine model sees both stories simultaneously as well as the way these stories interact and coevolve. From this perspective, the question, "What are they making together?" might be answered like this: Duffy and Yousef were making more terrorists, more Americans who don't understand why "they" hate us, more acts of terrorism, and more victims. In short, more of the same.

Shifting the scene from a New York courthouse to the streets of Gaza, the way conflicts like this "make" more terrorists was described by Israeli Brigadier General Ya'acov "Mendy" Orr. He tells this story from his time as a division commander in the Gaza Strip during the *intifada*:

I was walking down a street and I saw this little boy—I think he was a boy—he wasn't much more than one year old. He had just learned to walk. He had a stone in his hand. He could barely hold on to it, but he was walking around with a stone to throw at someone. I looked at him and he looked at me, and I smiled and he dropped the stone. I think it was probably too heavy for him. I'm telling you, he had just learned to walk. I went home and he went home. I thought about it later, and I thought, For that little kid, anger is a part of his life, a part of growing up—as much as talking or eating. He still didn't know exactly against whom he was angry; he was too young for that. He will know after a while. But for now, he knew he was supposed to be angry. He knew he was supposed to throw a stone at someone. . . . He had just learned to walk. (quoted by Friedman, 1990, p. 374)

According to some of those involved in it, the Palestinian *intifada* began as an incoherent expression of anger and only later became a sophisticated strategy for liberation (Friedman, 1990, pp. 373–374). But however started, the *intifada* became the social world into which a new generation was born and in which identities, motives, and habits were formed. Friedman (1990) interpreted General Orr's story as evidence of "just how deep and pervasive was the anger that had burst spontaneously from inside Palestinians" (p. 374).

Another way of understanding it, closer to the narrative itself, is as a description of how the continuing hatred and conflict is made. The conflict may be seen as a factory, mass producing a next generation ready to take their turns as fighters. As General Orr noted, this little boy will soon learn at whom to direct his anger as well as how and when to show his anger. He will develop rich stories about himself, the relationship between the Palestinians and Israelis, and the sequence of events that led to his being who and where and what he is. Someday he, like Yousef, might proudly claim to be a terrorist.

The study of the interactions between the New Religious Right in American politics and those they call "secular humanists" is the largest and most sustained project of critical research in the CMM tradition. In addition to seeking to understand each groups' social worlds and describing the pattern of their interaction, we evaluated these interactions. For example, despite the stories told about "tolerance" and "civility," we found that neither worldview contains sufficient resources to understand and communicate productively with the other, hence we deemed the quest for civility "quixotic" (Pearce, Littlejohn, & Alexander, 1987). In our book, *Moral Conflict: When Social Worlds Collide* (Pearce & Littlejohn, 1997), Stephen and I generalized from this and other research to the observation that there exists a category of conflicts in which the cultural resources of the participants differ so much that neither provides a sufficient guide for how to resolve the conflict. In these conflicts between incommensurate social worlds, a minimal requirement of satisfactory performance includes an awareness of one's own cultural resources, a willingness to move beyond them, and the ability to find ways of cooperatively dealing with the conflict that transcend the social worlds of the participants.

With this generalization in mind, I am distressed by conflicts in which the participants employ strategies of "more of the same" in attempts to "win," with the result of perpetuating and escalating the conflict. Based on CMM analyses, I am critical when people involved in unsatisfactory patterns of interaction only blame the other without sharing the responsibility for what they are making and/or when their stories about what they are making are narrow and shortsighted. CMM is grounded in pragmatism, however, not only by its interest in what people actually say and do (rather than abstractions such as attitudes, power, values, etc.), but also in its spirit of wanting to do something constructive in the social worlds that it interprets and critiques.

Since 1980, I've had the opportunity to work as a communication theorist and researcher with professionals who improve patterns of communication. These include therapists, mediators, national economic development officials, organizational consultants, and large-group facilitators. We've explored several ways in which their practice and my theoretical contributions could be mutually beneficial. I began in an observer's position, literally behind one-way mirrors watching therapists and mediators at work. Later, my relationship with practitioners became more symmetrical as they learned more about CMM and I learned more about their practice. In recent years, I've integrated the roles of practice and theorist in my work with Pearce Associates and the Public Dialogue Consortium. My shift in these roles has paralleled the evolution of CMM as a practical theory.

CMM AS A PRACTICAL THEORY

The primary purpose of a practical theory is to join with the people in various systems and situations to articulate the knowledge needed to act constructively. This purpose stands in marked contrast to that of developing propositions describing situations or the relationships among variables (Cronen, 2001, p. 14). The orienting question for CMM as a practical theory is, "How can we make better social worlds?"

Having done quite a few interpretive and critical studies, I'm struck by how complex even mundane instances of communication are, and how what communicators actually say and do underrepresents this complexity. One way of making better social worlds is to help people enrich the communication patterns of which they are a part and to intervene so that the participants see previously obscured possibilities.

For example, some CMM-ers and some therapists were working with family violence. The perpetrators repeatedly said something to the effect, "I had to hit him [her]! In a situation like that, a person like me has no choice! I had to do it!" You'll recognize this as a description of a powerful deontic logical force, heavily weighted toward contextual and prefigurative forces, and naming the episode ("situation") and self as levels of embedded contexts.

We chose to treat statements like these as honest descriptions of persons' social worlds from a first-person, insider's perspective. But from our third-person, observer's perspective, it was clear that the perpetrator had many other options. The practitioner's task was to help the perpetrator discover that there are other options and learn how to select them. My colleague Peter Lang developed the technique of asking questions like these: "Why didn't you go ahead and kill her?" In the case I observed, the husband recoiled and said, "I'd never do that! I love my wife!" "Ah," Peter replied, "then how did you decide how hard to hit her? Would it have been alright if you had just broken her arm?" "No!" And so on. Peter's purpose was to help the abusive husband discover that he was in fact making choices while telling himself that he was out of control. Once the husband's decision-making process was brought into the conversation, Peter could follow up with a line of interviewing focusing on other options. The role of the practical theorist is to help develop a vocabulary for describing situations like this that can be used by other practitioners in other cases. Many of the models in CMM have this function.

The hierarchy model suggests a variety of places for intervention. I was struck by the questions not asked and the statements not made in the interaction between Yousef and Duffy. I'm convinced that Duffy was constrained by the "episode" of the criminal court. But what if they had been in a different context? One of the things that the Public Dialogue Consortium does best is to design meetings that facilitate forms of communication that don't often occur in public places. What might have happened if, under the patient guidance of a facilitator, the "episode" had been redefined so that Duffy could have responded to Yousef's denunciation of the United States something like this: "You know, you're right about some things. For a peace-loving nation, we have been in a lot of wars and we've done some pretty horrible things in those wars. And the economic embargoes do hurt innocent people. But we live in a dangerous world and there are nations who seek to harm us, just as you did. So, from your perspective, how might the United States guarantee its security without doing harm to others?" No one can tell how a conversation like this might turn out, but (using the serpentine model as a guide) it would certainly have created a different interpersonal logic of action. It is at least possible that Yousef might have made a suggestion more articulate than a bomb, and that suggestion just might have trickled up to appropriate decision makers, leading to changes that would have reduced the number of bombs that have been exploded since Yousef had his day in court.

The daisy model, shown in Figure 2.2, is another CMM tool for exploring the richness of a communication situation. This model is designed to remind us of the multiple conversations that are occurring in each moment. The exchange between Duffy and Yousef was not just between two people; it was a specific "turn" in many conversations, including some with people who were not in the courthouse. As a practitioner, you might use this model by

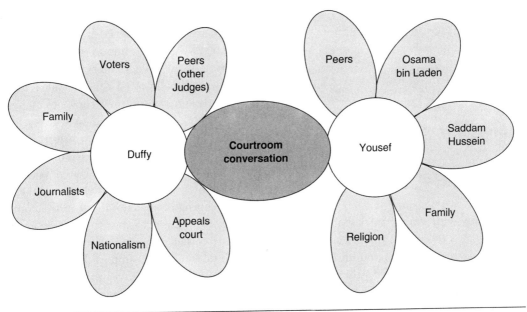

Figure 2.2   An Analysis of the Conversation Between Judge Duffy and Convicted Terrorist Yousef Using CMM's Daisy Model

putting Duffy and Yousef's conversation in the middle of the model and begin to trace out some of the other conversations of which it is a part. One petal on the daisy model might be a conversation including Osama bin Laden. To what extent was the exchange between Duffy and Yousef a "turn" in longer conversations that led to the plans that destroyed the World Trade Center 3½ years later? Was Yousef really the intended audience for Duffy's remarks? Or was he speaking to Yousef but, more important, in front of his family members, other judges, and perhaps the voters in the next election for his office? And to whom was Yousef really speaking? Was he using this opportunity to speak through the media to the girl he left behind, to other young men and women who might rally to his call to oppose the United States' hypocrisy and terrorism, or to Saddam Hussein, who provided financial compensation to the families of martyrs? As you foreground each of these conversations, the meaning of what is said differs, as well as the deontic logical force that explains why they said it.

Another CMM model, called LUUUTT (see Figure 2.3) as an acronym of its components, also helps practitioners enrich specific instances of communication (Pearce & Pearce, 1998). The components are stories Lived, Untold stories, Unheard stories, Unknown stories, stories Told, and storyTelling.

If we take the role of a practitioner seeking to enrich the conversation through the LUUUTT model, we might begin with the two T's: stories Told and the manner of storyTelling. In the UCA/LUC meeting, the participants told stories that included cultural differences and a readiness to adapt to the other culture, and, as it turned out, to adapt again to the specific form that the interaction took in the first encounter. In the confrontation between Yousef and Duffy, the participants told stories that had no provisions for uncertainty or alternative perspectives, and they told these stories in an accusatory manner. As a practitioner, I'd applaud the UCA/LUC participants but feel that Duffy and Yousef present a real challenge.

The accusatory mode of storytelling often leads to an escalation of the loudness and

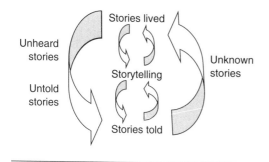

Figure 2.3 The LUUUTT Model

dogmatism with which stories are told; an unwillingness to express one's doubts, reservations, or uncertainties; and an inability to hear nuances in what the other says (e.g., "unheard stories"). Knowing this, mediators or facilitators will often intervene by interrupting; asking the participants to clarify what they are saying; and following up with questions about their uncertainties, perceptions of the other, or persons/situations not included in the talk that has just gone on. By doing this, mediators and facilitators slow things down, change the interpersonal deontic logical force that is driving the exchange, relieve the participants of the obligation to respond immediately to the Other, invite hearing previously unheard stories and telling previously untold stories, and provide a model of listening to and questioning rather than denouncing the Other. All of this is an attempt to change the mode of storytelling to one that has more opportunities for good things to happen.

In my description of the two events, I named some of the untold, unheard, and unknown stories. After doing a LUUUTT analysis, a practitioner should have some ideas about where to start to enrich the communication. For example, the elephant-sized untold story in the LUC/UCA meeting was that the United States overtly supported the Salvadoran military government with money, arms, and training during 10 years of bitter warfare against its own citizens and routinely turned a

blind eye to the government's violations of human rights. At least I felt guilty as I met former FMLN (Farabundo Marti National Liberation) guerrilla fighters and UCA staff who bravely supported the guerrillas' legitimate grievances if not their choice of tactics. I was surprised to be greeted so warmly, particularly during a trip we took behind FMLN lines. Belatedly, I realized that the only Americans these people had seen were like our Loyola colleague (not invited to make this trip) who had inserted himself in the combat zone on several occasions to help the guerrillas. They had not seen that portion of the $100 billion in U.S. support during the 1980s that came from my taxes that purchased the bullets and bombs used against them. So I was carrying around a tremendous amount of guilt that was never expressed. I never found out whether the UCA department chairs with whom we met were supporters of the government or the guerrillas. Had our conversation included this untold story, it would have changed the pattern of our interaction in ways that can only be guessed.

BEYOND CULTURAL PATTERNS OF COMMUNICATION

I began this chapter by quoting Berger's (2001) description of a dialectic, fueled by modernity, between fanaticism and relativism. This description is similar to Barber's (1995) contrast of "jihad vs. McWorld" and Friedman's (1999) paired symbols of the Lexus and the olive tree. These analyses depict a restless dynamic that is present within all ethnic and national cultures, each side imperiling that which the other holds most dear. When threatened, human beings tend to fight, and the gravest danger to humankind as a species is that the barbarians among us—or, more disturbing yet, the barbarian within each of us—will destroy us all while trying to protect us from the satanic Other.

Like the victors in the overthrow of the Tyrant of Sicily, we have the choice to continue to do more of the same—that is, to fight, now with each other rather than the deposed common enemy—or to develop new ways of communicating with each other. The political, economic, and technological world in which we live throws most of us, whether we want to or not, into contact with people who are not (and will not become) like us, many of whom do not like us. And this characterization holds no matter which "us" we have in mind. The contemporary challenge is to find ways of acting together that create a social world that does not take the form of culture wars but, instead, creates a framework within which individuals and groups can find the comfort and stability of their traditions without denying the same privilege to those in other traditions or even those who transcend their traditions.

If it were up to each of us to figure out how to act into this situation, we would have to summon the patience of saints, wisdom of sages, flexibility of diplomats or traveling salespersons, and altruism of consultants or therapists. That sets the bar too high, particularly in those crunching moments of life when circumstances diminish our capacity for acting at our best. I don't know what gave the citizens of Sicily the idea that it is better to resolve differences through sharpened wits rather than by sharpened weapons and the ability to translate that idea into social habits and institutions, but I hope that communication theory can provide an enabling scaffold on which we can lean as we confront the challenges of our era.

In this final section, I summarize some maxims and values embedded in CMM in the hope that they provide a means for making the kind of social world in which we want to live. After this, I identify some of what I see as the promising directions for the continued evolution of communication theory.

CMM'S CONTRIBUTION TO MAKING BETTER SOCIAL WORLDS

According to the story with which I began this chapter, the study of communication began with the rhetorical question of what the good reasons are for making decisions among conflicting claims. As I see it, the task for contemporary communication theorists is to answer the question of how we can make better social worlds when those involved in the process are grounded in traditions that frequently have been treated as if they are mutually exclusive.

As Yankelovich (1999) puts it, the issue is one of both will and skill. I'm assuming that the descriptions of the two situations earlier in this chapter are sufficient to summon your will to make better social worlds, and that the issue is that of skill. The CMM models—hierarchy, serpentine, daisy, LUUUTT, and others—can help us understand the complexity of and identify some opportunities in specific instances of communication. However, they don't address the question of how to act into those specific situations.

I'm not a fan of trying to raise anyone's skill in making social worlds by individual effort. My preference for working with groups and institutions is based on Vygotsky's (1978) concept of the "zone of proximal development." In his studies of how we learn to do all sorts of things, Vygotsky noted that, at any given time, there is a range of things we can do even without help and/or when circumstances are not favorable (e.g., hitting a routine slice backhand into the middle of the tennis court) and a range of things that we can't do no matter how much help we have (e.g., hitting a running topspin backhand around the post down the line for a winner). Between these is (a moving) zone of proximal development: things we can do if we have sufficient support.

Having the help of a skilled facilitator is perhaps the best way for us to practice better world-making skills in our zone of proximal development. As coach, model, and skillful interaction partner, a facilitator can enable us, however briefly, to communicate at a level that we could not achieve unaided. The experience of communicating in this way is both skill building (we become less dependent on the facilitator's help) and addictive (most people want to be involved in this quality of communication again). The Public Dialogue Consortium is the organization in which I've worked as facilitator and through which I've learned a lot about putting communication theory into practice and vice versa (Littlejohn & Domenici, 2000; Pearce, 2002; Spano, 2001).

In the absence of a facilitator, memorable maxims may function as supports for skills in making better social worlds. The following are my attempts to work out such maxims based on the key terms in CMM.

Coordination

The term *coordination* calls our attention to the fact that whatever we do does not stand alone. As shown in the serpentine model, it always intermeshes with the interpretations and actions of other people. Both Duffy and Yousef treated their actions (imposing sentence; bombing the World Trade Center) as if they were the final turns in a sequence. I wonder if they would have acted differently if either had been more mindful about the responses that would have been elicited in all of the conversations depicted in the daisy model.

Being aware of the inevitability of coordination does not, however, imply a commitment to coordinate smoothly with others. Gandhi's social-change producing tactics of civil disobedience were calculated refusals to coordinate within oppressive practices. Some patterns of coordination are simply richer in opportunities than others: a repetitive "hello"—"hello" between neighbors is well coordinated but has within it very limited opportunities for richer forms of relationships. To equip us to make better social worlds, these maxims might help:

- Be mindful that you are participating in a multiturn process.
- Be mindful that you are part of, but only one part of, a multiperson process.
- Be mindful that the process involves reciprocally responding to and eliciting responses from other people.
- Be mindful that this process creates the social world in which we all live.

Management of Meaning: Coherence and Mystery

CMM uses two terms to describe what we can do to manage our meanings: coherence and mystery. Coherence directs our attention to the stories that we tell that make our lives meaningful. Its opposite is something like vertigo, a loss of orientation. Mystery directs our attention to the fact that the universe is far bigger and subtler than any possible set of stories that we might develop. Whatever we think, there's more to it than that; it's not a riddle to be solved but a mystery to explore. These maxims for making better social worlds can be derived from the concepts of coherence and mystery:

- Treat all stories, your own as well as others, as incomplete, unfinished, biased, and inconsistent.
- Treat your own stories as "local," dependent on your own perspective, history, and purposes.
- Treat stories that differ from your own as "valid" within the framework of the other person's perspective, history, and purposes.
- Be curious about other people's stories.

Value Commitments

Theories that intend to describe the world rather than to change it may claim the values of objectivity and detachment; critical and practical theories like CMM cannot. CMM is part of a cluster of schools in philosophy and social theory that recognize that every theory "about" social worlds is also a part "of" those social worlds and as such should not pretend to be an objective mirror that only reflects them. Paralleling the principles for practice described in the preceding section, these are some of the commitments or responsibilities implied by CMM's view of communication.

- Develop sufficient self-awareness of the "localness" of your own stories to treat other peoples' stories with curiosity and respect.
- Develop habits and skills of articulating what you think, know, believe, and value in ways that enable and encourage others to articulate what they think, know, believe, and value, particularly if they disagree with you.
- Assume responsibility for authoring the most important stories in your interactions with others instead of allowing those stories to author you. Sometimes this will require changing your stories and/or the way you tell those stories.
- Develop abilities to think in terms of patterns, relationships, and systems, not just in terms of specific acts, your own intentions, and the way the world appears from your own perspective.
- Develop habits and skills of listening to other people so that you understand them and that they know that you have listened to and understood them.
- Develop the ability to move among perspectives, understanding situations from the perspective of other people involved and from the perspective of observers as well as from your own, first-person, perspective.
- Develop sufficient understanding of yourself, and confidence in your abilities, to be able to enter into high-quality relationships with others, even under less than optimal conditions.
- Realizing that you as a person are made by the same process that you are a part of making, be committed to improving existing social worlds, preventing the realization of unwanted social worlds, and calling into being better social worlds.

IMPLICATIONS FOR THE CONTINUING EVOLUTION OF COMMUNICATION THEORY

There is no disrespect for my intellectual forebears implied in my belief that the theories that they developed in response to the challenges confronting them do not necessarily serve us well in confronting the challenges of the contemporary era.

Toward a Rhetoric of Contextual Reconstruction

The first formulations of the art of persuasion were culture specific without being aware of it. The notion was that tests of evidence and forms of valid reasoning were universal. Bitzer's (1968) notion of "the rhetorical situation" was a major step forward, arguing that the arts of persuasion had to be tailored to the exigencies of specific situations. The case for the relativity of persuasion (and other forms of communication) has been further strengthened by studies of cultural patterns of communication (e.g., Carbaugh, 1996; Philipsen, 1997). Nearly 20 years later, I am even more convinced of the argument (Branham & Pearce, 1985) that contemporary challenges require us not only to adapt to different situations, but also to construct and reconstruct the situations that we encounter. For example, I've critiqued the interaction between Duffy and Yousef fairly thoroughly. But the context they were in—a criminal trial—imposed significant limits on what they could do as individuals. In my judgment, many of the institutions and practices of our society are functionally autonomous (Allport, 1937). That is, they served some good function when they were originally developed, but have lingered on—held in place by habits and laws—even though they no longer serve those functions. Communication theory and training, I believe, should focus not only on individual skills within contexts but also on abilities to analyze, critique, and reconstruct contexts.

Toward Transformative Communication Skills

Earlier in this chapter, I referred to a nascent social, systemic ethic, saying that it was necessary but far from adequately developed. McNamee and Gergen (1998) have begun to explore what this type of ethic would look like in contexts of informal interpersonal relations. Is it possible to extend this thinking to corporate, government, and/or legal contexts? If we could, I think that we would see Yousef's trial for bombing the World Trade Center as, for the most part, an irrelevant ritual. What if we were to pose the questions, "How can we construct a world in which sincere young men and women would never think of blowing up buildings?" rather than, or in addition to, the question "Is the defendant innocent or guilty?"

The literature on transformative learning provides an underpinning to the development of these skills of thought and action. As Mezirow (2000) describes it, transformative learning is

the process by which we transform our taken-for-granted frames of reference (meaning perspectives, habits of mind, mind-sets) to make them more inclusive, discriminating, open, emotionally capable of change, and reflective so that they may generate beliefs and opinions that will prove more true or justified to guide action. Transformative learning involves participation in constructive discourse to use the experience of others to assess reasons justifying these assumptions, and making an action decision based on the resulting insight. . . . Transformative learning . . . demands that we be aware of how we come to our knowledge and as aware as we can be about the values that lead us to our perspectives. Cultural canons, socioeconomic structures, ideologies and beliefs about ourselves, and the practices they support often conspire to foster conformity and impede development of a sense of responsible agency. (pp. 7–8)

Just as the rhetoricians of Sicily noted that some people are better persuaders and asked, "How do they do that?" our research might profitably note that some people are better able to understand their own beliefs and cultural patterns, and ask the same question.

Study What Works

One of the underlying concepts of "appreciative inquiry" (Cooperrider & Whitney, 2000) is the notion that what one studies, grows. If that is true, why should we want to study all the ways in which communication goes wrong? Why—except for the fact that agencies who fund research are set up that way—would we want to become experts in communication problems? Why wouldn't we want to become experts in what works well and to foster its development?

The good news is that the discipline of communication has always and continues to study "good communication." For example, Foss and Foss (1994) began the analysis of "invitational rhetoric," which recognizes that speaker and audience, and members of the audience, may have different cultural patterns of communication. And I'm very excited about the new emphasis on dialogue in many contexts (Anderson, Cissna, & Clune, 2003).

CONCLUSION

Sometimes I look back to the first 5 or 10 years of CMM's development with nostalgia. A closely knit group of us worked with high energy and creativity in the protective grasp of obscurity within a single department at a single university, itself a bit out of the mainstream in our discipline. The situation is very different now. The members of the original group are geographically dispersed; CMM (at least a very early form of it) has become one of the theories routinely included in survey textbooks in the United States; and, to my great pleasure, some of the most active sites where CMM is being developed are service-delivery centers in a variety of professions (for a reconnaissance of the ways CMM is being used, see Pearce, 2001).

I've described CMM's development as moving through three phases: interpretive, critical, and practical. I don't know what the next phase will be—perhaps it will stabilize as a practical theory, but maybe there will be another unforeseen development. A leader in a political party in Ireland and I recently discussed the possibility of establishing CMM as the Irish National Communication Theory, but perhaps because that conversation occurred over a few pints in a Dublin pub, no one has redesigned the Irish national flag to include the CMM crest and coat of arms. My more realistic hope is that there will be continued interactions between theorists and practitioners that will spur the evolution of CMM as a practical theory, and that it will provide useful resources on which we can all draw when confronting the communication challenges of our time.

NOTES

1. I learned this story through oral history—that is, it is what someone told me when I was a student. It may well be true, but, although I have not spent much time trying, I've not been able to verify it. For more and better information, see Enos (1993).

2. "9/11" refers to the terrorist attacks on the World Trade Center in New York City and the Pentagon in Washington, D.C., on September 11, 2001.

REFERENCES

Allport, G. W. (1937). The functional autonomy of motives. *American Journal of Psychology, 50,* 141–156.

Anderson, R., Cissna, K. N., & Clune, M. K. (2003). The rhetoric of public dialogue. *Communication Research Trends, 22,* 3–27.

Barber, B. R. (1995). *Jihad vs. McWorld: How the planet is both falling apart and coming together and what this means for democracy.* New York: Times Books.

Barge, J. K. (2001). Practical theory as mapping, engaged reflection, and transformative practice. *Communication Theory, 11,* 5–13.

Berger, P. L. (2001). Foreword. In R. C. Neville (Ed.), *The human condition* (pp. xi–xiv). Albany: State University of New York Press.

Bitzer, L. F. (1968). The rhetorical situation. *Philosophy and Rhetoric, 1,* 1–14.

Branham, R. J., & Pearce, W. B. (1985). Between text and context: Toward a rhetoric of contextual reconstruction. *Quarterly Journal of Speech, 71,* 19–36.

Carbaugh, D. (1996). *Situating selves: The communication of social identities in American scenes.* Albany: State University of New York Press.

Cooperrider, D., & Whitney, D. (2000). *Collaborating for change: Appreciative inquiry.* San Francisco: Barrett-Koehler.

Cronen, V. E. (2001). Practical theory, practical art, and the pragmatic-systemic account of inquiry. *Communication Theory, 11,* 14–35.

Enos, R. L. (1993). *Greek rhetoric before Aristotle.* Prospect Heights, IL: Waveland.

Foss, S. K., & Foss, K. A. (1994). *Inviting transformation: Presentational speaking for a changing world.* Prospect Heights, IL: Waveland.

Friedman, T. L. (1990). *From Beirut to Jerusalem.* New York: Anchor.

Friedman, T. L. (1999). *The Lexus and the olive tree: Understanding globalization.* New York: Farrar, Straus & Giroux.

Littlejohn, S. W., & Domenici, K. (2000). *Engaging communication in conflict: Systemic practice.* Thousand Oaks, CA: Sage.

McNamee, S., & Gergen, K. J. (1998). *Relational responsibility: Resources for sustainable dialogue.* Thousand Oaks, CA: Sage.

Mezirow, J. (2000). *Learning as transformation: Critical perspectives on a theory in progress.* San Francisco: Jossey-Bass.

Pearce, K. A. (2002). *Making better social worlds: Engaging in and facilitating dialogic communication.* Redwood City, CA: Pearce Associates.

Pearce, W. B. (1985). Scientific research methods in communication studies and their implications for theory and research. In T. Benson (Ed.), *Speech communication in the 20th century* (pp. 255–281). Carbondale: Southern Illinois University Press.

Pearce, W. B. (1994). *Interpersonal communication: Making social worlds.* New York: Harper-Collins.

Pearce, W. B. (2001). *CMM: Reports from users.* Redwood City, CA: Pearce Associates.

Pearce, W. B., & Benson, T. (1977). Alternative theoretical bases for human communication research: A symposium [Special issue]. *Communication Quarterly, 25.*

Pearce, W. B., Littlejohn, S. W., & Alexander, A. (1987). The New Christian Right and the humanist response: Reciprocated diatribe. *Communication Quarterly, 35,* 171–192.

Pearce, W. B., & Littlejohn, S. W. (1997). *Moral conflict: When social worlds collide.* Thousand Oaks, CA: Sage.

Pearce, W. B., & Pearce, K. A. (1998). Transcendent storytelling: Abilities for systemic practitioners and their clients. *Human Systems, 9,* 167–184.

Pearce, W. B., & Pearce, K. A. (2000). Extending the theory of the coordinated management of meaning ("CMM") through a community dialogue process. *Communication Theory, 10,* 405–423.

Philipsen, G. (1997). A theory of speech codes. In G. Philipsen & T. Albrecht (Eds.), *Developing communication theory* (pp. 119–156). Albany: State University of New York Press.

Spano, S. (2001). *Public dialogue and participatory democracy: The Cupertino Community Project.* Cresskill, NJ: Hampton.

Toulmin, S. (1990). *Cosmopolis: The hidden agenda of modernity.* Chicago: University of Chicago Press.

Vygotsky, L. S. (1978). *Mind in society: The development of higher psychological processes.* Cambridge, MA: Harvard University Press.

Wanniski, J. (2001). The mind of a terrorist. *FuturEdition, 4*(19).

Yankelovich, D. (1999). *The magic of dialogue: Transforming conflict into cooperation.* New York: Simon & Schuster.

3

Speech Codes Theory

Restatement, Revisions, and Response to Criticisms

GERRY PHILIPSEN

LISA M. COUTU

PATRICIA COVARRUBIAS

Speech codes theory is an original theory of human communication as considered from a cultural perspective. It was first published in prototypical form with an introduction to the concept of speech codes and a presentation of four empirically grounded principles about speech codes (Philipsen, 1992). Then it was presented as a formal theoretical statement with five empirically grounded propositions, four of which were carried over intact from the earlier version (Philipsen, 1997).

The present chapter has two purposes. One is to fill a gap. We do that here by re-presenting speech codes theory with six propositions. Five of these are carried over from the two previous presentations. One has been added on the basis of recently published empirical research that explicitly addresses the theory and that exposes a gap in it that we fill with the new proposition. Our second purpose is to respond to criticisms of the theory that have been published since its presentation in 1997

Authors' Note: The authors would like to acknowledge the thoughtful comments on weaknesses in Speech Codes Theory by Erica Erland, Nancy Bixler, Danielle Endres, and Jay Leighter, all of the University of Washington.

as a formal theoretical statement (Griffin, 2003; Stewart, 1997).

We begin with some background on speech codes theory, specifically with a consideration of the purpose of the theory, some of its defining characteristics as a theory, and the concept of code. Then, we re-present the theory with the newly added proposition. Finally, we turn to the published criticisms of the theory and our responses to them.

BACKGROUND TO SPEECH CODES THEORY

Why Speech Codes Theory Was Created

Speech codes theory was created for two purposes.

One purpose was to distill some of what might be learned from a large body of field-work research on culturally distinctive ways of speaking. When the first version of speech codes theory was written, there had been established a large body of fieldwork about cultural ways of speaking that had been conducted and published under the auspices of the ethnography of speaking (Hymes, 1968). Some 250 of these studies were cited in Philipsen and Carbaugh (1986). Focusing on selected exemplars from that body of work, Philipsen (1992, 1997) formulated a synthesis of (some of) what had been learned from studies of communicative conduct in its local and sociocultural contexts. Speech codes theory was that synthesis.

A second purpose was to provide a focus for further research and discussion. A distillation of what had been learned from extant data, cast in theoretical form, enhanced the likelihood that future research could be directed to the development of empirically grounded theory about communication. Cloaking that distillation in the mantle of theory enhanced the likelihood of evoking a critical response to those ideas.

Three Defining Characteristics of Speech Codes Theory

Speech codes theory is a particular type of theory of communication, and so we begin by setting forth three of its defining characteristics. We illustrate these characteristics by reference to Carbaugh (1999), a study that was conducted in a manner consistent with the precepts of speech codes theory.

One, speech codes theory is grounded in the observation of communicative conduct in particular times and places. For example, as part of a larger and long-term ethnographic project, Carbaugh (1999) reported, and interpreted, some uses by Blackfeet Indians (in the U.S.) of the word *listen* and the expression *sit down and listen*. Specifically, Carbaugh observed and reported in considerable, and considered, detail how a Blackfeet man used "listen" and "sit down and listen" in the course of teaching traditional Blackfeet ways, to outsiders as well as to Blackfeet people. Speech codes theory is concerned with such observed communicative conduct as its object of noticing, describing, interpreting, and explaining.

Two, speech codes theory posits a way to interpret or explain observed communicative conduct by reference to situated codes of meaning and value. For the Blackfeet, Carbaugh (1999) showed that the Blackfeet use of "listen" and "sit down and listen" expresses a complex system of meanings and values. These are meanings and values that pertain to Blackfeet places, to what it means to be a proper Blackfeet person, and to Blackfeet notions of the efficacy of communicative conduct in realizing their ideals. At the same time, when Carbaugh began to notice, describe, and interpret Blackfeet words, he drew from his previously acquired knowledge of Blackfeet beliefs, customs, and motives to provide his account of how it is that Blackfeet use of these implies a deeply cultured system of Blackfeet messages about communicative conduct. As the code of meaning and value was formulated, there was created the possibility for the interpretation and explanation of new instances of observed and experienced communicative conduct in the context of that community's discursive life. At the heart of speech codes theory is a concern with formulating local codes of interpretation and conduct and, in turn, with using those codes, as formulated, to interpret and explain situated communicative conduct.

Three, although the theory is based on studies of particular ways of speaking (e.g., those of Blackfeet), it provides a general understanding of communicative conduct. It is general in three ways. First, the theory presents a characterization of the nature of all speech codes. Propositions 1, 2, and 3 of the theory are empirical generalizations drawn from a consideration of a large body of descriptions of culturally distinctive speech codes. Second, speech codes theory contains a general answer to the question of how an observer might systematically try to learn about the particularities of particular, local ways of speaking. Proposition 5 of the theory provides an explicit and general answer to that question. Third, speech codes theory presents a general answer to the question of how speech codes relate to communicative conduct. In this way the theory enters the ongoing, interdisciplinary conversation about the use and force of codes in social life (Eliasoph & Lichterman, 2003; Harrison & Huntington, 2000; Swidler, 2001). It does this, in Proposition 4, with an argument as to how, in general, people use speech codes to interpret the meanings of communicative conduct, and in Proposition 6, with a specific proposition about the discursive force of speech codes.

The Concept of Code in Speech Codes Theory

Code is a key concept in the theory. Some critics misinterpreted the use of the word *code*, taking it to represent a rigid, fixed, one-to-one match of signal to point of meaning, as in Morse code. In the earlier formulations of code, the concept was treated deliberately and explicitly as something very different from these fixed senses of code. Here we reiterate the sense in which it was, and is, used in speech codes theory. Philipsen (1997) put it this way: "A speech code, then, is a system of socially-constructed symbols and meanings, premises, and rules, pertaining to communicative conduct" (p. 126). We discuss below two aspects of speech codes that are crucial to an understanding of how the concept of code is used in speech codes theory.

One, speech codes are constructs that observer-analysts formulate explicitly in order to interpret and explain communicative conduct in a particular speech community. The observer-analyst notices that participants in the discursive life of a speech community use particular resources to enact, name, interpret, and judge communicative conduct, and the analyst uses what she or he has noticed in order to construct a hypothesis as to the existence and nature of a system of resources that these participants use to do that enactment, naming, interpretation, and evaluation. That hypothesis is the observer-analyst's formulation of what in speech codes theory is called a speech code.

Two, the situated resources—symbols and meanings, premises, and rules pertaining to communicative conduct—that participants use to name, interpret, and judge communicative conduct are constructed by human beings in the course of social life. What humans construct, they can also deconstruct, or ignore, alter, and adapt to new purposes. Thus, these resources that people use are contingent, not deterministic; and they are open, not fixed. Proposition 6 in speech codes theory is addressed explicitly to the issue of whether speech codes are deterministic. Furthermore, Proposition 6 is addressed to how speech codes shape or influence communicative conduct.

THE SIX PROPOSITIONS
OF SPEECH CODES THEORY

In the present version of the theory there are six propositions. Each of these six propositions was built upon an extensive record of fieldwork data. Likewise, each is formulated so as to be amenable in principle to empirical evaluation, whether the evaluation takes the form of further substantiation, empirical elaboration, or empirical challenge. In this section, for each of the six propositions, we state the proposition, formulate the question that the proposition answers, state what we believe makes the proposition important theoretically and practically, and discuss the status of the extant evidence bearing on that proposition. The new proposition appears as Proposition 2, with the next four propositions now renumbered accordingly.

Proposition 1. Wherever there is a distinctive culture, there is to be found a distinctive speech code. Proposition 1 answers two questions about cultures. Before we state those questions, it will be important to be explicit about the definition of culture used in speech codes theory. The theory defines culture as a code and not as a geographic, political, or social unit. Such codes consist of a system of symbols, meanings, premises, and rules. These can be symbols, meanings, premises, and rules about many aspects of life; for example, types of people, ways of thinking, firewood, politics, and communicative conduct. Thus, when we speak of a culture we speak not primarily of a time or place, but of a code that was constructed, and is used, in some time or place.

If one thinks about such codes as we have described above, two questions can be asked. The first is: Does every culture (i.e., every socially constructed code) include symbols, meanings, premises, and rules about communicative conduct? This is a question about cultural systems in general—do all of them contain a subset that maps the domain of

communicative conduct? The second is: Do such codes differ in terms of the particular words, meanings, premises, and rules about communicative conduct that they include? Proposition 1 responds to both of those questions in the affirmative. It implies that everywhere people construct codes of life, the codes they construct include symbols, meanings, premises, and rules about communicative conduct. And it states directly that everywhere that people have constructed codes of communicative conduct, those codes—those systems of symbols, meanings, premises, and rules about communicative conduct—are distinctive.

Why is this proposition important to scholars, teachers, or practitioners of communication? It is important precisely because scholars, teachers, or practitioners of communication encounter cultures as codes, whether in research or in other modes of living. That is, in any given time and place where people have interacted enough to have formed systems of symbols, meanings, premises, and rules about something, they have also formed symbols, meanings, premises, and rules about communicative conduct. And in each time and place that such systems of symbols, meanings, premises, and rules about communicative conduct have been formed, those systems are distinctive. Thus to understand a particular culture, to teach it to someone else, or to use it in daily life, requires that one learn that culture as its own thing, because it is not precisely the same as other cultures. To study a particular speech code, to teach it to someone else, or to use it in daily life, requires that one learn that speech code, not assume what it will be, because it is not precisely the same as other speech codes.

When speech codes theory was first published, in 1992 and in 1997, there was a large body of empirical evidence based on ethnographic fieldwork that supported Proposition 1. Much of this evidence is contained in the more than 250 studies cited in Philipsen and Carbaugh (1986). Selected portions of this evidence are reviewed in detail in Braithwaite (1990), Carbaugh (1989), Goldsmith (1989/1990), Katriel (1986), and Philipsen (1989a, 1989b). Just prior to and since the publication of speech codes theory in 1997, there was a substantial body of new work published that supports Proposition 1 (including Carbaugh, 1996, 1999; Covarrubias, 2002; Fitch, 1998; Fong, 1994, 1998; Katriel, 1993; Miyahira, 1999; Winchatz, 2001).

Proposition 2. In any given speech community, multiple speech codes are deployed. Proposition 2 is concerned with speech codes as they are situated in a given place and time. Specifically, it responds to the question of whether there are, in any given speech community, two or more speech codes that are deployed by participants in social interaction.

Why is this proposition important to scholars, teachers, or practitioners of communication? It is important precisely because when scholars, teachers, or practitioners of communication encounter a speech code, whether in research or in other modes of living, they encounter it as something that articulates, in one way or another, with another code or with other codes. As will be shown below, this fact has important consequences for the learning, teaching, and practice of communicative conduct. In order to examine those consequences, it will be necessary to review some of the speech codes research that led to the formulation of Proposition 2.

Speech codes scholars have, in many instances of their research, found that they, and the people whom they studied, experienced, within the same life-world, different codes or at least traces of different codes pertaining to communicative conduct. Below we mention some examples of such findings.

Studies of the speech community labeled "Teamsterville" (Philipsen, 1975, 1976, 1986, 1992) emphasized a single local speech code. Nonetheless, that code was explicitly juxtaposed, in the speech of Teamstervillers, and in the ethnographic report of that speech, to another code or other codes. For example, Teamstervillers themselves defined their own ways of speaking by contrasting them with the ways of speaking of people who lived in the same city as they did but who lived in a different part of it, either north of their neighborhood (white people who were wealthier than Teamstervillers) or south of them (black people who were poorer than they were). They also thereby defined their own ways of speaking in contrast to the speech of people whom they described as being of a different social type from them (economically or racially). The juxtaposition of different ways of speaking, and of Teamstervillers' awareness of them, is made particularly stark in Philipsen (1986), a study of the critical engagement by outsiders of Teamsterville ways and critical engagement by Teamstervillers of the ways of the outsiders. One reader of Philipsen (1986) explicitly acknowledges that the interpretation presented there is grounded in "multiple codes of interpretation" (Rosteck, 1998).

Likewise in the early studies of "Nacirema" ways of speaking (Katriel & Philipsen, 1981; Philipsen, 1992, chaps. 4 & 5), there is evidence that the U.S. respondents whose communicative conduct was studied characterized their own communicative conduct by contrasting it with other ways of speaking. For example, the respondents M and K, in Katriel and Philipsen (1981), characterized their use of "communication" as different from the way of speaking of their parents or of the way of speaking of a former spouse. Likewise on a popular television show, the host and guests would characterize their present way of speaking ("really communicating") by reference to another way of speaking and another code of communicative conduct that they had now discarded.

Several fieldwork studies of ways of speaking in particular speech communities have contributed to a growing sense among speech codes scholars of the importance of focusing on the coexistence and interanimation of two or more codes in the same life-world. These include Baxter (1993) on two speech codes in the deliberations of a faculty and administration in a college, Huspek (1993, 1994, 2000; Huspek & Kendall, 1993) on the oppositional but essentially interdependent nature of two codes in a variety of field settings, Ruud (1995, 2000) on management and performer codes in the San Jose Symphony organization, Ruud and Sprague (2000) on two codes in an environmental dispute in California, Sequeira (1993) on two codes for personal address in the same church congregation and the negotiations of meanings that were attendant to the use of those two codes, Fitch (1998) on multiple codes for interpreting the use of personal address forms in Colombia, Winchatz (2001) on two systems of using and rationalizing the use of the personal pronoun of address *Sie* (English "you") in contemporary Germany, and Covarrubias (2002) on the use, contrapositionally, by workers in a Mexican company of two codes for the use of the personal pronouns of address *tu* and *usted*.

Early, as well as recent, speech codes studies report the presence and the mingling of two or more codes in the life of one community or in the life-worlds of particular people. Such possibilities were not denied but neither were they explicitly provided for in the earlier formulations of speech codes theory. Yet the emerging empirical record referred to above, as well as the theoretical arguments advanced by Huspek (particularly Huspek, 1993, 1994) led some scholars to address this gap directly. Here we turn to one recent study that was conducted with the extant propositions of speech codes theory clearly in mind, that acknowledges the heuristic influence of the theory (and of Huspek, 1993, 1994), and that set out in advance to examine a situation in which there would be two speech codes deployed within the same sustained discursive event.

Coutu's (2000) study of the discourse surrounding the publication of Robert S. McNamara's 1995 book, *In Retrospect: The Tragedy and Lessons of Vietnam*, explicitly employs speech codes theory (Coutu, 2000, p. 181) coupled with oppositional codes theory (see Huspek, 1993, 1994) to highlight the "organization of diversity" (Hymes, 1974, p. 433) present in speech communities or life-worlds. She found that, in the social discourse in and in response to McNamara's book, two competing codes are deployed—what she refers to as the codes of rationality and of spirituality. As Coutu wrote: "Although McNamara and his hearers shared one speech code, they each also endorsed distinctive speech codes to be used when discussing Vietnam" (p. 183). She argues that the codes, rather than representing two cultures, are two codes, oppositional in many of their meanings, present within the same speech community (pp. 182–183). In her study, Coutu capitalizes on the complexity of speech codes theory to illustrate the possibility of multiple codes within one community or life-world. In so doing she draws on much of the same literature as does Philipsen (1992, 1997), but develops a different perspective than he did on the presence of multiple codes within one community of discourse.

Proposition 2 says that speech codes do not appear in social life in isolation from other speech codes, but rather that they appear in social life with other speech codes. We have pointed here to multiple studies in the speech codes tradition that have reported, within one speech community, the deployment of more than one speech code. Many of these findings of multiple speech codes deployed within the same speech community were produced without the researcher explicitly looking and listening for multiple codes (although using a descriptive model, that of the ethnography of speaking, that provided for that possibility). We have also featured here one study in the speech codes tradition that explicitly set out to examine the discourse of a speech community with the possibility of finding two or more different speech codes deployed. Taken as a whole, we use this body of evidence to generate a new proposition for speech codes theory. Proposition 2 is that new proposition.

Proposition 3. A speech code implicates a culturally distinctive psychology, sociology, and rhetoric. Proposition 3 answers a question about the content of speech codes. To frame the question, one can ask about what is referred to, and furthermore what is suggested in, the symbols, meanings, premises, and rules of a speech code. Do such words, etcetera, refer neutrally or simply to aspects of communicative conduct or do they implicate something further? Proposition 3 answers that question by saying that the elements of a speech code implicate something more than communicative conduct narrowly conceived; they also implicate meanings about human nature (psychology), social relations (sociology), and strategic conduct (rhetoric). Specifically, wherever there is a situated vocabulary in use that pertains to communicative conduct (e.g., terms for talk), or a situated system of premises or rules pertaining to communicative conduct, there can be found in these situated vocabularies and systems of premises and rules, symbols and meanings that not only designate aspects of communicative conduct narrowly conceived but also aspects of the nature of persons, social relations, and the role of communicative conduct in linking persons in social relations.

Why is this proposition important to scholars, teachers, or practitioners of communication? It is important precisely because scholars, teachers, or practitioners of communication hear, in everyday talk, speech about communicative conduct. Such speech contains code elements, that is, symbols and expressions, and statements of premises and rules, about communicative conduct. Proposition 3 of speech codes theory states that in their reference to matters of communicative conduct, these code elements express and imply

notions of human nature, social relations, and strategic conduct, and that wherever and whenever one hears talk about communicative conduct one also hears talk about persons, society, and rhetoric. So that when one hears someone say that "communication" is necessary for a "relationship," as is said in much speech in the contemporary United States, one can hear in such talk traces of a code of personhood, social relations, and strategic action. Proposition 3 says that it is always the case that such talk about communicative conduct implicates meanings about persons, society, and rhetoric.

Proposition 3 also says that words and expressions about communicative conduct, and the notions they imply about persons, social relations, and strategic action, are *distinctive* across cultures. It says that wherever there is a distinctive culture, there is a distinctive system of symbols, meanings, premises, and rules about communicative conduct, and that these implicate a distinctive system of meanings about human nature, social relations, and strategic conduct.

Proposition 3 of speech codes theory can be confirmed or disconfirmed on the basis of empirical evidence. As with Proposition 1, however, there are few or no direct tests of this proposition, but rather an accumulation of evidence over time that is consistent with it. Such evidence consists of studies in which a scholar finds, in a given speech community, evidence of distinctive words and expressions pertaining to communicative conduct, and then shows that and how these words and expressions implicate a distinctive local psychology, sociology, and rhetoric. As with the evidence for Proposition 1, there was a substantial body of evidence available prior to the publication of speech codes theory in 1997, and there has been a substantial body of new evidence published in the years since. The sources cited for Proposition 1 apply to Proposition 3 as well. Philipsen (1975, 1976, 1986), Katriel and Philipsen (1981), Rosaldo

(1982), and Carbaugh (1988) provide early empirical cases that were crucial to the building of Proposition 3. Carbaugh (1989) is an important cross-case synthesizing paper in support of the proposition.

Proposition 4. The significance of speaking is contingent upon the speech codes used by interlocutors to constitute the meanings of communicative acts. Proposition 4 is concerned with the use (and force) of speech codes in the interpretive process. Specifically, it is concerned with how a participant in communicative conduct will interpret her or his own and others' communicative acts. If one thinks of a behavior that oneself or another emits or produces, one can also then ask what that behavior counts as, either to the producer or to someone else who observes or receives it. Does one's movement of the eyebrow, for example, count as a wink or as some other sort of movement and, if as a wink, then as what does that count, as an expression of conspiratorial solidarity, an invitation to intimacy, and so forth? Proposition 4 provides part of the answer to the general question thus implied: That what a given behavior counts as, for a given receiver and interpreter of it, is contingent upon the speech code that the interpreter uses to constitute it as one sort of action or another.

Proposition 4 is important to scholars, teachers, or practitioners of communication because it addresses something fundamental to the communication process—how people construe the meanings of communicative acts. It suggests that people construe the meanings of communicative acts as actions, at least in part, through the use of a speech code. Thus it makes interpretations of communicative acts, in terms of what action an act is taken to have performed, contingent upon the code(s) used to interpret them. For example, the Blackfeet man who taught Carbaugh (1999) about the action of "listening" in particular Blackfeet places, enjoined Carbaugh to "listen" and

then explained to him what it meant to "listen," that is, how to do it, but also what its existential significance is to one who does it, at least from the standpoint of the code that the Blackfeet man articulated on that and other occasions. Carbaugh reports that, prior to his learning the Blackfeet code, he would have constituted—heard and interpreted the acts he associated with listening—very differently from the way he eventually could constitute them having learned something of the Blackfeet code.

The evidence for Proposition 4 is based on several ethnographies of speaking, including Rosaldo (1982), Philipsen (1986, 1992), Carbaugh (1993), Pratt and Wieder (1993), and Winchatz (2001).

Proposition 5. The terms, rules, and premises of a speech code are inextricably woven into speaking itself. The question that Proposition 5 answers is as follows: Where should one look or listen to find evidence of a speech code? The answer that Proposition 5 provides is: Observe communicative conduct, because symbols, meanings, premises, and rules about communicative conduct are woven into communicative conduct. This proposition asserts that the key to noticing and describing speech codes is to watch communicative conduct and listen to it. Furthermore, the proposition directs the observer to pay attention to particular things. These are (1) meta-communicative words and expressions (e.g., words and expressions about communicative conduct), (2) the use of such words and expressions in particularly consequential interactive moments (rhetorical moments, one might say), (3) the contextual patterns of communicative conduct (e.g., as can be noticed and described in the terms of Hymes's descriptive framework [Hymes, 1961, 1968, 1972]), (4) and such special forms of communicative conduct as rituals, myths, and social dramas.

Proposition 5 was built up empirically, by learning from the published experience of ethnographers of speaking who have discovered and formulated speech codes on the basis of their fieldwork experience. It is formulated in such a way as to be subject to empirical critique and revision, that is, by learning from the experience of ethnographers of speaking who, using the framework, report in their studies ways to challenge its adequacy or to improve it by making it more parsimonious or more adequate to real cases of inquiry.

Philipsen (1976), Katriel and Philipsen (1981), Katriel (1986), and Carbaugh (1989) were instrumental in developing the strategy (initially suggested by Hymes, 1968) of attending to cultural vocabularies as a site for finding the deployment of culturally distinctive speech codes. Katriel and Philipsen (1981), Katriel (1986), and Philipsen (1986, and 1992, chap. 5) were instrumental in the construction of the portion of the descriptive strategy that relies on the use of such cultural forms as ritual, myth, and social drama as heuristic aids in the discovery and formulation of particular speech codes. Philipsen (1987) put together various elements of the strategy, and these are constructed as an integrative framework in Philipsen (1992, 1997).

Proposition 6. The artful use of a shared speech code is a sufficient condition for predicting, explaining, and controlling the form of discourse about the intelligibility, prudence, and morality of communicative conduct. The question that Proposition 6 answers is: How do speech codes influence communicative conduct? The answer that Proposition 6 provides is that (1) social actors *use* speech codes to label, interpret, explain, evaluate, justify, and shape their own and others' communicative actions; (2) when social actors use *shared* speech codes to frame their efforts to shape the conduct of others, such use is effective in shaping the responses of others; and (3) the rhetorical force of speech codes is *contingent* on the coherence, social legitimacy, and rhetorically artful use of the code so employed.

Proposition 6 is important to scholars, teachers, and practitioners of communication because it points to an important activity in human social life—the efforts by humans to shape the communicative conduct of themselves and of others. Proposition 6 furthermore points to a way that codes (or cultures) are used in humans' efforts to shape the communicative conduct of themselves and of others. It shows that such efforts are not necessarily successful in getting people to conform to codes but can be successful in shaping how people talk about the intelligibility, prudence, and morality of communicative conduct. It also shows why efforts to get people to talk about the intelligibility, prudence, and morality of conduct have the results that they do—it depends on the nature of the code used and on how artful the user is in using the code to shape her own or others' conduct.

There is a great deal of empirical evidence of various types that supports the claim that people experience a great deal of social pressure to make their behavior conform to social codes (Albert, 1964; Carbaugh, 1987; Coleman, 1989; Enker, 1987; Philipsen, 1975; Richman, 1988; Schwartz, 1973; Swidler, 1986; Turner, 1988). There is also a great deal of empirical evidence that humans who do indeed pay lip service to a cultural code do not always use it to guide and interpret their conduct (Hall, 1988/1989). There are several explanations for the slippage between culture and conduct: the open texture (Hart, 1961), essential incompleteness (Garfinkel, 1972), internal inconsistency in implications for action (Bilmes, 1976), indeterminacy (Wieder, 1974), susceptibility to change (Geertz, 1973), and multiplicity in the life-world (Huspek, 1993; Philipsen, 1992) of cultural codes.

Proposition 6 of speech codes theory enters the debate about the force of culture in conduct in two ways. First, its previous presentations (Philipsen, 1989a, 1992, 1997) acknowledge that cultures (and, by extension, socially constructed codes) are not fixed, unitary, and deterministic, but rather are dynamic, exist in life-worlds in which there are two or more cultures or codes that are used and that have existential force, and are resources that social actors deploy strategically and artfully in the conduct of communication. Second, speech codes theory nonetheless argues for the importance of culture in individual lives, in social life, and in scholarly efforts to understand individual lives and social life. It does this with Proposition 6, which captures what we believe is an empirically warranted resolution of the extant discussion. Proposition 6 presents a limited, but defensible and irreducible, role of culture in shaping communicative conduct.

There is a great deal of empirical evidence that supports Proposition 6's emphasis on a limited but important role of culture in the shaping of conduct. A great deal of anecdotal evidence could be pointed to as well, but here we will point instead to a few exemplary studies that have demonstrated a limited but important shaping effect. Bilmes (1976) shows that although social actors do not use codes deterministically, they nonetheless do employ them in pressing their case in community deliberations. Hopper (1993) shows that people who do not necessarily shape their actions to conform to their idea of what is culturally acceptable conduct, nonetheless appeal to cultural notions of acceptability in the process of retrospectively framing and evaluating their conduct as they explain it to others. Miller (1990) shows how justifications of conduct that are framed in the terms of a socially legitimated code are treated as more persuasive than those that are not so framed. What these studies have in common is an explicit acknowledgment of the limits of codes to shape conduct while such codes nonetheless are deployed strategically in communication about conduct and deployed in ways that have consequences for social interaction. Proposition 6 is designed to reflect this nuanced understanding of the role of codes in shaping communicative conduct.

We have here stated, clarified the presentations of, and assessed the state of evidence for the previously formulated propositions of speech codes theory. We have also, based on a consideration of an accumulating empirical record, formulated and presented a further theoretical proposition.

RESPONSES TO PUBLISHED CRITICISMS OF SPEECH CODES THEORY

Two sets of criticisms of speech codes theory have been published. One of these was authored by Stewart (1997), who wrote his criticisms as part of a commentary chapter in the volume in which Philipsen (1997) appeared. The second was authored by Griffin (2003) in prefatory materials for a chapter about speech codes theory that appears in his book that exposits and assesses several major theories of communication. Here we respond to what we distill to be the two key criticisms that these authors have expressed.

Criticism 1. Speech codes theory does not account for manifestations of power in discourse. This is a matter of omission in the theoretical assumptions, methodological framework, and examination of fieldwork materials.

The assumptive foundation of speech codes theory is derived from the assumptive foundation of the ethnography of speaking (see Hymes, 1968, and Philipsen, 1992). One of the cornerstones of that foundation is openness to the possibility that any dimension of social life, including power, be observed as manifested in discourse. Furthermore, the ethnography of speaking, and by extension speech codes theory, is grounded in a sociolinguistic perspective that explicitly acknowledges the universal possibility in any body of discourse of manifestations of power, solidarity, intimacy, and other fundamental dimensions of social life (see, for but one example,

Brown & Gilman, 1960, on the pronouns of power and solidarity, a study that ethnographers of speaking acknowledge as a fundamental source of insight into the possibilities of sociolinguistic enactment and social meaning). To say that the database on which speech codes theory is grounded is constructed from studies that were conducted without an open eye and a listening ear turned toward discourses of power is not consistent with our reading of the orienting literature.

For most speech codes researchers, their open eyes and listening ears are directed to what the people being studied, in a given inquiry, insert into the discourse they produce and find in the discourse they experience. Such researchers are concerned, fundamentally, with the means of communication that people use and experience and with the meanings those means have for those who use and experience them. Accordingly, we look at and listen to their conduct for evidence of what they do and of how they experience the communicative conduct of their life-world. For example, in his analysis of a social drama surrounding a speech by Chicago Mayor Richard Daley, Philipsen's (1986) interpretation of the speech points explicitly to the importance, in the Teamsterville code that is invoked and evoked in that speech, of, first, the honor-linked value of power. But he also finds evidence in that speech of such other honor-linked values as wealth, magnanimity, loyalty, precedence, sense of shame, glory, courage, excellence, and piety (p. 256). Indeed in interpreting the values that dominate the speech, Philipsen considers a very specific alternative to power as the dominating motive of the speaker and the speech, but concludes that power was the key motive or catalyst for rhetorical action in this particular case (p. 256). By following a model that directs the observer to give voice to the people being studied, rather than to the voice of the author herself or himself, power was found and invoked by the ethnographer on the basis of the evidence of the case itself, not on the basis of an a priori commitment to find that power is a dominant motive in all discourse.

The critics' charges, as we have heard or read them, are quite general and thus it is difficult to answer them in any concrete way. We can, however, point to multiple studies in the ethnography of speaking tradition and in the speech codes tradition that examine discourse and either (1) find evidence there of power as a dominant force in discourse (Philipsen, 1986, and Rosaldo, 1982, to cite just two key examples) or (2) systematically consider power as a key phenomenon but do not find the people being studied giving power the dominant interpretive role (Coutu, 2000; Covarrubias, 2002). We would welcome critiques of specific findings and claims as a productive starting point for constructive improvement of speech codes theory.

Criticism 2. Speech codes theory treats culture as overly deterministic. A corollary to this is that it reifies culture as a static entity.

Published expositions of the theory (including the present chapter) eschew any simplistic notion of cultural determinism or of cultures as static entities. Philipsen (1992) states, for example, "To say that speaking is structured is not to say it is absolutely determined. It is patterned, but in ways that its creators can circumvent, challenge, and revise" (p. 10). In the same paragraph Philipsen (1992) invokes Hymes's (1974) well-known characterization of a speech community as an "organization of diversity" (p. 433). Later, Philipsen (1997) states that "the people I observed did not behave as cultural automatons" and that "humans not only follow but also flout their cultures" (p. 147). That is, in each of the first two presentations of speech codes theory, as in the present restatement, there have been explicit statements that eschew notions of culture as static or deterministic.

Speech codes theory does, however, make a strong statement about the force of codes in shaping communicative conduct. To support this statement, which appears here as Proposition 6, a wide array of empirical data is cited that shows that culture does play an important role in shaping communicative conduct, and a wide array of empirical data and theoretical arguments is cited or summarized that shows that the role culture plays in shaping conduct is not simplistically deterministic. The discursive force proposition of the theory was formulated to raise the level of discussion of the matters of codes as static entities and deterministic forces. Specifically, a very specific, empirically grounded, and empirically testable proposition about these matters was formulated. As with our response to the first criticism indicated above, here we suggest that one effort at productive criticism would be to engage the specifics of speech codes theory, in this instance, the discursive force proposition, Proposition 6.

CONCLUSION

In this chapter we summarized and restated speech codes theory. Furthermore, we reviewed a substantial body of evidence that leads us to propose changing the theory by increasing its core propositions from five to six. This makes a substantial change and, we believe, improvement in the theory as a resource for interpreting and explaining culturally shaped communicative conduct and for guiding further study of speech codes. This change in the theory follows upon a substantial body of published field data that, we believe, warrants the proposed change in the theory. Finally, we distilled, and responded to, various published criticisms of the theory. In addition to pointing out what we believe to be some weaknesses in the principal criticisms lodged against the theory, we have emphasized that it is amenable to change in response to specific criticisms, either of the speculative-ratiocinative sort or of the sort warranted by an accumulation of case-based field evidence.

REFERENCES

Albert, E. M. (1964). "Rhetoric," "logic," and "poetics" in Burundi: Culture patterning of speech behavior. In J. J. Gumperz & D. Hymes (Eds.), The ethnography of communication. *American Anthropologist, 66,* pt. 2(6), 35–54.

Baxter, L. A. (1993). "Talking things through" and "putting it in writing": Two codes of communication in an academic institution. *Journal of Applied Communication Research, 21,* 313–326.

Bilmes, J. (1976). Rules and rhetoric: Negotiating social order in a Thai village. *Southwestern Journal of Anthropology, 32,* 44–57.

Braithwaite, C. (1990). Communicative silence: A crosscultural study of Basso's hypothesis. In D. Carbaugh (Ed.), *Cultural communication and intercultural contact* (pp. 321–327). Hillsdale, NJ: Lawrence Erlbaum.

Brown, R., & Gilman, A. (1960). The pronouns of power and solidarity. In T. A. Sebeok (Ed.), *Style in language* (pp. 252–276). Cambridge, MA: MIT Press.

Carbaugh, D. (1987). Communication rules in Donahue discourse. *Research on Language and Social Interaction, 21,* 31–62.

Carbaugh, D. (1988). *Talking American.* Norwood, NJ: Ablex.

Carbaugh, D. (1989). Fifty terms for talk: A cross-cultural study. In S. Ting-Toomey & F. Korzenny (Eds.), *Language, communication and culture* (International and Intercultural Communication Annual, Volume 13, pp. 93–120). Beverly Hills, CA: Sage.

Carbaugh, D. (1993). "Soul" and "self": Soviet and American cultures in conversation. *Quarterly Journal of Speech, 79,* 182–200.

Carbaugh, D. (1996). *Situating selves: The communication of social identities in American scenes.* Albany: State University of New York Press.

Carbaugh, D. (1999). "Just listen": "Listening" and landscape among the Blackfeet. *Western Journal of Communication, 63,* 250–270.

Coleman, J. (1989). Responses to the Sociology of Education award. *Academic Questions, 2,* 76–78.

Coutu, L. M. (2000). Communication codes of rationality and spirituality in the discourse of and about Robert S. McNamara's *In retrospect.*

Research on language and social interaction, 33, 179–211.

Covarrubias, P. (2002). *Culture, communication, and cooperation: Interpersonal relations and pronominal address in a Mexican organization.* Lanham, MD: Rowman & Littlefield.

Eliasoph, N., & Lichterman, P. (2003). Culture in interaction. *American Journal of Sociology, 108,* 735–794.

Enker, M. (1987). Attitudinal and normative variables as predictors of cheating behavior. *Journal of Cross-Cultural Psychology, 18,* 315–330.

Fitch, K. (1998). *Speaking relationally: Culture, communication, and interpersonal communication.* New York: Guilford.

Fong, M. (1994). *Chinese immigrants' interpretations of their intercultural compliment interactions with European Americans.* Unpublished doctoral dissertation, University of Washington, Seattle.

Fong, M. (1998). Chinese immigrants' perceptions of semantic dimensions of direct/indirect communication in intercultural compliment interactions with North Americans. *Howard Journal of Communication, 9,* 245–262.

Garfinkel, H. (1972). Remarks on ethnomethodology. In J. J. Gumperz & D. Hymes (Eds.), *Directions in sociolinguistics: The ethnography of communication* (pp. 301–324). New York: Holt, Rinehart & Winston.

Geertz, C. (1973). *The interpretation of cultures: Selected essays.* New York: Basic Books.

Goldsmith, D. (1989/1990). Gossip from the native's point of view: A comparative analysis. *Research on Language and Social Interaction, 23,* 163–194.

Griffin, E. (2003). *A first look at communication theory* (5th ed.). New York: McGraw-Hill.

Hall, B. (1988/1989). Norms, action, and alignment: A discursive perspective. *Research on Language and Social Interaction, 22,* 23–44.

Harrison, E., & Huntington, S. P. (Eds.). (2000). *Culture matters: How values shape human progress.* New York: Basic Books.

Hart, H. (1961). *The concept of law.* Oxford, UK: Clarendon.

Hopper, J. (1993). The rhetoric of motives in divorce. *Journal of Marriage and the Family, 55,* 801–813.

Huspek, M. (1993). Dueling structures: The theory of resistance in discourse. *Communication Theory, 3,* 1–25.

Huspek, M. (1994). Oppositional codes and social class relations. *British Journal of Sociology, 45,* 79–102.

Huspek, M. (2000). Oppositional codes: The case of the Penitentiary of New Mexico riot. *Journal of Applied Communication Research, 28,* 144–163.

Huspek, M., & Kendall, K. (1993). On withholding voice: An analysis of the political vocabulary of a "nonpolitical" speech community. *Quarterly Journal of Speech, 77,* 1–19.

Hymes, D. (1961). Functions of speech: An evolutionary approach. In F. C. Gruber (Ed.), *Anthropology and education* (pp. 55–83). Philadelphia: University of Pennsylvania Press.

Hymes, D. (1968). The ethnography of speaking. In J. Fishman (Ed.), *Readings in the sociology of language* (pp. 99-137). Paris: Mouton. (Reprinted from *Anthropology and human behavior,* pp. 13–53, by T. Gladwin & W. C. Sturtevant, Eds., 1962, Washington, DC: Anthropological Society of Washington)

Hymes, D. (1972). Models of the interaction of language and social life. In J. J. Gumperz & D. Hymes (Eds.), *Directions in sociolinguistics: The ethnography of communication* (pp. 35–71). New York: Holt, Rinehart & Winston.

Hymes, D. (1974). Ways of speaking. In R. Bauman & J. Sherzer (Eds.), *Explorations in the ethnography of speaking* (pp. 433–451). London: Cambridge University Press.

Katriel, T. (1986). *Talking straight: "Dugri" speech in Israeli Sabra culture.* Cambridge, UK: Cambridge University Press.

Katriel, T. (1993). Lefargen: A study in Israeli semantics of social relations. *Research on Language and Social Interaction, 26,* 31–54.

Katriel, T., & Philipsen, G. (1981). "What we need is communication": "Communication" as a cultural category in some American speech. *Communication Monographs, 48,* 302–317.

McNamara, R. S. (with VanDeMark, B.) (1995). *In retrospect· The tragedy and lessons of Vietnam.* New York: Times Books.

Miller, L. (1990). Violent families and the rhetoric of harmony. *British Journal of Sociology, 41,* 263–288.

Miyahira, K. (1999). Plotting a course of action: Ritual coordination of intercultural directive-response sequence in team-taught English classes. *Speech Communication Education, 2*, 151–172.

Philipsen, G. (1975). Speaking "like a man" in Teamsterville: Culture patterns of role enactment in an urban neighborhood. *Quarterly Journal of Speech, 61*, 13–22.

Philipsen, G. (1976). Places for speaking in Teamsterville. *Quarterly Journal of Speech, 62*, 15–25.

Philipsen, G. (1986). Mayor Daley's council speech: A cultural analysis. *Quarterly Journal of Speech, 72*, 247–260.

Philipsen, G. (1987). The prospect for cultural communication. In D. L. Kincaid (Ed.), *Communication theory: Eastern and Western perspectives* (pp. 245–254). San Diego, CA: Academic Press.

Philipsen, G. (1989a). An ethnographic approach to communication studies. In B. Dervin (Ed.), *Paradigm dialogues: Research exemplars* (pp. 258–268). Newbury Park, CA: Sage.

Philipsen, G. (1989b). Speaking as a communal resource in four cultures. In S. Ting-Toomey & F. Korzenny (Eds.), *Language, communication and culture* (International and Intercultural Communication Annual, Volume 13, pp. 93–120). Beverly Hills, CA: Sage.

Philipsen, G. (1992). *Speaking culturally: Explorations in social communication*. Albany: State University of New York Press.

Philipsen, G. (1997). A theory of speech codes. In G. Philipsen & T. L. Albrecht (Eds.), *Developing communication theories* (pp. 119–156). Albany: State University of New York Press.

Philipsen, G., & Carbaugh, D. (1986). A bibliography of fieldwork in the ethnography of communication. *Language in Society, 15*, 387–398.

Pratt, S., & Wieder, L. (1993). The case of *saying a few words* and *talking for another* among the Osage people: "Public speaking" as an object of ethnography. *Research on Language and Social Interaction, 26*, 353–408.

Richman, J. A. (1988). Deviance from sex-linked expressivity norms and psychological distress. *Social Forces, 67*, 208–215.

Rosaldo, M. (1982). The things we do with words: Ilongot speech acts and speech acts theory in philosophy. *Language in Society, 11*, 203–237.

Rosteck, T. (1998). Form and cultural context in rhetorical criticism: Re-reading Wrage. *Quarterly Journal of Speech, 84*, 471–490.

Ruud, G. (1995). The symbolic construction of organizational identities and community in a regional symphony. *Communication Studies, 46*, 201–221.

Ruud, G. (2000). The symphony: Organizational discourse and the symbolic tensions between artistic and business ideologies. *Journal of Applied Communication Research, 28*, 117–143.

Ruud, G., & Sprague, J. (2000). Can't see the [old growth] forest for the logs: Dialectical tensions in the interpretive practices of environmentalists and loggers. *Communication Reports, 13*, 55–65.

Schwartz, S. (1973). Normative explanations of helping behavior. A critique, proposal, and empirical test. *Journal of Experimental Social Psychology, 9*, 349–364.

Sequeira, D. (1993). Personal address as negotiated meaning in an American church community. *Research on Language and Social Interaction, 26*, 259–285.

Stewart, J. (1997). Developing communication theories. In G. Philipsen & T. L. Albrecht (Eds.), *Developing communication theories* (pp. 157–192). Albany: State University of New York Press.

Swidler, A. (1986). Culture in action: Symbols and strategies. *American Sociological Review, 51*, 273–286.

Swidler, A. (2001). *Talk of love: How culture matters*. Chicago: University of Chicago Press.

Turner, J. (1998). *A theory of social interaction*. Stanford, CA: Stanford University Press.

Wieder, D. (1974). *Language and social reality: The case of telling the convict code*. The Hague: Mouton.

Winchatz, M. R. (2001). Social meanings in German interactions: An ethnographic analysis of the second-person pronoun *Sie*. *Research on Language and Social Interaction, 34*, 337–369.

PART III

Theories Focusing on Cross-Cultural Variability in Communication

4

The Matrix of Face: An Updated Face-Negotiation Theory

STELLA TING-TOOMEY

A theory is a coherent set of explanations concerning the interconnected relationships between or among concepts. A well-designed intercultural communication theory provides a system of explanations for why certain cognitions, emotions, and/or behaviors occur in some intercultural encountering situations and under what conditions. A good theory of this kind can provide a deeper understanding of what happens in a given cultural context because of its explanatory richness. Overall, a sound intercultural theory should be a useful theory that can serve as a practical training framework to organize ideas together in a coherent fashion. A useful intercultural communication theory is a practical theory that can help individuals to communicate competently across a diverse range of cultural contexts.

The objective of this chapter is to provide an update of the face-negotiation theory from its 1998 version (Ting-Toomey & Kurogi, 1998). This chapter is organized in six sections. The first section covers the basic assumptions of the updated conflict face-negotiation theory. The second section addresses the core taxonomies of the theory. The third section discusses the cultural-level explanations of facework. The fourth section highlights individual-level factors of face-related conflict behaviors. The fifth section identifies relational and situational-level features that influence facework concerns. The final section maps out future research directions related to the testing of the conflict face-negotiation theory.

CONFLICT FACE-NEGOTIATION THEORY: CORE ASSUMPTIONS

Culture is a learned system of meanings that fosters a particular sense of shared identity and community among its group members. It is a complex frame of reference that consists of patterns of traditions, beliefs, values, norms, symbols, and meanings that are shared to varying degrees by interacting members of a community (Ting-Toomey, 1999a, p. 10). Culture affects communication, and communication affects culture (Hall, 1959, 1976). It is through communication that culture is learned, modified, and passed down from one generation to the next. Intercultural conflict takes place when our cultural group membership factors affect our conflict process with a member of a different culture on either a conscious or unconscious level.

The cultural membership differences can include deep-level differences such as cultural beliefs and values. Concurrently, they can also include the mismatch of applying different norms and expectations in a particular conflict scene. Conflict can be either an explicit or implicit interpersonal struggle process that entails perceived incompatible values, norms, goals, face orientations, scarce resources, interaction styles, and/or outcomes between two interdependent parties in an emotionally frustrating situation (Ting-Toomey & Oetzel, 2001).

Face Concerns and Intercultural Conflicts

Conflict of any kind is an emotionally laden, face-threatening phenomenon. Whether we choose to engage in or disengage from a conflict often depends on the differential weights we attribute to the different conflict goals. The perceived or actual conflict differences associated with our emotional frustrations often rotate around the following goal issues: content, relational, and identity (Wilmot & Hocker, 1998).

Content conflict goals refer to the substantive issues external to the individual involved. For example, intercultural business partners might argue about whether they should hold their business meetings in Mexico City or Los

Angeles. Recurrent content conflict issues often go hand in hand with relational conflict goals. *Relational conflict goals* refer to how individuals define, or would like to define, the particular relationship in that particular conflict episode. Nonintimate-intimate and formal-informal are two ways individuals might relate to one another. One business partner from the United States might opt to scribble a note and fax it to another international partner from Japan. The latter might well view this hastily prepared communication as a cavalier and unfriendly gesture. The Japanese partner may consequently perceive and experience face threat and relationship threat. The U.S. business partner, however, may not even realize that sending a message in this offhand manner was a faux pas. The U.S. American perceived the informal note as signaling affiliation or friendliness to minimize the formal relationship distance. *Identity-based goals* revolve around issues of identity confirmation-rejection, respect-disrespect, and approval-disapproval of the individuals in the conflict situation. Embedded identity conflict goals are often at the heart of many unresolved intercultural conflicts (Rothman, 1997). Identity conflict goals are directly linked to face-saving and face-honoring issues. When someone's face is threatened in a conflict episode, that person is likely to feel stressed, humiliated, shamed, aggravated, or embarrassed.

Identity conflict goals are broadly linked to the underlying beliefs and value patterns of the culture and the individuals. Thus, to reject someone's proposal or idea in a conflict can mean rejecting that person's deeply held beliefs and convictions. As an example, when an interfaith couple is arguing about which religious faith they should instill in their children, they are, at the same time, assessing which religious faith is more or less "worthwhile" in the family system. Likewise, in the case of deciding where the next Olympic Games should be held, the competing countries may be fighting over the merits and costs of a location site; however, they are also pushing and defending their national pride, honor, dignity, prestige, reputation, or *face* in the public arena. The decision to hold the Olympic Games in country X may be interpreted as enhanced power or increased status for the representatives of that country. In this way, identity goals are tied closely to culture-based face-orientation factors. At the heart of many recurring conflict problems often rest unresolved identity conflict needs.

The concept of *face* is about identity respect and other-identity consideration issues within and beyond the actual encounter episode. Face is tied to the emotional significance and estimated calculations that we attach to our own social self-worth and the social self-worth of others. It is therefore a precious identity resource in communication because it can be threatened, enhanced, undermined, and bargained over—on both an emotional reactive level and a cognitive appraisal level. On the emotional level, a face-threatening act in a conflict situation can arouse a mixed package of identity-linked vulnerable emotions. On the cognitive appraisal level, the degree of face threat or face disrespect is experienced when how we think we should be treated does not match with the reality of how the other person is actually treating us. If the discrepancy is great (i.e., between an individual's face need expectation vs. the actual encounter), he or she will then need to use different facework behaviors to manage the problematic episode.

Facework refers to the specific verbal and nonverbal behaviors that we engage in to maintain or restore face loss and to uphold and honor face gain. Face loss occurs when we are being treated in such a way that our expected identity claims in a conflict situation are challenged or ignored. A face-threatening episode is, in short, an identity expectancy violation episode. Face loss can be recouped via diverse conflict styles and facework strategies (see sections on "Conflict Communication Styles" and "Facework Interaction Strategies").

Theory Assumptions

While face and facework are universal phenomena, how we "frame" or interpret the situated meaning of face and how we enact facework differ from one cultural community to the next. In a nutshell, Ting-Toomey's (1985, 1988; Ting-Toomey & Kurogi, 1998) conflict face-negotiation theory assumes that

1. people in all cultures try to maintain and negotiate face in all communication situations;

2. the concept of face is especially problematic in emotionally vulnerable situations (such as embarrassment, request, or conflict situations) when the situated identities of the communicators are called into question;

3. the cultural variability dimensions of individualism-collectivism and small/large power distance shape the orientations, movements, contents, and styles of facework (see the section on "Face Orientations/Concerns and Cultural Value Dimensions");

4. individualism-collectivism shapes members' preferences for self-oriented facework versus other-oriented facework;

5. small/large power distance shapes members' preferences for horizontal-based facework versus vertical-based facework;

6. the cultural variability dimensions, in conjunction with individual (e.g., self-construal), relational (e.g., intimacy, status, ingroup/outgroup), and situational (e.g., topical salience) factors influence the use of particular facework behaviors in particular cultural scenes; and

7. intercultural facework competence refers to the optimal integration of knowledge, mindfulness, and communication skills in managing vulnerable identity-based conflict situations appropriately, effectively, and adaptively.

From these core assumptions, 32 theoretical propositions that account for the relationship between culture and face concerns, culture and conflict styles, and individual-level factors on face concerns were derived in the 1998 face-negotiation theory version (for a listing of past facework propositions, see Ting-Toomey & Kurogi, 1998). Since the 1998 version, many more research studies have been conducted on the relationship between culture-level factors and face concerns, culture-level factors and conflict styles, individual-level factors and face concerns, and individual-level factors and conflict styles. The results of some of these studies will be incorporated in this 2004 version of the conflict face-negotiation theory.

FACE MATRIX: CORE TAXONOMIES

To engage in competent facework negotiation, knowledge of facework taxonomies may pave the initial way to a constructive conflict dialogue process. Facework consists of five thematic clusters (Ting-Toomey, 1988; Ting-Toomey & Cole, 1990; Ting-Toomey & Kurogi, 1998):

1. face orientations or concerns—whether primary concern is for self, other, or both;

2. face movements or face moves' patterns—whether face is being defended/saved, maintained, or upgraded;

3. facework interaction strategies—the diverse verbal and nonverbal tactics to save or honor face;

4. conflict communication styles—the general behavioral tendencies used during the actual conflict negotiation process; and

5. face content domains—different face types or emphases.

In the following subsections, each thematic cluster will be discussed in detail.

Face Orientations/Concerns and Cultural Value Dimensions

The *orientation of face* determines the focus with which the face negotiator will direct her or his attention and energy of the subsequent conflict messages. *Self-face* is the protective concern for one's own image when one's own face is threatened in the conflict situation. *Other-face* is the concern or consideration for the other conflict party's image in the conflict situation. *Mutual-face* is the concern for both parties' images and/or the "image" of the relationship (Ting-Toomey, 1988, 1999b). While individualists or independents tend to be more concerned with protecting or preserving self-face images during an ongoing conflict episode, collectivists or interdependents tend to be more concerned with either accommodating the other-face images or saving mutual-face images in a conflict.

This line of reasoning is drawn from the value dimension of individualism-collectivism. Cultural value dimensions provide the underlying logic or motivational bases in framing why people behave the way they do in a cultural scene. Relational and situational features also assert a strong influence in terms of the foci and movements of face concerns and face efforts.

The value dimension of individualism-collectivism serves as an initial frame in explaining why individuals differ in their face expectations and face concerns in different cultures. Intercultural researchers (Fiske, 1991; Gudykunst & Ting-Toomey, 1988; Hofstede, 1991, 2001; Smith, Dugan, Peterson, & Leung, 1998; Triandis, 1994, 1995) in diverse disciplines have provided empirical evidence that the value spectrums of individualism and collectivism are indeed pervasive in a wide range of cultures. Basically, *individualism* refers to the broad value tendencies of a culture in emphasizing the importance of the "I" identity over the "we" identity, individual rights over group interests, and ego-focused emotions over social-focused emotions. In comparison, *collectivism* refers to the broad value tendencies of a culture in emphasizing the importance of the "we" identity over the "I" identity, ingroup interests over individual wants, and other-face concerns over self-face concerns (Ting-Toomey, 1985, 1988).

Individualistic and collectivistic value tendencies are manifested in everyday family, school, and workplace interactions. While both sets of value tendencies exist in the same culture and in each person, there are more situations in individualistic cultures that entail expectations for "I-identity" responses, and there are more situations in group-based cultures that call for "we-identity" responses. Hofstede's (1991, 2001) and Triandis's (1995) research indicates that individualism is a cultural pattern found in most northern and western regions of Europe and in North America. Collectivism refers to a cultural pattern common in Asia, Africa, the Middle East, Central and South America, and the Pacific Islands. Less than one third of the world's population resides in cultures with high individualistic value tendencies, and a little more than two thirds of the people live in cultures with high collectivistic value tendencies (Triandis, 1995). Within each culture, different ethnic communities can also display distinctive individualistic and collectivistic value patterns. Furthermore, distinctive forms and display styles of individualism and collectivism also reside within each unique ethnic/cultural grouping.

Beyond individualism-collectivism, another important value dimension we should take into consideration in explaining face negotiation is the dimension of power distance (Hofstede, 1991). In fact, the face-negotiation process entails a complex power interplay between the conflict parties. *Power distance,* from the cultural value analysis level, refers to the way a culture deals with status differences and social hierarchies. Cultures differ in the extent to which they view status inequalities (e.g., family background, age, birth order, gender, caste, occupation, education, wealth, and personal achievements) as good or bad, fair or unfair. People in *small power distance* cultures tend to value equal power distributions, symmetrical relations, and equitable rewards and costs based on individual achievement. People in *large power distance* cultures tend to accept unequal power distributions, asymmetrical

relations, and rewards and sanctions based on rank, role, status, age, and perhaps even gender identity. In small power distance work situations, power is evenly distributed. Subordinates expect to be consulted, and the ideal manager is a resourceful democrat. In large power distance work situations, the power of an organization is centralized in the upper management level. Subordinates expect to be told what to do, and the ideal manager plays a benevolent autocratic role. Small power distance index values are found, for example, in Austria, Israel, Denmark, New Zealand, Ireland, Sweden, and Norway. Large power distance index values are found in Malaysia, Guatemala, Panama, the Philippines, Mexico, Venezuela, and Arab countries (Hofstede, 1991).

While the United States scores on the low side of power distance, it is not extremely low. Hofstede (1991) explains that "U.S. leadership theories tend to be based on subordinates with medium-level dependence needs: not too high, not too low" (p. 42). Ting-Toomey and Oetzel (2001) observe that U.S. management style often follows a *status-achievement approach* because it emphasizes that via hard work, personal ambition, and competitiveness, status can be earned and displayed effectively and proudly (e.g., by driving expensive cars or having the spacious corner office). Two values that pervade this approach are freedom and earned inequality. Countries that predominantly reflect the status-achievement approach include some Latin nations (e.g., France and Italy) and to a moderate extent the United States and Great Britain. In comparison, many managers in other parts of the globe tend to see themselves as interdependent and at a different status level than others. That is, these managers think of themselves as people with connections to others and as members of a hierarchical network. They practice the *benevolent approach* of management style. Two values that pervade this approach are inequality and obligation to others. Countries that predominantly reflect the benevolent approach include most Latin American and South

American nations (e.g., Mexico, Venezuela, Brazil, Chile), most Asian nations (e.g., India, Japan, China, South Korea), most Arab nations (e.g., Egypt, Saudi Arabia, Jordan) and most African nations (e.g., Nigeria, Uganda).

For small power distance cultures, individuals often prefer horizontal-based facework interaction with the intent of minimizing status differences and social hierarchies. Comparatively, for large power distance cultures, individuals often prefer vertical-based facework interaction in accordance with titles, ranks, or hierarchical roles. For example, subordinates in large power distance organizations tend to trust and comply with the authority of their managers because of their implied status power, network connection, and long-term work experience. The different meanings, interpretations, and enactments of "power" and "trust" issues are tied closely to everyday facework practice in different cultures. Power distance value is often signaled through the linguistic habits of a cultural community. For example, many Mexicans tend to use the Spanish pronoun *usted* in formal situations and *tu* in informal-familiar situations. The use of *usted* is the formal application of the English pronoun *you* and forges a climate of *respeto*, or a respect-deference structure. The use of *tu* is the informal application of the English pronoun *you* and fosters a climate of relational intimacy and informality. Addressing someone by the improper form of *you* can pose serious face-threat problems in a diverse range of Mexican facework interactions (Garcia, 1996). Codes of honor and respect are tied closely to the everyday linguistic and nonverbal facework habits in each distinctive cultural community.

Interestingly, Hofstede (1991) has discovered that individualism and power distance are two separate conceptual dimensions, yet they are correlated. Countries that are high in individualism also tend to be low in power distance. Countries that are high in collectivism also tend to be high in power distance. The individualistic, small power distance cultural patterns can be found primarily in Northern European and North American regions. The collectivistic, large power distance cultural patterns can be found primarily in Latin American, African, and Asian regions (see also Gannon, 2004).

Face Movements or Face Moves' Patterns

The *face movement* cluster refers to the options that a negotiator faces in choosing whether to maintain, defend, and/or upgrade self-face versus other-face in a conflict episode (see Figure 4.1). Based on the conceptual dimensions of concern for self-face (high vs. low) and concern for other-face (high vs. low), there are four possible conflict movement options:

1. mutual-face protection moves: high concern for self-face and high concern for other-face movements;

2. mutual-face obliteration moves: low concern for self-face and low concern for other-face movements;

3. self-face defensive moves: high concern for self-face and low concern for other-face movements; and

4. other-face upgrading moves: low concern for self-face and high concern for other-face movements.

Maintaining one's own face or upholding another's face is what we usually do in our everyday social lives. Face maintenance, as a neutral starting point, is the civilized front with which we present ourselves to others via everyday politeness rituals (Goffman, 1959). To put it simply, face or interaction poise is sustained through everyday taken-for-granted communication routines. Face becomes more noticeable, however, when it is rendered problematic or threatened in diverse emotionally vulnerable situations. In almost all conflict situations, face-defending or face-saving strategies are needed when one's face is being threatened or attacked. When our face is under attack, emotional vulnerability or anxiety sets in, and associated emotions such as fear, anger,

Person A's Concern
for the Other's Face

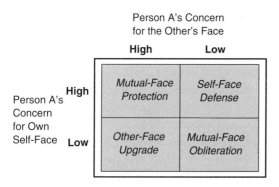

Figure 4.1   Dual-Concern Face Movements:
                   Four Options

humiliation, guilt, shame, disgust, and contempt follow closely. The need to recoup face loss and to restore equilibrium to face underlies some of these identity-based, fragile emotions.

In determining whether individuals would actually engage in face confrontation or flee the conflict scene altogether, interpersonal scholars (Brown & Levinson, 1987; Goffman, 1959; Guerrero, Andersen, & Afifi, 2001; Schlenker, 1985) have identified several conditions under which a face-threatening process (FTP) is perceived to be severe by the involved parties and, thus, shapes their use of diverse facework strategies. To connect their observations to face-based conflict situations, the scope conditions of facework strategies and, in conjunction, the use of different conflict styles are modified and extended as follows in this theoretical version:

1. the more important the culturally appropriate facework rule that is violated, the more severe the perceived FTP;

2. the larger the cultural distance between the conflict parties, the more mistrust or misunderstanding cumulates in the FTP;

3. the more important the conflict topic or imposition of the conflict demand, as interpreted from distinctive cultural angles, the more severe the perceived FTP;

4. the more power the conflict initiator has over the conflict recipient, the more severe the perceived FTP by the recipient;

5. the more harm or hurt the FTP produces, the more time and effort is needed to repair the FTP;

6. the more the actor is perceived as directly responsible for initiating the conflict cycle, the more that person is held accountable for the FTP; and

7. the more the actor is viewed as an outgroup member, the more severe the perceived FTP.

Face concern becomes incrementally more salient if several of these conditions are present in a face-threatening communication process.

From an individualistic cultural lens, the more severe the perceived FTP is in a conflict situation, the more likely the conflict communicators would engage in upfront, aggressive facework strategies to counter the direct face attacks. From a collectivistic cultural lens, however, the collectivistic communicators may opt to use high-context, avoidance strategies to wait for the conflict to simmer down and to buy time to recoup their hurt feelings. In addition, they may also turn to a third-party intermediary to mediate the conflict to avoid further head-on face-embarrassing collisions. A combination of some of the above FTP conditions, in conjunction with the situational face needs of the conflict negotiators, would determine the emotional tone, types, and particular strategies of facework management process in a conflict episode.

Facework Interaction Strategies

On a broad level, facework communicators can use either low-context or high-context verbal and nonverbal strategies to maintain face, to defend face, and/or to upgrade and honor someone else's face. Low-context communication emphasizes the importance of explicit verbal messages to convey personal thoughts, opinions, and feelings. High-context communication emphasizes the importance of multilayered contexts (e.g., historical context, social norms, roles, situational and relational contexts) that frame the interaction encounter

(Hall, 1976). Low-context style also emphasizes assertive, complementary nonverbal gestures to punctuate the important conflict points. High-context style, on the other hand, emphasizes nonverbal nuances and subtleties to signal conflict meanings.

While individualists tend to engage in low-context, direct styles (e.g., from verbal explicit style to verbal upfront style) of facework management, collectivists tend to engage in high-context, indirect styles (e.g., from verbal understated style to verbal effusive style) of facework negotiation (Ting-Toomey, 1985, 1997). Individualistic, low-context negotiators also tend to be able to separate the content goal issues from the conflict relationship, whereas collectivistic, high-context individuals are likely to see the person, the content goal, and the relationship conflict goal as an intertwined package.

Intercultural face-saving strategies can also span the range of dominating (e.g., defending and aggressive behaviors), avoiding (e.g., avoiding, giving in, seeking third-party help, and pretending), and integrating (e.g., apologizing, compromising, considering the other, private discussion, remaining calm, and talking about the problem) behaviors (Oetzel, Ting-Toomey, Yokochi, Masumoto, & Takai, 2000). *Dominating facework* focuses on presenting a credible image and wanting to win the conflict via competitive one-up/one-down strategies, to the use of defensive and aggressive interaction strategies. *Avoiding facework* emphasizes the preservation of relational harmony by not directly dealing with the conflict up front. Obliging the other person's needs, pretending to gloss over the conflict, passive-aggressive types of avoidance moves, and seeking third-party help are some avoiding facework tactics. *Integrating facework* emphasizes both the content resolution of the conflict and the importance of relationship preservation. Some integrative mutual-face protective strategies can include mindful listening, intentional reframing, collaborative dialogue, and mutual-interest problem solving (Ting-Toomey & Oetzel, 2001).

In approaching a conflict negotiation situation, facework serves a variety of communication functions. Facework can be used strategically to (a) defuse a conflict via avoidance and compromise tactics, (b) aggravate a conflict via direct and passive-aggressive tactics, (c) repair damaged images via excuses and justifications, and (d) mend broken relationships via apologies and third-party help. These functions are part of the process of maintaining, defending/saving, protecting/compensating, and upgrading and honoring face-image identity issues.

However, facework is not equivalent to conflict styles. According to Ting-Toomey and Oetzel (2001), in the context of U.S. conflict style research literature, conflict styles have often been studied from a content, problem-solving angle to the neglect of considering interaction identity or face-saving issues. Furthermore, conflict styles commonly have been referred to as specific behaviors used to engage in or disengage from a conflict situation. In the case of "face-saving" behaviors, however, face-saving strategies can be used before (preventive facework), during, or after (restorative facework) a conflict episode. They can also be used within a conflict relationship or beyond a conflict relationship via different face-saving stories to different interested third parties. Therefore, while conflict styles can include specific facework tactics, facework tactics or strategies can be used in a variety of identity-threatening and identity-protection situations. Furthermore, these situations can include, for example, requesting, embarrassment, performance feedback, and complimenting situations. Since face concerns and face strategies are concerned more with relational and face-identity issues (e.g., respect-disrespect, poise, shame, pride, composure, apology, forgiveness, etc.) above and beyond conflict content goal issues, two separate measurements of face concern dimensions and particular face-strategy types have been developed. The measurements together with reliability and validity issues are discussed in Ting-Toomey and Oetzel (2001).

Along a developmental time frame, when one's face is being threatened (or in anticipation of its being threatened), the typical facework strategies are preventive facework strategies and restorative facework strategies (Brown, 1977; Ting-Toomey & Cole, 1990). *Preventive facework strategies* (e.g., hedges and disclaimers) refer to communicative behaviors designed to soften or ward off the occurrence of face loss events that one anticipates will foster an appearance of weakness or vulnerability. It is also presumed that such events will potentially damage one's image or the image of those whom one represents (Brown, 1977). According to Cupach and Metts (1994), preventive facework can include some of the following strategy types:

1. credentialing: certification preface statements to certify one's status or role before sending potential face-hurting comments (e.g., "I have years of experience dealing with . . ." or "Since I'm your coach, that's why I'm telling you this . . .");

2. suspended judgment appeal: direct appeal statements for suspending premature judgment (e.g., "Before you make up your mind, hear me out");

3. pre-disclosure: relational solidarity/bonding statements in exchange for face support and understanding an actor's own self-disclosure (e.g., "Since we've all made fools of ourselves at different points in our lives, what I'm going to tell you . . .");

4. pre-apology: self-effacing or self-deprecating apologies to lower expectations and to alleviate potential face shame ("Before I start, please accept my apology for . . .";

5. hedging: preemptive, fudging phrases to minimize potential face loss (e.g., "I may be way off base here, but please hear me out . . ."); and

6. disclaimer: pre-handicapping statements used to cushion or circumvent potential face criticisms ("Since you are all experts in this area, and I'm only a novice in this field . . .").

Restorative facework strategies (e.g., excuses and justifications) refer to behaviors designed to repair damaged or lost face and occur in response to events that have already transpired. Restorative facework is past-oriented and is part of the important facework repair ritual. Restorative facework reflects behaviors designed to heal the damaged relationship or to reassert the individual's capability or strength after the person feels threatened (Brown, 1977). Restorative (or corrective) facework can include the following strategy types (Cupach & Metts, 1994):

1. direct aggression: includes verbal yelling, screaming, or physical violence to repair face loss;

2. excuses: accounts or explanations that minimize the personal responsibility of the actor for the offensive behavior (e.g., "I didn't want to sign the contract, but the other group manipulated me into signing . . .";

3. justifications: accounts or explanations that downplay the severity of the face loss behavior (e.g., "Yes, I signed the contract, but it's no big deal—It's only a three-month contract . . .";

4. humor: includes laughing at the actor's own mistakes or humoring the other person or encouraging the other person to lighten up;

5. physical remediation: attempts to repair physical damage (e.g., wipe up the coffee spill quickly);

6. passive aggressiveness: includes denial, forgetfulness, acting confused, passive blaming, sarcasm, complaining to third person, or acting verbally passive ("No, nothing is wrong") but nonverbally loaded (sulking, pouting, or slamming the door);

7. avoidance: topical avoidance to physical distancing from the face-loss situation; and

8. apologies: self-deprecating offerings to alleviate guilt or shame.

We can speculate here that individualists, because of their "I-identity" priority, would tend to use more self-face restorative strategies such as justifications and excuses to restore the perceived face loss in the conflict situation. On the other hand, collectivists, coming from face-salient cultures, would tend to use more proactive, self-face preventive strategies, such as disclaimers and pre-apologies, to ward off anticipated face threats. Furthermore, restorative facework strategies can include either situational attribution accounts or dispositional attribution accounts.

Attributions refer to the stories or reasons that we offer to explain why things occurred in the conflict situation. Individualists, when their face is complimented, would tend to use *positive dispositional accounts* to accept the face compliment. When their face is threatened, however, they would likely opt for *situational accounts* (i.e., external causes such as blaming generalized others or the situation) to save self-oriented face. Situational accounts refer to stories (e.g., car problems) that attribute the reasons of the conflict problem to external sources (i.e., external to one's ability, disposition, or competence). Conversely, collectivists, when their face is singled out and praised, would tend to use situational accounts (e.g., effort of teamwork and collaboration) to diffuse face attention. However, when their face is threatened, they may use dispositional accounts (e.g., "I should have been more careful in checking out the project details. I will try harder the next time around") to acknowledge the failed event, especially when the event affects ingroup team climate. Dispositional accounts refer to stories that locate the problematic event to one's failed effort, incompetence, or personality flaw. By engaging in self-criticism or self-effacing dispositional accounts, collectivists are acknowledging that there is a set of ingroup standards to be followed. To be competent facework negotiators, we need to develop a good knowledge base of face-negotiation taxonomies and apply them mindfully in a variety of face-sensitive communication situations.

Conflict Communication Styles

Overall, a conflict style is learned within the primary socialization process of a person's cultural or ethnic group. Many researchers have conceptualized conflict styles along two dimensions (Blake & Mouton, 1964; Putnam & Wilson, 1982; Thomas & Kilmann, 1974). Rahim (1983, 1992) bases his classification of conflict styles on the two conceptual dimensions of concern for self and concern for others. The first dimension illustrates the degree (high or low) to which a person seeks to satisfy her or his own interest. The second dimension represents the degree (high or low) to which a person desires to incorporate the other's conflict interest. The two dimensions are combined, resulting in five styles of handling interpersonal conflict: dominating, avoiding, obliging, compromising, and integrating.

Briefly, the *dominating* (or competitive/controlling) style emphasizes conflict tactics that push for a person's own position or goal above and beyond the other person's conflict interest. The *avoiding* style involves eluding the conflict topic, the conflict party, or the conflict situation altogether. The *obliging* (or accommodating) style is characterized by a high concern for the other person's conflict interest above and beyond a person's own conflict interest. The *compromising* style involves a give-and-take concession approach in order to reach a midpoint agreement concerning the conflict content issue. Finally, the *integrating* (or collaborative) style reflects a need for solution closure in conflict and involves high concern for one's self and high concern for the other in substantive conflict negotiation. It should be noted that in the U.S. conflict management literature, obliging and avoiding conflict styles often take on a Western slant of being negatively disengaged (i.e., "placating" or "flight" from the conflict scene). Collectivists, however, do not perceive obliging and avoiding conflict styles as negative. These two styles are typically employed to maintain mutual-face interests and relational network interests. Furthermore, the compromising style focuses more on the content goal negotiation process to the neglect of relational and identity-based respect and consideration issues (Ting-Toomey, 1988; Ting-Toomey & Kurogi, 1998).

Thus, while the five-style conflict model serves as a good initial probe of conflict style, it misses some other salient style factors such as emotions, third-party consultation or concern, and passive-aggressive types of conflict tactics. In examining U.S. ethnic-based conflict styles in four groups, Ting-Toomey et al. (2000) have added three more conflict styles to account for the potentially rich areas of cultural and ethnic differences in conflict: emotional expression, third-party help, and neglect. *Emotional expression* refers to using one's emotions to guide communication behaviors during conflict. *Third-party help* involves using an outsider to mediate the conflict. Especially in collectivistic, large power distance cultures, conflict is often managed via informal, third-party mediation. This third-party mediator is usually one who occupies a high-status position (perhaps a wise elder) and therefore has a credible reputation. The mediator also has a good relationship with both disputants. In order to "give face" to this high-status, third-party mediator, both collectivistic conflict parties may be willing to make concessions in the name of honoring the high-status mediator's "face" (and, thus, saving their own face). Finally, *neglect* is characterized by using passive-aggressive responses to sidestep the conflict but at the same time getting an indirect reaction from the other conflict party. Further conceptual discussions and measurements of these eight conflict styles can be found in Ting-Toomey et al.'s (2000) article on ethnic identity and conflict styles. In terms of specific ethnic conflict findings, Latino Americans and Asian Americans in the United States have been found to use avoiding and third-party conflict styles more than African Americans. Asian immigrants tend to use an avoiding style more than European Americans (Ting-Toomey et al.,

2000; see also Collier, 1991; Ting-Toomey, 1986). It is important to note that most of these studies have been conducted in acquaintance conflict relationships.

Face Content Domains

What are the possible content topics of face negotiation? Individuals have different face wants or face needs in a diverse range of communicative situations. Some face content domains include autonomy face, inclusion face, approval face, reliability face, competence face, and moral face (Bond, 1991; Brown & Levinson, 1987; Earley, 1997; Gao, 1998; Gao & Ting-Toomey, 1998; Katriel, 1986; Lim, 1994; Ting-Toomey, 1994a). *Autonomy face* is concerned with our need for others to acknowledge our independence, self-sufficiency, privacy, boundary, nonimposition, control issues, and vice versa (i.e., our consideration for the face needs of the other on the autonomy face domain, etc.). *Inclusion face* (or fellowship face) is concerned with our need for others to recognize that we are worthy companions, likeable, agreeable, pleasant, friendly, and cooperative. *Status face* is concerned with our need for others to admire our tangible or intangible assets or resources such as appearance, social attractiveness, reputation, position, power, and material worth. *Reliability face* is concerned with our need for others to realize that we are trustworthy, dependable, reliable, loyal, and consistent in our words and actions. *Competence face* (as in "communication competence") is concerned with our need for others to recognize our qualities or social abilities such as intelligence, skills, expertise, leadership, team-building skills, networking skills, conflict mediation skills, facework skills, and problem-solving skills. *Moral face* is concerned with our need for others to respect our sense of integrity, dignity, honor, propriety, and moral uprightness. The boundaries between face domains are permeable and overlapped such that in negotiating face reliability, we also need to tend to face competence. In dealing with face autonomy, we also need to tend to face fellowship or inclusion. Thus, the different face content domains exist in a three-dimensional, matrix-like space—in tight intersection with one another. When the need or expectation for one face content domain is not met, there will be repercussions for other face content domains. Concurrently, in dealing competently with one face content domain, the satisfied face domain may also have ripple effects on other face content domains.

On a deeper level of face content domain analysis, Hu (1944) describes two Chinese conceptualizations of face: *lien* and *mien-tzu*. *Lien* is the underlying moral face that involves a person's internalized notions or standards of shame, integrity, debasement, and honor issues. The loss of *lien* is associated with situations in which honor and, hence, integrity are in serious jeopardy. *Mien-tzu*, on the other hand, is the external social face that involves social recognition, position, authority, influence, and power. *Lien* and *mien-tzu* reciprocally influence one another. They are two interdependent constructs, with *lien* as the internalized moral compass and *mien-tzu* as the externalized social image. The Chinese concept of *lien* is equivalent to moral face as discussed here, while the concept of *mien-tzu* is related to the term *face* found in both past and current facework literature in psychology, sociology, sociolinguistics, diplomacy, and communication. Furthermore, the concept of *moral face* can include both culture-specific and culture-universal meanings, since concepts such as *morality* and *integrity* are tied so closely to the ethos of a culture.

 Drawing from the value dimensions of individualism-collectivism and small/large power distance, we can speculate that, comparatively speaking, while individualists would tend to emphasize the autonomy-face content domain, collectivists would tend to emphasize the inclusion-face domain. Individualists would also tend to emphasize more ego-focused emotions such as pride, personal hurt, personal insults, personal fairness, and individual justice issues. Collectivists, on the other hand, would focus more on social-focused emotions such as shame, public embarrassment, communal honor, and communal wrongdoing issues (Markus & Kitayama, 1991; Ting-Toomey, 1994b, 1994c). While both individualists and collectivists may experience a wide range of conflict emotions, they may internalize certain types of emotions with varying intensity in response to different face domains. For example, a collectivist might tend to experience a higher intensity of shame for the wrongdoings of a close relative than an individualist would on the fellowship face issue. The more we hold a particular face content domain in high regard, the more emotionally vulnerable we are in that face content domain. In sum, the more we hold a face domain in high esteem, the more we long for affirmation in that domain. The more we understand our own face needs and the face needs (plus the underlying face meanings) of the other conflict parties, the more we can validate and honor those valued face domains and the more competent we are as facework negotiators. The more severe the face transgression in particular face domains, the more defensive we become in our desire to save or protect the vulnerable spots in those valued assets.

CULTURAL-LEVEL THEORETICAL PROPOSITIONS

Cultural-Level Assumptions

Assumptions 1–5 cover cultural-level explanations in shaping our attitudes, expectations, and enactment of facework in a diverse range of cultures. Face is rendered problematic in communication dilemma situations when we are confronted with multiple options of maintaining our own face, defending our own face, and/or of upholding the other's face. Facework calculation is particularly active when self-interest and other-interest are at stake and when the interactions are played out in the international arena. Situations such as diplomatic negotiation, conflict negotiation, and crisis negotiation often entail active facework negotiation.

In relating national cultures with face concerns, research reveals that while individualists (e.g., U.S. respondents) tend to use more direct, self-face concern conflict behaviors (e.g., dominating/competing style), collectivists (e.g., Taiwan and China respondents) tend to use more indirect, other-face concern conflict behaviors (e.g., avoiding and obliging styles). Males (from both Japan and the U.S.) also reported the use of more dominating or competing conflict behaviors than females (Cai & Fink, 2002; Cocroft & Ting-Toomey, 1994; Ting-Toomey et al., 1991; Trubisky, Ting-Toomey, & Lin, 1991). In addition, other-/mutual-face concern has been found to relate positively with integrating facework strategies and conflict styles (Chen, 2002; Oetzel & Ting-Toomey, 2003; Oetzel et al., 2001).

In an organizational facework study, Oetzel, Myers, Meares, and Lara (2003)

examined face concerns and conflict styles in U.S. organizations. They surveyed 184 managers and employees and asked them to describe their reactions to typical conflicts with either a peer or a person of different status. It was found that *self-face concern* was associated positively with dominating and emotionally expressive styles. *Other-face concern* was associated positively with integrating, obliging, and compromising styles. *Mutual-face concern* was associated positively with integrating, obliging, and compromising styles. In addition, inclusion of face concerns provided a better prediction of which conflict style would be utilized than other relevant variables for six out of the eight conflict styles considered.

More recently, in a direct empirical test of the conflict face-negotiation theory (Oetzel & Ting-Toomey, 2003), the objective of the study was to test the underlying assumption of the face-negotiation theory that face is an explanatory mechanism for culture's influence on conflict behavior (see Figure 4.2). A questionnaire was administered to 768 participants in four national cultures (China, Germany,

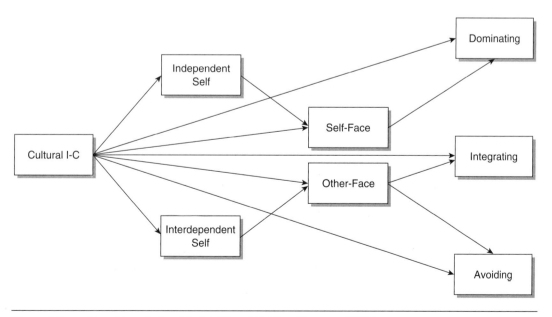

Figure 4.2   Face-Negotiation Model (Oetzel & Ting-Toomey, 2003)

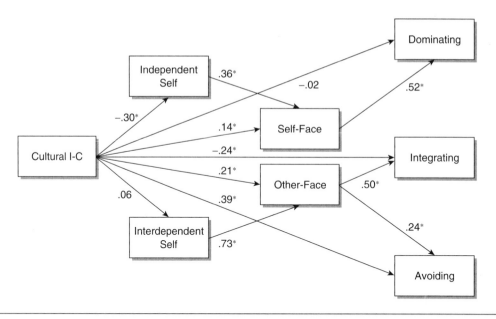

Figure 4.3   Results of the SEM Testing of the Face-Negotiation Model (Oetzel & Ting-Toomey, 2003)

Japan, and the U.S.) in their respective languages asking them to recall and describe a recent interpersonal conflict.

The major findings of the study are as follows: (a) cultural individualism-collectivism had direct effects on conflict styles, as well as mediated effects through self-construal and face concerns; (b) self-face concern was associated positively with dominating conflict styles, and other-face concern was associated positively with avoiding and integrating conflict styles; and (c) face concerns accounted for all of the total variance explained in dominating style, most of the total variance explained in integrating style, and some of the total variance explained in avoiding style when considering face concerns, cultural individualism-collectivism, and self-construals (see Figure 4.3).

Cultural-Level Propositions

Thus, based on past and recent studies, the revised cultural-level propositions of the face-negotiation theory are presented as follows:

Cultural-Level Propositions

Proposition 1: Members of individualistic cultures tend to express a greater degree of self-face maintenance concerns than members of collectivistic cultures.

Proposition 2: Members of collectivistic cultures tend to express a greater degree of other-face concerns than members of individualistic cultures.

Proposition 3: Members of collectivistic cultures tend to express a greater degree of mutual-face maintenance concerns than members of individualistic cultures.

Proposition 4: Members of individualistic cultures tend to use a greater degree of direct, dominating facework strategies in a conflict situation than members of collectivistic cultures.

Proposition 5: Members of collectivistic cultures tend to use a greater degree of avoidance facework strategies than members of individualistic cultures.

Proposition 6: Members of collectivistic cultures tend to use a greater degree of integrative facework strategies than members of individualistic cultures.

Proposition 7: Members of individualistic cultures tend to use more dominating/competing conflict styles than members of collectivistic cultures.

Proposition 8: Members of individualistic cultures tend to use more emotionally expressive conflict styles than members of collectivistic cultures.

Proposition 9: Members of individualistic cultures tend to use more assertive to aggressive conflict styles than members of collectivistic cultures.

Proposition 10: Members of collectivistic cultures tend to use more avoiding conflict styles than members of individualistic cultures.

Proposition 11: Members of collectivistic cultures tend to use more obliging conflict styles than members of individualistic cultures.

Proposition 12: Members of collectivistic cultures tend to use more compromising to integrating conflict styles than members of individualistic cultures.

INDIVIDUAL-LEVEL THEORETICAL EXPLANATIONS

Individual-Level Assumptions

Assumption 6 of the face-negotiation theory posits that the cultural value dimensions in conjunction with individual factors influence the use of specific facework behaviors in particular cultural scenes. Self-construal is one of the major individual factors that focuses on individual variation within and between cultures. *Self-construal* is one's self-image and is composed of an independent and an interdependent self (Markus & Kitayama, 1991, 1998). The independent construal of self involves the view that an individual is a unique entity with an individuated repertoire of feelings, cognitions, and motivations. In contrast, the interdependent construal of self

involves an emphasis on the importance of relational or ingroup connectedness.

Self-construal is the individual-level equivalent of the cultural variability dimension of individualism-collectivism. For example, Gudykunst et al. (1996), Oetzel (1998a, 1999), and Ting-Toomey, Oetzel, and Yee-Jung (2001) argue that independent self-construal is predominantly associated with people of individualistic cultures, while interdependent self-construal is predominantly associated with people of collectivistic cultures. However, both dimensions of self exist within each individual, regardless of cultural identity. In individualistic cultural communities, there may be more communication situations that evoke the need for independent-based decisions and behaviors. In collectivistic communities, there may be more situations that demand the sensitivity for interdependent-based decisions and actions. The manner in which individuals conceive of their self-images—independent versus interdependent selves—should have a profound influence on what types of facework they would use in a particular conflict episode. For example, in one study, Oetzel (1998b) found that a dominating/competing style was associated positively with independent self-construal, while avoiding/obliging and compromising styles were associated positively with interdependent self-construals. The integrating conflict style was associated with both self-construals, but more strongly with interdependence than independence. In a recent cross-national study, Oetzel and Ting-Toomey (2003) found that independent self-construal was associated positively with self-face concern. Interdependent self-construal, on the other hand, was associated positively with other-face concern. Self-face concern was found to relate positively with dominating/competing conflict tactics, while other-face concern was related positively with avoiding and integrating conflict tactics. In another interesting study (Ting-Toomey, Oetzel, & Yee-Jung, 2001), the authors examined the combination of the two self-construal dimensions that results in four self-construal types: biconstrual (high on both dimensions), independent orientation (high independent, low interdependent), interdependent orientation (low independent, high interdependent), and ambivalent orientation (low on both orientations).

They examined the self-construals and conflict styles of four ethnic groups in the United States who recalled an acquaintance conflict. The researchers found that (a) biconstruals use integrating and compromising conflict styles more than ambivalents; (b) biconstruals use an emotionally expressive style more than ambivalents; (c) biconstruals use a dominating/competing style more than ambivalents; (d) ambivalents use a third-party help style more than biconstruals; and (e) ambivalents use a neglecting (i.e., passive-aggressive) style more than biconstruals. Overall, it seems that the biconstruals have a wide range of conflict repertoires for dealing with different conflict situations, whereas ambivalents prefer to use the neglecting conflict style or complaining to a third party more than biconstruals, independents, and interdependents. Perhaps the role of "third-party" help needs to be further reconceptualized and researched in the conflict style literature—whether disputants seek third-party help constructively or passive-aggressively may mean different things to different members in different cultural communities. In sum, cultural individualism-collectivism had direct effects on conflict styles, as well as mediated effects through self-construals and face concerns.

Individual-Level Propositions

Thus, based on past and recent empirical studies on conflict face negotiation, here are the updated propositions:

Individual-Level Propositions

Proposition 13: Independent self is associated positively with self-face concern.

Proposition 14: Interdependent self is associated positively with other-face/mutual-face concern.

Proposition 15: Self-face maintenance is associated with dominating/competing conflict style.

Proposition 16: Other-face maintenance is associated positively with avoiding/obliging conflict style.

Proposition 17: Other-face maintenance is associated positively with compromising/integrating conflict style.

Proposition 18: Independent self-construal type is associated positively with dominating/competing conflict style.

Proposition 19: Interdependent self-construal type is associated positively with obliging/avoiding conflict style.

Proposition 20: Interdependent self-construal type is associated positively with compromising/integrating conflict style.

Proposition 21: Biconstrual type is associated positively with compromising/integrating conflict style.

Proposition 22: Ambivalent type is associated positively with neglect/third-party conflict style.

RELATIONAL AND SITUATIONAL EXPLANATIONS

Relational and Situational Assumptions

Cultural values and personal attributes influence the relational and situational norms that we use in a conflict interaction episode. Assumption 6 of the face-negotiation theory also assumes that the cultural variability and individual variability dimensions, *in conjunction with* relational and situational factors, influence the use of particular facework behaviors in particular cultural contexts. There are many relational and situational features we can consider when we theorize the influence of these factors on conflict competence behaviors. Relationship factors (e.g., relationship length, familiarity, intimacy, and power dynamics) along with situational factors (e.g., conflict salience, intensity, interaction goals, and public-private setting) can have a profound effect on face concerns and conflict styles. One of the relationship factors that has gained increased research attention is the concept of ingroup-outgroup (Oetzel, 1999; Ting-Toomey & Oetzel, 2002).

It is important to note that members of collectivistic cultures tend to make a greater distinction between ingroups and outgroups than members of individualistic cultures (Triandis, 1995). *Ingroups* are groups of individuals who perceive themselves as sharing some salient attributes (e.g., religious beliefs, values, or language), a strong emotional bond, and an interdependent fate. *Outgroups* are groups of individuals whom ingroup members consider as unconnected to them, as unfamiliar others, as existing on an unequal basis, and/or as threatening in some way. Individualists or independent-self personalities tend to have greater self-face concerns and less other-face concerns in dealing with both ingroups and outgroups during conflicts. Collectivists or interdependent-self personalities, on the other hand, tend to pay extra attention to other-face concerns with ingroup members because of long-term relational obligations and implications. They tend to focus, however, on self-face concern issues in outgroup conflict situations, especially when the conflict stake is high and the reward can benefit the ingroup as a whole. Of course, the initial facework scope conditions plus many other layered situational factors also influence the use of self-face concern versus other-face concern conflict strategies.

In addition, according to past research (Leung & Iwawaki, 1988), individualists tend to prefer the use of the *equity norm* in dealing with reward allocation. In comparison, collectivists prefer the use of the *communal norm* in reward allocation in dealing with ingroup task-based decisions. For example, individuals operating from an equity norm would tend to distribute points in a team project based on individual merit or contribution. Individuals operating from a communal norm, however, would tend to distribute points for a team project evenly—regardless of uneven personal contribution. The equity norm emphasizes the importance of personal reward and cost calculations. The communal norm, in contrast, stresses the importance of taking ingroup expectations, contexts, and long-term contributions into calculation. Vertical collectivists may also have to add the factor of seniority or status in distributing rewards, thus observing the hierarchical face needs of members in different status rankings.

Nevertheless, both individualists and collectivists have been found to prefer the use of the equity norm in *high-premium conflicts* when competing with outgroup members for needed scarce resources (Leung, 1999). For example, both individualistic and collectivistic managers from different companies would compete ferociously with each other for a contract by showing that they deserve it more than other bidders. However, for *low-grade to moderate-grade conflict situations* or when the conflict stake is low, collectivists tend to practice the "smoothing over" communal norm with both outgroup and ingroup members. They would opt for the mutual face-saving approach in preserving relational image or face and try to overlook any antagonistic irritations. The meanings and interpretations we attribute to whether a conflict event is salient (i.e., degree of importance) or nonsalient depend heavily on cultural, individual, relational, and situational factors.

Relational and Situational-Level Propositions

Based on the above discussions, the following two new theoretical propositions are presented as situational-level propositions.

Situational-Level Propositions

Proposition 23: Individualists or independent-self personalities tend to express a greater degree of self-face maintenance concerns and less other-face maintenance concerns in dealing with both ingroup and outgroup conflict situations.

Proposition 24: Collectivists or interdependent-self personalities tend to express a greater degree of other-face concerns with ingroup members and a greater degree of self-face maintenance concerns with outgroup members in intergroup conflict situations.

Altogether, 24 revised theoretical propositions are posed in this 2005 face-negotiation theory version. There are 12 culture-level propositions, 10 individual-level propositions, and 2 relational and situational-level facework propositions.

Finally, according to Assumption 7 of the face-negotiation theory, intercultural facework competence refers to the optimal integration of knowledge, mindfulness, and constructive conflict skills in managing vulnerable identity-based interaction scenes appropriately, effectively, and adaptively. Readers who are interested in the competence component of face negotiation may want to consult Ting-Toomey's (2004) article. With more empirical testing, new propositions on cross-cultural and intercultural facework competence can be posed in future update versions. The facework training article addresses the translation of the conflict face-negotiation theory into intercultural facework competence and application contexts.

CONFLICT FACE-NEGOTIATION THEORY: RESEARCH DIRECTIONS AND ISSUES

The previous discussion on the conflict face-negotiation theory reveals several areas that can benefit from additional research attention. The three suggested research directions are as follows: facework emotions, facework situations, and facework movements.

Facework Emotions Research

If we dig deeper, face concerns are linked directly to affective-based identity issues in conflict. We need more systematic studies in understanding the developmental ebbs and flows of facework emotions and facework emotional engagement. We need to understand the core metaphors, language, themes, psychosomatic changes, and nonverbal nuances that surround the onset of affective facework embarrassment and affective facework resolution.

Furthermore, we need to design more multi-methods studies on the affective aspects of respect, trust, dignity, and honor. For example, since "respect" is such an important concept in intercultural facework negotiation, we need to develop more complex models to analyze systematically the cognitive, affective, behavioral, and ethical dimensions of "facework respect" in different cultural communities.

Likewise, we know too little about the concept of "forgiveness." We need to conceptualize more deeply the role of forgiveness in the international arena. What does it mean in different cultures to "forgive" someone? How do we know we are "forgiven"? What are the particular cultural nuances, meanings, expectations, and assumptions about the concept of forgiveness in different cultures, especially in major conflict transgression episodes?

We also know too little about the culture-specific meanings of "trust" in facework trust-building sessions. What does it mean to "trust" someone in a cross-cultural comparative setting? What does it mean to "betray" someone in a cross-cultural arena? How do individuals in different cultures juggle the dual roles of "trust" and "betrayal" and rebuild trust again despite repeated trust transgressions?

The emotions of pride, shame, guilt, redemption, trust, betrayal, and disconfirmation are all powerful emotional concepts lacking sufficient treatment in the intercultural conflict literature. These are complex, affective responses generated and experienced in reaction to others and related to the cognitive appraisals of the worthiness of self-face and other-face issues. Facework emotional reactions and cognitive appraisals also always happen in some embedded facework situational systems.

Facework Situational Research

The study of face-negotiation in conflict would definitely benefit from an examination of the relationship between situations and different face content domains or face movements. For example, questions such as the following need more systematic research investigations: Under what situational conditions would facework negotiators be more concerned with inclusion face issues versus autonomy face issues? Under what specific situational conditions would conflict disputants be more interested in mutual-face protection versus self-face protection? Under what triggering mechanisms would conflict negotiators be more concerned with mutual-face protection versus mutual-face obliteration? What are the necessary and sufficient conditions that move the developmental trajectories of facework evolution—from self-interest to mutual-interest to universal-interest concerns?

There are a variety of situational features that can affect face concerns, facework, and conflict styles. Ting-Toomey and Oetzel (2001) propose a culture-based situational model of conflict. They focus on ingroup/outgroup boundaries, perceptual filters (e.g., ethnocentrism, stereotypes, and prejudice lenses), relational parameters, conflict goal assessments, and conflict intensity as situational features that frame diverse face behaviors and conflict styles. Further research work is needed to understand the situational effect on face and facework in cross-cultural and intercultural conflicts. More research is needed to

fine-tune the ingroup/outgroup dichotomous categories to finer, more complex distinctions. We can then relate the different face concerns and strategies with the more differentiated ingroup-outgroup parameters.

Facework Movements Research

Facework movements and temporality are also important dimensions for understanding how individuals complete the process of face-negotiation during and after the actual conflict negotiation process. The lack of investigations on face movements and temporality may be a by-product of the methods utilized for the majority of research on cross-cultural conflict. The majority of the studies on conflict facework have relied heavily on self-report measures of face behavior in hypothetical or recalled conflicts. The use of these methods does not allow researchers to examine the developmental process of face-negotiation—making it particularly difficult to study temporality. The study of conflict face-negotiation would benefit from examining actual interaction via procedures such as interaction analysis or discourse analysis to understand the diverse ways in which individuals defend and maintain face, as well as whether they are proactive or reactive in managing face. In addition, postconflict interviews or journal tracking can elicit the logic or narrative accounts that individuals use to justify their facework behaviors during a conflict.

In conclusion, there is a moderate amount of research on cross-cultural face concerns, facework, and conflict styles, especially in regard to individualism-collectivism and self-construals. However, more research is needed to determine the importance of affective and situational aspects of face concerns and conflict styles across ethnic groups and across a diverse range of cultures. Face movements, temporality, and competence are also important dimensions for cross-cultural conflict research. More studies are also needed to expand the research boundaries of cross-cultural conflict styles and to examine conflict transformational behaviors in a diverse range of intergroup and intercultural conflict settings. The future directions specified here will help to fine-tune the conflict face-negotiation theory, bringing us closer to understanding the complex matrix of face-on and face-off communication behaviors.

NOTE

1. I want to thank John Oetzel for all his collaborative work with me and with his graduate students in testing the conflict face-negotiation theory.

REFERENCES

Blake, R. R., & Mouton, J. S. (1964). *The managerial grid*. Houston, TX: Gulf.

Bond, M. (1991). *Beyond the Chinese face*. Hong Kong: Oxford University Press.

Brown, B. (1977). Face-saving and face-restoration in negotiation. In D. Druckman (Ed.), *Negotiations: Social-psychological perspectives* (pp. 275–299). Beverly Hills, CA: Sage.

Brown, P., & Levinson, S. (1987). *Politeness: Some universals in language usage*. Cambridge, UK: Cambridge University Press.

Cai, D. A., & Fink, E. L. (2002). Conflict style differences between individualists and collectivists. *Communication Monographs, 69,* 67-87.

Chen, G. M. (2002). The impact of harmony on Chinese conflict management. In G. M. Chen & R. Ma (Eds.), *Chinese conflict management and resolution* (pp. 3–17). Westport, CT: Ablex.

Cocroft, B., & Ting-Toomey, S. (1994). Facework in Japan and the United States. *International Journal of Intercultural Relations, 18*(4), 469–506.

Collier, M. J. (1991). Conflict competence within African, Mexican, and Anglo-American friendships. In S. Ting-Toomey & F. Korzenny (Eds.), *Cross-cultural interpersonal communication* (pp. 132–154). Newbury Park, CA: Sage.

Cupach, W., & Metts, S. (1994). *Facework*. Thousand Oaks, CA: Sage.

Earley, P. C. (1997). *Face, harmony, and social support: An analysis of organizational behavior across cultures*. New York: Oxford University Press.

Fiske, A. (1991). *Structures of social life: The four elementary forms of human relations*. New York: Free Press.

Gannon, M. J. (2004). *Understanding global cultures: Metaphorical journeys through 28 nations, clusters of nations, and continents* (3rd ed.). Thousand Oaks, CA: Sage.

Gao, G. (1998). An initial analysis of the effects of face and concern for "other" in Chinese interpersonal communication. *International Journal of Intercultural Relations, 22*(4), 467–482.

Gao, G., & Ting-Toomey, S. (1998). *Communicating effectively with the Chinese*. Thousand Oaks, CA: Sage.

Garcia, W. R. (1996). Respeto: A Mexican base for interpersonal relationships. In W. Gudykunst, S. Ting-Toomey, & T. Nishida (Eds.), *Communication in personal relationships across cultures* (pp. 137–155). Thousand Oaks, CA: Sage.

Goffman, E. (1959). *The presentation of self in everyday life*. Garden City, NY: Anchor/Doubleday.

Gudykunst, W. B., Matsumoto, Y., Ting-Toomey, S., Nishida, T., Kim, K. S., & Heyman, S. (1996). The influence of cultural individualism-collectivism, self construals, and individual values on communication styles across cultures. *Human Communication Research, 22,* 510–543.

Gudykunst, W. B., & Ting-Toomey, S. (1988). *Culture and interpersonal communication*. Newbury Park, CA: Sage.

Guerrero, L., Andersen, P., & Afifi, W. (2001). *Close encounters: Communicating in relationships*. Mountain View, CA: Mayfield.

Hall, E. T. (1959). *The silent language*. Garden City, NY: Doubleday.

Hall, E. T. (1976). *Beyond culture*. Garden City, NY: Doubleday.

Hofstede, G. (1991). *Culture and organizations: Software of the mind*. London: McGraw-Hill.

Hofstede, G. (2001). *Culture's consequences: Comparing values, behaviors, institutions, and organizations across cultures* (2nd ed.). Thousand Oaks, CA: Sage.

Hu, H. C. (1944). The Chinese concept of "face." *American Anthropologist, 46,* 45–64.

Katriel, T. (1986). *Talking straight: Dugri speech in Israeli Sabra culture.* Cambridge, UK: Cambridge University Press.

Leung, K. (Ed.). (1999). *Conflict management in the Asia Pacific.* New York: John Wiley.

Leung, K., & Iwawaki, S. (1988). Cultural collectivism and distributive behavior. *Journal of Cross-Cultural Psychology, 19,* 35–49.

Lim, T.-S. (1994). Facework and interpersonal relationships. In S. Ting-Toomey (Ed.), *The challenge of facework* (pp. 209–229). Albany: State University of New York Press.

Markus, H. R., & Kitayama, S. (1991). Culture and self: Implication for cognition, emotion, and motivation. *Psychological Review, 98,* 224–253.

Markus, H. R., & Kitayama, S. (1998). The cultural psychology of personality. *Journal of Cross-Cultural Psychology, 29,* 63–87.

Oetzel, J. G. (1998a). Culturally homogeneous and heterogeneous groups: Explaining communication processes through individualism-collectivism and self-construal. *International Journal of Intercultural Relations, 22*(2), 135–161.

Oetzel, J. G. (1998b). The effects of self-construals and ethnicity on self-reported conflict styles. *Communication Reports, 11,* 133–144.

Oetzel, J. G. (1999). The influence of situational features on perceived conflict styles and self-construals in small groups. *International Journal of Intercultural Relations, 23*(4), 679–695.

Oetzel, J. G., Myers, K., Meares, M., & Lara, E. (2003). Interpersonal conflict in organizations: Explaining conflict styles via face-negotiation theory. *Communication Research Reports, 20,* 105–155.

Oetzel, J. G., & Ting-Toomey, S. (2003). Face concerns in interpersonal conflict: A cross-cultural empirical test of the face-negotiation theory. *Communication Research, 30*(6), 599–624.

Oetzel, J., Ting-Toomey, S., Masumoto, T., Yokochi, Y., Pan, X., Takai, J., & Wilcox, R. (2001). Face behaviors in interpersonal conflicts: A cross-cultural comparison of Germany, Japan, China, and the United States. *Communication Monographs, 68,* 235–258.

Oetzel, J., Ting-Toomey, S., Yokochi, Y., Masumoto, T., & Takai, J. (2000). A typology of facework behaviors in conflicts with best

friends and relative strangers. *Communication Quarterly, 48,* 397–419.

Putnam, L., & Wilson, C. E. (1982). Communicative strategies in organizational conflicts: Reliability and validity of a measurement scale. In M. Burgoon (Ed.), *Communication yearbook 6* (pp. 629–652). Beverly Hills, CA: Sage.

Rahim, M. A. (1983). A measure of styles of handling interpersonal conflict. *Academy of Management Journal, 26,* 368–376.

Rahim, M. A. (1992). *Managing conflict in organizations* (2nd ed.). Westport, CT: Praeger.

Rothman, J. (1997). *Resolving identity-based conflict in nations, organizations, and communities.* San Francisco: Jossey-Bass.

Schlenker, B. R. (Ed.). (1985). *The self and social life.* New York: McGraw-Hill.

Smith, P. B., Dugan, S., Peterson, M. F., Leung, K. (1998). Individualism, collectivism and the handling of disagreement: A 23 country study. *International Journal of Intercultural Relations, 22*(3), 351–367.

Thomas, K. W., & Kilmann, R. H. (1974). *Thomas-Kilmann Conflict Mode Instrument.* Tuxedo, NY: XICOM.

Ting-Toomey, S. (1985). Toward a theory of conflict and culture. In W. Gudykunst, L. Stewart, & S. Ting-Toomey (Eds.), *Communication, culture, and organizational processes* (pp. 71–86). Beverly Hills, CA: Sage.

Ting-Toomey, S. (1986). Conflict communication styles in black and white subjective cultures. In Y. Kim (Ed.), *Current research in interethnic communication* (pp. 75–88). Newbury Park, CA: Sage.

Ting-Toomey, S. (1988). Intercultural conflicts: A face-negotiation theory. In Y. Kim & W. Gudykunst (Eds.), *Theories in intercultural communication* (pp. 213–235). Newbury Park, CA: Sage.

Ting-Toomey, S. (Ed.). (1994a). *The challenge of facework: Cross-cultural and interpersonal issues* (pp. 1–14). Albany: State University of New York Press.

Ting-Toomey, S. (1994b). Managing conflict in intimate intercultural relationships. In D. Cahn (Ed.), *Intimate conflict in personal relationships* (pp. 47–77). Hillsdale, NJ: Lawrence Erlbaum.

Ting-Toomey, S. (1994c). Managing intercultural conflicts effectively. In L. Samovar & R. Porter (Eds.), *Intercultural communication: A reader* (7th ed., pp. 360–372). Belmont, CA: Wadsworth.

Ting-Toomey, S. (1997). Intercultural conflict competence. In W. Cupach & D. Canary (Eds.), *Competence in interpersonal conflict* (pp. 120–147). New York: McGraw-Hill.

Ting-Toomey, S. (1999a). *Communicating across cultures*. New York: Guilford.

Ting-Toomey, S. (1999b). Face and facework. In J. Mio, J. Trimble, P. Arredondo, H. Cheatham, & D. Sue (Eds.), *Key words in multicultural interventions* (pp. 125–127). Westport, CT: Greenwood.

Ting-Toomey, S. (2004). Translating conflict face-negotiation theory into practice. In D. Landis, J. Bennett, & M. Bennett (Eds.), *Handbook of intercultural training* (3rd ed., pp. 217–248). Thousand Oaks, CA: Sage.

Ting-Toomey, S., & Cole, M. (1990). Intergroup diplomatic communication: A face-negotiation perspective. In F. Korzenny & S. Ting-Toomey (Eds.), *Communicating for peace: Diplomacy and negotiation across cultures* (pp. 77–95). Newbury Park, CA: Sage.

Ting-Toomey, S., Gao, G., Trubisky, P., Yang, Z., Kim, H. S., Lin, S. L., & Nishida, T. (1991). Culture, face maintenance, and styles of handling interpersonal conflict: A study in five cultures. *International Journal of Conflict Management, 2,* 275–296.

Ting-Toomey, S., & Kurogi, A. (1998). Facework competence in intercultural conflict: An updated face-negotiation theory. *International Journal of Intercultural Relations, 22*(2), 187–225.

Ting-Toomey, S., & Oetzel, J. (2001). *Managing intercultural conflict effectively*. Thousand Oaks, CA: Sage.

Ting-Toomey, S., & Oetzel, J. (2002). Cross-cultural face concerns and conflict styles: Current status and future directions. In W. Gudykunst & B. Mody (Eds.), *Handbook of international and intercultural communication* (2nd ed., pp. 143–163). Thousand Oaks, CA: Sage.

Ting-Toomey, S., Oetzel, J., & Yee-Jung, K. (2001). Self-construal types and conflict management styles. *Communication Reports, 14,* 87–104.

Ting-Toomey, S., Yee-Jung, K., Shapiro, R., Garcia, W., Wright, T., & Oetzel, J. (2000). Ethnic/cultural identity salience and conflict styles in four U.S. ethnic groups. *International Journal of Intercultural Relations, 24*(1), 47–81.

Triandis, H. C. (1994). *Culture and social behavior.* New York: McGraw-Hill.

Triandis, H. C. (1995). *Individualism and collectivism.* Boulder, CO: Westview.

Trubisky, P., Ting-Toomey, S., & Lin, S.-L. (1991). The influence of individualism-collectivism and self-monitoring on conflict styles. *International Journal of Intercultural Relations, 15*(1), 65–84.

Wilmot, W., & Hocker, J. (1998). *Interpersonal conflict* (5th ed.). Boston: McGraw-Hill.

5

Culture-Based Conversational Constraints Theory

Individual- and Culture-Level Analyses

MIN-SUN KIM

Understanding how language functions is one of the main goals in cross-cultural communication research. "Why do people from different cultures say what they say?" or "Why do members of different cultural groups bother to choose one strategy over another?" Typically, studies explain away the stereotypical communication differences as some "cultural" differences such as being Asian or American. Norms have been a mainstay of cultural analyses. The influence of norms, customs, and rules can be applied only according to a given situation, and thus, has a limited explanatory power. The central focus of conversational constraints relates not to *what is said*, but rather to *how what is said is to be said*. Interactive constraints are fundamental concerns regarding *the manner in which a message is constructed*. They tend to affect the general character of every conversation one engages in, and an individual's conversational style in general (Kellermann, 1989; Wilensky, 1983). Given that constraints are conceived of as general rules of interaction, they provide theoretical accounts for fundamental structural distinctions that underlie cultural contrasts in expressive patterns.

Much of past research on cross-cultural strategic choices is descriptive in nature. In an attempt to go beyond mostly descriptive research on cross-cultural strategy choice, I have introduced the notion of culture-based conversational constraints (Kim, 1993, 1995). In the 12 years since then, we have conducted research on various aspects of culture-based conversational constraints. The major goal of this research program has been to understand, from a goals perspective, *why* a particular alternative is chosen cross-culturally. This issue has been studied in terms of conversational constraints (social appropriateness and efficiency) in interpersonal communication contexts (Kellermann, 1989; Kellermann & Kim, 1991). The focus of the current program of research, however, has been to understand the cultural underpinnings of choices of communication strategies among people of different cultural backgrounds.

In the first section of this chapter I outline a goals approach to human communication, in particular intercultural communication, as contrasted with a rule- or norms-based approach. The notion of conversational constraints is defined and explained, referring to the distinction between cross-cultural pragmatic approaches and other interpersonal communication literature. Then the cross-cultural findings on conversational constraints are presented. After that, I introduce the concept of the interdependent, relational self as contrasted with the separated, independent self. I then review recent burgeoning literature on cultural variations in ways of being and the implications for conversational constraints. This chapter ends with a discussion of the advantages of applying both individual-level and cultural-level approaches to the study of cross-cultural communication behavior.

PROBLEM OF NORMS-BASED EXPLANATIONS

Comparing findings in different cultures is frequently used to examine the impact of culture on communication behavior. Although useful in evaluating whether cross-cultural differences exist, it is far less helpful in explaining why culture has an effect. For example, if one found with this method that people in the United States used more dominating conflict styles than people from Korea, there would be little direct evidence that the different results in the two cultures were attributable to cultural values. Perhaps the most important criticism of much of this research is that explanations for cross-cultural differences are frequently post hoc, and there is no direct assessment of any intervening variables that are presumed to affect the dependent variable. There is in general within this literature a lack of theoretical analysis underlying different communication practices and the relevance of cultural conditioning to that process.

Specifically, much of the accumulated research testifies that cross-cultural communication competence can be characterized as a general impression of communication quality, with particular reference to the nature of strategy choices. However, most of the research is descriptive in nature. Typically, such investigations have attempted to describe various communicative strategies or classes of tactics that people might use across cultures in the pursuit of some interaction goals. While this research provides an important and rich descriptive base, two fundamental problems stand out: (1) understanding and (2) prediction of strategy choices.

First, why are certain types of verbal strategies preferred by a cultural group? Why, would, say, an average Korean prefer to choose "hint" and an average American "request" as a favor-asking strategy? Typically, studies do not deal with the theoretical reason *why* a particular alternative is chosen. A few researchers attempt to explore the origins of preferred communicative strategies by relying on norms, rules, and conventions. For instance, some researchers in communication and sociology have generated a corpus of rules (e.g., Collier, 1989; Cronen, Chen, & Pearce, 1988). Norms and rules, being specific to particular social situations, have a severely limited explanatory role in comparative research, since the findings and bits of information on the choice of strategies frequently appear as isolated entities without connection to other situations. The appeal to certain norms and rules, therefore, runs the risk of not being applicable to other situations. Jacobs (1985) argues that a conventional rule-based logic cannot capture (a) the ways in which actors infer beyond the information given to achieve coherence, and (b) the ways in which actors organize communication functionally.

The second problem in most cross-cultural studies in strategic communication styles relates to the *predictability* of communicative strategy choices. Expressing interaction patterns declaratively restricts their predictability in other situations. We can imagine such scenarios as "what to say when a policeman pulls you over for speeding in Saudi Arabia" or "how to refuse a request from a best friend in Japan." Knowledge to handle such situations would be readily available if the interaction situations described were the ones frequently encountered by an individual. However, not all situations occur in standardized packages (i.e., script-like), and, of course, we cannot describe every possible strategy choice so as to account for every possible interaction goal across cultures.

A major purpose of cross-cultural communication competence research is to improve communication and understanding between members of different cultural groups. Thus, understanding others' intentions and predicting others' strategy choices should be the critical endeavors in cross-cultural strategic competence. In order to understand we must predict, and in order to predict there must be background knowledge of why specific strategy choices are made across cultures and how general impressions of competence are formed. Thus, researchers recognize that there is a need to go beyond the descriptive portrayal of different people, toward discovering the underlying reasons for communicative behavior that may be shared to some extent among them.

Conversational constraints are essentially cognitive generators of tactical preferences (see Kim, 1993, 1995). Without these overarching concerns, people's choices of tactics would appear as isolated entities without connection to the rest of their knowledge. The conversational constraints seem self-evident to native speakers but in fact are culturally specific. This chapter reviews a program of research that provides a theoretical framework that can systematically explain how the conversational constraints guide the cultural preference of communication tactics and the perceptions of intercultural communicative competence. The different interests served by each conversational constraint will affect the priority attached to the constraints, the different modes or approaches to achieving social goals, and, ultimately, overall impressions of cross-cultural strategic competence.

GOALS APPROACH TO SOCIAL INTERACTION

In everyday social interaction, people have various social goals (i.e., gaining compliance, seeking affinity, seeking favor, seeking information, revealing information, etc.). Goals are end states people desire to attain or maintain (Read & Miller, 1989; Schank & Abelson, 1977). To achieve those goals, people must have strategic competence—the procedural knowledge necessary to reach their goals. In considering structures for understanding social behavior and strategic competence, a number of cognitive and social theorists (e.g., Miller, Galanter, & Pribram, 1960; Schank & Abelson, 1977; Wilensky, 1983) have argued that social interaction and the perceptions of competence can be analyzed in terms of people's goals and the plans and strategies necessary to achieve those goals. Over the years, numerous terms related to "goals" have been used as the ends governing actions: "motive" (McClelland, 1985); "personal strivings" (Emmons, 1989); "values" (Rokeach, 1973); "end-beliefs" (Read & Miller, 1989).

Much of the knowledge about communication goals (or objectives of a conversation) has been formulated in terms of the degree of abstractness (see Kellermann, 1989; McCann & Higgins, 1988; Read & Miller,

1989; Street & Cappella, 1985; Wilson & Putnam, 1990). The knowledge of interaction goals is cast at three principal levels of abstraction that are hierarchically organized from specific and concrete to general, abstract, and global elements: (1) tactical or strategic goals, (2) primary communication goals (outcome of a conversation), and (3) global constraints.

At the most specific, basic level, Kellermann (1989) posits that tactical goals are concerned with desires for specific behavioral action (e.g., desiring to ask a question). These goals pertain to short periods of time, such as a single turn or adjacency pair in a conversation. The idea of "strategy" and "tactics" has been postulated in describing relatively concrete communicative actions (Miller et al., 1960; von Cranach, Kalbermatten, Indermuhle, & Gugler, 1982). Generally, *strategies* are viewed as action sequences that are used to attain goals, and *tactics* as specific behavioral actions that persons manifest in their goal-directed interactions with others (see Berger, 1987; Street & Cappella, 1985). Asking a question, breaking eye contact with someone, and turning away from someone are all examples of tactics.

The next level of goals consists of the numerous outcomes or primary goals that may be desired from an entire interaction. An overall strategy and specific tactics for carrying out that strategy are implemented only if we select a functional outcome desired from interaction. Recently, interest has emerged in identifying and classifying a variety of situation-specific interaction outcomes or goals, such as gaining compliance, seeking information, de-escalating relationships, correcting others, and testing affinity (see McCann & Higgins, 1988; Schank & Childers, 1984). The situation-specific interaction goals are functional outcomes of a conversation, for which a wide range of different tactical goals can be used (Kellermann, 1989; Read & Miller, 1989). For instance, if one has the interaction goal of seeking information, there are a number of different tactics (i.e., hinting, asking, keeping eye contact with the partner, etc.) one can use.

At the most abstract, global level, several authors have argued for cross-situational goals that serve as criteria for making a choice between tactics in the pursuit of interaction goals. As people pursue primary communication goals such as gaining compliance, seeking information, or altering relationships they generate messages within a variety of constraints. These higher-level goals or constraints have been named "meta-goals," "meta-plans" (Berger, 1987; Kellermann, 1989; Wilensky, 1981, 1983), "supergoals" (von Cranach et al., 1982), "life theme" (Schank & Abelson, 1977), "cross-situational goals" (Street & Cappella, 1985), "supermaxims" (Grice, 1975), "meta-strategies" (van Dijk & Kintsch, 1983), "ritual-constraints" (Goffman, 1967), and "sociopragmatic interactional principles" (Spencer-Oatey & Jiang, in press). The global constraints are different from tactics and interaction goals because they tend to affect the general character of every conversation one engages in. When a primary goal exists, it generates only a sequence of tactics specific to the nature of the interaction. Global constraints, on the other hand, are usually responsible for generating the strategies and actions that guide an individual's conversational style in general (Kellermann, 1989; Kellermann & Kim, 1991; Wilensky, 1983).

To account for cross-cultural similarities and differences in the choice of conversational strategies affecting perceptions of strategic competence, it is necessary to have available a limited set of shared interactive constraints (or "conversational concerns"). Many researchers, from communication, artificial intelligence, psychology, linguistics, and other related fields, have suggested two major dimensions that may serve as global constraints in conversational and planning situations: "clarity" and "face-support" (Blum-Kulka, 1987; Brown & Levinson, 1978; Grice, 1975). Clarity in conversational behavior is conceptualized as a concern about achieving a primary goal in the most explicit and the shortest way possible. On the other hand, face support is conceptualized as a concern about achieving a primary goal without hurting the hearer's desired social image and feelings.

In the past, several authors have suggested similar interactive constraints that are "motivating forces" in communication: "Be clear" and "Be polite" (Lakoff, 1977); "Concern for clarity" and "Concern with support" (Greene & Lindsey, 1989); "Directness" and "Politeness" (Blum-Kulka, 1987; Holtgraves, in press); and "Efficiency" and "Social appropriateness" (Kellermann & Kim, 1991). Brown and Levinson (1978) posit such wants as: (1) wanting to be efficient or to indicate urgency, and (2) wanting to maintain hearer's face to some degree. Grice (1975) also put forward the "Maxim of manner" in the use of language (e.g., be clear, be brief, try to avoid obscurity), which can be seen as a guideline for direct communication.

According to Holtgraves (in press), it is clearly possible that maxims people follow in communicating cooperatively may vary over cultures, perhaps reflecting differences in what is regarded as "rational" interaction. Similarly, our research proposes that the major overarching interactive constraints are anchored to predominant types of cultural orientations. In the following section I discuss how we came up with five conversational constraints instead of focusing on the two broad dimensions of social appropriateness (face support, politeness) and efficiency (effectiveness, task accomplishment, directness) that were developed in the field of interpersonal communication.

Beyond the Two Dimensions of Interpersonal Communication Competence: Culture-Based Conversational Constraints

Most theorists seem to have accepted, either implicitly or explicitly, the importance of appropriateness and effectiveness (or efficiency) in defining communication competence (Canary & Spitzberg, 1989; Kellermann & Kim, 1991). Borrowing these dimensions of interpersonal communication competence,

much of the current literature on intercultural communication competence proceeds by a practice that can be cynically referred to as the "list" technique. While many researchers conceptualize intercultural communication competence as either appropriate (the ability to demonstrate a knowledge of the socially appropriate communicative behavior) or effective (the degree to which personal or relationship goals are achieved), the skills lists are overlaid with Western values: "extroversion" (Guthrie & Zenicki, 1967); "open-mindedness" (Matveev & Nelson, 2003), "honesty" and "outgoingness" (Hawes & Kealey, 1981), and others. Furthermore, most items are cast at such a level as to be uninformative about communication: "ability to effectively communicate" (Matveev & Nelson, 2003), "ability to adjust to different cultures" (Abe & Wiseman, 1983).

The items listed above essentially miss the important "how" questions. For instance, "be polite" appears to be a rule of behavior that applies to members of diverse ethnic groups, but the particular behaviors that are defined as "polite" for each cultural group differ substantially. Similarly, in situations where people's conceptions of effectiveness and social appropriateness differ from one another, the problem is not the "ability to effectively or appropriately communicate," but "how to communicate effectively and appropriately" across cultures and how and why people think of the same actions differently in terms of appropriateness and effectiveness. Communication breakdown typically occurs because interactants disagree about the effectiveness or social appropriateness of one another's communication strategies.

As discussed above, several authors suggest that two cross-situational constraints are motivating forces in communication. In their well-known theory of politeness, Brown and Levinson (1978) posit that speakers balance the need to be efficient or indicate urgency, and the need to maintain the hearer's face. Dillard (1990), in an analysis of interpersonal influence situations, argues that gaining compliance (i.e., task effectiveness) is the primary or defining goal and that other concerns (e.g., self-presentational and relational concerns) are secondary issues that shape how a speaker accomplishes the primary one. Consistent with these conceptualizations, empirical evidence in the field of interpersonal communication suggests that appropriateness and efficiency are two critical and often conflicting dimensions that determine people's choice of conversation strategies (Douglas, 1987; Kellermann & Kim, 1991).

The notion of "social appropriateness" as a communication constraint, however, presupposes some accepted standards of what constitutes appropriate communication performance. It inherently requires a culturally homogenous community. Thus, "appropriateness" runs the risk of being meaningless in cross-cultural comparisons. When people do not share social conventions, their notions of appropriateness are different. Thus, a use of a request strategy by a person from one culture, where the choice would be appropriate, may be considered inappropriate when used with a person from another culture. Furthermore, "appropriateness" can be part of social as well as task dimensions of an interaction, with the emphasis gravitating to one or the other depending on cultural preferences.

CONTENTS OF CONVERSATIONAL CONSTRAINTS

We proposed a set of culture-based conversational constraints to account for the use of different conversational strategies in different cultures (Kim, 1995; Kim & Wilson, 1994). Social constraints are broken down into three more-specific social-relational categories (imposition, other's feelings, and negative evaluation). Two other constraints are added (clarity and effectiveness). The resulting five conversational constraints are (1) *Concern for clarity*, (2) *Concern for minimizing imposition*,

(3) *Concern for avoiding hurting the hearer's feelings*, (4) *Concern for avoiding negative evaluation by the hearer*, and (5) *Effectiveness*. Conversational constraints are best viewed as *general and overarching criteria* for choosing conversational strategy (Kim, 1993). They tend to affect the general character of every conversation one engages in, and an individual's conversational style in general. Thus, they contribute to consistent conversational performances across varying contexts (Wilensky, 1983). This section defines each dimension.

Clarity. Clarity is defined as the likelihood of an utterance making one's intention clear and explicit. Clarity is discussed frequently in the literature on conversation (Brown & Levinson, 1978; Leech, 1983). For instance, Grice's (1975) "Maxim of manner" (e.g., be clear, be brief, avoid obscurity) can be seen as a guideline for clear communication. For instance, the typology of request strategies varies on a clarity dimension. If one's primary goal is to request an action, direct imperatives (e.g., "Repay the loan" or "Lend me your book") make the speaker's illocutionary point explicit. The hint strategy should be least clear, since illocutionary force is not derivable from the literal meaning of the utterances.

Minimizing Imposition. This dimension pertains to the degree to which an utterance avoids imposing on the hearer's autonomy or interfering with the hearer's freedom of action. This type of concern has been referred to in more abstract terms, such as "negative politeness" (Brown & Levinson, 1978) or "deference politeness" (Scollon & Scollon, 1981), that avoid making imposition on others. Concern for minimizing imposition, thus, has primarily been conceived of as a means of protecting the hearer's negative face. Several authors (Scollon & Scollon, 1981; Ting-Toomey, 1988) argue that in the Western world the notion of "politeness" usually is associated with "showing deference" by not assuming the hearer's cooperation and by leaving the hearer options for noncompliance. While the salience of this constraint might differ between cultures, prior research confirms the importance of minimizing imposition in many cultures (Blum-Kulka, 1987; Holtgraves & Yang, 1992).

Consideration for the Other's Feelings. When making a request, people also may consider how their projected action will affect the hearer's feelings. "Concern for the other's feelings" relates to the speaker's perceived obligation to help the hearer claim and sustain positive self-images (Brown & Levinson, 1978). The degree to which a strategy shows a consideration for the hearer's feelings has been proposed under various labels, including "positive face" (Brown & Levinson, 1978), "identity goals" (Wilson & Putnam, 1990), and "concern with support" (Greene & Lindsey, 1989). Direct statements with a lack of request mitigation (e.g., "Do X!") may risk a higher chance of hurting the other's feelings than hints, by conveying the implicit message that the speaker is not concerned about the relationship but only with accomplishing the instrumental outcome.

Risking Disapproval for Self. This dimension represents the desire to avoid negative evaluation by the conversational partner. According to self-presentation theory (Weary & Arkin, 1981), self-conceptions are formed by how people believe others perceive them. Individuals in turn attempt to behave in ways that avoid devaluation by others. This constraint is consistent with Brown and Levinson's (1978) notion of a speaker's desire to save his or her own positive face. In recent years, several authors have suggested similar interactive constraints in communication, including "impression management goals" (Street & Cappella, 1985) and "approval-seeking strategies" (Ting-Toomey, 1988). Although people in any culture will have a general desire to minimize negative evaluation

by others, it has been speculated that members of collectivistic cultures tend to use more approval-seeking strategies than do members of individualistic cultures (Ting-Toomey, 1988). The direct statement strategy potentially could risk devaluation for self since it is more demanding than the hint strategy.

Effectiveness. Effectiveness is another major dimension that influences choices of conversational tactics and strategies. If speakers undertake communicative acts to accomplish a primary goal, then it seems likely that they are concerned whether that goal will be accomplished. Judgments of communicative competence are related to the effectiveness with which primary goals are pursued (Canary & Spitzberg, 1989). While effectiveness alone is not a sufficient condition of competence, it nonetheless indicates the importance of this constraint in social interaction. Table 5.1 lists the scales for measuring each of the five conversational constraints.

THE QUESTION IS *HOW* TO BE APPROPRIATE AND *HOW* TO BE EFFECTIVE

Traditional models of interpersonal communication competence have focused on appropriateness and effectiveness. The lack of shared knowledge on "how" to be effective and appropriate was not seriously addressed. For instance, Lustig and Spitzberg (1993) argue that,

> If interpersonal competence is defined in terms of appropriateness and effectiveness, then it becomes incumbent upon researchers of intercultural communication to ascertain the salience of these criteria in the population observed. Furthermore, given that some cultures may value one criterion more than another in any set of episode types, researchers may need to permit subjects to provide their own subjective weightings of these standards of competence. (p. 155)

Table 5.1   List of Culture-Based Conversational Constraints: Scale Items

Concern for clarity

1. In this situation, I feel it is very important to make my point as clearly and directly as possible.
2. In this situation, I want to come directly to the point while conveying my message.

Concern for not hurting the other's feelings

1. In this situation, I feel it is very important to avoid hurting the other's feelings.
2. In this situation, being considerate of the other's feelings is a major concern to me.

Concern for nonimposition

1. In this situation, it is very important *not* to intrude upon the other person.
2. In this situation, it is very important to avoid inconveniencing the other.

Concern for avoiding negative evaluation by the hearer

1. In this situation, it is very important that the other person does *not* see me in a negative light.
2. In this situation, it is very important that my message does *not* cause the other person to dislike me.

Concern for effectiveness

1. In this situation, it is very important to get the other person to do what I want.
2. In this situation, making the other person comply with my request is very important.

NOTE: Adapted from Kim (1994).

Kim, M.S., "Cross-Cultural Comparisons of the Perceived Importance of Conversational Constraints." *Human Communication Research*, 1994 21(1), pp. 128–151. Reprinted by permission of Oxford University Press.

We reasoned that the salience of "effectiveness" and "social appropriateness" would be essentially the same, regardless of cultural context. The essential idea, however, is that for people accustomed to different social conventions, the means for being "effective" or "appropriate" are different. The two factors of appropriateness and effectiveness are supposed to account for communication behaviors in a single culture. Thus, effectiveness and appropriateness, as major dimensions of competence, are too general to be useful in an intercultural context.

We have found support for this reasoning in several studies (Kim, 1994; Kim & Bresnahan, 1994; Kim & Wilson, 1994). In Kim's (1994) study, participants were given scenarios such as the following:

Imagine that one of your female friends, whom you have known for several years,

has the habit of borrowing money and then not repaying it for long periods of time. In fact, it seems that she has been late not only in repaying money borrowed from you but also from other people. Two weeks ago, she borrowed 20 dollars from you and again did not repay it as promised. You waited a few days more but found that you really needed some money. Now you want to ask her to pay it back.[1]

After being presented with such a request situation, participants rated the perceived importance of each constraint in that situation. The participants were a total of 892 undergraduates studying in Korea ($N = 296$), in Hawaii ($N = 297$), and in the mainland United States ($N = 299$). While there were significant cultural differences in the ratings of the perceived importance of the other three constraints, the data did not support the two hypotheses relating to the importance of effectiveness and of avoiding negative evaluation (central to social appropriateness). One plausible explanation could be that certain levels of concern for avoiding negative evaluation and for effectiveness are essential for successful interaction in any culture. While there are significant cultural differences regarding which tactics are perceived as effective, people in any culture may be equally concerned about effectiveness in general.

Another plausible explanation is that the two constraints that are apparently unaffected by cultural values may be confounded with the remaining three constraints. That is, the two constraints cannot be treated as equivalent to, and separate from, the remaining three categories. The concerns for clarity, avoiding imposition, and avoiding hurting the hearer's feelings seem to be conceptually confounded by the last two (avoidance of negative evaluation, and being effective). In other words, people are concerned about the first three categories in order to achieve minimum negative evaluation and maximum effectiveness.

To investigate this possibility, we tested a process model of request tactic evaluation in two different cultures (Kim & Bresnahan, 1994). We examined possible links between the perceptions of conversational constraints and the likelihood of using specific tactics. Data to test the proposed model were drawn from undergraduates studying in Korea and the mainland United States. The results indicated that in both cultures perceived effectiveness functions as a mediating variable between the four conversational constraints and the perceived likelihood of use. Among Korean participants, two social-relational constraints (concern for avoiding negative evaluation by the hearer, and concern for avoiding hurting the other's feelings) contribute substantially to the prediction of effectiveness. On the other hand, among the U.S. participants, clarity was an extremely strong predictor of perceived effectiveness of tactics. Perceived effectiveness played an equally important role in the prediction of likelihood of use in both cultures.

Although these findings are preliminary, a series of studies found that there were no significant cultural differences in the perceived importance of two conversational constraints: effectiveness, and avoidance of negative evaluation by others (which is the central theme underlying "social appropriateness"). This research, then, suggests that the two popularly accepted dimensions of intercultural communication competence (effectiveness and appropriateness) may not suffice to account for cultural differences in "competent" behavior. Any theory of competence that is intended to account for behavior in multicultural settings must take into consideration the "how" of appropriateness and the "how" of effectiveness, rather than presuming that people share some common knowledge. In sum, this is a reminder that simplistic attempts to apply to other cultures the factors of interpersonal competence developed within the United States would seriously hinder the development of intercultural communication research.

The above point was indirectly confirmed by Kim and Wilson's (1994) study that identified cross-cultural similarities and differences in people's implicit theories of requesting. Implicit theories are conceptualized as containing information about five conversational constraints that influence choices about requests. Our paper compared how these five constraints are perceived and rated across cultures, and it traces possible links between the constraints and perceptions of the likelihood of using various request strategies. Participants were undergraduate students from Korea and the mainland United States. After reading a hypothetical request situation, participants evaluated request strategies along the five constraint dimensions as well as for likelihood of use. The rank ordering of the request strategies along the dimensions were similar across cultures except for effectiveness of strategies.

Striking cross-cultural differences were found in the rank and mean strategy ratings for effectiveness judgments: U.S. participants considered the direct statement strategy as the most effective way of making a request, while Korean participants rated it as the least effective strategy. Regarding the incompatibility among conversational constraints, U.S. participants saw clarity to be closely related to effectiveness of strategies; for Korean participants clarity of strategies was counterproductive to effectiveness.

According to Gumperz and Tannen (1979), intercultural interactions are more difficult to carry out efficiently precisely because interlocutors lack shared background knowledge. The lack of shared understanding should precisely be the focus of intercultural communication competence. The basic constraints of being effective in interactions appear to be essentially the same across cultures and language regardless of which means or strategies one decides to choose. However, adherence to such constraints as concerns about clarity, imposition, and avoiding hurting the hearer's feelings is culture specific. The current list of constraints, even though the theory is in obvious need of further testing and theoretical refinement, can serve as useful dimensions of intercultural communication competence.

CULTURAL VARIABILITY IN THE PERCEIVED IMPORTANCE OF CONVERSATIONAL CONSTRAINTS

Another major issue that we have pursued involves linking the differences between "individualist" and "collectivist" communication styles to the importance of the conversational constraints. Individualism-collectivism has been considered the single most important dimension of cultural difference in social behavior (Triandis, 1988). Its popularity for cross-cultural communication derives from its use as a culture-level explanation for observed cultural differences in behavior.

The main purpose of Kim's (1994) study was to investigate how cultural groups may differ in the structure and content of their perceptions about preferred communication behavior, focusing on the importance attached to interactive concerns in conversation. Several hypotheses were formulated regarding the relationships between the conversational constraints and the cultural dimension of individualistic-collectivistic orientation. Specifically, constraints concerned with relational support (avoiding hurting the hearer's feelings, avoiding negative evaluation by the hearer, and minimizing imposition) were postulated to be closely connected with collectivistic traits and with concern for clarity and effectiveness with individualistic traits, respectively. In the main study, the participants were a total of 892 undergraduates studying in Korea ($N = 296$), in Hawaii ($N = 297$), and in the mainland United States ($N = 299$). After being presented with six request situations, participants rated the perceived importance of each constraint in each situation. The results indicated that the dimension of individualism-collectivism (as operationalized by nationality) is systematically related to the perceived importance of clarity, avoiding hurting the hearer's feelings, and minimizing imposition. On the other hand, the perceived importance of avoiding negative evaluation by the hearer and of effectiveness did not differ significantly across the three cultural groups. This research extends our knowledge about what kinds of general conversational constraints shape peoples' beliefs concerning competent behavior.

Extending this work, Miyahara and Kim (1993) compared the perceived importance of conversational constraints in two traditionally "collectivist" countries. Traditionally, Koreans and Japanese have been considered collectivistic in their communication behavior, in comparison to U.S. Americans. However, the important cultural differences (possibly subtle) in conflict management styles between the two "collectivist" cultures have been overlooked.

We aimed to explore how Japanese and Koreans might differ in their preferences for different conflict management styles, focusing on the importance attached to conversational constraints in conflict situations. Several hypotheses were formulated based on the origins of the conversational constraints in relation to the cultural orientations of Japanese and Koreans. A total of 534 undergraduate students, studying in Japan ($N = 235$) and Korea ($N = 299$), participated in the study. Each participant was provided descriptions of three conflict situations and was asked to rate the perceived importance of each constraint in each conflict situation. The main findings of this study point to a picture that Koreans are more collectivistic in conflict communication styles than Japanese. Specifically, the results of this study seem to suggest different processes of conflict management in the two cultures: Japanese as focusing on clarity constraints (conveying the message clearly and efficiently) more than Koreans, and Koreans focusing on social-relation constraints (avoiding imposition on the hearer or loss of face by the hearer) more than Japanese.

Our earlier research (Kim, 1994; Kim & Wilson, 1994) has focused on one specific type of speech act (i.e., requesting). Focusing on conflict management strategies, Miyahara, Kim, Shin, and Yoon (1998) tested whether culture affects the perceived importance of conversational constraints and whether the perceived importance of conversational constraints affects the likelihood of using various conflict management strategies. Several hypotheses were formulated based on the origins behind the conversational constraints and the preferred use of conflict strategies. A total of 746 undergraduate students, studying in Korea ($N = 215$), Hawaii ($N = 203$), and the mainland United States ($N = 328$), participated in the study. Each participant was provided descriptions of one of the three conflict situations and was asked to rate the perceived importance of each constraint in the conflict situation, as well as the scales

measuring conflict styles. The main findings of this study point to a picture that Koreans are more collectivistic in conflict communication styles than participants from Hawaii or the mainland United States. Specifically, the results of this study seem to suggest different processes of conflict management in the three groups: the mainland U.S. participants as focusing on clarity constraints (conveying the message clearly and efficiently) more than the participants from Korea and Hawaii, and Koreans focusing on social-relation constraints (avoiding imposition on the hearer or loss of face by the hearer) more than participants from Hawaii and the mainland United States. Similar to previous results on requesting, the perceived importance of effectiveness did not differ significantly across the three cultural groups.

Taken together, the results were very clear. There seem to be systematic cultural variations in the perceived importance of conversational constraints and perceptions regarding communication strategies along the dimensions of conversational constraints. Our research provided a theoretical framework and data that can systematically explain how the conversational constraints guide cultural preferences for communication tactics and the perceptions of intercultural communicative competence. Claims of cultural distinctions between East Asians and U.S. Americans on relationship-orientation versus task-orientation abound in the literature (see Argyle, Bond, Iizuka, & Contarello, 1986). Our research shows that the popular claims regarding relationship-orientation (East Asian) versus task-orientation (U.S. American) in verbal styles are in fact grounded in shared cognitive knowledge about communication behavior, and that this culturally shared knowledge can explicitly be shown to distinguish one from the other.

BEYOND NATIONALITY

Following Verschueren (1996), one can accept that contrastive pragmatics (assuming an explanatory goal) is "risky business" (p. 589). Certainly, the dangers of overgeneralization exist here. The above line of research has been guided by the cultural dimensions of individualism and collectivism. In the above studies, we have operationalized cultural variability primarily by using the dimension of individualism-collectivism (e.g., the U.S. as an individualistic culture, Taiwan as a collectivistic culture). This operationalization runs the risk of being too vague and general. What can be said of the individual within a particular culture? While conceptually one can expect culture-level and individual-level value dimensions to be related, it is still an empirical question whether the culture-level description can be translated at an individual level. The analytic gap between culture and individual behavior can be bridged with the study of individual-level correlates of cultural dimensions. Given the theoretical significance of studying the relationship of one's conversational patterns and culture, studying the cognitive correlates of individualism-collectivism (e.g., independent and interdependent self-construals; Markus & Kitayama, 1991) is very important.

Individualism and collectivism have been proposed as typical "East Asian" and "U.S." value orientations influencing communication styles. One reason for the criticism of individualism-collectivism is that it is (mis)used as a stand-in for a variety of social and cultural independent variables in the explanation and prediction of behavior (Kagitçibasi, 1996). The typical method of comparing findings in different cultures is frequently used to examine the impact of culture on communication behaviors. Although useful in evaluating whether cross-cultural differences exist, it is far less helpful in explaining why culture has an effect. A better way to evaluate the effect of culture on communication behavior is to examine the mediating role of self-concepts (e.g., self-construals).

Self-concepts are the mental representations of those personal qualities used by individuals for the purpose of defining themselves and regulating their behavior (Niedenthal & Beike, 1997). The entire set of concepts used to describe the self is usually referred to as the self system (Markus & Wurf, 1987). Self-concepts are thought to contain information about the characteristic features of the self in specific situations, temporal contexts, and moods, as well as the relations among the features (Niedenthal & Beike, 1997). Views of the acquisition and structure of self-concepts, however, are based on two philosophical positions. The two positions differentially emphasize the idea that concepts of self derive meaning through relationships with other people. That is, some theorists have argued that identity develops from social relationships and that relationships with others actually constitute identity, whereas other theorists suggest that identity develops as the individual separates from primary relationships and that features and experiences unique to him or her constitute identity (Markus & Kitayama, 1991).

Cultural contexts diverge in their cultural practices and in their ways of life. The ways of being a person are patterned according to the means and practices of a given cultural community, and communities are maintained by these ways of being in the world. Each person is embedded within a variety of sociocultural contexts or cultures (e.g., country, ethnicity, religion, gender, family, etc.). Each of these cultural contexts makes some claim on the person and is associated with a set of ideas and practices (i.e., a cultural framework) about how to be a "good" person (Markus & Kitayama, 1998). According to Smith (1991), "selfhood" is a label for the criterial features of the human condition, and over the millennia since people became *self*-consciously aware of their special place in the world it has been the prime puzzle (along with the cosmological puzzle) to which myth, religion, and philosophy have been addressed. Smith (1991) calls it the "universal features of being a person" (p. 20).

In describing the culture-specific nature of self, Markus, Mullally, and Kitayama (1997) suggest that cultural and social groups in every historical period are associated with characteristic patterns of sociocultural participation, or, more specifically, with characteristic ways of being a person in the world. They call these characteristic patterns of sociocultural participation *selfways*. By extension of the notion of selfways, we can also suggest that there are culture-specific ways of being a "communicating" person.

According to Markus and Kitayama (1991), the main difference between the two self-construals is the belief one holds regarding how the self is related to others. Those with highly developed independent construals see themselves as separate from others; those with highly developed interdependent construals see themselves as connected with others. These beliefs of separateness and connectedness differentiate the two self-construals. The normative imperative of the independent self-construal is to achieve independence and self-actualization. A goal of social maturity, in this view, is to be self-sufficient, not dependent on anyone. Those with this view also strive to know themselves and to express their unique strengths. In contrast, the normative imperative of the interdependent self-construal is to maintain connectedness and harmony with significant others. To be mature, in this view, would be to internally control or suppress abilities, opinions, emotions, or goals in deference to normative behaviors, specific to the current social context, that promote interdependence.

How do we live with the powerful pulls between the experiences of relatedness and autonomy, connection and separateness? This is not merely a question only about theory, but speaks to deeply rooted sensibilities regarding what it means to exist as a human being. The notion of self-construals is of great interest to a wide range of researchers. Increasing numbers of intercultural communication researchers are recognizing the importance of conceptualizing culture along meaningful dimensions of sociopsychological variability and developing ways to measure these dimensions at the individual level.

LINKING CULTURE- AND INDIVIDUAL-LEVEL ANALYSES OF CONVERSATIONAL CONSTRAINTS

Many papers have been written on the topic of cultural differences in communication styles. For instance, a preference for direct, open communication over indirect, ambiguous communication has been an often-noted attribute of U.S. conversational styles in contrast to East Asian conversational styles (for review, see Gudykunst & Ting-Toomey, 1988). Most papers, however, describe cultures in simplistic terms such as "individualistic" or "collectivistic." The papers implicitly assume that all individuals within a culture are identical in regard to the topic discussed.

Suppose the stereotypic model were true. If all individuals in a culture were alike, then there would be no need to spell out the causal pathway linking behavior to culture. Indeed, there would be little need to distinguish between measurement of behavior and measurement of culture. As it happens, empirical data have consistently shown the stereotypic model to be false. On any behavioral dimension there is massive variation within cultures. Furthermore, in comparisons across cultures, the distributions for behavior show very considerable overlap. The mean differences between cultural groups are usually relatively modest (for further discussion see Smith & Bond, 1998).

The prior cross-cultural studies reviewed here (e.g., Kim, 1994; Miyahara & Kim, 1993) involved only the cultural level, that is, those factors that lead people in one culture to communicate similarly to or differently from people in other cultures. In other words, the model was based on a culture-level analysis.

A solid theory of intercultural communication, however, should be based on individual- as well as culture-level analyses. For a theory to be broadly applicable, it must be supported by individual as well as cultural data (see Leung, 1989). The field of intercultural communication research is dominated by the culture-level approach and has also been extremely influenced by the ecological level, or the cross-cultural level of explanation only.

As an example of analyses at both the cultural and individual levels, Kim et al. (1996) tested a theoretical path model linking the cultural dimensions of individualism and collectivism to independent and interdependent self-construals, respectively. This relationship would, then, result in the use of either other-oriented or outcome-oriented constraints, whereby interdependents would prefer to use other-oriented constraints, and independents would favor the use of more outcome-oriented constraints. Results from this study indicated that culture-level individualism indeed influenced independent self-construals, which, in turn, correlated positively with the two outcome-oriented constraints (clarity and effectiveness). Furthermore, results also indicated that culture-level collectivism affected interdependent self-construals and, in turn, correlated positively with the three relational constraints. This study further supports the notion that independents tend to be more task-oriented, whereas interdependents focus more on relational aspects. On the whole, viewing conversational constraints from both culture- and individual-level perspectives allows for a more detailed understanding of cross-cultural communication.

In addition, our results provided important theoretical insights into the relationship between effectiveness and perceived likelihood of use of requesting strategies. According to the results for effectiveness ratings, no striking differences were found between the two groups in the rank orderings of the three strategies. The likelihood of use ratings, however, revealed strikingly different patterns between independents and interdependents. The rank ordering of strategies according to interdependents was the exact opposite of the rank ordering according to the independents: Independents rated the direct statement strategy the most likely to be used, followed by query strategy. The hint strategy was rated least likely to be used for both initial and second-attempt requests. On the other hand, interdependents preferred the hint strategy most, then the query strategy, followed by the direct statement strategy in both first and second-attempt requests.

INTRACULTURAL VARIABILITY

Our interest has also extended to intracultural variability in the perceived importance of conversational constraints. According to Markus and Kitayama (1991), on the average, relatively more individuals in Western cultures will hold independent self-construals than will individuals in non-Western cultures. Within a given culture, however, individuals will vary in the extent to which they are "typical" and construe the self in the "typical" way. Thus, not all people who are part of an individualistic culture will possess primarily independent self-construals, nor will all those who are part of a collectivistic culture possess primarily interdependent self-construals.

At least some of the remarkable variation among people results because they are unlikely to participate in the identical configuration of group memberships. Culture is NOT uniform within what we nominally designate as one "culture." This is obvious in the case of a country like India, where so many cultural details differ between linguistic groups and religions, and even within religions across castes. It is less obvious in other countries, but our analysis of all the countries that we know well suggests that heterogeneity of culture is true for most current countries. Furthermore, the ways in which individuals participate in culture reflect their position and status in society (i.e., gender, socioeconomic status, age, ethnicity, etc.), so that the effects of cultural participation will seldom be totalizing or uniform (Markus et al., 1997).

To test for the intracultural variability of self-construals and the perceived importance of conversational constraints, Kim, Sharkey, and Singelis (1994) attempted to extend the findings of Kim (1993) by comparing how conversational constraints are perceived across individuals with individualistic and collectivistic orientations within a culture. We hypothesized that interdependent self-construals would correlate positively with concern for other's feelings and concern for avoiding devaluation by the hearer and that independent self-construals would correlate positively with concern for clarity. Participants included individuals from diverse ethnic backgrounds (a total of 308 undergraduates) studying at the University of Hawaii at Manoa. After being presented with four conversational situations, participants rated the perceived importance of each constraint in relation to each situation. They then completed the Ego-Task Analysis Scale (Breckler, Greenwald, & Wiggins, 1986) to measure the independent and interdependent dimensions of their self-construals. The results indicate that the degree of independent and interdependent construals of self systematically affect the perceived importance of conversational constraints.

Going beyond student populations, Kim and Sharkey (1995) aimed to explain the cultural interaction patterns in multicultural organizational settings. The study focuses on the dimensions of independent and interdependent construals of self, the individual-level equivalent of individualism and collectivism. Specifically, the paper investigates the relationship between one's orientation toward independent and interdependent self-construals and the perceived importance of three conversational constraints in "bind" organizational communication situations. Participants were individuals, from diverse

ethnic backgrounds (N = 266), working at multicultural organizations based on Oahu and Maui, Hawaii. After being presented with three bind communication situations in an organizational setting, participants rated the perceived importance of each constraint in relation to each situation. After that, the participants completed scales measuring the independent and interdependent dimensions of self-construals. The data, collected from organizations with a multicultural workforce in Hawaii, were consistent with the predictions made in three hypotheses: (a) the higher the level of independent self-construal, the greater the concern for clarity; and the greater the individual's construal of self as interdependent, (b) the higher the perceived importance of not hurting the hearer's feelings and of (c) having a concern for negative evaluations in the pursuit of organizational communication goals.

Taken together, self-construals appear well suited to account for both the between- and within-culture variation in the expression of communication behavior. The line of research mentioned above attempts to disentangle both the cultural and psychological aspects of cultural communication styles. Using this individual-level approach to cross-cultural differences in conjunction with our prior culture-level approach (Kim, 1993, 1994), hypotheses can be examined both intraculturally and cross-culturally so that explanatory variables may be tested at two levels (Berry & Dasen, 1974). Following the terminology of Leung and Bond (1989), this correspondence (between individual-level and culture-level dimensions) is called a "strong etic" relationship, and a theory based on this relationship is called a strong etic theory. The theoretical framework proposed by Kim et al. (1996), combined with the prior culture-level approach (Kim, 1994), allows the examination of effects at both levels (individual and cultural) simultaneously and the comparison of their relative importance.

Similar mediation models have been adopted for explaining communication processes across cultures, including low- and high-context communication styles (Gudykunst et al., 1996; Kim et al., 2000; Singelis & Brown, 1995). To understand individual behavior, both culture-level individualism and collectivism as well as individual-level factors that mediate the influence of culture must be taken into consideration (see Gudykunst et al., 1996). To do so, we need to isolate the individual-level factors that mediate the influence of culture-level individualism and collectivism on communication behaviors.[2] Table 5.2 presents the Revised Self-Construal Scale (Leung & Kim, 1997) that we have used in our recent studies.

It should be noted that there is some debate about the construct validity of self-construals and the scales measuring them (Gudykunst & Lee, 2003; Kim & Raja, 2003; Levine et al., 2003). Self-construal constructs and the scales measuring them are in their infancy, and the nature and dimensionality of self-construals continue to be hotly debated. The current self-construal scales are evolutionary developments of the original unidimensional scales. Dimensionality of selves, such as independent, relational, interdependent, collective, and many other closely related terms, can vary markedly between investigators (see Kim & Raja, 2003; Sedikides & Brewer, 2001).

MULTICULTURAL IDENTITY

Although impressive in both the breadth of cultures covered and the general convergence of the findings by different research groups, the dimensional approach confronts some methodological and conceptual problems. First, although the utility of the constructs is indisputable, there is still the tendency to conceive of individualism-collectivism as a pure dichotomy in many contexts. Hofstede (1980) defined *individualism* as a tendency to place one's own needs above the needs of one's ingroup and *collectivism* as a tendency to place the needs of one's ingroup above one's own needs. Since the advent of cultural psychology, those definitions of individualism and collectivism as mutually exclusive have gone largely unchallenged (see Kim & Raja, 2003). It is rather understandable, given the fact that not so long ago the world was "us" versus "savages" ("noble" at times). The "others" were "foreign devils" or "barbarians," and we "the center of the universe and civilization."

Around 25 years ago, Hofstede (1980) proposed individualism and collectivism as opposite poles of a value dimension that differentiates world cultures. He empirically derived "individualism" as a unidimensional construct at the cultural level. Hofstede forced a single bipolar dimension of individualism and saw collectivism as an absence of individualism. Similarly, in dealing with self-construals (as individual-level correlates of individualism and collectivism), there has been a tendency to treat them as bipolar opposites. Many existing measures of cultural identity are unidimensional. However, some scholars have suggested that individuals can possess both orientations (Gudykunst et al., 1996; Kim et al., 1996; Singelis, 1994). The self-construal scale was originally developed at a time when the unidimensional model of cultural identity was still popular with most researchers. Gradually, scholars began to speculate that independent and interdependent self-construals might be unrelated to one another, not polar opposites as their verbal labels might imply.

Despite the intuitive appeal of dichotomies such as individualism-collectivism, at least one other pair of personality constructs defined as dichotomous by Hofstede (1980), namely masculinity-femininity, already had been redefined conceptually and empirically (Bem, 1974) as orthogonal dimensions in the mid-1970s. Perhaps it is not surprising that some authors have begun to call for a redefinition of individualism and collectivism as orthogonal constructs (e.g., Kim et al., 1996; Oyserman,

Table 5.2   Leung and Kim's (1997) Revised Self-Construal Scale

---

Directions: Using the scale below, indicate to what degree you disagree/agree with each statement provided. It may be helpful to think of "groups" as your peer group.

strongly disagree   1   2   3   4   5   6   7   strongly agree.

1. I should be judged on my own merit.
2. I voice my opinions in group discussions.
3. I feel uncomfortable disagreeing with my group.
4. I conceal my negative emotions so I won't cause unhappiness among the members of my group.
5. My personal identity, independent of others, is very important to me.
6. I prefer to be self-reliant rather than dependent on others.
7. I act as a unique person, separate from others.
8. I don't like depending on others.
9. My relationships with those in my group are more important than my personal accomplishments.
10. My happiness depends on the happiness of those in my group.
11. I often consider how I can be helpful to specific others in my group.
12. I take responsibility for my own actions.
13. It is important for me to act as an independent person.
14. I have an opinion about most things: I know what I like and I know what I don't like.
15. I enjoy being unique and different from others.
16. I don't change my opinions in conformity with those of the majority.
17. Speaking up in a work/task group is not a problem for me.
18. Having a lively imagination is important to me.
19. Understanding myself is a major goal in my life.
20. I enjoy being admired for my unique qualities.
21. I am careful to maintain harmony in my group.
22. When with my group, I watch my words so I won't offend anyone.
23. I would sacrifice my self-interests for the benefit of my group.
24. I try to meet the demands of my group, even if it means controlling my own desires.
25. It is important to consult close friends and get their ideas before making decisions.
26. I should take into consideration my parents' advice when making education and career plans.
27. I act as fellow group members prefer I act.
28. The security of being an accepted member of a group is very important to me.
29. If my brother or sisters fails, I feel responsible.

Reprinted by permission from Leung, T. & Kim, M.S. (1997). A revised self-construal scale. Department of Speech, University of Hawaii at Manoa.

1993). In our study (Kim et al., 1996), we allow for the possibility that the two constructs are uncorrelated rather than negatively correlated. By redefining individualism and collectivism so that persons can be viewed as high or low on either dimension, we are in a position to avoid constraining individuals to score on only one dimension.

It is important to note here that empirical research has demonstrated the coexistence of both independent and interdependent self-construals in individuals (Brewer & Gardner, 1996; Gudykunst et al., 1996; Kim et al., 1996; Singelis & Brown, 1995). Furthermore, there is a growing awareness of the identity challenges and communication patterns in the life of the bicultural or multicultural person. Whether through immigration, sojourning, marriage, adoption, or birth, a wide range of people are actively carrying the frame of reference of two or more cultures (see Bennett, 1993). Thus, in discussing the two types of self-construal, we do not wish to stereotype or classify individuals. Rather, the descriptions illustrate the extremes of the two types of self-construal that coexist in each individual. The strength of the tendencies is, in part, enabled and developed according to cultural background.

The latter part of Kim et al.'s (1996) study was built around the assumption that individuals may identify with both independent and interdependent characteristics. Four types of culture orientation were identified: bicultural (high association with both independent and interdependent characteristics), independent (high association with independent and low association with interdependent characteristics), interdependent (low association with independent and high association with interdependent characteristics), and marginal (low association with both characteristics).

There was a significant main effect of cultural orientation, with bicultural individuals expressing the highest level of overall conversational concern, followed by interdependent, then independent, and, finally, marginal individuals expressing the lowest level of concern. While bicultural individuals showed the highest levels of overall conversational concern in all cultures, the mean for biculturals did *not* significantly differ from the mean for interdependents. Such findings imply a tendency for bicultural and interdependent individuals

to be more adaptive than independent or marginal individuals in intercultural conversational settings. We are not sure, however, why interdependents also showed higher levels of conversational concern than independents or marginals. The fact that the percentage of biculturals was the highest in Hawaii, however, lends some support to our conceptualization of bicultural persons as those who identify with both independent and interdependent characteristics. Various ethnic and cultural groups live in Hawaii, with no single group forming a majority in this pluralistic social milieu. While different ethnic groups seem to preserve their cultural identity to varying degrees, a unique "local" culture, which blends aspects of many cultures, has developed in Hawaii. We need to investigate further the specific ways in which self-construals may determine the flexibility in actual conversational strategy choices across different cultural settings.

PRACTICAL IMPLICATIONS

The ability to achieve conversational goals successfully depends in large measure on being able to make accurate predictions about the effectiveness of communication strategies. Much-abused terms, such as "communication breakdown" and "cross-cultural miscommunication" (Coupland, Giles, & Wiemann, 1991), can often be attributed to different perceptions regarding the choices of communication tactics. For instance, "communication breakdown" typically occurs because interactants disagree about the effectiveness or social appropriateness of one another's conflict strategies. An individual's beliefs about the appropriateness of communication strategies are apt to affect what communication tactics and strategies the individual chooses, and what inferences the individual makes about her or his own and others' communication behavior. The current review implies that different cultural orientations seem to cause one to have drastically different ideas about what constitutes an appropriate communication strategy or tactic.

The concept of culture-based conversational constraints can help explain cultural differences in judgments of communicative competence. The prevailing culture determines whose speech style will be seen as normal; who will be required to learn the communication style and interpret the meaning of the other; and whose language style will be seen as deviant, irrational, and inferior. Also, due to their different implicit theories about conversational styles, cultural groups may disagree about appropriate choices of conversational strategies. As Koester and Olebe (1988) put it, as cultures vary, so do the specific behaviors that represent the underlying components of effectiveness. Our major concern has been to investigate how definitions and enactments of communicative competence may vary culturally. For example, comparisons of the perceived importance of constraints are presumably describing patterns of competent communication in different cultures. Individuals form impressions of others' communicative behavior, and then use these expectations as guidelines to judge their own and others' behaviors.

The main practical implication of this research is that when speakers of different cultural backgrounds interact, the problems that develop in communication can be accounted for by the salience of each other's global goals or constraints in conversation. Given that global constraints contribute to consistent performances across different contexts, the concept of the different restraining forces of various conversational constraints can provide a useful framework for explaining intercultural communication and misunderstandings. We have created a series of exercises for multicultural training that applies the concept of "culture-based conversational constraints" (see Kim, 1997). These exercises were designed for use in diverse settings, such as classrooms, teacher training, manager training, freshman seminars, and so forth. Understanding each other's conversational styles and the motives behind them is a first move in overcoming intercultural misunderstanding.

CONCLUSION

Not very long ago the world was "us" versus "savages." Understanding strangers' communication styles constitutes an essential step in going beyond that dichotomy. In this chapter I have reviewed some of our attempts to substantiate cultural communication styles empirically from a psychological perspective. Attention to culture can increase the validity of research on communication competence in general. Cross-cultural issues become the test case for a theory of competence. What is clear from the series of research on conversational constraints theory is that interaction style is individually goal-driven yet socially structured. Stereotypical descriptions of communication behaviors are reflections of an individual's preference for certain conversational constraints. Future understanding of how people produce and hearers understand conversations may continue to alter our view of the nature of intercultural communication competence.

Furthermore, our research indicates that culture influences mediating processes (e.g., self-construals) that affect the perceived importance of conversational constraints. Stated differently, cultural variability does not directly impact on the perceived importance of conversational constraints per se; rather its influences are indirect, through other processes. Recent between-culture analyses that included self-construal provided converging evidence of the critical role played by self-construal (Gudykunst et al., 1996; Kim et al., 1996; Singelis & Brown, 1995). Self-construals provide a parsimonious explanation of differences between cultures in the impact of self-related variables and communication behavior. The notion of self-construals (as individual-level correlates of individualism and collectivism) potentially clarify and elaborate the "fuzzy" construct of culture, not only providing more concise, coherent, integrated, and empirically testable dimensions of cultural variations but also linking psychological phenomena to cultural dimensions (see Kim, Triandis, Kagitçibasi, Choi, & Yoon, 1994). Coherent theoretical efforts can be made only through the logical connection between cultural level analysis on the one hand, and individual level analysis on the other.

In previous comparisons of selves in different cultural contexts the focus has been on the contrast between those patterns of cultural participation that construct the person as an independent, autonomous entity and those that construct the person as an interdependent part of a larger social order. However, we argue that elements of both worldviews may exist at the cultural and individual levels. There is growing evidence supporting the view that these concepts do not necessarily form opposite poles and may coexist in individuals or groups in different situations. The common tendency to pit independence against interdependence is not warranted. The unidimensional model of cultural identity has been significantly limited in its vision of human potential. Awareness of this is a crucial preparation for a genuine understanding of cultural identity and human communication. This theme is developed further in Kim (2002).

In conclusion, the data indicate that behaviors evidenced by members of different cultures are not simply surface representations of their cultural background, but rather are deeply tied to the values and self-identity possessed by the individual members. Our research raised the larger issues of what kinds of general conversational constraints shape interaction beliefs, and how these constraints are based in the wider social structure. The conversational constraints serve as "pressures" that shape and give rise to distinct social interaction patterns.

Limitations and Future Directions

Several potential limitations of the present approach should be noted. First, it should be noted that the current approach does not explore actual language use, but rather the conversational constraints that underlie people's use of language. Linguistic research has shown that there can be significant differences in what people think they say and what they actually say. Will the perceptions of the conversational constraints influence actual communication performance and outcome? Additional studies should be conducted to test how perceptions of the conversational constraints influences actual communication performance and outcome.

Our research has been limited primarily to the particular communication phenomenon of "requesting." While requests are particularly interesting (as they constitute face-threatening acts and can stretch over large parts of conversations), future studies should attempt empirical documentation of conversational behavior in other interaction goals (e.g., apologies, refusals, criticisms) and compare them across different speech communities. The current list of conversational constraints has the potential to account for cross-cultural similarities as well as differences in the manifestation of conversational constraints across a wide variety of primary goals, such as giving criticism, terminating a relationship, seeking information, eliciting promises, and more.

Third, it should be noted that specific cross-cultural and cross-linguistic studies, including the current one, tend to focus on two or three cultural and linguistic systems at most. Furthermore, in many cases English serves as the yardstick for comparison. While the cultures studied are very different indeed, and can therefore provide a preliminary basis for tentative generalizations, a wider variety of languages and of different populations with differing linguistic and sociocultural backgrounds should be investigated. In addition, relatively few studies to date have been conducted on nonnative speech act performance. There is a clear and definite need for studies examining second-language learner populations.

Finally, Spencer-Oatey and Jiang (in press) noted that our conversational constraints are presumed rather than extracted from factor analyses of those dimensions. So they asked participants to rate the perceived importance of specific goals that participants considered important during conversations in hypothetical situations, and then extracted the dimensions of interactional concerns through factor analysis. The factors extracted in their research were: concern for task, concern for clarity, nonentitlement-based concern for face, and entitlement-based concern for face (Spencer-Oatey & Jiang, in press). These interactional concerns fell mainly into two broad areas, communicative goal and speech design characteristics. Interactional goals falling into the category of communicative goals were those relating to task achievement, problem resolution, preservation of face, maintenance of a smooth relationship, and observation of rights or obligations; interactional concerns involving speech design characteristics were those relating to clarity, directness, friendliness, or lightheartedness of speech. However, Spencer-Oatey and Jiang's research design has some limitations. The distinction between the two main categories of factors seems unclear. For instance, I do not see how friendliness, which was listed under speech design characteristics, is very different from preservation of face or maintenance of a smooth relationship, which is listed under communicative goal. Furthermore, some of the Interactional Principles that were extracted are probably too general to elicit cultural differences (e.g., lightheartedness of speech).

Recent years have seen developments in the notion of higher-level constraints in interaction. The notion of conversational constraints is an important topic, eminently worthy of further theoretical and empirical investigation. What will the future bring to this area of investigation? More careful and critical examinations of conversational constraints and related concepts will probably occur. Undoubtedly the list of conversational constraints introduced in this chapter should be further refined and clarified. Some methodological advances and better ways to measure and assess importance of conversational constraints and self-construals and related concepts than are presently available should also develop.

NOTES

1. In general, we have not found significant differences between different types of situations (due to status of interactants, gender, etc.) in this study or in others. Accordingly, the differences due to situations are not discussed.

2. The increased attention to individual-level cultural dimensions was a further healthy step. Some began asking whether new or complementary theories, constructs, and methodologies could be teased from the collective worldview (see Kim, 2001, 2002).

REFERENCES

Abe H., & Wiseman, R. L. (1983). A cross-cultural confirmation of the dimensions of intercultural effectiveness. *International Journal of Intercultural Relations, 7,* 53-68.

Argyle, M., Bond, M., Iizuka, Y., & Contarello, A. (1986). Cross-cultural variations in relationship rules. *International Journal of Psychology, 21,* 287-315.

Bem, S. L. (1974). The measurement of psychological androgeny. *Journal of Consulting and Clinical Psychology, 42,* 155-162.

Bennett, J. M. (1993). Cultural marginality: Identity issues in intercultural training. In M. Paige (Ed.), *Education for the intercultural experience* (pp. 109-135). Yarmouth, ME: Intercultural Press.

Berger, C. R. (1987). Planning and scheming: Strategies for initiating relationships. In R. Burnett, P. McGhee, & D. D. Clarke (Eds.), *Accounting for relationships: Explanation, representation and knowledge* (pp. 158-174). London: Methuen.

Berry, J. W., & Dasen, P. R. (1974). *Culture and cognition: Readings in cross-cultural psychology*. London: Methuen.

Blum-Kulka, S. (1987). Indirectness and politeness in requests: Same or different? *Journal of Pragmatics, 11*, 131-146.

Breckler, S. J., Greenwald, A. G., & Wiggins, E. C. (1986, April). *Public, private, and collective self-evaluation: Measurement of individual differences*. Paper presented at the International Research and Exchange Board (IREX) Conference on Self and Social Involvement, Princeton, NJ.

Brewer, M. B., & Gardner, W. (1996). Who is this "we"? Levels of collective identity and self representations. *Journal of Personality and Social Psychology, 71*, 83-93.

Brown, P., & Levinson, S. (1978). Universals in language usage: Politeness phenomena. In E. N. Goody (Ed.), *Questions and politeness* (pp. 56-289). Cambridge, UK: Cambridge University Press.

Canary, D. J., & Spitzberg, B. H. (1989). A model of the perceived competence of conflict strategies. *Human Communication Research, 15*, 630-649.

Collier, M. J. (1989). Cultural and intercultural communication competence: Current approaches and directions for future research. *International Journal of Intercultural Relations, 13*, 287-302.

Coupland, N., Giles, H., & Wiemann, J. M. (1991). *"Miscommunication" and problematic talk*. Newbury Park, CA: Sage.

Cronen, V. E., Chen, V., & Pearce, W. B. (1988). Coordinated management of meaning: A critical theory. In Y. Y. Kim & W. B. Gudykunst (Eds.), *Theories in intercultural communication* (pp. 66-98). Newbury Park, CA: Sage.

Dillard, J. P. (Ed.). (1990). *Seeking compliance: The production of interpersonal influence messages* (pp. 41-56). Scottsdale, AZ: Gorsuch-Scarisbrick.

Douglas, W. (1987). Affinity-testing in initial interactions. *Journal of Social and Personal Relationships, 4*, 3-15.

Emmons, R. A. (1989). The personal striving approach to personality. In L. Pervin (Ed.), *Goal concepts in personality & social psychology*. Hillsdale, NJ: Lawrence Erlbaum.

Goffman, E. (1967). *Interaction ritual*. Garden City, NY: Doubleday/Anchor.

Greene, J. O., & Lindsey, A. E. (1989). Encoding processes in the production of multiple-goal messages. *Human Communication Research, 16*, 120-140.

Grice, H. P. (1975). Logic and conversation. In P. Cole & J. Morgan (Eds.), *Syntax and semantics 3: Speech acts* (pp. 107-142). New York: Academic Press.

Gudykunst, W. B., & Lee, C. (2003). Assessing the validity of self construal scales: A response to Levine et al. *Human Communication Research, 29*, 253-274.

Gudykunst, W. B., Matsumoto, Y., Ting-Toomey, S., Nishida, T., Kim, K., & Heyman, S. (1996). The influence of cultural individualism-collectivism, self-construals, and individual values on communication styles across cultures. *Human Communication Research, 22*, 510-543.

Gudykunst, W. B., & Ting-Toomey, S. (1988). *Culture and interpersonal communication*. Newbury Park, CA: Sage.

Gumperz, J. J., & Tannen, D. (1979). Individual and social differences in language use. In C. J. Fillmore & W. S.-Y. Wang (Eds.), *Individual differences in language ability and language behavior* (pp. 305-325). New York: Academic Press.

Guthrie, G. M., & Zenicki, N. (1967). Predicting performance in the Peace Corps. *Journal of Social Psychology, 71*, 11–21.

Hawes, F., & Kealey, D. J. (1981). Canadians in development: An empirical study of Canadian technical assistance. *International Journal of Intercultural Relations, 5*, 239–258.

Hofstede, G. (1980). *Culture's consequences: International differences in work-related values*. Beverly Hills, CA: Sage.

Holtgraves, T. (in press). Comprehending speaker meaning. In W. B. Gudykunst (Ed.), *Communication yearbook 26*. Mahwah, NJ: Lawrence Erlbaum.

Holtgraves, T., & Yang, J. N. (1992). Interpersonal underpinnings of request strategies: General principles and differences due to culture and gender. *Journal of Personality and Social Psychology, 62*, 246-256.

Jacobs, C. S. (1985). Language. In M. L. Knapp & G. R. Miller (Eds.), *Handbook of interpersonal communication* (pp. 313-343). Beverly Hills, CA: Sage.

Kagitçibasi, C. (1996). *Family and human development across cultures: A view from the other side.* Hillsdale, NJ: Erlbaum.

Kellermann, K. (1989). *Understanding tactical choice: Metagoals in conversation.* Unpublished manuscript, Department of Communication, Michigan State University.

Kellermann, K., & Kim, M. S. (1991). *Tactical choices in the pursuit of social goals.* Paper presented to the Information Systems Division of the International Communication Association, Chicago.

Kim, M. S. (1993). Culture-based conversational constraints in explaining cross-cultural strategic competence. In R. L. Wiseman & J. Koester (Eds.), *Intercultural communication competence* (pp. 132-150). Newbury Park, CA: Sage.

Kim, M. S. (1994). Cross-cultural comparisons of the perceived importance of conversational constraints. *Human Communication Research, 21,* 128-151.

Kim, M. S. (1995). Toward a theory of conversational constraints. In R. L. Wiseman (Ed.), *Intercultural communication theory* (pp. 148-169). Thousand Oaks, CA: Sage.

Kim, M. S. (1997). Conversational constraints as a tool for understanding communication styles. In T. Singelis (Ed.), *Teaching about culture, ethnicity, and diversity: Exercises and planned activities* (pp. 101-109). Thousand Oaks, CA: Sage.

Kim, M. S. (2001). Perspectives on human communication: Implications for transcultural theory. In V. H. Milhouse, M. K. Asante, & P. O. Nwoso (Eds.), *Transcultural realities* (pp. 3-31). Thousand Oaks, CA: Sage.

Kim, M. S. (2002). *Multicultural perspectives on human communication: Implications for theory and practice.* Thousand Oaks, CA: Sage.

Kim, M. S., & Bresnahan, M. (1994). A process model of request tactic evaluation. *Discourse Processes, 18,* 317-344.

Kim, M. S., Hunter, J. E., Miyahara, A., Horvath, A., Bresnahan, M., & Yoon, H. J. (1996). Individual- vs. culture-level dimensions of individualism and collectivism: Effects on preferred conversational styles. *Communication Monographs, 63,* 29-49.

Kim, M. S., Klingle, R. S., Sharkey, W. F., Park, H. S., Smith, D. H., Yuego, G., & Cai, D. (2000). A test of a cultural model of patient's motivation for verbal communication in patient-doctor interactions. *Communication Monographs, 67,* 262-283.

Kim, M. S., & Raja, N. S. (2003). When validity testing lacks validity: Comment on Levine et al. *Human Communication Research, 29,* 275-290.

Kim, M. S., & Sharkey, W. F. (1995). Independent and interdependent construals of the self: Explaining cultural patterns of interpersonal communication in multi-cultural settings. *Communication Quarterly, 43,* 20-38.

Kim, M. S., Sharkey, W. F., & Singelis, T. M. (1994). The relationship between individual's self-construals and perceived importance of interactive constraints. *International Journal of Intercultural Relations, 18,* 117-140.

Kim, M. S., & Wilson, S. R. (1994). A cross-cultural comparison of implicit theories of requesting. *Communication Monographs, 61,* 210-235.

Kim, U., Triandis, H. C., Kagitçibasi, C., Choi, S.-C., & Yoon, G. (1994). *Individualism and collectivism: Theory, method, and applications.* Thousand Oaks, CA: Sage.

Koester, J., & Olebe, M. (1988). The behavioral assessment scale for intercultural communication effectiveness. *International Journal of Intercultural Relations, 12,* 233-246.

Lakoff, R. T. (1977). What you can do with words: Politeness, pragmatics and performatives. In A. Rogers, B. Wall, & J. Murphy (Eds.), *Proceedings of the Texas Conference on Performatives, Presuppositions and Implicatures* (pp. 79-105), Arlington, VA: Center for Applied Linguistics.

Leech, G. N. (1983). *Principles of pragmatics.* New York: Longman.

Leung, K. (1989). Cross-cultural differences: Individual-level vs. culture-level analysis. *International Journal of Psychology, 24,* 703-719.

Leung, K., & Bond, M. H. (1989). On the empirical identification of dimensions for cross-cultural comparison. *Journal of Cross-Cultural Psychology, 20,* 133-151.

Leung, T., & Kim, M. S. (1997). *A revised self-construal scale.* Unpublished manuscript, Department of Speech, University of Hawaii at Manoa.

Levine, T. R., Bresnahan, M. J., Park, H. S., Lapinski, M. K., Wittenbaum, G. M., Shearman, S. M., Lee, S. Y., Chung, D. H., & Ohashi, R. (2003). Self-construal scales lack validity. *Human Communication Research, 29,* 210-252.

Lustig, M. W., & Spitzberg, B. H. (1993). Methodological issues in the study of intercultural communication competence. In R. L. Wiseman & J. Koester (Eds.), *Intercultural communication competence* (International and Intercultural Communication Annual, Volume 17, pp. 153-167). Newbury Park, CA: Sage.

Markus, H. R., & Kitayama, S. (1991). Culture and the self: Implications for cognition, emotion, and motivation. *Psychological Review, 98,* 224-253.

Markus, H. R., & Kitayama, S. (1998). The cultural psychology of personality. *Journal of Cross-Cultural Psychology, 29,* 63-87.

Markus, H. R., Mullally, P. R., & Kitayama, S. (1997). Selfways: Diversity in modes of cultural participation. In U. Neisser & D. A. Jopling (Eds.), *The conceptual self in context* (pp. 13-59). Cambridge, UK: Cambridge University Press.

Markus, H. R., & Wurf, E. (1987). The dynamic self-concept: A social psychological perspective. *Annual Review of Psychology, 38,* 299-337.

Matveev, A. V., & Nelson, P. E. (2003, May). *Improving management: Perceptions of intercultural communication competence by American and Russian managers.* Paper presented at the annual conference of the International Communication Association, San Diego, CA.

McCann, C. D., & Higgins, E. T. (1988). Motivation and affect in interpersonal relations: The role of personal orientations and discrepancies. In L. Donohew, H. Sypher, & T. Higgins (Eds.), *Communication, social cognition, and affect* (pp. 53-79). Hillsdale, NJ: Lawrence Erlbaum.

McClelland, D. C. (1985). *Human motivation.* Glenview, IL: Scott, Foresman.

Miller, G. A., Galanter, E., & Pribram, K. H. (1960). *Plans and the structure of behavior.* New York: Holt, Rinehart & Winston.

Miyahara, A., & Kim, M. S. (1993). Requesting styles among "collectivists" cultures: A comparison between Japanese and Koreans. *Intercultural Communication Studies, 6,* 104-128.

Miyahara, A., Kim, M. S., Shin, H. C., & Yoon, K. (1998). Conflict resolution styles among "collectivist" cultures: A comparison between Japanese and Koreans. *International Journal of Intercultural Relations, 22,* 505-525.

Niedenthal, P. M., & Beike, D. R. (1997). Interrelated and isolated self-concepts. *Personality and Social Psychology Review, 1,* 106-128.

Oyserman, D. (1993). The lens of personhood: Viewing the self and others in a multicultural society. *Journal of Personality and Social Psychology, 65,* 993-1009.

Read, S. J., & Miller, L. C. (1989). Inter-personalism: Toward a goal-based theory of persons in relationships. In L. Pervin (Ed.), *Goal concepts in personality and social psychology* (pp. 413-472). Hillsdale, NJ: Lawrence Erlbaum.

Rokeach, M. (1973). *The nature of human values.* New York: Free Press.

Schank, R. C., & Abelson, R. P. (1977). *Scripts, plans, goals, and understanding.* Hillsdale, NJ: Lawrence Erlbaum.

Schank, R. C., & Childers, P. G. (1984). *The cognitive computer.* Reading, MA: Addison-Wesley.

Scollon, R., & Scollon, S. (1981). *Narrative, literacy and face in interethnic communication.* Norwood, NJ: Ablex.

Sedikides, C., & Brewer, M. B. (Eds.). (2001). *Individual self, relational self, collective self.* Philadelphia: Psychology Press.

Singelis, T. M. (1994). The measurement of independent and interdependent self-construals. *Personality and Social Psychology Bulletin, 20,* 580-591.

Singelis, T. M., & Brown, W. J. (1995). Culture, self, and collectivist communication: Linking culture to individual behavior. *Human Communication Research, 21,* 354-389.

Smith, M. B. (1991). *Values, self, and society: Toward a humanist social psychology.* New Brunswick, NJ: Transaction Publishers.

Smith, P. B., & Bond, M. H. (1998). *Social psychology across cultures.* London: Prentice Hall.

Spencer-Oatey, H., & Jiang, W. (in press). Explaining cross-cultural pragmatic findings: Moving from politeness maxims to sociopragmatic interactional principles. *Journal of Pragmatics.*

Street, R. L., & Cappella, J. N. (1985). Sequence and pattern in communicative behavior: A model and commentary. In R. L. Street & J. N. Cappella (Eds.), *Sequence and pattern in communicative behavior*. Baltimore, MD: Edward Arnold.

Ting-Toomey, S. (1988). Intercultural conflict styles: A face-negotiation theory. In Y. Y. Kim & W. B. Gudykunst (Eds.), *Theories in intercultural communication* (pp. 213-238). Newbury park, CA: Sage.

Triandis, H. C. (1988). Collectivism vs. individualism: A reconceptualization of a basic concept in cross-cultural psychology. In G. Verma & C. Bagley (Eds.), *Cross-cultural studies of personality, attitudes and cognition*. London: Macmillan.

van Dijk, T., & Kintsch, W. (1983). *Strategies of discourse comprehension*. New York: Academic Press.

Verschueren, J. (1996). Contrastive ideology research: Aspects of pragmatic methodology. *Language Science, 18,* 589-603.

von Cranach, M., Kalbermatten, U., Indermuhle, K., & Gugler, B. (1982). *Goal-directed action*. London: Academic Press.

Weary, G., & Arkin, R. M. (1981). Attitudinal self-presentation. In J. H. Harvey, W. J. Ickes, & R. Kidd (Eds.), *New directions in attribution theory and research 3*. Hillsdale, NJ: Lawrence Erlbaum.

Wilensky, R. (1981). Meta-planning: Representing and using knowledge about planning in problem solving and natural language understanding. *Cognitive Science, 5,* 197-233.

Wilensky, R. (1983). *Planning and understanding: A computational approach to human reasoning*. Reading, MA: Addison-Wesley.

Wilson, S. R., & Putnam, L. L. (1990). Interaction goals in negotiation. In J. A. Anderson (Ed.), *Communication yearbook 13*, (pp. 374-427). Newbury Park, CA: Sage.

PART IV

Theories Focusing on Adaptations in Interactions

6

Communication Accommodation Theory

A Look Back and a Look Ahead

CINDY GALLOIS

TANIA OGAY

HOWARD GILES

Theories aim to capture the complexity of life in formalized conceptualizations. As time goes by, our understanding widens and at the same time becomes more precise. Theories undergo a continuous process of revising and refining; some disappear and are replaced by better-adapted ones. Theories are not only about life, they also have their own lives. For theories as for people, milestones like the turn of a century (or a millennium) or the completion of decades (see Giles, Mulac, Bradac, & Johnson, 1987) are occasions for a critical reappraisal of accomplishments and a look toward the future. As a theory that has investigated the links between language, context, and identity for three decades,

communication accommodation theory (CAT) is at a stage where it is timely for a look back at its history, which should help to set the agenda for its future development.

This chapter documents the trajectory of CAT, which has been particularly (but not solely) developed in the context of intercultural communication since its inception in the 1970s. Indeed, it has been reviewed in many intercultural communication texts and handbooks (e.g., Gallois & Callan, 1997; Gudykunst & Kim, 1992; Gudykunst & Lee, 2002; Gudykunst & Nishida, 1989; Martin & Nakayama, 2002) as well as in interpersonal communication and language texts (e.g., Bull, 2002; DeVito, 2004; Holtgraves, 2002;

Robinson, 2003) and in general communication theory texts more widely (e.g., Littlejohn, 2002; Miller, 2002). In addition, its cross-disciplinary impact has moved beyond social psychology and communication into handbooks and texts in sociolinguistics (e.g., Coupland, 1995; Giles, 2001; Giles & Powesland, 1997; see also Meyerhoff, 1998) as well as being adopted to provide explanatory weight to such linguistic phenomena as semicommunication (Braunmüller, 2002), code switching and mixing (e.g., Bissoonauth & Offord, 2001), language contact and dialect change (Trudgill, 1986), and hypercorrection (Giles & Williams, 1992).

In our view, CAT is a theory of both intergroup and interpersonal communication, invoking the dual importance of both factors in predicting and understanding intergroup interactions (see Gallois & Giles, 1998). As such, intercultural encounters provide perhaps the richest basis for understanding the theory, even though each intergroup context has its unique characteristics (e.g., Fox, Giles, Orbe, & Bourhis, 2000; Watson & Gallois, 2002; Williams, Giles, Coupland, Dalby, & Manasse, 1990). We examine CAT here on the basis of the different sets of propositions that have been formulated since the early 1970s (Ball, Giles, Byrne, & Berechree, 1984; Gallois, Franklyn-Stokes, Giles, & Coupland, 1988; Gallois, Giles, Jones, Cargile, & Ota, 1995; Giles et al., 1987; Street & Giles, 1982; Thakerar, Giles, & Cheshire, 1982). As we shall see, the evolution of CAT's propositions during these three decades raises a number of issues. The extensive amount of research and theory development around CAT has made parsimony a major concern, and, consequentially, recent overviews of the theory have been more discursive and have not invoked propositional formats (see Gallois & Giles, 1998; Giles & Noels, 1997; Giles & Ogay, in press; Giles & Wadleigh, 1999; Shepard, Giles, & Le Poire, 2001). Indeed, working toward the reduced number of propositions in the final

section has been a major challenge. In order to conserve space and avoid redundancy with other reviews of communication accommodation, references to the many experimental results that support the theory are in general left out of this chapter. Interested readers should consult the above-mentioned sources, as well as Giles, Coupland, and Coupland (1991) and, for more recent reviews, Shepard and colleagues (2001), Giles and Ogay (in press), Sachdev and Giles (in press) and Williams, Gallois, and Pittam (1999).

Background and Foundations

During the 1970s, social psychologists (Giles, 1973, 1977, 1979b; Giles, Taylor, & Bourhis, 1972) laid the foundations of what was then named speech accommodation theory (SAT) out of a dissatisfaction with sociolinguistics and its descriptive (rather than explanatory) appraisal of linguistic variation in social contexts (see Beebe & Giles, 1984), as well as to provide the burgeoning study of language attitudes with more theoretical bite (Giles & Powesland, 1975). Street and Giles (1982) put SAT in propositional form for the first time, although precursors to this had already appeared in the parallel-evolving ethnolinguistic identity theory (ELIT; e.g., Giles, 1978, 1979a; Giles & Johnson, 1981). Thakerar and colleagues (1982) revised the propositions and restated them. Could these authors have imagined then the developments the theory would undergo? Probably not, if one considers the modest scope of the theory in the early papers that formulated propositions:

> SAT was devised to explain some of the motivations underlying certain shifts in people's speech styles during social encounters, and some of the social consequences arising from them. More specifically, it originated in order to elucidate the cognitive and affective processes underlying speech convergence and divergence. (Thakerar et al., 1982, p. 207)

SAT soon generated a plethora of research and related theories, resulting in an expansion of its scope:

> SAT presents a broad and robust basis from which to examine mutual influences in communication, taking account of social and cognitive factors, and having the scope to cover the social consequences of speech shifts as well as their determinants and the motivations underlying them. Furthermore, it is applicable to a broad range of speech behaviors, and nonverbal analyses potentially, with the flexibility of relevance at both interpersonal and intergroup levels. (Giles et al., 1987, p. 34)

The latest presentation of the theory in propositional form indicates how much the scope of the theory widened in the ensuing years, exemplified by the change from "speech" to "communication accommodation theory" (CAT; Giles et al., 1987):

> Overall, CAT is a multifunctional theory that conceptualizes communication in both subjective and objective terms. It focuses on both intergroup and interpersonal features and, as we shall see, can integrate dimensions of cultural variability. Moreover, in addition to individual factors of knowledge, motivation, and skill, CAT recognizes the importance of power and of macro contextual factors. Most important, perhaps, CAT is a theory of intercultural communication that actually attends to communication. (Gallois et al., 1995, p. 127)

SAT was first formulated in order to explore the sociopsychological parameters underlying the moves speakers make in their speech behaviors. Central to it is the idea that communication is not only a matter of exchanging referential information, but that interpersonal as well as intergroup relationships are managed by means of communication. What are the motives and intentions behind speakers' conscious (or nonconscious)

linguistic choices? How do listeners perceive these choices and react to them?

Production and reception are thus the two basic facets of communication on which SAT first examined the original accommodative strategies of convergence and divergence/maintenance. *Convergence* is defined as a strategy through which individuals adapt their communicative behavior in such a way as to become more similar to their interlocutor's behavior. Conversely, the strategy of *divergence* leads to an accentuation of differences between self and other. A strategy similar to divergence is *maintenance*, in which a person persists in his or her original style, regardless of the communication behavior of the interlocutor. Central to the theory is the idea that speakers adjust (or accommodate) their speech styles in order to create and maintain positive personal and social identities.

SAT was derived in part from similarity-attraction theory (Byrne, 1971), which posits that an increase in perceived interpersonal similarity results in an increase in interpersonal attraction. Thus, convergence is a strategy that allows one person to become more similar to another (or, more precisely, to one's representation of the other) and therefore presumably more likeable to him or her. Giles (1978) also invoked Tajfel and Turner's (1979) social identity theory of intergroup relations (SIT), and SAT thereafter has largely (but not solely) relied on the framework of SIT to explain the motives behind the strategies of divergence and maintenance. Why should one choose to appear *dis*similar to another? Referring to similarity-attraction theory alone would mean that the motive driving divergence or maintenance behaviors would be to appear dislikable, or at least that the speaker's need for social approval is low. Invoking the intergroup context, SIT explains the adoption of these strategies through the desire to signal a salient group distinctiveness so as to reinforce a social identity.

Another fundamental resource for SAT is attribution theory (Heider, 1958; Kelley,

1973), which inspired the propositions on the reception side. How are accommodative strategies perceived and evaluated by interlocutors? Attribution theory suggests that we explain and appreciate people's behavior in terms of the motives and intentions that we think caused it: in other words, those to which we attribute the behavior. In general, we evaluate a person who performed a desired behavior more favorably when we attribute the behavior to an internal cause (e.g., intention to act in this way), rather than to an external one (e.g., situational pressure). Conversely, we evaluate a person who performed an undesirable behavior less negatively when we attribute the behavior to an external than to an internal cause (e.g., malevolent intention).

Propositions of SAT and CAT in Historical Perspective

During its development, SAT/CAT has received broad empirical support. As Table 6.1 indicates, two phases can be distinguished in the articles where propositions have been formulated:

- a first phase (speech accommodation theory) of definition and refinement of the initial set of propositions, focused on the strategies of convergence and divergence of speech styles during social encounters;

- a second phase (communication accommodation theory), characterized by a major extension of the focus from the two accommodation strategies of convergence and divergence to the whole process of communication in a number of intergroup contexts, along with the integration of satellite theories developed to account for communication between ethnic groups (Giles & Johnson, 1981), second-language acquisition (Beebe & Giles, 1984), and communication between generations (Coupland, Coupland, & Giles, 1991; Williams & Nussbaum, 2001).

Furthermore, CAT, along with some of the satellite theories, was the foundation for independent models (themselves subject to their own later refinements and elaborations) in which accommodative processes and dilemmas were embedded within wider social forces. These models include the communicative predicament model of aging (e.g., Ryan, Giles, Bartolucci, & Henwood, 1986), the group vitality model (Harwood, Giles, & Bourhis, 1994), the intergenerational contact model (Fox & Giles, 1993), the model of multiculturalism (Sachdev & Bourhis, 2001), the workplace gender nonaccommodation cycle model (Boggs & Giles, 1999), and the communication management effects model of successful aging (Giles & Harwood, 1997).

Table 6.1   Number of Propositions in Versions of SAT (Phase 1) and CAT (Phase 2)

Authors and Date of Paper	Number of Propositions
Phase 1: SAT	
Street and Giles (1982)	6
Thakerar et al. (1982)	6 (revision of Street & Giles)
Ball et al. (1984)	6
Giles et al. (1987)	6
Phase 2: CAT	
Gallois et al. (1988)	16 (revised, integrates satellite theories)
Gallois et al. (1995)	17

It is now time for a third phase, in which CAT is consolidated and revised in a clearer manner. Gallois and Giles (1998) noted that CAT's focus is most appropriately around the extent to which interlocutors apprehend the interaction in intergroup or interpersonal terms. Everything else, from motives to strategies to actual behavior to evaluations of behavior, flows from this. We adopt a similar approach in this reformulation.

PHASE 1: SPEECH ACCOMMODATION THEORY

The first presentation of SAT's propositions per se was in Street and Giles (1982), and a revised set appeared in the same year in Thakerar et al. (1982). The early propositions follow a symmetrical structure for the strategies of convergence and divergence/maintenance, exploring motives for the strategies and magnitude on the production side, and evaluation of them on the reception side.

Production

- *Convergence:* People are more likely to converge toward the speech patterns of their recipients when they desire recipients' approval and when the perceived costs for doing so are proportionally lower than the anticipated rewards.
- *Divergence/Maintenance:* People are more likely to maintain their speech patterns or diverge them away from those of their interlocutors' either when they define the encounter in intergroup terms and desire a positive ingroup identity, or when they wish to dissociate personally from another in an interindividual encounter.

Magnitude

- *Convergence:* The magnitude of speech convergence is a function of the extent of speakers' repertoires and the factors (personality and environmental) increasing the need for approval.

- *Divergence/Maintenance:* The magnitude of speech divergence is a function of the extent of speakers' repertoires, as well as contextual factors increasing the salience of group identification and the desire for a positive ingroup identity, or undesirable characteristics of another in an interindividual encounter.

Reception

- *Convergence:* Speech convergence is positively evaluated by recipients when the resultant behavior is perceived to be at an optimal sociolinguistic distance from them and is attributed with positive intent.
- *Divergence/Maintenance:* Speech maintenance and divergence are unfavorably evaluated by recipients when they attribute them to negative intent, but favorably evaluated by observers of the encounter who define the interaction in intergroup terms and who share a common, positively valued group membership with the speaker.

Functions of Accommodation

In its early days, SAT explained convergence in terms of the need for approval, and divergence in terms of the need for positive distinctiveness. Another function of convergence and divergence rapidly emerged, however. Thakerar et al. (1982) introduced into the propositions the idea that accommodation strategies have not only an affective function (i.e., of identity maintenance), but also a cognitive one involving speakers' organizing their output to take account of the requirements of listeners, and hence facilitating comprehension. Thakerar and colleagues mentioned the cognitive organization function only for convergence, however.

Street and Giles (1982) brought to the propositions the idea that divergence can also be enacted in order to facilitate comprehension, rather than being only an expression of the desire to show distinctiveness. For example, a bilingual may purposely exaggerate his or her accent or pretend to have difficulty in finding words in order to remind his or her interlocutor that any breaking of norms (linguistic, but also interactional and social) should be attributed not to intention but to the speaker's foreignness. In other contexts, divergence can function as a strategic move to encourage interlocutors to change their speech patterns, for instance when therapists diverge in their quantity of talk to encourage their patients to talk more. Street and Giles introduced only this second function for divergence in their revised propositions, as did Giles et al. (1987); the self-handicapping tactic was incorporated without being theorized in the propositions (see Gallois & Giles, 1998).

Following Thakerar and colleagues (1982), subsequent presentations of SAT added the cognitive goal "attaining communicational efficiency" to the two original affective goals of accommodation: "evoking listeners' social approval" for convergence and "maintaining speakers' positive social identities" for divergence/maintenance. It was not clear, however, whether this new goal should be linked only to convergence or to both strategies. This ambiguity can be resolved, as we have done here, by situating more clearly the different goals on the two dimensions of functions of accommodation introduced by Giles, Scherer, and Taylor (1979)—the cognitive dimension of cognitive organization and the affective dimension of identity maintenance:

Cognitive Function:
Cognitive Organization

- *Convergence:* Speaker (S) converges to Recipient's (R) speech characteristics in order to facilitate comprehension.
- *Divergence/Maintenance:* S diverges from R's speech characteristics in order to remind R of their nonshared group memberships and hence prevent misattributions, *or* S diverges in order to encourage R to adopt a more situationally appropriate speech pattern.

Affective Function:
Identity Maintenance

- *Convergence:* S converges to R's speech characteristics in order to appear more similar and thus more likeable.
- *Divergence/Maintenance:* S diverges from R's speech characteristics in order to emphasize distinctiveness, and thus reinforce S's positive sense of identity.

Exploring the goals of accommodation leads us to the subjective dimension of communication, reflecting interactants' perceptions of their own and their counterparts' goals and behaviors in an interaction. Thakerar et al. (1982) investigated the incongruity between objective speech (i.e., speech as observed by an outsider such as the researcher) and its perception by interactants. They observed that, in dyads characterized by status inequality, high-status participants slowed their speech rates and made their accents less standard, while lower-status speakers increased rate and produced more standardized accents. On objective measures, the dyads were diverging, but they actually *thought* that they were converging. Lower-status speakers did not accommodate to the actual speech patterns of their partners, but to their stereotype of high-status speakers talking faster and having a more standard accent. Therefore Thakerar and colleagues brought an important modification to the original propositions, stating that one does not converge toward (or diverge from) the *actual* speech of the recipient, but toward (from) *one's stereotypes* about the recipient's speech.

Types of Accommodation

Thakerar et al. (1982), thus, elaborated the distinction between linguistic accommodation (referring to actual speech behavior) and psychological accommodation (referring to speakers' motivations and intentions to converge or diverge). A further distinction was introduced by dividing linguistic accommodation into an objective and a subjective dimension: While speakers' linguistic shifts can objectively be described as diverging (or converging), speakers may *believe* that they are converging (or diverging). Thus we can account for cases like the one above, where linguistic divergence is observed while interlocutors intend to converge and attain psychological integration. Such a mismatch between linguistic and psychological accommodation happens in many role-defined situations characterized by status discrepancy, like interactions between doctors and patients, professors and students, or men and women. In cooperative situations involving people of different status, interlocutors may contribute through different speech patterns to the attainment of a common goal. Social norms in these types of settings require "speech complementarity" (Giles, 1980) rather than convergence. Differences correspond to an optimal sociolinguistic distance and are psychologically acceptable to both participants.

Prior research had mostly assumed equivalence between speakers' intentions, what they actually do, and what they think they are doing. With these subtle (yet crucial) distinctions, SAT opened up the complexity of communication, underscoring the importance of elucidating both cognitive and affective processes underlying a wide range of verbal and nonverbal behaviors (Giles et al., 1991; Giles & Wadleigh, 1999). Perhaps most significant, SAT accorded central importance to the sociopsychological processes of communication, conceptualizing communication as a negotiation of personal and social identities. This affective function of accommodation represents the historical core of SAT. It allows predictions about speakers' accommodative moves as a function of the interpersonal or intergroup salience of the interaction for them—in other words, their perception of how much their personal and social identities are called into question by the interaction.

Interpersonal and Intergroup Accommodation

Even though convergence leads to an increase in similarity, and divergence to an increase in distinctiveness, it should not be concluded that convergence is linked *only* to the interpersonal dimension of communication or that divergence is linked *only* to the intergroup dimension. This would allow for only interpersonal convergence and intergroup divergence. It is true that most SAT research on divergence is about intergroup contexts, as this strategy is a powerful means for interactants to differentiate from relevant outgroup members and to reinforce their social identities. Yet both strategies can in principle be either person-based or group-based, depending on the salience of the interpersonal or intergroup dimensions for the interactants, as well as their motivation (see Gallois & Giles, 1998, for a discussion of this and related issues). Gallois et al. (1988) noted, however, that interpersonal and intergroup accommodation are likely to involve different behaviors (i.e., personal and group markers, respectively).[1] Hornsey and Gallois (1998) followed this issue up empirically in the context of intercultural communication by examining evaluations of cultural ingroup (Australian) and outgroup (Chinese) speakers who converged to an Australian speaker's personal style, converged to typical Australian speech markers, or who diverged from interpersonal or intergroup markers. They found a tendency for some evaluators to be more responsive to interpersonal and others to intergroup convergence and divergence.

It is also likely that convergence has often been considered as interpersonal and divergence/maintenance as intergroup because these concepts were originally explained by reference to different theoretical frameworks: convergence to similarity-attraction and divergence to social identity theory. It is important to explain these two concepts using the same theory, because they are theorized as psychologically opposing strategies. SIT, and the concepts of social and personal identity in particular, allows for this possibility, but similarity-attraction theory probably does not; thus, CAT can be theorized more completely through social identity processes.

Reception of Accommodation

On the reception side, early SAT research (e.g., Giles, 1973) found that convergence generally evokes positive reactions in its recipients and divergence evokes negative reactions. According to Street and Giles (1982), "that convergence functions to establish optimal speech patterns represents a basic tenet of SAT" (p. 211). Converging speakers have been found to be perceived as more competent, attractive, warm, and cooperative; convergence is also appreciated by recipients because it means a reduction of the cognitive effort they have to provide in the interaction.

Other research has specified the antecedent conditions for these evaluations, demonstrating that convergence is not positively evaluated in all situations, and that divergence is not always negatively evaluated. For example, Simard, Taylor, and Giles (1976) investigated attribution processes in the evaluation of accommodation strategies. They found that listeners perceived convergence favorably when they attributed it to speakers' intent to break down cultural barriers (internal attribution of positive intent), but when speakers attributed the act to situational pressure (external attribution), their reaction was not positive. Conversely, when divergence was attributed to situational pressures, the response to it was less negative than when divergence was internally attributed, for example to a lack of effort on the part of the speaker. In the same vein, Ball et al. (1984) investigated the influence of situational constraints on the evaluation of divergence and convergence. Their results showed that, in a context where strong social norms operate (such as a job interview), adherence to sociolinguistic norms determines the positive or negative evaluation of the speaker, not the display of convergence or divergence itself (see Gallois & Callan, 1997, and Giles & Johnson, 1987, for extended discussions of the role of norms).

The propositions in these papers, thus, state that convergence is positively evaluated when it is attributed positive intent, and that divergence is negatively evaluated when it is attributed negative intent. These propositions do not indicate how convergence is evaluated when perceived intent is negative, or how divergence is evaluated when perceived intent is positive. Even so, Street and Giles (1982) argued that we should not conclude that "the relationship between degree of convergence and positive evaluation is necessarily linear" (p. 212). They named attribution processes as well as "listeners' tolerance or preference levels for various magnitudes and rates of speech discrepancies and adjustments" as moderating variables of the evaluation of convergence and divergence. Furthermore, Ball and colleagues (1984) stated that convergence is negatively evaluated when "prevailing situational norms define the convergent act as a violation of them" (p. 126). These papers open up the potential for the same strategy to be evaluated differently in different circumstances, which became a key part of CAT.

The next revision of SAT (Giles et al., 1987) went back to the original structure, stating that convergence is positively evaluated when perceived as adhering to a valued norm, and that divergence is negatively evaluated when perceived as departing from a valued norm. They noted in the text that "in some cases this sort of divergence that adheres to a valued norm would be expected to produce positive evaluations in fact. Similarly, convergence that departs from a valued norm should produce attenuated positive or even negative evaluations" (p. 39). Overall, the thrust has

Table 6.2   Attributions and Evaluations of Convergence and Divergence/Maintenance

	Internal Attribution by Recipient R of Speaker S		*External Attribution by R*
Convergence	Benevolent Intent by S e.g., R thinks that S is converging because S wants them to become friends.	Malevolent Intent by S e.g., R thinks that S is converging because S is making fun of R's accent.	Situational Constraints e.g., R thinks that S is converging because of social role and is forced to do so.
Divergence/ maintenance	Benevolent Intent by S e.g., R thinks that S is diverging/maintaining because S wants to remind R that this is not S's mother tongue (perceived self-handicapping strategy by S).	Malevolent Intent by S e.g., R thinks that S is diverging/maintaining because S wants to show disdain or disinterest in the interaction	Situational Constraints e.g., R thinks that S is diverging/ maintaining because S has not had an occasion to learn how to behave appropriately in another culture.
	Positive evaluation	Negative evaluation	Less negative evaluation

been that *both* convergence and divergence/maintenance can involve affective as well as cognitive functions, and that *both* can be attributed internally (to a positive or a negative intent) or externally, so that *both* can lead to positive or negative evaluations—perceptions and attributions are privileged over actual behavior. Nevertheless, statements of the propositions have maintained the original form. In this chapter, we address this issue by first stating the general tendency to evaluate convergence positively and divergence negatively, and then specifying the moderating variables (or "conflicting variables"; Giles et al., 1987, p. 39) that may change the valence of these evaluations.

Furthermore, the propositions in SAT mention only internal attributions (to a positive or negative intent) and not external attributions (to situational pressures), as investigated by Simard et al. (1976; see also Ball et al., 1984; Gallois & Callan, 1991). SAT and CAT have theorized the role of norms as constraints to accommodative processes, but social and situational norms and pressures have not yet received the attention they deserve. Table 6.2 illustrates the diversity of possible attributions (and, therefore, evaluations) for convergence and divergence/maintenance.

Other research has also investigated the errors in attribution processes. This research shows that we do not attribute meaning objectively to the behaviors we evaluate, but that attributions are biased. The "fundamental attribution error" describes our tendency to overestimate the influence of internal factors (personality, effort, intent) over external ones. The "ultimate attribution error" (Hewstone, 1990) adds intergroup processes to the attributional biases. If we are interacting with ingroup members, we tend to attribute their desirable behaviors to internal factors and their undesirable behaviors to external ones (situational constraints). Conversely, when we interact with outgroup members, we tend to attribute their desirable behaviors to external factors, and their undesirable behaviors to internal ones. The assumption of SAT is that convergence in general reflects desirable behavior and divergence/maintenance undesirable behavior, so that the integration of the ultimate attribution error leads to the following attributions: convergence by ingroup members attributed internally to benevolent intent; convergence by outgroup members attributed externally to situational constraints (and thus as less desirable); divergence by outgroup members attributed internally to malevolent intent; divergence by ingroup members attributed externally (and thus as less undesirable).

From SAT to CAT

In their 1987 paper, Giles et al. assessed the first decade of SAT and presented a reformulation of its propositions in light of recent research, renaming the theory communication accommodation theory (CAT). As can be seen from Table 6.3, the propositions still followed the original structure, with the exception of the order of presentation.

These revised propositions introduce the processes of self-presentation and impression management (see Baumeister, 1982, 1993; Giles & Street, 1994) as another theoretical resource. Indeed, the production and reception of language behaviors can be understood in terms of the image that individuals want to convey to others. According to self-presentation theory, communication is a process by which individuals manage the impressions they make on others, attempting in particular to create a positive impression on socially influential others (e.g., by adopting speech features, like deep pitch, fast speech rate, standard accent, that social knowledge associates with competence). This positive impression is crucial for the acquisition and maintenance of social power and influence, and hence for positive self- and group-esteem (see Ng & Bradac, 1993).

A comparison of these revised propositions to the first set shows how much subtler, and at the same time broader, the theory had become. Speech and linguistic features are no longer the

only focus of the theory, which progressively has grown into a theory of communication. A significant number of new theoretical concepts have been inserted into the six original propositions. Furthermore, proposals for further research and refinements abound in the papers reviewed so far, which would lead to even more complex propositions. As Giles et al. stated, the challenge for SAT in 1987 was

> whether or not SAT can be expanded comfortably to accommodate more and more complexity in its propositional format. At the same time, another challenge that will have to be met involves *explaining* this increased propositional complexity in terms of a parsimonious and unique set of integrative principles. (p. 41)

In the next section, we consider how the newly named CAT managed these challenges.

PHASE 2: COMMUNICATION ACCOMMODATION THEORY

Since 1987, CAT has been expanded into an interdisciplinary model of relational and identity processes in interaction (Coupland & Jaworski, 1997, pp. 241-242). It has been applied to communication between different social groups (cultures, generations, genders, abilities) and within and between organizations, in face-to-face interactions, as well as through different media (radio, telephone, e-mail, etc.), in different countries, and by researchers of diverse cultural and language backgrounds (for a review of this variety, see Giles & Ogay, in press). In particular, communication between generations (Coupland, Coupland, Giles, & Henwood, 1988; Fox & Giles, 1993), along with communication between cultures and linguistic groups (Gallois et al., 1988; Gallois et al., 1995), has been significantly considered in the theoretical development of CAT (in the further area of intergender communication, see Abrams, Hajek, & Murachver, in press, for a review).

Table 6.3   SAT/CAT's Revised Propositions (after Giles et al., 1987)

	Convergence	*Divergence / Maintenance*
Production	1. Speakers attempt to converge toward the speech AND NONVERBAL PATTERNS *believed to be characteristic* of their message recipients, BE THE LATTER DEFINED IN INDIVIDUAL, RELATIONAL, OR GROUP TERMS, when speakers: (a) desire recipients' social approval (and the perceived costs of acting in an approval-seeking manner are proportionally lower than the perceived rewards); *(b) desire a high level of communicational efficiency;* (C) DESIRE A SELF-, COUPLE-, OR GROUP PRESENTATION SHARED BY RECIPIENTS; (D) DESIRE APPROPRIATE SITUATIONAL OR IDENTITY DEFINITIONS; WHEN THE RECIPIENTS' (E) ACTUAL SPEECH IN THE SITUATION MATCHES THE BELIEF THAT THE SPEAKERS HAVE ABOUT RECIPIENTS' SPEECH STYLE; (F) SPEECH IS POSITIVELY VALUED, THAT IS, NONSTIGMATIZED; (G) SPEECH STYLE IS APPROPRIATE FOR THE SPEAKERS AS WELL AS FOR RECIPIENTS.	3. Speakers attempt to maintain their communication patterns, or even diverge away from their message recipients' SPEECH AND NONVERBAL BEHAVIORS when they (A) DESIRE TO COMMUNICATE A CONTRASTIVE SELF-IMAGE; (b) desire to dissociate personally from the recipients or the recipients' definition of the situation; (c) define the encounter in intergroup or relational terms WITH COMMUNICATION STYLE BEING A VALUED DIMENSION OF THEIR SITUATIONALLY SALIENT IN-GROUP OR RELATIONAL IDENTITIES; (d) desire to change recipients' speech behavior, for example, moving it to a more acceptable level; WHEN RECIPIENTS (E) EXHIBIT A STIGMATIZED FORM, THAT IS, A STYLE THAT DEVIATES FROM A VALUED NORM, WHICH IS (F) CONSISTENT WITH SPEAKERS' EXPECTATIONS REGARDING RECIPIENT PERFORMANCE.
Magnitude	2. The magnitude of such convergence is a function of: (a) the extent of speakers' repertoires, and (b) individual, RELATIONAL, SOCIAL, and contextual factors that may increase the needs for social comparison, social approval, *and/or high communicational efficiency.*	4. The magnitude of such divergence is a function of (a) the extent of the speakers' repertoires, and (b) individual, RELATIONAL, SOCIAL, and contextual factors increasing the salience of the cognitive and affective functions in (3) above.
Reception	5. Convergence is positively evaluated by message recipients, THAT IS, WILL LEAD TO HIGH RATINGS FOR FRIENDLINESS, ATTRACTIVENESS, AND SOLIDARITY when recipients PERCEIVE (A) A MATCH TO THEIR OWN COMMUNICATIONAL STYLE; (B) A MATCH TO A LINGUISTIC STEREOTYPE FOR A GROUP IN WHICH THEY HAVE MEMBERSHIP; (c) the speaker's convergence to be optimally distant sociolinguistically, AND TO BE PRODUCED AT AN OPTIMAL RATE, LEVEL OF FLUENCY, AND LEVEL OF ACCURACY; **(d) the speaker's style to adhere to a valued norm;** ESPECIALLY WHEN (E) PERCEIVED SPEAKER EFFORT IS HIGH; (F) PERCEIVED SPEAKER CHOICE IS HIGH; (g) perceived intent is altruistic or benevolent.	6. Divergence is negatively rated by recipients when they perceive (A) A MISMATCH TO THEIR OWN COMMUNICATIONAL STYLE; (B) A MISMATCH TO A LINGUISTIC STEREOTYPE FOR A GROUP IN WHICH THEY HAVE MEMBERSHIP; (C) THE SPEAKER'S DIVERGENCE TO BE EXCESSIVELY DISTANT, FREQUENT, FLUENT, AND ACCURATE; **(d) the speaker's style to depart from a valued norm;** especially when (E) PERCEIVED SPEAKER EFFORT IS HIGH; (F) PERCEIVED SPEAKER CHOICE IS HIGH; (g) perceived intent is selfish or malevolent.

NOTE: The additions by Thakerar et al. (1982) are italicized; those by Street and Giles (1982) are underlined, the additions inspired by Ball et al. (1984) are in **bold font**; and those by Giles et al. (1987) are in SMALL CAPS.

Working in the intergenerational context, Coupland and colleagues (1988) replaced the original structure of SAT's propositions with a model of the communication process as a path, starting with the psychological orientations of speakers; going through their goals and sociolinguistic strategies; and ending with evaluations of the interaction, which are dynamically related to orientations in subsequent encounters. This model was taken up again by Gallois et al. (1988), who developed CAT for the context of intercultural communication, and also incorporated propositions from ELIT (Giles & Johnson, 1981, 1987). In 1995, a second elaboration of CAT was presented (Gallois et al., 1995).

In the vast literature produced within CAT's framework, the two papers by Gallois and colleagues in 1988 and 1995 are the only publications to continue the task of developing CAT's propositions, although a number of other papers present formal models of the accommodation process, particularly in the contexts of health, emotions, and intergenerational communication (e.g., Williams et al., 1990). By problematizing issues of miscommunication and sociopsychological processes in communication, CAT is especially relevant to the study of intercultural communication and represents an alternative to the approach of communication effectiveness (see Gallois & Giles, 1998). Moreover, cultural groups (or groups with different linguistic codes or accents) were the most frequent ones studied in the early days of the theory; from the start, this gave SAT and CAT an intercultural flavor.

Figure 6.1 presents the full CAT model, incorporating concepts and variables from all its variants. As can be seen, intergroup encounters are theorized as occurring in a sociohistorical context, which is a key influence on the initial orientation of speakers to treat each other in intergroup terms, interpersonal terms, or both. This part of the model shows the influence of SIT and ELIT. In the immediate interaction situation, which is governed by norms that may enhance or inhibit accommodative moves, speakers take a psychological accommodative stance, depending upon the salience of affective or cognitive motives and social or personal identities. As the interaction proceeds, their addressee foci, strategies, behavior, and tactics change as a function of changing identity salience and the behavior of the other speaker, as well as of their perceptions and attributions about the other's behavior. Finally, speakers take their evaluations of the other person and the interaction away with them, leading to future intentions about interactions with the other or members of his or her ingroup.

It is worth asking whether this model should really be constrained to intercultural contexts alone. Indeed, the "interculturalness" of the model is limited to the dimension of individualism-collectivism, all other variables being applicable in other intergroup contexts. Individualism-collectivism describes the relative importance attached by a cultural group to the individual versus the group (e.g., Triandis, 1995). According to Gallois and colleagues (1995), individualism-collectivism helps to characterize the strength and exclusiveness of identification with ingroups. Collectivists belong to few ingroups and share strong beliefs about ingroup identification and loyalty, whereas individualists belong to many ingroups and have weaker beliefs about identification and loyalty. Collectivists emphasize group identity and thus tend to make sharper distinctions between ingroup and outgroup. In contrast, individualists value group identities less and personal identity more. They have multiple and changing group identifications, and make more interpersonal than intergroup comparisons.

These characterizations of individualists and collectivists have implications for the study of communication accommodation processes. For example, individualists may react to convergence from outgroup interlocutors in a relatively positive manner, and converge toward outgroup speakers reciprocally as well. With softer intergroup boundaries,

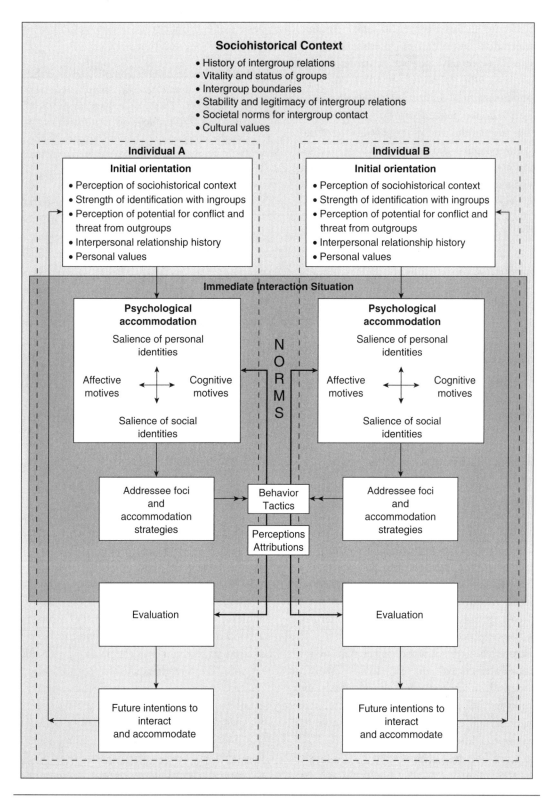

Figure 6.1   Full Model of Communication Accommodation Theory, Containing All Variables From Previous Versions of the Model

their thresholds for allowing linguistic penetration by outgroup members may be lower. Conversely, people from collectivistic cultures, who perceive harder intergroup boundaries, may react to attempts at communicative convergence from outgroup members more negatively, and diverge from them more if they perceive the convergence as overstepping a valued cultural or national boundary. In general, speakers from collectivistic cultures are likely to diverge more from outgroup interlocutors, both psychologically and linguistically, than their individualistic counterparts (Gallois et al., 1995; see Giles, 1979a, for the introduction of the ethnic boundary model).

The dimension of individualism-collectivism is centrally interesting and important to intercultural communication. Nevertheless, other concepts in the theory can probably do the same work as this variable, in a more generic way. For example, to characterize how individuals relate to their ingroups, both the 1988 and 1995 versions of CAT refer to dependence on the ingroup (available alternatives for ingroup identification; cf. Giles & Johnson, 1981) and solidarity with it (strength of identification to the ingroup and satisfaction with it). More generally, the concepts of social categorization and comparison processes, personal and social identity, and permeability and softness of group boundaries have already been integrated in CAT and can probably incorporate individualism and collectivism. This would be compatible with Gallois and Giles's (1998) presentation of CAT as "a systematic attempt to take account of intergroup *and* interpersonal variables, at macro and micro levels, in accounting for behavior in intergroup interactions" (pp. 157-158).[2] This is not to deny how central intercultural communication is to CAT, however, both as a key context of intergroup encounters and as the most fully developed context of the theory.

According to Shepard et al. (2001), while researchers first tended to apply CAT to a wide range of contexts, they are now formulating "specific context-driven theories using basic CAT propositions" (p. 41). Gallois and Giles (1998) noted that

> CAT has become very complex, so that the theory as a whole probably cannot be tested at one time. This means that researchers using CAT must develop mini-theories to suit the contexts in which they work, while at the same time keeping the whole of the theory in mind. (p. 158)

Given the complexities of CAT's history, it is not crystal clear what "basic CAT propositions" (Shepard et al., 2001) or the "whole of the theory" (Gallois & Giles, 1998) refer to. For example, Gallois et al. (1988; Gallois et al., 1995) adopted the hierarchical conceptual structure proposed by Coupland et al. (1988). Accommodation is the big picture; when people want to accommodate, they use "attuning strategies." There are four strategies: interpretability, discourse management, interpersonal control, and approximation; Giles et al. (1991) suggested two more—emotional expression or relationship-maintenance strategies and face-related strategies—that have recently begun to be studied. Under the approximation strategy, we find the original convergence, divergence, maintenance, and speech complementarity. This structure and the underlying terminology are not always represented consistently in texts and propositions, however. We attempt in this chapter to make the language of CAT more consistent and clear.

Overall, it seems timely to consider the achievements made so far in order to produce a revised set of propositions that can be considered as the general theory, and to which specific context-driven subtheories can be related. A general cross-contextual theory is even more important because theories focused on specific contexts entail the risk of considering one group membership (culture, generation, gender) on its own, thereby overlooking the multiplicity of identities that are negotiated through communication (Gallois & Giles, 1998; Gallois & Pittam, 1996).

TOWARD PHASE 3

This final section moves from the issues discussed above into a revised formulation of CAT. The challenge is to formulate propositions that respect the principle of parsimony as much as possible, while making allowance for the richness of research findings. The revised model is presented in Figure 6.2. Like previous models, it situates intergroup encounters in a sociohistorical context. This version highlights intergroup and interpersonal history, along with norms and values. The model features an interaction between two individuals, including what they bring into the interaction (their

initial orientation) and what they take out of it (their evaluations and future intentions for the partner and his or her social group). Within the norm-constrained immediate interaction situation, speakers derive a psychological accommodative stance, including the aspects of the interlocutor they are attending to (previously called addressee focus), which influences the accommodative and nonaccommodative strategies they adopt. We posit that behavior and tactics happen in a dynamic environment, influenced by the other's behavior as well as changing motives and identities. In addition, behavior leads to perceptions of the interlocutor and attributions about his or her motives,

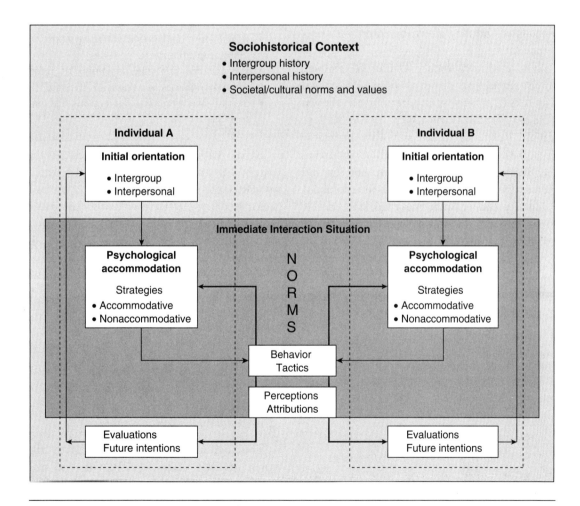

Figure 6.2   Revised Model of Communication Accommodation Theory as a General Theory of Intergroup Communication

which in turn influence evaluations and future intentions. In our view, this revised model foregrounds the key variables in CAT, leaving other variables for more specific contexts.

The present version of CAT is formulated as a general framework for intergroup communication. Specific contexts generate sub-theories within CAT, for example for intergenerational (Coupland et al., 1988; Giles, Coupland, Coupland, & Williams, 1992) or organizational (Gardner, Paulsen, Gallois, Callan, & Monaghan, 2001) communication. As such, CAT highlights the fact that intergroup encounters are never exclusively or permanently intercultural, intergenerational, or other per se, but that *different* group memberships may become salient during the same encounter and may affect the communication process.

Social identity theory (Tajfel & Turner, 1979) remains the major theoretical reference for CAT, along with attribution theory (Heider, 1958; Hewstone, 1990; Kelley, 1973). Reference to the similarity-attraction hypothesis (Byrne, 1971), which inspired earlier formulations, has been left out, as the perception of intergroup and interpersonal similarity and distinctiveness has since developed into an important topic within social identity theory (e.g., Brewer, 1991; Jetten, Spears, & Manstead, 1999). In addition, we have omitted references to anxiety/uncertainty management theory (e.g., Gudykunst, 1995), which also influenced earlier versions of CAT.

Assumptions

CAT is based on three general assumptions (A):

A.1: Communicative interactions are embedded in a sociohistorical context.

As stressed by sociolinguists (e.g., Gumperz, 1992), communication never occurs in a vacuum, but within a sociohistorical context. The influence of context on communication operates at two levels: a direct influence through the opportunities for intergroup contact that are provided, and, more important for CAT, an indirect influence by means of interactants' perceptions of the context. A range of macro-level factors delineates the intergroup power configuration reflected in the interaction:

- History of relations between the groups with which interactants identify;
- Vitality of these groups (Giles, Bourhis, & Taylor, 1977). A group's vitality is influenced by three structural factors: status (in terms of economic and sociocultural prestige), demography, and the institutional support enjoyed by the group. Giles et al. call vitality "that which makes a group likely to behave as a distinctive and active collective entity in intergroup situations" (p. 308).
- Permeability (or impermeability) of intergroup boundaries (see Giles, 1979a); and
- Stability and legitimacy of intergroup relations (see Giles, 1978).

Along with the value priorities of the culture (for a review of cross-cultural research on values, see Smith & Schwartz, 1997), these factors contribute to the establishment of societal norms for intergroup contact that specifies with whom, when, and how it is appropriate to interact. In particular, societies where two or more ethnolinguistic groups of unequal vitality are in contact tend to establish norms regarding bilingualism, diglossia, and code-switching.

A.2: Communication is about both exchanges of referential meaning and negotiation of personal and social identities.

This assumption refers directly to the origin of CAT (Giles, 1973). Giles pointed to the affective as well as cognitive functions of communicative behavior. Personal and social identities are negotiated throughout the communication process, whereby interactants regulate the social distance between themselves. As formulated in social psychology by Brewer (1991; Brewer & Roccas, 2001) and in intercultural communication by Ting-Toomey (1993), interactants strive for a compromise between two antagonistic identity needs: the need for assimilation (or, in Ting-Toomey's terms, desire to belong) and the need for differentiation (desire for uniqueness).

A.3: Interactants achieve the informational and relational functions of communication by accommodating their communicative behavior, through linguistic, paralinguistic, discursive, and nonlinguistic moves, to their interlocutor's perceived individual and group characteristics

Accommodation is the process through which interactants regulate their communication (adopting a particular linguistic code or accent, increasing or decreasing their speech rate, avoiding or increasing eye contact, etc.) in order to appear more like (accommodation) or distinct from each other (nonaccommodation, including counter-accommodation through divergent or hostile moves, underaccommodation through maintenance and unempathetic moves, and over-accommodation through oftentimes patronizing or ingratiating moves). These processes occur at the level of communicative behavior per se (termed "linguistic accommodation" by Thakerar et al., 1982), as well as at the psychological level (speakers' motivations and perceptions). The two levels may not coincide, for example, in situations characterized by status discrepancy requiring complementarity (cf. Giles, 1980). In addition, objective linguistic accommodation does not always equate to subjective linguistic accommodation (as perceived by interactants; Giles et al., 1991). This distinction highlights the importance of interactants' perceptions, which are privileged in CAT. Interactants have expectations regarding optimal levels of accommodation, based on stereotypes about outgroup members as well as prevailing social and situational norms.

Scope of CAT

These assumptions help to describe the scope of the theory: what CAT does, and what supplementary theory CAT relies on. First, CAT theorizes communication (and thence accommodation) as motivated. The motivation in a specific communicative encounter may be intergroup, interpersonal, both (see Giles & Hewstone, 1982), or neither (although the latter two are not included in the propositions below), and is influenced by the sociohistorical context and more directly by the initial orientations of participants.

Second, CAT theorizes accommodative strategies, motivated by initial orientation and the salience of particular features of the interaction like the desire to appear similar or identify, to be clearly understood and to understand, to maintain face, to maintain the relationship, to direct the flow of discourse, and to maintain interpersonal control. Like initial orientation, accommodation is in part a function of the context, salient societal and situational norms, and salient behaviors. Overall, motivation and perceptions are privileged over behavior as measured by outside observers. Even so, behavior is important because it is a major influence on the perceptions of recipients, which lead to attributions for behavior, evaluations of the other person and the encounter, and future intentions toward the other person and his or her group (see Figures 6.1, 6.2).

CAT allows for the role of conversational tactics—the ongoing behavioral moves that are driven by norms, the behavior of others, and so forth. This means that there is no one-to-one correspondence between strategy and behavior, or between behavior and evaluation (Gallois et al., 1995; Jones, Gallois, Callan, & Barker, 1999). In addition, motivation and accommodative strategies can change throughout the course of an interaction as a consequence of behavior or tactics (Gallois & Giles, 1998, give examples of such changes in terms of accommodative dilemmas). Overall, there is a cycle beginning with initial orientation and progressing through an interaction to future intentions, which influence initial orientation in the next iteration.

This scope is large, but many processes are inevitably left out and must be described by other theories. First, it is important to have a well-developed theory of social norms or rules. CAT theorizes norms as part of the societal and situational context, taking them as read but emphasizing that intergroup and interpersonal histories and initial orientation influence tolerance about their application. Norm theories should themselves deal with social rules as a function of the group memberships of interactants. Second, CAT relies on a thorough taxonomy of verbal and nonverbal behavior, in terms of both function and meaning. CAT assumes the existence of intergroup and interpersonal communicative markers, which have different impacts, but the task of describing these is left to other theory and research. Finally, CAT relies crucially on attribution theory. CAT deals with attributions as moderators (e.g., evaluation of behavior is exaggerated when attributions are internal; behavior is attributed more favorably when the other is an ingroup member).

Propositions

The propositions (P) below account for the process of communication accommodation in an intergroup encounter. They are written with reference to Speaker A and Partner B; of course, from B's perspective, A is the partner. Encounters take place in a context that includes a salient intergroup history involving good or bad relations, social equality or inequality, and so forth. The context may be one of permeable or less permeable boundaries, and an intergroup status that is perceived to be more or less stable and legitimate. The context also includes salient cultural values. Further, there is an interpersonal history

involving anything from no previous interaction to a long-term relationship of intimacy or enmity, and including salient personal values and identities. Thus, in the encounter, individuals are predisposed to a more intergroup or more interpersonal orientation to each other.

Initial Orientation. This part of the model concerns the extent to which A is predisposed to have an intergroup or interpersonal orientation toward B, and thus with A's motivation to accommodate or not to perceptions of B's personal and group characteristics.

P.1: A speaker A is predisposed to have an intergroup orientation toward interacting with a partner B, and be motivated toward nonaccommodation with B's perceived group characteristics when:

- There is a salient negative intergroup history between A's and B's ingroups AND
- A identifies strongly with one or few ingroups and perceives this ingroup's vitality to be low or makes insecure social comparisons with B's group OR
- A has had an earlier negative interaction with another member of B's group whom A perceived as typical of B's group.

However,

A is predisposed to have an intergroup orientation but be motivated to accommodate to B's perceived group characteristics when:

- A is a member of a subordinate group with which A identifies weakly, perceives the group's vitality to be low and intergroup boundaries to be soft, and perceives intergroup relations to be legitimate and stable OR
- A is a member of a dominant ingroup with high subjective vitality and perceives intergroup relations as legitimate and stable OR
- A has had an earlier positive interaction with a member of B's group whom A perceived as typical of B's group.

P.2: A speaker A is predisposed to have an interpersonal orientation toward interacting with a partner B and be motivated to accommodate to B's perceived personal characteristics when:

- A and B share a positive interpersonal history AND
- A identifies weakly with salient ingroups or there are no salient ingroups.

However,

A is predisposed to have an interpersonal orientation but be motivated toward nonaccommodation with B's perceived personal characteristics when:

- A and B share a negative interpersonal relationship history.

Psychological Accommodation. Here, we enter the interaction itself. Speaker A's initial orientation is transformed into A's immediate and ongoing intention to accommodate or not to B, through A's experience of the interaction. A's psychological accommodation is shaped by A's perception of the salience of personal and social identities in the interaction and by A's conversational motives. Perceived situational norms for contact and accommodation, as well as norms for other salient roles or group memberships, place constraints on the forms accommodation can take (Ball et al., 1984; Gallois & Callan, 1991).

Both the cognitive motive of facilitating comprehension and the affective motive of identity maintenance or development correspond to a dialectic about the amount of distance (or difference) to be expressed through communication. On the cognitive side, comprehension may be facilitated by either increasing similarity (e.g., adopting the same language), or in other situations by increasing dissimilarity (e.g., exaggerating one's foreign accent). On the affective side, identity maintenance or development can be attained either by trying to assimilate to the other (and thus be recognized as an intimate or ingroup member), or by trying to differentiate from the other (and thus gain a positive sense of

identity based upon comparisons with B or B's groups). The relative importance of cognitive and affective motives in determining psychological accommodation is especially significant when they do not coincide; for example, when the aim of facilitating comprehension requires emphasizing similarity but the aim of identity maintenance requires differentiation.

P.3: When A perceives that personal identities are salient in the interaction, A's psychological accommodation is directed at the perceived personal characteristics of B;

Whereas,

When A perceives that social identities are salient in the interaction, A's psychological accommodation is directed at the perceived group characteristics of B.

P.4: When A has an intergroup orientation, A is likely to perceive narrower, more constraining norms for the behavior of outgroup members and wider, more tolerant norms for ingroup behavior;

Whereas,

When A has an interpersonal orientation, A is likely to perceive similar norms for ingroup and outgroup members.

P.5: When affective motives predominate for A in the interaction, and A feels a need for assimilation, A is likely to accommodate psychologically even at the cost of facilitating comprehension;

However,

When affective motives predominate for A but A feels a need for differentiation, A is likely to nonaccommodate psychologically, even at the cost of facilitating comprehension.

P.6: When cognitive motives predominate for A in the interaction, and A feels that comprehension would be facilitated through increasing similarity with B, A is likely to accommodate psychologically, even at the cost of identity maintenance or development;

However,

When cognitive motives predominate for A and A feels that comprehension would be facilitated through differentiating from B, A is likely to nonaccommodate psychologically, even at the cost of identity maintenance or development.

P.7: In a status-stressing situation, A is likely to accommodate psychologically to the sociolinguistic markers and behavior of the dominant group.

Focus, Accommodative Strategies, and Behavior. The motivational force of psychological accommodation leads to the adoption of communicative strategies through A's focus on the needs or behaviors of B (earlier referred to as addressee focus). These strategies were called "attuning strategies" in earlier formulations of CAT, following Coupland et al. (1988); we have instead used the term *accommodative strategies* to be more consistent with the whole course of SAT and CAT. Strategies may change across the course of an interaction as a function of tactics and behavior. Indeed, as represented in Abrams, O'Connor, and Giles's (2002) transactional model of the relationship between communication (accommodation) and identity, the very perception of accommodative behaviors can trigger a social or personal identity. Furthermore, foci and strategies may be mixed in a single interaction (not to mention across time).

Several main foci have been proposed, including productive behavior, conversational competence, conversational needs, role and power relations (Coupland et al., 1988), emotional and relational needs, and face maintenance (Giles et al., 1991; Williams et al., 1990). When the focus is on B's productive language and communication, A may employ approximation strategies of convergence, divergence, or maintenance, which involve mutual perceived behavioral influence. The other foci may involve nonapproximation strategies (Coupland et al., 1988). The first of these is interpretability, resulting from a focus on B's interpretive (mainly decoding) competence or stereotypes about it, leading among other things to slower or simpler speech, more use of questions to check understanding, and the choice of familiar topics.

The second nonapproximation strategy, discourse management, results from a focus on B's conversational needs, and leads among other things to sharing of topic choice and development, as well as shared conversational register. Interpersonal control results from a focus on role relations, and leads to use of interruptions, honorifics, and the like, to keep the other person in role or to allow freedom to change roles. Emotional expression, resulting from a focus on B's emotional or relational needs, includes expressions of reassurance, care, warmth, and so forth (e.g., Watson & Gallois, 2002). Finally, face strategies, resulting from a focus on face maintenance, include positive and negative face threats and face maintenance moves (cf. Brown & Levinson, 1987).

These strategies, alone or in combination, are used to manage the psychological and sociolinguistic distance between interactants, making them more equal or emphasizing intergroup or interpersonal differences. While there is some association between strategies and behavior, there is no necessary connection between them. For example, discourse management is often reflected in topic development and turn-taking behaviors, but may be reflected in other behaviors, while topic development and turn taking can also reflect interpersonal control or interpretability strategies (Jones et al., 1999). Thus the model describes strategies and behaviors separately: Strategies remain covert; only behaviors are apparent in the situation. Behavior is the focal point through which the dynamic of the communicative process develops.

In CAT, there is one main path to accommodation: treating the other person more as an individual or ingroup member, and less as a function of the other's outgroup membership. Accommodation may involve any (or all) of the foci and strategies, but the underlying process is the same. On the other hand, nonaccommodation can take a number of forms. The first is counter-accommodation (an elaboration of the original divergence). When speakers counter-accommodate, they utilize the strategies to maximize the difference between themselves and the interlocutors as individuals and, when intergroup relations are salient, as group members. This often involves negative and even hostile behavior.

In many interactions, however, nonaccommodation takes a less obvious but also powerful form. One way this can happen involves under-accommodation (an elaboration of the original maintenance), in which speakers simply maintain their own behavior and discourse without moving at all toward the behavior or conversational needs of interlocutors. Coupland et al. (1988) described this process for intergenerational communication (see also Williams & Giles, 1996). In the intercultural context, it can involve in extreme cases the maintenance of a speaker's language even when the speaker is aware that the other person cannot speak the language and the speaker is competent in the other's language.

Finally, nonaccommodation can take the form of over-accommodation (an elaboration of negatively perceived convergence). In this case, speakers accommodate to their stereotypes about interlocutors' groups. Once again, over-accommodation has been articulated particularly for intergenerational communication, mainly as patronizing talk or secondary baby talk (e.g., Hummert & Ryan, 2001). In

intercultural contexts, a striking example involves foreigner talk, in which speakers "help" foreigners to understand by using a simplified—and unknown (often incomprehensible)—version of their language, frequently accompanied by exaggerated intonation and loud volume. Over-accommodative behavior is paradoxical in that the speaker may have good intentions (or appear to), but behave in an inappropriate way. Similarly, the receiver may interpret the behavior interpersonally and thus evaluate it positively as accommodation. This interpretation frequently occurs when intergroup relations are not salient and the interpersonal history is positive. When intergroup relations are salient and when speakers' behavior is perceived as not accommodating to the receiver's own behavior or needs, it is likely to be interpreted as nonaccommodative, whatever the speaker's intention. An important task for research is to specify and predict the conditions in which each form of nonaccommodation—counter, under, or over—is most likely to occur or be perceived to occur.

Attributions, Evaluations, and Future Intentions. The final part of the model concerns reception, although we again highlight the *transactive* nature of accommodative processes (Abrams et al., 2002). Essentially, CAT proposes that, all things being equal, accommodative behavior is attributed internally, evaluated positively, and results in positive future intentions toward interactions with the other person. In addition, when the other person is considered to be a typical member of his or her ingroup, these positive intentions are generalized to the whole group (cf. Hewstone, 1990). Likewise, nonaccommodation is attributed internally, evaluated negatively, and results in negative future intentions toward interactions with the other person (and the other person's group if it is an outgroup).

Of course, most of the time all things are *not* equal. As we noted above, social norms may dictate how behavior is initially perceived. For example, convergence that violates social norms is not labeled as accommodative (and may be perceived as over-accommodative; cf. Ball et al., 1984). In the same way, norm-following behavior is likely to be attributed more externally, and evaluated less extremely, than behavior that does not seem to be dictated by the situation. Third, all behavior by ingroup members tends to be evaluated more positively than the same behavior by outgroup members, at least when intergroup relations are salient. Finally, future intentions toward an outgroup generalize to interpersonal intentions toward the interlocutor only when the interlocutor is perceived as a typical member of his or her group.

These caveats lead to a plethora of propositional permutations on the path from behavior to future intentions. Gallois and colleagues (1988; Gallois et al., 1995) derived a large number of propositions in an attempt to capture this complexity. Looking back, this may be why it has been difficult to develop hypotheses that test the propositions (see Gallois & Giles, 1998). In this presentation, we have tried to cut through the complexity by relying on attribution theory. We believe the propositions below capture the essential characteristics but leave the nuances to context-specific models and empirical research.

P.8: When a speaker B accommodates to a receiver A, A is likely to interpret the behavior and evaluate B positively, especially when:

- A attributes B's behavior internally to benevolent intent OR
- B is a member of A's ingroup.

P.9: When a speaker B nonaccommodates to a receiver A, A is likely to interpret the behavior and evaluate B negatively, especially when

- A attributes B's behavior internally to malevolent intent OR
- B is a member of a salient outgroup for A.

P.10: When A evaluates B positively in an interaction, A is likely to have positive intentions toward

- Interpersonal interactions with B as an individual or as an ingroup member;
- Interactions with other members of B's group when A considers B to be a typical member of this group;

However,

When A evaluates B's behavior positively, A is likely to maintain A's original intentions toward B's group when A considers B to be an atypical group member.

P.11: When A evaluates B negatively in an interaction, A is likely to have negative intentions toward

- Interpersonal interactions with B as an individual;
- Interactions with other members of B's group, especially when A considers B to be a typical member of this group;

However,

When A evaluates B's behavior negatively, A is likely to maintain A's original intentions toward B's group when A considers B to be an atypical group member.

These 11 propositions together delimit the CAT model, with one caveat. The process of accommodation, like the process of communication (cf. Harwood & Giles, in press), is dynamic. Thus, something may happen in an interaction—sudden awareness (or change) of the situation or relevant norms, unexpected behavior (positive or negative) by the other person, a change to a more intergroup or interpersonal frame of reference, and so forth—that shifts a speaker from an interpersonal to an intergroup orientation (or vice versa) or from an accommodative to a nonaccommodative stance (or vice versa). The accommodative dilemmas in Gallois and Giles (1998) go some way toward describing this phenomenon. This means that the path from initial orientation to future intentions has many twists and turns, and predicting it will never be a simple task.

CONCLUSIONS AND FUTURE DIRECTIONS

So where are we now, after three decades with communication accommodation theory, and where do we go from here? It is fair to say that CAT has stood the test of time in that it is still generating research up to the present day. It has also spun off a number of more specific theories, of which communication predicament of aging theory (Ryan et al., 1986) is perhaps the most fully developed and productive example; in the health arena, Street's (2001) linguistic model of patient participation in care is also gaining momentum. It has provided the impetus for research in intercultural communication, as well as intergenerational, intergender, interability, and organizational communication. In all these contexts, CAT highlights the intergroup aspects of communication, something that many theories of interpersonal communication neglect.

In the case of intercultural communication, the intergroup aspects of interactions are always there. Intercultural encounters take place in the context of an intergroup as well as an interpersonal history, and in the context of different (and sometimes contradictory) social norms. Effective or good communication depends crucially on these factors. For this reason, the communication skills models that have been so prevalent in intercultural communication training are frequently likely to fail (cf. Cargile & Giles, 1996; Gallois, 2003; Gallois & Giles, 1998; Hajek & Giles, 2003). It is essential both for theory development and for effective applications that researchers take full account of the intergroup aspect of intercultural, and indeed all, communication.

CAT provides a comprehensive way to do this without neglecting the interpersonal and idiosyncratic aspects of conversation.

We have attempted in this chapter to clarify the propositions of CAT to at least some extent. We have reduced their number from 17 in 1995 to 11 here. In doing this, we have acknowledged the scope of CAT, invoked supporting theories explicitly, and tried to make the use of terms consistent. Our aim is to make CAT more accessible and easier for researchers to use to derive testable hypotheses. In addition, we have tried to make CAT more generic, so that researchers can develop more specific models for particular contexts. These models may invoke extra variables like values and personality, and situational characteristics such as formality, task orientation, and uncertainty management.

A great deal of work is still to be done before we understand the process of accommodation fully and in detail. There is a need to explore the strategies beyond approximation, especially the more recently theorized strategies of emotional expression and face maintenance. It will also be important to elaborate the impact of social norms as against intergroup relations. The role of multiple identities is a key factor that has hardly been explored using CAT, but that CAT can handle (see Jones et al., 1999). Finally, there are many important intergroup contexts where CAT has not been developed at all, involving interactions in institutionally driven contexts and elsewhere. Our hope is that CAT will be useful in all this research, and that in 30 years we (or others) will be able to take stock of it again.

NOTES

1. Sometimes "accommodation," which at the inception of SAT included both convergent and divergent moves, became rather loosely associated with convergence. "Nonaccommodative" moves included everything else: maintenance/divergence, and later under- and over-accommodation. See Giles, McCann, Ota, and Noels (2002) for the

invocation of this distinction (following Williams & Giles, 1996) in the sphere of cross-cultural inter-generational communication.

2. Gallois and Giles (1998) do not present propositions, but four "cases" showing how the elements of the model interplay.

REFERENCES

Abrams, J., Hajek, C., & Murachver, T. (in press). An intergroup analysis of sexual and gender identity. In J. Harwood & H. Giles (Eds.), *Intergroup communication: Multiple perspectives.* Berlin & New York: Peter Lang.

Abrams, J., O'Connor, J., & Giles, H. (2002). Identity and intergroup communication. In W. B. Gudykunst & B. Mody (Eds.), *Handbook of international and intercultural communication* (2nd ed., pp. 225-240). Thousand Oaks, CA: Sage.

Ball, P., Giles, H., Byrne, J. L., & Berechree, P. (1984). Situational constraints on the evaluative significance of speech accommodation: Some Australian data. *International Journal of the Sociology of Language, 46,* 115-129.

Baumeister, R. F. (1982). A self-presentation view of social phenomena. *Psychological Bulletin, 91,* 3-26.

Baumeister, R. F. (1993). Self-presentation: Motivational, cognitive, and interpersonal patterns. *Personality psychology in Europe* (Vol. 4, pp. 257-279). Tilburg, the Netherlands: Tilburg University Press.

Beebe, L. M., & Giles, H. (1984). Speech-accommodation theories: A discussion in terms of second-language acquisition. *International Journal of the Sociology of Language, 46,* 5-32.

Bissoonauth, A., & Offord, M. (2001). Language use of Mauritian adolescents in education. *Journal of Multilingual and Multicultural Development, 22,* 381-392.

Boggs, C., & Giles, H. (1999). "The canary in the coal mine": The nonaccommodation cycle in the gendered workplace. *International Journal of Applied Linguistics, 22,* 223-245.

Braunmûller, K. (2002). Semicommunication and accommodation: Observations from the linguistic situations in Scandinavia. *International Journal of Applied Linguistics, 12,* 1-12.

Brewer, M. B. (1991). The social self: On being the same and different at the same time. *Personality and Social Psychology Bulletin, 17,* 475-482.

Brewer, M. B., & Roccas, S. (2001). Individual values, social identity, and optimal distinctiveness. In C. Sedikides & M. B. Brewer (Eds.), *Individual self, relational self, collective self* (pp. 219-235). Philadelphia: Psychology Press/Taylor & Francis.

Brown, P., & Levinson, S. (1987). *Politeness: Some universals in language usage.* Cambridge, UK: Cambridge University Press.

Bull, P. (2002). *Communication under the microscope.* London: Routledge.

Byrne, D. (1971). *The attraction paradigm.* New York: Academic Press.

Cargile, A. C., & Giles, H. (1996). Intercultural communication training: Review, critique, and a new theoretical framework. In B. Burleson (Ed.), *Communication yearbook 19* (pp. 385-423). Thousand Oaks, CA: Sage.

Coupland, N. (1995). Accommodation theory. In J. Verschueren, J.-O. Ostman, & J. Blommaert (Eds.), *Handbook of pragmatics* (pp. 21-26). Amsterdam: John Benjamins.

Coupland, N., Coupland, J., & Giles, H. (1991). *Language, society and the elderly.* Oxford, UK: Blackwell.

Coupland, N., Coupland, J., Giles, H., & Henwood, K. (1988). Accommodating the elderly: Invoking and extending a theory. *Language in Society, 17,* 1-41.

Coupland, N., & Jaworski, A. (1997). Relevance, accommodation, and conversation: Modeling the social dimension of communication. *Multilingua, 16,* 235-258.

DeVito, J. A. (2004). *The interpersonal communication book* (10th ed). Boston: Pearson.

Fox, S. A., & Giles, H. (1993). Accommodating intergenerational contact: A critique and theoretical model. *Journal of Aging Studies, 7*(4), 423-451.

Fox, S. A., Giles, H., Orbe, M. P., & Bourhis, R. Y. (2000). Interability communication: Theoretical perspectives. In D. O. Braithwaite & T. L. Thompson (Eds.), *Handbook of communication and people with disabilities: Research and application* (pp. 193-222). Mahwah, NJ: Lawrence Erlbaum.

Gallois, C. (2003). Reconciliation through communication in intercultural encounters: Potential or peril? *Journal of Communication, 53,* 5-15.

Gallois, C., & Callan, V. J. (1991). Interethnic accommodation: The role of norms. In H. Giles, J. Coupland, & N. Coupland (Eds.), *Contexts of accommodation: Developments in applied sociolinguistics* (pp. 245-269). Cambridge, UK: Cambridge University Press.

Gallois, C., & Callan, V. J. (1997). *Communication and culture: A guide for practice.* London: Wiley.

Gallois, C., Franklyn-Stokes, A., Giles, H., & Coupland, N. (1988). Communication accommodation in intercultural encounters. In Y. Y. Kim & W. B. Gudykunst (Eds.), *Theories in intercultural communication* (pp. 157-185). Newbury Park, CA: Sage.

Gallois, C., & Giles, H. (1998). Accommodating mutual influence in intergroup encounters. In M. T. Palmer & G. A. Barnett (Eds.), *Mutual influence in interpersonal communication: Theory and research in cognition, affect and behavior* (Vol. 20, Progress in Communication Science, pp. 135-162). Stamford, UK: Ablex.

Gallois, C., Giles, H., Jones, E., Cargile, A. C., & Ota, H. (1995). Accommodating intercultural encounters: Elaborations and extensions. In R. L. Wiseman (Ed.), *Intercultural communication theory* (pp. 115-147). Thousand Oaks, CA: Sage.

Gallois, C., & Pittam, J. (1996). Communication attitudes and accommodation in Australia: A culturally diverse English-dominant context. *International Journal of Psycholinguistics, 12,* 193-212.

Gardner, J., Paulsen, N., Gallois, C., Callan, V. J., & Monaghan, P. (2001). Communication in organizations: An intergroup perspective. In W. P. Robinson & H. Giles (Eds.), *The new handbook of language and social psychology* (pp. 561-584). Chichester, UK: Wiley.

Giles, H. (1973). Accent mobility: A model and some data. *Anthropological Linguistics, 15*(2), 87-109.

Giles, H. (1977). Social psychology and applied linguistics: Towards an integrative approach. *I.T.L.: Review of Applied Linguistics, 33,* 27-42.

Giles, H. (1978). Linguistic differentiation between ethnic groups. In H. Tajfel (Ed.), *Differentiation between social groups: Studies in the social psychology of intergroup relations* (pp. 361-393). London: Academic Press.

Giles, H. (1979a). Ethnicity markers in speech. In K. R. Scherer & H. Giles (Eds.), *Social markers in speech* (pp. 251-289). Cambridge, UK: Cambridge University Press.

Giles, H. (1979b). A new theory of the dynamics of speech. *Diogenes, 106,* 119-136.

Giles, H. (1980). Accommodation theory: Some new directions. In S. de Silva (Ed.), *Aspects of linguistic behavior* (pp. 105-136). York, UK: York University Press.

Giles, H. (2001). Speech accommodation. In R. Mesthrie (Ed.), *Concise encyclopaedia of sociolinguistics* (pp. 193-196). Oxford, UK: Elsevier.

Giles, H., Bourhis, R. Y., & Taylor, D. M. (1977). Towards a theory of language in ethnic group relations. In H. Giles (Ed.), *Language, ethnicity and intergroup relations.* London: Academic Press.

Giles, H., Coupland, J., & Coupland, N. (Eds.). (1991). *Contexts of accommodation: Developments in applied sociolinguistics* (Studies in Emotion and Social Interaction). Cambridge, UK: Cambridge University Press.

Giles, H., Coupland, N., Coupland, J., & Williams, A. (1992). Intergenerational talk and communication with older people. *International Journal of Aging & Human Development, 34*(4), 271-297.

Giles, H., & Harwood, J. (1997). Managing intergroup communication: Lifespan issues and consequences. In S. Eliasson & E. Jahr (Eds.), *Language and its ecology: Essays in memory of Einar Haugen* (pp. 105-130). Berlin: Mouton de Gruyter.

Giles, H., & Hewstone, M. (1982). Cognitive structures, speech and social situations: Two integrative models. *Language Sciences, 4,* 187-219.

Giles, H., & Johnson, P. (1981). The role of language in ethnic group relations. In J. C. Turner & H. Giles (Eds.), *Intergroup behavior* (pp. 199-243). Oxford, UK: Basil Blackwell.

Giles, H., & Johnson, P. (1987). Ethnolinguistic identity theory: A social psychological approach to language maintenance. *International Journal of the Sociology of Language, 68,* 69-99.

Giles, H., McCann, R., Ota, H., & Noels, K. (2002). Challenging intergenerational stereotypes across Eastern and Western cultures. In M. S. Kaplan, N. Z. Henkin, & A. T. Kusano (Eds.), *Linking lifetimes: A global view of intergenerational exchange* (pp. 13-28). Honolulu: University Press of America.

Giles, H., Mulac, A., Bradac, J. J., & Johnson, P. (1987). Speech accommodation theory: The first decade and beyond. In M. McLaughlin (Ed.), *Communication yearbook 10* (pp. 13-48). Newbury Park, CA: Sage.

Giles, H., & Noels, K. (1997). Communication accommodation in intercultural encounters. In J. Martin, T. Nakayama, & L. Flores (Eds.), *Readings in cultural contexts* (pp. 139-149). Mountain View, CA: Mayfield.

Giles, H., & Ogay, T. (in press). Communication accommodation theory. In B. B. Whaley & W. Samter (Eds.), *Explaining communication: Contemporary theories and exemplars.* Mahwah, NJ: Lawrence Erlbaum.

Giles, H., & Powesland, P. F. (1975). *Speech style and social evaluation.* London: Academic Press.

Giles, H., & Powesland, P. F. (1997). Accommodation theory. In N. Coupland & A. Jaworski (Eds.), *A sociolinguistics reader* (pp. 232-239). Basinstoke, UK: Macmillan.

Giles, H., Scherer, K. R., & Taylor, D. M. (1979). Speech markers in social interaction. In K. R. Scherer & H. Giles (Eds.), *Social markers in speech* (pp. 343-381). Cambridge, UK: Cambridge University Press.

Giles, H., & Street, R. L., Jr. (1994). Communicator characteristics and behavior: A review, generalizations, and model. In M. Knapp & G. Miller (Eds.), *The handbook of interpersonal communication* (2nd ed., pp. 103-161). Thousand Oaks, CA: Sage.

Giles, H., Taylor, D. M., & Bourhis, R. Y. (1972). Toward a theory of interpersonal accommodation through language: Some Canadian data. *Language in Society, 2,* 177-192.

Giles, H., & Wadleigh, P. M. (1999). Accommodating nonverbally. In L. K. Guerrero, J. A. DeVito, & M. L. Hecht (Eds.), *The nonverbal communication reader: Classic and contemporary readings* (2nd ed., pp. 425-436). Prospect Heights, IL: Waveland.

Giles, H., & Williams, A. (1992). Accommodating hypercorrection: A communication model. *Language and Communication, 12,* 343-356.

Gudykunst, W. B. (1995). Anxiety/uncertainty management theory: Current status. In R. Wiseman (Ed.), *Intercultural communication theory* (pp. 8-58). Thousand Oaks, CA: Sage.

Gudykunst, W. B., & Kim, Y. Y. (1992). *Communicating with strangers: An approach to intercultural communication.* New York: McGraw-Hill.

Gudykunst, W. B., & Lee, C. M. (2002). Cross-cultural communication theories. In W. B. Gudykunst & B. Mody (Eds.), *Handbook of international and intercultural communication* (2nd ed., 25-30). Thousand Oaks, CA: Sage.

Gudykunst, W. B., & Nishida, T. (1989). Theoretical perspectives for studying intercultural communication. In M. K. Asante & W. B. Gudykunst (Eds.), *Handbook of international and intercultural communication* (pp. 17-46). Newbury Park, CA: Sage.

Gumperz, J. (1992). Contextualization and understanding. In A. Duranti & C. Goodwin (Eds.), *Rethinking context: Language as an interactive phenomenon* (pp. 229-252). Cambridge, UK: Cambridge University Press.

Hajek, C., & Giles, H. (2003). Intercultural communication competence. A critique and alternative model. In B. Burleson & J. Greene (Eds.), *Handbook of communicative and social skills* (pp. 935-957). Mahwah, NJ: Lawrence Erlbaum.

Harwood, J., & Giles, H. (Eds.). (in press). *Intergroup communication: Multiple perspectives.* Berlin & New York: Peter Lang.

Harwood, J., Giles, H., & Bourhis, R. Y. (1994). The genesis of vitality theory: Historical patterns and discoursal dimensions. *International Journal of the Sociology of Language, 108,* 168-206.

Heider, F. (1958). *The psychology of interpersonal relations.* New York: John Wiley.

Hewstone, M. (1990). The ultimate attribution error: A review of the literature on intergroup causal attribution. *European Journal of Social Psychology, 20,* 311-355.

Holtgraves, T. M. (2002). *Language as social action.* Mahwah, NJ: Lawrence Erlbaum.

Hornsey, M., & Gallois, C. (1998). The impact of interpersonal and intergroup communication accommodation on perceptions of Chinese students in Australia. *Journal of Language and Social Psychology, 17,* 323-347.

Hummert, M. L., & Ryan, E. B. (2001). Patronizing talk. In W. P. Robinson & H. Giles (Eds.), *The new handbook of language and social psychology* (pp. 253-269). Chichester, UK: Wiley.

Jetten, J., Spears, R., & Manstead, A. S. R. (1999). Group distinctiveness and intergroup discrimination. In N. Ellemers, R. Spears, & B. Doosje (Eds.), *Social identity: Context, commitment, content* (pp. 107-126). Oxford, UK: Blackwell.

Jones, E., Gallois, C., Callan, V. J., & Barker, M. (1999). Strategies of accommodation: Development of a coding system for conversational interaction. *Journal of Language and Social Psychology, 18,* 123-152.

Kelley, H. H. (1973). The process of causal attribution. *American Psychologist, 28,* 107-128.

Littlejohn, S. W. (2002). *Theories of human communication* (7th ed.). Belmont, CA: Wadsworth.

Martin, J. N., & Nakayama, T. K. (2002). *Intercultural communication in contexts* (2nd ed.). Mountain View, CA: Mayfield.

Meyerhoff, M. (1998). Accommodating your data: The use and abuse of accommodation theory in sociolinguistics. *Language and Communication, 18,* 205-221.

Miller, K. (2002). *Communication theories.* New York: McGraw-Hill.

Ng, S.-H., & Bradac, J. J. (1993). *Power in language: Verbal communication and social influence.* Newbury Park, CA: Sage.

Robinson, W. P. (2003). *Language in social worlds.* Oxford, UK: Blackwell.

Ryan, E. B., Giles, H., Bartolucci, G., & Henwood, K. (1986). Psycholinguistic and social psychological components of communication by and with the elderly. *Language and Communication, 6,* 1-24.

Sachdev, I., & Bourhis, R. Y. (2001). Multilingual communication. In W. P. Robinson & H. Giles (Eds.), *The new handbook of language and social psychology* (pp. 407-428). Chichester, UK: Wiley.

Sachdev, I., & Giles, H. (in press). Bilingual speech accommodation. In T. K. Bhatia (Ed.), *Handbook of bilingualism.* Oxford, UK: Blackwell.

Shepard, C. A., Giles, H., & Le Poire, B. A. (2001). Communication accommodation theory. In W. P. Robinson & H. Giles (Eds.), *The new handbook of language and social psychology* (pp. 33-56). New York: John Wiley.

Simard, L., Taylor, D. M., & Giles, H. (1976). Attribution processes and interpersonal accommodation in a bilingual setting. *Language and Speech, 19,* 374-387.

Smith, P. B., & Schwartz, S. H. (1997). Values. In J. W. Berry, M. H. Segall, & C. Kagitçibasi (Eds.), *Handbook of cross-cultural psychology: Vol. 3. Social behavior and applications* (pp. 77-118). Boston: Allyn & Bacon.

Street, R. L. (2001). Active patients as powerful communicators. In W. P. Robinson & H. Giles (Eds.), *The new handbook of language and social psychology* (pp. 541-560). Chichester, UK: Wiley.

Street, R. L., & Giles, H. (1982). Speech accommodation theory: A social cognitive approach to language and speech behavior. In M. E. Roloff & C. R. Berger (Eds.), *Social cognition and communication* (pp. 193-226). Beverly Hills, CA: Sage.

Tajfel, H., & Turner, J. C. (1979). An integrative theory of intergroup conflict. In W. G. Austin & S. Worchel (Eds.), *The social psychology of intergroup relations* (pp. 33-53). Belmont CA: Wadsworth.

Thakerar, J. N., Giles, H., & Cheshire, J. (1982). Psychological and linguistic parameters of speech accommodation theory. In C. Fraser & K. R. Scherer (Eds.), *Advances in the social psychology of language* (pp. 205-255). Cambridge, UK: Cambridge University Press, & Paris: Editions de la Maison des Sciences de l'Homme.

Ting-Toomey, S. (1993). Communicative resourcefulness: An identity negotiation perspective. In R. L. Wiseman & J. Koester (Eds.), *Intercultural communication competence* (International and Intercultural Communication Annual, Volume 17, pp. 72-111). Newbury Park, CA: Sage.

Triandis, H. C. (1995). *Individualism & collectivism.* Boulder, CO: Westview.

Trudgill, P. (1986). *Dialects in contact.* Oxford, UK: Blackwell.

Watson, B., & Gallois, C. (2002). Patients' interactions with health providers: A linguistic category model approach. *Journal of Language and Social Psychology, 21,* 32-52.

Williams, A., Gallois, C., & Pittam, J. (Eds.). (1999). *Communication accommodation theory in context* [Special section]. *International Journal of Applied Linguistics, 9*(2).

Williams, A., & Giles, H. (1996). Intergenerational conversations: Young adults' retrospective accounts. *Human Communication Research, 23,* 220-250.

Williams, A., Giles, H., Coupland, N., Dalby, M., & Manasse, H. (1990). The communicative contexts of elderly social support and health: A theoretical model. *Health communication, 2*(3), 123-143.

Williams, A., & Nussbaum, J. N. (2001). *Intergenerational communication across the lifespan.* Mahwah, NJ: Lawrence Erlbaum.

7

Cross-Cultural and Intercultural Applications of Expectancy Violations Theory and Interaction Adaptation Theory

JUDEE K. BURGOON

AMY S. EBESU HUBBARD

That all cultures have communication expectancies seems patently obvious. Whether cast as cultural display rules (Ekman & Friesen, 1969) or cognitive schemata for processing social information (Planalp, 1985; Schank & Abelson, 1977; Taylor & Crocker, 1981), every culture has guidelines for human conduct that carry associated anticipations for how others will behave. Those guidelines and anticipations manifest in interactions between people. Intercultural communication, then, involves communicators adjusting and influencing the behaviors of each other, partly through the lens of expectations. The question for communication scholars is whether greater understanding of human relations within and between cultures can be achieved by examining the patterns of adaptation that occur in such

Authors' Note: Portions of this research were supported by funding from the U.S. Air Force Office of Scientific Research under the U.S. Department of Defense University Research Initiative (Grant #F49620-01-1-0394). The views, opinions, and/or findings in this report are those of the authors and should not be construed as an official Department of Defense position, policy, or decision.

interactions and the effects of people's adherence to and deviations from those expectations.

Two theories that answer the question in the affirmative are expectancy violations theory (EVT; Burgoon, 1978, 1983, 1986, 1992, 1993; Burgoon & Hale, 1988; Burgoon & Le Poire, 1993); Hale & Burgoon, 1984; Le Poire & Burgoon, 1994) and interaction adaptation theory (IAT; Burgoon, Stern, & Dillman, 1995). Historically speaking, in 1978 EVT was originally developed to explain the effect of proxemic violations in interactions. This theory was later expanded to include a variety of verbal and nonverbal violations. In 1995, IAT was formally explicated. This relatively new theoretical framework incorporates and extends the explanatory calculus of EVT (by integrating other biological, arousal/affect, social norm, and communication/cognitive approaches to adaptation patterns in interactions) to predict the interpersonal communication patterns of convergence, matching, reciprocation, compensation, and maintenance. As with EVT, a central concept in IAT is the role of expectations in interactions and responses to violations of expectations.

Considerable communicological, sociological, and psychological literature has implicitly or explicitly endorsed the importance of confirming or disconfirming expectations. For example, in his prolific sociological writings on self-presentation, Goffman (1959) asserted that successful performances depend upon discerning the norms or expectations for a given situation and conforming to those expectations. Further, he claimed that failure to conform would result in stigmatization and spoiled identities. Most training manuals and programs preparing employees for international work implicitly embrace the same assumption by enumerating a given culture's norms and advising workers to abide by them. Books on intercultural communication often prescribe determining and then adapting and moving toward a target culture's communication norms (Axtell, 1998; Novinger, 2001).

Seemingly bolstering the same conclusion is research documenting the negative consequences of committing nonverbal violations such as personal space invasions (see Burgoon & Jones, 1976).

Yet, some psychological and marketing work has argued just the opposite, that violating expectations can be beneficial. For example, the multiple plausible causes framework (summarized in Eagly & Chaiken, 1993) proposes that unexpected persuasive messages are more successful than expected ones. Marketing researchers have similarly concluded that customer satisfaction is maximized by positively violating customer expectations rather than conforming to them (see, e.g., Brandt, 1988; Cadotte, Woodruff, & Jenkins, 1987; Kopalle & Lehmann, 2001; Sirgy, 1984; Spreng & Chiou, 2002; Tse & Wilton, 1988).

The importance of framing communication events according to expectancies is thus tacit in a wide array of research. What has yet to be resolved is when expectancy violations are harmful or helpful and whether conclusions about the effects of violations generalize beyond Western cultures. To date, EVT and IAT principles have rarely been applied or tested beyond the scope of mainstream U.S. culture (for exceptions, see Burgoon, 1992, 1993; Burgoon et al., 1998; Ebesu Hubbard, 2000; Gudykunst & Ting-Toomey, 1988; Lobdell, 1990). Our objectives in this chapter are (a) to describe the key principles of EVT and IAT and (b) to articulate some of the cross-cultural and intercultural applications of the theories.

EXPECTANCY VIOLATIONS THEORY (EVT)

The focal constructs in the theory that have special relevance for cross-cultural and intercultural interactions are expectancies, expectancy violations, communicator valence, and behavior valence.

Communication Expectancies

Communication expectancies are enduring patterns of anticipated verbal and nonverbal behavior (Burgoon & Walther, 1990). Expectancies comprise (a) socially normative patterns of behavior applicable to an entire speech community or subgroup plus (b) person-specific knowledge related to another's typical communication patterns. When individuating information is absent or open to interpretation, expectancies tend to be stereotypic (Hamilton, Sherman, & Ruvolo, 1990). Inasmuch as most stranger and intercultural interactions entail very little personalized knowledge about other interactants, expectancies revert to cultural or subcultural norms and stereotypes.

There are actually two different senses of "expected." One reflects the regularity with which a behavioral pattern occurs, that is, its central tendency. *Expectancy* in this sense refers to communicative acts that are modal (most typical) in a given culture or subculture. The other meaning of expectancy reflects the degree to which a behavior is regarded as appropriate, desired, or preferred. It refers to idealized standards of conduct rather than actual communicative practice. Staines and Libby (1986) labeled these two conceptualizations as, respectively, *predictive* and *prescriptive expectations*. Like expectancy-value theories in the social influence arena (e.g., Fishbein & Ajzen, 1975), EVT assumes that expectancies (and beliefs) entail both a predictive and a prescriptive component. This permits arraying expectancies on a valence continuum ranging from good to bad. Jackson (1966), in an insightful analysis of social norms and roles, showed that behaviors occurring most frequently are often, but not always, the most preferred. Thus, the relationship between a behavior's frequency and its evaluation need not be linear. For example, although moderate proximity may be the modal pattern in noncontact cultures, close proximity may be preferred, especially with

favorably regarded others. Operationally, this means that understanding communication through an expectancy lens requires knowing both a behavior's typicality and its valence.

Predictive communication expectancies are shaped by three classes of factors: (a) characteristics of individual communicators, (b) characteristics of the relationship between sender and receiver, and (c) features of the communication context itself. *Communicator factors* include all those salient features of individual actors, such as sociodemographics, personality, physical appearance, social skills, language style, and so on, that are the basis for categorizing people and that carry associated anticipations about how such people will communicate. For example, females are expected to be more affiliative than males. *Relationship factors* include interpersonal characteristics such as degree of familiarity, liking, attraction, similarity, or status equality between interactants that also lead to anticipated communication patterns. For example, where status or power asymmetries exist, the less powerful person is expected to show deference toward the more powerful one. *Context characteristics* include environmental constraints and definitions of the situation—such as its privacy, formality, or task requirements—that prescribe or proscribe certain interaction behaviors. These three classes of elements combine to form primary interaction schemata that should be activated in all human encounters, irrespective of culture.

The presence of such expectancies does not imply that expectancies will be identical across cultures. To the contrary, the *content* of each culture's interactional expectancies will vary substantially along such cultural dimensions as collectivism-individualism, uncertainty avoidance, power distance, masculinity-femininity, ascription versus achievement orientations, time and activity orientation, universalism-particularism, degree of face concern, and high- versus low-context communication (see FitzGerald, 2003; Gudykunst, 1997;

Gudykunst & Kim, 1997; Kim, 2002). Collectivist cultures such as Japan and China may expect greater verbal indirectness, politeness, and nonimmediacy than individualistic cultures such as the United States, Canada, and Australia (Baker, 1989; Kim, 1993). People from cultures that are more expressive and assertive (e.g., Australians, Indians, Pakistanis, Iranians, Israelis, Italians, and Spaniards) may expect others to be more talkative and dominant than do those from cultures that are more inexpressive and reticent conversationally (e.g., Japanese, Koreans, Swedes, Norwegians, and the British; Ito, 1989b; Kim, 2002; Matsumoto & Ekman, 1989). Noncontact cultures may expect greater interaction distances than contact cultures (Hall, 1966, 1981), and so forth. But each culture will have its own set of expectancies for a given type of encounter.

Cultures may also vary in the extent to which expectancies are rigidly or loosely defined. This might be conceptualized statistically as the size of the confidence interval around the mean expected behavior. However, because expectancies are better conceived as ranges than point estimates, the diffuseness or precision of the expectancies might be better visualized as the size of the tolerance range for a given act beyond which the act is considered a violation and may invoke sanctions or disapprobation. An example is gum-chewing—an act that is commonplace in the United States, frowned upon in Germany, and illegal in Singapore. It may be that ideological societies, which rely on rules and laws to minimize conflict, may have more narrow expectancy bandwidths than human relations societies, which are more concerned with group harmony than with conforming to prescriptions and principles (Ito, 1989a, 1989b). Alternatively, human relations cultures may be the more restrictive, given the importance they place on obedience, status differentials, and interpersonal harmony (Chu, 1988). In line with this latter possibility, Gudykunst and Ting-Toomey (1988) conjectured that cultures low in power distance and uncertainty avoidance (such as the U.S.) have fewer rules and norms regulating proxemic behavior than do cultures high in power distance and uncertainty avoidance (such as Japan). Although the empirical evidence leads us to disagree that proxemic norms are minimal in the United States (see, e.g., Burgoon, Buller, & Woodall, 1996; Hayduk, 1978), it may be that, relatively speaking, such cultures are less norm-bound. Regardless of which cultures have narrower or wider tolerance ranges, the larger principle here is that cultures are not uniform in the degree to which communication behavior is regulated by rules and social norms.

Where rules and norms are less explicit, cultures may also vary in the degree of tentativeness or certainty with which communication expectancies are held (Gudykunst, 1998; Heinemann, Pellander, Vogelbusch, & Wojtek, 1981). Japanese, for example, have greater attributional confidence about how strangers from their own and disparate cultures will behave than do North Americans (Gudykunst & Nishida, 1984). Too, cultures may differ on the degree of intracultural homogeneity. For example, if distinctly different expectancies are held for different subgroups, a single expectancy cannot be identified that has culture-wide applicability. The different expectancies for ingroups and outgroups in Greece is illustrative: Ingroup members are expected to be warm, cooperative, polite, reliable, and truthful, whereas outgroup members are expected to be hostile, competitive, untrustworthy, and deceitful (Broome, 1990).

As a counterpoint to all these claims for cultural differences, at some fundamental level there must be some commonalities present that enable shared meanings and coordinated interchanges. Without them, communication would be impossible. These commonalities reflect collective norms or expectations about communicative practices, many of which transcend culture (see Graumann, 1995). Further systematic study of the foundations of communicative exchange may reveal many points of similarity.

If so, expectancy-based predictions will not require as much culture-specific adjustment.

Regardless of how well defined and homogeneous or heterogeneous the predictive expectancies are, all expectancies theoretically should have an associated valence that defines their prescriptive aspect. Predictive components of expectancies are arrayed on a frequency continuum; prescriptive components are arrayed on a valence continuum. The answer to the question, Is the expected range of behavior viewed as good, bad, or neutral? dictates where on the valence continuum the range is located. Its size reflects the latitude of acceptable variability (i.e., the magnitude of departure from the midpoint of the range that is tolerated before the valence changes).

Expectancy valences may vary significantly from one culture to the next. To illustrate, collectivist cultures place more positive value on communicative indirectness and restrained expressiveness than do individualist cultures. Hence, members of such cultures may be more distressed by forthrightness and flamboyance than would members of individualist cultures. Japanese, for example, suppress emotional expressiveness so as to avoid insulting the group (Matsumoto, 1993). Valences may also be specific to particular communicator, relationship, or context characteristics within cultures. In Mediterranean cultures, for instance, public handholding is a positive and accepted display of friendship when exhibited by same-sex friends but unacceptable when displayed by heterosexual pairs; in North America, the opposite is true (Morris, 1971). Even though our current state of knowledge is such that the valences for many communicative behaviors are unrecognized or ambiguous at present, they are all theoretically subject to empirical verification.

To summarize, despite variability in the content, stability, intracultural homogeneity, and evaluations associated with expectancies, predictive and prescriptive communicative expectancies should be ubiquitous *within* cultures.

But, what about communication expectancies *between* cultures? If expectancies are a fundamental principle of social organization or social information processing, it follows that they should also exist for interactions between unfamiliar and dissimilar people. The form such intercultural expectancies take probably coincides with the character of most intergroup interactions, such that people respond primarily to one another according to social categories and ingroup-outgroup distinctions (Tajfel, 1978). The degree to which a culture is individualist or collectivist is known to affect perceptions of, and interactions with, ingroup versus outgroup members (Gudykunst et al., 1992). For example, Kupperbusch et al. (1999) summarized research that compared the Japanese (collectivists) and Americans (individualists) with ingroups and outgroups on the expression of emotion. The findings suggested that the most appropriate emotion expressions depended on the interaction between individualism and ingroups/outgroups. Collectivists interacting with outgroup members expressed more negative feelings than did individualists interacting with outgroup members, and individualists interacting with ingroup members expressed more negative feelings than did collectivists. Prior experience with a given group should also determine the extent to which communication expectancies are grounded in stereotypes or whether any well-formulated expectancies even exist (Manusov & Hegde, 1993). With highly limited knowledge, expectancies may be very tentative and/or aligned with whatever outgroup the individual appears to most closely resemble. To the extent that expectancies are linked to outgroup stereotypes, they may also be more negatively valenced than expectancies for those from familiar or similar cultural backgrounds.

With repeated interactions, intercultural expectations presumably should shift from heavy reliance on cultural- and sociological-level data to greater emphasis on psychological, particularized, and idiosyncratic data;

that is, they should evolve from being "noninterpersonal" to "interpersonal" (see Miller & Steinberg, 1975). If such interactions follow uncertainty reduction theory principles, greater familiarity simultaneously should foster increased certitude associated with the expectancies (Gudykunst, 1985; Gudykunst & Nishida, 1984). According to Gudykunst's anxiety/uncertainty management (AUM) theory (1993, 1998), when people feel confident in their ability to predict the behaviors and thoughts of members of another culture and when anxiety is low when interacting with members of another culture, then adaptive behaviors are likely. However, when confidence is low and anxiety is high, then maladaptive behaviors are likely. When Hullett and Witte (2001) applied the extended parallel process model to test anxiety/uncertainty management theory, they found that favorable day-to-day contact reduced anxiety and was related to more adaptive behaviors. Thus, intercultural expectancies should parallel longitudinally the evolution of expectancies among strangers within the same culture.

Expectancy Violations

Expectancy violations refer to actions sufficiently discrepant from the expectancy to be noticeable and classified as outside the expectancy range. In psychology, such behavior is frequently referred to as behavioral disconfirmation.

Just as rules are partly defined by their exceptions, so are expectancies partly recognized by their violations. Thus, if cultures have expectancies, by definition they must also have expectancy violations. In some cases, such violations may even invoke legal sanctions or other social means of enforcement, but more often they are "legislated" tacitly. Cultures vary in how deviant a behavior must become before it is recognized as a violation. For example, cultures high in uncertainty

avoidance are intolerant of deviant behavior (Hofstede, 1980). Such cultures should be quicker to declare a given nonnormative behavior as a violation than cultures that are more tolerant of individual variability.

The manner in which people respond to violations should also differ. Gudykunst and Ting-Toomey (1988), for instance, theorized that individualistic cultures would respond to proxemic violations with aggressive behavior, whereas collective cultures will respond to such violations with withdrawal. EVT proposes a more complex set of predictions that are a function of the valencing of the violation, discussed below.

Of course, expectancy violations are not just within-culture phenomena. Because intercultural interactions typically fall at the heterogeneous end of a homogeneity-heterogeneity continuum, they are prototypical cases of potential expectancy violations. Fundamental differences in philosophies, values, and social organization, coupled with widespread ignorance about cultural differences, makes intercultural encounters prime candidates for colliding expectancies. The countless anecdotes about misunderstandings and failed communication often translate into pitting one culture's norms against the quaint, peculiar, or "deviant" acts of another culture.

Communicator Valence

A key premise of EVT is that communication expectations are influenced by communicator characteristics, and more specifically, the valences attached to those characteristics. We know from the proxemic literature, for example, that close proximity is regarded as desirable when interacting with attractive and familiar interactants but not when interacting with unattractive others or strangers. With the former, proximity may communicate such positive meanings as liking, interest, and approval-seeking but with the latter may be seen as threatening and/or overbearing.

The communicator's positive or negative characteristics are posited to moderate how distance and other violations are interpreted and evaluated.

The salient aspect of communicator characteristics is encapsulated in EVT as *communicator reward valence,* or more simply, communicator valence. That communicator characteristics affect communication practices is axiomatic to communication scholars. But social scientists have had great difficulty prioritizing communicator variables in terms of importance or impact. The stance taken in EVT is that what unifies innumerable and disparate communicator characteristics is their net valence—whether, on balance, a communicator is deemed rewarding or not and, by extension, an interaction with that person is expected to be pleasurable/useful/gratifying or not. The importance of communicator valence is echoed by social exchange and attraction theories (e.g., Byrne, 1971; Thibaut & Kelley, 1959), which postulate that communicators size up the costs and rewards associated with another and attempt to maximize rewards relative to costs.

Just as communicator, relationship, and context factors are posited to affect expectancies, so are they also posited to govern communicator valence. All prior knowledge or observable information about a communicator, plus that individual's behavior during the interaction, feeds into the communicator valence quotient. For example, an individual may be reputed to have task expertise (a pre-interactional, externally attributed communicator characteristic) or may actually demonstrate that task knowledge during the interchange (an internally derived, interactional characteristic). Although features inevitably will vary in how heavily they are weighted for each given circumstance, the key point is that they yield a net positive or negative valence assigned to the communicator.

To date, factors that have been operationalized and verified as relevant components of communicator valence within U.S. culture include physical attractiveness, task expertise and knowledge, socioeconomic status, an authoritative demeanor, giving positive or negative feedback, possession of appealing personal attributes, similarity, familiarity, and status equality (see Burgoon & Hoobler, 2002, for a summary).

Apart from the direct effects that communicator valence exerts on communication patterns and outcomes (which is by no means a postulate unique to EVT), its special importance in EVT arises from its moderating role in valencing communication behaviors generally and violations specifically. It does so by influencing one or both parts of an interpretation-evaluation process.

Behavior and Violation Valence

Deviant and unexpected behaviors, by virtue of their novelty or unusualness, are known to be alerting or arousing and to trigger finer-grained information processing (Burgoon & Hale, 1988; Hilton, Klein, & von Hippel, 1991; Le Poire & Burgoon, 1996; Newtson, 1973). This attention-diverting feature of expectancy violations is posited to intensify responses relative to expectancy confirmations by potentiating communicator valence and activating an otherwise latent interpretation-evaluation process. Specifically, attention should be drawn to the violator and the violation act itself. The heightened awareness of communicator characteristics should magnify their positive or negative value. At the same time, the increased attention to the violation behavior should instigate an appraisal process to "make sense" of the violation. This appraisal process is posited to include assessment of (a) the meaning associated with a given violative act (*interpretation*) amid the range of possible meanings and (b) the act's desirability (*evaluation*).

Interpretations and evaluations hinge partly on constraints imposed by the context but also partly on who has committed the violation, that is, on communicator valence. When a violation's meaning is ambiguous or subject to multiple interpretations, communicator valence may influence which interpretations are selected. An abrupt departure, without the usual leave-taking ritual and no available situational information to explain it, is a violation. If committed by a person who is highly regarded, it may be perplexing but the perceiver may make more charitable attributions about its cause than if the act is committed by a poorly regarded communicator. For example, the departure may be excused as necessitated by some urgent problem, an attribution that would further reinforce the communicator's perceived power and status. It is unlikely to be interpreted as an intentional slight (unless the receiver suffers from low self-esteem). However, the same act committed by a disliked other may be interpreted as an affront, as rude, or as indicative of the communicator's social incompetence. Thus, when alternative readings are possible, the "who" committing the act becomes an essential factor in narrowing the range of interpretations considered plausible.

Communicator valence may also moderate evaluations, with or without having affected interpretations. In the leave-taking example, even though the act itself is normally not evaluated positively, the fact that it is committed by someone held in high regard may result in its being evaluated neutrally. By contrast, the same act by the poorly regarded communicator is more likely to be evaluated severely and classified as a negative violation of expectations. Gaze serves as another example. A high degree of gaze generally carries positive interpretations and evaluations in Western cultures (Burgoon, Coker, & Coker, 1986). But such gaze from a stranger, if prolonged, is likely to become disconcerting and to be judged as unpleasant.

The interpretive analysis of communicative behaviors may precede evaluation, follow it, or occur instantaneously and simultaneously with it. Regardless of the temporal ordering, the end result of this appraisal process should be a valence, ranging from positive to negative, that is attached to the violation. (Expected behaviors are also assumed to undergo an appraisal process over the course of their numerous instantiations, but their interpretations and evaluations are likely to remain at a much more subconscious level as long as the interaction is "humming along.")

The current state of knowledge of what interpretations and evaluations are attached to various behaviors has until now rested largely on an anecdotal and intuitive base. To give expectancy- and violation-based predictions the necessary empirical grounding, our own work within U.S. culture has been investigating systematically the expectations, meanings, and evaluations associated with various nonverbal behaviors and composites (see Burgoon & Hoobler, 2002, for a summary). Our results have shown that some behaviors have consensual interpretations and evaluations, whereas others are moderated by communicator valence (Burgoon, 1992; Burgoon et al., 1986; Burgoon, Newton, Walther, & Baesler, 1989; Burgoon, Walther, & Baesler, 1992). For example, nearly constant gaze is interpreted as dominant when exhibited by a highly regarded male but as submissive when exhibited by a highly regarded female. An open, relaxed posture is also viewed as dominant when exhibited by an attractive same-sex partner but submissive when exhibited by an unattractive one. Various forms of touches are evaluated differently depending on the attractiveness of the communicator, and proximity is evaluated differently depending on the status equality or inequality between participants (Burgoon & Walther, 1990; Lannutti, Laliker, & Hale, 2001). In many other cases, communicator valence has an additive effect on evaluations, that is, the more rewarding the communicator, the more desirable his or her behavior is judged to be.

Similar undertakings are needed within other cultures and for intercultural interactions, because what is considered appropriate in U.S. culture may be considered inappropriate elsewhere. Novinger (2001) provided an example of a Frenchman considering a North American who makes eye contact, smiles, and nods while passing a stranger in a safe neighborhood as flirtatious rather than friendly. Another case in point is the way in which intimacy was manipulated in an experiment by Guerrero, Jones, and Burgoon (2000). Romantic partners were instructed to increase intimacy by being more flirtatious and "warm" in their conduct. Although such behavior is typically welcome in the United States from a romantic partner, it might be regarded as offensive to display in public by cultures that place a premium on privacy and public decorum. That said, knowledge of linguistic and nonverbal norms (e.g., Burgoon et al., 1989; Kim, 1993) may permit drawing inferences about which kinds of violations might be positively or negatively valenced and hence produce positive or negative consequences within different cultures. To illustrate, Gudykunst and Ting-Toomey (1988) contend that high-context, ambiguous, and indirect communication typifies collectivist cultures. Such behavior presumably is also preferred. If so, verbal directness and immediacy may constitute negative violations that lead to unpleasant interactions and outcomes.

The same kind of inferential analysis can also be applied to intercultural interactions. Take, for example, an American working in Japan. Politeness is expected and preferred, but a Japanese businessman may expect (stereotypically) a U.S. businessman to be very forthright and opinionated. If, instead, the U.S. businessman displays a great deal of tact and forbearance, this may serve as a positive violation. The result should be more agreeable interaction than had the American been expected to be polite in the first place. As another illustration, consider an interchange between an American and an Israeli. Although Americans and Israelis both value "straight

talk" as sincere, Americans have an upper threshold beyond which candor is seen as rude and overbearing. Israelis, for whom a highly direct speech pattern known as *dugri* is normative (see Katriel, 1986), may find themselves committing negative violations when interacting with North Americans because their discourse is overly direct. The severity of such violations is likely to be even greater when interacting with Japanese or Chinese.

Not only are individuals aware of the communication norms within their culture, but people may also hold expectations for the communication norms of other cultures. For example, in Hess, Blairy, and Kleck's (2000) comparison of judgments of facial emotion displays by Caucasian and Japanese people, they found that ratings of dominance and affiliation varied depending on how likely a Caucasian or Japanese person was expected to display anger facially. Inferences regarding positive or negative violations in different cultures, thus, must attend to communication norms for a particular culture, as well as knowledge of, or stereotypes about, communication norms for other cultures.

Despite a myriad of differences cross-culturally on what communicative behaviors qualify as positive or negative violations, there may be some superordinate forms of communication that prompt universally positive or negative evaluations. One illustration comes from tests of nonverbal expectancy violations by Aune and colleagues (Aune, Ching, & Levine, 1996; Aune, Levine, Ching, & Yoshimoto, 1993; Levine et al., 2000). Their multicultural sample judged unexpected (stereotypically deceptive-appearing) behaviors as more deceptive than expected (stereotypically truthful) behaviors and perceived the most deceptiveness when the message source was unattractive rather than attractive. In other words, they found an interaction between reward valence and expectancy violations. As another illustration, Chinese and North Americans are highly similar in how they display discontent when disputed, wronged, or disappointed (Ma, 1990). It seems likely that many communicative acts that are negatively valenced in U.S. culture—betrayals of trust, insults, excessive familiarity by a stranger, or angry outbursts—are negatively valenced in most other cultures as well. Similarly, some positively valenced communication acts—compliments, gift-giving, humor, unexpectedly positive feedback—should generalize beyond North American culture.

Because of the predilection to assign more socially desirable interpretations and evaluations to the behaviors of positively valenced communicators, the probability might appear much higher for them to engage in more positive violations than negatively valenced communicators. But this is an empirical question, and two factors mitigate against this always occurring. One is that positive-valence communicators are granted a wider latitude in deviating from social norms before their behavior is regarded as unexpected. This larger bandwidth of expected behavior (akin to idiosyncrasy credits in the small groups literature) means that positive-valence communicators may have to engage in more extreme behaviors before their actions qualify as positive violations. Second, the standards of conduct for positive-valence communicators may be much higher than for negative-valence communicators. If expected and enacted behaviors are placed along a continuum from extreme positive valence to extreme negative valence, then the gap between the expected and enacted behavior might be quite small for a positive-valence communicator, but quite large for a negative-valence one, making it easier for a negative-valence communicator to commit a positive violation and a positive-valence communicator to commit a negative violation. Thus, positive violations are not uniformly associated with positive-valence communicators or negative violations with negative-valence ones. It is quite possible for positively regarded

communicators to commit negative violations and negatively regarded communicators to commit positive violations.

Effects of Violations

The last aspect of EVT is its predictions of how positive and negative violations or confirmations relate to interaction processes and interaction outcomes. With regard to interaction patterns, EVT predicts whether interactions should be involving, pleasant, and synchronized or not. Routine interactions that are progressing smoothly should exhibit, among other things, synchronization of verbal and nonverbal activity between speaker and listener, rapid turn-switches between speakers, and reciprocity of communication styles (see Bernieri & Rosenthal, 1991; Burgoon, Stern, & Dillman, 1995). EVT predicts the conditions under which interactants should adapt their interaction behaviors to one another in the form of reciprocity or compensation (Burgoon, Le Poire, & Rosenthal, 1995; Burgoon, Olney, & Coker, 1988; Hale & Burgoon, 1984; Le Poire & Burgoon, 1996) and when they should exhibit nonaccommodation. Like communication accommodation theory (Giles, Coupland, & Coupland, 1991), EVT posits that under some circumstances, interactants will converge toward or match each other's communicative behavior (reciprocity) and in other circumstances, diverge (compensation). The pattern depends on the valences of the communicator and the violation. For example, increased involvement by a rewarding partner is hypothesized to be reciprocated because it is a behavior pattern with positive connotations that should be welcomed from such a partner. Decreased involvement by the same partner is hypothesized to elicit compensatory increases in involvement because low involvement connotes disinterest or dislike, is unpleasant, and should motivate the person to restore the interaction to its previous involvement level.

With a nonrewarding partner, the reverse should be true. Increased involvement should be unwanted, thus prompting a compensatory response, whereas decreased involvement, the preferred pattern, should prompt a reciprocal decrease in involvement. The net effect is that interactants should follow another's lead when that person moves the interaction in a desired direction but resist when that person moves it in an undesired one. This general prediction should hold true regardless of which culture is involved and whether the interaction is between or within cultures.

As for interaction outcomes, the proposed relationship is as follows: Positive violations are predicted to yield more favorable interaction outcomes than conforming to expectations; negative violations are predicted to yield more unfavorable consequences than conforming to expectations. For example, people may be expected to learn more when high-reward communicators commit positive violations than if they conform to expectations. Conversely, learning should be impaired when a low-reward communicator commits a negative violation compared to the same communicator behaving normally (i.e., committing a behavioral confirmation).

One important outcome is the definition of the interpersonal relationship among interactants. Present in all human interactions is an ever-present subtext defining the nature of people's interpersonal relationships. Verbal statements, language choice, and nonverbal behaviors may all serve as relational messages that convey liking, friendship, dominance, formality, distrust, or animosity statements. Expectancy violations are posited to bring implicit relational messages to the foreground. Given that people typically rely on nonverbal channels to conduct relational "business," the greater importance a culture invests in nonverbal forms of expression, the greater the chances of violations reinforcing the relational interpretations associated with them. Hence, collectivist and homogeneous cultures (e.g.,

China and Japan) that are oriented toward interpersonal relationships, that incline toward ambiguous language and high reliance on nonverbal cues to exchange relational messages, may be especially subject to violations having relational implications. For example, one of the cardinal principles of Confucianism is promoting warm human feelings and "proper social relationships" (Yum, 1994). Indirection, commonly used as a means of preserving face and minimizing conflict, forces greater reliance on nonverbal behavior (Doi, 1973; Reischauer, 1977). Yet even an individualist, heterogeneous culture such as the United States exhibits high consensus on the relational meanings associated with certain nonverbal cues (Burgoon & Newton, 1991). We can surmise, then, that expectancy violations may affect relational communication in all cultures, albeit to different degrees, even though the content of those messages will vary from culture to culture. A self-effacing act that is interpreted as appropriate deference in one culture may be interpreted instead as spineless sycophancy in another. The particular meanings associated with violations, then, will be culture-specific, but relational interpretations of some sort will still be attached to the interactional behaviors.

A question that arises is whether cultures with rigid role and rule structures ever assign positive interpretations to violations and hence valence them positively. In discussing proxemic violations, Gudykunst and Ting-Toomey (1988) contended that in high power distance and collectivist cultures, a high-status person engaging in a personal space violation would be behaving totally outside ascribed role behavior and that such an action would inevitably produce stress and anxiety—a negative outcome. The implication of this example is that all forms of violations would carry negative relational attributions in such cultures. This is an empirical question, and the speculation runs counter to common intuition that unexpected acts such as shows of kindness or affiliation might be viewed as liking or approval—a positive relational interpretation which is likely to lead to other positive outcomes. While we cannot assume that what constitutes a positive violation in U.S. culture will be a positive violation elsewhere, EVT makes no such an assumption. It only postulates that if (a) an act is unexpected, (b) it is assigned favorable interpretations, and (c) it is evaluated positively, it will produce more favorable outcomes than an expected act with the same interpretations and evaluations. Making predictions within any given culture requires knowing what interpretations and evaluations are assigned to communicative behaviors *in that culture*.

In intercultural encounters an additional factor may need to be taken into account: uncertainty. Dissimilarities between participants may heighten ambiguities associated with the relational meaning of violations. A study of sojourners reentering their home culture is illustrative. Lobdell (1990) examined friends' and family's reactions to sojourners who return from their travels with new mannerisms, dress, and values at odds with those of their home culture. These expectancy violations, which may be analogous to the situation confronting interactants in intercultural encounters, proved to be a source of uncertainty and were often evaluated negatively. White (1989), in analyzing the role of expectancy violations in relationship development, similarly found that violations, especially negative ones, typically increase uncertainty. Thus, to the extent that violations increase rather than decrease relational ambiguities and are accompanied by discomfort or negative affect, they may lead to unfavorable relational attributions.

However, this need not be the case. White (1989) conjectured that unexpected behavior, especially in newer relationships, may also create opportunities to learn more about another. This would be especially true of intercultural interchanges, which are often an occasion for gaining greater knowledge about

another culture and lifestyle. Under such circumstances, violations may take on positive rather than negative valence. Interactants may be inclined to give more favorable "readings" to the other's behaviors, or they may suspend relational interpretations until more information is forthcoming. Because of the greater uncertainty associated with intercultural interactions, participants may also give those from a different culture a "wider berth" to deviate from expectations without regarding the other's behavior as a violation. That is, the expectancy bandwidth may be expanded to tolerate a wider range of behavior. How long interactants are willing to remain in an elevated state of uncertainty before reverting to their own culture's expectancies and relational interpretations would determine the persistence or transience of favorable reactions to the novelty and uncertainty. It is possible that as the newness of interacting with an unfamiliar other wears off, the expectancy bandwidth may also lose its elasticity such that behaviors once tolerated would now fall outside the acceptance region, and behaviors initially interpreted as "quaint" might now be seen as annoying. These conjectures argue for more empirical investigation of what expectancies people hold for interactions with those from dissimilar cultures and what range of interpretations they are willing to assign to dissimilar communication patterns.

In summary, expectancies exert significant influence on people's interaction patterns, on their impressions of one another, and on the outcomes or their interactions. Violations of expectations in turn may arouse and distract their recipients, shifting greater attention to the violator and the meanings of the violation itself. People who can assume that they are well regarded by their audience are safer engaging in violations and more likely to profit from doing so than are those who are poorly regarded. When the violation act is one that is likely to be ambiguous in its meaning or to carry multiple interpretations that are not uniformly positive or negative, then the reward valence of the communicator can be especially significant in moderating interpretations, evaluations, and subsequent outcomes. Examples of this type of violation include, in the nonverbal realm, conversational distance and various types of touch. In other cases, violations have relatively consensual meanings and valences associated with them, so that engaging in them produces similar effects for positive- and negative-valence communicators. Examples of this type of nonverbal violation are gaze and nonverbal involvement.

Despite the contributions of EVT to understanding interaction patterns and the outcomes of interaction, EVT's interaction predictions have received minimal testing outside U.S. culture. Beyond this fact, it is also useful to consider two shortcomings of the theory noted by Burgoon, Stern, and Dillman (1995). First, EVT does not fully account for the overwhelming prevalence of reciprocity that has been found in interpersonal interactions. Second, EVT is silent on whether communicator valence supersedes behavior valence or vice versa when the two are incongruent (such as when a disliked partner engages in a positive violation). As a corrective, Burgoon, Stern, and Dillman (1995) developed a new theory, interaction adaptation theory (IAT), that builds upon many EVT principles, but also incorporates biological and sociological pressures toward reciprocity as part of its explanatory calculus. We turn to IAT next.

INTERACTION ADAPTATION THEORY (IAT)

Extending EVT, IAT is intended to provide a comprehensive account of multiple concurrent adaptation patterns (Burgoon, Stern, & Dillman, 1995; Burgoon & White, 1997). The theory increases the scope of previous adaptation models by highlighting the strong entrainment effect that occurs in normal interactions and by incorporating a broader range of communication behaviors and functions.

Principles

There are nine underlying principles that guide IAT. The first is that humans are predisposed to adapt to each other. As social beings, the meshing of people's interaction patterns with others may help to fulfill needs for survival, communication, coordination of activities, and socialization. The second principle is that, at a biological level, there are strong pressures toward entrainment and synchrony, except in situations where physical safety and comfort are jeopardized. Entrainment (picking up another's behavioral pattern) and synchrony (coordinating, meshing, and pacing the timing of interaction behaviors) most likely occur rapidly and with a low level of awareness. From an intercultural standpoint, there should be no culturally relevant exceptions to these two principles. In other words, regardless of cultural background, people adjust and adapt their behaviors to each other and exhibit an inherent tendency to become entrained with each other. The exception is when safety or comfort is at stake. Then a pattern of compensation—behaving in a manner opposite the other person's—is the more likely. For example, if one person moves too close for comfort, the other should withdraw; if an actor stares at a target, the target will likely avert gaze rather than stare back.

The third principle is that approach and avoidance drives function as dialectical tensions as people cycle between competing needs for closeness and separation. These drives are not static or fixed and may be shaped by culture such that people from different cultures may exhibit different drive states at different times in their interactions. To illustrate, whereas some cultures choose to congregate to grieve a death, that is, the approach drive predominates, other cultures choose solitude, that is, the avoidance drive predominates. Communicators' cycling between approach and avoidance may coincide with each other or may be staggered.

The fourth principle of IAT is that, at a social level, there is pressure toward matching and reciprocity during routine, polite conversations. That is, people will typically exhibit highly similar nonverbal communication patterns and language use. Matching refers to linguistic, vocal, kinesic, proxemic, chronemic, and appearance similarities, irrespective of cause, such as two people tapping their feet nervously while waiting for the outcome of a competition; reciprocity refers to changes toward greater similarity with another that is contingent on, and directed toward, the other's behavior, such as increasing one's level of involvement in response to the other's increase in involvement. Matching and reciprocity as the default condition in interaction should also be a fairly universal principle, as behavioral similarity is a means of signaling common ground. Tendencies toward matching and reciprocity should be tempered, however, by other social and cultural prescriptions related to power, status, and relational familiarity, some of which may dictate a compensatory pattern, as in the case of showing deference to a superior by avoiding direct gaze.

The fifth principle of IAT is that, at a communication level, because participants have more awareness and are more mindful of their actions, both reciprocity and compensation may occur. In other words, communication goals play an important role in assessing when reciprocity and compensation may be intentionally and deliberately used. In intercultural interactions, native speakers who desire to provide directions to liked, nonnative speakers may adapt their behavioral pattern accordingly.

The sixth principle of IAT is that the degree to which adaptation can occur is limited by (a) tendencies toward consistency and constancy in an individual's own behavioral style, (b) internal causes for adjustment, (c) self- or partner-monitoring skill, (d) performance adjustment ability, and (e) cultural differences in communication practices and expectations. Thus, in regard to the latter, conversations between strangers from different cultural backgrounds may be characterized by some dissynchrony. For example, in societies with high power distance, role relationships might dictate compensatory patterns. An interesting research question becomes how intense the pressure is to match and reciprocate one another's behavior in intercultural encounters and what factors influence nonaccommodation to another (see communication accommodation theory for deeper consideration of these factors). This sixth principle of IAT recognizes that each culture has its own standards for social conduct, and those standards may not mesh with other cultures.

The seventh principle of IAT is that biological, psychological, and social forces combine to create boundaries within which patterns such as matching, synchrony, and reciprocity will occur. Interaction behaviors outside of those boundaries will often be characterized by nonaccommodation. The eighth principle of IAT is that there are many pre-interactional factors such as one's cultural background or the physical setting for an encounter that may systematically moderate interaction adaptation. Still, factors within the interaction itself, such as each person's conversation style, will be the most proximate influence on adaptation patterns. Finally, the ninth principle of IAT is that functional groupings of behaviors will be associated with more accurate analyses than single behaviors considered in isolation from their communication function.

Key Concepts

With the nine principles as the foundation of IAT, the predictions offered under IAT are based on analysis of five key concepts: requirements, expectations, desires, interaction position, and actual position. The first three concepts in the model are interrelated and not independent of each other. *Requirements* (R) refer to the required behavioral level needed to fulfill basic human needs for survival, comfort, safety, affiliation, and the like. *Expectations* (E) refer to the anticipated behaviors of self and others. Expectations are largely based on social factors (e.g., social norms, knowledge of the other's behavior, and the communication function or goal in the situation) and are equivalent to the predictive aspect of expectancies discussed under EVT. *Desires* (D) refer to wants or preferences in the interaction. They are person-specific and capture personal likes, dislikes, and idiosyncratic goals. Because they may be influenced by social and cultural backgrounds, they are equivalent to the concept of prescriptive expectations discussed under EVT; that is, they reflect valenced cognitions about current or impending interactions. These three factors, R, E, and D, can be arranged hierarchically, with R given highest priority, followed by E, and then D. Biological needs must be met before expected and desired elements come into play.

The fourth concept is *interaction position* (IP). The IP represents the melding of all the R, E, and D elements into one net value. It captures the communication behavioral pattern that is needed, anticipated, and preferred in a given interaction. For example, if a fearful child needs comforting, expects parents to be nurturing, and desires hugs and a soothing voice from the parent, the anticipated IP for the parent is one of physical proximity, touch, eye contact, and a quiet, comforting voice. Similar to EVT, in IAT the IP is compared to the *actual* (A) communication behavior exhibited, the fifth concept. Based on this comparison, IAT makes two elegant predictions. If the IP is a more positively valenced behavior than A, then the anticipated interpersonal pattern is divergence, compensation, or maintenance. If, in the parenting example, the parent is aloof, the child will not match that pattern but instead compensate, perhaps climbing in the

parent's lap, in hopes of eliciting the desired closeness from the parent. Conversely, if A is a more positively valenced behavior than IP, then the anticipated interpersonal pattern is convergence, matching, and reciprocity. If the parent is typically nondemonstrative and in this case is particularly loving, then the child will reciprocate with shows of affection.

In order to understand R, E, D, IP, and A more fully in intercultural interactions, the R, E, and D factors need to be assessed. These analyses should be conducted with the largest ethnic or cultural group in a single country or location as well as among multiple cultural and ethnic groups within a single country. Based on the previous discussion of EVT, it is likely that prescriptive expectations will vary among people from different cultures and subcultures. However, it is also possible that certain patterns may be pan-cultural. Ebesu Hubbard (1996, 2001) investigated the generally held relational prescriptive expectations (desires) for what should happen during conflicts between dating partners. Although not designed as intercultural studies, both of her studies had ethnically diverse samples, with the majority of participants describing themselves as Asian in descent (i.e., Japanese, Chinese, and Filipino) and only a small minority describing themselves as being of Caucasian descent. Ebesu Hubbard (1996) found highly consistent beliefs among participants that their partners should convey relational messages of intimacy, equality, and composure. On the other hand, there was less consistency among participants' desires for how much dominance and formality should be exhibited by their partners during conflicts. In the second study, Ebesu Hubbard (2001) again found considerable agreement in that participants generally believed their partners should show affiliation during conflicts. However, she also found more variable responses with regard to desires (prescriptive expectations) for dominance displays. These findings offer insight into how the IP may be determined for various groups of people as well as present some tentative evidence that cultural variation and similarity exist for prescriptive expectations.

Tests and Application of IAT to Intercultural and Cross-Cultural Interactions

IAT and intercultural and cross-cultural interactions are particularly well suited to each other because the combination of the two allows us to understand more fully the nature of adaptation in communication situations in which the adaptation may be nonroutine, difficult, awkward, or disrupted. The research conducted to date on IAT has generally been supportive of the tenets of the theory (e.g., Andersen, Guerrero, Buller, & Jorgensen, 1998; Burgoon, Le Poire, & Rosenthal, 1995; Guerrero & Burgoon, 1996; Guerrero, Jones, & Burgoon, 2000). In initial tests of IAT in an intercultural context, Burgoon, Ebesu et al. (1998) and Ebesu Hubbard (2000) conducted an experiment in which a U.S. student was paired with another U.S. student or with an international student (Asian, Mediterranean, or Hispanic), based on the participant's self-classification into the cultural category. These communicators conducted two discussions. The first discussion was held without an experimental manipulation. During the second discussion, one participant became a confederate who maintained either a responsive interaction style or adopted a nonresponsive one. Results showed that matching, reciprocity, and coordination are the standard patterns exhibited generally in interpersonal interactions. Their results also indicated that when U.S. participants interacted with other U.S. participants, they displayed more interpersonal coordination than when the U.S. participants interacted with international student participants. When more interpersonal matching and synchrony were displayed between partners, regardless of national origin, the participants evaluated the interaction more favorably.

In addition, the findings from this investigation indicated that social skill was an important individual difference factor to consider when examining interpersonal coordination, especially in intercultural interactions. In both Gudykunst's (1993) and Spitzberg's (1994) theoretical discussions of effective intercultural communication and competence, a communicator's skill was thought to be an important variable because skill can enhance the ability to adjust to the behavior of others. Kim (1993) has suggested that intercultural communication competence may be related to the ability to achieve synchrony. The results from Ebesu Hubbard's (2000) study provide some initial evidence supporting these ideas. The overall pattern was such that when one or both interactants were more socially skilled, conversations exhibited more interpersonal coordination.

Moreover, because researchers such as Kempton (1980) have hypothesized that "synchronization occurs as a result of both interactants sharing *mutually known rhythmic patterns*" (p. 71), we might expect that interactants who do not share a common culture may exhibit less interactional synchrony. Indeed, Burgoon, Ebesu et al. (1998) found that when people from different cultures were conversing, they tended to exhibit less interpersonal coordination than when people from the same culture were conversing. A question arising from these results was: Which is more important, intercultural differences or social skills? Ebesu Hubbard's (2000) post hoc analyses indicated that social skill might be the more potent variable. When social skill was covaried out of an analysis comparing the interpersonal coordination displayed by same-culture and mixed-culture dyads, culture type was not significant. In other words, interpersonal coordination was more closely associated with social skill than differences in cultural background.

In other tests of IAT, Le Poire and Yoshimura (1999) found support for one of the key principles of IAT, namely that reciprocity occurs in social-polite interactions. In their study, they had participants engage in a mock medical interview. During the interview, participants responded to nonverbal displays of pleasantness in kind. The universality of the reciprocity of pleasant behaviors in social-polite situations could be tested in intercultural interactions. Communicating pleasantness may be met with pleasantness. However, when desires and expectancies are factored in, some exceptions to the reciprocity of pleasantness are likely.

For example, Floyd and colleagues (Floyd & Burgoon, 1999; Floyd, & Voloudakis, 1999) investigated nonverbal indicators of liking in stranger dyads. They found that when people first met each other and the actual communication was congruent or exceeded the projected interaction position, liking was reciprocated. When the actual communication was more undesirable than the interaction position (e.g., participants wanted their partners to dislike them and leave them alone, such that their IP was for disaffiliation but partners' actual behavior, A, instead showed liking), participants tended to compensate by behaving in an unpleasant and detached fashion. When IP was more positively valenced than A (e.g., participants wanted to be liked but the partner instead expressed disliking), participants also tended to compensate. This investigation thus demonstrated that desires to be liked (or disliked) were stronger influences on behavioral responses to expressions of liking (or dislike) than expectations of liking (or dislike). A useful extension of this work in intercultural interactions would be to examine conversation between members of different cultures who vary in their desires to be liked by others, their expectations for members of different cultures, and their liking behavior. For example, if an Iraqi generally expects to be liked but prefers to be disliked by Americans, following the explanatory calculus of IAT, the Iraqi should respond to any shows of liking from the American with compensatory displays of dislike yet reciprocate a countryman's show of liking with similar displays of liking.

White and Burgoon's (2001) application of IAT principles in their investigation of deception adds further insight into the patterns of communication between members of different cultures. In their study, White and Burgoon found that the initial interaction positions of truthtellers and deceivers differed because of anxiety and self-presentational concerns. Deceivers showed less involvement than truthtellers. Kim (2002) points out that truthtelling is seen more as a moral imperative in independent cultures than in collectivistic cultures. In collectivistic cultures, tact and sensitivity to others' feelings are more valued goals than stating the truth. Thus, interaction positions are likely to vary according to the independent or collectivistic nature of one's native culture. For example, imagine the situation in a diverse classroom setting where students are called upon to provide feedback to a student who gave a poorly delivered speech. The Korean (collectivist) classmate may attempt to "soften the blow" by engaging in deception (giving positive feedback to the speaker) while an American (independent) classmate feels that the speaker needs to hear the honest truth (giving the speaker negative feedback). Because of the different views on truthtelling, there may not be a different level of initial conversational involvement between the Korean telling the lie and the American telling the truth. It is also possible that an American being less than truthful will show similar levels of conversational involvement as a Korean who is being truthful.

Comstock (1999) applied IAT principles to the instructional setting. She found support for the prediction that students' nonverbal involvement affected teacher involvement. In particular, teachers reciprocated decreased involvement from their students. Analysis of classroom adaptation patterns in different cultural settings would be very useful because evaluations and preferences for student nonverbal involvement are likely to vary. In addition, as classrooms become increasingly diverse, teacher behaviors may be differentially affected by their students' involvement. For example, in a multicultural classroom, there may be students from cultures that believe that making eye contact with a professor is a sign of disrespect and students who believe that making eye contact shows that they are paying attention to the professor. How a teacher will adapt in this setting is unclear.

SUMMARY OF BOTH THEORIES

In sum, the evidence is persuasive that within Western cultures, positive expectancy violations can be more efficacious than positive expectancy confirmations when the objective is to enhance self-image, develop favorable interpersonal relationships, create a smooth-flowing conversation, or influence another. But will violations be equally efficacious in all cultures or in intercultural interchanges? Ridgeway and Berger (1986) contend that high-status members' greater license to violate group norms does not include violating status-linked performance expectations. They claim there is greater risk violating those behavioral expectations that are markers of status and affirm the legitimacy of a status position (e.g., participating more, influencing the group, speaking with a firm voice, and looking at others directly while talking). This qualification might apply to other cultures as well, although the status-linked cues themselves would vary.

However, the previous EVT findings implicitly challenge the necessity of powerful and high-status people adhering to these stereotypic profiles. Ultimately, the answer will lie in further research. If favorable impressions and influence are attainable by virtue of violations galvanizing attention to positive or negative qualities of communicators and their behavior, then positive violations should gain more desirable consequences and negative violations less desirable ones, regardless of culture.

As for IAT, the relative newness of the theory means that it has yet to be subjected to extensive empirical testing, particularly in cross-cultural and intercultural contexts. Nonetheless, the essentiality of coordinated interaction as the foundation upon which effective and efficient social commerce is erected speaks to the importance of understanding the conditions under which adaptation is accomplished or thwarted. If, as IAT postulates, biological, sociological, and cultural forces together encourage matching and reciprocity as the default settings for most human interchanges, future cross-cultural and intercultural research can fruitfully refine knowledge of the circumstances under which nonadaptation and compensatory patterns prevail and with what consequences. IAT's distinctions among individual requirements, expectations, and desires, as well as the comparison between an actor's required/expected/desired interaction position and another's actual communication behavior may prove to be useful and universal heuristics for understanding interaction trajectories and their ultimate outcomes.

REFERENCES

Andersen, P. A., Guerrero, L. K., Buller, D. B., & Jorgensen, P. (1998). An empirical comparison of three theories of nonverbal immediacy exchange. *Human Communication Research, 24,* 501-535.

Aune, R. K., Ching, P. U., & Levine, T. R. (1996). Attributions of deception as a function of reward value: A test of two explanations. *Communication Quarterly, 44,* 478-486.

Aune, R. K., Levine, T. R., Ching, P. U., & Yoshimoto, J. M. (1993). The influence of perceived source reward value on attributions of deception. *Communication Research Reports, 10,* 15-27.

Axtell, R. E. (1998). *Gestures: Do's and taboos of body language around the world.* New York: John Wiley.

Baker, J. M. (1989). *Privacy regulation mechanisms in Japan and the United States.* Unpublished master's thesis, Arizona State University.

Bernieri, F. J., & Rosenthal, R. (1991). Interpersonal coordination: Behavior matching and interactional synchrony. In R. S. Feldman & B. Rimé (Eds.), *Fundamentals of nonverbal behavior* (pp. 401-432). Cambridge, UK: Cambridge University Press.

Brandt, D. R. (1988). How service marketers can identify value-enhancing service elements. *Journal of Services Marketing, 2(3)*, 35-41.

Broome, B. J. (1990). "Palevome": Foundations of struggle and conflict in Greek interpersonal communication. *Southern Communication Journal, 55*, 260-275.

Burgoon, J. K. (1978). A communication model of personal space violations: Explication and an initial test. *Human Communication Research, 4*, 129-142.

Burgoon, J. K. (1983). Nonverbal violation of expectations. In J. M. Wiemann & R. P. Harrison (Eds.), *Nonverbal interaction* (pp. 77-111). Beverly Hills, CA: Sage.

Burgoon, J. K. (1986, February). *Expectancy violations: Theory, research, and critique.* Paper presented at the annual meeting of the Western States Communication Association, Tucson.

Burgoon, J. K. (1992). Applying a comparative approach to nonverbal expectancy violations theory. In J. Blumler, K. E. Rosengren, & J. M. McLeod (Eds.), *Comparatively speaking* (pp. 53-69). Newbury Park, CA: Sage.

Burgoon, J. K. (1993). Interpersonal expectations, expectancy violations, and emotional communication. *Journal of Language and Social Psychology, 12*, 30-48.

Burgoon, J. K., Buller, D. B., & Woodall, W. G. (1996). *Nonverbal communication: The unspoken dialogue.* New York: McGraw-Hill.

Burgoon, J. K., Coker, D. A., & Coker, R. A. (1986). Communicative effects of gaze behavior: A test of two contrasting explanations. *Human Communication Research, 12*, 495-524.

Burgoon, J. K., Ebesu, A. S., White, C. H., Koch, P., Alvaro, E. M., & Kikuchi, T. (1998). The multiple faces of interaction adaptation. In M. T. Palmer & G. A. Barnett (Eds.), *Progress in communication sciences: Vol. 14. Mutual influence in interpersonal communication: Theory and research in cognition, affect, and behavior* (pp. 191-220). Stamford, CT: Ablex.

Burgoon, J. K., & Hale, J. L. (1988). Nonverbal expectancy violations theory: Model elaboration and application to immediacy behaviors. *Communication Monographs, 55*, 58-79.

Burgoon, J. K., & Hoobler, G. D. (2002). Nonverbal signals. In M. L. Knapp & J. Daly (Ed.), *Handbook of interpersonal communication* (pp. 240-299). Thousand Oaks, CA: Sage.

Burgoon, J. K., & Jones, S. B. (1976). Toward a theory of personal space expectations and their violations. *Human Communication Research, 2*, 131-146.

Burgoon, J. K., & Le Poire, B. A. (1993). Effects of communication expectancies, actual communication, and expectancy disconfirmation on evaluation of communicators and their communication behavior. *Human Communication Research, 20*, 67-96.

Burgoon, J. K., Le Poire, B. A., & Rosenthal, R. (1995). Effects of preinteraction expectancies and target communication on perceiver reciprocity and compensation in dyadic interaction. *Journal of Experimental Social Psychology, 31*, 287-322.

Burgoon, J. K., & Newton, D. A. (1991). Applying a social meaning model to relational message interpretations of conversational involvement: Comparing observer and participant perspectives. *Southern Communication Journal, 56*, 96-113.

Burgoon, J. K., Newton, D. A., Walther, J. A., & Baesler, E. J. (1989). Nonverbal expectancy violations and conversational involvement. *Journal of Nonverbal Behavior, 13*, 97-120.

Burgoon, J. K., Olney, C. A., & Coker, R. (1988). The effects of communicator characteristics on patterns of reciprocity and compensation. *Journal of Nonverbal Behavior, 11*, 146-165.

Burgoon, J. K., Stern, L. A., & Dillman, L. (1995). *Interpersonal adaptation: Dyadic interaction patterns.* Cambridge, UK: Cambridge University Press.

Burgoon, J. K., & Walther, J. B. (1990). Nonverbal expectancies and the evaluative consequences of violations. *Human Communication Research, 17*, 232-265.

Burgoon, J. K., Walther, J. B., & Baesler, E. J. (1992). Interpretations, evaluations, and consequences of interpersonal touch. *Human Communication Research, 19*, 237-263.

Burgoon, J. K., & White, C. H. (1997). Researching nonverbal message production: A view from interaction adaptation theory. In J. O. Greene (Ed.), *Message production: Advances in communication theory* (pp. 279-312). Mahwah, NJ: Lawrence Erlbaum.

Byrne, D. (1991). *The attraction paradigm*. New York: Academic Press.

Cadotte, E. R., Woodruff, R. B., & Jenkins, R. L. (1987). Expectations and norms in models of consumer satisfaction. *Journal of Marketing Research, 24,* 305-314.

Chu, L. L. (1988). Mass communication theory: A Chinese perspective. In W. Dissanayake (Ed.), *Communication theory: An Asian perspective* (pp. 126-138). Singapore: Asian Mass Communication and Information Centre.

Comstock, J. (1999, November). *Mutual influence in teacher-student relationships: Applying IAT to assess teacher adaptation to student classroom involvement.* Paper presented at the annual meeting of the National Communication Association, Chicago.

Doi, L. T. (1973). The Japanese patterns of communication and the concept of *amae. Quarterly Journal of Speech, 59,* 180-185.

Eagly, A. H., & Chaiken, S. (1993). *The psychology of attitudes.* Fort Worth, TX: Harcourt Brace Jovanovich.

Ebesu Hubbard, A. S. (1996). *Examination of relational responsiveness and empathy during conflict in dating relationships.* Unpublished doctoral dissertation, University of Arizona.

Ebesu Hubbard, A. S. (2000). Interpersonal coordination in interactions: Evaluations and social skills. *Communication Research Reports, 17,* 95-104.

Ebesu Hubbard, A. S. (2001). Conflict between relationally uncertain romantic partners: The influence of relational responsiveness and empathy. *Communication Monographs, 68,* 400-414.

Ekman, P., & Friesen, W. V. (1969). The repertoire of nonverbal behavior: Categories, origins, usage, and coding. *Perceptual and Motor Skills, 24,* 711-724.

Fishbein, M., & Ajzen, I. (1975). *Belief, attitude, intention, and behavior: An introduction to theory and research.* Reading, MA: Addison-Wesley.

FitzGerald, H. (2003). *How different are we? Spoken discourse in intercultural communication.* Clevendon, UK: Cromwell Press.

Floyd, K., & Burgoon, J. K. (1999). Reacting to nonverbal expressions of liking: A test of interaction adaptation theory. *Communication Monographs, 66,* 219-239.

Floyd, K., & Voloudakis, M. (1999). Affectionate behavior in adult platonic friendships: Interpreting and evaluating expectancy violations. *Human Communication Research, 25,* 341-369.

Giles, H., Coupland, N., & Coupland, J. (1991). Accommodation theory: Communication, context, and consequence. In H. Giles, J. Coupland, & N. Coupland (Eds.), *Contexts of accommodation: Developments in applied sociolinguistics* (pp. 1-68). Cambridge, UK: Cambridge University Press.

Goffman, E. (1959). *The presentation of self in everyday life.* Garden City, NY: Anchor Books/Doubleday.

Graumann, C. F. (1995). Commonality, mutuality, reciprocity—A conceptual introduction. In I. Markovà, C. F. Graumann, & K. Foppa (Eds.), *Mutualities in dialogue.* Cambridge, UK: Cambridge University Press.

Gudykunst, W. B. (1985). The influence of cultural similarity, type of relationship, and self-monitoring on uncertainty reduction processes. *Communication Monographs, 52,* 203-217.

Gudykunst, W. B. (1993). Toward a theory of interpersonal and intergroup communication: An anxiety/uncertainty management (AUM) perspective. In R. Wiseman & J. Koester (Eds.), *Intercultural communication competence* (pp. 33-71). Newbury Park, CA: Sage.

Gudykunst, W. B. (1997). Cultural variability in communication: An introduction. *Communication Research, 24,* 327-348.

Gudykunst, W. B. (1998). Applying anxiety/uncertainty management (AUM) theory to intercultural adjustment training. *International Journal of Intercultural Relations, 22,* 227-250.

Gudykunst, W. B., Gao, G., Schmidt, K. L., Nishida, T., Bond, M. H., Leung, K., Wang, G., & Barraclough, R. A. (1992). The influence of individualism-collectivism, self-monitoring, and predicted-outcome value on communication in ingroup and outgroup relationships.

Journal of Cross-Cultural Psychology, 23, 196-213.

Gudykunst, W. B., & Kim, Y. Y. (1997). *Communicating with strangers* (3rd ed.). New York: McGraw-Hill.

Gudykunst, W. B., & Nishida, T. (1984). Individual and cultural influences on uncertainty reduction. *Communication Monographs, 51,* 23-36.

Gudykunst, W. B., & Ting-Toomey, S. (1988). *Culture and interpersonal communication.* Newbury Park, CA: Sage.

Guerrero, L. K., & Burgoon, J. K. (1996). Attachment styles and reactions to nonverbal involvement change in romantic dyads: Patterns of reciprocity and compensation. *Human Communication Research, 22,* 335-370.

Guerrero, L. K., Jones, S. M., & Burgoon, J. K. (2000). Responses to nonverbal intimacy change in romantic dyads: Effects of behavioral valence and degree of behavioral change on nonverbal and verbal reactions. *Communication Monographs, 67,* 325-346.

Hale, J. L., & Burgoon, J. K. (1984). Models of reactions to changes in nonverbal immediacy. *Journal of Nonverbal Behavior, 8,* 287-314.

Hall, E. T. (1966). *The hidden dimension* (2nd ed.). Garden City, NY: Anchor/Doubleday.

Hall, E. T. (1981). *Beyond culture.* Garden City, NY: Anchor/Doubleday.

Hamilton, D. L., Sherman, S. J., & Ruvolo, C. M. (1990). Stereotype-based expectancies: Effects on information processing and social behavior. *Journal of Social Issues, 46*(2), 35-60.

Hayduk, L. A. (1978). Personal space: An evaluative and orienting overview. *Psychological Bulletin, 85,* 117-134.

Heinemann, W., Pellander, F., Vogelbusch, A., & Wojtek, B. (1981). Meeting a deviant person: Subjective norms and affective reactions. *European Journal of Social Psychology, 11,* 1-25.

Hess, U., Blairy, S., & Kleck, R. E. (2000). The influence of facial emotion displays, gender, and ethnicity on judgments of dominance and affiliation. *Journal of Nonverbal Behavior, 24,* 265-283.

Hilton, J. L., Klein, J. G., & von Hippel, W. (1991). *Attention allocation and impression formation.* Manuscript submitted for publication.

Hofstede, G. (1980). *Culture's consequences.* Beverly Hills, CA: Sage.

Hullett, C. R., & Witte, K. (2001). Predicting intercultural adaptation and isolation: Using the extended parallel process model to test anxiety/uncertainty management theory. *International Journal of Intercultural Relations, 25,* 125-139.

Ito, Y. (1989a). A non-Western view of the paradigm dialogues. In B. Dervin, L. Grossberg, B. J. O'Keefe, & E. Wartella (Eds.), *Rethinking communication* (pp. 173-177). Newbury Park, CA: Sage.

Ito, Y. (1989b, May). *Socio-cultural backgrounds of Japanese interpersonal communication style.* Paper presented at the annual meeting of the International Communication Association, San Francisco.

Jackson, J. (1966). A conceptual and measurement model for norms and roles. *Pacific Sociological Review, 9,* 35-47.

Katriel, T. (1986). *Talking straight: Dugri speech in Israeli Sabra culture.* Cambridge, UK: Cambridge University Press.

Kempton, W. (1980). The rhythmic basis of interactional micro-synchrony. In M. R. Key (Ed.), *The relationship between verbal and nonverbal communication* (pp. 150-167). New York: Oxford University Press.

Kim, M. (1993). Culture-based interactive constraints in explaining intercultural strategic competence. In R. L. Wiseman & J. Koestner (Eds.), *Intercultural communication competence* (pp. 132-150). Newbury Park, CA: Sage.

Kim, M. (2002). *Non-Western perspectives on human communication: Implications for theory and practice.* Thousand Oaks, CA: Sage.

Kopalle, P. K., & Lehmann, D. R. (2001). Strategic management of expectations: The role of disconfirmation sensitivity and perfectionism. *Journal of Marketing Research, 38,* 386-395.

Kupperbusch, C., Matsumoto, D., Kooken, K., Loewinger, S., Uchida, H., Wilson-Cohn, C., & Yrizarry, N. (1999). Cultural influences on nonverbal expressions of emotion. In P. Philippot, R. S. Feldman, & E. J. Coats (Eds.), *The social context of nonverbal behavior* (pp. 17-44). New York: Cambridge University Press.

Lannutti, P. J., Laliker, M., & Hale, J. L. (2001). Violations of expectations and social-sexual communication in student/professor interactions. *Communication Education, 50,* 69-82.

Le Poire, B. A., & Burgoon, J. K. (1994). Two contrasting explanations of involvement violations: Expectancy violations theory versus discrepancy arousal theory. *Human Communication Research, 20,* 560-591.

Le Poire, B. A., & Burgoon, J. K. (1996). Usefulness of differentiating arousal responses within communication theories: Orienting response or defensive arousal within nonverbal theories of expectancy violations. *Communication Monographs, 63,* 208-230.

Le Poire, B. A., & Yoshimura, S. M. (1999). The effects of expectancies and actual communication on nonverbal adaptation and communication outcomes: A test of interaction adaptation theory. *Communication Monographs, 66,* 1-30.

Levine, T. R., Anders, L. N., Banas, J., Baum, K. L., Endo, K., Hu, A. D. S., & Wong, N. C. H. (2000). Norms, expectations, and deception: A norm violation model of veracity judgments. *Communication Monographs, 67,* 123-137.

Lobdell, C. L. (1990, June). *Expectations of family and friends of sojourners during the reentry adjustment process.* Paper presented at the annual meeting of the International Communication Association, Dublin, Ireland.

Ma, R. (1990). An exploratory study of discontented responses in American and Chinese relationships. *Southern Communication Journal, 55,* 305-318.

Manusov, V., & Hegde, R. (1993). Communicative outcomes of stereotype-based expectancies: An observational study of cross-cultural dyads. *Communication Quarterly, 41,* 338-354.

Matsumoto, D. (1993). Ethnic differences in affect intensity, emotion judgements, display rule attitudes, and self-reported emotional expression in an American sample. *Motivation and Emotion, 17,* 107-123.

Matsumoto, D., & Ekman, P. (1989). American-Japanese cultural differences in intensity ratings of facial expressions of emotion. *Motivation and Emotion, 13,* 143-157.

Miller, G. R., & Steinberg, M. (1975). *Between people.* Chicago: SRA.

Morris, D. (1971). *Intimate behavior.* New York: Random House.

Newtson, D. (1973). Attribution and the unit of perception of ongoing behavior. *Journal of Personality and Social Psychology, 28,* 28-38.

Novinger, T. (2001). *Intercultural communication: A practical guide.* Austin: University of Texas Press.

Planalp, S. (1985). Relational schemata: A test of alternative forms of relational knowledge as guides to communication. *Human Communication Research, 12,* 3-29.

Reischauer, E. (1977). *The Japanese.* Cambridge, MA: Harvard University Press.

Ridgeway, C. L., & Berger, J. (1986). Expectations, legitimation, and dominance behavior in task groups. *American Sociological Review, 51,* 603-617.

Schank, R. C., & Abelson, R. P. (1977). *Scripts, plans, goals and understanding.* Hillsdale, NJ: Lawrence Erlbaum.

Sirgy, M. J. (1984). A social cognition model of consumer satisfaction/dissatisfaction. *Psychology & Marketing, 1*(2), 27-44.

Spitzberg, B. H. (1994). A model of intercultural communication competence. In L. A. Samovar & R. E. Porter (Eds.), *Intercultural communication: A reader* (7th ed., pp. 347-359). Belmont, CA: Wadsworth.

Spreng, R. A., & Chiou, J. (2002). A cross-cultural assessment of the satisfaction formation process. *European Journal of Marketing, 36,* 829-840.

Stacks, D. W., & Burgoon, J. K. (1981). The role of nonverbal behaviors as distractors in resistance to persuasion in interpersonal contexts. *Central States Speech Journal, 32,* 61-73.

Staines, G. L., & Libby, P. L. (1986). Men and women in role relationships. In R. D. Asmore & F. K. Del Boca (Eds.), *The social psychology of male-female relations* (pp. 211-258). New York: Academic Press.

Tajfel, H. (1982). *Human groups and social categories.* Cambridge, UK: Cambridge University Press.

Taylor, S. E., & Crocker, J. (1981). Schematic bases of social information processing. In E. T. Higgins, C. P. Herman, & M. P. Zanna (Eds.),

Social cognition: The Ontario Symposium (Vol. 1, pp. 89-134). Hillsdale, NJ: Lawrence Erlbaum.

Thibaut, J. W., & Kelley, H. H. (1959). *The social psychology of groups.* New York: John Wiley.

Tse, D. K., & Wilton, P. C. (1988). Models of consumer satisfaction formation: An extension. *Journal of Marketing Research, 25,* 204-212.

Watzlawick, P., Beavin, J. H., & Jackson, D. D. (1967). *Pragmatics of human communication.* New York: Norton.

White, C. H. (1989). *Effects of expectancy violations on uncertainty in interpersonal interactions.* Unpublished master's thesis, Texas Tech University.

White, C. H., & Burgoon, J. K. (2001). Adaptation and communicative design: Patterns of interaction in truthful and deceptive conversations. *Human Communication Research, 27,* 9-37.

Yum, J. O. (1994). The impact of Confucianism on interpersonal relationships and communication patterns in East Asia. In L. A. Samovar & R. E. Porter, (Eds.), *Intercultural communication: A reader* (7th ed., pp. 75-86). Belmont, CA: International Thomson Publishing.

8

From the Margins to the Center

Utilizing Co-Cultural Theory in Diverse Contexts

MARK P. ORBE

REGINA E. SPELLERS

Two individuals who brought diverse perspectives to the project author this chapter on co-cultural theory. While both of us identify as co-cultural group members, our experience with co-cultural theory varies considerably. Over the past several years, the first author has dedicated a significant amount of his research activities to investigating the communicative experiences of those persons traditionally on the margins of dominant societal structures (Orbe, 1996, 1997, 1998a, 1998b, 1998c). Through this line of research, co-cultural communication theory has emerged. The second author has considerably less experience with the theory, yet has identified it as a productive framework for her primary area of research (Spellers, 2000; Spellers,

Sanders, & Orbe, 2003). In this regard, our coauthored chapter reflects a dual perspective of two scholars with varying degrees of immediacy with the theory. Within this chapter, we reflect on the origins of co-cultural theory, summarize some of the existing work in this area, and point to specific implications for future research, theorizing, and practice.

CO-CULTURAL THEORY: AN OVERVIEW

In its most general form, co-cultural communication refers to interactions among underrepresented and dominant group members. The vast majority of work in this area derives from the perspectives of underrepresented group members, including people of color; women; people with disabilities; those from a lower socioeconomic status; and gays, lesbians, and bisexuals (Orbe, 1998c). It is important to note, however, that instances of co-cultural communication are defined from the perspective of the underrepresented group members when they perceive cultural differences as salient during any given interaction. This may, in fact, include instances of intragroup communication in that another aspect of one's co-cultural identity becomes a salient issue (e.g., an African American woman with a disability interacting with an able-bodied African American woman). A co-cultural theoretical approach to communication is designed to speak to the issues of traditionally underrepresented group members as they function within societal structures governed by cultural groups that have, over time, achieved dominant group status (Orbe, 1998c).

Co-cultural theory, as described by Orbe (1998a), assists in understanding the ways in which persons who are traditionally marginalized in dominant societal structures communicate in their everyday lives. Grounded in muted group (e.g., Kramarae, 1981) and standpoint theories (e.g., Smith, 1987) and cultural phenomenology (Husserl, 1964; Lanigan, 1988; Orbe, 2000), co-cultural communication theory is derived from the lived experiences of a variety of "nondominant" or co-cultural groups, including people of color, women, persons with disabilities, gays/lesbians/bisexuals, and those from a lower socioeconomic background.

Co-cultural theory is embedded in five epistemological assumptions (Orbe, 1998a), each of which reflects its theoretical foundation. First, a hierarchy exists in each society that gives privilege to certain groups of people. In the United States, these groups include men, European Americans, heterosexuals, the able-bodied, and the middle and upper classes. Second, dominant group members, on the basis of these varying levels of privilege, occupy positions of power that they use to create and maintain communication systems that reflect, reinforce, and promote their field of experience. Third, dominant communication structures, directly and indirectly, impede the progress of those persons whose lived experiences are not reflected in the public communicative systems. Fourth, co-cultural group members' experiences will vary; however, they will also share a similar societal position that renders them marginalized and underrepresented within dominant societal structures. Fifth and finally, co-cultural group members strategically adopt certain communication behaviors to negotiate oppressive dominant structures.

In its most basic form, co-cultural theory lends insight into the process by which co-cultural group members negotiate their "cultural differentness" with others (with others both like, and unlike, themselves). For researchers and practitioners interested in the experiences of underrepresented group members, co-cultural theory offers a framework to understand the process by which individuals come to select how they are going to interact with others in any given specific context. While many existing interpersonal and intercultural theories offer general approaches to study such phenomena, co-cultural theory is one of only a few that is grounded in the lived experiences of the persons it seeks to describe. In this regard, it approaches the study of co-cultural communication from the perspective of those traditionally marginalized in societal structures (as well as communication research and theory).

Co-cultural theory, as originally described by Orbe (1996, 1998a), was developed inductively from a series of studies that explored how underrepresented group members communicate within dominant societal structures. Three of these four foundational studies focused on different co-cultural groups: African American graduate students (Ford-Ahmed & Orbe, 1992), African American men (Orbe, 1994), and gay men (Roberts & Orbe, 1996). The fourth (Orbe, 1996) specifically sought to explore co-cultural communicative experiences more generally and included people of color, gays/lesbians/bisexuals, and women, as well as those from a lower socioeconomic status. Despite the different foci, the consistent thread that ran through each of these studies was twofold. First, each sought out opportunities to explore inductively the communicative experiences of traditionally marginalized groups from their own cultural standpoints. Second, each shared a common methodological framework, what has become regarded as cultural phenomenology (Orbe, 2000).

In short, the fundamental concepts of the theory are grounded in four phenomenological research projects involving diverse co-cultural group members from across the United States. While each of these studies had been reported individually (Ford-Ahmed & Orbe, 1992; Orbe, 1994, 1996; Roberts & Orbe, 1996), the emergence of co-cultural theory represents an advanced point of self-reflexivity where the data collected from these studies were re-viewed as a means to generate new insight. From a phenomenological perspective, co-cultural theory was birthed out of a hermeneutic spiral that was put in place by each of these four studies, and extended through the synergistic force of all four collectively.

CO-CULTURAL COMMUNICATION CORE CONCEPTS

Co-Cultural Practices

In the early stages of research that led to the emergence of a co-cultural communication model (Orbe, 1996), the focus was on specific practices that co-cultural groups used during their interactions with dominant group members. Table 8.1 provides a brief description of each co-cultural communicative practice identified. The initial purpose for identifying and explicating these practices was not necessarily to advance a definitive collection of mutually exclusive communication

behaviors. The design, instead, was to give voice to various ways in which co-cultural group members negotiated larger dominant structures (Orbe, 1998b). Consequently, the identification of specific practices—and ongoing research concerning these communication behaviors—generated additional insight into how co-cultural group status is constantly reinforced, augmented, and/or challenged through everyday discursive interaction (Herring, Johnson, & DiBenedetto, 1995).

Co-Cultural Factors

Once an inventory of co-cultural communicative practices was established, the focal point of scholarly inquiry shifted to the ways in which persons came to select certain practices over others. Central to co-cultural theory is the explication of six interrelated factors that influence the process by which underrepresented group members communicate within dominant societal structures. Each of these is described within this section.

Preferred Outcome. One of the fundamental factors that influences the practices that co-cultural group members use is the preferred outcome for their interaction. Each person asks herself or himself the following question: "What communication behavior will lead to the effect that I desire?" To this end, co-cultural group members typically, consciously or unconsciously, consider how their communication behaviors affect their ultimate relationship with dominant group members. Three primary interactional outcomes exist for underrepresented group members: assimilation, accommodation, and separation.

Assimilation involves attempts to eliminate cultural differences, including the loss of any distinctive characteristics, in order to fit in with dominant society. The reasoning behind assimilation is simple: In order to participate effectively in dominant society, you must conform to dominant society. The

Table 8.1   Practices and Orientations Summary*

Examples of Practices	Brief Description
	Nonassertive Assimilation
Emphasizing commonalities	Focusing on human similarities while downplaying or ignoring co-cultural differences
Developing positive face	Assuming a gracious communicator stance where one is more considerate, polite, and attentive to dominant group members
Censoring self	Remaining silent when comments from dominant group members are inappropriate, indirectly insulting, or highly offensive
Averting controversy	Averting communication away from controversial or potentially dangerous subject areas
	Assertive Assimilation
Extensive preparation	Engaging in an extensive amount of detailed (mental/concrete) groundwork prior to interactions with dominant group members
Overcompensating	Conscious attempts—consistently enacted in response to a pervasive fear of discrimination—to become a "superstar"
Manipulating stereotypes	Conforming to commonly accepted beliefs about group members as a strategic means to exploit them for personal gain
Bargaining	Striking a covert or overt arrangement with dominant group members where both parties agree to ignore co-cultural differences
	Aggressive Assimilation
Dissociating	Making a concerted effort to elude any connection with behaviors typically associated with one's co-cultural group
Mirroring	Adopting dominant group codes in attempt to make one's co-cultural identity more (or totally) invisible
Strategic distancing	Avoiding any association with other co-cultural group members in attempts to be perceived as a distinct individual
Ridiculing self	Invoking or participating in discourse, either passively or actively, that is demeaning to co-cultural group members
	Nonassertive Accommodation
Increasing visibility	Covertly, yet strategically, maintaining a co-cultural presence within dominant structures
Dispelling stereotypes	Myths of generalized group characteristics and behaviors are countered through the process of just being one's self

Examples of Practices	Brief Description
	Assertive Accommodation
Communicating self	Interacting with dominant group members in an authentic, open, and genuine manner; used by those with strong self-concepts
Intragroup networking	Identifying and working with other co-cultural group members who share common philosophies, convictions, goals
Utilizing liaisons	Identifying specific dominant group members who can be trusted for support, guidance, and assistance
Educating others	Taking the role of teacher in co-cultural interactions; enlightening dominant group members of co-cultural norms, values, etc.
	Aggressive Accommodation
Confronting	Using the necessary aggressive methods, including ones that seemingly violate the "rights" of others, to assert one's voice
Gaining advantage	Inserting references to co-cultural oppression as a means to provoke dominant group reactions and gain advantage
	Nonassertive Separation
Avoiding	Maintaining a distance from dominant group members; refraining from activities and/or locations where interaction is likely
Maintaining barriers	Imposing, through the use of verbal and nonverbal cues, a psychological distance from dominant group members
	Assertive Separation
Exemplifying strength	Promoting the recognition of co-cultural group strengths, past accomplishments, and contributions to society
Embracing stereotypes	Applying a negotiated reading to dominant group perceptions and merging them into a positive co-cultural self-concept
	Aggressive Separation
Attacking	Inflicting psychological pain through personal attacks on dominant group members' self-concept
Sabotaging others	Undermining the ability of dominant group members to take full advantage of their privilege inherent in dominant structures

*Note: These communicative practices are examples of tactics enacted to promote each orientation. It is important to recognize that, depending on the other personal, interpersonal, or organizational factors, one tactic (e.g., communicating self) can be used innovatively to promote more than one communication orientation.

*SOURCE: Orbe, 1998c.

preferred outcome of accommodation, in comparison, believes that communication is most effective when individuals can retain some of their cultural uniqueness. Consequently, the goal of accommodation is to transform existing dominant structures so that a "cultural pluralism without hierarchy" (Asante, 1991, p. 271) exists. Separation provides a third alternative for co-cultural group members. Those embracing this stance reject the notion of forming a common bond with dominant group members. Instead, the goal of separation is to join other co-cultural group members and create social communities and organizations that are reflective of their own values, mores, and norms.

Field of Experience. Field of experience, as a factor in the co-cultural communication process, refers to the sum of an individual's lived experiences. The influence of one's past experiences is an important consideration in the constant, cyclical process of contemplating, choosing, and evaluating co-cultural communication practices. Through a lifelong series of experiences, co-cultural group members learn how to enact a variety of practices, and also come to realize the consequences for using certain tactics in different situations. Within an individual's field of experience, each co-cultural group member is engaged in a dynamic process of constructing, and subsequently deconstructing, the perceptions of what constitutes appropriate and effective communication with dominant group members.

Abilities. One factor that must be acknowledged in the co-cultural communication process is the person's relative ability to enact different practices. Most practices described in Table 8.1, given some thoughtfulness, rehearsal, and motivation, appear to be accessible to all co-cultural group members. However, the ability to use some practices may vary greatly depending on the individual characteristics and situational circumstances.

For example, some individuals may not have the natural ability to engage in verbal abuse, personal attacks, or confrontational tactics. Others might lack any reasonable opportunity to network with other co-cultural group members or have difficulty in identifying dominant group members who can be utilized as liaisons. Consequently, the assumption that all co-cultural group members have equal abilities to enact each practice cannot be made.

Situational Context. The issue of situational context is also central to co-cultural communication. Co-cultural group members do not typically select one practice, or cluster of practices, to use for all interactions with dominant group members (Orbe, 1998b). Instead, the specifics of the situational context—where the interaction occurs, who is present, and the particular circumstances that facilitate the interaction—help to inform the selection of particular co-cultural practices. In this regard, co-cultural group members may adopt different practices within one general setting (e.g., work), depending on the particular set of circumstances.

Perceived Costs and Rewards. Over time, co-cultural group members come to recognize that certain costs and rewards are associated with different communication practices. Within this context, it is important to recognize that each communicative behavior has some potential advantages and disadvantages associated with it, albeit sometimes difficult to calculate. These potential advantages and disadvantages, however, are not perceived as the same for all co-cultural group members. Instead, perceptions of the costs and rewards associated with each co-cultural practice—as well as the satisfaction from each strategic decision—depend largely on the field of experiences of individual co-cultural group members. For example, the same outcome (e.g., social approval) may be regarded as positive or negative, contingent on the individual's preferred outcome.

Communication Approach. The final factor that emerged as influential in the process of co-cultural practice selection is communication approach. In one regard, communication approaches can be described as nonassertive, assertive, or aggressive (Wilson, Hantz, & Hanna, 1995). From the perspective of co-cultural group members, nonassertive behavior would include actions in which individuals are inhibited and nonconfrontational while putting the needs of others before their own. Aggressive communicative behaviors would describe actions more hurtfully expressive, self-promoting, and controlling (putting self needs before the needs of others). Representing a balance between the extremes of nonassertiveness and aggressiveness, assertive behaviors encompass self-enhancing, expressive communication that takes into account the needs of both self and others.

As illustrated through the brief descriptions provided here, these six co-cultural factors are inherently interdependent and, taken collectively, represent points of contention for co-cultural strategic decisions. Whereas co-cultural group members engage in processes at varying levels of consciousness, the ways in which these influential factors affect co-cultural communication also varies. This notwithstanding, these factors help articulate the basic idea behind co-cultural theory:

> Situated within a particular *field of experience* that governs their perceptions of the *costs and rewards* associated with, as well as their *capability* to engage in, various communicative practices, co-cultural group members will adopt certain communication orientations—based on their *preferred outcomes* and *communication approaches*—to fit the circumstances of a specific *situation*. (Orbe, 1998b, p. 19)

Co-Cultural Orientations

The description of co-cultural communication shared above contains the term *communication orientation,* a concept referring to specific stances that underrepresented group members assume during their everyday interactions. Each communication orientation is situated primarily within a specific preferred outcome (assimilation, accommodation, or separation) and communication approach (nonassertive, assertive, or aggressive), but is also directly influenced by the four remaining factors (field of experience, perceived costs and rewards, capability, and situational context). In this regard, co-cultural group members may assume one or more orientations during their everyday interactions with others. Table 8.2 depicts nine different co-cultural orientations, each of which is briefly described in this section.

Nonassertive Assimilation. When co-cultural group members use a nonassertive approach in communicating with dominant group members, three basic options exist, depending on their preferred outcome. One is that of adopting a nonassertive assimilation orientation. As illustrated in the upper right-hand cell in Table 8.2, a nonassertive assimilation stance typically embraces co-cultural communicative practices like emphasizing commonalties and censoring self as a means to blend into the dominant society. These efforts are enacted in a seemingly, yet sometimes strategically, inhibited manner.

Assertive Assimilation. Similar to their nonassertive counterparts, persons adopting an assertive assimilation orientation strive to downplay co-cultural differences and try to become absorbed into the dominant society. Instead of doing so in presumably passive stance, however, this co-cultural orientation adopts a more assertive communication approach. Through such practices as bargaining, overcompensating, and extensive preparation (see middle right cell in Table 8.2), co-cultural group members attempt to fit into dominant structures by highlighting the quality of their contributions as individuals.

Table 8.2   Co-Cultural Orientations

		Preferred Outcome		
		Separation	*Accommodation*	*Assimilation*
	Nonassertive	Nonassertive Separation Orientation	Nonassertive Accommodation Orientation	Nonassertive Assimilation Orientation
Communication Approach	*Assertive*	Assertive Separation Orientation	Assertive Accommodation Orientation	Assertive Assimilation Orientation
	Aggressive	Aggressive Separation Orientation	Aggressive Accommodation Orientation	Aggressive Assimilation Orientation

Aggressive Assimilation. An aggressive assimilation orientation to co-cultural communication takes a determined, sometimes belligerent, approach to efforts at being seen as one of the dominant group. Using such practices as mirroring or strategic distancing (lower right cell in Table 8.2), co-cultural group members who use this primary orientation place great importance on fitting in—to the extent that other's rights and beliefs are viewed as less important in comparison. The practice of self-ridicule illustrates the magnitude to which some co-cultural group members will go in order to be perceived as like dominant group members.

Nonassertive Accommodation. Individuals who adopt a nonassertive accommodation

orientation to co-cultural communication attempt to invoke change through a seemingly constrained and nonconfrontational manner. As displayed in Table 8.2 (upper middle cell), this co-cultural orientation includes such practices as increasing visibility and dispelling stereotypes. Although some instances of these strategic efforts may be considered more assertive than nonassertive, most co-cultural group members describe using the practices as a delicate means to influence dominant group members so that they will not react with defensiveness or caution.

Assertive Accommodation. While a nonassertive accommodation orientation privileges the needs of dominant group members, an assertive accommodation co-cultural orientation creates a balance between self and others' needs in attempts to transform societal structures. Several different co-cultural practices appear to seek accommodation through an assertive voice (center box in Table 8.2). Through such tactics as communicating self and educating others, co-cultural group members are able to work with others—both co-cultural group and dominant group members—in order to change existing dominant structures.

Aggressive Accommodation. The focus for those persons adopting an aggressive accommodation orientation is to become part of dominant structures and then work from within to promote change. At times, their efforts may be perceived as self-promoting or pushy; however, co-cultural group members who use this primary communication orientation are not overly concerned with dominant group perceptions. Using confrontational tactics and power moves to gain advantage (see lower middle cell in Table 8.2) are two co-cultural practices associated with this orientation. While these practices are perceived by co-cultural group members as aggressive, they also reflect a genuine desire to work with, and not necessarily against, dominant group members.

Nonassertive Separation. For some co-cultural group members, separation from others who are different is a naturally occurring reality. Still others use subtle communicative practices to maintain a separation orientation during co-cultural group interactions. As illustrated in the upper left-hand cell in Table 8.2, co-cultural communicative practices like avoiding and maintaining interpersonal barriers can be used to facilitate co-cultural separation. For those who use this primary orientation, physical avoidance is implemented whenever possible. However, when some interaction with dominant group members is unavoidable, co-cultural group members find themselves subtly enacting certain behaviors that create psychological distance between the two groups.

Assertive Separation. Whereas a nonassertive separation approach can reflect an inherent inclination, an assertive separation orientation is a more conscious choice. As such, individuals adopting an assertive separation orientation are more self-assured in their attempts to create co-cultural structures exclusive of dominant group members. Practices that can effectively establish an assertive separation orientation include exemplifying strengths and embracing stereotypes (see left middle cell, Table 8.2). From the standpoint of co-cultural group members, other practices such as communicating self and intragroup networking appear useful for both assertive separation and assertive accommodation orientations. The consequences of these co-cultural practices, in relation to the achievement of a particular outcome, are contingent on other influential factors like situational context.

Aggressive Separation. An aggressive separation orientation is a primary communication orientation when co-cultural segregation is a top urgency. As depicted in the lower left cell in Table 8.2, this particular orientation seeks to exert personal power through the use of co-cultural communicative practices like verbal attacking and sabotaging dominant group efforts. While the levels of co-cultural personal power do not match the societal power bases of dominant group members, they do enable some individuals to confront the pervasiveness of dominant structures on a smaller level.

EXISTING WORK ON CO-CULTURAL THEORY

Since the initial publications describing co-cultural theory, scholars across the world have adopted it as a framework for a variety of research projects. Much of this research has advanced co-cultural theoretical applications in areas where the theory was originally situated. For instance, one of the earliest articles on co-cultural theory focused on its applicability to understanding how underrepresented group members functioned as outsiders within organizations (Orbe, 1998b). Drawing from this article, several organizational scholars have utilized co-cultural theory in their research. Buzzanell's (1999) research on nondominant perspectives to employment interviews is a good case in point. She adopts a co-cultural approach to this phenomenon and then utilizes the "communication processes aligned with nondominant membership" (p. 149) to help shape both theorists' and practitioners' understanding.

While Buzzanell's (1999) research uses co-cultural theory to speak to the organizational experiences of underrepresented groups generally, other researchers have focused specifically on people of color. These have included research on African Americans generally (Phillips-Gott, 1999), African American women specifically (Orbe, 1999; Parker, 2003), as well as both African Americans and Latino/as (Greer-Williams, 2000) and multiracial persons (Heuman, 2001). In addition, Spellers et al. (2003) conducted a co-cultural analysis of how black professional women negotiate their aesthetic representations in dominant culture organizations. Specifically, the authors utilized co-cultural theory (Orbe 1998a, 1998b) as a framework to understand the ways in which black women enact particular co-cultural practices (see Orbe, 1998a, pp. 14–16) representing a particular communication orientation in terms of their hair/bodies/clothing. The authors explored the following research question: *What co-cultural practices did black women enact when negotiating the body politics of corporate America?* Individual interviews and focus group interviews were conducted with 15 women of African descent employed at various levels in different organizations. Three communication orientations were discussed as strategies black women adopted while negotiating their aesthetic images in their particular workplaces:

nonassertive assimilation—even though casual dress attire is permitted in the organization, black women often purposely dress more formally in order to avoid reinforcing certain negative stereotypes about blacks; assertive accommodation—black women often find themselves educating others in the organization about the black body in general and, more specifically in their everyday organizational life, address a barrage of questions about their hairstyles, particularly when the hair is worn in a natural state such as locks; and, assertive assimilation—in order to reduce the potential of material consequences, black women often attempt to downplay aesthetic differences between dominant and subordinate groups by changing their hair or attire to blend in with the dominant culture. Overall, findings suggest that in the context of dominant culture organizations, there is a common theme. Women of African descent construct their aesthetic representations in the midst of a dominant gaze (Spellers, 2000; Spellers et al., 2003). Here, co-cultural theory provided a productive framework for studying how underrepresented groups navigate organizational settings where they are traditionally positioned as "outsiders within."

Alone or combined with other perspectives, co-cultural theory appears a useful tool to explore issues of assimilation, access to opportunity, and advancement for people of color in organizations. In her study of how African American women and men interact with others in organizations, Gates (2003), for example, utilized feminist standpoint theory (Allen, 2000; Bullis, 1993) and co-cultural theory (Orbe, 1998a, 1998b) to argue that African Americans and other co-cultural groups oftentimes are oppressed in their organizations as a result of their race, gender, class, and the like. Her study examined how co-cultural groups address these challenging interactions, which ultimately affect how they learn the ropes in an organization and become socialized. Findings suggested that in organizational interactions between African Americans and other organizational members, power shifts depending on one's race, gender, class, age, and position. Here, both African American men and women sought creative communication tactics to cope with and to resist their oppression, including (1) checking yourself, (2) isolation, (3) speaking out, (4) remaining silent, (5) journaling, (6) intimidation, and (7) using flattery. As Gates (2003) notes, several of these tactics appear closely aligned with existing co-cultural practices (e.g., checking yourself and censoring self, remaining silent and averting controversy, and using flattery and developing positive face). Still others, like journaling, may point to other communicative co-cultural practices not included in existing co-cultural theory literature. Additional analyses are needed to clarify co-cultural practices, and we agree with Gates (2003), who challenges scholars to look more closely at how co-cultural communication processes influence organizational socialization as well as other areas of organizational life.

Recently, scholars have also drawn from co-cultural theory to explore lived experiences of underrepresented group members outside of an organizational context. This has included research on people with disabilities (Fox, Giles, Orbe, & Bourhis, 2000; Orbe & Greer, 2000), native Hawaiians (Miura, 2001), as well as Israeli women (First & Lev-Aladgem, 2000), Israeli gay men (Kama, 2002), and the homeless (Harter, Edwards, McClanahan, Hopson, & Carson-Stern, 2003). Interestingly, not all of the "texts" of these studies have been transcripts of interviews, focus groups, or other public meetings. Some have used co-cultural theory to analyze editorial cartoons (Sewell, 1999), community theater (First & Lev-Aladgem, 2000), and homeless street journals (Harter et al., 2003). For instance, First and Lev-Aladgem describe how actors may use community theater as a site for expressing the politics of identity for co-cultural group members:

The Israeli "community theater" endures from its early days and on, a complicated "politics of identity" that operates in a constant conflict between its external, given identity and its internal, created self-identity. The actors always identify the "community theater" as a representative devise of their co-culture; a platform to exhibit their particular, oppositional expression to the dominant culture. (p. 5)

The fundamental ideas of co-cultural theory are being used as a foundation to explore relationships of culture, power, and communication in contexts that extend the initial point of focus. In no uncertain terms, these additions/extensions affirm the heuristic value of the theory. Recently, we learned that one scholar from Israel has translated the term co-culture into Hebrew (*Bo-tarbut*), which has helped others to embrace its implications for research and practice (personal communication, Amit Kama, 2000). Making the concepts of co-cultural theory accessible to practitioners has been an important development; consequently, it is the focus of our next section.

CO-CULTURAL THEORY INTO MEANINGFUL PRACTICE

Although not the focus of this chapter, we would be remiss if we did not mention the practical value of co-cultural theory in various contextual settings. Dixon (2001) insightfully recognizes that a co-cultural perspective assists in obtaining a greater "knowledge of others." In this regard, it can serve as an important avenue for greater understanding. Like Heuman (2001), we have had great success in using co-cultural theory to facilitate an understanding of the centrality and connectedness of racism, sexism, classism, heterosexism, and ableism for our students. Likewise, DeCarlo (2000-2001) has found practical value in a co-cultural perspective to group counseling of inner-city youth. In particular, he utilized a co-cultural orientation to offer therapists a practical and culturally empowering tool, "rap therapy," to working with urban adolescents. In addition, scholars (e.g., Orbe, 1997) have begun to utilize the theory in various diversity facilitations in corporations and institutions of higher learning with great success.

One project in particular represents an outstanding example of engaged scholarship (Applegate, 2001) whereby communication theory—in this case co-cultural theory—research, and practice meet to address an important social issue. The primary objective of the Civil Rights Health (CRH) Project was "to create and promote the use of a meaningful, non-judgmental, community-based assessment model that will allow individual communities to systematically discern the state of civil rights health in their respective communities" (Orbe, 2003, p. 2). Over a 2-year period (September 2000–December 2002), this project involved a university research team working with four different community-based committees composed of city officials; community activists; and leaders from the corporate, education, financial, and social services sectors. The objective was to organize community-based discussions and focus groups in order to evaluate and determine the current civil rights health of specific communities in Michigan with the goal of informing strategic planning on civil rights initiatives.

Co-cultural theory played a critical role in helping CRH project organizers maximize the ways in which community members discussed their experiences with civil rights issues (Orbe, 2003). Specifically, it provided organizers with a key theoretical foundation to acknowledge the ways in which traditional structures marginalized the voices of certain community members. For example, as a framework that encourages recognition of the Other, co-cultural theory assisted organizers and participants alike in understanding the direct and indirect means by which a person's field of experience influenced how he or she communicated about civil rights issues and, in the most ideal scenario, the particular costs and rewards that informed said comments.

Co-cultural theory also provided guidance in how the CRH project was structured (Orbe, 2003). The CRH steering committee, for example, recognized that having discussions within familiar community locations (community centers, churches, etc.) and taking into consideration other logistical decisions—such as time, who was invited, availability of daycare, whether or not the location was accessible to persons with disabilities, and so on—was vital to maximizing participation and contribution of underrepresented group members.

Further, co-cultural theory also provided the CRH project facilitators with important concepts to better understand certain dynamics that took place during attempts at civil rights dialogue (Orbe, 2003). For instance, the CRH project brought together people from diverse backgrounds, perceptions, concerns, and experiences with civil rights issues. Through the application of co-cultural theory many CRH project planners could come to recognize the fact that individuals would also bring to the discussion different preferred outcomes. By using a co-cultural theoretical framework, facilitators were not only able to acknowledge each preferred outcome, but they were also able to develop practices to engage participants in valuing each others' desired results.

Another theoretical concept that provided an important foundation to the CRH project was the co-cultural factor of communication approach. As noted earlier in this chapter, three primary communication approaches are used in co-cultural communication: aggressive, nonassertive, and assertive. Sometimes the diversity of communication approaches within the public forums and focus group discussions organized by the CRH project created potentially difficult dialogues. Through the use of co-cultural theory, CRH project planners and facilitators came to recognize that in order to address the problem of civil rights health in the community effectively, diverse communication approaches must be valued. As can be seen in the brief description provided here, co-cultural theory offers important concepts, structures, and models for practical, applied projects.

CURRENT AND FUTURE RESEARCH AND THEORIZING

As described earlier, co-cultural theory is highly interdisciplinary in that it combines work from a number of disciplines. Its most direct influences are rooted in feminist sociology (muted group theory and standpoint theories) and philosophy (phenomenology). Current work, as well as that which we anticipate in the near future, continues in this eclectic approach to exploring the lived experiences of underrepresented group members. In this section, we outline four specific areas that focus on developments in co-cultural research and theorizing.

Clarifying Co-Cultural Practices

As outlined earlier, co-cultural theory has been researched in a variety of contexts. One of the results of many of these applications is the emergence of additional co-cultural practices. In Orbe (1998a), 26 practices, which were affiliated across nine different co-cultural communication orientations, were described. However, this initial list was never meant to be exclusive. The expectation was that future research on co-cultural communication would do two things. First, additional practices would be identified through subsequent research on various co-cultural groups. Second, those practices already identified would be clarified, extended, and possibly altered to best capture the lived experiences of underrepresented group members. Earlier, we described how the work of Gates (2003) fulfilled these expectations.

While the potential for extending the ways in which we understand the complexities of

how these co-cultural practices are negotiated can be seen within all co-cultural studies, research by Miura (2001) probably serves as another strong example of specific contributions in this area. His research examined what he termed "the defiant discourse" (p. 4) of the Native Hawaiian people during reconciliation hearings with representatives of the federal government in 1999. His analysis revealed a renewed sense of ethnic pride among Native Hawaiians, one that was reflected clearly in their comments during these public hearings. Specifically, Miura discusses several examples of communication practices that are not explicitly discussed by Orbe (1998a), including the negotiation of labels and identity (see also Dixon, 2001), as well as a refusal to negotiate with those not in positions to change policy.

Over the years, anonymous reviewers of manuscripts that covered the basics of co-cultural theory would occasionally ask, "What about the dominant group members' communication?" These comments were grounded—and rightly so—in the transactional perspective of communication that assumes that co-cultural group communication is best understood alongside dominant group communication. Because the initial work on co-cultural communication explicitly sought insight into the communication of underrepresented group members from their own cultural standpoints, such an inclusion did not seem appropriate at the time. Now, however, dominant group communication—especially that which is perceived as a response to co-cultural communication practices—appears a fruitful area of exploration. In fact, Miura's (2001) analysis reveals some interesting insight into some of the ways that dominant group members respond to aggressive accommodation and aggressive separation co-cultural orientations. Other scholars have questioned whether or not dominant group members also use co-cultural communication practices. In other words, does co-cultural theory, as Todd-Mancillas

(2000) asks, "extend beyond the intercultural communication domain to encompass important interpersonal communication considerations" (p. 476)? Future research in these particular areas has great promise for advancing our understanding of communicative interactions where culture and power differences have great saliency.

Co-Cultural Correlations

The initial work that ultimately became the foundation of co-cultural theory was completed to help fill a gap in intercultural communication (Dixon, 2001), namely research that featured unheard voices and honored the experiential as much as the experimental (Houston Stanback, 1989). Despite efforts to situate co-cultural theory and research as a much-needed *complement* to existing [largely] social scientific research, some scholars such as Todd-Mancillas (2000) take issue with what they perceive as "cavalier and inaccurate criticisms made of conventional social scientific methods" (p. 477). The intent of co-cultural theory has never been to criticize traditional empirical research and position more critical/interpretative research as "superior." Research completed through different epistemological paradigms contributes different types of insights into communication phenomena. In previous articles, we have tried to articulate the need for our discipline to value more experientially based scholarship in research related to culture and communication (Orbe, 2000; Spellers, 2000). Critical interpretative research alone, however, is also not adequate. Clearly, we need multiple methodological perspectives. This idea is eloquently articulated by Dixon (2001), who calls specifically for critical perspectives to research that "provide alternate— not substitute—paths" (p. 9) to co-cultural understanding.

In this vein, Lapinski and Orbe (2002) have worked to create a series of co-cultural measurement tools. Specifically, they sought to develop instruments that allow researchers to assess—via self-report questionnaires—primary co-cultural communication orientations as well as their use of different co-cultural practices. Within this work, an initial pool of items was developed based on the definitions of co-cultural concepts and reexamination of initial phenomenological studies. Survey data were then subjected to confirmatory factor analysis in order to ascertain whether or not the data were consistent with the a priori specified measurement models. The analysis provided preliminary evidence for the construct validity of the Co-Cultural Theory Scales (C-CTS). In particular, the initial tests of initial consistency and parallelism used by Lapinski and Orbe (2002) indicated that empirical data were consistent with the three unidimensional factors measuring communication approach and the three unidimensional factors measuring preferred outcomes. In this regard, preliminary evidence exists in terms of the construct validity and reliability for the factors directly influencing co-cultural communication orientations.

C-CTS are invaluable for efforts that seek to understand the differences and similarities of co-cultural communication among and within various co-cultural groups. For instance, Lapinski and Orbe (2002) anticipate using the tools to explore the effects of co-cultural visibility (e.g., a person of color or a woman vs. someone gay or lesbian or with a hidden disability) on communicative practices. Being able to quantify co-cultural lived experiences successfully has a number of inherent difficulties, especially in regard to the ability to quantify the centrality of the situational context and the varying degrees of saliency in co-cultural communication. However, the benefits of creating an effective measurement tool are clear and abundant.

Even within the basic level, a series of co-cultural measurements will allow some clarification of the initial framework. For instance, research in this area will provide insight into the correlations between particular co-cultural practices and specific communication orientations. It will also help clarify existing assumptions, including the belief that some practices (e.g., intragroup networking) can be used as part of more than one communication orientation. As scholars, we share concerns with other scholars (Gonzalez, Houston, & Chen, 2000) who criticize social scientific research as producing a "universal iconography" of racial/ethnic groups (see also, Orbe, 1995, 2000). Consequently, this line of research has been approached with some caution. Yet, such efforts are simultaneously engaged with a certain degree of enthusiasm in that they represent an ideal form of triangulation, one that vividly illustrates how interpretative and social scientific research can work to directly inform one another.

Theoretical Connections/Intersections

Several scholars, like Greer-Williams (2000), Gates (2003), and Heuman (2001), have used phenomenological inquiry as the methodology of choice for their co-cultural research. The fit between this methodology and co-cultural theory is "natural" and productive, largely because phenomenology represents the tool that was used to construct co-cultural theory. Yet other scholars have revealed additional theoretical connections and intersections that provide the most productive sets of lenses for the phenomenon that is the focus of their research.

In the final chapter of *Constructing Co-Cultural Theory,* Orbe (1998a) highlights a couple of different theoretical frameworks that might serve as valuable partners with co-cultural research. These include rhetorical sensitivity (Hart & Burks, 1972; Hart, Carlson, & Eadie, 1980) and communication accommodation theory (Giles, Mulac, Bradac, & Johnson, 1987). To date, no research has used these theoretical approaches in tandem with co-cultural theory. Interestingly, however,

several scholars have created their own unique theoretical connections. For instance, Harter et al. (2003) used Fisher's narrative paradigm and co-cultural theory to explore the lived experiences of homeless people via street journals. Given their topic and focus, such a theoretical union appears especially productive. Miura (2001) recognized the parallels between Deetz's (1992) view of a corporate mentality and what Native Hawaiians face in dealing with the U.S. government. His use of Deetz's work on democracy and the politics of everyday life, in tandem with co-cultural theory, is fascinating. Finally, Kama (2002) takes a multitheoretical approach in his study of Israeli gay men and media consumption, drawing from co-cultural theory, cultural studies, symbolic interactionism, and queer studies.

In reflection, co-cultural theory was birthed out of triangulated theory (muted group theory, standpoint theory, phenomenology); therefore it makes sense that it would also facilitate additional theoretical intersections. As articulated by Dixon (2001), theoretical connections can be made with more established *and* emerging theories: "The expanded vision of researchers should incorporate theories and methods successfully used in the past while embracing new theories that answer questions and interpret data in enlightening ways" (p. 9).

Complications of Co-Cultural Identity

Co-cultural communication is traditionally used to describe the interactions among the diverse collections of persons who call the United States "home" (Orbe, 1998a, p. 30). According to Dixon (2001), this area of research assists in centralizing the communicative life experiences of those groups underrepresented in communication research and theory. An area of study that focuses on interactions between "dominant" and "co-cultural" groups appears easily defined; however, as the complexities of identity become more visible, the task of defining co-cultural communication becomes more complex. Therefore, efforts to explore the complications that come with co-cultural identities appear as a "natural" development as the theory emerges. As Duster (1993) reminds us, "the closer one is to the phenomenon, the more likely one is to see internal differences" (p. 238).

The question here centers on the saliency of cultural markers within the interaction, as defined through multiple perspectives (self and other). Co-cultural communication can be differentiated from interpersonal communication in that one person perceives an aspect of his or her identity to be salient within an interaction. What is the usefulness of co-cultural theory, then, when both persons perceive themselves to be at a social disadvantage in the same interaction? Such could certainly be the case during a conversation between an African American man and a European American woman, where one feels that race is the most salient marker of the interaction but the other perceives gender to be the defining factor. To date, co-cultural theory has not been used to explore the complexities of this phenomenon or how saliency might shift before, during, and after specific episodes. The potential to shed light into the "deep structures" (Pennington, 1979) of this intriguing area of communication is unlimited.

Recent work on culturally diverse groups of first-generation college (FGC) students helps to gain insight into the complex ways that co-cultural identities are negotiated (Orbe & Groscurth, in press). Three specific research questions guided this project: (a) How do FGC students describe their experiences during their undergraduate years?; (b) What co-cultural strategies do they enact at home and on campus?; and (c) What similarities and differences exist among the experiences of FGC students related to other facets of their identities (e.g., age, race/ethnicity, gender, socioeconomic status, and type of institution)? This project utilized co-cultural theory to explore how

students navigate the "alien culture" (Chaffee, 1992) of academia without the experiential support of their families, and the context of home once their status as a college student positioned them, in some regard, as the Other. In terms of the issue raised earlier, the third research question facilitates significant insight into the varying levels of saliency that different cultural markers play in different contexts. Analyses of focus group transcripts revealed that FGC student status is a central identity marker for some, but largely a nonissue for others. Much of it depends on context (e.g., being at a community college vs. a selective university) as well as other cultural markers (e.g., nontraditional student or student of color). This research project, as others like it (e.g., Jeffries, 2003), holds significant promise for advancing research that increases our understanding of the dynamic nature of co-cultural identities.

As discussed earlier, the genesis of co-cultural theory is in the lived experiences of underrepresented group members. Consequently, the theoretical framework that emerged from this line of research provided understanding in terms of how specific (micro) practices were chosen and used by co-cultural group members. Additional work is still needed to obtain a fuller (macro) understanding of the deep structures that inform co-cultural communication. Hopson (2002), whose work focused on the communicative experiences of African American men in dominant societal organizations, took an important step toward an advanced level of understanding. His current research works to identify dialectical tensions specific to the African American male experience in organizations; in doing so, he will also work to reveal how these tensions are negotiated via specific co-cultural practices. For instance, one tension seems to be between "playing the part" and "being true to yourself" (Hopson, 2002). Understanding how these larger dialectical tensions inform how African Americans approach co-cultural communication and choose specific practices is an important step in advancing the development of co-cultural theory. As demonstrated by Hopson (2002), utilizing existing theoretical frameworks, such as dialectical theory, assists in addressing the complications of co-cultural identity negotiation across contexts.

CONCLUSION

In its infancy, co-cultural theory represented a framework that emerged out of the communicative experiences of underrepresented group members. Within the past decade, scholars have utilized, extended, and critiqued co-cultural theory in ways that extend the initial scope of the theory. Without question, scholars are applying co-cultural theory to areas of research that seem to "fit" with the mission of the theory, but that were not initially anticipated.

Reviewing the various applications and extensions of co-cultural theory has prompted one conclusion: Any real advancement of theory occurs not through the work of the original contributor but through the research, scholarship, and theorizing of others. This may or may not be true for all theories. The growth that co-cultural theory is experiencing, however, is very much the product of other scholars—whether working independently or with the theory originator—via various collaborative efforts. In this regard, we have one challenge for each scholar who finds valuable linkages with co-cultural theory: Go beyond simple theoretical applications and answer the ever-so-valuable "So What?" question. Think creatively, critically, and experientially to determine how your research extends, critiques, or refutes existing research on co-cultural theory. The true test of the value of a theory is, in part, its longevity. Co-cultural theory—and its utility for understanding relationships among culture, power, and communication—can stand the test of time only if scholars and practitioners continue to extend beyond the theory's original intent and purpose.

REFERENCES

Allen, B. J. (2000). "Learning the ropes": A black feminist standpoint analysis. In P. Buzzanell (Ed.), *Rethinking organizational and managerial communication from feminist perspectives* (pp. 177–208). Thousand Oaks, CA: Sage.

Applegate, J. L. (2001, September). Engaged graduate education: Skating to where the puck will be. *Spectra*, pp. 2–5.

Asante, M. K. (1991). The Afrocentric idea in education. *Journal of Negro Education, 60*(2), 170–180.

Bullis, C. (1993). Organizational socialization research: Enabling, constraining, and shifting perspectives. *Communication Monographs, 60*, 10–17.

Buzzanell, P. M. (1999). Tensions and burdens in employment interviewing processes: Perspectives of non-dominant group members. *Journal of Business Communication, 36*(2), 143–162.

Chaffee, J. (1992). Transforming educational dreams into education reality. In L. S. Zwerling & H. B. London (Eds.), *First-generation students: Confronting the cultural issues* (pp. 81–88). San Francisco: Jossey-Bass.

DeCarlo, A. (2000–2001). Rap therapy?: An innovative approach to groupwork with urban adolescents. *Journal of Intergroup Relations, 27*, 40–48.

Deetz, S. (1992). *Democracy in an age of corporate colonization: Developments in communication and the politics of everyday life.* Albany: State University of New York Press.

Dixon, L. D. (2001, April). *Naming issues in the future of intercultural communication research: The contributions of Mark Orbe's co-cultural theory.* Paper presented at the annual meeting of the Central States Communication Association, Cincinnati, OH.

Duster, T. (1993). The diversity of California at Berkeley: An emerging reformulation of "competence" in an increasingly multicultural world. In B. W. Thompson & S. Tyagi (Eds.), *Beyond a dream deferred: Multicultural education and the politics of excellence* (pp. 231–255). Minneapolis: University of Minnesota Press.

First, A., & Lev-Aladgem, S. (2000). *An Israeli community theater as a site of feminine self-image reconstruction.* Paper presented at the annual meeting of the International Communication Association, Acapulco, Mexico.

Ford-Ahmed, T., & Orbe, M. (1992, November). *African American graduate students, their majority host institution and ethnic prejudice: A bright side?* Paper presented at the annual meeting of the Speech Communication Association, Chicago.

Fox, S., Giles, H., Orbe, M., & Bourhis, R. Y. (2000). Interability communication: Theoretical perspectives. In D. O. Braithwaite & T. L. Thompson (Eds.), *Handbook of communication and people with disabilities: Research and application* (pp. 193–222). Mahwah, NJ: Lawrence Erlbaum.

Gates, D. (2003). Learning to play the game: An exploratory study of how African American women and men interact with others in organizations. *Electronic Journal of Communication, 13*(4/5).

Giles, H., Mulac, A., Bradac, J. J., & Johnson, P. (1987). Speech accommodation theory: The first decade and beyond. In M. L. McLaughlin (Ed.), *Communication yearbook 10* (pp. 13–48). Newbury Park, CA: Sage.

Gonzalez, A., Houston, M., & Chen, V. (Eds.). (2000). *Our voices: Essays in culture, ethnicity, and communication.* Los Angeles: Roxbury.

Greer-Williams, N. (2000, November). *Diversity and organizations: A smooth mixture.* Paper presented at the annual meeting of the National Communication Association, Seattle, WA.

Hart, R. P., & Burks, D. M. (1972). Rhetorical sensitivity and social interaction. *Speech Monographs, 39,* 75–91.

Hart, R. P., Carlson, R. E., & Eadie, W. F. (1980). Attitudes toward communication and the assessment of rhetorical sensitivity. *Communication Monographs, 47,* 1–22.

Harter, L. M., Edwards, A., McClanahan, A., Hopson, M., & Carson-Stern, E. (2003, November). *Exploring street journals from a co-cultural perspective: The case of Street-Wise.* Paper presented at the annual meeting of the National Communication Association, Miami, FL.

Herring, S., Johnson, D. A., & DiBenedetto, T. (1995). "This discussion is going too far!": Male resistance to female participation on the Internet. In K. Hall & M. Bucholtz (Eds.), *Gender articulated: Language and the socially constructed self* (pp. 67–96). New York: Routledge.

Heuman, A. (2001, April). *Multiracial/ethnic identity: A co-cultural approach.* Paper presented at the annual meeting of the Central States Communication Association, Cincinnati, OH.

Hopson, M. C. (2002). *Playing the game: The value of exploring dialectical tensions and identifying co-cultural communication strategies of black males in predominantly white organizational structures.* Unpublished master's thesis, Western Michigan University, Kalamazoo.

Houston Stanback, M. (1989). Feminist theory and black women's talk. *Howard Journal of Communications, 1,* 187–194.

Husserl, E. (1964). *The idea of phenomenology.* The Hague: Martinus Nijhoff.

Jeffries, T. (2003, November). *Intersections of race, identity, and co-cultural practices: A content analysis of a "white black woman."* Paper presented at the annual meeting of the National Communication Association, Miami, FL.

Kama, A. (2002). The quest for inclusion: Jewish-Israeli gay men's perceptions of gays in the media. *Feminist Media Studies, 2*(2), 195–212.

Kramarae, C. (1981). *Women and men speaking.* Rowley, MA: Newbury House.

Lanigan, R. L. (1988). *Phenomenology of communication: Merleau-Ponty's thematics in communicology and semiology.* Pittsburgh, PA: Duquesne University Press.

Lapinski, M., & Orbe, M. (2002, July). *Preliminary evidence for the construct validity and reliability of the Co-Cultural Measurement Scales.* Paper presented at the annual meeting of the International Communication Association, Seoul, Korea.

Miura, S. Y. (2001). New identity, new rhetoric: The Native Hawaiian quest for independence. *Journal of Intergroup Relations, 28*(2), 3–16.

Orbe, M. (1994). "Remember, it's always whites' ball": Descriptions of African American male communication. *Communication Quarterly, 42*(3), 287–200.

Orbe, M. (1995). African American communication research: Toward a deeper understanding of interethnic communication. *Western Journal of Communication, 59*(1), 61–78.

Orbe, M. (1996). Laying the foundation for co-cultural communication theory: An inductive approach to studying non-dominant communication strategies and the factors that influence them. *Communication Studies, 47,* 157–176.

Orbe, M. (1997). A co-cultural communication approach to intergroup relations. *Journal of Intergroup Relations, 24,* 36–49.

Orbe, M. (1998a). *Constructing co-cultural theory: An explication of culture, power, and communication.* Thousand Oaks, CA: Sage.

Orbe, M. (1998b). From the standpoint(s) of traditionally muted groups: Explicating a co-cultural communication theoretical model. *Communication Theory, 8,* 1–26.

Orbe, M. (1998c). An "outsider within" perspective to organizational communication: Explicating the communicative practices of co-cultural group members. *Management Communication Quarterly, 12*(2), 230–279.

Orbe, M. (1999, November). *Negotiating multiple identities in and around organizational margins: A case study in co-cultural theory.* Paper presented at the annual meeting of the National Communication Association, Chicago.

Orbe, M. (2000). Centralizing diverse racial/ethnic voices in scholarly research: The value of phenomenological inquiry. *International Journal of Intercultural Relations, 24,* 603–621.

Orbe, M. (2003, July). *Community networking as engaged scholarship: Practical applications of communication theory and research methodology in the area of civil rights.* Paper presented at the biennial meeting of the World Communication Association, Haninge, Sweden.

Orbe, M., & Greer, C. M. (2000, April). *Recognizing the diversity of lived experience: The utility of co-cultural theory in communication and disabilities research.* Paper presented at the annual meeting of the Central States Communication Association, Detroit, MI.

Orbe, M., & Groscurth, C. R. (in press). A co-cultural theoretical analysis of communicating on campus and at home: Exploring the negotiation strategies of first generation college (FGC) students. *Qualitative Research Reports in Communication, 5.*

Parker, P. (2003). Learning leadership: Communication, resistance, and African American women's executive leadership development. *Electronic Journal of Communication, 13*(4/5).

Pennington, D. L. (1979). Black-white communication: An assessment of research. In M. K. Asante, E. Newmark, & C. A. Blake (Eds.), *Handbook of intercultural communication* (pp. 383–402). Beverly Hills, CA: Sage.

Phillips-Gott, P. C. (1999, November). *African American communication, organizations, and assimilation: A co-cultural perspective.* Paper presented at the annual meeting of the National Communication Association, Chicago.

Roberts, G., & Orbe, M. (1996, May). *"Creating that safe place among faculty": Exploring intergenerational gay male communication.* Paper presented at the annual meeting of the International Communication Association, Chicago.

Sewell, E. H. (1999, November). *Editorial cartooning in the gay press.* Paper presented at the annual meeting of the National Communication Association, Chicago.

Smith, D. E. (1987). *The everyday world as problematic: A feminist sociology of knowledge.* Boston: Northeastern University Press.

Spellers, R. E. (2000). *Cornrows in corporate America: Black female hair/body politics and socialization experiences in dominant culture workplace organizations.* Unpublished doctoral dissertation, Arizona State University.

Spellers, R. E., Sanders, F. L., & Orbe, M. P. (2003, November). *The business of black hair/body politics: A co-cultural analysis of black professional women's aesthetic representations in a contested site of workplace culture.* Paper presented at the annual meeting of the National Communication Association, Miami, FL.

Todd-Mancillas, W. (2000). Constructing co-cultural theory by M. Orbe and Communication and identity across cultures edited by D. V. Tanno and A. Gonzalez [book review]. *Communication Theory, 10*(4), 475–480.

Wilson, G. L., Hantz, A. M., & Hanna, M. S. (1995). *Interpersonal growth through communication.* Dubuque, IA: WCB Brown & Benchmark.

PART V

Theories Focusing on Identity

9

Identity Management Theory

Facework in Intercultural Relationships

TADASU TODD IMAHORI

WILLIAM R. CUPACH

Is there a culture-general definition of intercultural communication competence? Or does it have to be defined differently in each culture (i.e., is it culture-specific)? In 1989, we were invited to present a conference paper that dealt with these questions. We then proposed that intercultural communication competence was both culture-general and culture-specific, and furthermore, culture-synergistic (Cupach & Imahori, 1989). Specifically, we argued that people's ability to behave effectively (i.e., achieve personal goals) and appropriately (i.e., treat others politely) are culturally universal standards for intercultural competence. Different cultures, however, have different expectations regarding which communicative behaviors are considered effective and socially appropriate. Moreover, we maintained that intercultural communication competence is also culture-synergistic because relational partners are able to negotiate their own idiosyncratic ways of behaving competently within their relationship (Imahori & Lanigan, 1989; Spitzberg & Cupach, 1984, 1989) and this relationally negotiated competence reflects a synergy between the individual partners' distinct cultural expectations for competence.

Identity management theory (IMT; Cupach & Imahori, 1993) was then conceptualized based on this relational and culture-synergistic view of competence. It was also heavily influenced by other identity-based theories of intercultural communication, such as identity negotiation theory (Ting-Toomey, 1988, 1993) and, particularly, cultural identity

195

theory (Collier, 1998; Collier & Thomas, 1988). According to Wiseman (2002), IMT is akin to cultural identity theory, and both theories share ontological bases regarding "actors' meanings, interpretations, and the rules governing their behavior" (p. 216).

Similar to others with identity-based theories, we argue that communication competence requires the ability of individuals "*to successfully negotiate mutually acceptable identities in interaction*" (Cupach & Imahori, 1993, p. 118). However, IMT is unique in at least in two different ways. First, we contend that competence entails the effective management of relational as well as cultural identities. Second, we postulate that face is the communicative reflection of people's relational and cultural identities, and thus effective identity management requires competent facework. The inclusion of face and facework in IMT was stimulated by our shared metatheoretical interest in symbolic interactionism, and particularly the work of Goffman (1967).

Since the introduction of IMT, several studies have been conducted to apply the theory in various types of intercultural interactions and to test the validity of its propositions. This chapter begins by sketching the theoretical scope and assumptions of IMT. Next we consider the current status of its theoretical propositions based on recent empirical research. We conclude the chapter by addressing future directions for research and application.

THEORETICAL SCOPE

IMT attempts to explain how cultural identities are negotiated through development of an interpersonal relationship (Cupach & Imahori, 1993). The theory explains competent identity management across the developmental stages of a relationship, ranging from initial acquaintance to a relationship with deep intimacy and commitment. Although the theory pays particular attention to people's cultural identities,

it is not restricted to intercultural relationships because cultural identities are present in all types of relationships—intracultural, intercultural, or interpersonal. The theory limits its application to dyads, and does not address intergroup relations. Regarding culture, IMT's theoretical premises can be applied to various types of cultures, including cultures of nation, ethnicity, region, socioeconomic class, sexuality, presence or absence of disabilities, and so forth. Since the introduction of IMT, it has been applied to interethnic relationships (Imahori, 1999, 2001, 2002, 2003) and to relationships between people with and without disabilities (Merrigan, 2000).

METATHEORETICAL AND THEORETICAL ASSUMPTIONS

Identity management theory involves several key concepts, including competence, identity, cultural and relational identities, face, and facework. Our definitions and ontological assumptions regarding these key concepts are discussed below.

IMT is based on a particular view of competence. Competence requires both appropriate and effective behavior that is mutually satisfying to the participants in a relationship (Cupach & Imahori, 1993; Imahori & Lanigan, 1989; Spitzberg & Cupach, 1984, 1989). Although Collier (1998) argues that competence is "based on implicit privilege" (p. 142) and thus is often defined by the dominant culture, we argue that in a particular intercultural relationship, competent negotiation of cultural identities requires cultural identity support that is mutually satisfying. We acknowledge that a member of the dominant culture would benefit from the influence of social standards for competence that exist in the dominant culture. However, it is theoretically possible for any two individuals to achieve mutually satisfying identity negotiation that transcends the social standards of competence.

Following cultural identity theory (Collier, 1998; Collier & Thomas, 1988), IMT views cultural identity as a focal element in intercultural communication. Identity is defined as "self-conception—one's theory of oneself" (Cupach & Imahori, 1993, p. 113). Identity serves as a framework for understanding one's self and the surrounding world. Identity is formed through mechanisms such as self-categorization into social groups (Tajfel & Turner, 1979; Turner, Hogg, Oakes, Reicher, & Wetherell, 1987) and identification with particular social roles such as husband, wife, teacher, student, and so on (McCall & Simmons, 1978; Stryker, 1980; for a review, see Stets & Burke, 2000).

Identity is a complex construct. An individual's total identity is made up of numerous overlapping aspects or subidentities. Not as an exhaustive list, identities may be related to nationality, ethnicity, region, sex, sexuality, age or generation, occupation, political affiliation, various social groups such as groups of common hobby, common experience (e.g., survivors of the Holocaust, Vietnam veterans, Japanese American internees), and groups engaged in illegal activities including drug use and street violence. Furthermore, identity reflects that aspect of self that is defined in terms of a particular interpersonal relationship, that is, a relational identity (Cupach & Imahori, 1993). IMT concerns itself specifically with cultural and relational identities.

Cultural identity is defined "as identification with and perceived acceptance into a group that has shared systems of symbols and meanings as well as norms/rules for conduct" (Collier & Thomas, 1988, p. 113). It encompasses all types of identities associated with social and cultural groups. *Relational identity* is born out of shared relational culture, that is, "a privately transacted system of understandings" that helps people coordinate meanings and behaviors (Wood, 1982, p. 76). It is a specific sense of "we" rather than "you and I" that is shared in a given relationship. Montgomery (1992) explains,

As with cultures in general, a relational culture arises when a couple develops a meaning system and evaluative norms that set them apart from other couples. These unique ways of engaging in, interpreting, and evaluating communication behavior represent and reinforce the unique identity of the couple in comparison with others. (p. 485)

Collier and Thomas (1988) explain the complexity of identity by using three dimensions of identity: scope, salience, and intensity. Scope is tantamount to the size of the group of people who share the same identity. Relational identity is extremely small in scope as it is shared between only the individuals in a specific relationship (e.g., husband–wife, best friends, etc.). Salience refers to the relative psychological importance an individual feels with respect to the various aspects of identity in a specific interaction, whereas intensity refers to how openly and explicitly an individual expresses an aspect of identity in a given interaction. Intensity is tantamount to the concept of activation in identity theory, which pertains to the enactment of an identity in a social situation (Stets & Burke, 2000).

Although scope is a relatively stable dimension, salience and intensity fluctuate across situations, rendering identity highly amorphous. Depending on the person with whom one is communicating, the topic of conversation, and the social context, one or more aspects of identity become highly salient. In turn, the salience of identity can motivate its expression with relatively high or low intensity. For example, a Japanese person who is asked about the atomic bombing of Hiroshima and Nagasaki is likely to experience Japanese cultural identity as highly salient. If the Japanese person prefers to minimize avowing Japanese identity, then low intensity could be demonstrated by shifting the topic of conversation.

An abundance of research demonstrates that salient identities influence the expectations for and interpretations of social interactions, as well as motivate social behavior (see Hecht, Collier, & Ribeau, 1993; Stets & Burke, 2000). Moreover, identity salience determines whether communication is characterized as intercultural, intracultural, or interpersonal. IMT defines intercultural communication as occurring when people's cultural identities are experienced as salient and distinct, whereas intracultural communication occurs when people's cultural identities are salient and similar. On the other hand, when relational identity is more salient than cultural identity, then communication becomes interpersonal. Since identity salience can fluctuate momentarily, the type of communication two people are sharing can vary both within and between interaction episodes. Consequently, it is important not to confuse types of relationships with types of communication. Although two people from two different cultural groups may form an intercultural relationship, their communication may be intercultural in one instance, but shift to interpersonal or intracultural communication in another. For this reason, any relationship, whether interpersonal, intercultural, or intracultural, involves interpersonal, intercultural, and intracultural communication. Thus, IMT does not regard the strict differentiation of these types of relationships to be important.

During these interpersonal, intercultural, or intracultural interactions, identities are "played out" as individuals avow (via self-presentation; Goffman, 1959) the particular identities they wish to assume for themselves, and ascribe (via altercasting; Weinstein & Deutschberger, 1963) the identities they assign to other interlocutors (Collier & Thomas, 1988). Each person's socially situated identity is referred to as his or her *face* (Tracy, 1990). The maintenance of face is a natural taken-for-granted condition of interactions because it promotes orderliness and civility. Normally one cooperates in supporting the face of another to ensure that the other supports one's own face (Brown & Levinson, 1978; Goffman, 1967). In this way,

the logical utility of reciprocal face support provides a structuring mechanism for interactions that allow people to meet their goals and accomplish their tasks in ways that are consistent with face. It is only when the mechanism breaks down by accident or design that face maintenance becomes the explicit objective. (Metts, 2000, p. 80)

Brown and Levinson (1978) proposed two distinct face wants that people possess. Positive face refers to the desire for acceptance and approval from others. "To have regard for others' positive face is to show approval of their personality, attributes, accomplishments, appearance, and so forth, as well as to show that they are considered likeable and worthy to be a friend and companion" (Metts, 2000, p. 84). Negative face, on the other hand, refers to an individual's desire for autonomy and freedom from imposition. Addressing one with tact, as well as avoiding intrusive and constraining actions, demonstrates respect for one's negative face.

Whenever a person engages in behavior that runs contrary to one's own or another's face needs, one is said to be committing a face-threatening act (Brown & Levinson, 1978). Threats to a person's face challenge that person's situated identity, thereby undermining the working agreement of mutual identity support upon which smooth interactions are predicated. Communicators employ a variety of devices that are designed to counteract or mitigate threats to their own and others' positive and negative face; that is, they behave in ways that avoid face threats, and they endeavor to restore face when it has been lost or discredited. These communicative behaviors are collectively referred to as *facework* (Goffman, 1967). Skill at facework is an essential ingredient of interpersonal competence (e.g., Cupach & Metts, 1994; Goffman, 1967; Weinstein, 1969). Situated identities represent the source of rewards and costs for social actors in all but the most impersonal of encounters (Weinstein, 1969). Facework validates situated identities and promotes the mutual achievement of personal goals. Moreover, facework enables mutual respect. "This supports the ritual order of social interactions, allowing encounters between people to be relatively smooth and enjoyable, rather than disruptive and distressing" (Cupach & Metts, 1994, p. 15).

THEORETICAL PROPOSITIONS AND RESEARCH EVIDENCE

Identity management theory offers specific propositions regarding what identity issues are involved in intercultural relationships and how they are likely to be managed. Before testing these specific propositions, previous studies (Imahori, 1999, 2001) tested whether identities are indeed significant factors of intercultural communication competence. Imahori (1999) measured Japanese perceptions of various intercultural competence factors suggested by IMT, anxiety and uncertainty management theory (Gudykunst, 1993, 1995), and identity negotiation theory (Ting-Toomey, 1993). He found that cultural, relational, and personal identity management are perceived by Japanese as important factors of intercultural communication in conjunction with other factors of competence proposed by the other theories. In the second study, Imahori (2001) compared Japanese perceptions of identity management in hypothetical intraethnic (Japanese-Japanese) and interethnic (Japanese-white American) interactions. The results indicated that Japanese perceived management of cultural and relational identities as significant in interethnic and intraethnic interactions, and that relational identity was perceived as more important in interethnic than intraethnic interaction.

Although cultural and relational identities are both important aspects of identity management, intercultural interlocutors are particularly vulnerable to committing and receiving face threats related to their cultural identities. These face-related problems are reviewed in the section that follows.

Propositions Regarding Face Problematics and Dialectics

IMT proposes that *people experience four specific types of face problematics related to cultural identity management (Proposition 1).* First, *people may experience face threat when their cultural identities are constrained because of being stereotyped or being seen only as a person with a particular cultural identity (Proposition 1a).* This face threat occurs because people in early phases of intercultural relationships lack detailed knowledge about each other (e.g., Gudykunst, 1993, 1995). Since cultural memberships constitute the first type of information people obtain about each other through readily accessible cues (e.g., accent, clothing, and physical features), they tend to see each other only as members of their respective cultures and to ignore other aspects of each other's identity. We refer to this face-threatening tendency as "identity freezing." Identity freezing obviously threatens the other person's negative face since it constrains the other's desire to avow an identity that differs from the one ascribed. Moreover, identity freezing also threatens the other's positive face insofar as it disregards characteristics the other person values.

Research indicates that identity freezing is commonly experienced. Recently, Imahori (2002) conducted extensive interviews with more than 120 individuals in real intercultural relationships varying from acquaintance to marriage. Through open-ended interviews with an ethnically diverse sample in the San Francisco Bay Area, he assessed whether respondents experienced various face problematics and dialectical tensions, and how they coped with them. He found 22.3% of the respondents experienced identity freezing by their intercultural partners. Furthermore, previous studies on interethnic communication in North America (Hecht et al., 1993; Hecht & Ribeau, 1984, 1987; Hecht, Ribeau, & Alberts, 1989) found that African Americans experience a "powerlessness" that is similar to identity freezing. This powerlessness entails feeling trapped, manipulated, or controlled by the other in a conversation.

Related to identity freezing, stereotyping is also commonly experienced in intercultural relationships. People may not only see each other as members of their respective cultures, but also try to interact with each other based on beliefs about each other's culture. Such stereotyping ignores the unique characteristics of an individual and forces a person into a predefined category. Consequently, the stereotyped person's negative face is threatened, whether the stereotype is favorable or pejorative in nature. Prior studies on interethnic communication provide ample evidence for the occurrence of stereotyping (Collier, 1988, 1991; Collier, Ribeau, & Hecht, 1986; Hecht et al., 1993; Hecht, Larkey, & Johnson, 1992; Hecht & Ribeau, 1984, 1987; Hecht et al., 1989; Hecht, Ribeau, & Sedano, 1990). In a recent interview study of real intercultural relationships (Imahori, 2002), 66% of the interview respondents admitted experiencing stereotyping from their relational partners.

Although these studies have generally reported that negative stereotyping is more commonly experienced by ethnic minority groups, even people from a dominant cultural group can experience identity freezing and stereotyping if they are perceived solely in terms of their cultural group. In this sense, IMT considers identity management issues of dominant groups and oppressed groups to be similar, even though identity freezing and stereotyping may be subjectively experienced in different ways and to different degrees by the two groups.

An obvious corollary to the identity freezing problem is when one's cultural identity is not sufficiently supported. This may occur because experienced intercultural communicators are quite aware of the danger of stereotyping and identity freezing, and thus try to see each other more as individuals than as members of their respective cultures. This can result in virtually ignoring each other's cultural identities. Thus, *when people's cultural identities are ignored, they experience threats to their positive face. We refer to this as the nonsupport problematic (Proposition 1b)*[1].

In addition to these face problematics, intercultural interlocutors face a dialectical choice between supporting one's own face and the other's face. This face dialectic becomes increasingly difficult to resolve as the cultural identities of intercultural partners become more distinct. Supporting one's own cultural identity legitimizes one's own cultural norms or values, which may be at considerable odds with the partner's cultural norms or values, thus threatening the partner's cultural identity. On the other hand, supporting the partner's cultural identity may require sacrificing feelings of belongingness and pride with respect to one's own culture. In short, *intercultural communicators experience a "self-other face dialectic," that is, dialectical tension between supporting one's own face versus the partner's face related to their cultural identities (Proposition 1c)*. According to Imahori (2002), this face dialectic is commonly experienced in intercultural relationships, as approximately 60% of his interview respondents stated that they experienced this dialectical tension.

In addition to the self-other face dialectic, *intercultural communicators experience a positive-negative face dialectic, "that is, a dialectical tension between supporting the partner's negative face or positive face" (Proposition 1d)*. In supporting the other's cultural identity by making it a conversational focus or by directly issuing a compliment about it, one incurs the risk of constraining the other's identity to that particular cultural identity, thus threatening the partner's negative face. In other words, this dialectic tension is experienced if one is afraid of freezing the other person's identity but at the same time wants to show approbation regarding the other's cultural identity. In Imahori's (2002) interview study, 22.3% of the respondents reported experiencing this dialectic.

freezing -vs- legitimizing = tension

Although the original version of IMT (Cupach & Imahori, 1993) identified three of these face problematics and dialectics, it did not specify what types of facework strategies are employed to cope with them. However, a recent interview study by Imahori (2002) was able to delineate a typology of facework strategies used to cope with each type of face problematic/dialectic proposed in the original version of IMT. In general, Imahori (2002) found that people use a full range of facework strategies designed to support positive or negative face of the self, the other, or both self and other. One exception was that a strategy that is designed solely to protect self's negative face did not appear in his study. Tables 9.1 through 9.3 summarize the specific facework strategies used to counteract face threats in intercultural interactions. These strategies are briefly identified below.

In coping with the identity freezing problematic, Imahori (2002) identified four sets of strategies: self positive face support,[2] mutual positive face support, other positive face support, and mutual negative face support. Self positive face support strategies are used to protect one's own face when it is threatened by stereotypes or identity freezing. Mutual positive face support strategies attempt to support both one's own and the partner's face. Other positive face support strategies aim to uphold the partner's face. Finally, mutual negative face support is designed to honor each other's autonomy by avoiding interactions that express stereotypes. Previous studies on African American–European American

Table 9.1   List of Facework Strategies for Coping With Identity Freezing Problematic

Strategies	*Brief Definitions*
Self Positive Face Support	
Education	Educating about the stereotype/identity freezing
Disregard	Discounting validity of the stereotype/identity freezing
Request simple	Asking to stop stereotyping/identity freezing
Request empathy	Asking to empathize about being stereotyped/identity frozen
Request confirmation	Asking to confirm if the partner really meant to stereotype or freeze identity
Mutual Positive Face Support	
Laughter	Laughing off the stereotype/identity freezing
Humorous interchange	Joking back to the partner
Humorous retaliation	Joking back with a stereotype applicable to the partner
Other Positive Face Support	
Acceptance	Accepting the stereotype as true, a compliment, or advice
Apology	Apologizing for oneself being true to the other's stereotype/identity freezing comment
Mutual Negative Face Support	
Avoidance	Avoiding interaction about the stereotype/identity freezing

Table 9.2   Facework Strategies for Coping With Self-Other Face Dialectic

Strategies	Brief Definitions
Other Positive Face Support	
Other orientation	Supporting the partner's face while sacrificing own face
Reciprocity expectation	Supporting the partner's face with an expectation that the partner will reciprocate
Advice acceptance	Accepting the partner's comment that created dialectic tension as advice for one to change (e.g., not making an excuse for being a foreign student)
Self Positive Face Support	
Assertion	Asserting one's own identity over the partner's identity (e.g., refusing to learn the partner's language)
Justification	Justifying supporting one's own identity (e.g., arguing that one's own religious belief is correct)
Reliance	Supporting one's own identity by relying on the partner's other-face support strategy (e.g., "my partner likes my culture better than his own.")
Mutual Positive Face Support	
Mutual support	Supporting both one's own and the partner's identities in alternate areas or alternate occasions
Mutual adaptation	Adapting to each other's cultural ways of doing things
Adaptation facilitation	Not changing one's own cultural way of doing things but helping the partner to adapt to one's own culture
Adaptation facilitation request	Asking the partner to help one's adaptation toward the partner's culture
Mutual Negative Face Support	
Avoidance	Avoiding interaction that causes the dialectic tension
Difference recognition	Recognizing the differences in identities and in some cases choosing to behave in separate ways

communication have reported similar strategies of confronting the other about the stereotype, treating the other as an individual, educating the other about the stereotype (Martin, Moore, Hecht, & Larkey, 2001), and avoidance (Martin, Hecht, & Larkey, 1994).

For coping with the self-other face dialectic, Imahori (2002) found four sets of strategies: other positive face support, self positive face support, mutual positive face support, and mutual negative face support. Other face support strategies try to support the partner's culture rather than the self's. Self positive face support is a set of strategies specifically designed to increase self-approbation. Mutual positive face support strategies are designed to alternately support each other's identities, adapt toward each other's culture, or facilitate the other's adaptation toward one's own culture. Finally, mutual negative face support avoids culture-related interactions or simply accepts cultural differences.

Table 9.3   Facework Strategies for Coping With Positive-Negative Face Dialectic

Strategies	Brief Definitions
Other Negative Face Support	
Bouncing past	Supporting the partner's identity within the partner's comfort zone that was learned from past interactions
Bouncing explicit	Supporting the partner's identity until she or he says explicitly to stop
Bouncing sign	Supporting the partner's identity until she or he shows signs of discomfort
Focus shift	Avoiding imposition on the partner's face by shifting focus away from the partner's cultural identity
Self support	Allowing time and space for the partner to support partner's own identity (e.g., letting the partner go back to home country)
Subtle nonverbal support	Engaging in nonverbal acts that support the partner's identity (e.g., using artifacts from the partner's culture)
Mutual Negative Face Support	
Avoidance	Avoiding interaction that causes the dialectic tension
Mutual Positive Face Support (in combination with Bouncing)	
Apology	Apologizing for threatening the partner's negative face
Justification	Justifying why one imposed upon the partner's identity

In coping with the positive-negative face dialectic, Imahori (2002) reported three sets of strategies. Other negative face support includes strategies that are all intended to avoid impositions on the partner's autonomy, such as "bouncing" off the other's autonomy boundary (e.g., avoiding certain topics). Mutual negative face support avoids interactions that cause positive-negative face tensions. Mutual positive face support includes apologizing for or justifying threat to partner's negative face. Offering an apology supports one's own positive face by showing that one is competent enough to admit one's own fault.

In addition to these facework strategies, IMT proposes that both self-other face and positive-negative face dialectics may be resolved if a relational identity can be emphasized and mutually supported (Cupach & Imahori, 1993). In the following section, we discuss identity management in the context of relationship development.

Propositions Regarding Identity Management Phases

IMT suggests that people manage their identities differently at different junctures of their relationships. The theory proposes that *there are three highly interdependent and cyclical phases of intercultural relationships based on unique features of identity management in each phase: trial, enmeshment, and renegotiation* (Proposition 2).

Trial. Cultural differences are often evident early in intercultural relationships, and, thus, people experience their cultural identities as different and as salient. Moreover, their cultural differences are often seen as barriers to their communication and relationships because of differences in language, communication styles, and cultural norms. Due to these differences, intercultural partners in this early phase of identity management strongly experience the self-other face dialectic or the nonsupport problematic. In addition, they may face the identity freezing problematic because their initial knowledge of each other's cultures may be based on stereotypical information or images. Finally, they may demonstrate excessive interest in each other's culture, resulting in identity freezing or the positive-negative face dialectic.

People tend to react to these face challenges in at least two ways. First, they may simply decide that costs stemming from their cultural differences are too great for them to maintain an intercultural relationship. Second, they may try to build their relationship based on commonalities they can find, such as common interests, joint activities, mutual need fulfillment, and the like. IMT calls this early phase of identity management "trial" because trial and error experimentation is required to identify such commonalities.

In addition to identifying commonalities, people also go through a trial-and-error process in identifying boundaries for each other's face support and face threats. For example, in showing interest toward the partner's culture, an individual may engage in stereotyping or identity freezing. However, the partner may then react with facework strategies such as education (see Table 9.1). In turn, one learns to discern, not stereotype, the partner's comfortable negative face boundary. As this example illustrates, one's incompetent act leads to discovering competent ways of dealing with the face threat.

In summary, the following two propositions are relevant for the trial phase of identity management:

Proposition 2a: Identity management in the trial phase necessitates balancing the self-other face dialectic and the positive-negative face dialectic while avoiding the nonsupport problematic and the identity freezing problematic.

Proposition 2b: Identity management in the trial phase necessitates certain degrees of face threat to discover the balancing point for various face dialectics and problematics.

Enmeshment. Intercultural partners will proceed to a relationship phase called "enmeshment" if they are able to find enough commonality between them during the trial phase (Cupach & Imahori, 1993). In this phase, *increased coactions around commonalities between intercultural partners result in convergence of symbols and rules, further enmeshing the partners' interpretive framework for understanding each other and their relationship (Proposition 2c).* Interpersonal communication theory and research have claimed that people develop symbolic interdependence (Stephen, 1986; Wood, 1982) or symbolic union (Duck, 1991) in close relationships. Specifically, Baxter (1987) identified five types of symbolic systems that are shared between relational partners. These shared systems were found for symbols related to verbal and nonverbal actions (e.g., nicknames), prior events or times, physical objects (e.g., stuffed animals), special places (e.g., meeting places for the partners), and cultural artifacts (e.g., songs, music, books, films) that have special meanings for the partners.

In addition to converging on symbols, partners converge on rules they follow in communicating with each other (Shimanoff, 1980). Partners increasingly share expectations regarding what behaviors are considered obligated, prohibited, and preferred in the context of the shared relationship. Partners improvise and negotiate their own relational standard for competent communication with each other. Montgomery (1992) suggests that, "Creative standards are a unique set of mutually held beliefs that partners develop about what constitutes competent interaction between them. They are distinguished by being decidedly different from more global, societal standards and by being the product of negotiation and agreement between partners" (p. 485).

The increased convergence in symbols and rules, in turn, leads to the development of a shared relational identity. Although intercultural partners in the enmeshment phase are able to begin developing a strong sense of relational bonding, IMT claims that their relational identity is not yet fully developed. Furthermore, they are still not entirely comfortable with their cultural differences in this phase. Rather, they tend to ignore or de-emphasize their cultural differences because they are buoyed by the personal commonality they have been able to discover. In summary, *identity management in the enmeshment phase is characterized by de-emphasis on cultural identities and emphasis on developing a relational identity (Proposition 2d)*.

According to IMT, face problematics and dialectics are not entirely resolved in this phase, either. Even with their increased symbolic and rule convergence, intercultural partners encounter new kinds of cultural differences as their relationship develops. For example, intercultural (platonic) friends normally do not have to deal with cultural differences in sexual expectations, customs, and rituals. If they become romantic partners, however, they may discover unexpected differences in rules regarding public displays of affection or in expectations regarding who initiates sexual advances. Thus, they must deal with the self-other face and the positive-negative face dialectics in this phase.

Renegotiation. The third phase of identity management is characterized by the increased ability of intercultural interlocutors to work out face problematics and dialectics based on salient relational identity, and increased symbolic and rule convergence (Proposition 2e). As the intercultural partners develop a stronger sense of relational identity, it serves as a newly shared interpretive framework, or what Stephen (1986) calls "relationship worldview." Through this relational identity the relational partners are able to view their relationship, each other, and the world outside

of their relationship in similar ways. This shared relational perspective allows the intercultural communicators to reinterpret their distinct cultural identities as an asset and as integral to their relationship rather than as a relational barrier.

By using a facework strategy that relies on this increasingly bonded sense of relational identity, the self-other face dialectic can be resolved because the distinct cultural identities are recognized as integral components of the shared relational identity. Furthermore, close intercultural partners have less need for positive face support regarding their cultural identities because emphasis shifts to giving and receiving support for positive face associated with the shared relational identity. Consequently, intercultural interlocutors can now afford to emphasize the negative face rather than the positive face related to the partner's cultural identity, resolving the positive-negative face dialectic.

In addition to managing face problematics and dialectics successfully, *intercultural partners in the renegotiation phase are able to deal directly with cultural differences that were skirted during the enmeshment phase because the cultural differences are now seen as integral and positive aspects of their relationship (Proposition 2f)*. Intercultural dating couples, for example, may have avoided dealing with cultural differences regarding marital ceremonies due to fear of conflict. As their relationship grows with increased relational identity and symbolic and rule convergence, however, they may reinterpret their cultural differences as unique assets of their relationship, an opportunity to have a wedding ceremony like nobody else's. As this example suggests, intercultural partners in this phase are not only able to perceive their cultural differences positively, but also to integrate their cultural differences as positive aspects of their relationship. Furthermore, their ability to integrate their cultural differences into their relationship leads them to view their cultural differences as smaller or less significant compared to the way they viewed the differences in the earlier phases.

Although IMT proposes that the three phases of trial, enmeshment, and renegotiation are sequential, the pace at which people go through these phases may or may not correspond to development of other relational factors such as closeness, interdependence, commitment, and satisfaction. Moreover, these identity management phases may be experienced repeatedly and cyclically because intercultural partners may go back to earlier phases after reaching the later phases if they discover new areas of cultural identity differences that need to be managed.

Abrams, O'Connor, and Giles (2002) criticize IMT as "overly optimistic" (p. 228) in its assumption that enmeshment of relational identity is possible. We do acknowledge that "individual identities cannot be totally isomorphic" (Cupach & Imahori, 1993, p. 128). Enmeshment occurs in degrees, and the establishment of relational identity does not resolve all identity management problems in the life of that relationship. Competent intercultural partners must continue to grapple with various face problematics and dialectics as they encounter growing and ever-changing cultural and relational identities. "Indeed, the more two individuals interact and become interdependent, the more complex their relationship becomes and, therefore, the more aspects of identity will have to be negotiated and renegotiated" (Cupach & Imahori, 1993, p. 129).

Research Evidence Related to Identity Management Phases. IMT's propositions regarding the identity phases have gained partial empirical support. For example, studies on interethnic communication have demonstrated the importance of a common identity (Hecht et al., 1993; Hecht & Ribeau, 1984, 1987; Hecht et al., 1989). Furthermore, an investigation of opposite-sex relationships found that strength of relational identity was associated with constructive relational outcomes such as

positive thoughts about one's relationships and relational satisfaction (Acitelli, Rogers, & Knee, 1999).

Imahori (2003) recently measured perceptions of likelihood of use, appropriateness, and effectiveness of facework strategies in dealing with identity-related face-threatening situations in a cross-sectional survey of 973 respondents residing in the San Francisco Bay Area in various stages of intercultural relationships. He specifically explored how facework strategies were associated with relational identity, relationship types (i.e., acquaintances, casual friends, friends, best friends, dating partners, and cohabiting/engaged/married couples), and symbolic and rule convergence. Results generally found that intercultural partners were more likely to use mutual positive face support strategies and to perceive them as competent if their relationships were developed with significant relational identity. On the other hand, Imahori (2003) found that people tended to emphasize mutual negative face support via avoidance in less developed intercultural relationships. These results suggest that with increased relational identity, people are able simultaneously to support each other's cultural identity with less tension stemming from the self-other face dialectic (Proposition 2e).

Imahori (2003) also found that intercultural dating couples and best friends with stronger relational identity were more likely to view other negative face support strategies as effective in dealing with the positive-negative face dialectic than were casual friends and friends. This finding supports that with stronger relational identity, there is less need for emphasizing positive face support of cultural identity (Proposition 2e).

Imahori (2003) additionally reported partial support for IMT's proposition that cultural differences are avoided in the enmeshment phase (Proposition 2d). Best friends with the stronger relational identity tended not to avoid cultural issues, whereas friends tended to use strategies that focused on their relationship and individuality. This finding, however, was mixed with a contradictory result for cohabiting/engaged/married couples, who also tended to favor strategies that focused on relationships and individuality rather than on culture. These contradictory findings seem to suggest that there are two different motivations for avoiding cultural differences. We speculate that cohabiting/engaged/married partners "avoid" cultural issues since they are "beyond" their cultural differences as they have established significant relational identity. On the other hand, friends are still in the trial phase, and are therefore busy identifying commonality not related to their cultures, and consequently they are avoiding cultural issues. This speculation is supported by another finding that friends in the self-other face dialectic situation rated another avoidance strategy of *mutual negative face support* more appropriate and effective than did cohabiting/engaged/married partners and best friends.

In terms of rule and symbolic convergence, Imahori (2003) found only weak associations with specific facework strategies. Rule convergence was associated with the mutual positive face support strategies (for perceptions of use and effectiveness) in the positive-negative face dialectic situation. As IMT claims, one of the rules that must be converged for competent intercultural identity management is the rule regarding stroking the other's positive identity while keeping the other's autonomy intact. Symbolic convergence was correlated with *self face support by request* facework in the stereotyping/identity freezing situation. This suggests that symbolic convergence allows intercultural partners to emphasize their own identities over the other's because they share many symbols of relational unity.

Imahori (2003) also found that the identity freezing dialectic was consistently managed with self positive face support strategies regardless of the nature of relationship or the perceived significance of relational identity. It

appears that identity freezing is a problematic experienced throughout the three phases of identity management, and the protection of self's face seems to override emphasis on relational identity in dealing with this dialectic.

Finally, Imahori's (2003) study failed to provide evidence that views on cultural differences would become more positive as relational identity develops (Proposition 2f). Instead, Imahori (2003) found that intercultural partners, regardless of the nature of the relationship or the degree of perceived relational identity, tended to view cultural differences either as good or as an insignificant part of their relationship.

CONCLUSION

Identity management theory has been able to contribute to the understanding of competent intercultural communication by clarifying the relationship between identity management and facework strategies within the context of relational development. The theory's tenets have mostly withstood criticisms and gained some research support.

Nevertheless, the theory is still in its infancy and needs a lot of maturing. Although Imahori's studies (2002, 2003) were able to identify a typology of facework strategies for managing face problematics and dialectics, and further investigated how relational identity, relationship type, and symbolic and rule convergence affected facework strategies, these studies did not longitudinally follow intercultural partners through their relational development process. To test the validity of IMT's propositions fully, longitudinal research must be conducted.

IMT was proposed as a heuristic framework to aid our understanding of the complex process of identity management in intercultural interactions. Although not designed to be prescriptive, IMT suggests a set of principles to promote competent communication between intercultural partners: (a) establish relational identity through increased coactions, symbolic convergence, and coordination of relationship rules; (b) view cultural differences as assets rather than barriers; and (c) recognize that identity management and relationship management represent two sides of a single coin. We are confident that additional "research regarding the processes of face management in intercultural couples can provide insight into how intercultural partners overcome the cultural barriers that can undermine the formation of a successful close relationship" (Cupach & Metts, 1994, p. 103).

NOTES

1. This proposition was not included in the original version of identity management theory (Cupach & Imahori, 1993).

2. In the original study, Imahori (2002) used the label self face restoration.

REFERENCES

Abrams, J., O'Connor, J., & Giles, H. (2002). Identity and intergroup communication. In W. B. Gudykunst & B. Mody (Eds.), *Handbook of international and intercultural communication* (2nd ed., pp. 225-240). Thousand Oaks, CA: Sage.

Acitelli, L. K., Rogers, S., & Knee, C. R. (1999). The role of identity in the link between relationship thinking and relationship satisfaction. *Journal of Social and Personal Relationships, 16,* 591-618.

Baxter, L. A. (1987). Symbols of relationship identity in relationship cultures. *Journal of Social and Personal Relationships, 4,* 261-280.

Brown, P., & Levinson, S. (1978). Universals in language usage: Politeness phenomena. In E. N. Goody (Ed.), *Questions and politeness* (pp. 56-289). Cambridge, UK: Cambridge University Press.

Collier, M. J. (1988). A comparison of intracultural and intercultural communication among acquaintances: How intra- and intercultural competencies vary. *Communication Quarterly, 36,* 122-144.

Collier, M. J. (1991). Conflict competence within African, Mexican, and Anglo American friendships. In S. Ting-Toomey & F. Korzenny (Eds.), *Cross-cultural interpersonal communication* (pp. 132-154). Newbury Park, CA: Sage.

Collier, M. J. (1998). Researching cultural identity. In D. V. Tanno & A. González (Eds.), *Communication and identity across cultures* (pp. 122-147). Thousand Oaks, CA: Sage.

Collier, M. J., Ribeau, S., & Hecht, M. L. (1986). Intercultural communication rules and outcomes within three domestic cultural groups. *International Journal of Intercultural Relations, 10,* 439-457.

Collier, M. J., & Thomas, M. (1988). Cultural identity: An interpretive perspective. In Y. Y. Kim & W. B. Gudykunst (Eds.), *Theories in intercultural communication* (pp. 94-120). Newbury Park, CA: Sage.

Cupach, W. R., & Imahori, T. T. (1989, November). *Intercultural communication competence: Culture-general, culture-specific, and culture-synergistic.* Paper presented at the annual meeting of the Speech Communication Association, San Francisco.

Cupach, W. R., & Imahori, T. T. (1993). Identity management theory: Communication competence in intercultural episodes and relationships. In R. L. Wiseman & J. Koester (Eds.), *Intercultural communication competence* (pp. 112-131). Newbury Park, CA: Sage.

Cupach, W. R., & Metts, S. (1994). *Facework.* Thousand Oaks, CA: Sage.

Duck, S. (1991, May). *New lamps for old: A new theory of relationships and a fresh look at some old research.* Paper presented at the Third Annual Conference of the International Network on Personal Relationships, Normal/ Bloomington, IL.

Goffman, E. (1959). *The presentation of self in everyday life.* Garden City, NY: Anchor.

Goffman, E. (1967). *Interaction ritual: Essays on face to face behavior.* Garden City, NY: Anchor.

Gudykunst, W. B. (1993). Toward a theory of effective interpersonal and intergroup communication: An anxiety/uncertainty management (AUM) perspective. In R. L. Wiseman & J. Koester (Eds.), *Intercultural communication competence* (pp. 33-71). Newbury Park, CA: Sage.

Gudykunst, W. B. (1995). Anxiety/uncertainty management (AUM) theory: Current status. In R. L. Wiseman (Ed.), *Intercultural communication theory* (pp. 8-58). Thousand Oaks, CA: Sage.

Hecht, M. L., Collier, M. J., & Ribeau, S. (1993). *African American communication: Ethnic identity and cultural interpretation.* Newbury Park, CA: Sage.

Hecht, M. L., Larkey, L. K., & Johnson, J. N. (1992). African American and European American perceptions of problematic issues in interethnic communication effectiveness. *Human Communication Research, 19,* 209-236.

Hecht, M. L., & Ribeau, S. (1984). Ethnic communication: A comparative analysis of satisfying communication. *International Journal of Intercultural Relations, 8,* 133-151.

Hecht, M. L., & Ribeau, S. (1987). Afro-American identity labels and communicative effectiveness. *Journal of Black Studies, 21,* 501-513.

Hecht, M. L., Ribeau, S., & Alberts, J. K. (1989). An Afro-American perspective on interethnic communication. *Communication Monographs, 56,* 385-410.

Hecht, M. L., Ribeau, S., & Sedano, M. V. (1990). A Mexican American perspective on interethnic communication. *International Journal of Intercultural Relations, 14,* 31-55.

Imahori, T. T. (1999). Theoretical validation of intercultural communication competence in Japan: An exploratory study. *Studies in English Language and Literature, Seinan Gakuin University, 39*(3), 25-58.

Imahori, T. T. (2001). Validation of identity management theory in Japan: A comparison of intraethnic and interethnic communication. *Studies in English Language and Literature, Seinan Gakuin University, 42*(2), 25-50.

Imahori, T. T. (2002, November). *Facework strategies for identity management in real intercultural relationships: An extensive interview study.* Paper presented at the annual meeting of the National Communication Association, New Orleans.

Imahori, T. T. (2003, November). *Relational development and identity management facework strategies in intercultural relationships.* Paper presented at the annual meeting of the National Communication Association, Miami, FL.

Imahori, T. T., & Lanigan, M. (1989). Relational model of intercultural communication competence. *International Journal of Intercultural Relations, 13,* 269-286.

Martin, J. N., Hecht, M. L., & Larkey, L. K. (1994). Conversational improvement strategies for interethnic communication. *Communication Monographs, 61,* 236-255.

Martin, J. N., Moore, S., Hecht, M. L., & Larkey, L. K. (2001). An African American perspective on conversational improvement strategies. *Howard Journal of Communications, 12,* 1-27.

McCall, G. J., & Simmons, J. L. (1978). *Identities and interactions.* New York: Free Press.

Merrigan, G. (2000). Negotiating personal identities among people with and without identified disabilities: The role of identity management. In D. O. Braithwaite & T. L. Thompson (Eds.), *Handbook of communication and people with disabilities: Research and application* (pp. 223-238). Mahwah, NJ: Lawrence Erlbaum.

Metts, S. (2000). Face and facework: Implications for the study of personal relationships. In K. Dindia & S. Duck (Eds.), *Communication and personal relationships* (pp. 77-93). New York: John Wiley.

Montgomery, B. M. (1992). Communication as the interface between couples and culture. In S. A. Deetz (Ed.), *Communication yearbook 15* (pp. 475-507). Newbury Park, CA: Sage.

Shimanoff, S. (1980). *Communication rules: Theory and research.* Beverly Hills, CA: Sage.

Spitzberg, B. H., & Cupach, W. R. (1984). *Interpersonal communication competence.* Beverly Hills, CA: Sage.

Spitzberg, B. H., & Cupach, W. R. (1989). *Handbook of interpersonal competence research.* New York: Springer.

Stephen, T. (1986). Communication and interdependence in geographically separated relationships. *Human Communication Research, 13,* 191-210.

Stets, J. E., & Burke, P. J. (2000). Identity theory and social identity theory. *Social Psychology Quarterly, 63,* 224-237.

Stryker, S. (1980). *Symbolic interactionism: A social structural version.* Menlo Park, CA: Benjamin Cummings.

Tajfel, H., & Turner, J. C. (1979). An integrative theory of intergroup conflict. In W. G. Austin &

S. Worchel (Eds.), *The social psychology of intergroup relations* (pp. 33-47). Monterey, CA: Brooks-Cole.

Ting-Toomey, S. (1988). Identity and interpersonal bonding. In M. K. Asante & W. B. Gudykunst (Eds.), *Handbook of international and intercultural communication* (pp. 351-373). Newbury Park, CA: Sage.

Ting-Toomey, S. (1993). Communicative resourcefulness: An identity negotiation perspective. In R. L. Wiseman & J. Koester (Eds.), *Intercultural communication competence* (pp. 72-111). Newbury Park, CA: Sage.

Tracy, K. (1990). The many faces of facework. In H. Giles & W. P. Robinson (Eds.), *Handbook of language and social psychology* (pp. 209-226). New York: John Wiley.

Turner, J. C., Hogg, M. A., Oakes, P. J., Reicher, S. D., & Wetherell, M. S. (1987). *Rediscovering the social group: A self-categorization theory.* New York: Basil Blackwell.

Weinstein, E. A. (1969). The development of interpersonal competence. In D. A. Goslin (Ed.), *Handbook of socialization theory and research* (pp. 753-775). Chicago: Rand McNally.

Weinstein, E. A., & Deutschberger, P. (1963). Some dimensions of altercasting. *Sociometry, 4,* 454-466.

Wiseman, R. L. (2002). Intercultural communication competence. In W. B. Gudykunst & B. Mody (Eds.), *Handbook of international and intercultural communication* (2nd ed., pp. 207-224). Thousand Oaks, CA: Sage.

Wood, J. T. (1982). Communication and relational culture: Bases for the study of human relationships. *Communication Quarterly, 30,* 75-83.

10

Identity Negotiation Theory: Crossing Cultural Boundaries

STELLA TING-TOOMEY

Individuals acquire and develop their identities through interaction with others in their cultural group. Through interaction with others on a daily basis, we acquire the meanings, values, norms, and styles of communicating. Two very common questions we often ask ourselves in our daily lives are: Who am I? and, Who are you? The struggle to answer both questions is profoundly influenced by our cultural socialization, family socialization, and acculturation and identity change processes.

For many, the result is a struggle between an individual's perception of being "different" coupled with the inability to blend in with either the dominant cultural group or her or his ethnic heritage group. While culture plays the larger role in shaping our view of ourselves, it is through multiple channels that we acquire and develop our own ethics, values, norms, and ways of behaving in our everyday lives. For example, through the direct channel of family, values and norms are transmitted and passed on from one generation to the next. Parents teach their children about right and wrong, and acceptable and unacceptable ways of behaving through the words they use and through their role modeling actions.

The chapter is organized in five sections. The first section addresses the theme of family and gender socialization in shaping identity development. The second section discusses the content and salience (i.e., degree of importance) of cultural and ethnic identity formation issues. The third section explains the core assumptions of the identity negotiation theory. The fourth section addresses two ethnic identity development models. The final section outlines the components, criteria, and outcomes of intercultural identity competence.

FAMILY AND
GENDER SOCIALIZATION

Children in their early years internalize what to value and devalue, what to appreciate and reject, and what goals are important in their culture through the influence of their family system. In addition, teenagers and young adults may be influenced, to a certain extent, by the pervasive messages from the popular culture and the contemporary media scenes. It is through the pervasive cultural value patterns—as filtered through the family and media systems—that the meanings and values of identities such as ethnicity, gender, and identity types are defined.

The term *identity* is used in this chapter as the reflective self-conception or self-image that we each derive from our family, gender, cultural, ethnic, and individual socialization process. Identity basically refers to our reflective views of ourselves and other perceptions of our self-images—at both the social identity and the personal identity levels (Mead, 1934; Stryker, 1987, 1991; Tajfel, 1981; Tajfel & Turner, 1986). *Social identities* can include cultural or ethnic membership identity, gender identity, sexual orientation identity, social class identity, age identity, disability identity, or professional identity, to name a few. *Personal identities*, on the other hand, can include any unique attributes that we associate with our individuated self in comparison to those of others. In collectivistic group-oriented cultures, for example, people may be more concerned with communal or social-based identity issues. In individualistic cultures, however, people may be more concerned with individuated-based personal identity issues (Hofstede, 1991, 2001; Triandis, 1995). Regardless of whether we may or may not be conscious of these identities, they influence our everyday behaviors in both a generalized and a particularized manner. In this section, we explore some important ideas about family and gender socialization processes. In the next section, we discuss cultural and ethnic identity formation process.

Family Socialization
and Interaction Patterns

Family is the fundamental communication system in all cultures. People in every culture are born into a network of family relationships. First and foremost, for example, we acquire some of the beliefs and values of our culture via our primary family system. The rules that we acquire in relating to our parents, grandparents, siblings, and extended families contribute to the initial blueprint of our formation of role, gender, and relational identities. For example, through our family socialization process, we learn to deal with boundary issues such as space and time. We also learn to deal with authority issues such as gender-based decision-making activities (e.g., who does what household chores?) and power dynamics (e.g., which parents or siblings hold what status power?). We also acquire the scripts for emotional expressiveness or restraint, as well as for nonverbal eloquence or stillness, within our family system.

We can also think of two possible family types in the family decision-making process: personal family system and positional family system. Some of the major characteristics of a *personal family system* include the emphasis on personal, individualized meanings, negotiable roles between parents and child, and an emphasis on interactive discussions within the family (Bernstein, 1973; Haslett, 1987). Democratic families try to emphasize different family members as unique individuals. Democratic parents are consultative in their decision-making process. They hold family meetings to solicit inputs in major family decision issues. They are explicit in their communication styles, and they encourage experimentations and individual initiatives in their children. They try to foster individualistic and small power distance value patterns in the family system. They act more like friends to their children than authority figures (Guerrerro, Andersen, & Afifi, 2001). Comparatively, a *positional family system* emphasizes communal meanings, ascribed roles and statuses between parents and child, and family rule conformity. Positional families emphasize the importance of holding the hierarchical power structure in the family exchange process. Individuals have different status-based authorities and responsibilities in a positional family system. Authoritarian parents, from a positional family framework, are demanding and directive. They expect their children to obey family rules without question. They do not believe in explaining the reasons behind their disciplinary actions to their children (Guerrerro et al., 2001; see also Koerner & Fitzpatrick, 2002). Many positional family systems exist in collectivistic, larger power distance cultural regions (Hofstede, 1991, 1998).

As a result of our interaction with our family and our peers, we directly and indirectly acquire the various value patterns in our culture. While no single family can transmit all the value patterns in a culture, families who share similar cultural and ethnic ties do have some family value patterns in common. Family serves as the primary value socialization channel that creates a lasting imprint in our communicative behavior. It also cues our perceptions and interpretations concerning appropriate gendered-based interpersonal behaviors.

Gender Socialization and Interaction Patterns

The gender identities we learned as children affect our communication with others. They affect how we define ourselves, how we encode and decode gendered messages, how we develop intimate relationships, and how we relate to one another. Gender identity, in short, refers to the meanings and interpretations we hold concerning our self-images and expected other-images of "femaleness" and "maleness."

For example, females in many cultures are expected to act in a nurturing manner, to be more affective, and to play the primary caregiver role. Males in many cultures are expected to act in a competitive manner, to be

more emotionally reserved, and to play the breadwinner role. The orientations toward femaleness and maleness are grounded and learned via our own cultural and ethnic practices. Children learn appropriate gender roles through rewards and punishments they receive from their parents in performing the "proper" or "improper" gender-related behaviors. In the United States, feminine-based tendencies such as interdependence, cooperation, and verbal relatedness are often rewarded in girls, whereas masculine-based tendencies such as independence, competition, and verbal assertiveness are often promoted in boys.

Gender researchers observe that young girls and boys learn their gender-related behaviors in the home and school, and in childhood games. For example, in the United States, girls' games (e.g., playing house, jump rope) tend to involve either pairs or small groups. The girls' games often involve fluid discussion about who is going to play what roles in the "playing house" game, for example, and usually promote relational collaboration. Boys' games (e.g., baseball, basketball), on the other hand, involve fairly large groups and have clear objectives, distinct roles and rules, and clear win-lose outcomes. The process of playing, rather than the win-lose outcome, is predominant in girls' games in the larger U.S. culture (Maltz & Borker, 1982; Tannen, 1990, 1994).

From such research observations, another scholar (Wood, 1996, 1997) concludes that girls' games enable U.S. females to form the expectation that "communication" is used to create and maintain relationships and to respond to the other's feelings empathetically rather than with individual competitiveness. In comparison, boys' games prompt U.S. males to form the expectations that "communication" is used to achieve some clear outcome, attract and maintain an audience, and compete with others for the "talk stage."

Moving beyond the U.S. cultural context, to illustrate, in traditional Mexican culture, child-rearing practices also differ significantly in socializing girls and boys. At the onset of adolescence, the difference between girls and boys becomes even more markedly apparent. The female is likely to remain much closer to home and to be protected and guarded in her contact with others beyond the family. The adolescent male, however, following the model of his father, "is given much more freedom to come and go as he chooses and is encouraged to gain much worldly knowledge and experience outside the home" (Locke, 1992, p. 137). Gender identity and cultural/ethnic identity intersect and form part of an individual's composite self-conception.

Our gender identities are created, in part, via our communication with others. They are also supported and reinforced by the existing cultural structures and practices.

CULTURAL-ETHNIC IDENTITY FORMATION

Our family scripts and gender role expectations influence our evaluations of how females or males "should" or "should not" behave in a given situation. Structural and historical constraints and practices also assert a strong influence in the shaping and construction of our multifaceted identity (Weinreich, 2003). Our cultural and ethnic identities that we acquired during our childhood and adolescent years also influence whom we befriend, what holidays we celebrate, what language or dialect we are comfortable with, and what nonverbal styles we are at ease with in communicating with others. Lastly, our individual motivations to change, in interaction with the larger systems-level environment, will also propel an identity transformation process in multiple directions.

For the purpose of this chapter, issues surrounding cultural and ethnic identity conceptualization will be the focus. There are many other important identities, such as spiritual identity, social class identity, age identity, disability identity, sexual orientation identity,

body identity, and the like, that await deeper exploration by other authors. In being aware and increasing our knowledge of our own multifaceted self-conception, we can also develop a fuller awareness of the multifaceted identities of culturally different others. We begin our discussion with cultural identity.

Cultural Identity Conceptualization

All individuals are socialized within a larger cultural membership group. For example, everyone born and/or raised in the United States has some sense of being an "American" (in this chapter, to avoid ambiguity, I will use the term "U.S. American"). Minority group members or biracial members, however, may need to answer the question, "Where're you from?" more often than mainstream white Americans. Alternatively, if you look like everyone else in the mainstream culture, you may not even notice the importance of your cultural membership badge until someone asks you, "What is your nationality?" or "Where do you come from?" in your overseas travels.

We acquire our cultural group memberships through the guidance of primary caretakers and peer associations during our formative years. Furthermore, physical appearance, racial traits, skin color, language usage, self-appraisal, and other-perception factors all enter into the cultural identity construction equation. The meanings and interpretations that we hold for our culture-based identity groups are learned via direct or mediated contacts (e.g., mass media images) with others. *Cultural identity* is defined as the emotional significance we attach to our sense of belonging or affiliation with the larger culture. To illustrate, we can talk about the larger Brazilian cultural identity, or the larger Canadian cultural identity. To understand cultural identity more specifically, we need to discuss two issues: content and salience. *Value content* refers to the standards or expectations that people hold in their mind-set in making evaluations. One way to understand the content of cultural identity is to look at the value dimensions that underlie people's behavior. While there are many value content dimensions in which cultural groups differ, one dimension that has received consistent attention from intercultural researchers around the world is individualism-collectivism (Hofstede, 1991, 2001). In order to negotiate mindfully with people from diverse cultures, it is critical that we understand the value contents of their cultural identities (for a discussion of individualism-collectivism, see Ting-Toomey, Chapter 4 in this volume).

Cultural identity salience refers to the strength of affiliation we have with our larger culture. Strong associations of membership affiliation reflect high cultural identity salience. Weak associations of membership affiliation reflect low cultural identity salience. The more strongly our self-image is influenced by our larger cultural value patterns, the more we are likely to practice the norms and communication scripts of the dominant, mainstream culture. Salience of cultural identity can operate on a conscious or an unconscious level. We should also clarify here that while the concept of "national identity" refers to one's legal status in relation to a nation, the concept of "cultural identity" refers to the sentiments of belonging or connection to one's larger culture. To illustrate: As an immigrant society, residents in the United States may mix some of the larger cultural values with those of their ethnic-oriented values and practices. In order to negotiate cultural and ethnic identities mindfully with diverse cultural/ethnic groups, we need to understand in depth the content and salience of cultural *and* ethnic identity issues.

Ethnic Identity Conceptualization

An individual who is associated with a particular ethnic group may not actually behave in accordance with her or his ethnic norms or behaviors. In other words, skin color does not automatically guarantee ethnic ingroup membership. While many ethnic minority U.S. Americans strive hard to be an "American," they are constantly reminded by the media or in actual interactions that they are not part of the fabric of the larger U.S. society.

Ethnic identity is "inherently a matter of ancestry, of beliefs about the origins of one's forebears" (Alba, 1990, p. 37). Ethnicity can be based on national origin, race, religion, or language. For many people in the United States, ethnicity is based on the countries from which their ancestors came (e.g., those who can trace their ethnic heritage to an Asian or a Latin American country). Most Native Americans—descendants of people who settled in the Western Hemisphere long before Columbus, sometime between 25,000 and 40,000 years ago—can trace their ethnic heritage based on distinctive linguistic or religious practices.

Most African Americans, however, may not be able to trace their precise ethnic origins because of the pernicious slavery codes (e.g., a slave could not marry or meet with an ex-slave; it was forbidden for anyone, including whites, to teach slaves to read or write) and the uprootedness coerced upon them by slaveholders beginning in the 1600s (Hecht, Jackson, & Ribeau, 2003; Schaefer, 1990). Lastly, many European Americans may not be able to trace their ethnic origins precisely because of their mixed ancestral heritage. This phenomenon stems from generations of intergroup marriages (say, Irish American and French American marriages, or mixed Irish/ French American and Polish American marriages, etc.) starting with the great-grandparents or grandparents (Waters, 1990; Yinger, 1994).

Ethnicity, of course, is based on more than the country of origin. It involves a subjective sense of belonging to or identification with an ethnic group across time. In order to understand the significance of someone's ethnicity, we also need to understand the content and the salience of that person's ethnic identity in particular. For example, with knowledge of the individualism-collectivism value tendencies of the originating countries, we can infer the *ethnic value content* of specific ethnic groups. Most Asian Americans, Native Americans, and Latino/a Americans, for example, who identify strongly with their traditional ethnic values, would tend to be group oriented. Those European Americans who identify strongly with European values and norms (albeit on an unconscious level) would tend to be oriented toward individualism. African Americans might well subscribe to both collectivistic and individualistic values—in blending both ethnic African values and assimilated U.S. values—for purposes of survival and adaptation (Jackson, 1999, 2002; Orbe, 1998).

Beyond ethnic value content, we should address the issue of ethnic identity salience. The role of *ethnic identity salience* is linked closely with the intergroup boundary maintenance issue across generations (e.g., third-generation Cuban Americans in the U.S.). Ethnic identity salience is defined as the subjective allegiance and loyalty to a group—large or small, socially dominant or subordinate—with which one has ancestral links (Edwards, 1994). Ethnic identity can be sustained by shared objective characteristics such as shared language or religion. There is also a subjective sense of "ingroupness" whereby individuals perceive of themselves and each other as belonging to the same ingroup through shared historical and emotional ties. Many ethnic minority group members living in the larger U.S. society, however, are constantly struggling between the perception of their own ethnic identity issue and the perception of others' questioning of their ethnic heritage or role. Oftentimes, this results in a sense of both ethnic and cultural rootlessness. On the other hand, selective resilient or constructive marginals (J. Bennett, 1993) may be able to utilize all the resources within and beyond themselves to create a "double consciousness" state. Through identity crisis and stretch, or in Kim's (2001, 2004) term a *stress-adaptation-growth* experience, some of them are able to re-create a

dynamic identity that functions effectively to bridge between the mainstream culture and their ethnic heritage culture.

Thus, ethnic identity has both objective and subjective layers. Ethnicity is, overall, more a subjective phenomenon than an objective classification. While a political boundary (e.g., delimiting Chechnya—formerly the Chechno-Ingush Autonomous Soviet Socialist Republic—from Russia) can change over generations, the continuation of ethnic boundaries is an enduring, long-standing phenomenon that lasts in the hearts and minds of its members. Ethnicity is basically an inheritance wherein members perceive each other as emotionally bounded by a common set of traditions, worldviews, history, heritage, and descent on a psychological and historical level.

By understanding how we define ourselves and how others define themselves ethnically and culturally, we can communicate with culturally different others with more sensitivity. We can learn to lend appropriate self-conception support in terms of ethnic and cultural identity issues. Uncovering and supporting others' self-conceptions requires mindful identity-support work. Moving beyond general cultural and ethnic identity issues, many majority-minority group identity models have been developed to account for the identity change process of immigrants and minority group members. We first discuss some of the underlying factors that affect immigrants' acculturation experience and then explore two perspectives on ethnic-cultural identity developmental processes.

INGROUP/OUTGROUP MEMBERSHIP: INTERCULTURAL BOUNDARY-CROSSING

The intercultural boundary-crossing journey, from identity security to insecurity, and from identity membership inclusion to exclusion, can be a turbulent or exhilarating process. The route itself has many ups and downs, and twists and turns. In such a long, demanding journey, an incremental process of identity change or transformation is inevitable (Ting-Toomey, 1997). This section identifies the core assumptions of the identity negotiation process and then discusses strangers' acculturation experience as examples to highlight the basic theoretical assumptions.

Identity Negotiation Theory: Core Assumptions

While human beings in all cultures desire identity respect in the communication process, what constitutes the proper way to show identity respect and consideration varies from one culture to the next. The identity negotiation perspective emphasizes particular identity domains in influencing our everyday interactions. There are many more identities (e.g., social class, sexual orientation, age, disability) that people bring into an interaction. For the purposes of this chapter, however, I will emphasize cultural and ethnic identity conceptualizations.

In order to engage in mindful identity negotiation work, we have to increase our knowledge base, our attunement level, and our honesty in assessing our own group membership and personal identity issues. Concomitantly, we have to understand the content and salience issues of identity domains in direct correspondence with how others view themselves in a variety of situations. The theoretical assumptions I pose in this section are cast as a set of basic human needs that carry both culture-general and culture-specific meanings.

The identity negotiation theory emphasizes that identity or reflective self-conception is viewed as the explanatory mechanism for the intercultural communication process. *Identity* is viewed as reflective self-images constructed, experienced, and communicated by the individuals within a culture and in a particular interaction situation. The concept *negotiation* is defined as a transactional interaction process whereby individuals in an intercultural situation attempt to assert, define, modify, challenge, and/or support their own and others' desired self-images. Identity negotiation is, at a minimum, a mutual communication activity. At the same time the communicators attempt to evoke their own desired identities in the interaction, they also attempt to challenge or support the others' identities. While some individuals are relatively mindless (or act on "automatic pilot") about the identity negotiation process, other individuals are relatively mindful about the dynamics of that process. Mindfulness is, moreover, a learned process of attuning to self-identity reactive issues plus engaging in intentional attunement to others' salient identity issues. The present section is devoted to (a) the core theoretical assumptions of the identity negotiation theory and (b) an explanation of these key theoretical assumptions.

Core Theoretical Assumptions

In the context of the identity negotiation theory, competent identity negotiation focuses on ways to obtain accurate knowledge of the identity domains of the self and others in the intercultural encounter. In a nutshell, the theory assumes that human beings in all cultures desire both positive group-based and positive person-based identities in any type of communicative situation. How we can enhance identity understanding, respect, and mutual affirmative valuation of the other is the essential concern of this approach. For example, J. H. Turner (1987, 1988) asserts that failure to meet the basic human needs of security, predictability/trust, and inclusion can lead to diffuse anxiety and frustration in our everyday life. He concludes that our efforts to sustain a coherent self-conception are directly fueled by the three following motivation dimensions of social-based and person-based identity communication process: (1) the need to feel secure that things are as they appear; (2) the need to feel included or actually be included; and (3) the need to experience a certain amount of predictability and to trust the responses of others.

However, how we go about establishing security, inclusion, trust, and connection in ourselves and others depends heavily on culture-sensitive knowledge and competent identity-based communication skills. On a positive note, the theory assumes that while the efforts of both communicators are needed to ensure competent identity negotiation, the effort of one individual can set competent communication in motion. The theory consists of the following 10 core assumptions that explain the antecedent, process, and outcome components of intercultural communication:

1. The core dynamics of people's group membership identities (e.g., cultural and ethnic memberships) and personal identities (e.g., unique attributes) are formed via symbolic communication with others.

2. Individuals in all cultures or ethnic groups have the basic motivation needs for identity security, inclusion, predictability, connection, and consistency on both group-based and person-based identity levels. However, too much emotional security will lead to tight ethnocentrism, and, conversely, too much emotional insecurity (or vulnerability) will lead to fear of outgroups or unfamiliar strangers. The same underlying principle applies to identity inclusion, predictability, connection, and consistency. Thus, an optimal range exists on the various identity negotiation spectrums.

3. Individuals tend to experience identity emotional security in a culturally familiar environment and experience identity emotional vulnerability in a culturally unfamiliar environment.

4. Individuals tend to feel included when their desired group membership identities are positively endorsed (e.g., in positive ingroup contact situations) and experience identity differentiation when their desired

group membership identities are stigmatized (e.g., in hostile outgroup contact situations).

5. Individuals tend to experience interaction predictability when communicating with culturally familiar others and interaction unpredictability (or novelty) when communicating with culturally unfamiliar others—thus, identity predictability leads to trust, and identity unpredictability leads to distrust, second-guessing, or biased intergroup attributions.

6. Individuals tend to desire interpersonal connection via meaningful close relationships (e.g., in close friendship support situations) and experience identity autonomy when they experience relationship separations—meaningful intercultural-interpersonal relationships can create additional emotional security and trust in the cultural strangers.

7. Individuals tend to experience identity consistency in repeated cultural routines in a familiar cultural environment, and they tend to experience identity change (or at the extreme, identity chaos) and transformation in a new or unfamiliar cultural environment.

8. Cultural, personal, and situational variability dimensions influence the meanings, interpretations, and evaluations of these identity-related themes.

9. A competent identity negotiation process emphasizes the importance of integrating the necessary intercultural identity-based knowledge, mindfulness, and interaction skills to communicate appropriately and effectively with culturally dissimilar others.

10. Satisfactory identity negotiation outcomes include the feelings of being understood, respected, and affirmatively valued.

Drawing from the core assumptions of the identity negotiation theory, the following themes underscore the development of the discussions that follow: identity security-vulnerability, inclusion-differentiation,

Table 10.1 Identity Dialectics: Five Boundary-Crossing Themes

Identity Security	- -	Identity Vulnerability
Identity Inclusion	- -	Identity Differentiation
Identity Predictability	- -	Identity Unpredictability
Identity Connection	- -	Identity Autonomy
Identity Consistency	- -	Identity Change

predictability-unpredictability, connection-autonomy, and consistency-change (see Table 10.1). We turn now, in the following subsections, to a summary discussion of Assumptions 1 through 3, then Assumptions 4 and 5, Assumption 6, and Assumptions 7 and 8. I will discuss Assumptions 9 and 10 in the last section "Identity Negotiation Competence." The background arguments that frame these assumptions are more fully developed elsewhere (Ting-Toomey, 1986, 1988, 1989a, 1989b, 1993, 1999, 2005).

Assumptions 1 Through 3

The basic idea concerning Assumption 1 is that people in all cultures form their reflective self-images, such as cultural identity and ethnic identity, via their enculturation process. Through the content of their cultural, ethnic, and family socialization experiences, they acquire the values, norms, and core symbols of their cultural and ethnic groups. Through their identity content and salience levels, their respective group-based and person-based identities shape their thinking, emotions, and communication patterns when interacting with culturally dissimilar others.

Thus, in order to understand the person with whom you are communicating, you need to understand the identity domains that she or he deems salient. For example, if she strongly values her cultural membership identity and

gender membership identity, you need to find ways to validate and be responsive to her cultural and gender identities; or if he strongly values his personal identity above and beyond his cultural or gender group membership, you need to uncover ways to affirm his positively desired personal identity. Through mindful communication, we can discover salient identity issues that are desirable to the individuals in our everyday intercultural encounters.

The identity negotiation perspective posits that individuals in all cultures have similar basic human needs for identity security, inclusion, predictability, connection, and consistency in their communication with others (Turner, 1987, 1988). The thematic pairs of the respective needs include identity vulnerability, differentiation, unpredictability, autonomy, and change. Since Assumption 3 is a specific extension of Assumption 2, I discuss both theoretical assumptions here.

According to Assumptions 2 and 3, we often experience emotional insecurity or vulnerability because of a perceived threat or fear in a culturally estranged environment. On the other hand, we experience emotional security in a culturally familiar environment. Emotional issues are tied closely to self-conception or identity issues. Thus, identity security refers to the degree of emotional safety concerning one's sense of both group-based membership and person-based identities in a particular cultural setting. Identity vulnerability refers to the degree of anxiousness or ambivalence in regard to group-based and person-based identity issues.

In an unfamiliar cultural environment, it is inevitable that most individuals would fall back on their familiar ethnocentric nets or habits and put on their stereotypic lens to help them to adapt more efficiently to an unfamiliar cultural environment.

Assumptions 4 and 5

Assumptions 4 and 5 are about the themes of ingroup/outgroup-based boundary maintenance issues. Assumption 4, the identity inclusion and differentiation assumption, refers to membership-based boundary maintenance issues. Identity inclusion is conceptualized as the degree of our perceived nearness (i.e., emotional, psychological, and spatial proximity) to our ingroups and outgroups. Identity inclusion is an ingroup/outgroup boundary maintenance issue in which our self-image is attached to some emotionally significant group membership categories (e.g., racial or ethnic identification). Identity differentiation is defined as the degree of remoteness (i.e., emotional, psychological, and spatial distance) we perceive in regulating our group-based boundary with either ingroup or outgroup members.

Mindful boundary regulation helps to satisfy ingroup inclusion and intergroup differentiation needs (Brewer, 1991, 1996; Brewer & Miller, 1996). To the extent that one's salient ingroup (e.g., one's ethnic group) compares favorably with other relevant social/cultural groups, one may consider one's membership group positively. Conversely, to the extent that one's salient ingroup compares unfavorably, one would choose different options. Such options can include changing one's identity group (if possible), changing the comparative criteria dimensions, reaffirming one's own group value, or downgrading the comparative group.

For example, drawing from social identity theory, Brewer (1991) argues that "social identity derives from a fundamental tension between human needs for validation and similarity to others (on the one hand) and a countervailing need for uniqueness and individuation (on the other)" (p. 477). The identity needs for both appropriate inclusion and differentiation exist as dualistic motivations to the intergroup communication process. Too much group-based inclusion may cause us to ponder the significance and meanings of our person-based identity. Too much group-based differentiation, however, may cause us to feel unwelcome or excluded.

Assumption 5 emphasizes interaction predictability or trust versus interaction unpredictability or distrust issues. According to Assumption 5, to the extent that an individual experiences identity predictability when interacting with familiar others, a reliable interaction climate is developed. To the extent that an individual experiences interaction unpredictability or uncertainty, anxiety sets in and a defensive interaction climate may be established (Gudykunst, 1995, 2004; see also Chapter 13 in this volume). We experience identity trust in interacting with familiar others because expected norms and routines occur with a high degree of frequency. Comparatively, we experience identity awkwardness or estrangement in interacting with unfamiliar others because unexpected behaviors (e.g., nonverbal violations behavior) occur frequently and intrusively.

Assumption 6

Assumption 6 is about the theme of relational boundary regulation issues of autonomy and connection in significant close relationships (see Baxter & Montgomery, 1996; Ting-Toomey, 1989a, 1989b, 1999). Assumption 6 concerns the thematic pair of identity autonomy and identity connection. Identity autonomy-connection is defined as an interpersonal relationship boundary regulation issue (e.g., from an autonomy-privacy lens to a relational connection lens). Cultural values such as individualism and collectivism influence our interpretations and evaluations of concepts such as "autonomy" and "connection."

For example, in an intercultural romantic relationship, an individualistic partner (e.g., an Australian boyfriend) may emphasize personal autonomy or privacy issues, while a collectivistic partner (e.g., a Vietnamese girlfriend) may invest more energy in regulating connection issues with the surrounding family network issues. Furthermore, the theme of identity autonomy-connection is clearly manifested through a culture's language usage and nonverbal emotional expression issues (Ting-Toomey, 1999).

For a deeper understanding of the relational theme of autonomy-connection, we need to have a strong grasp of the cultural, ethnic, gender, and relational value orientations that frame the motif of autonomy and connection. We also need to pay mindful attention to the verbal and nonverbal message styles of people in different individualistic, collectivistic, and hybrid cultural communities.

Assumptions 7 and 8

Assumption 7 is concerned with identity consistency and change issues over time. Identity consistency refers to a sense of identity continuation or stability through time as practiced through repeated daily routines or familiar cultural/ethnic interaction rituals (e.g., politeness rituals such as "complimenting," "requesting," and "requesting refusal" rituals). Identity change refers to a sense of identity dislocation and stretch in the spiraling cross-boundary intercultural contact experiences (Ting-Toomey, 1993, 1999).

For example, the identity change process of immigrants often involves subtle change to overt change. *Acculturation* involves the long-term conditioning process of newcomers in integrating the new values, norms, and symbols of their new culture, and developing new roles and skills to meet its demands. *Enculturation*, on the other hand, often refers to the sustained, primary socialization process of strangers in their original home (or natal) culture wherein they have internalized their primary cultural values. Many factors influence the immigrants' acculturation process—from systems-level factors (e.g., receptivity of the host culture), to individual-level (e.g., individual expectations) and interpersonal-level factors (e.g., formation of social networks; see Kim, 1995, 2001; Ting-Toomey, 1999).

The combined systems-level factors can create either a favorable or unfavorable climate for the newly arrived strangers. Obviously, the more favorable and receptive the cultural climate for the arrival of strangers, the easier it is for the strangers to adapt to the new culture (Kim, 2001, 2004). The more help the newcomers receive during the initial cultural adaptation stages, the more positive are their perceptions of their new environment. Lastly, the more realistic expectations the newcomers have concerning the new environment, the more they are psychologically prepared to handle the external and internal pressures of their new adventure.

In any effective intercultural cross-boundary journey, members of the host culture need to act as gracious hosts while newcomers need to act as willing-to-learn guests. Without collaborative effort, the hosts and the new arrivals may end up with great frustrations, miscommunications, and identity misalignments. In addition, the more an individual cultivates an optimal level of identity security, inclusion, interaction predictability, connection, and consistency, the more she or he is likely to be open to constructive identity change. The more an individual experiences identity threats or frustrations (e.g., identity exclusion, disconnection, and prolonged identity chaos), the more he or she is likely to cling to old, familiar identity habits. Overall, there exists a tolerable range of identity consistency or rootedness and identity change or rootlessness in an intercultural identity transformation process. All these identity themes are cast in dialectics' contrastive and complementary terms. Too much of one dialectical pole is not a good thing. Going to an extreme or stagnating along the dialectical spectrum is also not a good idea (Ting-Toomey, 1989a, 1989b, 1993).

For example, too much identity rootedness will turn a person into a highly ethnocentric being. Too much identity change (resulting in identity chaos) will turn a person into a highly marginal type with no moral center. However, a self-system without change will also stagnate. A balanced pendulum-like swing (as in a horizontal "figure 8" dance) between an identity rootedness process and an identity change process will help to promote dynamic identity growth and adaptation (see Yoshikawa, 1988). Conjointly, a "yin-yang" complementary perspective in viewing the identity thematic pairs—emotional security-vulnerability, membership inclusion-differentiation, interaction predictability-unpredictability, relational connection-autonomy, and identity consistency-change—in a mindful direction will help us to be aware of the identity fluidity issues within ourselves and in unfamiliar others. Competent intercultural communication is achieved via a joint function of both communicators successfully meeting all these mutual identity needs, expectations, attunements, and cravings.

Assumption 8 posits that cultural/ethnic, personal, and situational variability dimensions influence the meanings, interpretations, and evaluations of these identity-related themes. The needs and thresholds for emotional security and vulnerability, or group membership inclusion and differentiation differ from one cultural group to the next, from one personality type to the next, and from one situation to the next. Cultural beliefs and values (see Ting-Toomey, 1988; Ting-Toomey & Kurogi, 1998; and Chapter 4 in this volume) provide the implicit standards for evaluating and enacting different identity-related practices. Cultural membership and hence its cultural values direct how we think about our "identities," how we construct the identities of others, and how

these interactive identities play out in verbal and nonverbal symbolic interaction.

Situational norms and rules influence the appropriate delivery of identity lines or role enactments (Collier, 1996; Collier & Thomas, 1988). In "loose" cultures (e.g., Australia and the United States) or personal family systems, deviation from situational norms (e.g., crossing against red lights and jaywalking) and proper role performance is tolerated. In "tight" cultures (e.g., Greece and Japan) or positional family systems, individuals are expected to follow closely the sociocultural norms, the situational rules, and the interaction scripts of the larger cultural community (Triandis, 1995). Deviation from appropriate role performance often evokes disapproval and sanctions from others. Macro- to micro factors shape the identity-based conforming behaviors to identity-based expectancy violations' behaviors. On the macro level, factors such as cultural heterogeneity/homogeneity, low/high population density, institutional climate, and geographic mobility shape the "looseness" or "tightness" of a cultural situation (Triandis, 1995). On the micro level, cultural traveling experience, peer group attitudes, mass media channels, classroom learning, and family openness or security issues will act as a combined holistic effect in crafting an individual's identity transformation and stretching process (see Phinney, 1990, 1991, 1992).

Finally, personality trait factors and personal ability factors such as tolerance for ambiguity, personal flexibility, openness to experience, field independence versus field dependence, and construal of self (see Markus & Kitayama, 1991) also shape the meanings and expectations of identity enactment issues. Individuals who have higher degrees of tolerance for ambiguity or risk taking, for example, have less fear when in approaching cultural strangers or crossing ingroup/outgroup boundaries than individuals with lower degrees of tolerance for ambiguity (Ward, 2004; Ward, Bochner, & Furnham, 2001). Individuals with personal flexibility are more ready to experiment with new knowledge, cognitions, and skills than individuals with personal inflexibility in an unfamiliar cultural environment (Tharp, 2003). Individuals who take the time to reflect and increase their knowledge about cross-boundary identity issues may also stand a greater chance of challenging their own identity assumptions than individuals who stay in an ethnocentric state of denial or defense (M. Bennett, 1993; see also Bennett & Bennett, 2004).

Interestingly, immigrants and ethnic minority group members, in the context of intergroup relations, tend to be keenly sensitive to the intersecting issues of ethnicity and cultural identity issues. For ethnic minority members, the perceived imbalanced power dimension within a society often leads them to draw clear boundaries between the dominant "powerholder" group and the nondominant "fringe" group. For example, Orbe (1998) explains a variety of strategies that minority group members (or in his term, "co-culture members") use to deal with diverse identity issues in a dominant culture. The two conceptual dimensions in his co-culture theory are (a) whether the minority group member acts nonassertively, assertively, or aggressively, and (b) whether the minority group member takes the stance of separation (a maintenance of co-culture or minority culture views), accommodation (a combination of dominant and co-culture views), or assimilation (adopting the dominant culture's views). With these two dimensions, many intergroup communication strategies are made possible (e.g., intragroup networking, using liaisons, overcompensating) to deal with complex intergroup relation issues. Similarly, Cross, Smith, and Payne (2002) have also generated an interesting list of identity strategies (i.e., identity buffering, identity code-switching, identity bonding, identity bridging, and identity individuation) in accounting for how minority group members communicate with dominant group members. All these researchers are especially attuned to sociostructural constraint factors and sociohistorical practices that shape the

construction of a multifaceted, minority membership identity.

On the middle-level unit of analysis concerning ethnic and cultural identity issues, the one perspective that seems to capture the essence of the immigrants' and minority adaptation process is that of Berry and associates' fourfold identity typological model (Berry, Kim, & Boski, 1987). I review two ethnic/cultural identity development models in the next section.

TWO ETHNIC AND CULTURAL IDENTITY DEVELOPMENT MODELS

Ethnic-Cultural Identity Typology

In order to understand how ethnic individuals see themselves in relation to both their ethnic group (traditional ethnic group) and the society at large, ethnic and cultural identity salience can be viewed as a fourfold model that emphasizes an individual's adaptation option regarding ethnic identity *and* larger cultural identity maintenance issues (see Figure 10.1). Berry and his associates developed this model based in large part on Gordon's (1964) discussion of assimilation. While Gordon's work emphasizes the structural variables that determine minority group members' gradual assimilation into the dominant group, Berry's research emphasizes more of the psychological aspects of acculturation.

According to Berry (1994, 2004), immigrants who identify strongly with their ethnic traditions and values and weakly with the values of the dominant culture subscribe to the traditional-based or *ethnic-oriented identity* option. These individuals emphasize the value of retaining their ethnic practice and avoid interacting with the dominant group. As a result, there is an implication of a higher degree of stress that occurs through contact with the dominant group. Individuals who identify strongly with ethnic tradition maintenance and at the same time incorporate values and practices of the larger society internalize the *bicultural identity* or integrative option.

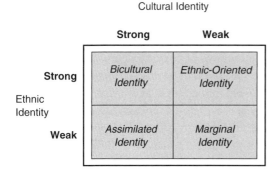

Cultural Identity

Figure 10.1   A Cultural-Ethnic Identity
                 Typology Model

SOURCE: Adapted from Berry, Kim, and Boski
(1987).

Integrated individuals feel comfortable being members of both cultural groups.

Individuals who identify weakly with their ethnic traditions and values and identify strongly with the values and norms of the larger culture tend to practice the *assimilated identity* option. Finally, individuals who identify weakly with their ethnic traditions and also weakly with the larger cultural worldviews are in the *marginal identity* state. They basically have disconnected ties to both their ethnic group and the larger society and often experience feelings of ambiguity, invisibility, and alienation.

For example, a second-generation Asian American or Latino/a American can commit to one of the following four ethnic/cultural identity salience categories: Asian or Latino(a) primarily, American primarily, both, or neither (Chung & Ting-Toomey, 2001; Espiritu, 1992). Systems-level antecedent factors—situational, individual, and interpersonal factors—add together as a net influence on immigrants' adaptive experience and identity change process (Yinger, 1994).

Racial/Ethnic Identity Development Model

Alternatively, from the racial/ethnic identity development framework, various models have

been proposed to account for racial or ethnic identity formation of African Americans (e.g., Cross, 1978, 1995; Hecht et al., 2003), Asian Americans (e.g., Sodowsky, Kwan, & Pannu, 1995; Sue & Sue, 1999), Latino/a Americans (e.g., Ruiz, 1990), and European Americans (e.g., Rowe, Bennett, & Atkinson, 1994). Racial/ethnic identity development models tend to emphasize the oppressive-adaptive nature of intergroup relations in a pluralistic society.

From this framework, racial/ethnic identity salience concerns the development of racial or ethnic consciousness along a linear, progressive pathway of identity change. For example, Cross (1991) has developed a five-stage model of African American racial identity development that includes pre-encounter (stage 1), encounter (stage 2), immersion-emersion (stage 3), internalization (stage 4), and internalization-commitment (stage 5). Helms and her associates (e.g., Helms, 1993; Parham & Helms, 1985) have amended and refined this five-stage model (i.e., integrating the concept of "worldview" in each stage) into four stages: pre-encounter, encounter, immersion-emersion, and internalization-commitment (see Figure 10.2).

The *pre-encounter stage* is the high cultural identity salience phase wherein ethnic minority group members' self-concepts are influenced by the values and norms of the larger culture. In this stage, individuals are naïve, unaware of being an ethnic group member, and may define themselves as "Canadian," "American," or "Australian." The *encounter stage* is the marginal identity phase when new racial/ethnic realization is awakened in the individuals because of a "racially shattering" event (e.g., encountering racism), and minority group members realize that they cannot be fully accepted as part of the "white world." The *immersion-emersion* stage is the strong racial/ethnic identity salience phase when individuals withdraw to the safe confines of their own racial/ethnic groups and become ethnically conscious. Lastly, the *internalization-commitment stage*

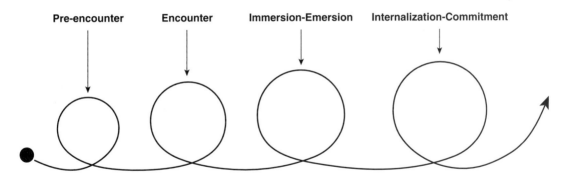

Figure 10.2   Racial/Ethnic Identity Development Model

SOURCE: Adapted from Helms (1993).

is the phase in which individuals develop a secure racial/ethnic identity that is internally defined and at the same time are able to establish genuine interpersonal contacts with members of the dominant group and other multiracial groups.

From the identity negotiation perspective, we can predict that individuals who can creatively handle the challenges of the identity dialectics of security-vulnerability, inclusion-exclusion, predictability-unpredictability, connection-autonomy, and consistency-change would be the ones who become dynamic biculturalists or dynamic cultural transformers. A dynamic biculturalist or transformer is one who has struggled to and worked out a comfortable and coherent sense of identity through trials and errors, and through the creative management of identity security and vulnerability, and identity inclusion-differentiation issues. Only when individuals have cultivated the dynamic, comfortable zone of emotional security and vulnerability, for example, can they begin to accept and understand those who are culturally different from them and their struggles for emotional security and inclusion efforts. While many individuals can arrive at being functional biculturalists (i.e., they can function adaptively through different behavioral or nonverbal code-switching strategies), dynamic cultural transformers have worked through the dynamic tensions of cognitive, affective,

behavioral, and ethical struggles in a deep manner. Dynamic cultural transformers can function fluidly in an "effortlessly mindful" state of shifting among multiple cultural mindscapes and multiple cultural/ethnic identity issues (see Ting-Toomey, 1999; Ting-Toomey & Chung, 2005).

With the increase in minority groups living in the United States, the question of identification with group membership is an important concern. One of the common threads is trying to figure out who we as U.S. Americans are in the context of being seen as a culturally pluralistic nation. How can we all learn to grow and stretch with each other side by side? How can we reconcile intergroup identity struggles? How can we utilize the dynamic tensions from diverse groups to construct a meaningful "U.S. American" culture or a meaningful common-ground culture that takes into account all the identity diversity and richness? These are some of the important issues that await us in our development toward becoming dynamic cultural transformers in the 21st century.

INTERCULTURAL IDENTITY NEGOTIATION COMPETENCE

Assumption 9 of the identity negotiation theory emphasizes two ideas: The first is that mindful intercultural communication has three components: knowledge, mindfulness, and identity negotiation skills; the second is that mindful intercultural communication refers to the appropriate, effective, and satisfactory management of desired shared identity meanings and shared identity goals in an intercultural episode. Competent identity negotiation emphasizes the importance of creatively integrating knowledge and positive attitudinal factors, and putting them into mindful practice in everyday intercultural interactions (Ting-Toomey, 1999, 2004). Assumption 10 posits that competent identity negotiation outcomes include the feelings of being understood, respected, and affirmatively valued.

This section covers the components, criteria, and outcomes of identity negotiation competence. The components and criteria of competent identity negotiation are presented in Assumption 9, and identity competence outcomes are identified in Assumption 10.

Identity Knowledge Component

In order to understand the person with whom you are communicating, you need to understand the identity domains that she or he deems as salient. For example, if she or he strongly values her or his cultural membership identity, you need to find ways to validate and be responsive to her or his cultural identities; or if she or he strongly values her or his personal identity above and beyond her or his cultural membership, you need to uncover ways to affirm her or his positively desired personal identity.

Without culture-sensitive knowledge, cultural communicators may not be able to match cultural value issues with identity-related behaviors. Knowledge here refers to the process of an in-depth understanding of certain phenomena via a range of information gained through conscious learning and personal experiences and observations. In order to manage cultural differences mindfully, for example, we must take other people's cultural membership and personal identity factors into consideration.

If others are collectivists, we may want to pay extra attention to their "process-oriented" (i.e., relationship-based) assumptions about communication. If others are individualists, we may want to be sensitive to their "outcome-oriented" (i.e., instrumental result-based) assumptions about communication (see Ting-Toomey, 1999; Ting-Toomey & Oetzel, 2001). Both culture-general and culture-specific knowledge can enhance our positive attitudes and constructive interaction skills in dealing with people who are culturally different.

To increase our knowledge, we need to be mindful of what is going on in our own thinking, feelings, and experiencing. The concept of "mindfulness" can serve as the first attunement step in raising our awareness of our own systems of thinking and judging. In addition, through mindfulness we can learn to be more aware of the commonalities and differences that exist between dissimilar individuals and groups.

Mindfulness Component

Langer's (1989, 1997) concept of mindfulness encourages individuals to tune in conscientiously to their habituated mental scripts and preconceived expectations. Mindfulness means the readiness to shift one's frame of reference, the motivation to use new categories to understand cultural or ethnic differences, and the preparedness to experiment with creative avenues of decision making and problem solving (Tharp, 2003). The concept of mindfulness can serve as the first intentional step in integrating our theoretical knowledge with identity-based process and outcome dimensions.

Mindlessness, on the other hand, is the heavy reliance on familiar frames of reference, old routinized designs or categories, and customary ways of doing things. It means we are operating on "automatic pilot," without conscious thinking or reflection. It means we are at the "reactive" stage rather than the intentional "proactive" stage. To engage in a state of mindfulness in transformative intercultural communication, individuals need to be aware that both differences and similarities exist between the membership groups and the communicators as unique human individuals.

To be mindful communicators, individuals need to recognize the value systems that influence others' self-conceptions. They need to be open to a new way of identity construction. They need to be prepared to perceive and understand a behavior or a problem from others' cultural and personal standpoints. Mindful communicators need to be on the alert for the multiple perspectives that typically exist in interpreting a cultural collusion episode (Ting-Toomey, 2004).

Identity-Negotiation Skills' Component

The term *skills* refers to the actual operational abilities to perform those behaviors that are considered appropriate and effective in a given cultural situation. Adaptive interaction skills help us to communicate mindfully in an intercultural situation. Many interaction skills are useful in promoting appropriate and effective identity-based competent communication.

Some of these, for example, are values clarification skills, mindful observation skills, mindful listening skills, verbal empathy skills, nonverbal sensitivity skills, identity support skills, facework management skills, conflict reframing skills, collaborative dialogue skills, and transcultural competence skills (see Ting-Toomey, 1999, 2004; Ting-Toomey & Chung, 2005).

We can discover salient identity issues that are desirable to the individuals in our everyday intercultural encounters through practicing two particular identity negotiation competence skills: mindful listening and identity validation. Mindful listening demands that we pay intentional attunement to both the verbal and nonverbal messages of the speaker before responding. It means listening attentively with all our senses and noticing and checking responsively for the accuracy of our meaning

decoding process on multiple identity and contextual levels. We have to learn to listen responsively or *ting* (the Chinese word for listening means attending delicately with our ears, eyes, and a focused heart) to the sounds, tones, gestures, movements, nonverbal nuances, pauses, silences, and identity meanings in a given intercultural situation. Mindful listening essentially involves a fundamental shift of perspective. It means taking into account not only how things look from my identity perspective, but how they look and feel from the other's identity framing perspective.

When a person perceives authentic and positive identity validation, she or he would tend to view self-images positively. When a person perceives identity rejection, he or she would tend to view self-images negatively. There are, of course, macro- and micro-level factors that mediate between our perceptions or mental filters and the behaviors that we have experienced or observed. In addition, positive identity validation is typically expressed through verbal and nonverbal confirming behaviors and postures. For example, confirming communication involves recognizing others with important group-based and person-based identities, responding sensitively to other people's moods and affective states, and accepting other people's experiences and stories as real. Disconfirmation, on the other hand, is the process through which individuals do not recognize the existence of the others, do not respond sensitively to cultural strangers, and do not accept others' experiences as valid (Cissna & Sieburg, 1981). By verbally and nonverbally confirming the desired identities of the cultural stranger, we reaffirm the intrinsic worthiness of the dissimilar other. Identity valuation skill can be conveyed through a word, a glance, a gesture, or a responsive silence.

Identity Negotiation Process: Criteria

Mindful intercultural communication involves the appropriate management of shared identity meanings and effective achievement of desired identity goals. Spitzberg and Cupach (1984) and Cupach and Imahori (1994) propose that communication competence has two criteria: appropriateness and effectiveness. Appropriateness refers to the degree to which behaviors are regarded as proper and match the expectations generated by the culture. Effectiveness refers to the degree to which communicators achieve shared meanings and desirable outcomes in a given situation. Using these two criteria in evaluating intercultural identity-based competence, we can define mindful intercultural communication as the process and outcome of how two dissimilar individuals negotiate shared identity meanings and achieve desired, conjoint identity outcomes through appropriate and effective behaviors in an intercultural episode.

Shared identity meanings involve an acute awareness of meaning encoding and decoding on the cultural, gender, social class, sexual orientation, age, or personal identity level. Interaction identity goals (or facework goals; see Ting-Toomey, 1988, 2004, and Chapter 4 in this volume) refer to how individuals would like to be treated in the intercultural interaction episode. Self-presentation goals or interactional identity goals refer to the personal or social images that we want to sustain or impress (e.g., as intelligent, credible, or with high social status) and want others to respect as a consequence of our interaction. Identity goals are closely related to relationship goals and are subject to constant emotional strains and turmoil on both sociocultural membership and personal levels (Rothman, 1997).

Thus, competent intercultural communication emphasizes the importance of integrating the necessary intercultural knowledge, mindfulness, and interaction skills to manage identity-based issues adaptively and to achieve desired identity outcomes creatively. Desired identity outcomes can include mutual identity respect, differentiating identity space, or conjoint identity synchrony.

Furthermore, intercultural communication competence relies heavily on the perceptions of the communicators in evaluating each other's communicative performance. What may appear effective (e.g., starting a public presentation with a joke) in one cultural context can be viewed as ineffective and inappropriate from another cultural perspective. Likewise, what may appear as appropriate (e.g., speaking apologetically or metaphorically) in one cultural context can be interpreted by another culture as inappropriate and ineffective. To communicate competently, individuals have to enhance their cultural knowledge and mindful commitment in applying elastic verbal and nonverbal negotiation skills in the intercultural encounter process.

Identity Negotiation Competence: Outcomes

According to the identity negotiation theory, satisfactory outcomes include the feeling of being understood, the feeling of being respected, and the feeling of being affirmatively valued. Together, they serve as the identity outcome facets. The accomplishment of a satisfactory identity negotiation process is contingent on the perceptions of the communicators in the interaction scene. It also depends on our willingness and commitment to practice mindfulness in our interactions with dissimilar others.

To the extent that communicators perceive that desired identities have been authentically understood, accorded due respect and courtesy, and affirmatively valued and supported, the involved parties should experience a high sense of identity satisfaction. To the extent that the communicators perceive that desired identities have been mindlessly bypassed, misunderstood, and/or insulted, the involved parties should experience a low sense of identity satisfaction. Thus, the construct of identity satisfaction acts as an essential criterion of identity negotiation competence. As one scholar indicates (Cahn,

1987, 1992), the *feeling of being understood* is one of the most powerful means of being validated on both group membership and personal identity levels.

The feeling of being understood connotes an illuminating understanding voice out there that clearly can act as a reflective mirror for one's thinking, feeling, and behaving. The comprehending voice does not necessary have to agree, but it has to have empathetic emotional impact (i.e., "I truly understand where you're coming from"). Identity understanding begins with gathering accurate identity-based information and being culturally sensitive in probing identity-based layers in the intergroup negotiation process. It also means the willingness to share facets of our own self-conceptions with others in a culturally and personally resonating manner.

The *feeling of being respected* connotes that our desirable identity-based behaviors and practices are being deemed legitimate, credible, and on an equal footing with members of other groups. Identity respect connotes the mindful monitoring of one's verbal and nonverbal attitudes in interacting with dissimilar others. It means empowering oneself to dig deeper to discover unmet identity needs and unmet identity wants issues. It also means recognizing what is important to others on multiple identity levels (Bush & Folger, 1994). It further means getting to the heart of the matter through the use of collaborative, respectful dialogue and treating others' salient identities with courtesy, respect, and dignity (Littlejohn & Domenici, 2001).

The *feeling of being affirmatively valued* refers to our sense of being positively endorsed and being affirmatively embraced as "worthwhile" individuals despite having different group-based identities or stigmatized identities. Positive identity endorsement is typically expressed through verbal and nonverbal confirming messages. Confirmation is the "process through which individuals are recognized, acknowledged, and endorsed" (Laing,

1961, p. 83). Confirming communication involves recognizing others with important sociocultural identities and person-based identities and conveying in a sensitive manner your positive valuation of the other person's self-valued identities. Disconfirming communication, on the other hand, involves the display of aloof, patronizing, rejective, and/or hostile attitudes to the cultural strangers and a lack of awareness and sensitivity toward the central identities of the cultural strangers. In confirming others on an authentic basis, we use identity-support messages to affirm others' alternative or marginalized worldviews, values, feelings, stories, and/or experiences. In disconfirming others, we use indifferent or apathetic messages (e.g., verbally and nonverbally dissociating from culturally different others) and discrediting or hostile messages (e.g., patronizing language, overgeneralized stereotyping messages, demeaning language or racist jokes) to discount the others' feelings, thoughts, experiences, and personhoods.

We affirm others by the words and nonverbal actions we use in our communication with them. In communicating mindfully, our messages convey our understanding, respect, and affirmative valuation of dissimilar others on a holistic and humane level. In interacting mindlessly, our messages convey ignorant or hostile intergroup attitudes, doubts, and distrust. The positive or negative consequences of the identity negotiation process, ultimately, affect the development of quality intergroup and interpersonal relationships. Competent intercultural communicators are resourceful individuals who are attuned to both self-identity and other-identity negotiation issues (Ting-Toomey, 1993). They are mindful of the antecedent, process, and outcome factors that shape the dynamic interplay of the intercultural identity negotiation process. They are also attuned to the structural, historical, and situational scripts in shaping a multifaceted identity. A competent identity negotiator is one who is able to hold two polarized value systems and be at ease with the dynamic tensions that exist between the vulnerability spectrum and the security spectrum in the double-swing dance. She or he is able to use multiple cultural frames of reference to interpret a problematic, cultural collusion situation. He or she is able to use multiple communication styles to listen, to empathize, to resonate, to code-switch, and to convey positive affirmation to members of diverse cultural and ethnic groups. A competent identity negotiator is a dynamic ice skater who can maintain an optimal sense of balance and grace as she or he waltzes through the maze of identity chaos and the identity discovery process.

REFERENCES

Alba, R. (1990). *Ethnic identity: The transformation of White America*. New Haven, CT: Yale University Press.

Baxter, L. A., & Montgomery, B. M. (1996). *Relating: Dialogues and dialectics*. New York: Guilford.

Bennett, J. (1993). Cultural marginality: Identity issues in intercultural training. In R. M. Paige (Ed.), *Education for the intercultural experience*. Yarmouth, ME: Intercultural Press.

Bennett, J., & Bennett, M. (2004). Developing intercultural sensitivity: An integrative approach to global and domestic diversity. In D. Landis, J. Bennett, & M. Bennett (Eds.), *Handbook of intercultural training* (3rd ed.). Thousand Oaks, CA: Sage.

Bennett, M. (1993). Toward ethnorelativism: A developmental model of intercultural sensitivity. In R. M. Paige (Ed.), *Education for the intercultural experience*. Yarmouth, ME: Intercultural Press.

Berry, J. (1994). Acculturation and psychological adaptation. In A. Bouvy, F. van de Vijver, P. Boski, & P. Schmitz (Eds.), *Journeys into cross-cultural psychology*. Lisse, The Netherlands: Swets & Zeitlinger.

Berry, J. (2004). Fundamental psychological processes in intercultural relations. In D. Landis, J. Bennett, & M. Bennett (Eds.), *Handbook of intercultural training* (3rd ed.). Thousand Oaks, CA: Sage.

Berry, J., Kim, U., & Boski, P. (1987). Psychological acculturation of immigrants. In Y. Y. Kim & W. B. Gudykunst (Eds.), *Cross-cultural adaptation: Current approaches*. Newbury Park, CA: Sage.

Berstein, B. (1973). *Class, codes, and control* (Vol. 1). London: Routledge.

Brewer, M. (1991). The social self: On being same and different at the same time. *Personality and Social Psychology Bulletin, 17,* 475–482.

Brewer, M. (1996). When contact is not enough: Social identity and intergroup cooperation. *International Journal of Intercultural Relations, 20,* 291–303.

Brewer, M., & Miller, N. (1996). *Intergroup relations*. Pacific Grove, CA: Brooks/Cole.

Bush, R., & Folger, J. (1994). *The promise of mediation: Responding to conflict through empowerment and recognition*. San Francisco: Jossey-Bass.

Cahn, D. (1987). *Letting go: A practical theory of relationship disengagement and reengagement*. Albany: State University of New York Press.

Cahn, D. (1992). *Conflict in intimate relationships*. New York: Guilford.

Chung, L. C., & Ting-Toomey, S. (2001). Ethnic identity and relational expectations among Asian Americans. *Communication Research Reports, 16,* 157–166.

Cissna, K., & Sieburg, E. (1981). Patterns of interactional confirmation and disconfirmation. In C. Wilder-Mott & J. Weakland (Eds.), *Rigor and imagination*. New York: Praeger.

Collier, M. J. (1996). Communication competence problematics in ethnic friendships. *Communication Monographs, 63,* 314–336.

Collier, M. J., & Thomas, M. (1988). Identity in intercultural communication: An interpretive perspective. In Y. Y. Kim & W. B. Gudykunst (Eds.), *Theories of intercultural communication*. Newbury Park, CA: Sage.

Cross, W., Jr. (1978). The Thomas and Cross models on psychological nigrescence: A literature review. *Journal of Black Psychology, 4,* 13–31.

Cross, W., Jr. (1991). *Shades of black: Diversity in African-American identity*. Philadelphia: Temple University Press.

Cross, W., Jr. (1995). The psychology of nigrescence: Revising the Cross model. In J. Ponterotto, J. Casas, L. Suzuki, & C. Alexander

(Eds.), *Handbook of multicultural counseling.* Thousand Oaks, CA: Sage.

Cross, W., Jr., Smith, L., & Payne, Y. (2002). Black identity: A repertoire of daily enactments. In P. Pedersen, J. Draguns, W. Lonner, & J. Trimble (Eds.), *Counseling across cultures* (5th ed.). Thousand Oaks, CA: Sage.

Cupach, W., & Imahori, T. (1994). Identity management theory: Communication competence in intercultural episodes and relationships. In R. Wiseman & J. Koester (Eds.), *Intercultural communication competence.* Newbury Park, CA: Sage.

Edwards, J. (1994). *Multilingualism.* London: Routledge.

Espiritu, Y. (1992). *Asian American panethnicity.* Philadelphia: Temple University Press.

Gorden, M. (1964). *Assimilation in American life.* Oxford, UK: Oxford University Press.

Gudykunst, W. B. (1995). Anxiety/uncertainty management (AUM) theory: Current status. In R. Wiseman (Ed.), *Intercultural communication theory.* Thousand Oaks, CA: Sage.

Gudykunst, W. B. (2004). *Bridging differences: Effective intergroup communication* (4th ed.). Thousand Oaks, CA: Sage.

Guerrerro, L., Andersen, P., & Afifi, W. (2001). *Close encounters: Communicating in relationships.* Mountain View, CA: Mayfield.

Haslett, B. (1987). *Communication: Strategic action in context.* Hillsdale, NJ: Lawrence Erlbaum.

Hecht, M., Jackson, R., & Ribeau, S. A. (2003). *African American communication: Exploring identity and culture.* Mahwah, NJ: Lawrence Erlbaum.

Helms, J. (1993). Introduction: Review of racial identity terminology. In J. Helms (Ed.), *Black and white racial identity: Theory, research, and practice.* Westport, CT: Praeger.

Helms, J., & Parham, T. (1993). Black Racial Identity Attitude Scale (Form WRIAS). In J. Helms (Ed.), *Black and white racial identity: Theory, research, and practice.* Westport, CT: Praeger.

Hofstede, G. (1991). *Cultures and organizations: Software of the mind.* London: McGraw-Hill.

Hofstede, G. (1998). *Masculinity and femininity: The taboo dimension of national culture.* Thousand Oaks, CA: Sage.

Hofstede, G. (2001). *Culture's consequences* (2nd ed.). Thousand Oaks, CA: Sage.

Jackson, R. L. (1999). *The negotiation of cultural identity.* Westport, CT: Praeger.

Jackson, R. L. (2002). Cultural contracts theory: Toward an understanding of identity negotiation. *Communication Quarterly, 50,* 359–367.

Koerner, A., & Fitzpatrick, M. A. (2002). Understanding family communication patterns and family functioning: The roles of conversation orientation and conformity orientation. In W. B. Gudykunst (Ed.), *Communication yearbook 26.* Mahwah, NJ: Lawrence Erlbaum.

Kim, Y. Y. (1995). Intercultural adaptation. In R. Wiseman (Ed.), *Intercultural communication theory.* Thousand Oaks, CA: Sage.

Kim, Y. Y. (2001). *Becoming intercultural: An integrative theory of communication and cross-cultural adaptation.* Thousand Oaks, CA: Sage.

Kim, Y. Y. (2004). Long-term cross-cultural adaptation: Training implications of an integrative theory. In D. Landis, J. Bennett, & M. Bennett (Eds.), *Handbook of intercultural training* (3rd ed.). Thousand Oaks, CA: Sage.

Laing, D. (1961). *The self and others.* New York: Pantheon.

Langer, E. (1989). *Mindfulness.* Reading, MA: Addison-Wesley.

Langer, E. (1997). *The power of mindful learning.* Reading, MA: Addison-Wesley.

Littlejohn, S., & Domenici, K. (2001). *Engaging communication in conflict: Systematic practice.* Thousand Oaks, CA: Sage.

Locke, D. (1992). *Increasing multicultural understanding: A comprehensive model.* Newbury Park, CA: Sage.

Maltz, D., & Borker, R. (1982). A cultural approach to male-female communication. In J. Gumperz (Ed.), *Language and social identity.* Cambridge, UK: Cambridge University Press.

Markus, H., & Kitayama, S. (1991). Culture and the self: Implications for cognition, emotion, and motivation. *Psychological Review, 2,* 224–253.

Mead, G. H. (1934). *Mind, self, and society.* Chicago: University of Chicago Press.

Orbe, M. (1998). *Constructing co-culture theory: An explication of culture, power, and communication.* Thousand Oaks, CA: Sage.

Parham, T., & Helms, J. (1985). The relationship of racial identity attitudes to self-actualization of black students and affective states. *Journal of Counseling Psychology, 32,* 431-440.

Phinney, J. (1990). Ethnic identity in adolescence and adulthood: A review. *Psychological Bulletin, 108,* 499–514.

Phinney, J. (1991). Ethnic identity and self-esteem: A review and integration. *Hispanic Journal of Behavioral Sciences, 13,* 193–208.

Phinney, J. (1992). The multigroup ethnic identity measure: A new scale for use with diverse groups. *Journal of Adolescent Research, 7,* 156–176.

Rothman, J. (1997). *Resolving identity-based conflict in nations, organizations, and communities.* San Francisco: Jossey-Bass.

Rowe, W., Bennett, S., & Atkinson, D. (1994). White racial identity development models: A critique and alternative proposal. *Counseling Psychologist, 22,* 129–146.

Ruiz, A. (1990). Ethnic identity: Crisis and resolution. *Journal of Multicultural Counseling, 18,* 29–40.

Schaefer, R. (1990). *Racial and ethnic groups* (4th ed.). New York: HarperCollins.

Sodowsky, G., Kwan, K.-L., & Pannu, R. (1995). Ethnic identity of Asians in the United States. In J. Ponterotto, J. Casas, L. Suzuki, & C. Alexander (Eds.), *Handbook of multicultural counseling.* Thousand Oaks, CA: Sage.

Spitzberg, B., & Cupach, W (1984). *Interpersonal communication competence.* Beverly Hills, CA: Sage.

Stryker, S. (1987). Identity theory: Developments and extensions. In K. Yardley & T. Honess (Eds.), *Self and society: Psychosocial perspectives.* Chichester, UK: Wiley.

Stryker, S. (1991). Exploring the relevance of social cognition for the relationship of self and society: Linking the cognitive perspective and identity theory. In J. Howard & P. Callero (Eds.), *Self-society dynamic: Emotion, cognition and action.* Cambridge, UK: Cambridge University Press.

Sue, D. W., & Sue, D. (1999). *Counseling the culturally different: Theory and practice* (3rd ed.). New York: John Wiley.

Tajfel, H. (1981). *Human groups and social categories.* Cambridge, UK: Cambridge University Press.

Tajfel, H., & Turner, J. (1986). The social identity theory of intergroup relations. In S. Worchel &

W. Austin (Eds.), *Psychology of intergroup relations.* Monterey, CA: Brooks/Cole.

Tannen, D. (1990). *You just don't understand: Women and men in conversation.* New York: William Morrow.

Tannen, D. (1994). *Talking 9 to 5.* New York: William Morrow.

Ting-Toomey, S. (1981). Ethnic identity and close friendship in Chinese American college students. *International Journal of Intercultural Relations, 5,* 383–406.

Ting-Toomey, S. (1986). Interpersonal ties in intergroup communication. In W. B. Gudykunst (Ed.), *Intergroup communication.* Baltimore, MD: Edward Arnold.

Ting-Toomey, S. (1988). Intercultural conflict styles: A face-negotiation theory. In Y. Y. Kim & W. B. Gudykunst (Eds.), *Theories in intercultural communication.* Newbury Park, CA: Sage.

Ting-Toomey, S. (1989a). Culture and interpersonal relationship development: Some conceptual issues. In J. Anderson (Ed.), *Communication yearbook 12.* Newbury Park, CA: Sage.

Ting-Toomey, S. (1989b). Identity and interpersonal bonding. In M. Asante & W. B. Gudykunst (Eds.), *Handbook of international and intercultural communication.* Newbury Park, CA: Sage.

Ting-Toomey, S. (1993). Communicative resourcefulness: An identity negotiation perspective. In R. Wiseman & J. Koester (Eds.), *Intercultural communication competence.* Newbury Park, CA: Sage.

Ting-Toomey, S. (1997). An intercultural journey: The four seasons. In M. Bond (Ed.), *Working at the interface of cultures: Eighteen lives in social science.* London: Routledge.

Ting-Toomey, S. (1999). *Communicating across cultures.* New York: Guilford.

Ting-Toomey, S. (2004). Translating conflict face-negotiation theory into practice. In D. Landis, J. Bennett, & M. Bennett (Eds.), *Handbook of intercultural training* (3rd ed.). Thousand Oaks, CA: Sage.

Ting-Toomey, S., & Chung, L. C. (2005). *Understanding intercultural communication.* Los Angeles: Roxbury.

Ting-Toomey, S., & Kurogi, A. (1998). Facework competence in intercultural conflict: An updated face-negotiation theory. *International Journal of Intercultural Relations, 22,* 187–225.

Ting-Toomey, S., & Oetzel, J. (2001). *Managing intercultural conflict effectively*. Thousand Oaks, CA: Sage.

Tharp, T. (2003). *The creative habit: Learn it and use it for life*. New York: Simon & Schuster.

Triandis, H. (1995). *Individualism and collectivism*. Boulder, CO: Westview.

Turner, J. H. (1987). Toward a sociological theory of motivation. *American Sociological Review, 52*, 15–27.

Turner, J. H. (1988). *A theory of social interaction*. Stanford, CA: Stanford University Press.

Ward, C. (2004). Theories of culture: Contact and implications. In D. Landis, J. Bennett, & M. Bennett (Eds.), *Handbook of intercultural training* (3rd ed.). Thousand Oaks, CA: Sage.

Ward, C., Bochner, S., & Furnham, A. (2001). *The psychology of culture shock* (2nd ed.). London: Routledge.

Waters, M. (1990). *Ethnic options: Choosing identities in America*. Berkeley: University of California Press.

Weinreich, P. (2003). Identity structural analysis. In P. Weinreich & W. Saunderson (Eds.), *Analysing identity: Cross-cultural, societal and clinical contexts*. London: Routledge.

Wood, J. (1996). Gender, relationships, and communication. In J. Wood (Ed.), *Gendered relationships*. Mountain View, CA: Mayfield.

Wood, J. (1997). *Gendered lives: Communication, gender, and culture* (2nd ed.). Belmont, CA: Wadsworth.

Yinger, M. (1994). *Ethnicity*. Albany: State University of New York Press.

Yoshikawa, M. (1988). Cross-cultural adaptation and perceptual development. In Y. Y. Kim & W. B. Gudykunst (Eds.), *Cross-cultural adaptation*. Newbury Park, CA: Sage.

11

Theorizing Cultural Identifications

Critical Updates and Continuing Evolution

MARY JANE COLLIER

As a scholar/instructor/practitioner, my work is best understood as a collaborative enterprise: contingent and temporary, continually evolving, and an integration of my experiences with different ideologies, social institutions, and norms of practice, my relationships with diverse scholars, respondent/collaborators living in places and speaking/acting from locations quite different from my own, as well as my experiences as a human being with a heart, spirit, political orientations, emotional needs, and ego. I'm grateful to Bill Gudykunst for inviting me to reflect upon and provide a synthesis of my work on cultural identifications over the past 20 years. In this chapter I select out a few significant ways in which my assumptions about culture, cultural identifications, and context have and are evolving, what orientations I now bring to inquiry, and my own ways of being

in the world and engaging others and the environment.

I approach theorizing and researching as engaged and interrelated sets of practices and experiences. My earliest work on cultural identity theory was characterized by a goal of developing a set of interrelated testable propositions. Currently I think of theorizing as offering proposals of contingent understandings that reflect and engage my multiple cultural group identifications, histories, and socialization; my aspirations as a scholar; and all my experiences in the continuously changing contexts in which I live and interact with others. I am committed to developing tentative understandings of praxis, or practical wisdom. As Stewart and Zediker (2000) explain, this kind of knowledge is dialogic, situated, and mediates between universal and particular, between cultural and individual (after Dunne,

1993). I also seek to build knowledge based on examining relationships among and between structures and situated texts from critical and interpretive perspectives. In this chapter I select out a few significant moments, and share stories of the twists and turns along the way.

Enduring Premises and Goals

My intentions as a scholar/practitioner/instructor/interlocutor working with communication and multiple cultural groups continue to be based upon a desire to better understand social interaction, relationships, and group processes, and particularly how conflict emerges, and relationships and connections between individuals and groups occur. I am drawn to understand how we, as individuals, come to be aligned with different groups, and to understand who we are as cultural beings and also as unique spiritual beings. I am moving in a direction to explore transcendent and spiritual principles that parallel and intersect with cultural identifications and contextual factors and to discover new locations for dialogue to provide an alternative to violence. I am also committed to increase my awareness and change my own behavior, as well as to collaborate with others, to change our communication conduct, norms, policies, and institutions ultimately to pursue social justice and create alternative spaces to engage a wider array of voices, adopt ethical standards, and transform our social worlds.

My goal is to live, work, and have my conduct reflect what Yep (in Collier, Hegde, Lee, Nakayama, & Yep, 2002) calls the embodiment of social justice: ethics and progressive social change. I seek to orient my work toward relevant social issues and life experiences; as Hegde (in Collier et al., 2002) notes, "We need to relate our work to the material realities of life outside" (p. 274). I am working to recognize the ways in which I most certainly benefit from a range of privileges based upon my national citizenship, my race, ethnic

affiliations, class level, educational status, sexual orientation, and physical abilities, among others, while so many others live in conditions that threaten their lives, emotions, and spirits. My goal in contributing to knowledge about intercultural communication is to turn our attention to peoples' lives and livelihoods and demonstrate that what we study and teach reflects whom we are and has the potential to be a tool for transformation.

Because of these general goals, my orientations as a scholar/practitioner include being open and reflexive to ways in which I have privilege and to uncover taken-for-granted assumptions. In so doing I recognize scholarship as political and the engaged nature of theorizing. I choose to share my journey in this personal way to show my continuing struggle to recognize and work with the privileges with which I am accorded and work toward my goal of learning how to maximize relationships that promote inclusion and social justice. In addition, I hope to help readers better understand the utility of a critical orientation and the value of scholarly evolution.

Theorizing about cultural identifications in my own work has and continues to evolve over the past 20 years because the location from which I speak and act is changing. Who I am as a scholar/practitioner/instructor/interlocutor is a compilation of multiple cultural identifications that continue to shape, and be shaped by, the educational institutions where I received my training and where I have been employed, and my travels along a political and professional path that includes an itinerary and a history.

For example, I have expanded conceptualizations of culture from a historically transmitted system of symbols, meanings, and norms, to being enactments of group identity(ies) observable in patterns of contextualized social interaction. Due in part to dialogue with Wenshu Lee and other colleagues about culture as itinerary (see Collier et al., 2002) I am now exploring a conception of cultures as a combination of contextual identifications, representations, and relationships; a position along a path that provides an orientation for speaking, acting, and producing; a view of the past and histories; and a contingent and changing direction of movement for the present and future. Cultural identifications are shared locations and orientations evidenced in a variety of communication forms, including conduct of groups of people, discourse in public texts, mediated forms, artistic expressions, commodities and products, and individual accounts and ascriptions about group conduct. More specifically, in this chapter I refer to my experiences and current research about cultural identifications in three international sites: the United States, South Africa, and the region of Palestine and Israel.

A JOURNEY IN WHICH THE PERSONAL MEETS THE POLITICAL

The assumptions grounding my work have changed over time partly because of my desire to remain relevant to the dynamics of evolution characterizing our environment and social worlds and concomitant expanding bases of knowledge and orientations to inquiry. Also, I have changed as a person due to my own rich experiences with communities of people having very different locations and identifications than mine. In my senior year of undergraduate studies at the University of Colorado, Boulder, as I was finishing up my combined majors in Communication and Education in 1974, I became a student teacher at East High School in Denver, Colorado. At this time, many students were required to ride buses across town in order to ensure that the student population was "integrated."

From the Latina/o and African American students in my classrooms and during Forensics Team practice and tournaments, I learned that what I had been taught and read about the culture of "ethnic groups" (defined then as "minority, non-whites") wasn't consistent with how many of my students lived their lives. Some

of my students told me that although they could see I was trying to understand, I "didn't really have a clue about their 'cultures.'" One African American student asked me after school one day, "Why did you come here to teach? What makes you think you know what we need?" Another Chicano student chose to show his reaction to the information on interpersonal relationship development I was teaching by going to the first-floor window, opening it wider, and making his way out of the classroom. These were some of my first lessons in the need to question the relevance of what we teach and the value of an interpretive perspective to better understand insider experiences and lived cultures across contexts.

I spent the other part of my senior year of college living on the Navaho Reservation, staying with a Navaho family, and teaching at Chinle High School. I wrote a senior thesis, an attempted ethnography of communication, about my experiences as a participant/ observer living with a Navaho family and teaching Navaho students. This was another important set of experiences that broadened my awareness of the importance of fully engaging different ways of living, and alternative values and norms. I was learning both to increase and to question what I counted as knowledge by making what was initially strange and new with regard to Navaho culture more familiar, and beginning to question what had been familiar and I had taken for granted by beginning to see myself, the stranger, the "white eyes," through the eyes and hearts of others (after Geertz, 1983).

Each one of the family members with whom I lived did the "being" (Sacks, 1984) of Navaho differently than the others. Grandmother and Grandfather lived more "traditional" lives in a hogan, speaking Navaho exclusively, and raising sheep. I was introduced to the power of ritual and integrating the spiritual into daily life by being allowed to observe their ways of being in the world. The parents and children lived in a small duplex with color television and telephone. The youngest daughter, 11 years old, didn't want to speak Navaho and spoke English at home.

With regard to the policies and practices of the educational system as an institution, the teachers at Chinle High School were all "white eyes," like me; the only Navahos in view were the cafeteria staff, janitors, and an artist and jewelry maker who visited once or twice a month. The principal told me that there weren't any "qualified" Navaho teachers available and refused permission when I asked to organize a "field trip" with elders and community members. There were no courses in Navaho language, oral history, or art, and in the history texts that were used, no mention of Bureau of Indian Affairs policies or the hegemonic and imperialistic residential school practices during the earlier part of the century, and minor mention in the curriculum of historical events such as the Long Walk. There were, however, unannounced locker and book bag inspections searching for alcohol.

These examples, among others, demonstrated clearly how an educational system, steeped in a history of Bureau of Indian Affairs policies of assimilation, continued to reinforce norms privileging English only, the limited European American views of history, and ideologies and standards of achievement based in Whiteness. Enforcement of these standards was reflected in the printed versions of policies and staff requiring that only English be spoken and written. Advisors encouraged students to develop skills and pursue jobs enabling them to move off the reservation as quickly as possible.

The family with whom I lived attended several churches as well as attended what they described as "traditional" Navaho ceremonies to which I was not invited. When I asked if the family was "trying out" different religious affiliations, it took more than one conversation for the eldest daughter to make clear to me that we had different ideas about what constituted spiritual practices. She explained that the family was not going to choose

between the church affiliations. She asked, "Why not celebrate things that different Christian churches and the Navaho way have in common?" This was one of my first experiences seeing how institutions such as religion can be redefined in what I'd now call a counter-hegemonic way. She also moved beyond the dualism in my questions regarding choosing one religion and excluding all the rest. This was an introduction to thinking about both/and, and finding a broader alternative and third space for conceptualizing spiritual values and practices; this was a moment of witnessing the engagement of practical wisdom and finding a transcendent, third space.

My experiences continued to shape my academic interest in culture, communication, and relationships. During graduate school I was privileged enough to think I could, and fortunate enough to find a faculty member here and there to support my venturing into new territory. My first adventure in integrating theoretical perspectives is evident in my dissertation, in which I studied culture through integrating rules and systems theoretical perspectives. In that project I examined cultural competencies (within group) and intercultural competencies (between groups) in order to see if and how conduct differed when interacting with someone defined to be an "insider" in terms of ethnic identification, and with one who was defined as an "outsider."

I did discover some trends in what was considered "competent" impressions of appropriate and effective conduct. For instance, respondents in my study who identified as African American and European American changed their descriptions about what was considered appropriate and effective conduct in cultural and intercultural conversations, and respondents identifying as Mexican American did not. I also discovered that conversational conduct is complex and norms and outcomes are multileveled, contextual, relational, and gender based, as well as ethnically oriented. As my work on cultural and intercultural competence evolved, I began to recognize the identity politics and status hierarchies that constitute what is considered competent, as well as who decides what is competent, and who benefits from conduct deemed to be "appropriate and/or effective."

My experiences as a faculty member and visitor at different institutions in the United States and abroad have also become part of my history and scholarly journey. In the 1980s, California State University, Los Angeles, was an ethnically diverse campus; the average age of students was 29, most worked full-time and contributed or were the sole providers for their families, and many were the first in their family to earn a college degree.

One of the first principles I learned from the students was that individuals who identified with one ethnic group such as "Latino/a" followed diverse norms of conduct in different situations. Some respondents explained that they spoke Spanish exclusively at home with grandparents and said little in discussions of U.S. and California politics, but when attending a La Raza meeting on campus spoke Spanish and argued vehemently about politics, and when at work, spoke English and followed the norms of conduct outlined by their employer. In addition, some did not question the need for adapting their conduct and code-switching between languages, while others found ways to resist the dominant group norms by speaking Spanish covertly at work. From their descriptions I began to see that valid claims about cultural and intercultural competencies had to consider political, institutional, and organizational contexts and personal relationship contexts, as well as situated interactions.

My respondents and students helped me understand the importance of selecting labels when describing cultural conduct and creating representations of their groups. When I was drafting surveys and asking for recommendations from my students, they told me that the check-the-box technique for identifying ethnicity or nationality often is not an accurate measure of ethnic and national heritage, let alone that such sweeping categories correlate with their enacted and situated cultural identities. They noted that sometimes their preferred labels do not appear as an option on demographic lists. Many students also had parents from different national, racial, and ethnic groups and asked me why they had to choose between them.

Students also pointed out that labels signify contested political locations. As Tanno (2000) describes, Chicano/a, Mexican American, Mexicano/a, and Latino/a signify different political standpoints. To further complicate the use of identity labels by interactants as well as researchers, more than one identity label may apply to members of groups across situations, regions of the country, and at different stages of life. This is the point at which I began to ask respondents on surveys and in interviews to fill in their own labels for their ethnic, racial, and national groups.

My work with Milt Thomas (Collier & Thomas, 1988) led me to try to understand cultural identities as they were formed in interactions with others. From his training in ethnography of communication as well as philosophy of communication and what were precursors of social constructivism, we developed working principles characterizing cultural identities. We theorized about cultural identities that could emerge in communication texts within or across groups and proposed the following properties. First, individuals have a range of cultural identities that may emerge in conduct, including national, racial, ethnic, class-related, sex- and gender-based, political, religious, and more. Cultural identities come to be when a pattern of conduct across individuals demonstrates membership in a group or groups. Second, from the perspective of individuals, these diverse cultural identities differ in salience across situational contexts and also vary over time and interactions. Third, cultural identities vary in scope, referring to how widely held and generalizable they are. Fourth, cultural identities are formed through processes of avowal (self views) and ascription (views communicated by others). Fifth, the intensity with which particular cultural identities are avowed and ascribed differs depending upon situation, context, topic, and relationship. Sixth, cultural identities both endure over time and space, and change in significant ways. Seventh, cultural identities have both content and relational aspects.

Applying cultural identity theory in a collaborative research project in South Africa in 1992, I examined avowed descriptions of cultural identities, cultural ascriptions, and intercultural relationships (Collier & Bornman, 1999). My South African White Afrikaner coauthor and I analyzed discursive examples from focus groups showing the ease with which members of higher status groups such as Afrikaner- and English-identified whites expressed negative stereotypes and racist and classist categorizations about blacks. We also identified themes that characterized the norms for individuals in our study identifying as Afrikaner, British, Asian/Indian, Coloured, and Black, aligning with various groups.

My work on the book about African American communication with Michael Hecht and Sidney Ribeau (Hecht, Collier, & Ribeau, 1993) is an example of another valuable collaboration. Each of us brought experience from different scholarly paradigms, and we aligned with different racial, ethnic, religious, male, and female cultural identifications. Rather than "speaking for," our goal was to provide a space for African American voices to be heard. We argued that multivocality was present as well as patterns of conduct evidencing ethnic identity, and we defined ethnic identity as a "problematic event" that was situated and negotiated in social interaction. We also illustrated the utility of examining ethnic cultural identity from individual, relational, and communal frames (Philipsen, 1987). We pointed to "insider" avowed and "outsider" ascribed descriptions of ethnic identities in order to provide a broader view

of the communication through which African American ethnic identities are negotiated.

In the years immediately after the book was published, colleagues pointed out to me that cultural identity theory in its initial version seemed to minimize issues of unequal privilege, and be based on assumptions of equal agency across individuals. Marsha Houston also raised questions in her comments during a National Communication Association conference in 1994 about our implied view of individuals freely choosing a cultural identity in chameleon-like fashion, which is not consistent with such identity categories as race and sex that are not viewed as easily changed, and that our view neglects broader social hierarchies, power, and contextual constraints. Such comments called me to reflect on our ontological assumptions about how individuals enacted and experienced consequences from enacting their identities.

My experiences, therefore, became characterized by interactions with people and texts in diverse geographical places and political spaces; these included my collaborative experiences with scholars and practitioners having different national affiliations from mine, those who identify and are identified as persons of color, lesbians and gays, and those who bring critical voices and questions to intercultural communication. These experiences can be summed up as a continued call for reflexivity. A more current example of my attempt to be self-reflexive and uncover biases with help from my friends and colleagues can be found in the cyberdialogue chapter about ferment in intercultural communication (Collier et. al., 2002).

Editing volumes 23 through 25 of *the International and Intercultural Communication Annual* gave me the opportunity to work with scholars with newer and alternative theoretical orientations and to participate in dialogue forums with established scholars and practitioners about issues of concern to those of us who study culture and communication. The cyberdialogue chapter (Collier et al.,

2002) with Radha Hegde, Wenshu Lee, Tom Nakayama, and Gust Yep was a stimulating and challenging scholarly exchange because their arguments and questions alternatively challenged my assumptions, showed the need for consistent clarification, and unquestionably reaffirmed the need for intercultural scholars to make our work not only relevant but also oriented toward social justice.

These points along my journey, and reading, reviewing, and engaging in dialogue with scholars approaching culture from a critical perspective, have contributed to my growth as a scholar and my intention to understand and add a critical perspective to my own research program. In the remainder of this chapter I cite theoretical assumptions and contingent conclusions followed by discursive examples from four current studies. Taken together, these reflect my current epistemological location as an intercultural researcher. I outline several tentative theoretical claims and then offer situated conclusions evidenced by selected findings. My goal is to demonstrate the value of integrating critical and interpretive perspectives in dialectic fashion (Martin, Nakayama, & Flores, 2002) to increase our understanding of cultural identifications and relationships as contextual negotiation, and show the consequences of enacted cultural dominance, patriarchy, and racism on groups inside and outside of the United States.

WORKING ASSUMPTIONS AND TENTATIVE CLAIMS ABOUT CULTURAL IDENTIFYING AND RELATING

Theorizing as Intimate Engagement. To reiterate, I recognize my intimate engagement with scholarly inquiry, teaching, and practice (Collier, 1998). As the previous examples illustrate, who I am, what I experience, and what I've been taught become part of the ontological, epistemological, and axiological lenses that frame my work. As well, I benefit from dialogue

with colleagues who speak from alternative locations to illuminate biases that limit the relevance and applicability of my research.

Uncovering Biases and Levels of Privilege: A Continuing Challenge. I work to integrate self-reflexivity and reflexive dialogue with others to uncover and examine my own biases, privileges, and hidden assumptions that I bring to my scholarship and instruction. In my earlier work on intercultural competence, for example, I presumed that individuals enacting different salient identities such as African American young female and European American older male could talk through and agree upon mutually appropriate and effective conduct. Now I see that this "negotiation" process is characterized by hierarchy, and individuals from marginalized groups take greater risks and experience different consequences from speaking up and expressing their preferences and emotions. See Collier (1988, 1998, 2003a) and Collier et al. (2002).

I acknowledge the need to reexamine who and what benefits accrue from my work. Because of what I have seen, felt, heard, and experienced in South Africa, Palestine, Israel, England, and the United States, and the challenging times in which we live, I believe that those of us with more status and privilege have a moral responsibility to initiate action about social problems. Intercultural scholars have much to contribute to work that focuses on lived experiences, social injustice, overcoming oppression, and emancipation. I am concerned when my friends and colleagues read intercultural communication scholarship and judge it as irrelevant at best, or misrepresentative, essentializing, and subjugating, at worst. Chen and Starosta (2003) and Shin and Jackson (2003) make the same point. Also see Collier et al. (2002).

Expanding View of Culture. Because of what I've learned from respondents, colleagues, and friends, my views of culture have become more complex and expanded. For example, I think of cultural systems as having broader time frames, important histories, and itineraries of travel, and I emphasize structural factors such as social institutions and norms, dominant ideologies, and status, privilege, hierarchy, and agency. My working orientation to culture is now that of a communicative location, a shared and contested alignment created by individuals, groups, organizations, or institutions; the location includes a history and itinerary and is both constrained by social structures and constructed through situated interaction.

Integrating Theoretical/Metatheoretical Perspectives. My orientations to the study of culture and communication in relationships and groups have therefore also evolved. Acknowledging a bit of oversimplification for purposes of this discussion, my itinerary has unfolded from what was more prescriptive (with attention to intercultural competence), to an interpretive (with attention to cultural identities), to a critical/interpretive orientation with attention to cultural identifications and communication in relationships and groups. I continue to be interested in building contingent understandings of cultural identification systems and intercultural relationships as lived, situated experiences. Valid and relevant knowledge of this kind must include attention to structures, institutions, representations, and ideologies that constrain agency, and are the root of injustice, patriarchy, and oppression. As well, I am committed to inquiry that moves us toward transformation of institutions, structures, norms, and relationships.

Positionality of researchers, respondents, and audiences for research has become an important issue in my work. As mentioned previously, in my earlier research I gave attention to prescriptions and cultural and intercultural competence (Collier, 1988, 1991, 1996), and I now question presumptions of equal agency that are foundational in most competence

research. I recognize that negotiating mutually appropriate and effective conduct occurs in a larger context of historical inequality and structural constraints, and that the risk of experiencing negative consequences is higher for members of historically marginalized groups.

CURRENT RESEARCH AS CONTINGENT AND CONTEXTUALLY RELEVANT

During the past 10 years, I have been collecting discursive data in two international sites outside of the United States. In South Africa I have spent time in townships as well as major cities and met and interviewed respondents whose racial/ethnic/linguistic identifications are Black Zulu, Xhosa, Tswana, and Swazi, among others, Coloured (mixed race), Asian Indian, White Afrikaners, and White "British" English-speaking, and spent time at "Black" Vista Universities, universities enrolling Afrikaans speakers, and UNISA, which is based in distance education. I also made three trips and traveled in Israel and Palestine and worked with a peace building program bringing young women from the Middle East and United States to Colorado.

One study is a retrospective analysis of interviews with young women identifying as Palestinian, Israeli, and Palestinian-Israeli who participated in a peace building camp in the United States in 1997 and 1998 (Collier, 2003b). A second analyzes interviews with respondents identifying with varied groups in South Africa during two points during the political transition from apartheid to a working democracy (Collier, 2003c). I also cite examples from two additional collaborative projects, both founded in critical/interpretive perspectives. The first (Myers & Collier, 2003) focuses upon a feminist and critical interpretive analysis of subjugating ascriptions evident in interview discourse of judges, attorneys, and advocates regarding women applying for restraining orders in domestic abuse court cases. The study features conduct in and around a courtroom in the Midwestern area of the United States. The fourth study cited here (Thompson & Collier, 2003) is a critical/interpretive analysis of negotiated relationship and cultural identifications in discourse from couples who volunteered to participate in multiple, joint interviews about their interracial relationships.

These four studies exemplify an epistemological both/and dialectic of critical and interpretive perspectives that the three of us, among others, are applying to understand a range of social problems including racism, sexism, and classism, and the role of privilege and hierarchy related to identity and relationship negotiation. All four studies have a common intention to build understanding of the intersecting ways that privilege and social context are implicated in respondents' locations of speaking and acting and the situated negotiation of their multiple cultural identifications.

More specifically the first study (Collier, 2003b) is a retrospective view of interviews with current and past participants in a program called Building Bridges for Peace that brought young women from Israel and Palestine to join U.S. American young women in the United States for a 2-week program on peace building. I interviewed 19 past participants in Israel and Palestine during the spring of 1997, and then became a facilitator for the program during the summer of 1997. A research assistant interviewed nine pairs of young women from the Middle East who were paired as "allies" for specific activities at the end of the 2-week peace building program in the United States. Another research assistant interviewed 10 past participants in Israel and Palestine in the spring of 1998. Questions addressed such topics as what the allies talked about, how they dealt with disagreements, when they were aware of talking as members of particular groups and as individuals, and, for the past participants, what they liked and disliked about the program, what kind of contact they had with other participants, how

they were using the communication tools they learned, and their predictions about peace in the Middle East. Interviews were videotaped and audiotaped.

The second study (Collier, 2003c) is a retrospective analysis of discourse from focus group interviews with young adults in 1992 and in 1999. Respondents identified as Afrikaner White, and as Black aligned with groups including Tswana, Xhosa, Zulu, Swazi, and Swati. I facilitated the interviews with the groups varying in size from 5 to 10 participants. Open-ended questions addressed views about their own group, other race/ethnic groups in South Africa, their friendships with individuals who held different cultural identifications, and their views about the current political situation, policies such as Affirmative Action, and their predictions for the political climate and future of South Africa. Interviews were held at the Human Sciences Research Council in Pretoria, and at universities in the surrounding areas. Interviews were videotaped and audiotaped.

In the third study (Myers & Collier, 2003) my coauthor and I concentrate on data from 16 in-depth qualitative interviews conducted by the first author with four judges, six attorneys, and six advocates. Interviews were held in 2001 in convenient locations near the courtroom devoted to Restraining Order cases. The data featured in this study focus on responses to interview questions such as: "Please tell me about the women who come into your courtroom. What are your perceptions of them? Do you perceive any general similarities across the women who appear? How does ethnic/cultural background play a role in communication processes in your courtroom, if at all?" The first author transcribed all of the audiotaped interviews.

The fourth study (Thompson & Collier, 2003) is an analysis of responses from interviews conducted by the first author in a Midwestern city of the United States with 12 couples who volunteered to be interviewed jointly to discuss their interracial relationship and cultural identifications. The first author met twice with each couple and asked questions about how they met, how their courtship and relationship developed, the responses of friends and family to their relationship over the years, any experiences with discrimination, views of their own and their partner's cultural identifications, and child-rearing practices. Couples had been married on average 9 years. Eight of the couples were composed of husbands identifying as black and wives identifying as white, two included biracial husbands with wives identifying as white, and two of husbands who identified as white with wives identifying as black. The wives were 34 years old, on average, and the husbands were 38. Two couples categorized themselves as upper class/privileged, and 10 as middle class. Interviews with each couple were audiotaped, and from 2 to 5 hours of discourse was obtained from each couple.

I refer readers to the complete version of each study for specific details about the goals, context, methodologies, and interpretive procedures used. Below I include selected discursive examples from focus groups and interviews in the four studies so that readers have a clearer picture of some of the data from which our interpretations emerged.

Differing Levels of Agency Affecting Intercultural Relationships

Attempting to move beyond the kind of "ontological and political erasure" that occurs when factors such as historically reified and socially reinforced status hierarchies are overlooked, agency is an important consideration. Agency is approached here as the freedom and ability to choose and enact a range of actions, including the enabling and constraining factors such as patriarchal ideologies and histories of oppression that comprise part of the context. Identity politics and agency affecting cultural identification negotiation are showcased in the following examples from interviews with young women from the Middle East. In the first a Palestinian describes her feelings of not having an "identity" as represented by a passport. She argues that because Palestinian passports are not recognized by Israelis at checkpoints, Palestinian-Israelis who have Israeli passports have more freedom to travel and therefore are more "comfortable than me."

Faten[1]:   I just get offended whenever I talk to a person who has an identity because I don't.

Interviewer: I don't understand.

Faten: I am Palestinian but I don't have either a Palestinian passport or an Israeli passport. . . . If I take the Palestinian passport the Israeli government would prevent me from entering Jerusalem and Jerusalem is a part of my soul. I just can't NOT enter it. And of course, I'm not taking an Israeli passport, so . . . I get frustrated when I talk to people and especially Palestinians who have Israeli passports . . . when talking with people WITH identity, especially Palestinians with Israeli identity. . . . I just get like kind of offended because I think they're more comfortable than me.

The comments below show Palestinian past participants after returning home after the peace building program discussing ideas about how to resist the dominant political status quo. The views of the three respondents about the need for and the difficulty of taking action rather than just talking emerged when they were asked about follow-up program activities. Several Palestinian past participants voiced comments addressing the need for organizing small marches or demonstrations in order to express views publicly.

Rinad: I think we will not do dialogues; we will stop that because we had enough, we had enough in America.

Maissallun: We had enough. We have to work.

Rinad: So I think we have now to work. To do things. To, for example, to meet together . . . for example, Netanyahu is going to make a settlement and both, we both don't want this kind of action. So we have both to go and make a little demonstration to express ourselves.

Muna: We were thinking about doing something when the problem of Abu-Ganam Mountain started just to show the whole world that the youth of these two nations are against settlements and against taking land. But there was no chance. So we COULD really do something, I mean like a peaceful demonstration, or you know, something that shows the whole world our opinion and this is very good and it will influence the policy and it will influence others' ideas.

Class Privilege, Whiteness, and Subjugating Ascriptions

Myers and Collier (2003) present discourse from judges and attorneys that, when examined as an overall picture, includes cultural ascriptions evidencing patriarchy and ideologies reflecting normative standards that are based in part on unnamed Whiteness, ethnic, and class privilege. In Restraining Order courtrooms such ascriptions from judges and attorneys form an interpretive frame that is applied to the conduct and lives of women plaintiffs; this frame may act as a constraint upon the abilities of plaintiffs to tell their stories in full and have the context of their stories understood. Some cultural ascriptions take the form of essentializing generalizations about groups such as women, women plaintiffs,

members of various race and ethnic groups, and those who are poor; such frames have the potential to affect questions asked, guidance offered and/or not offered, and ultimate decisions made by court personnel.

Attorney Katia: I think victims of domestic violence they're—they're too focused on the other person. I think in general they are women who are—they're used to taking care of other people and not themselves. So in the court process they're always very willing to just agree, agree, agree. So if the other side says, "you know this Restraining Order is getting in the way," or if they don't have an attorney or it's a different attorney who may not be keyed into those issues, sometimes the Restraining Orders get dropped or they get modified really weird to where they're ineffective because the client is not assertive enough, they're not strong enough.

Judge Abel: They [police] come out seeing it as the woman really is disagreeable to the point where you can understand why the guy took a swing at her um the officer isn't going to want to—he's gonna want to settle it the way he does any kind of an altercation. . . . Some women are really obnoxious and the officers on the street see that.

Judge Carol: My perception is that they're [Women] mostly trying to be honest, but their honesty is so driven with doubt and stuff it's very difficult to go along with someone and feel like you feel comfortable with your decision. Particularly if you are yourself the decision maker in a linear, analytical frame. 'Cuz you're made up of mostly lawyers, who are more likely to be analytical. The women are also emotional and that makes a lot of decision makers extremely uncomfortable. And again I can observe it without being sure what to do about it. There is real fear of women out of control, there is real anger that you can't tell the story without making me feel bad. We like our victims un-angry, we white knights like to rescue damsels in distress, not damsels who are pissed off.

Subjugating views consistent with ideologies depicting women as overly emotional were revealed. Some views reflected that respondents recognized more complex and intersecting group identifications linking sex, race or ethnicity, and class; however, women identified as belonging to marginalized ethnic groups were also described as passive and meek, or angry and scary, indicating that there are multiple ideologies at work. As van Dijk (1997) argues, "Ideologies are developed by dominant groups in order to reproduce and legitimate their domination" (p. 25). The ideologies displayed reveal standards of judgment that are consistent with patriarchal standards as well as judges claiming the individual right to define what constitutes just the right amount of assertiveness, emotion, and specific evidence to be offered by women plaintiffs in their courtroom. Such presumption of their individual agency to flexibly define what is appropriate for women plaintiffs is consistent with an ideology of individualism that is a cornerstone of many institutions in the United States, including the justice system.

Respondents' comments indicate how women identified with marginalized race and ethnic groups who are seeking help in leaving abusive relationships are further oppressed in the patriarchal court system. For instance, negative ascriptions were applied to members of varied groups, and race and ethnic background labels were used as if they were signs of conduct, values, and psychological states. Hispanic and Asian women were described as being influenced by expectations from their cultural and family communities that discourage them from seeking help outside of their families or communities. Such ascriptions

reflect what Moon (1999) calls "Whitespeak," in which the race of others becomes abstractly defined, agency of others is erased, and subjects are disembodied.

Judge Abel: It's hard with Hispanic people 'cuz they're often missing my, you know, interactions with other people, and they're very willing to accept what somebody in authority says . . .

Judge Denise: I think the Hispanic women are much more passive, uh, and it takes more assistance on the part of the court to bring out the facts of the case. I think that may be due to embarrassment or the acculturation that they're not as important as their male companion assuming the relationship is of that nature.

Attorney Katia: . . . the Vietnamese population, I find that domestic violence is really bad because I think it's cultural, the women are really, they're really meek—the victims we get, moreso than other women.

Court representatives' discourse also revealed that when respondents spoke about effects of cultural categorizations such as sex, race, ethnicity, and class influencing communication in court they nearly always referenced those constructs in terms of how other people's identifications affected interactions without acknowledging how their own cultural identifications are influential in shaping communication. This trend is not surprising given that Whiteness ideology has an element of invisibility to insiders (Martin, Krizek, Nakayama, & Bradford, 1996):

Whites as the privileged group take their identity as the norm or standard by which other groups are measured, and this identity is therefore invisible, even to the extent that many Whites do not consciously think about the profound effect being white has on their everyday lives. (p. 125)

Thompson and Collier (2003) also identified Whiteness ideologies in the discourse from interviews with interracial couples. One way the pervasiveness of Whiteness ideology is illustrated is in the way several couples disassociate themselves from the label "interracial." Couples pre-empt this categorization and its relevance to their relationship by saying they "never think about it," constructing alternative identities such as "normal" and as being unique individuals, and using discourse of colorblindness.

These discursive forms function as strategies where couples exercise agency to reinforce a view of the couple as both unique and ordinary as well as to reinforce partners' unique individuality. At times the forms also function to maintain the invisibility of Whiteness and power relations and/or to resist the inequality of the power structure without directly addressing it.

Richard: (black male) Yeah it's been an interesting ride. . . . One of the reasons I was curious about your involvement in this study is that I've never really thought of myself as [in] an interracial couple. I mean, I really look at us just being a couple. And not looked at anything as questionable or abnormal or wondering what would be in Ella's past that she would marry someone who's not of the same race. It just all seems so natural. And I don't know if our friends question it or not because they would never say anything to me, of course. And I don't know if they ever have to Ella, but I've never heard anything to that regard.

Ella: (white female) I shared with [name of interviewer] that, you know, just the very few things I could remember where somebody has said something to us and one was one of your bankers, I think. In Chicago, that black woman who (to Richard) asked you why you married a white woman and you said I didn't marry a white woman, I married

Ella: . . . You know the nice thing was our parents were supportive without coming out and saying we . . . we are supportive of this biracial marriage. They *never* said anything. . . . We . . . we have never had . . . I mean, we are not aware of people looking at us, um, as a biracial couple, I think because we're both tall and, you know, we're striking in appearance that people are probably are . . . you know, look at us. We've never been mistreated, not even in the South where we might expect to run into some . . . challenges.

Jim: (black male) I'm not sure I look at us as an interracial couple . . .

Karen: (white female) I've never really thought about it. It never enters my mind. I forget sometimes . . .

Jim: Sometimes I did kid her a little bit about it. But that's . . .

Karen: Oh yeah. You know we joke about things sometimes. But, I've never really thought about it. It never enters my mind. I forget sometimes that I'm white and Jim's black and, we're just us.

The above examples illustrate how identifications are negotiated and emergent in social and relational contexts. Examining the salience of one or more avowed cultural identities from the point of view of individual descriptions of recalled conversations, for example, would not have reflected the role of relational collaboration and ambivalence with which one partner "never even thinks about" race and the other "did kid her a little about it." Below, the couple says that worries about discrimination against them as an interracial couple were an issue for only a small minority of "individual people" and that society is progressing enough that it is "[not] a huge problem anymore" and Corrine doesn't have to think about it at all. These comments illustrate the partners' exercise of agency to maximize their experience as generalizable to all interracial couples.

Mat: (white male) It's kind of like my mom said, "It's not even an issue anymore." For us, I don't think it ever was an issue, except for our parents. And Corrine says there's going to be individual people that have problems with it. And our as society progresses, they're more and more the minority. So I don't really think it is a huge problem anymore.

Corrine: (black female) I forget about it. I don't even . . . it used to be, um, when we first started dating, it was, at least for me, it was a day-to-day thing. I would consciously think about it, you know, *every day*. Am I going to *run* into somebody who doesn't like it? And what *am* I going to do and you know, just that whole thing. And *after,* you know; now it's like nine years later, *almost,* and I don't think about it at all.

Tensions between group and individually unique identifications are evident at some points in the discourse of the various studies. In the comments above, the interracial partners articulate a preference for how things are "now" in which they erase race; Corrine says "I don't think about it at all," and Mat notes that the issue of individual people who have a "problem" with racial differences isn't a "huge problem" anymore. By using race-evasive discourse (Frankenburg, 1993) the couple implies that being able to "forget" about their races is better than having racial difference be an issue.

Along with race-evasiveness, discourses praising "individuation" and explicit preferences for acting as an individual are widely visible and establish the power of this norm as a preferred standard of conduct for members identifying with higher status groups. Preferences for speaking and acting as "an individual" are also found in the discourse of U.S. college students with higher status (Haspel & Collier, 2000). Consider the

following comments from White Afrikaner young adults in South Africa in 1999 in which respondents talk about "individualizing" and pursuing a future:

Robert: The other thing is, sorry, it may be a bit idealistic, that I think one of the big problems is labeling because as soon as you have labels and okay black people are now at the top in merit over white people or whatever and you have this whole thing of investing in the economy as well. As soon as you get rid of that we can start functioning as a nation uhm with all of our individualizing it would be a great way to see things.

Esther: Our country has to grow up and stop blaming everything on the past and looking to the future and what we can achieve.

Hentie: It is important to have history in the culture but not to the extent where you limit yourself and end up not pursuing a future.

In 1999, the following exchange among black young adult respondents names Whiteness and describes the forms it takes in South Africa.

Joseph: There are black people in this country who still worship white people, still, everything white is good. "I want to be like a white person, I want to own a house in a nice suburb and drive a Range Rover." And uh, you know.

Funeka: Yea. Uh huh.

Joseph: It's still if you are white, you are good. If you are black, you are probably a thief or rapist or whatever.

Edna: Even in lectures, if you ask a question, the lecturer goes "Oh, is that how you speak here?" . . . students do not say jack in class, they are so complacent . . .

Phineas: Well, I think it's because most of what we are has been so drummed out of us, uhm, I don't know. I was, I was reading this one philosophy book on African philosophy and I realized that, uhm, there is no real African philosophy, that everything has just been snatched, boom, during the reign.

It is important to mention that a few respondents did reflexively address their own privilege and how it functions in their favor. For example, one judge reflects on her views regarding plaintiffs' cultural identifications:

Judge Carol: I think in this society the boogie person is a really angry, large, black person . . . we need to worry about whether we have white rules or black rules, not so much in a conscious way but if a few black women . . . sometimes I'll make it personal, it feels very "alright, you go girl!" I mean . . . but I also feel like my initial gut is, "Good heavens, that's unladylike." And so I think to myself, hmmm, so I expect white women to be ladylike, maybe I think black women shouldn't be so ladylike. You know I've got some categories going here that I need to be pretty aware of to get past that initial gut sense of okay, blah, blah, blah, fair and reason. Is it self-defense?

Also, in 1999, an Afrikaner male acknowledges the privileges experienced by his group.

Christo: As white people we are used to that as well. I don't know about the rest [of you] but most people aren't against a black woman coming into the house doing all the washing, the ironing, and cleaning the house and stuff so then I certainly think we're a bit lazy too. And that's maybe why this, oh, ah, thing with less jobs for white males and white females is a good thing; maybe we can

start to work for a change. I'm not saying that it's always that we have been entirely lazy but we got used to the idea that things work our way and now for a change I think it's good to work harder . . .

Intersecting Cultural Identifications and Contextual Forces

Multiple cultural identifications as shared locations of speaking/acting/producing that reflect an itinerary and past and tentative path for the future are evident in the discourse of all four studies. Allies and past participants from the Middle East spoke from multiple and contradictory cultural group identifications and locations. One Israeli ally describes the complexity and range of her group and individual identifications and summarizes her location of speaking as an individual.

Tal: I am not just Israeli, I'm also Jewish but I'm also, for example, a woman, or a sister, or a friend. I have parts of me that are individual but some I do belong to groups. I'm not denying that, but I'm SICK of speaking in the name of people. I want to say what I (!) think. What others say doesn't always match what I think. . . . I can't speak for our government. It's not possible for me. . . . I don't speak in the name of my whole country because I can't. I simply can't.

A Palestinian past participant describes the existence of multivocality and her disagreements with other Palestinians about politics.

Faten: In the university there is a lot of political groups and political parties you know. And you know some of these groups just don't believe in peace and they don't want peace. And I can't prevent myself from not being a friend to a person just because of his political view. . . . And sometimes, anything happens like a terrorist attack . . . or a closure, they'll come to me and say "Is this the kind of peace you're talking about?" . . . We talk sometimes but not, you know, not deeply, because I know that it's very hard problem . . . and a lot of my friends were in prisons in Israel, so it's hard to talk to them.

Not only do individuals speak from multiple locations and enact different cultural identifications, but the salience of different group identifications differs across situations. The following comment by an Israeli past participant demonstrates her exercise of agency in choosing to claim an Israeli identity and/or a new immigrant identity "when the situation is right."

Noa: And, I don't know. I think I'm kind of more Israeli now. And, I feel like a new immigrant. I was only a year and a half in Israel but uhm, I was kind of sliding between new immigrant and, and, Israeli. And I think it's more fixed now. I mean I think . . . I know I'm an Israeli. I mean, (louder) I know I'm an Israeli and I know I am a new immigrant. . . . I'm able to, to, to make a distinction between the two of them, and to, to behave and to acknowledge the fact that I'm one or the other, at times, I mean when the situation is right.

One of the past participants from the previous year described the difficulties in being Palestinian-Israeli: "It is difficult to be in the middle. Is it my fault that my parents chose to stay where they were born? I don't want to hear the question, 'Are you Palestinian?' It is obvious." Another Palestinian-Israeli past participant said, "Sometimes we have to be Israeli girls, and sometimes Palestinian girls, but all the time we have to be Israeli/Arab girls . . . the ones who understand the problems with Jerusalem and understand what's happening in Tel Aviv and everything. To be between two sides."

Another past participant's struggle with identifications shows the importance of not only acknowledging multiple identifications but also the salience of cultural identifications that may change across situations depending upon such contextual factors as agency and

hierarchy. As well, the Palestinian-Israeli invokes not only her ancestry but also the history "before '48," in reference to the period before Israel was designated a nation-state by the United Nations.

Sinay: We were enroute to . . . and there were arguments there. And the Israelis just can't accept that the Palestinian-Israelis, the Arabs who live in Israel, are Palestinian. It's like they totally can't accept it. And I found myself, that's when I recognized (small laugh) that I had, I found myself defending my . . . (long breath) . . . I mean I am Palestinian before '48. My grandparents were here and my grandparents are still here. And, wow! I'm turning Palestinian.

In another example, in 1999, South African White Afrikaners articulate the following tensions and conflicting views about their multiple identifications and which identifications are salient. Christo points to diversity within groups as problematic, and Louise describes Afrikaans speakers as having limited agency due to fear of being "harassed."

Pierre: I think it is more important to feel South African because uhm the country has changed, there are so many different groups you feel more that you should hum relate to bigger pictures, being South African and looking internationally maybe say you are South African instead of . . . Afrikaans; You're black. You're Xhosa . . . I think that is where we meet in the present.

Christo: I think only if you feel secure in your own culture, Afrikaner, or Xhosa, or whatever, they can finally begin to feel South African. That to me is the whole problem, is that diversity in the group itself.

Louise: I think for now especially for Afrikaans speaking people it's harder because they are not as assertive in saying, "This is who I am, and, this is what I believe."

Because they are sort of scared that somebody will pull back and harass them. So you are very selective about what you say about your boss, and who you are and what you believe. But most of the time you keep quiet.

In another part of the discussion in which the topic of affirmative action was raised, the following comments illustrate the importance of contextualizing interpretations of discourse about identifications.

Esther: [Affirmative action] it makes you work harder for what you want.

Several   Ya.
voices:

Wynand: At the beginning I felt this is so unfair ... but after awhile I feel this is going to give me the power to, to, go out on top. I will be there, I will study hard and I will be successful in my career.

Pierre: It may reverse on you. A few years back there were people ... black people or whatever, Coloured people, that came out on top even though the situation was difficult. And if they can do anything then there is no excuse for us not to be able to do it now.

The struggle to speak as an individual and/or group member within a context of historically intractable conflict and different levels of agency becomes evident in the interaction between an Israeli and a Palestinian, below. The contradictions and tensions are negotiated as the two respondents, who are paired as allies in the program, talk about their positions.

Lilach: I think I always talked as an individual. It was kind of hard for me because I mean, I'm an individual but I also represent a certain group and sometimes I feel like I am not representing it the way I should have. ... It was hard for me and I think it's the same for her that I felt we talked as individuals. We didn't talk as, I don't know, fighters for our country or something like this. We talked as an individual person who wants to have peace in their life and stuff like that.

Maissallun: I personally talked as an individual but I actually tried to convey the ideas of my delegation or my community as a whole. I mean I told her that, for example, I didn't like these terrorist attacks, or I didn't like this shooting of people, but I also tried to explain for her why these people do this, I mean the terrorist attacks. These people don't come from out of the middle of nowhere and just bomb these people ... they have their own reasons. I tried to explain, for in a way I was saying "they think" (putting her fingers up to signify quotation marks) not "I think." Whenever I was saying "I think" then I would put in only my opinion.

Cultural ascriptions about Others often took the form of subjugating and essentializing views along with contrastive comparisons of "them" as negative compared with "us" or "my experience" as positive. These serve the function of reifying privilege. See Myers and Collier (2003) and Collier (2003c). Negative stereotypes of particular ethnic groups emerged and were described in the form of descriptions of Others. Often there was an implied standard of comparison and preference for dominant group standards. The views below are representative of interview discourse in which court personnel speak for plaintiffs, overgeneralize, and use generic pronouns. Such characterizations illustrate the limiting interpretive frames that judges and attorneys may apply to plaintiffs' testimonies, based on their expectations for members of those groups.

Judge Denise: I think the Hispanic women are much more passive, uh, and it takes more assistance on the part of the court to bring out the facts of the case. I think that may be due to embarrassment or the acculturation that they're not as important ah as their male companion assuming if the relationship is of that nature. And I think it does affect the information that is provided to the court.

Advocate Suzanna: I think with the Spanish clients they are . . . their culture is that their private life should be private they really don't want to talk about it. They think—if he wants to—she should do that because she is married to him. Uhm it's sort of like slavery. He does whatever he wants with her . . . especially if she doesn't work . . . she doesn't know the language, he's the one that supports her and the kids. Uhm and they don't know domestic violence. The history of domestic violence or the education on domestic violence. I think it's very hard, if they do go through it they're often stuck—having to work and support themselves and the kids with little or no help.

Cultural identifications intersect with structurally and socially produced representations and forces such as racism, sexism, classism, and other ideologies. Racism, in particular, emerges through a discursive form of ambivalence in discourse of higher status groups (discourse of judges and attorneys in U.S. Restraining Order courtrooms and of Afrikaner respondents in 1999). See Myers and Collier (2003) and Collier (2003c).

An additional form of patriarchy is evident in the form of group comparisons articulated by a judge in the Restraining Order courtroom, below. This example is representative of responses illustrating ambivalence in expressed views about plaintiffs while simultaneously presenting views of themselves as fair-minded.

Judge Bob: Some of these men and women communicate differently in the sense that you've got to be listening from a different perspective. When you're talking about time frames, for example, when you ask, "when did that happen?" a man's liable to sit there and tell you, "well it happened on December 22, 1998," or something like that, whereas a woman is more apt perhaps to relate to an event, "well I was pregnant at the time with my second child." So that's where they're coming from to begin with in terms of the way they tell their story. Ah and you have to be sensitive to that type of a situation, and you can't as a judge necessarily sit there and say, well just because she can't tell me the exact date like the man can or something like that doesn't necessarily mean that she's any more forgetful of the date she's just relating to it in a different sense rather than the numerical significance. So that's one of the things we have to adjust our hearing, shall we say, to the different people. Which actually makes sense because you start off with what might be ah considered a gender stereotype: men talk this way and women talk this way or something like that, but what you're really saying is regardless of who comes up in front of you, realize that this person has a different way of communicating with you than anybody else, so you have to view each case individually.

Identifications are overlapping and problematic, and are negotiated through multiple discursive and dialectic tensions in personal relationships. These include advancing and resisting cultural identifications, tensions between individual uniqueness and identification with cultural groups, as well as tensions between different intersecting cultural identifications such as sex, class, ethnic/racial, political, and religious groupings, both constraining and enabling historical events, norms, and institutional practices. Negotiating this tension is related to agency, as illustrated in the interaction of a Palestinian and an Israeli, below, as is their negotiation of their views of each other as allies and as individuals from different sides in the conflict.

Tamara: Well, we were talking about . . . the checkpoints.

Rawan: Yea.

Tamara: And I was saying that I think they are necessary for the safety of (looks straight ahead and away from ally and interviewer) Israeli citizens and . . . uhm . . . that, that was my point of view. And (gestures to ally) . . .

Rawan: And my point of view is that they don't just stop the men and they stop sometimes pregnant women. (tone gets progressively softer) They stop old women and old men. So this is what I think. I disagree.

Interviewer: So how did you feel when you had that disagreement?

Rawan: I didn't feel that I am talking to my, my ally.

Interviewer: What did you feel like?

Rawan: I just called her another name in my mind and I felt like I was talking to an Israeli and when we finished this, this, uhm, discussion, I just forget about it and forget that it came from her.

Interviewer: (to other ally) How about for you?

Tamara: Well it wasn't nice to find something we disagree on, but it was obvious to me that we come to a certain point (tone gets very soft) and disagree . . .

In summary, enactment of cultural identifications occurs through varied discursive and textual forms and serves multiple functions to constitute, reinforce, as well as resist institutional structures, ideologies, and social norms, and group, relational, and individual identifications. Cultural identifications are situated and contingent, and imagined, and endure over time and space.

IMPLICATIONS AND APPLICATIONS

From expanding the focus of inquiry to include broader contextual forces comes a richer and more valid picture of cultural identifications as they are negotiated and experienced. Cultural identifications are not only constituted by but also constitute institutions and structures because communication is the means through which individuals and groups define themselves, relate to each other, and struggle over issues of status and power. Individuals as members of groups and organizations discursively negotiate their relationships and their identifications while simultaneously navigating the complex contexts in which they live.

A critical theoretical perspective points researchers to acknowledge that a part of this negotiation is constrained and enabled by social histories and forces. For instance, racism and subjugating ascriptions appear in many overt and less visible forms, sometimes emerging from courtroom personnel who pride themselves on being "objective," and sometimes evident in comments from wives who identify as white in interracial marriages. As well, views of Other may be expressed in contradictory ways and reflect ambivalence and dialectic tension. For example, at one point in the interview both spouses in an interracial marriage insist that race and being a biracial couple is just not relevant to their present lives nor to their relationship, and a short time later the wife, who identifies as white, critiques discriminatory and racist treatment of her husband by a supervisor at work, and still later expresses blatantly racist views about her husband's first wife who identifies as black. Another dialectic tension very evident in the discourse is related to orientations to the past and present/future. Understanding the ways in which political histories are described as an essential part of the scene by respondents of marginalized groups, those identifying as black in South Africa as well as the Palestinians in the peace building program, for instance, and how they are juxtaposed with responses from White Afrikaners and Israelis whose comments show a preference for orienting to the future provides useful information about relationship negotiation. In addition, pinpointing how examples of discourse point to invisible standards based on Whiteness and class privilege and how these function to reinforce and extend the status and resources of particular groups is critically important not only to enable scholars/practitioners to uncover systems of oppression, but also identify what can be changed.

Contradictions and nuances of group and relationship identifications demonstrate the complexity and importance of understanding the broader social structures and norms as well as the situated and local negotiation process as a problematic.

Methodological evolution within my program of research is also evident. While I'm still drawn to understand peoples' experiences of their multiple identifications and relationships, I also believe that overlaying critical and interpretive perspectives and/or probing for views to uncover bases of status and privilege, and analyzing discourse through examining ideological forms, resistance, and counterhegemony is important.

Since researcher reflexivity as well as cultural validity and relevance of the research and findings to respondents' experiences are critical to my current research, interpretation and coding procedures in the four studies involve multiple coders in dialogue with one another working with transcriptions from video and audiotapes. As well, as Tanno and Jandt (2002) argue, combining insider and outsider interpretations of conduct can provide a broader view of cultural systems and can also help uncover invisible assumptions made by researchers and/or coders who are members of dominant groups. Whenever possible, multiple interviews and/or time to develop a collaborative relationship with respondents and significant time in the site in which residents reside are essential in order to grapple better with the contextual factors. Both set the scene and tone and are reflected in the respondents' discourse cited in the four studies above.

If the goal of interpretive scholarship is understanding culture as lived experience, and the goal of critical scholarship is uncovering communicative forms of power at work in cultural systems in order to enable emancipation and change, I am very hopeful about the abilities of intercultural communication scholars to build relevant bodies of knowledge about lived experiences and to transform oppressive structures, institutions, and relationships. With regard to the four studies cited, examples of collaborating with communities and taking results back to communities for application include the following. Myers is developing a report and "manual" for women plaintiffs, judges, attorneys, and court advocates related to communication in the Restraining Order courtroom. Thompson is synthesizing her findings from respondents she interviewed to guide a larger group discussion among the interracial couples. I summarized my findings from interviews with participants in the peace building program and presented them with recommendations for changing the program structure to coordinators of the program, and I'm collaborating with a South African colleague to extend and apply our research in community service organizations.

It is also noteworthy that discourse from respondents with historically and socioeconomically privileged identifications in several of the studies acknowledged their unearned status, including one judge in the Restraining Order court (Myers & Collier, 2003) and an Afrikaner identified respondent (Collier, 2003c). Informal and published dialogues among scholars and editors about the value of applying critical perspectives, and integrating theoretical perspectives, are becoming more common (see Collier, 2003a; Collier et al., 2002). I look forward to engaging in further collaborations to continue and begin new projects in the future related to topics such as relating as allies in intercultural conflict and negotiating third spaces for dialogue.

NOTE

1. Names of respondents have been changed to protect confidentiality.

REFERENCES

Chen, G. M., & Starosta W. J. (2003). "Ferment," an ethic of caring, and the corrective power of dialogue. In W. J. Starosta & G. M. Chen (Eds.), *Ferment in the intercultural field* (International and Intercultural Communication Annual, Volume 26, pp. 3–23). Thousand Oaks, CA: Sage.

Collier, M. J. (1988). A comparison of conversations among and between domestic culture groups: How intra- and intercultural communication competencies vary. *Communication Quarterly, 36,* 122–144.

Collier, M. J. (1991). Conflict competence within African, Mexican and Anglo American friendships. In S. Ting-Toomey & F. Korzenny (Eds.), *Cross-cultural interpersonal communication* (International and Intercultural Communication Annual, Volume 15, pp. 132–154). Thousand Oaks, CA: Sage.

Collier, M. J. (1996). Communication competence problematics in ethnic friendships. *Communication Monographs, 63,* 314–336.

Collier, M. J. (1998). Research on cultural identity: Reconciling post-colonial and interpretive approaches. In D. Tanno (Ed.), *Cultural identity and intercultural communication* (International and Intercultural Communication Annual,

Volume 21, pp. 122–147). Thousand Oaks, CA: Sage.

Collier, M. J. (2003a). Negotiating intercultural alliance relationships: Toward transformation. In M. J. Collier (Ed.), *Intercultural alliances: Critical transformation* (International and Intercultural Communication Annual, Volume 25, pp. 1–16). Thousand Oaks, CA: Sage.

Collier, M. J. (2003b). *Contextual negotiation of cultural identifications and relationships: Discourse of Middle Eastern identified young women in a U.S. program.* Manuscript submitted for publication.

Collier, M. J. (2003c). *Negotiating cultural identifications during political transition: Discursive themes of agency and privilege among South Africans in 1992 and 1999.* Manuscript submitted for publication.

Collier, M. J., & Bornman, E. (1999). Intercultural friendships in South Africa: Norms for managing difference. *International Journal of Intercultural Relations, 23,* 133–156.

Collier, M. J., Hegde, R. S., Lee, W., Nakayama, T. K, & Yep, G. (2002). Dialogue on the edges: Ferment in communication and culture. In M. J. Collier (Ed.), *Transforming communication about culture: Critical new directions* (International and Intercultural Communication Annual, Volume 24, pp. 219–280). Thousand Oaks, CA: Sage.

Collier, M. J., & Thomas, M. (1988). Cultural identity: An interpretive perspective. In Y. Y. Kim & W. B Gudykunst (Eds.), *Theories in intercultural communication* (International and Intercultural Communication Annual, Volume 12, pp. 99–120). Thousand Oaks, CA: Sage.

Dunne, J. (1993). *Back to the rough ground: Practical judgment and the lure of technique.* Notre Dame, IN: University of Notre Dame Press.

Frankenburg, R. (1993). *White women: Race matters: The social construction of whiteness.* Minneapolis: University of Minnesota Press.

Geertz, C. (1983). *Local knowledge.* New York: Basic Books.

Haspel, K., & Collier, M. J. (2000, May). *Individualization in the construction of cultural identities and inequities in conversations about public issues.* Paper presented at the

International Communication Association conference, Acapulco, Mexico.

Hecht, M. L., Collier, M. J., & Ribeau, S. (1993). *African American communication: Ethnic identity and cultural interpretation.* Thousand Oaks, CA: Sage.

Martin, J. N., Krizek, R. L., Nakayama, T. K., & Bradford, L. (1996). Exploring whiteness: A study of self-labels for white Americans. *Communication Quarterly, 44,* 125–144.

Martin, J. N., Nakayama, T. K., & Flores, L. A. (2002). A dialectical approach to intercultural communication. In J. Martin, T. Nakayama, & L. Flores (Eds.), *Readings in intercultural contexts* (pp. 1–12). Boston: McGraw-Hill.

Moon, D. (1999). White enculturation and bourgeois ideology: The discursive production of "good (white) girls." In J. Martin & T. Nakayama (Eds.), *Whiteness: The communication of social identity* (pp. 177–197). Thousand Oaks, CA: Sage.

Myers, M., & Collier, M. J. (2003). *Cultural ascriptions in a restraining order court: Implicating patriarchy and Whiteness ideologies.* Paper presented at the National Communication Association conference, Miami, FL. (Submitted for publication)

Philipsen, G. (1987). The prospect for cultural communication. In D. L. Kincaid (Ed.), *Communication theory: Eastern and Western perspectives* (pp. 245–254). New York: Academic Press.

Sacks, H. (1984). On doing "being ordinary." In J. M. Atkinson & J. Heritage (Eds.), *Structures of social action: Studies in conversation analysis* (pp. 413–429). Cambridge, UK: Cambridge University Press.

Shin, C. I., & Jackson, R. L. (2003). A review of identity research in communication theory: Reconceptualizing cultural identity. In W. J. Starosta & G. M. Chen (Eds.), *Ferment in the intercultural field* (International and Intercultural Communication Annual, Volume 26, pp. 211–242). Thousand Oaks, CA: Sage.

Stewart, J., & Zediker, K. (2000). Dialogue as tensional, ethical practice. *Southern Communication Journal, 65*(2 & 3), 224–242.

Tanno, D. V. (2000). Names, narratives, and the evolution of ethnic identity. In A. Gonzalez, M. Houston, & V. Chen (Eds.), *Our voices: Essays in culture, ethnicity and communication* (pp. 25–30). Los Angeles: Roxbury.

Tanno, D. V., & Jandt, F. E. (2002). Redefining the "other" in multicultural research. In J. Martin, T. Nakayama, & L. Flores (Eds.), *Readings in intercultural communication* (pp. 378–385). Boston: McGraw-Hill.

Thompson, J., & Collier, M. J. (2003). *Interracial couples in the U.S. negotiating cultural and relationship identifications: A critical/interpretive perspective.* Manuscript submitted for publication.

Van Dijk, T. A. (1987). Discourse as interaction in society. In T. A. van Dijk (Ed.), *Discourse as social interaction: Vol. 2. Discourse studies: A multidisciplinary introduction* (pp. 1–35). London: Sage.

Van Dijk, T. A. (1997). *Discourse as structure and process.* Thousand Oaks, CA: Sage.

12

The Communication Theory of Identity

Development, Theoretical Perspective, and Future Directions

MICHAEL L. HECHT

JENNIFER R. WARREN

EURA JUNG

JANICE L. KRIEGER

One of the challenges for scholars studying communication and culture has been the ubiquitous nature of theory. Communication studies has traditionally drawn upon theories from other disciplines (Berger, 1991). In the process Communication has been labeled as schizophrenic and its disciplinary status challenged due to its interdisciplinary legacy. Berger, in issuing what can be viewed as a call-to-arms in theory development in communication, fundamentally believes that the "future growth and well-being of the field depend upon the ability of communication researchers to advance ideas and theories that are taken seriously by colleagues in other disciplines" (p. 102). Of course, there are a myriad of unique theories that have been advanced in our field, such as interpersonal and intergroup communication theory (Gudykunst, 1988) and identity negotiation theory (Ting-Toomey, 1999). Complementing this trend, the communication theory of identity (CTI) offers a distinctive contribution that has the potential to move effortlessly across disciplines, in addition to motivating its own wave of theoretical development. In this chapter we start with a review of the genesis and development of the communication theory of identity. Next we present recent trends in research utilizing the theory, and then conclude by exploring some of the future directions.

IDENTITY ACROSS TIME AND SPACE

The theory emerged out of several trends in social knowledge, not the least of which are those focusing on self and identity. In attempting to understand who we are as human beings, social scientists and humanists have observed patterns of behavior steeped in sociocultural significance. Their discoveries acknowledge that concepts of self and personal identity are universal, while noting cultural variance (Hecht, Collier, & Ribeau, 1993). Thus, culture and society provide two interpretative lenses for individual understandings of the self. Although many diverse and unique cultures across the globe provide their own understandings of identity, Ancient Greece, Asia, and Africa represent three cradles of civilizations from which our contemporary understandings of the self are often conceptualized. Each of these great civilizations maintains a metaphysical understanding of identity, as well as positioning the self in relation to others.

Self in African Cultures. The enduring sense of self permeating many of Africa's multiple and distinct cultures reflects individual and collective harmony. Based upon Dogon philosophy, *ntu* is a predominate influence in understanding African identity as a force in which, "Beings and beings coalesce" (Jahn, 1961, p. 101). Both humanity and Superhumans (i.e., Gods, ancestors) are conceived as existing in concert. Accordingly, nothing exists apart from this force, for it is harmonizing and universal. In African societies *ntu* reflects a holism of being that is manifested through *sudicism*, "the spiritual commitment to an ideological

view of harmony" (Asante, 1998, p. 200). Identity is salient as a product of what one does on the journey to achieve balance and is conceived of in relation to one's ancestors and the internal strength they provide the individual (Asante, 1998). *Ntu* celebrates the interdependence of all things, which fundamentally influences the ways in which many African identities are constructed and perceived (Jahn, 1961; Woodyard, 2003).

Self in Asian Cultures. Asian understandings of identity are profoundly influenced by Confucian philosophy. While there are just as many East Asian cultures as there are varying philosophies, Confucianism appears to move across Korean, Chinese, and Japanese worldviews (Yum, 1998). Similar to the African view of a situated identity, Confucianism situates the self in the collectivity and de-emphasizes the importance of individual human beings. As a core value, the concept of *jen* is based on reciprocity with others in an individual's daily life (Yum, 1998). Accordingly, identity is the culmination of an individual's relationships with others. *Jen* is also understood as human heartedness. The self should be restrained, disciplined, and in harmony with everything (Yum, 1998). In addition, Confucianism promotes ideals of the self that are rooted in tradition. The ethic to conform in every way by living in harmony with cosmic law and the orderliness of the societal structure is one of the keys to understanding identity in Asian culture (Wei-ming, 1985). As a means of teaching these principals, paradoxes are employed to encourage the view that differing forces do not exclude each other, a concept akin to dialectical thinking in Western thought.

Self in Greek Culture. Polarity is a predominant feature of the Classical Greek worldview and the crux of their identity. The "Greek" way of defining the self is through "negative polar opposition to a whole series of 'others'— the unfree, minors, females, and non-Greeks, not to mention . . . the gods" (Cartledge, 2002, p. 4). Defined in opposition, the self is a combination of "spirit and intelligence" that is inextricably linked with an identity that is free, male, Greek, and a citizen. In contrast to collectivist understandings of identity, the self was viewed primarily as an individual entity. However, the *polis* or city-state was highly lauded, and to be a citizen or *polities* was also a fundamental aspect of one's identity. The *polis* was constructed upon commonalities, such as race, language, religion, and worldview (Cartledge, 2002). Classical Greek understandings of identity have profoundly influenced our views within mainstream U.S. culture.

CTI draws upon all three of these classical influences. Invoking the notion of paradox from Confucionism, CTI conceptualizes identity as including all of these elements (individual, polis, collectivity) as well as the interplays between and among them. The theory attempts to integrate the holism from Asian and African conceptions, polarity from the Greeks, harmony from African views, collectivism from Asian ideas, and the individual orientation in the Greek perspective.

The CTI conceptualization of identity has more recent origins as well, however, with modernity and postmodernity posing shifting perspectives. On the heels of the Enlightenment's need to control the seeming arbitrariness of nature and to break from the immutability of the past, modernism emerged as an era of "untrammeled individualism" and the "search for [individual] realization" (Harvey, 1990, p. 19). Accordingly, the modern identity sought purpose through a search for "truth" within. It was scientific inquiry turned in on the self, with the individual longing to select the correct means to represent the true self—a self that is centered (Bewes, 1997; Harvey, 1990). From this perspective, CTI incorporated the notion of identity located in the individual.

Conversely, postmodernism is "an extension of the freely chosen and multiple identities of the modern self that accepts and affirms

an unstable and rapidly mutating condition" (Kellner, 1992, p. 158). Within this perspective there is no ultimate truth and authority is questioned. The stability afforded by modernism is diminished as our society changes due to technology, immigration, and advancing transportation systems affording an increased potential to engage diverse and multiple relationships outside of our immediate social and cultural circles (Gergen, 1996, p. 5).

As we encounter diverse ways of envisioning reality, identities become increasingly complex. From postmodernism, CTI conceptualized a fluid, multilayered self as well as the dynamic interplay between stability and change. The theory also imported the notion that different aspects of self were interpenetrated—that is, infused into each other.

Up to this point, the chapter has traced the roots of CTI in classical civilizations and their views of identity as well as more recent macro-theoretical or philosophical trends. CTI also traces its heritage to two related theories of identity, social identity theory and identity theory.[1] These approaches, particularly social identity theory, have set the agenda for much of the theorizing about identity and thus it is not surprising that they influenced CTI. Below we briefly discuss these theories and show their influence on CTI.

Social Identity Theory (SIT). The primary focus of SIT is identity formation as a product of social categorization (Hogg, 1993; Hogg & Abrams, 1988; Turner, 1991). Social categories, such as ethnicity, gender, and political affiliation, are parts of a structured society. Individuals belong to various social categories and form identities based on memberships of social categories. Through this process, society is internalized by individuals in the form of social identities on the basis of social categories. Social identities, in turn, connect individuals to society through group memberships influencing individuals' beliefs, attitudes, and behavior in their relationships with members of other social groups. As a result, the basic unit by which the individual–society relation is examined is a social group. SIT emphasizes social aspects more than individual aspects, whereas identity theory pays more attention to individual aspects in the society–individual relationship.

Identity Theory. As a product of symbolic interactionism, identity theory explains the relationship between society and individuals on the basis of roles. Within this framework, a role refers to "the functions or parts a person performs when occupying a particular position within a particular social context" (Schlenker, 1985, p. 18). A person's role is a pattern of social behavior that appears appropriate to the expectations of others and to the demands of the situation (Banton, 1965). Roles are internalized and form role identities. Identity is formed in opposition to and in relation to others; hence roles have inherently social aspects.

This view has a long history. Cooley (1902, p. 152) coined the phrase "looking-glass self" to emphasize a self formed through our impressions of how others perceive us, and Mead (1934) spoke of a self that emerges in relation to a "generalized other" represented by communal attitudes (p. 152). Role is also acknowledged as how closely an individual's behavior and status conform to the ideal within societies having fixed and/or rigid social positions (Jackson, 1972). Goffman (1959, 1963, 1967) conceives of role taking or playing as a dynamic process whereby identity is conceptualized through a theatrical metaphor, that is, backstage and front stage. Individuals wield control over which role will be performed, although this negotiation of the self has various personal and social constraints. Individuals do, however, have some flexibility in determining with which roles they choose to identify. Roles can be multiple and change throughout an individual's life. In this research identity is conceptualized as a product of social interaction in

which the self, influenced by the norms and mores of Western society, is constituted by and usually adheres to the expectations of others.

While research focusing on roles acknowledges identity as relational, that is, constituted in social interaction, it does not necessarily conceptualize how role or identity is communicated. The theory sees the self as communicated but not as communication. In other words, identity theory sees communication as playing a role in identity development and as a means for expressing identity, but *not* as identity. CTI breaks with this approach, seeing social behavior, itself, as an aspect of self—the enacted identity. That is, a person's sense of self is part of his or her social behavior, and the sense of self emerges and is defined and redefined in social interaction. CTI complements role research in centering identity as relational and takes into consideration identity as discursive.

CTI utilizes the notion of group-based identities and categorization (from social identity theory) and social roles and ascriptions (from identity theory). CTI sees the group and social roles as important aspects of the self, and the categorization and ascription processes as one of the bases by which identity is established and enacted.

Both social identity theory and identity theory, as well as other approaches to self and identity, see the individual and society as inseparable and interdependent (Meltzer & Petras, 1972). They are mutually interactive and reflective, change constantly through the mutual interaction, and, thus, should be understood in the context of each other (Schlenker, 1985). The mutual interaction between an individual and society is reflected in identity. An individual's social environments can be internalized as the individual's identity. The individual's identity, in turn, can affect the individual's social behavior and subsequently his or her social environments. Consequently, identity can be regarded as a pivotal point interrelating individual with society.

While many approaches to identity recognize these dynamic tensions, CTI differs from most in locating communication as the process through which the individual and social environment interact. Most other theories focus on social roles or the social structures rather than the processing of identity through interaction. This becomes a key point at which CTI departs from other theories. Having traced the theoretical legacy of CTI, we now describe how it evolved through a series of related research projects.

THE DEVELOPMENT OF CTI

The communication theory of identity developed out of a line of research investigating ethnic differences in communication as well as describing the nature of intra- and interethnic communication. Michael Hecht and his colleagues were particularly interested in African American and Mexican American ethnic cultures. The projects they initiated described the intra-ethnic and interethnic communication of these groups from a within-group perspective and compared the perspectives of European Americans, African Americans, and Mexican Americans. Closely allied with work manifesting from the intergroup perspective but with an "interpretive twist," their research began to include "ethnic identity" as a construct, first describing interpretations of African American identity labels and then moving on to examine the relationship between identity and communication. The goal was for this line of work to provide some understanding of ethnic similarities and differences in effective and competent communication. Working from the perspective of African Americans (see the summary in Hecht, Jackson, & Ribeau, 2003) and Mexican Americans (Collier, Ribeau, & Hecht, 1986; Hecht, Ribeau, & Sedano, 1990), Hecht and colleagues started by identifying the problematic issues in communication (e.g., what were the main obstacles to effective communication?) as well as strategies for dealing with these

issues, which were called communication improvement strategies. In a sense, they were hoping to include ethnicity in a theory of effective communication. It was in this last move that an anomaly emerged.

The general model from which the researchers worked presented identity as prior to and influencing communication issues and improvement strategies that, in turn, had an influence on outcomes. This model can be expressed as follows:

Identity → Communication → Communication Satisfaction

When this model was tested, the path analyses did not support the overall model (Hecht, Larkey, & Johnson, 1992). The model works well, however, when modified to lump identity with communication as in:

Identity/Communication → Communication Satisfaction

With this change the findings were quite dramatic, with identity and communication issues accounting for more than 80% of the variance in communication satisfaction for both African Americans and European Americans. While the groups differed in how the issues and identity were related to satisfaction, it appeared that we had identified a successful model of effective interethnic communication for these groups.

However, this did not explain why identity was not an exogenous variable that was prior to or caused communication. In puzzling through this question, the beginnings of CTI emerged. Hecht reasoned that identity was not separate from communication. Indeed, these issues were so salient to personhood (e.g., acceptance, powerlessness, stereotyping) that the communication was, itself, an *enactment* of identity. Concurrently, a request came to submit a paper to *Communication Monographs* articulating directions for future study. Hecht chose this new way of looking at identity as the basis for this contributed piece, and the communication theory of identity was born.

COMMUNICATION THEORY OF IDENTITY

Identity has been studied in various areas, such as psychology, sociology, and anthropology. The studies in these areas focus on the individual, role, social, and communal aspects of identity (Hecht, 1993). CTI extends these studies by integrating communication. The theory sees identity as communicative. Identity is formed, maintained, and modified in a communicative process and thus reflects communication (Hecht, 1993; Hecht et al., 1993; Hecht et al., 2002). Identity, in turn, is acted out and exchanged in communication. Thus, communication externalizes identity.

Communication and Identity

Hecht et al. (1993) posit two ways through which communication is internalized as identity. First, symbolic meanings of social phenomena are created and exchanged through social interaction. Identity is formed when relevant symbolic meanings are attached to and organized in an individual in various situations through social interaction, a perspective adopted from identity theory. Social interaction is internalized as identity when one forms symbolic meanings and associates these meanings with self. Second, when people place themselves in socially recognizable categories, as noted by social identity theory, they confirm or validate through social interaction whether these categories are relevant to them. Thus, identity is formed and reformed by categorization through social interaction. Identity, in turn, is manifested in social interaction through expectations and motivations (Hecht et al., 1993). Specific identities entail specific expectations, and these expectations influence the person's communication.

Conversely, the ascriptions and categorizations that are communicated to a person also shape her or his identity. Hence, identity is internalized from, as well as externalized to, social interaction through expectations attached to identities and other social categories.

Four Layers of Identity

In light of the direct relationship between identity and communication, the theory posits various loci of identity involving not only an individual but social interaction (Hecht, 1993; Hecht et al., 2003). Here the theory borrows from postmodernism (the layering notion), the three ancient civilizations, as well as social identity and identity theories. In American culture, identity tends to be placed in the individual as a separate entity (Carbaugh, 1989). Identity resides in an individual as a cognitive schema by which the individual understands and interprets the social world (Markus & Sentis, 1982). From the perspective of social interaction as the locus of identity, identity is a social process, exists in the social world between and among people, and, thus, resides in social interaction (Burke & Reitzes, 1981; Pearce, 1989). Hecht (1993) embraced both positions of the individual and social interaction as the loci of identity. This idea of multiple loci of identity is further refined in four layers of identity in CTI.

The four layers of identity are the personal, enacted, relational, and communal. These four layers refer to the four loci where identity resides. Identity resides in a person, communication, a relationship, and/or a group. The four identities located in the four layers represent different aspects of an individual's identity. These layers sometimes match each other but sometimes are contradictory. However, the four layers cannot exist isolated from each other. They are interpenetrated with each other. Following are the basic notions of the four layers and relationships among them (Hecht 1993; Hecht et al., 2003).

Personal Layer. A personal layer refers to the individual as a locus of identity. Identity is stored in a personal layer as self-concept, self-image, self-cognitions, feelings about self, and/or spiritual sense of self-being. Identity as a personal layer provides "understanding how individuals define themselves in general as well as in particular situations" (Hecht et al., 1993, pp. 166–167).

Enactment Layer. Identity is enacted in communication through messages. The self is seen as a performance, as expressed. Thus, communication is the locus of identity in the enactment layer.

Relational Layer. In this layer, relationship is the locus of identity. Identity is a mutual product, jointly negotiated and mutually formed in relationships through communication. The relational layer has three levels. First, an individual constitutes his or her identities in terms of other people through social interaction. The formation and ongoing modification of a person's identity is influenced by other people's views of the individual, especially their ascriptions and categorizations. An individual shapes how to enact his or her identity partially in response to his or her interaction partners. Second, an individual identifies him- or herself through his or her relationships with others, such as marital partners, coworkers, and friends (e.g., I am a husband, accountant, friend). Social roles are particularly important in shaping this aspect of identity. Third, a relationship itself is a unit of identity. Thus, a couple as a unit, for instance, can establish an identity.

Communal Layer. A group is also a place where identity exists. Group members usually share common characteristics and have collective memories. Members of a group establish common group identities on the basis of common characteristics and history. The common group characteristics function to form the contents of the group's identities.

Interpenetration of Layers. The four layers of identity are not separate from each other. They are interpenetrated. While they can be seen as functioning independently of each other for analytical purposes, they actually work together. Thus, analyses are enriched if they consider the layers two at a time, three at a time, or all four at once. In some situations, each or some of the layers may be contradictory to or exclusive of each other. In other situations, some or all of the layers are integrated. With the separation and/or integration, that is, interpenetration, the four layers of identity show various aspects of identity in various situations.

Propositions of CTI

Focusing on the direct association between communication and identity as well as the interpenetration of all four layers of identity, CTI summarizes characteristics of identity in 18 testable/observable propositions, many of which are traceable directly to its historical, philosophical, and theoretical roots. As presently conceptualized, 10 of these are the basic, overall assumptions of CTI, while the others are related to the personal, enactment, relational, or communal layers. Following are the propositions in each category. The Basic Propositions are as follows:

- Identities have individual, social, and communal properties.
- Identities are both enduring and changing.
- Identities are affective, cognitive, behavioral, and spiritual.
- Identities have both content and relationship levels of interpretation.
- Identities involve both subjective and ascribed meaning.
- Identities are codes that are expressed in conversations and define membership in communities.
- Identities have semantic properties that are expressed in core symbols, meanings, and labels.

- Identities prescribe modes of appropriate and effective communication.
- Identities are a source of expectations and motivations.
- Identities are emergent.

The proposition for the personal layer is:

- Identities are hierarchically ordered meanings attributed to self as an object in a social situation.

The proposition for the enactment layer is:

- Identities are enacted in social behavior and symbols.

Propositions for the relational layer are:

- Identities emerge in relationship to other people.
- Identities are enacted in relationships.
- Relationships develop identities as social entities.
- Identities are meanings ascribed to the self by others in the social world.
- Identities are hierarchically ordered social roles.

The proposition for the communal layer is:

- Identities emerge out of groups and networks.

CTI RESEARCH

Ethnic Labeling and Ethnicity

The CTI emerged out of research focusing on ethnic identity and interethnic communication. This research led to reconceptualizing identity through a communicative lens. The theory, in turn, guided additional research on ethnic identity. In this section we discuss the role of CTI in our understanding of ethnic identity.

One of the most salient issues in ethnic identity literature involves specifying the nature of the construct. Much of the research on identity revolves around two approaches: ethnic labeling and ethnicity or ethnic salience.

Ethnic labeling focuses on group membership (e.g., which overall group a person identifies or associates with) and is typically measured utilizing a checklist of ethnic terms or labels. These lists resemble those used by the census, placing people in broad, ethnic categories. The "ethnicity" approach distinguishes different ways in which people conceptualize themselves as group members (e.g., social identity, political identity, ethnic pride) and/or the degree to which these memberships are salient to their own identity. The ethnicity approach typically uses multidimensional scales to operationalize identity.

A number of critiques have been leveled at the ethnic labeling approach because it places people in broad ethnic categories (e.g., African American, European American, Asian American, Mexican American). These critiques argue that labeling approaches ethnicity in a "garbled" and "unsophisticated" way, using homogenous ethnic group labels as a crude proxy for the complex relationships between ethnicity and behaviors (Collins, 1995; Longshore, 1998; Trimble, 1995). "Ethnic glosses" (Collins, 1995; Trimble, 1995), or conceptualizations of ethnicity as homogenous categories, may be problematic for several reasons. Williams, Lavizzo-Mourey, and Warren (1994), for example, question the utility of racial taxonomies for understanding behavior substantively. Such categories were built on an outdated racial paradigm, assuming that people with different skin color were biologically or genetically different and therefore could be expected to behave differently. These biological conceptualizations are without scientific basis (Gould, 1996; Montagu, 1997) and have limited predictive power as determinants of health (Gold, Thomas, & Davis, 1987). One-dimensional ethnic labels may obfuscate the differences within groups and create overinclusive categories that are meaningless for understanding behavior (Beauvais, 1998; Cheung, 1993; Longshore, 1998). Phinney (1996) concludes that the variation within ethnic groups on such factors as education, family structure, and social class makes predicting behaviors by ethnic group membership alone untenable. Ethnic labels also may obscure the role of other variables, such as socioeconomic status, that have a more potent effect on behavior (Cheung, 1990-1991). Failure to identify these proximal factors can reinforce ethnic prejudices and perpetuate racist stereotypes.

Currently there is a broader acceptance of the ethnicity paradigm, recognizing the importance of culture over phenotypical (racial) differences (Wallace, Bachman, O'Malley, & Johnson, 1995). The CTI, however, stresses the interpretive processes involved in groups, focusing on the meanings associated with identities. The theory points to the role of core symbols in guiding interpretations. Given the realities of race relations around the world and in the United States, ethnic labels are meaningful categories to people and may, in fact, function as core symbols (Witteborn, 2003). In addition, the theory stresses the layered nature of reality and the importance of understanding how group membership positions interpretations of the social world. Finally, the theory links identity to modes of behavior, arguing that there are functional implications. Thus, the theory predicts that ethnic labels and ethnicity are meaningful and functional but not unproblematic. These concerns led to a line of research attempting to understand how ethnic identity functions. The research involved describing the dimensions of identity for various groups and examining the relationship between labels and ethnicity.

The first studies in this sequence were conducted among adults. These studies had three themes. The first theme examined how labels were used by members of an ethnic group to describe the range of identities within the group and linked these identities to interpretations and communication. These studies established three labels most commonly used by African Americans (African American, black American, black) and demonstrated that

each was associated with different meanings and forms of expression (Hecht et al., 2003; Larkey & Hecht, 1995; Larkey, Hecht, & Martin, 1993). Thus, consistent with the theory, the labels were meaningful to group members as well as functional (i.e., related to communication).

Second, this work sought to identify the dimensions of ethnicity and compare these dimensions across cultures (Larkey & Hecht, 1995). Following the work of White and Burke (White, 1989; White & Burke, 1987), we examined the personal, social, and political elements of identity. This work demonstrated that African Americans perceived a more differentiate notion of identity, with two factors (personal/social, political) emerging for this group compared to a single, overall identity salience factor for European Americans. Larkey and Hecht (1995) also showed that ethnicity was differentially related to communication, with a negative relationship between identity and interethnic communication satisfaction (stronger identity associated with lower satisfaction) for European Americans, while a positive relationship was observed for African Americans.

The positive correlation for African Americans is in part a product of the other orientation that often emerges from being an outgroup member (Hecht et al., 1992; Hecht, Ribeau, & Alberts, 1989; Martin, Hecht, & Larkey, 1994). Generally, the salience of white ethnic identity is comparatively minimal. There can be for some an overawareness of one's African American ethnic identity and the ways in which problematic interethnic communication can be instigated by racial attitudes and perceived power issues. It is further complicated by competing understandings of messages, context, and conversational rules. Thus, ethnicity is not only defined differently in the two communities, but it functions differently as well.

The latter two themes, defining the dimensions of ethnicity and examining the functions of labels and ethnicity, also were pursued in research among adolescents. First, a series of studies was conducted to describe ethnic similarities and differences in adolescent communication about drugs. Specifically, these studies described how Mexican American, African American, and European American adolescents were offered drugs and how they resisted those offers (Hecht, Trost, Bator, & MacKinnon, 1997; Moon, Hecht, Jackson, & Spellers, 1999; Moon, Jackson, & Hecht, 2000). Small but consistent differences were reported across the groups. Probably more significant, however, a study was conducted to compare the effects of ethnic labels and ethnicity (Marsiglia, Kulis, & Hecht, 2001). This study demonstrated an independent effect for ethnic labels but not ethnicity (ethnic identity salience), consistent with the CTI view that labels are meaningful, core symbols of identity. More important, however, significant interactions were observed that supported the complexity of identity as well as the conclusion that ethnic identity functions differently for different groups. In this study, different dimensions of ethnicity were identified for adolescents; not surprising, because identity is seen as developmental in CTI. For adolescents, identity involves ethnic pride and typicality (the degree to which one's behavior is typical of one's group). Among African Americans and Mexican Americans, higher pride and lower typicality were associated with less substance use. Among European Americans, however, the opposite pattern was observed; lower pride and higher typicality were associated with less use. One outcome of this research was a successful, multicultural middle school drug prevention program (Hecht et al., 2003).

These studies demonstrate the value of the multilayered approach taken by CTI. It recognizes both enduring and changing elements (e.g., in the dimensions of ethnicity that differ between adolescents and adults), and sees communication as an essential aspect of identity, not merely an outcome or effect. The line of research emerging from this dynamic conceptualization demonstrates the complexity of identity, both as an interpretive framework as well as in functional relationships to important behaviors.

Identity Negotiation

Adding to this complexity is the dynamism in the interpenetration between and among the four layers of identity. As the layers of identity play out in social life, they not only interpenetrate each other, but also the identities of other social actors as well as communal representation. Although one layer may at times be more salient than another, the other layers are never static or irrelevant. Moreover, there may be conflict between and among layers that the individual struggles to put into perspective. Identity is not exclusively a dialectic among the self and society (Hecht et al., 1993).

CTI uses the metaphor of negotiation to describe these interplays.[2] Negotiation captures the give and take as people face the challenge of calibrating enactments to personal layers, one's personal layer to a partner's relational layer for the individual, as well as a relational identity (e.g., how a couple defines itself) in the context of how a community views that relationship type.[3] This complexity provides a challenge to CTI research, one that requires techniques such as multilevel statistical analyses, layered qualitative methods, and/or multimethod research.

A recent line of research on Jewish American identity yields insight into the fluidity and give and take inherent within identity negotiation. The closetable and potentially stigmatized nature of this identity provides a unique opportunity to observe the negotiation among the personal, the enacted, relational, and communal layers (Hecht & Faulkner, 2000; Hecht et al., 2002).

Golden, Niles, and Hecht (1998) note modernism's effect on Jewish identity. Through a modernist lens, many Jewish Americans are observed as moving away from being defined by their closed religious communities. They celebrate this individualism by making their own choices in constructing their personal identity as Jews. Marsiglia and Hecht (1999) take the negotiation between communal and personal identity farther by looking at gendered Jewish American identity. Their autoethnographic exploration presents the complex negotiation process between the communally ascribed and self-avowed female Jewish identity. Community stereotypes of Jewish women provide boundaries for the ways in which gendered identity is enacted. Thus, there is a dialectical tension between the personal and communal layers of gender, which some Jewish American women resolve through the appropriation of various core symbols, meanings, and labels at the expense of others.

In addition to supporting many of the previous issues, a study of television representations of Jewish identity described how some Jewish Americans negotiate the challenge of being both an insider and an outsider group (Hecht & Faulkner, 2000; Hecht et al., 2002). Specifically, Jewish Americans negotiate a privileged U.S. identity (i.e., the "model minority" that now also plagues many Asian American groups) in opposition to anti-Semitism (e.g., Jews remain among the most frequent victims of hate crimes in the U.S.). Unlike many ethnicities, however, Jewish Americans have the ability to hide their identities or to choose not to identify with the group. Originally developed to describe how members of gay and lesbian communities manage their identities, closeting is especially salient during problematic interactions where their group membership will be devalued. There are, however, varying levels and difference of identity enactment for Jewish Americans, even though they may "share personal labels and identification" (Hecht et al., 2002, p. 868). The reverse is also true, whereby enacted identities are shared while personal identities differ. Regardless, it appears that Jewish Americans consider the centrality of their own identities as well as the severity of the consequences as they manage

their privacy boundaries (Hecht & Faulkner, 2000). Specific strategies for revealing their identity align along an explicit/implicit dimension that is influenced by the relationship type (especially the presence of romance) and in the greater societal context of isolation and "otherness" (Hecht & Faulkner, 2000). Clearly, identity negotiation has a dialectical as well as fluid nature as Jewish Americans reveal the interpenetrable nature of CTI's four layers.

NEW DIRECTIONS IN CTI

Negotiation of Cultural Identity

Stemming in part from the work on negotiation in Jewish identity and evolving further from a study of African American communication, Hecht et al. (1993) acknowledge the importance of more directly exploring the negotiation processes implicated by the CTI framework. Taking them up on their challenge, Jackson (1999) examines "cultural identity as a relationally-driven negotiation process" in intercultural communication (p. 4). Drawing on the scholarship of Ting-Toomey (1999) in addition to utilizing various aspects of the CTI, Jackson (2002a) developed cultural contracts theory (CCT). CCT conceptualizes the *negotiation of cultural identity* as a contractual process (Jackson, 2002a). Every "signed" or agreed-upon cultural contract has a direct impact on one's identity because identity attributes (i.e., core symbols, meanings, labels) are "bargaining chips." Hence, cultural contracts serve as a means to protect and define the self as well as stipulating our behavior and perceptions during relational communication.

Jackson (2002b) stipulates three types of cultural contracts. *Ready-to-sign* contracts have been already established and are nonnegotiable. The individual enacting this type of agreement expects others to conform to the individual's perspective and ways of communicating. In *quasi-completed* contracts there is room for partial negotiation of identities and their relational coordination. Lastly, *co-created* contracts are completely negotiable. Difference is valued and relational partners seek communication satisfaction.

CCT emerged out of a study addressing the negotiation of cultural identity for and between African Americans and European Americans, examining communication and negotiation via "core symbols, codes, prescriptions, and community" (Jackson, 1999, p. 102). Although individuals in each group negotiate cultural identity to varying degrees, the findings suggest cultural negotiation often functions at a subconscious level for both groups. This study also revealed dominant groups usually maintain ready-to-sign contracts. They are not necessarily motivated to redefine and negotiate their cultural identities, while it is expected minority groups will realign their worldviews, communication styles, and behavior to fit the majority.

Jackson and colleagues (Jackson & Crawley, in press; Jackson & Simpson, in press) utilize CCT to explore further the cultural contracts that are negotiated by whites. In the student-teacher context (Jackson & Crawley, in press), whites moved through each type of contract in reflecting on their white identity in relation to their black male professor, as they moved more toward co-created contracts. They still retained their conservative views on social reality, however, and ultimately were reluctant to completely deny the value of ready-to-sign contracts in their dealings with racialized identities. This latter point echoes Jackson and Simpson's (in press) analysis of whiteness in a broader context. Thus, it appears that, at times, whites will negotiate cultural contracts with African Americans, particularly where whites are in low power positions, but negotiating quasi or co-created contracts is not the most frequent or easiest form for them to adopt.

At the same time, the negotiation process is equally problematic for minorities (Jackson (2002b), especially in the common situation in which persons, institutions, and cultures marginalize their identities. Quasi-completed contracts are often utilized in these situations

to align their identities temporarily with mainstream practices and protect their well-being. Implicating a *layered approach* to identity, this perspective focuses on the dialectical tensions among the layers of the CTI, asserting that if goals and interests are not aligned, the result is identity conflict (Hecht, Jackson, Lindsley, Strauss, & Johnson, 2001; Jackson, 2002a). This type of identity negotiation is also salient when moving through multiple cultural contexts (e.g., homeland vs. foreign host country; Onwumechili, Nwosu, Jackson, & James-Hughes, 2003). Not only are the individuals negotiating, the coordination of relationships is intimately tied to and further negotiated through cultural contracts with a larger entity.

Teaming up with Hecht and Ribeau in the release of the second edition of *African American Communication,* Jackson (see Hecht et al., 2003) utilizes CCT to explicate more precisely the negotiation processes and dialectical tensions between African American self-avowed and socially ascribed identities, in addition to the negotiation process moving through CTI's multilayered layers of identity. Jackson's growing scholarship on CCT is not a derivative of CTI. It has a number of other origins, as well, and effectively fills in some of the gaps of negotiated identity in relational communication among the various layers of CTI.

Identity Gaps

CTI describes the relationships among the four layers of identity as "interpenetration." Among various possible types of interpenetration is the discrepancy or contradiction between and among the different layers of identity. For example, the personal and relational layers of identity, or the personal and enacted layers of identity, can be different for an individual. These discrepancies between or among the four layers are defined as an "identity gap" (Jung, 2003).

Identity gaps can exist between and among any of the identity layers. Overall, the possible number of identity gaps is six when discrepancies between two layers are counted, and five more are added if discrepancies among three and four layers are considered. Among these possible identity gaps, Jung and Hecht (2003) studied the gaps between personal and relational layers and personal and enacted layers.

The personal-relational identity gap refers to discrepancies between how an individual views him- or herself (personal identity) and his or her perception of how others view him or her (a type of relational identity). The idea that identity includes the views of others and differences exist between self-view and others' view was suggested in various theories, including Cooley (1902), Mead (1934), self-verification theory (Giesler & Swann, 1999; McNulty & Swann, 1994), control theory (Carver & Scheier, 1982; Powers, 1973), and identity theory (Burke, 1991; Stryker & Burke, 2000). All of these theories describe a "gap-like" construct and posit a drive to reduce or avoid the differences. Further, related research shows that discrepancies or gaps are associated with feeling lack of pride and interest, loneliness, and insecurity (Higgins, 1987; Higgins, Bond, Klein, & Strauman, 1986; Higgins, Klein, & Strauman 1985).

An individual's personal identity also can differ from his or her enacted identity. One's expressed self in communication can be different from one's self-concepts. Hence, the definition of "personal-enacted identity gap" is the discrepancy between an individual's self-view and the same individual's enactment of self in communication with others. Ideas related to the difference between personal and enacted identities appear in a number of theories, including Goffman's (1959) dramaturgical approach, Petronio's (1991, 2000) communication boundary management theory, and Jack's (1991) silencing the self theory. For example, women's enactment of inauthentic selves suppressing their real selves to meet culturally defined standards of femininity seemed to cause feelings of hopelessness and eventually depression (Jack, 1999).

Although ideas similar to personal, relational, and enacted identities and the gaps between them were suggested in various theories, these theories tended to overlook communicative characteristics of the three aspects of identity and the role of communication in developing gaps. Jung and Hecht (2003) conceptualized the identity gaps—personal-relational and personal-enacted gaps—as communication variables or the results of communication. This conceptualization was supported by high correlations between each of the two identity gaps and communication outcomes, such as communication satisfaction, feeling understood, and conversational appropriateness and effectiveness in their study. Further research is also needed to specify the nature of these relationships. For example, gaps may mediate the relationship between communication inputs (e.g., communication style, communication competence) and message strategies or communication outcomes. Gaps may also be related to psychological and behavioral issues.

Thus far in this chapter we have emphasized the implications of CTI for racial, ethnic, and cultural identities. Although race, ethnicity, and culture obviously play important roles in shaping the self, they are not the sole basis for our identification with others. Promising future directions for the development of CTI include examining its contribution to understanding other aspects of our identities, such as age or health, as well as its contribution to identity and technology. The next section will take a brief look at health identity and identity in computer-mediated communication for the purposes of elucidating the applications of CTI in new contexts.

FUTURE DIRECTIONS

Applying CTI to Illness Identity

In addition to traditional contexts for identity research such as race, ethnicity, and gender, there is a growing interdisciplinary interest in the identity functions of health status. In general, this research has focused on describing the identity transformations that accompany particular types of long-term illness, such as for people with cancer (Mathieson & Stam, 1995), cardiac patients (Kundrat & Nussbaum, 2003), HIV/AIDS (Tewksbury & McGaughey, 1998), and mental illness (Onken & Slaten, 2000). While some authors claim that illness identity formation includes "identifiable states of transformation similar to the states contained in minority development models based on race, ethnicity, and sexual orientation" (Onken & Slaten, 2000, p. 104), others confirm that the health context offers new challenges to our understanding of the socially constructed nature of identity by utilizing constructs such as invisible illness (Kundrat & Nussbaum, 2003), contextual age (Clarke, 2001; Kundrat & Nussbaum, 2003), and "body talk" as a form of biographical disruption (Mathieson & Stam, 1995; Tewksbury & McGaughey, 1998). While most previous research assumes that individuals will make sense of their physical and mental health state based on personal ideas about what constitutes health and illness (Levine, 1999), recent research has begun to address the ways in which illness identity is constructed through social interaction (Kundrat & Nussbaum, 2003; Newton, 2001). As previously mentioned, the CTI assumes that identity is formed through interaction, making it a viable theoretical framework for advancing development of illness identity research. The following section provides examples of how illness identity research can be examined with reference to the four identity layers proposed by CTI: personal, enacted, relational, and communal.

The personal identity layer encompasses self-cognitions and is the layer most closely related to psychological perspectives on illness identity, such as explaining illness in terms of self-presentation problems (Schlenker, 2003) or patients who assume a "sick role" (e.g., Hamilton, Deemer, & Janata, 2003; Krahn,

Li, & O'Conner, 2003). Lack of consistency between physical ability and perceived age also would be included in this layer. For example, Clarke (2001) found that the experience of physical limitations associated with ageing served as a stimulus for older adult women to redefine the relationship between the body and self. These women described how they now differentiate between the "outside self" (i.e., the chronological age of the body) and the "inside self" (i.e., personality and feeling youthful).

The enacted layer in CTI refers to how identity is expressed through interactions with others. Enacting illness identity may take various forms, such as discussing one's sexual health history with a partner or participating in rallies for AIDS research. Newton (2001) provides numerous examples of how mentally ill adults enacted various aspects of their identities as they transitioned to community living. For instance, the very act of living in the community setting enabled one of the participants to enact a self-concept that was separate from mental illness. Another participant was able to enact an independent identity by conducting her weekly shopping without a list.

The relational layer describes the component of illness identity that is formed through relationships with other people. One way to illustrate this concept is to consider the context of invisible illness. Invisible illness refers to infirmity that is not easily detectable by appearances only, such as cardiovascular disease, cancer, HIV, and learning disabilities (Kundrat & Nussbaum, 2003). Thus, acquaintances, friends, and perhaps even family members are likely to be unaware of the illness unless the ill individual chooses to disclose this information to them. The context of invisible illness puts the ill individual in the uncomfortable position of determining the appropriate point in a relationship to disclose medical information, as well as dealing with the changes to relationships that are likely to accompany the disclosure (Kundrat & Nussbaum, 2003).

The last layer, communal, refers to the collective identity of a particular group with which an individual perceives affiliation. Onken and Slaten (2000) describe one of the paths to positive disability identity formation as the feeling of not belonging in an ableist society, and increased interaction with similarly disabled others to counteract feelings of isolation and alienation.

In sum, the CTI can be utilized to advance our understanding of the various aspects of illness identity, including personal, enacted, relational, and communal layers. Future research should build on this framework to identify explicitly the *unique characteristics* of health identity as compared with other aspects of identity, such as the potentially transient nature of illness identity (e.g., cancer survivors), and further elaborate a differentiation between illness identity (i.e., identity formed through illness), and health identity (i.e., identity associated with the absence of illness), as well as the *similarities* between health and illness identity development and other aspects of identity. In addition, research should investigate the interpenetration of the four layers of identity in various contexts. For example, one might ask how changing images of diseases such as HIV (communal identity) are related to self-image (personal) and family communication (relational and enacted).

Applying CTI to Technology

Postmodern ideations of identity effectively pave the way for understanding how identity becomes salient within a computer-mediated world and sets the stages for innovative applications of CTI. Computer mediated communication (CMC) is multifaceted (the Internet, instant messaging, gaming, etc.), and each facet has its unique place in identity processes.

In contrast to the face-to-face modality, online communication of individual and group identity is usually separated from physical representation. The communicator is shielded by the technology and, as a result, anonymity is facilitated to a much greater degree than in other forms of communication because individuals have the ability to create and/or reveal many sides of their identity (Barnes, 2001; Turkle, 1997a). For instance, skin color, ethnicity, gender, socioeconomic status, health, and sexual orientation may be hidden or modified if the communicator so chooses.

Potential anonymity is one of the key qualities of online communication and changes the dynamics of enacted identities. If an individual can portray him- or herself in relatively unlimited ways with little chance of disconfirmation, strategies for self-presentation, privacy management, and identity politics are almost unlimited. This added freedom creates a problematic event in which attributions and interpretations of messages become subject to rapid change.

Take, for example, an identity claim in a chat room. Someone who has taken on the screen name "DOC" has been making arguments about our nation's inner cities. DOC is challenged and responds by asserting membership in an oppressed group to gain a privileged voice on the topic. It would be difficult to challenge this claim without the sort of information normally available in face-to-face interaction (dress and other markers of socioeconomics, phenotypical characteristics, etc.).

Technology not only changes (and challenges) the geometry of identity enactment, it extends the reach of enactment and opens up possibilities for new relationships. While people establish relationships and join online communities based on textual exchanges related to various topics (e.g., chat rooms) and digital images, reasons that are similar to face-to-face and other more traditional relationships, online interactions may in fact take place with individuals and communities with which one may not feel quite comfortable interacting offline. Moreover, these relationships can transcend geographic boundaries into areas of the world interactants would not otherwise travel. Rather than identity being situated "in" the body and place, information and communication technologies create a "saturated self" in which identity is spread across networks of social relationships and roles (Gergen, 1991) as well as across space.

Online gaming provides an excellent example of this characteristic of technology. Turkle (1997a) argues that online multiuser computer games position individuals and technology in new relationships to each other by providing "evocative objects" for thinking about identity (p. 17). These innovative liaisons encourage a postmodern form of identity manifesting as multiple and fluid identities constructed through language and in interaction with the technology. For instance, Turkle (1997b) highlights the experiences of playing the text-based multiuser games known as multiuser dungeons or domains (MUD). MUDs allow players to construct virtual worlds collectively through text. The most popular is based on the fantasy game Dungeons and Dragons. In these virtual domains players can assume characters, build homes, create props, journey through towns, and interact with sometimes thousands of other players, all textually produced. One player, in particular, assumed the roles of multiple assertive females while interacting with other players. Through his experiences and experimentation with identity online, this player was able to overcome the communicative difficulties in his offline interactions when the assertive roles acted out online provided means to challenge his offline passive identity (Turkle, 1997b). As a result, Turkle (1984) contends, users learn from online interaction and are better able to control self-presentation and communicate more effectively than in face-to-face interpersonal settings. This perspective also applies to other online settings, such as virtual communities, personal home pages, discussion groups, e-mail, and the use of instant messaging.

As a result, online social interactions provide fertile contexts for thinking about the communication of identity and for the application of CTI. As we have seen, computer technology provides a rich and unique context for message exchange (Chayko, 2002; Kolko, 2000; Nass & Steuer, 1993). As the computer is endowed with sociocultural meanings through its designers and programmers, in addition to those who provide content online, it reflects various worldviews and understandings (Kolko, 2000). Its users conjointly bring myriad perspectives and identities to their interaction with the technology, centering the interpretation of layers active within CTI as implicated in an individual's computer use and in interpretations of computer content.

Human-computer interaction (HCI) is one context for exploring further uses of CTI. HCI has been viewed as the "social interaction with technology arising from the general psychological tendency of people to respond socially in situations in which they are reminded of their own humanity or social selves, or in which they form an attachment to another" (Kiesler, Sproul, & Waters, 1996, p. 3). People tend to treat computers as if they were real people and their online behavior as social (Reeves & Nass, 1996). CTI can address how individual and group identities are constructed, influenced, validated, or denied within this unique type of social interaction, and the research may consider the hardware, the software, or the Internet itself.

Usability of software interfaces provides another example of the potential for CTI research in this domain. Kolko (2000) describes the ways in which interfaces are made in the image of the designer as he or she delimits what type of representations and interactions the user has with the technology. Kolko argues that, in general, interfaces (as messages) do not acknowledge the diverse identities and perspectives people bring to their interaction with the computer. The majority of interfaces reflect a particular worldview that may marginalize some identities. In the analysis of the MUDs, Kolko notes that while the MUD interface allows users to access varying commands to describe their gender (@gender), age (@age), and interests (@interests), there is no similar command for denoting race (i.e., @race). This absence may signal race as not important or homogenous. However, the default race of the particular MUD LambdaMOO is assumed to be white based on the documentation of community member interaction. Clearly this points to assumptions designers have in the programming of particular interfaces.

This marginalization has cultural and political implications. It affects how individuals view who they are (personal, enacted, relational, communal) in attempting to establish a relationship with the technology. If cultural or racial identities are not considered as options in interaction with the technology, then individuals would have to deny aspects of their identity in the relationship. This devaluing may negatively influence self-image and interaction with the computer. Hence, it could dissuade one from even utilizing the technology, which further complicates the knowledge gap and digital divide.

There are a number of other ways CTI can further our understanding of the role technology plays in our lives. CTI can enhance the study of HCI by helping us describe the interpenetration of the layers of identity that individuals bring to computer use or how any one of the layers influences computer interaction. More important, CTI can broaden the discourse on the digital divide by focusing attention on the communication of cultural and racial identities (communal layer) in interaction with the computer. Clearly, CTI has the framework necessary for exploring the complex nature of identity in a multitude of contexts across disciplines.

CONCLUSION

The construction and advancement of theory is critical to all disciplines. From within communication studies, CTI presents an innovative framework for the study of identity that centralizes communication. While psychological and sociological theories are often "imported" to study communication, CTI is a communication-based theory. Emerging through culturally variant understandings of identity and shifting perspectives, the development of CTI moves the study of identity beyond the individual and society to performance and relationship, and provides a counterpoint to previous theories.

Emerging out of research examining effective intergroup communication, CTI conceptualizes identity as inherently connected to communication. A sense of self is defined and redefined in communicative process. In addition, communication performs and enacts identity. From this basic viewpoint, the theory identifies four layers—personal, enacted, relational, and communal. Each layer provides a lens through which to view the communication of identity, although identity is seen as the interpenetration of all layers. The layers are not separate, and analyses are enriched if all, two, or three are applied to a particular phenomenon.

Up to this point the application of CTI has centered on research on ethnic identity. Its contribution challenges one-dimensional understandings of ethnic categories. CTI focuses on the interpretative processes involved in groups, meanings associated with identity, the layered nature of reality, and how group membership positions understandings of the social world. CTI also connects behavior to identity. Considering the fluid and complex nature of identity, identity negotiation presents a clear case for the interpenetration of layers and the manner in which individuals may negotiate the layers of CTI in communicating who they are.

Extending the unique contributions of CTI are paradigms that seek to fill in the gaps and extend its layers for understanding identity. Cultural contract theory takes on the task of exploring more specifically the negotiation processes involved in CTI. Other research has conceptualized identity gaps as the inconsistencies and contradictions inherent in the interpenetration of layers or various layers of identity. Applications to closetable identities, including ethnic groups, computer-mediated communication, and human-computer interaction, explore the nuances of identity negotiation. Work in the health field has begun to demonstrate the practical utility of the theory. Each of these new directions is complemented by future applications, which center the concrete interdisciplinary nature of CTI.

This chapter summarizes the development and articulation of the communication theory of identity. We have attempted to describe its basic tenets and then demonstrate applications and future directions. Our goal was not only to inform, but also to enact the theory through this fluid and versatile exploration. It is telling that postmodern, interpretive, and behavioral applications are emerging from a theory that itself is multilayered.

NOTES

1. We use the label "identity theory" because it is the title most commonly used in this literature. It appears to us, however, that the theory might more aptly be titled "identity role theory," because it does not truly capture the full range or force of identity.

2. Related terms include managing identity and identity construction/reconstruction.

3. For another discussion of negotiation, see the work of Ting-Toomey (1993).

REFERENCES

Asante, M. K. (1998). *The Afrocentric idea.* Philadephia: Temple University Press.

Banton, M. (1965). *Roles: An introduction to the study of social relations.* New York: Basic Books.

Barnes, S. B. (2001). *Online connections: Internet interpersonal relationships.* Cresskill, NJ: Hampton Press.

Beauvais, F. (1998). Cultural identification and substance use in North America: An annotated bibliography. *Substance Use and Misuse, 33,* 1315–1336.

Berger, C. R. (1991). Chautauqua: Why are there so few communication theories? Communication theories and other curios. *Communication Monographs, 58,* 102–113.

Bewes, T. (1997). *Cynicism and postmodernity.* New York: Verso.

Burke, P. J. (1991). Identity processes and social stress. *American Sociological Review, 56,* 836–849.

Burke, P. J., & Reitzes, D. C. (1981). The link between identity and role performance. *Social Psychology Quarterly, 44,* 83–92.

Carbaugh, D. (1989). *Talking American: Cultural discourses on Donahue.* Norwood, NJ: Ablex.

Cartledge, P. (2002). *The Greeks: A portrait of self and others.* New York: Oxford University Press.

Carver, C. S., & Scheier, M. F. (1982). Control theory: A useful conceptual framework for personality—Social, clinical, and health psychology. *Psychological Bulletin, 92,* 111–135.

Chayko, M. (2002). *Connecting: How we form social bonds and communities in the Internet age.* Albany: State University of New York Press.

Cheung, Y. W. (1990-1991). Ethnicity and alcohol/drug use revisited: A framework for future research. *International Journal of Addiction, 25,* 581–605.

Cheung, Y. W. (1993). Approaches to ethnicity—Clearing roadblocks in the study of ethnicity and substance use. *International Journal of Addictions, 28*(12), 1209–1226.

Clarke, L. H. (2001). Older women's bodies and the self: The construction of identity in later life. *Canadian Review of Sociology and Anthropology, 38*(4), 441–464.

Collier, M. J., Ribeau, S. A., & Hecht, M. L. (1986). Intracultural communication rules and outcomes within three domestic cultural groups. *International Journal of Intercultural Relations, 10,* 439–457.

Collins, R. L. (1995). Issues of ethnicity in research on prevention of substance abuse. In G. J. Botvin, S. Schinke, & M. A. Orlandi (Eds.), *Drug abuse prevention with multiethnic youth* (pp. 28–45). Thousand Oaks, CA: Sage.

Cooley, C. H. (1902). *Human nature and the social order.* New York: Scribners.

Gergen, K. (1991). *Saturated self: Dilemmas of identity in contemporary life*. New York: Basic Books.

Gergen, K. (1996). Technology and the self: From the essential to the sublime. In D. Grodin & T. Lindlof (Eds.), *Constructing the self in a mediated world* (pp. 127–140). Thousands Oaks, CA: Sage.

Giesler, R. B., & Swann, W. (1999). Striving for confirmation: The role of self-verification in depression. In T. Joiner & J. C. Coyne (Eds.), *The interactional nature of depression* (pp. 189–218). Washington DC: American Psychological Association.

Goffman, E. (1959). *The presentation of self in everyday life*. Garden City, NY: Anchor/Doubleday.

Goffman, E. (1963). *Stigma: Notes on the management of spoiled identity*. Englewood Cliffs, NJ: Prentice Hall.

Goffman, E. (1967). *Interaction ritual*. New York: Pantheon.

Gold, R. S., Thomas, S. B., & Davis, D. (1987). The literature on prevention in minority communities: Some lessons to be learned. Minority Health Research Laboratory, Office of Minority Health (Report). Washington, DC: Centers for Disease Control and Prevention.

Golden, D., Niles, T. A., & Hecht, M. L. (1998). Jewish American identity. In J. N. Martin, T. K. Nakayama, & L. A. Flores (Eds.), *Readings in cultural contexts*. Mountain View, CA: Mayfield.

Gould, S. J. (1996). *The mismeasure of man* (Rev. & expanded ed.). New York: Norton.

Gudykunst, W. (1988). *Theories in intercultural communication*. Newbury Park, CA: Sage.

Hamilton, J. C., Deemer, H. N., & Janata, J. W. (2003). Feeling bad but looking good: Sick role features that lead to favorable interpersonal judgements. *Journal of Social & Clinical Psychology, 22(2)*, 253–274.

Harvey, D. (1990). *The condition of postmodernity: An enquiry into the origins of cultural change*. Cambridge, MA: Blackwell.

Hecht, M. L. (1993). A research odyssey: Towards the development of a communication theory of identity. *Communication Monographs, 60*, 76–82.

Hecht, M. L., Collier, M. J., & Ribeau, S. A. (1993). *African American communication: Ethnic identity and cultural interpretation*. Newbury Park, CA: Sage.

Hecht, M. L., & Faulkner S. L. (2000). Sometimes Jewish, sometimes not: The closeting of Jewish American identity. *Communication Studies, 51(4)*, 372–387.

Hecht, M. L., Faulkner S. L., Meyer, C. R., Niles, T. A., Golden, D., & Cutler, M. (2002). Looking through *Northern Exposure* at Jewish American identity and the communication theory of identity. *Journal of Communication, 52*, 852–870.

Hecht, M. L., Jackson, R. L., II, Lindsley, S., Strauss, S., & Johnson, K. E. (2001). A layered approach to ethnicity: Language and communication. In W. P. Robinson & H. Giles (Eds.), *The new handbook of language and social psychology*. New York: John Wiley.

Hecht, M. L., Jackson, R. L., II, & Ribeau, S. (2003). *African American communication: Exploring identity and culture* (2nd ed.). ahwah, NJ: Lawrence Erlbaum.

Hecht, M. L., Larkey, L. K., & Johnson, J. N. (1992). African American and European American perceptions of problematic issues in interethnic communication effectiveness. *Human Communication Research, 19*, 209–236.

Hecht, M. L., Marsiglia, F. F., Elek-Fisk, E., Wagstaff, D. A., Kulis, S., Dustman, P., & Miller-Day, M. (2003). Culturally-grounded substance use prevention: An evaluation of the keepin' it R.E.A.L. curriculum. *Prevention Science, 4*, 233–248.

Hecht, M. L., Ribeau, S., & Alberts, J. K. (1989). An Afro-American perspective on interethnic communication. *Communication Monographs, 56*, 385–410.

Hecht, M. L., Ribeau, S., & Sedano, M. V. (1990). A Mexican-American perspective on interethnic communication. *International Journal of Intercultural Relations, 14*, 31–55.

Hecht, M. L., Trost, M., Bator, R., & McKinnon, D. (1997). Ethnicity and gender similarities and differences in drug resistance. *Journal of Applied Communication Research, 25*, 75-97.

Higgins, E. T. (1987). Self-discrepancy: A theory relating self and affect. *Psychological Review, 3*, 319–340.

Higgins, E. T., Bond, R. N., Klein, R., & Strauman, T. (1986). Self-discrepancies and emotional vulnerability: How magnitude, accessibility, and type of discrepancy influence affect. *Journal of Personality and Social Psychology, 51,* 5–15.

Higgins, E. T., Klein, R., & Strauman, T. (1985). Self-concept discrepancy theory: A psychological model for distinguishing among different aspects of depression and anxiety. *Social Cognition, 3,* 51–76.

Hogg, M. A. (1993). Group cohesiveness: A critical review and some new direction. *European Review of Social Psychology, 4,* 85–111.

Hogg, M. A., & Abrams, D. (1988). *Social identifications: A social psychology of intergroup relations and group processes.* London: Routledge.

Jack, D. C. (1991). *Silencing the self: Women and depression.* Cambridge, MA: Harvard University Press.

Jack, D. C. (1999). Silencing the self: Inner dialogue and outer realities. In T. Joiner & J. C. Coyne (Eds.), *Interactional nature of depression* (pp. 221–246). Washington DC: American Psychological Association.

Jackson, J. A. (1972). *Role.* Cambridge, UK: Cambridge University Press.

Jackson, R. L., II. (1999). *The negotiation of cultural identity: Perceptions of European Americans and African Americans.* Westport, CT: Praeger.

Jackson, R. L., II. (2002a). Cultural contracts theory: Toward an understanding of identity negotiation. *Communication Quarterly, 50*(3 & 4), 359–367.

Jackson, R. L., II. (2002b). Exploring African American identity negotiation in the academy: Toward a transformative vision of African American communication scholarship. *Howard Journal of Communications, 13,* 43–57.

Jackson, R. L., II, & Crawley, R. (in press). White student confessions about an African American male professor: A cultural contracts theory approach to intimate conversations about race and worldview. *Journal of Men's Studies.*

Jackson, R. L., II, & Simpson, K. (in press). White positionalities and cultural contracts: Critiquing entitlement, theorizing and exploring the negotiation of white identities. *International Journal of Intercultural Relations.*

Jahn, J. (1961). *Muntu: African culture and the Western world.* New York: Grove Weidenfeld.

Jung, E. (2003). *Korean Americans' identity gaps in interethnic interaction and level of depression.* Manuscript in preparation, The Pennsylvania State University.

Jung, E., & Hecht, M. L. (2003). *Elaborating the communication theory of identity: Identity gaps and communication outcomes.* Manuscript under review.

Kellner, D. (1992). Popular culture and the construction of postmodern identities. In S. Lash & J. Friedman (Eds.), *Modernity and identity* (pp. 141–177). Cambridge, UK: Blackwell.

Kiesler, S., Sproul, L., & Waters, K. (1996). A Prisoner's Dilemma experiment on cooperation with people and human-like computers. *Journal of Personality and Social Psychology* [On-Line] 70(1), 1–25.

Kolko, B. E. (2000). Erasing @race: Going white in the (inter)face. In B. E. Kolko, L. Nakamura, & G. B. Rodman (Eds.), *Race in cyberspace.* New York: Routledge.

Krahn, L. E., Li, H., & O'Conner, M. K. (2003). Patients who strive to be ill: Factitious disorder with physical symptoms. *American Journal of Psychiatry, 160*(6), 1163–1168.

Kundrat, A. L., & Nussbaum, J. (2003). The impact of invisible illness on identity and contextual age across the lifespan. *Health Communication, 15*(3), 331–347.

Larkey, L. K., & Hecht, M. L. (1995). A comparative study of African American and European American ethnic identity. *International Journal of Intercultural Relations, 19*(4), 483–504.

Larkey, L. K., Hecht, M. L., & Martin, J. (1993). What's in a name? African American ethnic identity terms and self-determination. *Journal of Language and Social Psychology, 12*(4), 302–317.

Levine, R. M. (1999). Identity and illness: The effects of identity salience and frame of reference on evaluation of illness and injury. *British Journal of Health Psychology, 4*(1), 63–80.

Longshore, D. (1998). Desire for help among drug-using Mexican American arrestees. *Substance Use & Misuse, 33*(6), 1387–1406.

Markus, H., & Sentis, K. (1982). The self in information processing. In J. Suls (Ed.), *Psychological perspectives on the self* (Vol. 1, pp. 41–70). Hillsdale, NJ: Lawrence Erlbaum.

Marsiglia, F. F., & Hecht, M. L. (1999). The story of Sara: Raising a Jewish child around the Christmas tree. In D. O. Braithwaite & J. T. Woods (Eds.), *Case studies in interpersonal communication processes and problems* (pp. 44–51). Belmont, CA: Wadsworth/ Thomson Learning.

Marsiglia, F. F., Kulis, S., & Hecht, M. L. (2001). Ethnic labels and ethnic identity as predictors of drug use and drug exposure among middle school students in the Southwest. *Journal of Research on Adolescence, 11,* 21–48.

Martin, J. N., Hecht, M. L., & Larkey, K. L. (1994). Conversational improvement strategies for interethnic communication: African American and European American perspectives. *Communication Monographs, 61,* 236–255.

Mathieson, C. M., & Stam, H. J. (1995). Renegotiating identity: Cancer narratives. *Sociology of Health & Illness, 17*(3), 283–306.

McNulty, S. E., & Swann, W. (1994). Identity negotiation in roommate relationships: The self as architect and consequence of social reality. *Journal of Personality and Social Psychology, 67,* 1012–1023.

Mead, G. H. (1934). *Mind, self, and society from the standpoint of a social behaviorist.* Chicago: University of Chicago Press.

Meltzer, B. N., & Petras, J. W. (1972). The Chicago and Iowa schools of symbolic interactionism. In T. Shibutani (Ed.), *Human nature and collective behavior* (pp. 3–18). Englewood Cliffs, NJ: Prentice Hall.

Montagu, A. (1997). *Man's most dangerous myth: The fallacy of race* (6th ed.). Walnut Creek, CA: Altamira Press.

Moon, D. G., Hecht, M. L., Jackson, K. M., & Spellers, R. E. (1999). Ethnic and gender differences and similarities in adolescent drug use and refusals of drug offers. *Substance Use & Misuse, 34,* 1059–1083.

Moon, D. G., Jackson, K. M., & Hecht, M. L. (2000). Family risk and resiliency factors, substance use, and the drug resistance process in adolescence. *Journal of Drug Education, 30,* 373–398.

Nass, C., & Steuer, J. (1993). Voices, boxes, and sources of messages: Computers and social actors. *Human Communication Research, 19,* 504–527.

Newton, L. (2001). Self and illness: Changing relationships in response to life in the community following prolonged institutionalization. *Australian Journal of Anthropology, 12*(2), 166–181.

Onken, S. J., & Slaten, E. (2000). Disability identity formation and affirmation: The experiences of persons with severe mental illness. *Sociological Practice: A Journal of Clinical and Applied Sociology, 2*(2), 99–111.

Onwumechili C. N., Nwosu, P. O., Jackson, R. L., II, & James-Hughes, J. (2003). In the deep valley with mountains to climb: Exploring identity and multiple reacculturation. *International Journal of Intercultural Relations, 27,* 41–62.

Pearce, W. B. (1989). *Communication and human condition.* Carbondale: Southern Illinois University Press.

Petronio, S. (1991). Communication boundary management: A theoretical model of managing disclosure of private information between marital couples. *Communication Theory, 4,* 311–335.

Petronio, S. (2000). The boundaries of privacy: Praxis of everyday life. In S. Petronio (Ed.), *Balancing the secrets of private disclosures* (pp. 37–49). Mahwah, NJ: Lawrence Erlbaum.

Phinney, J. S. (1996). Understanding ethnic diversity: The role of ethnic identity. *American Behavioral Scientist, 40*(2), 143–152.

Powers, W. (1973). *Behavior: The control of perception.* Chicago: Aldine.

Reeves, B., & Nass, C. (1996). *The media equation: How people treat computers, television, and new media like real people and places.* New York: Cambridge University Press.

Schlenker, B. R. (1985). Introduction: Foundations of the self in social life. In B. R. Schlenker (Ed.), *The self and social life* (pp. 1–28) New York: McGraw-Hill.

Schlenker, B. (2003). Self-presentation. In M. Leary & J. P. Tangney (Eds.), *Handbook of self and identity.* New York: Guilford.

Stryker, S., & Burke, P. J. (2000). The past, present, and future of an identity theory. *Social Psychology Quarterly, 63,* 284–297.

Tewksbury, R., & McGaughey, D. (1998). Identities and identity transformation among persons with HIV disease. *Journal of Gay, Lesbian, and Bisexual Identity, 3*(3), 213–232.

Ting-Toomey, S. (1999). *Communicating across cultures*. New York: Guilford.

Trimble, J. E. (1995). Toward an understanding of ethnicity and ethnic identity, and their relationship with drug use research. In G. J. Botvin, S. Schinke, & M. A. Orlandi (Eds.), *Drug abuse prevention with multiethnic youth* (pp. 3–27). Thousand Oaks, CA: Sage.

Turkle, S. (1984). *The second self: Computers and the human spirit*. New York: Simon & Schuster.

Turkle, S. (1997a). Computational technologies and images of the self. *Social Research, 64*(3), 1093–1111.

Turkle, S. (1997b). *Life on the screen: Identity in the age of the Internet*. New York: Touchstone.

Turner, J. C. (1991). *Social influence*. Milton Keynes, UK: Open University Press.

Wallace, J. M., Jr., Bachman, J. G., O'Malley, P. M., & Johnson, L. D. (1995). Racial/ethnic differences in adolescent drug use: Exploring possible explanations. In G. J. Botvin, S. Schinke, & M. A. Orlandi (Eds.), *Drug abuse prevention with multiethnic youth* (pp. 81–104). Thousand Oaks, CA: Sage.

Wei-ming, T. (1985). Selfhood and otherness in Confucian thought. In F. D. A. J. Marsella & F. L. K. Huse (Eds.), *Culture and self: Asian and Western perspectives* (pp. 231–251). New York: Tavistock.

White, C. L. (1989). Measuring ethnic identity: An application of the Burke-Tully method. *Sociological Focus, 22,* 249–261.

White, C. L., & Burke, P. J. (1987). Ethnic role identity among black and white college students: An interactionist approach. *Sociological Perspectives, 30,* 310–331.

Williams, D. R., Lavizzo-Mourey, R., & Warren, R. C. (1994). The concept of race and health status in America. *Public Health Reports, 109*(1), 2641.

Witteborn, S. (2003). *On being an Arab woman before and after September 11th: The enactment of cultural identity in talk*. Paper presented at the 2003 Doctoral Honors Conference, Bowling Green, OH.

Woodyard, J. L. (2003). Africological theory and criticism: Reconceptualizing communication constructs. In R. L. Jackson, II, & E. B. Richardson (Eds.), *Understanding African American rhetoric: Classical origins to contemporary innovations* (pp. 133–154). New York: Routledge.

Yum, O. J. (1998). The impact of Confucianism on interpersonal relationships and communications patterns in East Asia. *Communication Monographs, 55,* 374–388.

PART VI

Theories Focusing on Effective Communication and Decisions

13

An Anxiety/Uncertainty Management (AUM) Theory of Effective Communication

Making the Mesh of the Net Finer

WILLIAM B. GUDYKUNST

> *Theories . . . are nets cast to catch what we call "the world": to rationalize, to explain. . . . We endeavor to make the mesh ever finer and finer.*
>
> Karl Popper

> *There is nothing so practical as a good theory.*
>
> Kurt Lewin

Author's Note: I want to thank Ron Perry for reading an earlier draft of this chapter. I also want to thank the people to whom I owe an intellectual debt in constructing AUM theory. Chuck Berger's writing on uncertainty initially stimulated me to develop the theory. Henri Tajfel's work convinced me of the importance of incorporating an intergroup perspective. Walter Stephan's and Cookie Stephan's research on intergroup anxiety laid the foundation for integrating cognitive and affective processes in the theory. Georg Simmel's concept of the stranger provided the link between interpersonal and intergroup behavior. Ellen Langer's work on mindfulness has allowed me to articulate things I learned subjectively sitting *zazen* while practicing Zen Buddhism. Harry Triandis' and Michael Bond's work convinced me of the importance of theorizing about cross-cultural variability. They also have provided feedback on my work over the years. Mitch Hammer collaborated on the first theory focusing on intercultural adjustment. Elizabeth Chua, Gao Ge, Sherrie Guerrero, Kimberly Hubbert, Karen Schmidt, Robin Shapiro, Lori Sodetani, and Junko Tominaga collaborated on the major studies I have conducted on anxiety/uncertainty management processes. Finally, Tsukasa Nishida and I have worked together since graduate school. I cannot imagine what my cross-cultural research would have been like without him as a collaborator and friend.

281

I have been working on developing a theoretical research program (Laktos, 1970) to explain intercultural communication since I finished graduate school. A theoretical research program is a set of interrelated theories, including theoretically based research designed to test the theories, as well as action research that applies the theories to individual or social change (Berger et al., 1974). At the present time, the program includes two interrelated theories: a theory of effective interpersonal and intergroup communication (discussed in this chapter), and a theory of intercultural adjustment (presented in Chapter 18 in this volume).

When I began conducting research, there was no theoretical work on effective communication or intercultural adjustment. I decided that one way to begin theorizing would be to adapt an existing theory. I selected uncertainty reduction theory (URT; e.g., Berger & Calabrese, 1975) as a starting point for several reasons. First, URT intuitively made sense to me. Second, URT includes concepts (e.g., similarity) that allowed a relatively straightforward extension from interpersonal to intercultural and intergroup contexts. Third, I could see direct applications of URT to improving the quality of communication.

I developed the anxiety/uncertainty management (AUM) theoretical research program in several stages. Initially, I developed a model of intergroup communication (Gudykunst, 1985b) by integrating URT and social identity theory (e.g., Tajfel, 1978, 1981). I choose to focus on intergroup communication because I see intercultural communication as one type of intergroup communication (e.g., when the main group membership influencing communication is our cultures). Next, Mitch Hammer and I (Gudykunst & Hammer, 1988b) developed a version of the theory that used uncertainty reduction and anxiety reduction to explain intercultural adaptation (this version contained 24 axioms; see Witte, 1993, for an alternative conceptualization). At about the same time, I incorporated Stephan and Stephan's (1985) work on anxiety into an abstract theory of effective interpersonal and intergroup communication and intercultural adaptation that also focused on anxiety and uncertainty reduction (Gudykunst, 1988; this version of the theory included 13 axioms, with 2 focusing on cross-cultural variability).

Neither of the 1988 versions of the theory were labeled AUM; both focused on reducing anxiety and uncertainty. Reducing anxiety and uncertainty, however, were not the "outcomes" explained in the theories; rather, effective communication and intercultural adaptation were the outcomes. Up to this point, the theory was relatively consistent with URT, but the outcomes were different. In 1990, I applied the 1988 version of the theory of effective communication to diplomatic communication. I also used this theory to guide the content of *Bridging Differences* (Gudykunst, 1991).

In 1993, I explicitly stated the metatheoretical assumptions in this version of the theory. In this version, I focused on anxiety and uncertainty management (e.g., maintaining anxiety and uncertainty between minimum and maximum thresholds to make effective communication possible), and incorporated the role of mindfulness in communicating effectively. I became aware of the importance of mindfulness from sitting *zazen* and reading Buddhist writing on the subject (e.g., Hahn, 1975; Rahula, 1974; Suzuki, 1970) and then looked for social science work on mindfulness to incorporate into the theory (e.g., Langer, 1989; Note: Thresholds and mindfulness were first discussed in Gudykunst, 1991). I also expanded the number of axioms, made the axioms more concrete than the 1988 version, and added axioms on cross-cultural variability (this version contained 49 axioms, with 11 focusing on cross-cultural variability).

The 1993 version of the theory focused on interpersonal and intergroup communication competence. It was the first version of the theory to be labeled AUM. A name may seem like a small thing, but this is not the case for theories. Until I named the theory, most writers assumed that it was totally consistent with URT and referred to the theory as a version of URT (and some still do). Unlike the 1988 version of the theory, the 1993 version of the theory was designed to be a practical theory (e.g., a theory that individuals could apply to improve the quality of their communication). The change in focus from anxiety and uncertainty reduction to anxiety and uncertainty management, as well as focusing on practical application instead of just explaining effective communication, changed the fundamental nature of the theory.

In 1995, I clarified several concerns raised about the 1993 version of the theory and expanded the discussion of cultural variability in AUM processes (i.e., this version contained 94 axioms, with one cross-cultural axiom for each axiom in the main part of the theory). This version of the theory incorporated ethnical aspects of communicating with strangers and maintained the goal of being a practical theory. I revised the intercultural adjustment version of the theory (Gudykunst & Hammer, 1988b) in 1998 (Gudykunst, 1998a), and outlined how it can be used to design intercultural adjustment training programs (this version contained 49 axioms, plus cross-cultural axioms). An updated version of this theory is presented in Chapter 18 in this volume. I update the 1995 version of the theory of interpersonal and intergroup communication effectiveness in this chapter. To put the theory in context, I begin with the scope of the theory.

SCOPE OF THE THEORY

A theory dealing with communication and culture should specify what is occurring at four levels of analysis and "articulate" how the levels are interrelated: individual, interpersonal, intergroup, and cultural (Doise, 1986). The individual level involves those factors that motivate us to communicate and influence the ways

we create and interpret messages (e.g., our needs for group inclusion, self-concept support). The interpersonal level includes those factors that influence our exchange of messages when we are acting as individuals (e.g., intimacy of relationships, social networks). The intergroup level involves the factors that influence our exchange of messages when we are acting based on our group memberships and the relations between the groups themselves (e.g., social identities, collective self-esteem). The cultural level involves those factors that lead people to communicate similarly or differently across cultures (e.g., dimensions of cultural variability).

This version of AUM theory is designed to explain interpersonal and intergroup communication effectiveness (defined below). There are two ways that interpersonal and intergroup processes can be differentiated. One way they can be differentiated is based on the type of data we use in making predictions about others' behavior: cultural (e.g., predictions based on regularities in others' behavior derived from their following cultural norms and rules), sociological (e.g., predictions based on others' group memberships and roles), and psychological (e.g., predictions based on personal information about the individual with whom we are communicating) (Miller & Steinberg, 1975). We use all three types of data in most interactions. When our predictions are based mainly on cultural and sociological data, however, intergroup behavior tends to take place. When our predictions are based mainly on psychological data, interpersonal behavior tends to take place.

An alternative way that interpersonal and intergroup behavior can be differentiated is based on the identities guiding our behavior: human (e.g., the views of ourselves we share with other humans), social (e.g., our views of ourselves that we share with members of specific ingroups such as ethnic groups, social classes, etc.), and personal (e.g., our views of ourselves that differentiate us from other ingroup members) (e.g., Tajfel, 1978; Turner et al., 1987). We tend to use all three types of identities in most interactions, but one identity tends to predominate at any given time (Turner, 1987). When our behavior is guided mainly by our social identities, intergroup behavior tends to take place. When our behavior is guided mainly by our personal identities, interpersonal behavior tends to take place.

We can draw distinctions between interpersonal and intergroup behavior, and interactions can be characterized as mainly interpersonal or intergroup. Most, if not all, interactions, however, involve both interpersonal and intergroup factors. I, therefore, believe that explaining effective communication requires that both levels of analysis must be included.

ASSUMPTIONS

In order to understand and evaluate theories, it is necessary to understand the assumptions theorists make. A theory's assumptions can be questioned, but they must be granted when the content of the theory is evaluated. In this section, I outline the metatheoretical assumptions (e.g., ontology) and the theoretical assumptions (e.g., linking concepts, thresholds) that I make, as well as the approach I use in constructing the theory.

Metatheoretical Assumptions

There are at least three metatheoretical issues about which any theorist must make assumptions: ontology (e.g., what is the nature of reality), epistemology (e.g., how do we gain knowledge), and human nature (e.g., what is the basis of human behavior) (e.g., Burrell & Morgan, 1979). In making metatheoretical assumptions, I avoid extreme "objectivist" and "subjectivist" assumptions (see the introductory chapter in this volume for an overview of the two positions). I believe both sets of assumptions are valid under different circumstances (i.e., "objectivist" assumptions hold when we are not mindful [e.g., consciously

aware of communication in the present moment], and "subjectivist" assumptions hold when we are mindful; see below).

With respect to ontology, I assume that names, concepts, and labels are artificial constructs we use to create our "subjective" realities (e.g., "nominalism"). Because of our socialization into our cultures and ethnic groups, we share a large portion of our intersubjective realities with other members of our cultures or ethnic groups. Our shared intersubjective realities are sufficiently stable that we tend to view the shared portions as an "objective" reality (e.g., "realism"). I assume that the basic processes of communication are the same across cultures, but that our cultures provide rules for how we should interpret the content of communication. This assumption is similar to Hamill's (1990) argument that we are endowed with innate logical structures, but our cultures create unique meanings out of this innate knowledge.

Epistemologically, I assume that our interpretations of our communication (e.g., "antipositivism") and external observations of our communication (e.g., "positivism") provide useful data for generating and testing theories. Meanings are not simply in the person, but are constructed when we communicate. As researchers, we need to search for underlying regularities in communication and, at the same time, recognize that our explanations will never be perfect because our subjective realities are different.

With respect to human nature, I assume that our communication is influenced by our cultures and group memberships, as well as structural, situational, and environmental factors (e.g., "determinism") when we are not highly conscious of our communication (e.g., we are mindless; Langer, 1989). We, nevertheless, have the ability to choose how we communicate (e.g., "voluntarism") when we are mindful (e.g., conscious of our behavior; see below). Fisher and Brown (1988) argue that one person can change a relationship based on how she or he chooses to communicate with her or his partners. One person, therefore, can influence the effectiveness of communication that occurs in a relationship if he or she is mindful (see below).

Theoretical Assumptions

I begin with the concept I use to link interpersonal and intergroup communication, the stranger. Following this, I present my assumptions about uncertainty, anxiety, effective communication, and being mindful.

Strangers. In earlier work (e.g., Gudykunst, 1991, 1998b; Gudykunst & Kim, 1997), I argue that the processes underlying communication between people from different groups (including cultures and ethnicities) are the same as the processes underlying communication between members of the same group. I refer to the common processes underlying our communication with people we do not know and who are in an environment unfamiliar to them as "communicating with strangers" (using Simmel's, 1908/1950, notion of the stranger; see Gudykunst & Kim, 1997, for a complete description of the concept; see Rogers, 1999, for a discussion of the role of the stranger in intercultural research).

Simmel (1908/1950) views strangers as possessing the contradictory qualities of being both near and far at the same time; "the unity of nearness and remoteness in every human relation is organized, in the phenomenon of the stranger, in a way which may be most briefly formulated by saying that in the relationship to him [or her], distance means that he [or she], who is also far, is actually near" (p. 402). Strangers represent both the idea of nearness in that they are physically close and the idea of remoteness in that they have different values and ways of doing things.

We do not share all of our group memberships with anyone and, therefore, everyone we meet is a potential stranger. Since everyone

is a potential stranger, both interpersonal and intergroup processes must operate in our interactions with them. Interacting with strangers is characterized by anxiety and uncertainty. Herman and Schield (1961) point out that "the immediate psychological result of being in a new situation is lack of security. Ignorance of the potentialities inherent in the situation, of the means to reach a goal, and of the probable outcomes of an intended action causes insecurity" (p. 165). Attempts to deal with the ambiguity of new situations involves a pattern of information seeking (managing uncertainty) and tension reduction (managing anxiety) (Ball-Rokeach, 1973). Managing uncertainty and anxiety, therefore, are central processes affecting our communication with strangers.

Since the stranger-ingroup relationship is a figure-ground phenomenon, it is necessary to take one perspective in stating axioms. I use the perspective of members of ingroups being approached by strangers in constructing the theory of effective interpersonal and intergroup communication. The theory, however, also is applicable from the perspectives of the strangers approaching ingroups. There are, nevertheless, some differences in strangers' and ingroup members' perspectives (e.g., strangers tend to be more mindful than ingroup members; Frable, Blackstone, & Sherbaum, 1990). These issues are discussed below. In constructing the theory of intercultural adaptation (see Chapter 18 in this volume), I use the perspective of strangers approaching host cultures (e.g., ingroups).

Uncertainty. Marris (1996) argues that "uncertainty is created by our own preconceptions . . . because events only appear uncertain in some context of purposes, and expectations of orderliness" (p. 16). He goes on to point out that "what constitutes uncertainty depends on what we want to be able to predict, what we can predict, and what we might be able to do about it" (p. 16). Watts (1951) suggests that complete predictability is an illusion because the world is basically unpredictable (also see Becker, 1971; Solomon et al., 1991). Similarly, Marris claims "uncertainty is a fundamental condition of human life" (p. 1). Grieve and Hogg (1999) "propose that uncertainty reduction is perhaps the most fundamental motivational process underlying group membership and group behavior" (p. 928).

Uncertainty is a cognitive phenomenon; it affects the way we think about strangers. Berger and Calabrese (1975) argue that predictive uncertainty involves our inability to predict strangers' attitudes, feelings, beliefs, values, and behavior. We need to be able, for example, to predict which of several alternative behavior patterns strangers will employ (Note: I focus on behavior in the axioms of the theory, but the axioms also apply to feelings, beliefs, attitudes, values, etc.). Explanatory uncertainty involves the uncertainty we have about explaining strangers' behavior, attitudes, feelings, thoughts, and beliefs (e.g., making causal attributions).

We experience more uncertainty when we communicate with members of outgroups (e.g., strangers) than when we communicate with members of our ingroups (Gudykunst, 1985b; Lee & Boster, 1991). Frequently, but not always, we try to manage uncertainty when strangers act in a deviant fashion, when they can provide us with rewards, and when we anticipate seeing them again in the future (Berger, 1979). Since we often do not see strangers as providing rewards or we do not anticipate seeing them again, we may not be motivated to manage our uncertainty about their behavior.

We do not always want to minimize our uncertainty. Weick (1979), for example, contends that equivocality can lead to creativity. We also may not be able to minimize our uncertainty because "ambiguous modes of expression are rooted in the very nature of language and thought" (Levine, 1985, p. 20), or strangers transmit equivocal messages (e.g., Bavelas et al., 1990). When communicating

with strangers we may be ambiguous on purpose. To illustrate, Levine contends that ambiguity allows us to protect ourselves through "opaqueness." Eisenberg (1984) also believes that ambiguity has benefits in some situations (e.g., it allows us to maintain power over strangers).

The extent to which we value uncertainty varies across cultures, ethnic groups, and individuals. Basso (1979), for example, points out that Western Apaches do not find uncertainty distressing. Keenan (1976) suggests that men in a Malagasy community generate messages to create uncertainty and value ambiguity in interactions. Lim and Choi (1996) also claim that Koreans sometimes create ambiguous messages so that others cannot "figure out their meanings" (p. 131). Morris (1981) argues that Puerto Rico is "a society of continuities where things are kept open, where things are not so clearly defined as to exclude other interpretations" (p. 119). In Puerto Rico, leaving interpretations open is viewed as a sign of respect. Within any culture, there are individuals who value uncertainty and those who do not (e.g., the personality characteristics tolerance for ambiguity [Budner, 1962] and certainty-uncertainty orientation [Sorrentino & Short, 1986], which are discussed below, can explain these differences).

We have minimum and maximum thresholds for uncertainty that are different across cultures and individuals (this idea was first introduced in Gudykunst, 1991). Our maximum thresholds are the highest amount of uncertainty we can have and think we can predict strangers' behavior sufficiently to feel comfortable interacting with them. Our minimum thresholds are the lowest amount of uncertainty we can have and not feel bored or overconfident about our predictions of strangers' behavior.

If our uncertainty is above our maximum thresholds or below our minimum thresholds, we cannot communicate effectively. When uncertainty is above our maximum thresholds, strangers' behavior is seen as unpredictable and we do not have confidence in our predictions or explanations of their behavior. When our uncertainty is below our minimum thresholds, we are likely to misinterpret strangers' messages because we do not consider the possibility that our interpretations of their messages are wrong. Where our minimum and maximum thresholds are located is a function of the general acceptance of uncertainty in our cultures (e.g., Hofstede's, 2001, uncertainty avoidance dimension of cultural variability; see the cross-cultural section below) and our tolerance for ambiguity (e.g., Budner, 1962) or uncertainty orientation (e.g., Sorrentino & Roney, 1999).

Communicating effectively requires that our uncertainty be between our minimum and maximum thresholds (Gudykunst, 1993). When our uncertainty is between the two thresholds, we have sufficient confidence in our ability to predict strangers' behavior that we feel comfortable, but our confidence is not sufficiently high that we become overconfident. Since we are not overconfident, we can recognize cues indicating potential misunderstandings when they occur, especially if we are mindful (see below).

Uncertainty fluctuates over time and within specific interactions (e.g., Planalp et al., 1988; Sodetani & Gudykunst, 1987). One way to view the fluctuation within interactions is as a dialectic between predictability and novelty (e.g., Baxter, 1988). Predictability is necessary to know how to expect strangers to behave, but novelty is needed to keep us from becoming overconfident about our predictions.

Anxiety. Anxiety is the affective (emotional) equivalent of uncertainty. We experience some degree of anxiety any time we communicate with others. Anxiety is a "generalized or unspecified sense of disequilibrium" (imbalance; Turner, 1988, p. 61). It stems from feeling uneasy, tense, worried, or apprehensive about what might happen (Note: the focus

here is on state anxiety, not trait anxiety; see Britt et al., 1996, for a discussion of trait intergroup anxiety). Anxiety is based on the anticipation of negative consequences (Stephan & Stephan, 1985). Anxiety is one of the fundamental problems with which we all must cope (Lazarus, 1991; May, 1977).

Schlenker and Leary (1982) argue that social anxiety occurs when we are motivated to present a particular impression in our interactions, but we doubt that we will be able to present that impression. The less we expect to receive the reaction from others that we want, the greater our anxiety. Intergroup interactions have the potential for creating intense social anxiety because we do not want to appear prejudiced or perceived as incompetent communicators (also see Plant & Devine, 2003). Our anxiety, therefore, tends to be higher in intergroup than interpersonal encounters (e.g., Ickes, 1984; Word et al., 1974). Interactions with strangers tend to lead to fear across cultures (e.g., Walbott & Scherer, 1986). Our explanations for why we experience anxiety can vary widely (e.g., because we do not want to appear prejudiced or because we have hostile feelings toward an outgroup; see data reported in Greenland & Brown, 2000).

We have minimum and maximum thresholds for anxiety (Gudykunst, 1991). Our maximum thresholds are the highest amount of anxiety we can have and feel comfortable interacting with strangers. If our anxiety is above our maximum thresholds, we are so uneasy that we do not want to communicate with strangers. When our anxiety is above our maximum thresholds, the source our anxiety may be unknown or "vague—but it is more powerful for its vagueness. As there is no definite threat or danger upon which we could act, it paralyzes action" (Riezler, 1960, p. 147; Turner, 1988, calls this "diffuse" anxiety). Of course, there also may be a specific source (e.g., we feel that our identities are threatened) that brings our anxiety above our maximum thresholds. No matter how our anxiety gets above our maximum thresholds, our attention focuses exclusively on the anxiety and not on the effectiveness of our communication when it is. When anxiety is above our maximum thresholds, we tend to process information in a simplistic fashion (Wilder & Shapiro, 1989).

Our minimum thresholds are the lowest amount of anxiety we can have and care about our interactions with strangers. If our anxiety is below our minimum thresholds, there is not enough adrenaline running through our system to motivate us to communicate effectively with strangers. Tuan (1979), for example, points out that our curiosity is primed by our anxiety. When our anxiety is below our minimum thresholds, we do not care what happens and we do not have any curiosity about what might happen.

Our anxiety has to be below our maximum thresholds and above our minimum thresholds for us to be motivated to communicate. Some anxiety, but not too much, can be "transformed into a type of useful highly-adaptive social response, which leaves the self protected from the impact of its own emotions and its own imperatives while it promotes the highest vigilance, albeit uncritical, toward the behavior of others" (Schneiderman, 1960, pp. 161–162). The argument being made here is consistent with Janis' (1958, 1971, 1985) theory of anticipatory fear. He argues that moderate levels of fear lead to adaptive processes, but low and high levels do not. My position also is compatible with Csikszentmihalyi's (1990) argument that there is an optimal level of anxiety that facilitates experiencing "flow," or having optimal experiences. The argument also is comparable with research suggesting there is a curvilinear relationship between anxiety and performance (e.g., Halvari & Gjesme, 1995; Pickersgill & Owen, 1992).

Managing anxiety over time is associated with developing trust. Trust is "confidence that one will find what is desired from another,

rather than what is feared" (Deutsch, 1973, p. 149). When we trust strangers, we expect positive outcomes from our interactions with them; when we have high levels of anxiety about interacting with strangers (e.g., above our maximum thresholds), we fear negative outcomes from our interactions with them. When we first meet strangers, "trust is often little more than a naive expression of hope" (Holmes & Rempel, 1989, p. 192). For relationships with strangers to become close, some minimal degree of trust is necessary. Anxiety can be viewed as a dialectic involving fear and trust.

The anxiety we experience when we communicate with strangers usually is based on negative expectations. Stephan and Stephan (1985) argue that we fear four types of negative consequences when interacting with strangers: we may fear negative consequences for our self-concepts, we may fear negative behavioral consequences, we may fear negative evaluations by strangers, and we may fear negative evaluations by members of our ingroups.

One of the behavioral consequences of anxiety is avoidance (Stephan & Stephan, 1985). We avoid strangers because it allows us to manage our anxiety. Schlenker and Leary (1982), however, argue that avoiding intergroup interactions has negative consequences for those experiencing anxiety (e.g., they do not develop the skills necessary for intergroup interactions). When we are experiencing anxiety and cannot avoid strangers, we tend to terminate the interaction as soon as we can (Stephan & Stephan, 1985). Schlenker and Leary also point out that social anxiety leads to individuals' being uncomfortable in intergroup interactions, which reinforces their viewing themselves as incompetent communicators. Devine et al. (1996) contend that being uncomfortable leads to nervous behavior, which can be perceived as prejudice by strangers. Crocker et al. (1998) also point out that "discomfort resulting from a desire to be nonprejudiced combined with the lack of confidence in one's ability to act appropriately may be misinterpreted [by strangers] as stemming from hostility and prejudice" (p. 515).

Cognitively, anxiety leads to biases in how we process information. The more anxious we are, the more likely we will focus on the behaviors we expect to see, such as those based on our negative stereotypes, and the more likely we are to confirm these expectations and not recognize behavior that is inconsistent with our expectations (Stephan & Stephan, 1985).

Fiske and Morling (1996) point out that the amount of anxiety we experience in intergroup interactions is partly a function of the degree to which we feel in control. The less powerful we feel in a situation, the more anxious we are. When we are anxious, we see strangers as easier to control than we are. We, therefore, often try to control strangers when we are highly anxious.

When our anxiety or uncertainty is too high or too low, we cannot communicate effectively. In the 1995 version of the theory, I suggested that our minimum and maximum thresholds are catastrophe points. That is, there are drastic changes in communication effectiveness when anxiety or uncertainty drop below our maximum thresholds or rise above our minimum thresholds. This position is based on the assumption of catastrophe theory (e.g., Tesser, 1980) that there can be sudden, discontinuous changes in one variable (e.g., effectiveness) when other variables (e.g., anxiety, uncertainty) reach a catastrophe point. In other words, anxiety and uncertainty are not related to effective communication above our maximum thresholds or below our minimum thresholds, but anxiety and uncertainty are related to effective communication between the two thresholds.

Effective Communication. Communication is a process involving the exchange of messages and the creation of meaning (Barnlund, 1962). Communication is effective to the extent that the person interpreting the message attaches a meaning to the message that is relatively similar to what was intended by the person transmitting it. Stated differently, communication is effective to the extent that we are able to maximize understandings (Gudykunst, 1993, 1995). This position is somewhat similar to Triandis' (1977) position that effectiveness involves trying to make "isomorphic attributions," and Powers and Lowrey's (1984) "basic communication fidelity"—"the degree of congruence between the cognitions of two or more individuals following a communication event" (p. 58). I assume, however, that making isomorphic attributions is impossible. Rogers and Kincaid (1981) use the term "mutual understanding" and McLeod and Chaffee (1973) use the term "accuracy" for what I call effective communication. Effective communication can occur through direct or ambiguous messages (Levine, 1985). (Note: alternative conceptualizations of communication effectiveness are discussed in the section on cross-cultural variability below.)

The vast majority of the time (i.e., when we are not mindful) we interpret strangers' messages using our own frames of reference and they interpret our messages using their frames of reference. When we interact with strangers, we may or may not recognize that communication is ineffective. It is possible that our interpretations of strangers' messages are different than they intend or that their interpretations of our messages are different than we intend and neither of us recognizes the difference. Alternatively, we may recognize that there are differences in meaning or strangers may perceive that there are differences in meaning. When the differences in meaning are recognized, we may or may not attempt to repair the problem. Correcting misinterpretations requires that we are mindful. When we are mindful, we need to negotiate meanings with strangers.

Mindfulness. Most of the time when we communicate we are not highly aware of our behavior. In other words, we communicate mindlessly or automatically (Langer, 1989). We do not, however, communicate totally on automatic pilot. Rather, we pay sufficient attention to recall key words in conversations we have (Kitayama & Burstein, 1988). Bargh (1989) contends that automatic information processing involves various combinations of attention, awareness, intention, and control. When we are consciously aware of our communication behavior, we become mindful to some extent (Bellah et al., 1991, and Csikszentmihalyi, 1990, refer to this as "paying attention"). Langer (1989) argues that mindfulness involves "(1) creation of new categories; (2) openness to new information; and (3) awareness of more than one perspective" (p. 62).

Langer (1989) contends that "categorizing is a fundamental and natural human activity. . . . Any attempt to eliminate bias by attempting to eliminate the perception of differences is doomed to failure" (p. 154). Being mindful involves making more, not fewer, distinctions. When we are mindless, for example, we tend to use broad categories to predict strangers' behavior (e.g., their cultures, ethnicities, genders, or roles). When we are mindful, we can create new categories that are more specific (e.g., we can subdivide the broad categories into more specific categories). The more subcategories we use, the more personalized the information we use to make predictions about strangers' behavior.

Mindfulness also involves being open to new information (Langer, 1989). When we are mindfully open to new information, we see aspects of our own and strangers' behavior that we do not see when we are mindless. Being open to new information involves focusing on the process of communication that is taking place, not the outcomes of our interactions. When we focus on the outcomes, we miss subtle cues in our interactions and this often leads to misunderstandings.

To be mindful, we must also recognize that strangers use different perspectives to understand or explain our interactions than we do

(Langer, 1989). When we are mindless, we tend to assume strangers interpret our messages the same way we intended. When we are mindful, in contrast, we can recognize that strangers interpret our messages differently than we do. Being mindful allows us to see the choices we have regarding how to communicate when interacting with strangers (Langer, 1989, 1997).

When we are mindful, we need to focus on negotiating meanings with strangers. That is, we need to mindfully try to understand strangers' meanings and try to make sure that they understand our meanings. One approach to negotiating meaning is Clark's (1996) "collaborative model," which suggests that meanings emerge in interactions. In this model, communicators try to make sure that they share similar meanings for each utterance before proceeding. Various conversational mechanisms are used to assure that meanings are negotiated (e.g., acts of reference). Negotiating meanings involves creating and reflecting identities (e.g., Tracey, 2002). The processes, therefore, are more complicated when the participants are native speakers of different languages (e.g., see Gass & Varonis, 1991) or come from different ethnic or social classes (e.g., Ellis, 1999), or one person is disabled (e.g., Coleman & DePaulo, 1991) than when the communicators are from the same group.

Theory Construction

Two types of theoretical statements are used in the theory: axioms and theorems. Axioms are "propositions that involve variables that are taken to be directly linked causally; axioms should therefore be statements that imply direct causal links among variables" (Blalock, 1969, p. 18, italics omitted). Some axioms do not apply in all situations. Boundary conditions specify when the axioms hold. The axioms can be combined to derive theorems. When combined the axioms and theorems form a "causal process" theory (Reynolds, 1971) that explains effective communication. Many of the relationships, however, are reciprocal, especially over time (e.g., unreported data from Hubbert et al., 1999, indicates that our perception of effective communication at one point in time influences our anxiety and uncertainty the next time we communicate). Dialectical processes influence much of our communication within specific interactions (e.g., Baxter, 1988; Vanlear, 1991). To illustrate, uncertainty involves a dialectic between predictability and novelty. In the present version of the theory, dialectics are incorporated as boundary conditions for the axioms where applicable.

There are a large number of axioms (47) in this working version of the theory, but they are not excessive (and they are only one half the number in the 1995 version). Reynolds (1971) points out that "in dealing with logical systems that are completely abstract . . . a common criteria is to select the smallest number of axioms from which all other statements can be derived, reflecting a preference for simplicity and elegance. There is reason to think that this is inappropriate for a substantive theory, particularly when it makes it more difficult to understand the theory" (p. 95). Since one of my concerns is applying the theory, I include a sufficient number of statements to make anxiety/uncertainty management processes clear to readers who may want to apply the theory to improve their communication effectiveness.

Lieberson (1985) suggests that we need to isolate the "basic causes" of the phenomenon under investigation. In generating the axioms for the theory, I assume that managing anxiety and uncertainty are "basic causes" influencing effective communication. Other variables (which are organized using the categories of self concepts; motivation; reactions to strangers; social categorization; situational processes; connections with strangers; ethical interactions; and anxiety, uncertainty, mindfulness, and effective

communication), therefore, are treated as "superficial causes" of effective communication. The influence of these "superficial causes" on effective communication is mediated through anxiety and uncertainty. Being mindful allows us to engage in anxiety and uncertainty management.

There are three ways that I deviate from the traditional social science construction of causal process theories; namely, I include ethical concerns and mindfulness in the theory, and the theory is designed to be applied. Johannesen (2001) argues that moral issues are inherent in the communication process, and that "ethical concerns have been central to communication theory and practice at least since Plato" (p. 202). In the 1995 version, I included two axioms dealing with ethical issues in the "connections with strangers" section. In this version, I add an additional axiom and discuss ethical concerns in a separate section to emphasize their importance. The inclusion of mindfulness makes at least part of the theory subjective in nature. When we are mindful, we choose how to communicate and our behavior is not determined by external factors or internal characteristics (e.g., identities, personality). Finally, the present theory is designed to be applied by individuals to improve the quality of their communication, not just explain effective communication.

A schematic summary of AUM theory is presented in Figure 13.1 (Note: not all of the superficial causes are listed in the figure). The figure involves only one person (i.e., the ingroup member). The stranger would be a mirror image of the ingroup member. I believe that the processes explained in the theory generalize across cultures and across types of interaction (e.g., intragroup and intergroup communication). There is, however, variability in the content of the processes (e.g., what constitutes uncertainty and how it is managed) across cultures. These issues are discussed in detail in the section on cross-cultural variability.

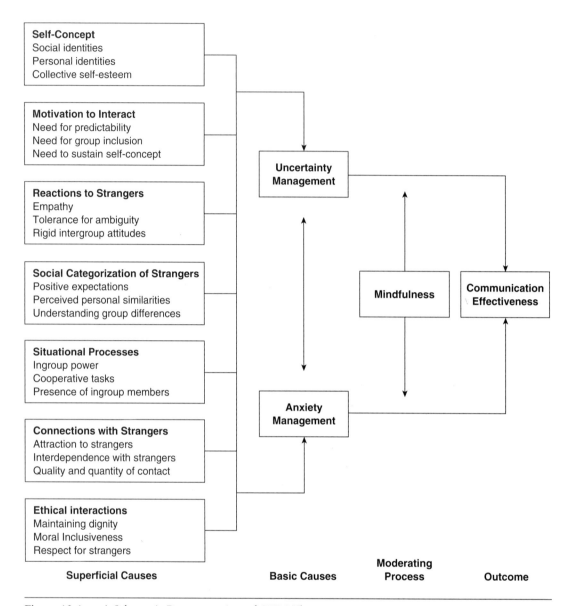

Figure 13.1   A Schematic Representation of AUM Theory

AN AUM THEORY OF EFFECTIVE COMMUNICATION

It is necessary to use some sort of schema to organize the axioms. To maintain consistency, I generally follow the organizational schema (i.e., the categories at the left of Figure 13.1) in this version that I used in the 1995 version (Note: the ethical interactions category was not used in 1995.) I begin by looking at how our self-concepts influence our anxiety and uncertainty management.

Self-Concepts

Our self-concepts are our views of ourselves. Turner et al. (1987) argue that we place ourselves in categories with others whom we see as similar to ourselves on some dimension and different from others on that dimension. Grieve and Hogg (1999) argue that "people apply social categorizations to themselves and others to clarify their perception of the social world and their place in it and thus render it more meaningful and predictable—identification reduces subjective uncertainty" (p. 926; also see Hogg & Mullin, 1999). Social categorizations lead to defining ourselves in terms of our social identities. Social identities are the major generative mechanisms for intergroup behavior, and personal identities are the major generative mechanisms for interpersonal behavior. Our social and personal identities, however, influence our behavior in virtually all of our interactions. In any particular situation, nevertheless, one identity tends to guide our behavior (Turner, 1987).

Our social identities tend to be activated when we communicate with strangers because we define strangers as being different from us in terms of some group membership. The social identity activated depends on how we categorize ourselves and the strangers with whom we are interacting. If we categorize ourselves or strangers based on ethnicity, for example, our ethnic identities are activated.

The strength of the social identities we use to guide our behavior facilitates our ability to manage our anxiety and uncertainty. This claim, however, has to be qualified. Gudykunst and Hammer (1988a) point out that the strength of our social identities reduces uncertainty only when we recognize that strangers are from other groups and when strangers are perceived to be typical members of their groups. When we perceive strangers to be atypical members of their groups, we do not treat them based on their group memberships (e.g., we see them as "exceptions to the rule"). In this case, our communication is guided by our personal identities, and we use information about the individual strangers with whom we are communicating to manage our uncertainty. How secure we feel in our identities also has to be taken into consideration. Jackson and Smith (1999), for example, report that individuals with insecure social identities engage in the ingroup bias more than individuals with secure social identities.

Our social identity complexity should affect how we communicate with strangers. Social identity complexity focuses on the extent to which our social identities are differentiated and integrated into one inclusive social identity (Roccas & Brewer, 2002). Roccas and Brewer argue that "having a complex social identity is dependent on two conditions: first, awareness of more than one ingroup categorization and second, recognition that the multiple ingroup categories do not converge" (p. 93). They contend that our complexity is "domain specific." We may be complex in one aspect of our self-concepts but not in others. The greater our social identity complexity, the more tolerant we are of outgroup members.

Our self-esteem, the positive or negative feelings we have about ourselves (e.g., Rosenberg, 1979), also influences our communication. Our self-esteem affects the way we process information and the amount of anxiety we experience. Burns (1985), for example, argues that low self-esteem leads us to distort cognitive processing of information about ourselves and strangers. When our self-esteem is high, in contrast, we are able to look for objective information about ourselves and strangers, even in stressful situations. Low self-esteem also leads us to be anxious about interacting with strangers. The greater our self-esteem, the better we are able to manage our anxiety (e.g., Becker, 1971; Cozzarelli & Karafa, 1998; Epstein, 1976).

The collective self-esteem associated with our group memberships also affects our communication with strangers. Collective self-esteem is the degree to which we evaluate our social groups positively (Luhtanen & Crocker, 1992). I believe that we have general and ingroup-specific collective self-esteem (e.g., the ingroup associated with the social identity generating our behavior). Individuals high in general collective self-esteem tend to be more biased toward their general ingroups than those low in general collective self-esteem (Crocker & Luhtanen, 1990). Ingroup-specific collective self-esteem, however, should operate similarly to individual-level self-esteem. That is, high ingroup-specific collective self-esteem should help us manage our anxiety and uncertainty and obtain objective information about strangers when this ingroup identity is activated. This suggests that the higher our ingroup-specific collective self-esteem, the lower our anxiety and the higher our accuracy in predicting strangers' behavior.

Social identity theory posits that we strive to have the most positive self-images we can (e.g., Tajfel, 1978). When our identities are threatened, we attempt to raise our esteem. Worchel and Coutant (1997) argue that threats to our identities may come from sources within our ingroups (e.g., our ingroups' failures) or from outgroups (e.g., outgroups attack our ingroups). They also contend that both types of threats to our social identities lead to discrimination against members of outgroups. Perceived threats to our social identities, therefore, should lead to intergroup anxiety and uncertainty.

How we define ourselves affects the way we communicate, as well as the way we manage the anxiety and uncertainty we experience when we communicate with strangers. Five axioms regarding self-concepts, therefore, are included in the theory:

Axiom 1: An increase in the degree to which our social identities guide our interactions with strangers will produce a decrease in our anxiety and an increase in our confidence in predicting their behavior. *Boundary Conditions:* This axiom holds only when we are secure in our social identities, we are not mindful, if strangers are perceived to be typical outgroup members, and when our anxiety and uncertainty are between our minimum and maximum thresholds.

Axiom 2: An increase in the degree to which our personal identities guide our interactions with strangers will produce a decrease in our anxiety and an increase in our ability to predict their behavior accurately. *Boundary Conditions:* This axiom holds only in individualistic cultures, when we are not mindful we are secure in our personal identities, and our anxiety and uncertainty are between our minimum and maximum thresholds.

Axiom 3: An increase in our self-esteem when interacting with strangers will produce a decrease in our anxiety and an increase in our ability to predict their behavior accurately. *Boundary Conditions:* This axiom holds only when our anxiety and uncertainty are between our minimum and maximum thresholds, and we are not mindful.

Axiom 4: An increase in our ingroup-specific collective self-esteem when interacting with strangers from outgroups based on the specific ingroup will produce a decrease in our anxiety and an increase in our ability to predict their behavior accurately. *Boundary Conditions:* This axiom holds only for the ingroups on which the collective self-esteem is based, when our anxiety and uncertainty are between our minimum and maximum thresholds, and when we are not mindful.

Axiom 5: An increase in perceived threats to our social identities when interacting with strangers will produce an increase in our anxiety and a decrease in our confidence in predicting their behavior. *Boundary Condition:* This axiom holds only when we are not mindful.

The identities we activate in specific encounters affect our motivation to communicate with strangers. If we are not motivated to communicate with strangers, we tend to avoid interactions with strangers rather than try to manage our anxiety and uncertainty. If we are motivated to communicate with strangers, in contrast, we try to manage our anxiety and uncertainty so we can interact with strangers comfortably.

Motivation

Turner (1988) suggests that when our needs are met, we are motivated to interact with strangers. Needs are "fundamental states of being that create feelings of deprivation" that mobilize us "to eliminate this sense of deprivation" if they are not satisfied (p. 59). Four needs are critical to AUM: (1) our need for a sense of predictability (or trust), (2) our need for a sense of group inclusion, (3) our need to avoid diffuse anxiety, and (4) our need to sustain our self-conceptions.

We "need to 'trust' others in the sense that, for the purposes of a given interaction, others are 'reliable' and their responses 'predictable'" (Turner, 1988, p. 56). When we categorize strangers, our stereotypes are activated. Our stereotypes of strangers' groups provide predictions of strangers' behavior. If strangers conform to our stereotypes, we see their behavior as predictable. If strangers do not conform to our stereotypes, we see their behavior as unpredictable if we are using only group-based information to predict their behavior. If we see strangers' behavior as reliable and predictable, it helps to confirm our self-concepts and helps us to feel included.

Our need for group inclusion results from *not* feeling involved in our relationships with strangers (Turner, 1988). When we do not feel included, we experience anxiety and uncertainty. The need for inclusion is related directly to how we see our social identities. Our social identities are derived from a tension between our need to be seen as similar to and to fit in with others and our need to be seen as unique people (Brewer, 1991; also see Brewer & Roccas, 2001). The need to be seen as similar allows us to identify with different groups and involves the general process of inclusion. Stevens and Fiske (1995) view belonging to groups as an important motive for our behavior because it removes ambiguity about ourselves and others and helps us plan our actions (also see Baumeister & Leary,

1995). The need to be seen as unique is expressed in the general process of differentiation. If our attempts to communicate with strangers are not successful, our need for group inclusion is unsatisfied. This leads to anxiety about ourselves and our standing in a group context (Turner, 1988).

Our anxiety and uncertainty are interrelated. Demerath's (1993) knowledge-based affect theory, for example, suggests that increases in uncertainty lead to negative affect (e.g., fear, anxiety). Turner's (1988) theory of motivation links lack of predictability (e.g., uncertainty) to anxiety. Increases in anxiety, however, also lead to increases in uncertainty (e.g., Hubbert et al., 1999).

Closely related to our need for inclusion is our need for self-concept confirmation. When our self-conceptions are confirmed, we feel secure in our identities. When we feel secure in our identities, we feel confident in our interactions with strangers. The more secure we are in our identities, the better able we are to manage our anxiety and the more confident we are in predicting strangers' behaviors. As our anxiety increases, our need for group inclusion and our need to sustain our self-conceptions increases (Turner, 1988).

If our needs are not met, we are not motivated to communicate with strangers. If our needs are met, in contrast, we tend to be motivated to manage our anxiety and uncertainty. Four axioms regarding our motivation to communicate with strangers, therefore, are included in the theory:

Axiom 6: An increase in our need for group inclusion when interacting with strangers will produce an increase in our anxiety. *Boundary Condition:* This axiom holds only when we are not mindful.

Axiom 7: An increase in our need to sustain our self-conceptions when interacting with strangers will produce an increase in our anxiety. *Boundary Condition:* This axiom holds only when we are not mindful.

Axiom 8: An increase in the degree to which strangers confirm our self-conceptions will produce a decrease in our anxiety. *Boundary Conditions:* This axiom holds only when our anxiety and uncertainty are between our minimum and maximum thresholds, and when we are not mindful.

Axiom 9: An increase in our confidence in our ability to predict strangers' behavior will produce a decrease in our anxiety; a decrease in our anxiety will produce an increase in our confidence in predicting strangers' behavior. *Boundary Conditions:* This axiom holds only when our anxiety and uncertainty are between our minimum and maximum thresholds, and when we are not mindful.

When our needs are met, we are motivated to interact with strangers. When we interact with strangers, how we react to them cognitively, affectively, and behaviorally influences our ability to manage our anxiety and uncertainty.

Reactions to Strangers

Cognitively complex people form impressions of strangers that are more extensive, more differentiated, and represent the behavioral variability of strangers more than cognitively simple people (O'Keefe & Sypher, 1981). There is a negative association between cognitive complexity and perceived uncertainty (Downey et al., 1977). The more we are able to process information complexly, the more we search for alternative explanations for strangers' behavior. Being able to isolate alternative explanations for behavior facilitates accurately predicting strangers' behavior.

When our attitudes are rigid and divisive (e.g., ethnocentrism, prejudice, racism, authoritarianism, sexism, ageism, dogmatism, social dominance orientation, closed-mindedness, etc.), we tend to be intolerant of strangers' viewpoints. Holding rigid attitudes leads us to need nonspecific closure when we are interacting with strangers (Kruglanski, 1989). If we have rigid attitudes, we prefer any form of closure to

ambiguity because closure provides "assured knowledge that affords predictability and a base for action" (Kruglanski, 1989, p. 14).

Rigid attitudes create negative expectations for our interactions with strangers. Stephan and Stephan (1985, 1989, 1992) point out that the more ethnocentric and prejudiced we are, the more anxiety we experience interacting with strangers. Devine et al. (1996) argue that individuals who are low in prejudice "are sincere in their efforts to behave without prejudice . . . even if the efforts are not particularly skillful or smooth" (p. 443). Because people low in prejudice are sincere, they experience low levels of anxiety when interacting with strangers. When we have rigid attitudes and have negative expectations, we do not look for new information about the strangers with whom we interact. The more rigid our attitudes, therefore, the lower our ability to predict strangers' behavior accurately.

Huber and Sorrentino (1996) argue that uncertainty orientation influences whether we try to manage our uncertainty (also see Sorrentino & Roney, 1999). Uncertainty-oriented individuals tend to be more accurate in their recall of past interactions (either positive or negative) and are less likely "to think in terms of categories and stereotypes" than certainty-oriented individuals (p. 607). More generally, uncertainty-oriented individuals try to deal with their uncertainty (e.g., resolve or manage it) more than certainty-oriented individuals. Huber and Sorrentino argue that certainty-oriented individuals tend "to maintain the certainty or clarity associated with their existing cognitions, rather than striving to resolve uncertainty" (pp. 592–593). Sorrentino et al. (2001) report that certainty-oriented individuals have a stronger ingroup bias than uncertainty-oriented individuals. Uncertainty-oriented individuals, therefore, should make more accurate predictions about strangers than certainty-oriented individuals.

Our tolerance for ambiguity affects the type of information we gather about strangers.

Budner (1962) argues that lack of tolerance for ambiguity involves perceiving ambiguous situations as threatening and undesirable. Smock (1955) contends that if we have a low tolerance for ambiguity, we tend to base our judgments of strangers on first impressions that are prematurely formed before all information is available. McPherson (1983) also points out that if we have a low tolerance for ambiguity, we tend to seek out information that is supportive of our belief systems when we interact with strangers. Pilisuk (1963) suggests that if we have a high tolerance for ambiguity, we tend to seek out "objective" information about the situation and the strangers with whom we interact. If we are high in tolerance for ambiguity, we also tend to be open to new information about ourselves and strangers.

Empathy also facilitates anxiety and uncertainty management. Bell (1987) points out that "cognitively, the empathic person takes the perspective of another person, and in so doing strives to see the world from the others' point of view. Affectively, the empathic person experiences the emotion of another; he or she *feels* the others' experiences" (p. 204). Stephan and Stephan (1992) report that an increase in empathy is associated with a decrease in intergroup anxiety. Stephan and Finlay (1999), however, point out that "empathy that is not accompanied by respect for the other group is clearly problematic" (e.g., it can lead to condescension) (p. 727). Since we are trying to understand strangers' perspectives when we empathize, the greater our ability to empathize, the more accurate our predictions should be (assuming we respect strangers).

We react favorably to strangers who linguistically converge toward us (Giles & Smith, 1979). Convergence, however, is not always viewed favorably. Giles and Byrne (1982) point out that as strangers begin to learn our speech styles, we may diverge in some way to maintain linguistic distinctiveness. Our reaction to strangers' speech convergence also depends on the intent ingroup members attribute to strangers (Simard et al., 1976). When we perceive strangers' intent to be positive, we tend to evaluate their convergence positively. If we are insecure in our social identities and/or we perceive threats from strangers, we perceive strangers' convergence toward us negatively (Gallois et al., 1995). Members of collectivistic cultures react more negatively to strangers' convergence than members of individualistic cultures (Gallois et al., 1995).

Our accommodation to strangers and strangers' accommodation to us affect our communication, but it is the strangers' accommodation to us that influences our anxiety and uncertainty. If strangers diverge from us, their behavior appears to be unpredictable and we have anxiety and uncertainty about communicating with them. If strangers converge to our communication styles and we perceive their intent to be positive, in contrast, it will facilitate managing our uncertainty and anxiety about communicating with them.

The way we think about strangers, our affective responses to strangers, and the ways we behave toward them affect our ability to manage our anxiety and uncertainty. Six axioms regarding how we react to strangers, therefore, are included in the theory:

Axiom 10: An increase in our ability to process information complexly about strangers will produce a decrease in our anxiety and an increase in our ability to predict their behavior accurately. *Boundary Conditions:* This axiom holds only when our anxiety and uncertainty are between our minimum and maximum thresholds, and we are not mindful.

Axiom 11: An increase in the rigidity of our attitudes toward strangers will produce an increase in our anxiety and a decrease in our ability to predict their behavior accurately. *Boundary Conditions:* This axiom holds only when our anxiety and uncertainty are between our minimum and maximum thresholds, and we are not mindful.

Axiom 12: An increase in our uncertainty orientation will produce an increase in our ability to predict strangers' behavior accurately. *Boundary Conditions:* This axiom holds only when our uncertainty is between our minimum and maximum thresholds, and we are not mindful.

Axiom 13: An increase in our tolerance for ambiguity will produce a decrease in our anxiety. *Boundary Conditions:* This axiom holds only when our anxiety and uncertainty are between our minimum and maximum thresholds, and we are not mindful.

Axiom 14: An increase in our ability to empathize with strangers will produce a decrease in our anxiety and an increase in our ability to predict their behavior accurately. *Boundary Conditions:* This axiom holds only when we respect strangers and when our anxiety and uncertainty are between our minimum and maximum thresholds, and we are not mindful.

Axiom 15: An increase in the degree to which strangers converge toward us will produce a decrease in our anxiety and an increase in our confidence in predicting their behavior. *Boundary Conditions:* This axiom holds only in individualistic cultures when we are secure in our social identities and we do not perceive threats from strangers, when our anxiety and uncertainty are between our minimum and maximum thresholds, and we are not mindful.

The way we react to strangers affects our ability to manage our anxiety and uncertainty. There are, however, many different ways we can react to strangers. Our reactions are dependent, in part, on how we categorize strangers.

Social Categorizations

Social categorizations refer to the way we order our social environments by grouping people into categories that make sense to us (Tajfel, 1978, 1981). In categorizing ourselves and strangers, we become aware of being members of ingroups and outgroups. Social categorization results in the activation of social identities and engaging in intergroup behavior with strangers. This leads to anxiety and uncertainty. If, however, we perceive that we share superordinate common ingroup identities with strangers, our anxiety levels will be similar to when we communicate with ingroup members (see research summarized in Gaertner et al., 1999).

We tend to view our ingroups as more differentiated than outgroups (e.g., strangers' groups; Linville et al., 1989). The more familiar we are with outgroups, however, the greater our perceived differentiation of these groups. The more variability we perceive in outgroups, the less our tendency to treat all members in a similar negative fashion (Johnston & Hewstone, 1990). Goffman (1959) argues that functional behavior in intergroup situations involves recognizing the differences between groups and using this information to try to make our interactions as smooth as possible.

When we categorize strangers, or think about strangers and their groups, we form expectations for strangers' behavior. Expectations involve our anticipations and predictions about how strangers will communicate with us. Negative expectations (e.g., based on ethnocentrism, negative stereotypes, prejudice) lead to uncertainty and intergroup anxiety (Hubbert et al., 1999). Positive expectations (e.g., based on positive stereotypes), in contrast, help us manage uncertainty and anxiety. Positive expectations lead us to behave in a positive manner toward strangers (see Hamilton et al., 1990, for a discussion of expectancy confirming processes). The more positive our expectations for strangers' behavior, the less our anxiety and the greater our confidence in predicting their behavior (Gudykunst & Shapiro, 1996; Hubbert et al., 1999; Plant & Devine, 2003). Positive expectations alone, however, do not necessarily lead to accurate predictions. To make accurate predictions, we need to have accurate information regarding strangers' cultures, group memberships, and the individual strangers with whom we are communicating.

Devine (1989) argues that mindfully managing our reactions when our negative stereotypes are activated is necessary to control our prejudiced response to strangers. She points out that "nonprejudiced responses are . . . a function of intentional controlled processes and require a conscious decision to behave in a nonprejudiced fashion. In addition, new responses must be learned and well practiced before they can serve as competitive responses to the automatically activated stereotype-congruent response" (p. 15). When we are mindful that our negative expectations are being activated, we can cognitively manage our reactions. Being mindful of negative expectations, therefore, allows us to manage our anxiety and increase our ability to predict strangers' behavior accurately.

We tend to base our categorizations of strangers on their skin color, dress, accents, and so forth (Clark & Marshall, 1981). The cues we use, however, are not always accurate ways to categorize strangers (e.g., an inaccurate categorization occurs when we put strangers in a category in which they do not place themselves in the interaction). Our predictions of strangers' behavior may not be accurate because the group memberships we use to categorize strangers may not be affecting their behavior in the situation. We might categorize strangers based on one group membership (e.g., ethnicity) and assume that the social identity based on this category is influencing their behavior. Strangers, however, may be basing their behavior on a different social identity (e.g., social class, gender, role). To make accurate predictions, we must understand which social identity is guiding strangers' behavior in a particular situation.

If strangers strongly identify with their groups, we must recognize their group memberships in order to support their self-concepts. If we ignore strangers' group memberships

when they identify strongly with their groups, they perceive our behavior as disconfirming. Knowledge of the similarities and differences between our groups and strangers' groups when the strangers strongly identify with their groups, therefore, is critical to effective communication. Group differences, in contrast, are not necessarily critical when strangers do not strongly identify with their groups.

Perceived personal similarities with strangers influence whether we will approach them or form relationships with them (see Berscheid, 1985). Perceived similarity is related to managing uncertainty (e.g., Gudykunst, Chua, & Gray, 1987; Hubbert et al., 1999) and anxiety (e.g., Hubbert et al., 1999; Stephan & Stephan, 1985). The greater the perceived differences between our groups and strangers' groups, the more intense the negative affect (e.g., anxiety) we have about interacting with them (Dijker, 1987).

The way we categorize strangers affects the amount of anxiety and uncertainty we experience when interacting with them. The way we categorize strangers also influences the accuracy of our predictions about their behavior. Seven axioms regarding social categorizations, therefore, are included in the theory:

Axiom 16: An increase in our understanding of similarities and differences between our groups and strangers' groups will produce a decrease in our anxiety and an increase in our ability to accurately predict their behavior. *Boundary Conditions:* This axiom holds only when our anxiety and uncertainty are between our minimum and maximum thresholds, we are not mindful, and only for strangers who strongly identify with their groups.

Axiom 17: An increase in the personal similarities we perceive between ourselves and strangers will produce a decrease in our anxiety and an increase in our ability to predict their behavior accurately. *Boundary Conditions:* This axiom holds only when our anxiety and uncertainty are between our minimum and maximum thresholds, and we are not mindful.

Axiom 18: An increase in our ability to categorize strangers in the same categories they categorize themselves will produce an increase in our ability to predict their behavior accurately. *Boundary Conditions:* This axiom holds only when our anxiety and uncertainty are between our minimum and maximum thresholds, and we are not mindful.

Axiom 19: An increase in the variability we perceive in strangers' groups will produce a decrease in our anxiety and an increase in our ability to predict their behavior accurately. *Boundary Conditions:* This axiom holds only when our anxiety and uncertainty are between our minimum and maximum thresholds, and we are not mindful.

Axiom 20: An increase in perceiving that we share superordinate ingroup identities with strangers will produce a decrease in our anxiety and an increase in our ability to predict their behavior accurately. *Boundary Conditions:* This axiom holds only when our anxiety and uncertainty are between our minimum and maximum thresholds, and we are not mindful.

Axiom 21: An increase in our positive expectations for strangers' behavior will produce a decrease in our anxiety and an increase in our confidence in predicting their behavior. *Boundary Conditions:* This axiom holds only when our anxiety and uncertainty are between our minimum and maximum thresholds, and we are not mindful.

Axiom 22: An increase in our ability to suspend our negative expectations for strangers' behavior when they are activated will produce a decrease in our anxiety and an increase in our ability to predict their behavior accurately. *Boundary Conditions:* This axiom holds only when we are mindful of the process of communication, and our anxiety and uncertainty are between our minimum and maximum thresholds.

The way we categorize strangers affects the amount of anxiety and uncertainty we experience interacting with them. The amount of anxiety and uncertainty we experience, however, is mediated by the situations in which we are interacting with strangers.

Situational Processes

One of the major ways that situations influence our behavior is in the scripts we activate in different situations. A script is "a coherent sequence of events expected by the individual, involving him [or her] either as a participant or an observer" (Abelson, 1976, p. 33). Scripts provide guides for the conversations we have in different situations, and help us manage the uncertainty we have about how to behave in various situations (Berger & Bradac, 1982).

Although we know thousands of scripts, most of us do not have scripts for communicating with strangers. When we do not have information about strangers' groups and do not have scripts for the interaction, we do not feel in control interacting with strangers and we experience anxiety (Britt et al., 1996). Our anxiety is a function of the strangers with whom we are interacting and the situation in which the interaction occurs (Britt et al., 1996). If we interact with strangers following our usual scripts, misunderstandings tend to occur because we assume strangers use the same perspectives we do when we communicate mindlessly. Some scripts, however, are useful in interacting with strangers. Activating an information seeking script, for example, reduces our anxiety about interacting with strangers (Leary et al., 1988).

The conditions under which we have contact with strangers influence our anxiety and uncertainty. Argyle (1991), for example, argues that cooperation leads to positive feelings toward the people with whom we cooperate. When we work on cooperative goals with strangers, and when there is institutional and normative support for interacting with strangers, we do not experience high levels of anxiety and we have confidence in our ability to predict their behavior. Also, we experience less anxiety when there are other members of our ingroups present in the situation than we are alone because there is security in numbers.

The situation also influences the power members of our ingroups and strangers have. Power is the ability to influence others (e.g., French & Raven, 1959). Lack of power leads to anxiety and attempts to cope with the anxiety (Fiske et al., 1996). Strangers tend to have less power than ingroup members. Strangers also tend to be more aware of power differences between groups than ingroup members (e.g., Gurin et al., 1999). The nature of the stranger-ingroup relationship influences strangers' and ingroups' power and the potential for conflict between them (Gudykunst, 1985c). The more power our ingroups have over strangers, the less anxiety we have about interacting with strangers. Power also leads to cognitive and evaluative biases (Goodwin et al., 1998) and, therefore, to inaccurate predictions of strangers' behavior.

The situations in which we interact with strangers affect the amount of anxiety and uncertainty we experience interacting with them. Four axioms regarding situational influences on anxiety and uncertainty management, therefore, are included in the theory:

Axiom 23: An increase in the cooperative structure of the tasks on which we work with strangers will produce a decrease in our anxiety and an increase in our confidence in predicting their behavior. *Boundary Conditions:* This axiom holds only when our anxiety and uncertainty are between our minimum and maximum thresholds, and we are not mindful.

Axiom 24: An increase in the normative and institutional support for communicating with strangers will produce a decrease in our anxiety and an increase in our confidence in predicting their behavior. *Boundary Conditions:* This axiom holds only when our anxiety and uncertainty are between our minimum and maximum thresholds, and we are not mindful.

Axiom 25: An increase in the percentage of our ingroup members present in a situation will produce a decrease in our anxiety. *Boundary*

Conditions: This axiom holds only when our anxiety and uncertainty are between our minimum and maximum thresholds, and we are not mindful.

Axiom 26: An increase in the power we perceive that we have over strangers will produce a decrease in our anxiety and a decrease in the accuracy of our predictions of their behavior. *Boundary Conditions:* This axiom holds only when our anxiety and uncertainty are between our minimum and maximum thresholds, and we are not mindful.

The situations in which we interact with strangers affect the nature of the contact we have with strangers. The nature of the contact we have with strangers, in turn, affects whether we form connections with them.

Connections to Strangers

Attraction, or liking, is one of the major factors contributing to the development of relationships with strangers. If we are not attracted to strangers, we will not want to form connections with them. We tend to be attracted to strangers we perceive to be similar to us. This is especially true before we interact with strangers (Sunnafrank & Miller, 1981). When we have a chance to interact with strangers we perceive to be dissimilar to us, however, we often become attracted to them. Attraction to strangers reduces our uncertainty (Berger & Calabrese, 1975; Gudykunst, Chua, & Gray, 1987) and anxiety (Stephan & Stephan, 1985).

Stephan and Stephan (1985, 1989, 1992) argue that the quality of contact with strangers affects the amount of anxiety we experience interacting with them. Islam and Hewstone (1993) contend that the quantity of contact we have with strangers also affects the amount of anxiety we experience. Britt et al. (1996) also report that trait and state anxiety are correlated negatively with overall contact with strangers.

The quantity and quality of contact we have with strangers also affects the amount of uncertainty we experience. Berger and Calabrese's (1975) URT, for example, posits that the more verbal communication in which we engage with strangers, the less uncertainty we have about their behavior. URT also suggests that the greater the intimacy of our communication with others (e.g., nonsuperficial contact), the less uncertainty we have about them. Extending URT implies that the more contact we have with strangers and the greater the quality of the contact (e.g., favorable contact), the more information we are able to collect about strangers and their groups, and the less uncertainty we have.

Our interdependence with strangers affects how we communicate with them. When we are interdependent with strangers, for example, we do not experience high levels of anxiety about interacting with them. When we are interdependent, we also tend to have confidence in our ability to predict their behavior. Fiske and Morling (1996) argue that "interdependence usually motivates accuracy in impression formation" (p. 324). Interdependence, therefore, should lead to accuracy in predicting strangers' behavior.

The intimacy of our relationships with strangers also affects how we communicate with them. As relationships between people from different groups become more intimate (i.e., move from initial interactions to close friends), communication becomes more personalized, more synchronized, and there is less difficulty (Gudykunst, Nishida, & Chua, 1987). Group similarities appear to have a major influence on our communication in the early stages of relationship development (i.e., initial interactions and acquaintance relationships), but not in later stages of relationship development (e.g., close friendships; Gudykunst, Chua, & Gray, 1987; Gudykunst & Shapiro, 1996).

Our relationships with strangers are embedded in social networks. Parks and Adelman (1983) argue that communication with members of others' social networks (e.g., their family and friends) helps us reduce uncertainty about them. The amount of uncertainty we experience when we communicate with strangers is influenced by the degree to which we share communication networks with the strangers (e.g., Gudykunst, Chua, & Gray, 1987). Shared networks also help us manage anxiety about strangers (e.g., Dyal & Dyal, 1981). The more we know the same people that the strangers with whom we are communicating know, the more we can manage uncertainty and anxiety interacting with those strangers.

The nature of the connections we have with strangers influences the amount of anxiety and uncertainty we experience interacting with them. Five axioms dealing with the nature of our connections with strangers, therefore, are included in the theory:

Axiom 27: An increase in our attraction to strangers will produce a decrease in our anxiety and an increase in our confidence in predicting their behavior. *Boundary Conditions:* This axiom holds only when our anxiety and uncertainty are between our minimum and maximum thresholds, and we are not mindful.

Axiom 28: An increase in the quantity and quality of our contact with strangers and members of their groups will produce a decrease in our anxiety and an increase in our ability to predict their behavior accurately. *Boundary Conditions:* This axiom holds only when our anxiety and uncertainty are between our minimum and maximum thresholds, and we are not mindful.

Axiom 29: An increase in our interdependence with strangers will produce a decrease in our anxiety and an increase in our ability to predict their behavior accurately. *Boundary Conditions:* This axiom holds only when our anxiety and uncertainty are between our minimum and maximum thresholds, and we are not mindful.

Axiom 30: An increase in the intimacy of our relationships with strangers will produce a decrease in our anxiety and an increase in our ability to predict their behavior accurately. *Boundary Conditions:* This axiom applies only to broad trends across stages of relationship development. Within any stage of relationship development or within specific conversations, anxiety and uncertainty fluctuate (i.e., act as dialectics). The axiom also holds only when we are not mindful.

Axiom 31: An increase in the networks we share with strangers will produce a decrease in our anxiety and an increase in our ability to accurately predict their behavior. *Boundary Conditions:* This axiom holds only when our anxiety and uncertainty are between our minimum and maximum thresholds, and we are not mindful.

As indicated in the discussion of interdependence, the nature of our connections with strangers does not directly affect our ability to predict their behavior accurately. Our ability to manage our anxiety and accurately predict strangers' behavior is dependent on our ability to be mindful of our communication when we interact with them. Our ability to be mindful moderates the influence of managing anxiety and uncertainty on effective communication.

Ethical Interactions With Strangers

Dignity involves a minimal level of self-respect, or feeling worthy, honored, and respected as a person (Pritchard, 1991). Being ethical or moral requires that we maintain our own and strangers' sense of dignity. Pritchard argues that the "overridingness of morality" requires that our "conduct be limited to what is morally acceptable" (p. 226). Behavior in early stages of interaction tends to be reciprocated (Gouldner, 1960); therefore, if we treat strangers with dignity, they will treat us with dignity. This should lead to low levels of anxiety about interacting with strangers.

Respecting strangers also is necessary to behave in a moral fashion (Gutmann, 1992). Pritchard (1991) also argues that "respect for persons" is an important component of moral

behavior. We need to interact with strangers on the basis of a "presumption of equal worth" (Taylor, 1992, p. 72). When we respect strangers, we unconsciously assume that strangers respect us (see Sampson, 1993, Selznick, 1992, and Smiley, 1992, for discussions of the importance of respect). This leads to low levels of anxiety about interacting with strangers.

When we respect strangers, we treat them in a morally inclusive fashion. Optow (1990) points out that "moral exclusion occurs when individuals or groups are perceived as outside the boundary in which moral values, rules, and considerations of fairness apply. Those who are morally excluded are perceived as nonentities, expendable, or undeserving" (p. 1, italics omitted). If strangers are perceived as nonentities, "harming them appears acceptable, appropriate, or just" (p. 1). When we are morally inclusive we assume that considerations of fair play apply to strangers, and we are willing to make sacrifices to help them.

Moral exclusion emerges from blaming strangers and distancing ourselves psychologically from them (Optow, 1990). It, therefore, leads to high levels of anxiety about interacting with strangers. We have high levels of anxiety because we do not expect those we treat morally exclusively to apply the rules of fair play to us. When we are morally inclusive toward strangers, in contrast, we expect strangers to apply the rules of fair play to us. When we expect to be treated fairly, we are not highly anxious about communicating with strangers.

Our ethical responsibilities toward strangers do not stop when we are bystanders to others' interactions with strangers. Staub (1989) claims that "bystanders can exert a powerful influence. They can define the meaning of events and move others toward empathy and indifference. They can promote values and norms of caring, or by passivity or participation in the system they can affirm the perpetrators" (p. 87). Blanchard et al.'s

(1991) research suggests that if we express anti-prejudice sentiments, others are not likely to express their prejudice toward strangers when we are present. We, therefore, can influence others' ethical behavior toward strangers.

Treating strangers ethically affects the anxiety we experience interacting with them. Three axioms regarding ethical treatment of strangers, therefore, are included in the theory:

Axiom 32: An increase in our ability to maintain our own and strangers' dignity in our interactions with them will produce a decrease in our anxiety. *Boundary Conditions:* This axiom holds only when our anxiety is between our minimum and maximum thresholds, and we are not mindful.

Axiom 33: An increase in our respect for strangers will produce a decrease in our anxiety. *Boundary Conditions:* This axiom holds only when our anxiety is between our minimum and maximum thresholds, and we are not mindful.

Axiom 34: An increase in our moral inclusiveness toward strangers will produce a decrease in our anxiety. *Boundary Conditions:* This axiom holds only when our anxiety is between our minimum and maximum thresholds, and we are not mindful.

For most of us, maintaining our own and strangers' dignity, respecting strangers, and being morally inclusive toward strangers requires that we be mindful. This is especially true when our anxiety is above our maximum thresholds.

Anxiety, Uncertainty, Mindfulness, and Effective Communication

To communicate effectively with strangers we must be able to understand strangers' perspectives. This requires mindfulness. As indicated earlier, Langer (1989) argues that mindfulness involves creating new categories, being open to new information, and recognizing strangers' perspectives. Communicating effectively with strangers requires that we develop mindful ways of learning about strangers. Langer (1997) contends this involves "(1) openness to novelty; (2) alertness to distinctions; (3) sensitivity to different contexts; (4) implicit, if not explicit, awareness of multiple perspectives; and (5) orientation in the present" (p. 23). These processes are all interrelated and lead us to be "receptive to changes in an ongoing situation" (p. 23).

Strangers tend to be more mindful in intergroup interactions than ingroup members. Frable et al. (1990) argue that strangers pay attention to how their interactions with ingroup members are going and are aware of alternative ways the interactions may develop. Often, strangers' mindfulness is a defensive strategy because they are unsure how ingroup members will respond to them (Frable et al., 1990). Further, strangers tend to be aware of ingroup members' perspectives more than ingroup members are aware of strangers' perspectives. Devine et al. (1996) suggest that this results in strangers' being able to "negotiate potentially problematic social interactions more effectively" than ingroup members (p. 444).

Devine et al. (1996) argue that the extent that ingroup members' mindfulness leads to effective interactions depends on strangers' biases and objectivity. They contend that "socially stigmatized members of society [e.g., many, but not all, strangers] are generally mistrusting and suspicious of majority group members' intentions and motives" (p. 445). Strangers' responses to ingroup members also are affected by strangers' "attributional ambiguity" (e.g., strangers may attribute ingroup members' behavior to ingroup members' personal qualities or ingroup members' stereotypes of strangers' groups; Crocker et al., 1991). Devine et al. suggest that strangers who expect to be treated negatively "may misperceive social anxiety as antipathy" (p. 449) even for ingroup members who are low in prejudice. There is no research on how strangers respond when ingroup members are mindful. I think that strangers' responses to ingroup members' mindfulness will lead to smooth interactions if strangers perceive that ingroup members are not highly prejudiced and ingroup members' intentions are positive. This should be the case if ingroup members are mindful of the process of communication rather than mindful of the outcome of their interactions.

If we interpret strangers' messages from our own perspectives, as we do when we communicate mindlessly, we tend to communicate ineffectively. The more we are able to learn how to describe strangers' behavior and the less evaluative we are, the more positive strangers will perceive our intentions to be. Describing strangers' behavior also helps us understand how strangers interpret messages because we do not automatically assume that strangers interpret messages the same way we do and we can try to understand strangers' interpretations. Our ability to differentiate strangers' interpretations of messages from our interpretations of messages leads to predicting strangers' behavior accurately.

Understanding strangers' languages or dialects also facilitates managing our anxiety and uncertainty, in large part, because it helps us understand strangers' perspectives. Second language competence, for example, increases our ability to cope with uncertainty in cultures where the language is spoken (Naiman et al., 1978). Knowledge of strangers' languages and dialects also helps us manage our anxiety (Stephan & Stephan, 1985).

Experiencing anxiety when we interact with strangers leads us to engage in social categorizations (e.g., create ingroups and outgroups; Greenland & Brown, 1999). The anxiety we experience also affects our ability to process information. Wilder and Shapiro (1989) point out that when anxiety is high (e.g., above our maximum thresholds), we tend to process information in a simplistic fashion. Wilder (1993) points out that high levels of anxiety

generate arousal, which leads to self-focused attention that distracts us from what is happening and decreases our ability to make differentiations regarding strangers. This line of reasoning suggests that we are not able to gather new or accurate information about strangers when our anxiety is high and, therefore, we are not able to make accurate predictions or explanations of strangers' behavior. Wilder and Shapiro (1989), however, point out that "integral anxiety" (e.g., anxiety attributed to strangers' groups) can facilitate information processing, but intense anxiety (e.g., anxiety from unknown sources) inhibits it.

Greenland and Brown (2000) propose that our strategies for coping with anxiety may depend on our explanations for why we experience anxiety. They contend that having a "positive" reason for experiencing anxiety (e.g., we do not want to appear to be prejudiced) should lead to processing information systematically and not engaging in stereotyping. Having a "negative" reason for experiencing anxiety (e.g., because we have hostile feelings toward strangers' groups), in contrast, should lead to simplistic information processing.

If our anxiety and uncertainty are above our maximum thresholds, we must first mindfully manage our anxiety (e.g., bring it below our maximum threshold) before we can accurately predict strangers' behavior (e.g., manage our uncertainty). Managing our anxiety requires controlling our bodily symptoms (e.g., shortness of breath) and controlling our worrying thoughts (Kennerley, 1990). Once we mindfully manage our bodily symptoms (e.g., by physically or mentally breaking from the situation), we can mindfully manage the worrying thoughts that cause the anxiety (e.g., all-or-nothing thinking; see Burns, 1989, for a discussion of cognitive distortions that can cause anxiety and how to manage them). Managing the worrying thoughts is important because if we do not manage them they will interfere with our ability to process information complexly about strangers (Fiske & Morling, 1996).

We cannot communicate effectively if our anxiety and uncertainty are too high or too low. The optimal level of anxiety and uncertainty that facilitates effective communication with strangers is somewhere between our minimum and maximum thresholds. For uncertainty, our optimal level is when we think that strangers' behavior is predictable, but we also recognize that we may not be able to explain their behavior accurately. For anxiety, our optimal level is when we feel comfortable interacting with strangers, but we still have sufficient anxiety that we are not complacent in our interactions with them.

When our anxiety and uncertainty are not at optimal levels, we can mindfully manage them to bring them between our minimum and maximum thresholds (Note: this notion of uncertainty management is different from Brashers' (2001) uncertainty management theory). When our anxiety and uncertainty are at optimal levels, we can communicate effectively, especially if we are mindful. We do not, however, want to be overly vigilant when we are mindful (Langer, 1997). If we engage in "soft vigilance," in contrast, we will be open to new information and aware of strangers' perspectives (Langer, 1997). We also can correct miscommunication that occurs.

Gass and Varonis (1991) isolate two types of miscommunication that occur in our interactions with strangers. "Misunderstandings" occur when we attach different meanings to messages than strangers but do not recognize it. "Incomplete understandings" occur when we attach different meanings to messages than strangers and one of us recognizes it. Gass and Varonis contend that misunderstandings are highly problematic because the communicators assume they understand each other. We, nevertheless, increase the likelihood we will recognize misunderstandings when we are mindful. We can manage pragmatic errors (e.g., errors due to using our perspectives when we should be using strangers' perspectives) that occur if we are mindful (e.g., by

using paraphrasing, clarifications, feedback, giving additional information, etc.). Successful management of pragmatic errors facilitates negotiating meanings that lead to effective communication.

When our anxiety and our uncertainty are between our minimum and maximum thresholds, we can communicate effectively with strangers when we are mindful. Five axioms summarize the relationships among anxiety, uncertainty, mindfulness, and effective communication:

Axiom 35: An increase in our ability to describe strangers' behavior will produce an increase in our ability to predict their behavior accurately. *Boundary Conditions:* This axiom holds only when we are mindful of the process of communication, we are not overly vigilant, and our anxiety and uncertainty are between our minimum and maximum thresholds.

Axiom 36: An increase in our knowledge of strangers' languages and/or dialects will produce a decrease in our anxiety and an increase in our ability to predict their behavior accurately. *Boundary Conditions:* This axiom holds only when our anxiety and uncertainty are between our minimum and maximum thresholds, and when we are not mindful.

Axiom 37: An increase in our mindfulness of the process of our communication with strangers will produce an increase in our ability to manage our anxiety and an increase in our ability to manage our uncertainty. *Boundary Condition:* This axiom holds only when we are not overly vigilant.

Axiom 38: An increase in mindfully recognizing and correcting pragmatic errors that occur in our conversations with strangers facilitates negotiating meaning with strangers (which will produce an increase in the effectiveness of our communication). *Boundary Conditions:* This axiom holds only when we are mindful of the process of communication and we are not overly vigilant, and our anxiety and uncertainty are between our minimum and maximum thresholds.

Axiom 39: An increase in our ability to manage our anxiety about interacting with strangers *and* an increase in the accuracy of our predictions and explanations regarding their behavior will produce an increase in the effectiveness of our communication. *Boundary Conditions:* This axiom holds only when we are mindful of the process of communication and we are not overly vigilant, and our anxiety and uncertainty are between our minimum and maximum thresholds.

These five axioms are critical for effective communication; they focus on the basic causes (i.e., anxiety and uncertainty management) and the processes (e.g., mindfulness) of effective communication. The preceding axioms (1–34) explain ways that we can manage our anxiety and uncertainty when we communicate with strangers (e.g., they focus on the superficial causes of effective communication).

Cross-Cultural Variability in AUM Processes

As indicated in my discussion of the scope of AUM theory, I believe that theories are not complete unless the cultural level of analysis is included. In the 1995 version of AUM theory, I included one axiom regarding cross-cultural variability in anxiety and uncertainty management processes for each axiom in the main part of the theory. Most of those axioms are plausible hypotheses for future research (Note: Kodiara, 2002, does not support axiom 50 of the 1995 theory). In 1995, I suggested that the cross-cultural axioms could be tested at either the cultural- or individual-levels of analysis (e.g., making comparisons across individualistic or collectivistic cultures or using self construals [e.g., the ways individuals conceive of themselves; Markus & Kitayama, 1991] as individual-level mediators of cultural individualism-collectivism). I no longer think this position is correct. I now believe that axioms regarding cultural variability should be tested only at the cultural level (see Gudykunst, 2002, for a discussion of this issue).

I am no longer convinced it is necessary to have one cross-cultural axiom for each axiom in the main part of the theory (axioms 1–39). It is likely that there will be position effects for culture (i.e., cultural differences in mean scores) in the superficial causes of effective communication. This does not, however, mean that there are pattern effects for culture (i.e., different correlations among the superficial causes and anxiety/uncertainty; see Leung & Bond, 1989, for a discussion of position and pattern effects). The cross-cultural research that exists suggests relatively similar patterns of correlations between other variables and uncertainty across cultures (e.g., Gudykunst et al.'s, 1985, cross-cultural test of URT). Cross-cultural research on anxiety (e.g., Kleinknecht et al., 1997) suggests that members of different cultures emphasize different types of anxiety, but these are not limited to specific cultures. Cultural factors, nevertheless, influence the prediction of anxiety across cultures. It is, therefore, important to address cross-cultural variability in the major components of the theory. In this section, I proffer axioms regarding cultural variability in stranger-ingroup relationships, anxiety, uncertainty, and effective communication. I also apply these axioms to intercultural communication with strangers.

To begin, there are differences in the nature of stranger-ingroup relationships across cultures. Triandis (1995) points out that members of collectivistic cultures (e.g., cultures that emphasize the ingroup over individuals) draw a sharper distinction between ingroups and outgroups than members of individualistic cultures (e.g., cultures that emphasize individual members over their ingroups). There is, however, at least one ingroup-outgroup distinction drawn in individualistic cultures that tends to be drawn sharply; namely, the distinctions among ethnic groups.

Members of collectivistic cultures tend to view both their ingroups and their outgroups as relatively homogeneous and do not pay a lot of attention to individuals' attributes (Triandis et al., 1990). Members of individualistic cultures, in contrast, tend to view their ingroups as more heterogeneous than outgroups. Members of collectivistic cultures tend to base their behavior on social identities more than members of individualistic cultures (see Gudykunst & Bond, 1997, for a summary of studies). There are greater differences in ingroup and outgroup anxiety and uncertainty management processes in collectivistic cultures than in individualistic cultures (e.g., Gudykunst et al., 1992). This line of reasoning suggests the following axiom:

> *Axiom 40:* An increase in cultural collectivism will produce an increase in the sharpness with which the stranger-ingroup distinction is drawn. *Boundary Conditions:* This axiom does not apply to stranger-ingroup relationships based on ethnicity, and when we are mindful.

This axiom implies that increases in cultural collectivism produce increases the anxiety and uncertainty ingroup members experience when they interact with strangers.

Cultural individualism-collectivism is not the only dimension of cultural variability that affects our communication with strangers. Hofstede (2001) argues that xenophobia is stronger in cultures high in uncertainty avoidance (e.g., cultures where uncertainty is viewed as dangerous) than in cultures low in uncertainty avoidance (e.g., cultures where uncertainty is viewed as interesting). Tolerance for diversity, in contrast, is higher in low uncertainty avoidance cultures than in high uncertainty avoidance cultures. Hofstede (2001) claims that members of high uncertainty avoidance cultures reject members of other groups as neighbors, think immigrants should be sent back to their native cultures, are suspicious of foreign managers, and are not prepared to travel abroad more than members of low uncertainty avoidance cultures. These differences suggest the following axiom:

> *Axiom 41:* An increase in cultural uncertainty avoidance will produce an increase in ingroup members' xenophobia about interacting with strangers. *Boundary Condition:* This axiom does not hold when we are mindful.

This axiom suggests that an increase in cultural uncertainty avoidance will produce an increase in the anxiety and uncertainty experienced when interacting with strangers from other cultures, races, or ethnic groups.

Specific types of stranger-ingroup relationships are influenced by other dimensions of cultural variability. The effect of the gender composition of the stranger-ingroup relationship on anxiety and uncertainty is affected by cultural variability in masculinity-femininity. Hofstede (2001) points out that members of masculine cultures (e.g., cultures with highly differentiated gender roles) are socialized with members of the same sex and have little contact with members of the opposite sex. Members of feminine cultures (e.g., cultures with little gender role differentiation), in contrast, are socialized with members of the same- and opposite sex. Members of masculine cultures, therefore, draw a sharper distinction between same- and opposite-sex relationships than members of feminine cultures. This leads to members of masculine cultures having greater anxiety and uncertainty in opposite-sex relationships than members of feminine cultures.

The effect of the status/power of strangers and ingroup members on anxiety and uncertainty is affected by cultural variability in power distance. Hofstede (2001) points out that members of high power distance cultures view power as being distributed unequally in society. Members of low power distance cultures, on the other hand, view power as distributed equally in society. Members of high power distance cultures, therefore, draw a sharper distinction between low- and high-status communicators than members of low power distance cultures. This leads to members of high power distance cultures having greater anxiety and uncertainty in relationships where individuals have different statuses than members of low power distance cultures.

Hofstede (2001) links generational attitudes to cultural uncertainty avoidance. He points out that favorable attitudes toward younger people and favorable attitudes toward older people are correlated positively with uncertainty avoidance at the cultural level. Hofstede argues that older people in high uncertainty avoidance cultures are "more likely to disapprove of the behavior of young people and to wait longer before leaving the responsibility in the hands of juniors" than older people in low uncertainty avoidance cultures (pp. 158–159). This leads to a larger generation gap in high uncertainty avoidance cultures than in low uncertainty avoidance cultures. It should be noted, however, that Hofstede (2001) contends that relationships between parents and children is influenced by cultural power distance. He claims, for example, that "respect for parents and older relatives is a basic virtue" in high power distance cultures and that "children treat parents and older relatives as equals" in low power distance cultures. The reasoning outlined here suggests three axioms:

Axiom 42: An increase in cultural masculinity will produce an increase in the sharpness of the stranger-ingroup distinction drawn for opposite-sex relationships. *Boundary Condition:* This axiom does not hold when we are mindful.

Axiom 43: An increase in cultural power distance will produce an increase in the sharpness of the stranger-ingroup distinction drawn for relationships involving unequal statuses. *Boundary Condition:* This axiom does not hold when we are mindful.

Axiom 44: An increase in cultural uncertainty avoidance will produce an increase in the sharpness of the stranger-ingroup distinction drawn based on age. *Boundary Conditions:* This axiom does not hold for intergenerational communication within families or when we are mindful.

The sharper the specific stranger-ingroup distinction that is drawn, the greater our anxiety and uncertainty when we communicate with strangers from the specific cultures, and the greater the difference in ingroup and outgroup communication. To illustrate, low status members of low power distance cultures will have greater anxiety and uncertainty communicating with high status members of high power distance cultures than with high status members of their own cultures.

The type of information that individuals use to manage their uncertainty is influenced by individualism-collectivism. Gudykunst and Nishida (1986), for example, report that members of individualistic cultures focus on person-based information (e.g., values, attitudes, beliefs) to manage uncertainty, and members of collectivistic cultures focus on group-based information (e.g., group memberships, age, status) to manage uncertainty. Similarly, Gelfand et al. (2000) observe that individuating information is used to make predictions in individualistic cultures more than in collectivistic cultures, and relational information is used to make predictions in collectivistic cultures more than in individualistic cultures. Norenzayan et al. (2002) also point out that members of collectivistic cultures use situation-based information to make social inferences more than members of individualistic cultures when situational information is salient (see Choi et al., 1999, and Norenzayan et al., 1999, for discussions of cultural differences in causal attributions; see Nisbett, 2003, for a summary of studies). This suggests the following axiom:

Axiom 45: An increase in cultural individualism will produce an increase in ingroup members' use of person-based information to manage uncertainty with strangers; an increase in cultural collectivism will produce an increase in ingroup members' use of group-based and situation-based information to manage uncertainty with strangers. *Boundary Condition:* This axiom does not hold when we are mindful.

The focus on person-based information leads members of individualistic cultures to look for personal similarities with strangers more than members of collectivistic cultures. The focus on group-based information and the firm ingroup-outgroup distinction, in contrast, leads members of collectivistic cultures to look for group differences and to pay attention to the situation more than members of individualistic cultures.

The general amount of anxiety and uncertainty experienced when communicating with strangers is influenced by cultural variability in uncertainty avoidance. Hofstede (2001) argues that members of high uncertainty avoidance cultures try to avoid uncertainty more, have higher levels of anxiety, and tolerate deviant behavior less than members of low uncertainty avoidance cultures. High uncertainty avoidance cultures, however, tend to have norms and rules for most situations, including intergroup interactions, in order to minimize the uncertainty and anxiety members of the culture experience. Intergroup interactions are perceived more negatively in low uncertainty avoidance cultures than in high uncertainty avoidance cultures because there are clear rules for intergroup interactions in high uncertainty avoidance cultures (Gudykunst et al., 1999). This suggests the following axiom:

> *Axiom 46:* When there are clear rules for stranger-ingroup interactions, an increase in cultural uncertainty avoidance will produce a decrease in the anxiety and uncertainty experienced communicating with strangers. When there are not clear rules for stranger-ingroup interactions, an increase in cultural uncertainty avoidance will produce an increase in the anxiety and uncertainty experienced interacting with strangers. *Boundary Condition:* This axiom does not hold when we are mindful.

Testing this axiom requires specifying the clarity of the rules for the specific stranger-ingroup interactions being studied.

Cultural variability in uncertainty avoidance also affects individuals' minimum and maximum thresholds. Since members of high uncertainty avoidance cultures try to avoid anxiety and uncertainty, their maximum thresholds for anxiety and uncertainty are lower than the maximum thresholds for members of low uncertainty avoidance cultures. In other words, members of high uncertainty avoidance cultures need their anxiety and uncertainty to be lower than members of low uncertainty avoidance cultures to feel comfortable communicating with strangers. Members of high uncertainty avoidance cultures minimum thresholds for anxiety and uncertainty also will be lower than those for members of low uncertainty avoidance cultures.

Finally, what is perceived as effective communication differs in individualistic and collectivistic cultures. Tominaga et al. (2003) report that U.S. Americans perceive effective communication to involve (from most to least frequent): (1) understanding (the focus is on understanding others' messages), (2) compatibility, (3) displaying positive behavior, (4) smoothness of communication, (5) positive outcomes, (6) positive nonverbal communication, and (7) adapting messages.

Tominaga et al. (2003) also report that Japanese perceive effective communication to involve: (1) compatibility, (2) appropriateness, (3) good relations between communicators, (4) positive outcomes, (5) smoothness of communication, (6) displaying positive behavior, (7) understanding (the focus is on understanding others' feelings), (8) positive nonverbal communication, and (9) clear messages. The first three themes for the Japanese focus on maintaining good emotional relations between communicators. This is consistent with the emphasis on maintaining harmony in collectivistic cultures (e.g., Triandis, 1995). The differences between the U.S. Americans and the Japanese also is compatible with Kim's (1994) research indicating that members of individualistic cultures are concerned with clarity in conversations more than members of collectivistic cultures, and that members of collectivistic cultures are more concerned with not hurting others' feelings and not imposing on others more than members of individualistic cultures. This research suggests the following axiom:

> *Axiom 47:* An increase in cultural individualism will produce an increase in the focus on cognitive understanding to communicate effectively with strangers. An increase in cultural collectivism will produce an increase in the focus on maintaining good relations between communicators to communicate effectively. *Boundary Condition:* This axiom does not hold when we are mindful.

Awareness of these differences obviously is critical to communicate effectively with strangers from other cultures.

Tominaga et al.'s (2003) study suggests that there are similarities and differences in what is perceived as effective communication in individualistic and collectivistic cultures. These differences, however, do not mean that AUM theory does not apply in collectivistic cultures like Japan; only that the conceptualization of effective communication that needs to be used to test the theory may be different. The differences in conceptualizations of effective communication also suggest that when we are communicating with strangers from other cultures, we need to be mindful that their conceptions of effective communication may be different from ours. The different conceptions should be clear if we are aware of strangers' perspectives and we can adapt our communication. We can choose, for example, to focus on good relations between communicators rather than understanding when we are mindful. When we are not mindful, we use our own conception of effective communication. Also, multiple outcomes can be accomplished simultaneously.

Theorems

Theorems can be generated by logically combining the axioms, but space does not

allow them to be presented here. If axioms 6 and 7 are combined, for example, the theorem that "there is a positive association between our need for group inclusion and sustaining our self-conceptions" can be generated. This theorem is consistent with Turner's (1988) theory of motivation. Some theorems generated will be consistent with previous research and some will form hypotheses for future research. To illustrate, combination of axioms 17 and 27 yields the similarity-attraction hypothesis (i.e., "the more similarities we perceive between ourselves and strangers, the more we are attracted to them"), which has received extensive empirical support (e.g., Byrne, 1971). Combination of axioms 10 and 11 yields the theorem that "the rigidity of our attitudes is related negatively to our ability to process information complexly," a hypothesis for future research.

Not all axioms should be combined to form theorems. The cross-cultural axioms (40–47), for example, should not be combined with the axioms in the main part of the theory (axioms 1–39). This would involve the ecological fallacy or the reverse ecological fallacy. Also, some combinations of axioms will involve the fallacy of the excluded middle and should not be generated. If A → C and B → C, for example, it can be deduced that A and B are related. The fallacy of the excluded middle involves not recognizing that there may be another variable mediating the relationships between the two variables (e.g., A → D → B).

RESEARCH SUPPORTING THE THEORY

Research cited in generating the axioms of AUM theory supports the theory. Several other studies provide support for the relationships between the superficial causes of effective communication (e.g., identities, networks, intimacy) and anxiety or uncertainty management (e.g., Gudykunst, 1985a; Gudykunst & Hammer, 1988a; Gudykunst et al., 1989; Gudykunst,

Nishida, & Chua, 1986; Gudykunst, Sodetani, & Sonoda, 1987; Guerrero & Gudykunst, 1997; Sodetani & Gudykunst, 1987; for a summary of several studies, see Gudykunst, 1989) and cross-cultural variability in anxiety and uncertainty management (e.g., Gudykunst, 1983; Gudykunst et al., 1992; Gudykunst & Nishida, 1984, 1986; Gudykunst et al., 1985), as well as the adjustment version of the theory (e.g., Gao & Gudykunst, 1990; Hammer et al., 1998). In this section, I focus on the most important components of the theory, the relationships among anxiety, uncertainty and perceived effectiveness.

Gudykunst and Shapiro (1996) observed correlations between anxiety and uncertainty ranging from .64 to .79 in interpersonal and intergroup relationships in the United States. Hubbert et al. (1999) examined the relationship between anxiety and uncertainty in two studies of intergroup communication over four points in time for European American and nonEuropean American participants. They found that 13 of the 16 correlations were above .60 (the other three were above .40).

Gudykunst, Nishida, and Chua (1986) found a positive relationship between attributional confidence (the inverse of uncertainty) and perceived effectiveness of communication in Japanese-U.S. American dyads. Gudykunst and Shapiro (1996) reported correlations between anxiety and uncertainty and perceived quality of communication (e.g., the extent to which communication is relaxed and smooth, and it involves understanding and attentiveness), a concept closely related to effective communication, ranging from – .58 to – .72 in interpersonal relationships and – .74 to – .83 in intergroup relationships.

Hubbert et al. (1999) examined the relationships among uncertainty, anxiety, and perceived effectiveness of communication in one of their two studies (Study 2). They found correlations between uncertainty and perceived effectiveness ranging from – .57 to – .71 across the four points in time. They also

observed correlations between anxiety and perceived effectiveness ranging from –.42 to –.61. Hubbert et al. also examined the associations between anxiety, uncertainty, and perceived quality of communication in both of their studies. Fourteen of the 16 correlations between uncertainty and perceived quality were greater than –.60 (the other two were above –.40). Fifteen of the 16 correlations between anxiety and perceived quality were above –.50 (the other was –.46).

Gudykunst and Nishida (2001) examined whether anxiety and uncertainty could predict perceived communication effectiveness in ingroup and outgroup relationships in Japan and the United States. The data indicate that there is a moderate, positive relationship between anxiety and attributional confidence (the inverse of uncertainty) across relationships and cultures. The results also reveal that anxiety negatively predicts perceived effectiveness and attributional confidence positively predicts perceived effectiveness across relationships and cultures. The measure of perceived effectiveness of communication used in this and other studies reported here was based on understanding. Future research is needed using other conceptualizations of effective communication (see the discussion in the cross-cultural variability section).

None of the studies presented here document that anxiety and uncertainty were between the respondents' minimum and maximum thresholds (i.e., one of the boundary conditions for axiom 39). Mean scores for anxiety and uncertainty in all of the studies were in the moderate range and standard deviations were not large, suggesting few extreme scores (e.g., scores that could logically be above maximum or below minimum thresholds). To date, a method for assessing our minimum and maximum thresholds for anxiety and uncertainty has not been developed. There is a need for future research in this area.

All of the studies discussed here focus on *perceived* effectiveness or quality of communication. Axiom 39, however, deals with actual effectiveness of communication. The research conducted to date, therefore, provides only indirect evidence supporting axiom 39. Future laboratory research is needed where interactions are videotaped. The participants need to be interviewed while watching the videotapes. Both participants need to be asked what they meant at selected points and how they interpreted the other person's messages. By comparing intentions and interpretations, the actual effectiveness (e.g., the extent to which they maximized understanding) can be assessed. Other conceptualizations of effectiveness could be examined as well in this type of study.

Another area where there is a need for future research is in assessing mindfulness. Gudykunst (1998b) presents a 10-item self-assessment scale. This scale, however, was developed for pedagogical purposes, not as a research instrument. In completing the items, respondents become mindful of their communication, at least to some extent. Langer's (1989, 1997) work may provide some suggestions for assessing mindfulness in future research.

APPLYING THE THEORY

AUM theory can be applied in several ways. The theory, for example, has clear implications for improving the effectiveness of our communication and helping sojourners adjust to new cultures. Given space limitations, I can provide only overviews here of how to apply the theory.

The theory of effective communication presented here has direct implications for improving the quality of our communication with strangers. Mindfully managing our anxiety so that it is below our maximum thresholds and above our minimum thresholds, for example, is necessary in order to make accurate predictions of strangers' behavior. The theory clearly suggests that if both anxiety and uncertainty

are above our maximum thresholds, we must manage our anxiety before we manage our uncertainty.

The theory also suggests that when we are mindful, we should create new categories for strangers (e.g., look for individuating information about strangers), be open to new information (e.g., things we do not already know about the strangers with whom we are communicating), and be aware of how strangers are interpreting messages. If we are able to accomplish these objectives, we will be able to make accurate predictions about and explanations for strangers' behavior. This is necessary to communicate effectively with strangers.

We also can change the superficial causes to influence the amount of anxiety and uncertainty we experience. We can focus, for example, on describing strangers' behavior rather than interpreting or evaluating their behavior. We also can mindfully choose to behave in ways that are different than our personality characteristics (e.g., uncertainty orientation, tolerance for ambiguity). To illustrate, certainty-oriented individuals can consciously choose to pay attention to their uncertainty and manage it rather than ignoring uncertainty like they tend to do if they are not mindful.

CONCLUSION

In presenting the theory here, I have dropped a large number of axioms (e.g., axioms regarding shame, adapting behavior, informality of situations, gathering appropriate information, self-monitoring; as well as most axioms dealing with cross-cultural variability), and I added several axioms dealing with intergroup processes (e.g., axioms focusing on power, threatened identities, collective self-esteem, common ingroup identities) and cross-cultural variability in stranger-ingroup relationships, anxiety, and uncertainty. The axioms I dropped are ones that I currently do not think are critical to managing anxiety and uncertainty. The axioms that I added increase the compatibility of AUM theory with social identity theory (e.g., Tajfel, 1978, 1981).

Huber and Sorrentino (1996) argue that there is an "uncertainty orientation" bias in theories of interpersonal and intergroup relations. As indicated earlier, Sorrentino and Short (1986) differentiate between uncertainty-oriented individuals and certainty-oriented individuals (e.g., this is an individual difference variable, a personality characteristic). Uncertainty-oriented individuals are motivated to resolve uncertainty about themselves and/or the environment, but certainty-oriented individuals are not. Huber and Sorrentino contend that certainty-oriented individuals "maintain certainty and clarity by avoiding or ignoring inconsistency or ambiguity" (p. 593). They also point out that "uncertainty-oriented people attend to and deal directly with uncertainty and inconsistency; whereas certainty-oriented people attend to and deal with the familiar and certain" (p. 593). Huber and Sorrentino, therefore, claim that URT (Berger & Calabrese, 1975) applies only to uncertainty-oriented individuals. They might make the same claim about the present version of AUM theory.

I do not think that AUM theory is limited to uncertainty-oriented individuals for three reasons. First, I incorporate uncertainty-orientation in the theory. Second, the factors that influence our uncertainty (e.g., the superficial causes) influence the amount of uncertainty that uncertainty- and certainty-oriented individuals experience. Third, I believe that our personality characteristics like uncertainty-orientation influence our behavior only when we are mindless. When we are mindful, we can choose to behave in ways that are not based on our personalities (e.g., certainty-oriented individuals can choose to manage their uncertainty if they want to communicate effectively when they are mindful).

Some readers may argue that the theory is too complicated with 47 axioms. It is, nevertheless, important to keep in mind that the goals of theories must be balanced with the number of theoretical statements when theories are constructed. Since one of the goals of AUM theory is to help improve the quality of our communication, the axioms cannot be highly abstract. Increasing the abstractness of the axioms could make the theory simpler, but it would decrease its applicability. The present form of the theory allows direct application in many practical areas including, but not limited to improving the effectiveness of communication and adapting to new cultural environments.

One area where additional specification is needed involves the relationships among anxiety and uncertainty management, effective communication, and being mindful. How can we, for example, recognize our optimal levels of uncertainty and anxiety? Given that we cannot be mindful of our communication all of the time, how can we recognize when we need to be mindful? To increase the practicality of the theory, it is necessary to isolate the cues that we can use to trigger mindfulness when we perceive that misunderstandings are occurring or might occur. We make choices, whether we are conscious of them or not, of when we want to communicate effectively. In those situations where we want to communicate effectively, we need to know when it is necessary to become mindful in order to increase the likelihood that our communication will be effective. Including these issues in future versions of the theory will improve its practical applicability.

To summarize, I have outlined the development of AUM theory and updated the axioms. The current version of the theory is not a finished product. Rather, the theory is in a constant state of revision. The current version, nevertheless, accomplishes its purpose; it makes the "mesh" of the "net" cast to "catch" effective communication "finer" than the 1995 version.

REFERENCES

Abelson, R. (1976). Script processing in attitude formation and decision making. In J. Carroll & J. Payne (Eds.), *Cognition and social behavior* (pp. 33–45). Hillsdale, NJ: Lawrence Erlbaum.

Argyle, M. (1991). *Cooperation.* London: Routledge.

Ball-Rokeach, S. (1973). From pervasive ambiguity to definition of the situation. *Sociometry, 36,* 378–389.

Bargh, J. (1989). Conditional automaticity. In J. Uleman & J. Bargh (Eds.), *Unintended thought* (pp. 3–51). New York: Guilford.

Barnlund, D. (1962). Toward a meaning centered philosophy of communication. *Journal of Communication, 2,* 197–211.

Basso, K. H. (1979). *Portraits of "the whiteman": Linguistic play and cultural symbols among the western Apache.* Cambridge, UK: Cambridge University Press.

Baumeister, R., & Leary, M. (1995). The need to belong: Desire for interpersonal attachments as a fundamental human motive. *Psychological Bulletin, 117,* 497–529.

Bavelas, J., Black, A., Chovil, N., & Mullett, J. (1990). *Equivocal communication.* Newbury Park, CA: Sage.

Baxter, L. A. (1988). A dialectical perspective on communication strategies in relationship development. In S. Duck (Ed.), *Handbook of personal relationships* (pp. 257–273). London: Wiley.

Becker, E. (1971). *The birth and death of meaning.* New York: Harper & Row.

Bell, R. (1987). Social involvement. In J. McCroskey & J. Daly (Eds.), *Personality and interpersonal communication* (pp. 195–242). Newbury Park, CA: Sage.

Bellah, R., Madsen, R., Sullivan, W., Swidler, A., & Tipton, S. (1991). *The good society.* New York: Basic Books.

Berger, C. R. (1979). Beyond initial interactions. In H. Giles & R. St. Clair (Eds.), *Language and social psychology* (pp. 122–144). Oxford, UK: Blackwell.

Berger, C. R., & Bradac, J. (1982). *Language and social knowledge.* London: Edward Arnold.

Berger, C. R., & Calabrese, R. (1975). Some explorations in initial interactions and beyond: Toward a developmental theory of interpersonal communication. *Human Communication Research, 1,* 99–112.

Berger, J., Conner, T., & Fisek, M. (Eds.). (1974). *Expectation states: A theoretical research program.* Cambridge, MA: Winthrop.

Berscheid, E. (1985). Interpersonal attraction. In G. Lindzey & E. Aronson (Eds.), *The handbook of social psychology* (3rd ed., Vol. 2, pp. 413–484). New York: Random House.

Blalock, H. (1969). *Theory construction.* Englewood Cliffs, NJ: Prentice Hall.

Blanchard, F., Lilly, T., & Vaughn, I. (1991). Reducing the expression of racial prejudice. *Psychological Science, 2,* 101–105.

Brashers, D. (2001). Communication and uncertainty management. *Journal of Communication, 51,* 477–497.

Brewer, M. B. (1991). The social self. *Personality and Social Psychology Bulletin, 17,* 475–485.

Brewer, M. B., & Roccas, S. (2001). Individual values, social identity, and optimal distinctiveness. In C. Sedikides & M. B. Brewer (Eds.), *Individual self, relational self, collective self* (pp. 219–237). Philadelphia: Psychology Press.

Britt, T., Boniecki, K., Vescio, T., Biernot, M., & Brown, L. (1996). Intergroup anxiety: A person × situation approach. *Personality and Social Psychology Bulletin, 22,* 1177–1188.

Budner, S. (1962). Intolerance of ambiguity as a personality variable. *Journal of Personality, 30,* 29–50.

Burns, D. (1985). *Intimate connections.* New York: Signet.

Burns, D. (1989). *The feeling good handbook.* New York: William Morrow.

Burrell, G., & Morgan, G. (1979). *Sociological paradigms and organizational analysis.* London: Heinemann.

Byrne, D. (1971). *The attraction paradigm.* New York: Academic Press.

Choi, I., Nisbett, R., & Norenzayan, A. (1999). Causal attributions across cultures. *Psychological Bulletin, 125,* 47–63.

Clark, H. (1996). *Using language.* Cambridge, UK: Cambridge University Press.

Clark, H., & Marshall, C. (1981). Definite reference and mutual knowledge. In A. Joshi, B. Webber, & I. Sag (Eds.), *Elements of discourse understanding* (pp. 10–63). Cambridge, UK: Cambridge University Press.

Coleman, L., & DePaulo, B. (1991). Uncovering the human spirit: Moving beyond disability and "missed" communication. In N. Coupland, H. Giles, & J. Wiemann (Eds.), *"Miscommunication" and problematic talk* (pp. 61–84). Newbury Park, CA: Sage.

Cozzarelli, C., & Karafa, J. (1998). Cultural estrangement and terror management theory. *Personality and Social Psychology Bulletin, 24,* 253–267.

Crocker, J., & Luhtanen, R. (1990). Collective self-esteem and the ingroup bias. *Journal of Personality and Social Psychology, 58,* 60–67.

Crocker, J., Major, B., & Steele, C. (1998). Social stigma. In D. Gilbert, S. Fiske, & G. Lindsey (Eds.), *Handbook of social psychology* (4th ed., Vol. 2, pp. 504–553). New York: McGraw-Hill.

Crocker, J., Voekl, K., Testa, M., & Major, B. (1991). Social stigma: The affective consequences of attributional ambiguity. *Journal of Personality and Social Psychology, 60,* 218–228.

Csikszentmihalyi, M. (1990). *Flow: The psychology of optimal experience.* New York: Harper & Row.

Demerath, L. (1993). Knowledge-based affect. *Social Psychology Quarterly, 56,* 136–147.

Deutsch, M. (1973). *The resolution of conflict.* New Haven, CT: Yale University Press.

Devine, P. (1989). Stereotypes and prejudice: Their automatic and controlled components. *Journal of Personality and Social Psychology, 56,* 5–18.

Devine, P., Evett, S., & Vasquez-Suson, K. (1996). Exploring the interpersonal dynamics of intergroup contact. In R. Sorrentino & E. T. Higgins (Eds.), *Handbook of motivation and cognition* (Vol. 3, pp. 423–464). New York: Guilford.

Dijker, A. (1987). Emotional reactions to ethnic minorities. *European Journal of Social Psychology, 17,* 305–325.

Doise, W. (1986). *Levels of explanation in social psychology.* Cambridge, UK: Cambridge University Press.

Downey, H., Hellriegel, D., & Slocum, J. (1977). Individual characteristics as sources of

perceived uncertainty variability. *Human Relations, 30,* 161–174.

Dyal, J., & Dyal, R. (1981). Acculturation, stress, and coping. *International Journal of Intercultural Relations, 5,* 301–328.

Eisenberg, E. (1984). Ambiguity as a strategy in organizational communication. *Communication Monographs, 51,* 227–242.

Ellis, D. (1999). *Crafting selves: Ethnicity, class, and communication theory.* Mahwah, NJ: Lawrence Erlbaum.

Epstein, S. (1976). Anxiety arousal and the self-concept. In I. Sarason & C. Spielberger (Eds.), *Stress and anxiety* (Vol. 3, pp. 185–224). New York: John Wiley.

Fisher, R., & Brown, S. (1988). *Getting together: Building relationships as we negotiate.* Boston: Houghton Mifflin.

Fiske, S., & Morling, B. (1996). Stereotyping as a function of personal control motives and capacity constraints: The odd couple of power and anxiety. In R. Sorrentino & E. T. Higgins (Eds.), *Handbook of motivation and cognition* (Vol. 3, pp. 322–346). New York: Guilford.

Fiske, S., Morling, B., & Stevens, L. (1996). Controlling self and others: A theory of anxiety, mental control, and social control. *Personality and Social Psychology Bulletin, 22,* 115–123.

Frable, D., Blackstone, T., & Sherbaum, C. (1990). Marginal and mindful. *Journal of Personality and Social Psychology, 59,* 140–149.

French, J., & Raven, B. (1959). The basis of social power. In D. Cartwright (Ed.), *Studies in social power* (pp. 150–167). Ann Arbor, MI: Institute for Social Research.

Gaertner, S., Dovidio, J., Nier, J., Ward, C., & Banker, B. (1999). Across cultural divides: The value of a superordinate identity. In D. Prentice & D. Miller (Eds.), *Cultural divides* (pp. 173–212). New York: Russell Sage.

Gallois, C., Giles, H., Jones, F., Cargile, A., & Ota, H. (1995). Accommodating intercultural encounters. In R. Wiseman (Ed.), *Intercultural communication theory* (pp. 115–147). Thousand Oaks, CA: Sage.

Gao, G., & Gudykunst, W. B. (1990). Uncertainty, anxiety, and adaptation. *International Journal of Intercultural Relations, 14,* 301–317.

Gass, S., & Varonis, E. (1991). Miscommunication in nonnative speaker discourse. In N. Coupland, H. Giles, & J. Wiemann (Eds.), *"Miscommunication" and problematic talk* (pp. 121–145). Newbury Park, CA: Sage.

Gelfand, M., Spurlock, D., Smilzek, J., & Shao, L. (2000). Culture and social prediction. *Journal of Cross-Cultural Psychology, 31,* 498–516.

Giles, H., & Byrne, J. (1982). An intergroup approach to second language acquisition. *Journal of Multilingual and Multicultural Development, 3,* 17–40.

Giles, H., & Smith, P. (1979). Accommodation theory. In H. Giles & R. St. Clair (Eds.), *Language and social psychology* (pp. 45–65). Oxford, UK: Blackwell.

Goffman, E. (1959). *The presentation of self in everyday life.* Garden City, NY: Doubleday.

Goodwin, S., Operario, D., & Fiske, S. (1998). Situational power and interpersonal dominance facilitates bias and inequality. *Journal of Social Issues, 54,* 677–698.

Gouldner, A. (1960). The norm of reciprocity. *American Sociological Review, 25,* 161–179.

Greenland, K., & Brown, R. (1999). Categorization and intergroup anxiety in contact between British and Japanese nationals. *European Journal of Social Psychology, 29,* 503–521.

Greenland, K., & Brown, R. (2000). Categorization and intergroup anxiety in intergroup contact. In D. Capozza & R. Brown (Eds.), *Social identity processes* (pp. 167–183). London: Sage.

Grieve, P., & Hogg, M. (1999). Subjective uncertainty and intergroup discrimination in the minimal group situation. *Personality and Social Psychology Bulletin, 25,* 926–940.

Gudykunst, W. B. (1983). Uncertainty reduction and predictability of behavior in low- and high-context cultures. *Communication Quarterly, 31,* 49–55.

Gudykunst, W. B. (1985a). The influence of cultural similarity, type of relationship, and self-monitoring on uncertainty reduction processes. *Communication Monographs, 52,* 203–217.

Gudykunst, W. B. (1985b). A model of uncertainty reduction in intercultural encounters. *Journal of Language and Social Psychology, 4,* 79–98.

Gudykunst, W. B. (1985c). Normative power and conflict potential in intergroup relations. In W. B. Gudykunst, L. Stewart, &

S. Ting-Toomey (Eds.), *Communication, culture, and organizational processes* (pp. 155–176). Beverly Hills, CA: Sage.

Gudykunst, W. B. (1988). Uncertainty and anxiety. In Y. Y. Kim & W. B. Gudykunst (Eds.), *Theories in intercultural communication* (pp. 123–156). Newbury Park, CA: Sage.

Gudykunst, W. B. (1989). Culture and the development of interpersonal relationships. In J. Anderson (Ed.), *Communication yearbook 12* (pp. 315–354). Newbury Park, CA: Sage.

Gudykunst, W. B. (1990). Diplomacy: A special case of intergroup communication. In F. Korzenny & S. Ting-Toomey (Eds.), *Communicating for peace* (pp. 19–39). Newbury Park, CA: Sage.

Gudykunst, W. B. (1991). *Bridging differences: Effective intergroup communication.* Newbury Park, CA: Sage.

Gudykunst, W. B. (1993). Toward a theory of effective interpersonal and intergroup communication: An anxiety/uncertainty management perspective. In R. L. Wiseman & J. Koester (Eds.), *Intercultural communication competence* (pp. 33–71). Newbury Park, CA: Sage.

Gudykunst, W. B. (1995). Anxiety/uncertainty management (AUM) theory: Current status. In R. L. Wiseman (Ed.), *Intercultural communication theory* (pp. 8–58). Thousand Oaks, CA: Sage.

Gudykunst, W. B. (1998a). Applying anxiety/uncertainty management (AUM) theory to intercultural adjustment training. *International Journal of Intercultural Relations, 22,* 227–250.

Gudykunst, W. B. (1998b). *Bridging differences: Effective intergroup communication* (3rd ed.). Thousand Oaks, CA: Sage.

Gudykunst, W. B. (2002). Issues in cross-cultural communication research. In W. B. Gudykunst & B. Mody (Ed.), *Handbook of international and intercultural communication* (2nd ed., pp. 165–177). Thousand Oaks, CA: Sage.

Gudykunst, W. B., & Bond, M. H. (1997). Intergroup relations across cultures. In J. Berry, M. Segall, & C. Kagitçibisi (Eds.), *Handbook of cross-cultural psychology* (2nd ed., Vol. 3, pp. 119–161). Boston: Allyn & Bacon.

Gudykunst, W. B., Chua, E., & Gray, A. (1987). Cultural dissimilarities and uncertainty reduction processes. In M. McLaughlin (Ed.),

Communication yearbook 10 (pp. 456–469). Newbury Park, CA: Sage.

Gudykunst, W. B., Gao, G., Schmidt, K., Nishida, T., Bond, M. H., Leung, K., Wang, G., & Barraclough, R. (1992). The influence of individualism-collectivism, self-monitoring, and predicted outcome values on communication in ingroup and outgroup relationships. *Journal of Cross-Cultural Psychology, 23,* 196–213.

Gudykunst, W. B., & Hammer, M. R. (1988a). The influence of social identity and intimacy of interethnic relationships on uncertainty reduction processes. *Human Communication Research, 14,* 569–601.

Gudykunst, W. B., & Hammer, M. R. (1988b). Strangers and hosts. In Y. Y. Kim & W. B. Gudykunst (Eds.), *Cross-cultural adaptation* (pp. 106–139). Newbury Park, CA: Sage.

Gudykunst, W. B., & Kim, Y. Y. (1997). *Communicating with strangers* (3rd ed.). New York: McGraw-Hill.

Gudykunst, W. B., & Nishida, T. (1984). Individual and cultural influences on uncertainty reduction. *Communication Monographs, 51,* 23–36.

Gudykunst, W. B., & Nishida, T. (1986). Attributional confidence in low- and high-context cultures. *Human Communication Research, 12,* 525–549.

Gudykunst, W. B., & Nishida, T. (2001). Anxiety, uncertainty, and perceived effectiveness of communication across relationships and cultures. *International Journal of Intercultural Relations, 25,* 55–72.

Gudykunst, W. B., Nishida, T., & Chua, E. (1986). Uncertainty reduction in Japanese-North American dyads. *Communication Research Reports, 3,* 39–46.

Gudykunst, W. B., Nishida, T., & Chua, E. (1987). Perceptions of social penetration in Japanese-North American dyads. *International Journal of Intercultural Relations, 11,* 171–189.

Gudykunst, W. B., Nishida, T., Koike, H., & Shiino, N. (1986). The influence of language on uncertainty reduction. In M. McLaughlin (Ed.), *Communication yearbook 9* (pp. 555–575). Newbury Park, CA: Sage.

Gudykunst, W., B., Nishida, T., Morisaki, S., & Ogawa, N. (1999). The influence of students' personal and social identities on their perceptions of interpersonal and intergroup

encounters in Japan and the United States. *Japanese Journal of Social Psychology, 15,* 47–58.

Gudykunst, W. B., Nishida, T., & Schmidt, K. (1989). Cultural, relational, and personality influences on uncertainty reduction processes. *Western Journal of Speech Communication, 53,* 13–29.

Gudykunst, W. B., & Shapiro, R. (1996). Communication in everyday interpersonal and intergroup encounters. *International Journal of Intercultural Relations, 20,* 19–45.

Gudykunst, W. B., Sodetani, L., & Sonoda, K. (1987). Uncertainty reduction in Japanese-American/Caucasian relationships in Hawaii. *Western Journal of Speech Communication, 51,* 256–278.

Gudykunst, W. B., Yang, S.-M., & Nishida, T. (1985). A cross-cultural test of uncertainty reduction theory. *Human Communication Research, 11,* 407–454.

Guerrero, S., & Gudykunst, W. B. (1997). A thematic analysis of intergroup communication over time. *Intercultural Communication Studies, 6*(2), 43–76.

Gurin, P., Peng, T., Lopez, G., & Nagda, B. (1999). Context, identity, and intergroup relations. In D. Prentice & D. Miller (Eds.), *Cultural divides* (pp. 133–170). New York: Russell Sage.

Gutmann, A. (1992). Introduction. In A. Gutmann (Ed.), *Multiculturalism and "the politics of recognition"* (pp. 3–24). Princeton, NJ: Princeton University Press.

Hahn, T. N. (1975). *The miracle of mindfulness.* Boston: Beacon.

Halvari, H., & Gjesme, T. (1995). Trait and state anxiety before and after performance. *Perceptual Motor Skills, 81,* 1059–1074.

Hamill, J. (1990). *Ethno-logic: The anthropology of human reasoning.* Urbana: University of Illinois Press.

Hamilton, D., Sherman, S., & Ruvolo, C. (1990). Stereotype-based expectancies. *Journal of Social Issues, 46*(2), 35–60.

Hammer, M. R., Wiseman, R. L., Rasmussen, J., & Bruschke, J. (1998). A test of uncertainty/anxiety reduction theory: The intercultural adaptation context. *Communication Quarterly, 46,* 309–326.

Herman, S., & Schield, E. (1961). The stranger group in cross-cultural interaction. *Sociometry*, 24, 165–176.

Hofstede, G. (2001). *Culture's consequences* (2nd ed.). Thousand Oaks, CA: Sage.

Hogg, M., & Mullin, B. (1999). Joining groups to reduce uncertainty: Subjective uncertainty and group identification. In D. Abrams & M. Hogg (Eds.), *Social identity and social cognitions* (pp. 249–279). Oxford, UK: Blackwell.

Holmes, J., & Rempel, J. (1989). Trust in close relationships. In C. Hendrick (Ed.), *Close relationships* (pp. 187–220). Newbury Park, CA: Sage.

Hubbert, K. N., Gudykunst, W. B., & Guerrero, S. L. (1999). Intergroup communication over time. *International Journal of Intercultural Relations*, 23, 13–46.

Huber, G., & Sorentino, R. (1996). Uncertainty in interpersonal and intergroup relations. In R. Sorrentino & E. T. Higgins (Eds.), *Handbook of motivation and cognition* (Vol. 3, pp. 591–619). New York: Guilford.

Ickes, W. (1984). Composition in black and white. *Journal of Personality and Social Psychology*, 47, 330–341.

Islam, M. R., & Hewstone, M. (1993). Dimensions of contact as predictors of intergroup anxiety, perceived out-group variability, and out-group attitudes. *Personality and Social Psychology Bulletin*, 19, 700–710.

Jackson, J., & Smith, E. (1999). Conceptualizing social identity. *Personality and Social Psychology Bulletin*, 25, 120–135.

Janis, I. (1958). *Psychological stress*. New York: John Wiley.

Janis, I. (1971). *Stress and frustration*. New York: Harcourt Brace Jovanovich.

Janis, I. (1985). Stress inoculation in health care. In A. Monat & R. Lazarus (Eds.), *Stress and coping* (pp. 330–355). New York: Columbia University Press.

Johannesen, R. L. (2001). Communication ethics. In W. B. Gudykunst (Ed.), *Communication yearbook 25* (pp. 201–235). Mahwah, NJ: Lawrence Erlbaum.

Johnston, L., & Hewstone, M. (1990). Intergroup contact. In D. Abrams & M. Hogg (Eds.), *Social identity theory* (pp. 185–210). New York: Springer.

Keenan, E. (1976). The universality of conversational postulates. *Language in Society*, 5, 67–80.

Kennerley, H. (1990). *Managing anxiety*. New York: Oxford University Press.

Kim, M. S. (1994). Cross-cultural comparisons of the perceived importance of conversational constraints. *Human Communication Research*, 21, 128–151.

Kitayama, S., & Burstein, E. (1988). Automaticity in conversations. *Journal of Personality and Social Psychology*, 54, 219–224.

Kleinknecht, R., Dinnel, D., Kleinknecht, E., Hiruma, N., & Haroda, N. (1997). Cultural factors in social anxiety. *Journal of Anxiety Disorders*, 11, 157–177.

Kodiara, W. (2002). *The influence of self construals on anxiety and uncertainty management in Japan and the United States*. Unpublished master's thesis, California State University, Fullerton.

Kruglanski, A. (1989). *Lay epistemics and human knowledge*. New York: Plenum.

Laktos, I. (1970). Falsification and the methodology of scientific research programs. In I. Laktos & A. Musgrave (Eds.), *Criticism and the growth of knowledge* (pp. 91–196). Cambridge, UK: Cambridge University Press.

Langer, E. (1989). *Mindfulness*. Reading, MA: Addison-Wesley.

Langer, E. (1997). *The power of mindful learning*. Reading, MA: Addison-Wesley.

Lazarus, R. (1991). *Emotion and adaptation*. New York: Oxford University Press.

Leary, M., Kowalski, R., & Bergen, D. (1988). Interpersonal information acquisition and confidence in first encounters. *Personality and Social Psychology Bulletin*, 14, 68–77.

Lee, H. O., & Boster, F. (1991). Social information for uncertainty-reduction during initial interaction. In S. Ting-Toomey & F. Korzenny (Eds.), *Cross-cultural interpersonal communication* (pp. 189–212). Newbury Park, CA: Sage.

Leung, K., & Bond, M. H. (1989). On the empirical identification of dimensions for cross-cultural comparisons. *Journal of Cross-Cultural Psychology*, 20, 133–151.

Levine, D. (1985). *The flight from ambiguity*. Chicago: University of Chicago Press.

Lieberson, S. (1985). *Making it count: The improvement of social research and theory*. Berkeley: University of California Press.

Lim, T.-S., & Choi, S.-H. (1996). Interpersonal relationships in Korea. In W. B. Gudykunst, S. Ting-Toomey, & T. Nishida (Eds.), *Communication in personal relationships across cultures* (pp. 122–136). Thousand Oaks, CA: Sage.

Linville, P., Fischer, G., & Salovey, P. (1989). Perceived distribution of the characteristics of ingroup and outgroup members. *Journal of Personality and Social Psychology, 57*, 165–188.

Luhtanen, R., & Crocker, J. (1992). A collective self-esteem scale. *Personality and Social Psychology Bulletin, 18*, 302–318.

Markus, H., & Kitayama, S. (1991). Culture and the self. *Psychological Review, 98*, 224–253.

Marris, P. (1996). *The politics of uncertainty.* New York: Routledge.

May, R. (1977). *The meaning of anxiety.* New York: Ronald.

McLeod, J., & Chaffee, S. (1973). Interpersonal approach to communication research. *American Behavioral Scientist, 16*, 469–499.

McPherson, K. (1983). Opinion-related information seeking. *Personality and Social Psychology Bulletin, 9*, 116–124.

Miller, G., & Steinberg, M. (1975). *Between people.* Chicago: Science Research Associates.

Morris, M. (1981). *Saying and meaning in Puerto Rico.* Oxford, UK: Pergamon.

Naiman, N., Frohlich, M., Stern, H., & Todesco, A. (1978). *The good language learner.* Toronto: Ontario Institute for Studies in Education.

Nisbett, R. (2003). *The geography of thought.* New York: Free Press.

Norenzayan, A., Choi, I., & Nisbett, R. (1999). Eastern and Western perspectives of causality for social behavior. In D. Prentice & D. Miller (Eds.), *Cultural divides* (pp. 239–272). New York: Russell Sage.

Norenzayan, A., Choi, I., & Nisbett, R. (2002). Cultural similarities and differences in social inference. *Personality and Social Psychology Bulletin, 28*, 109–120.

O'Keefe, D., & Sypher, H. (1981). Cognitive complexity measures and the relationship of cognitive complexity to communication. *Human Communication Research, 8*, 72–92.

Optow, S. (1990). Moral exclusion and injustice: An introduction. *Journal of Social Issues, 46*(1), 1–20.

Parks, M., & Adelman, M. (1983). Communication networks and the development of romantic relationships. *Human Communication Research, 10*, 55–80.

Pickersgill, M., & Owen, A. (1972). Mood-states, recall and subjective comprehensibility of medical information in non-patient volunteers. *Personality and Individual Differences, 13*, 1299–1305.

Pilisuk, M. (1963). Anxiety, self acceptance and open-mindedness. *Journal of Clinical Psychology, 19*, 386–391.

Planalp, S., Rutherford, D., & Honeycutt, J. (1988). Events that increase uncertainty in personal relationships II. *Human Communication Research, 14*, 516–547.

Plant, E., & Devine, P. (2003). The antecedents and implications of interracial anxiety. *Personality and Social Psychology Bulletin, 29*, 790–801.

Powers, W., & Lowry, D. (1984). Basic communication fidelity. In R. Bostrom (Ed.), *Competence in communication* (pp. 57–71). Beverly Hills, CA: Sage.

Pritchard, M. (1991). *On becoming responsible.* Lawrence: University of Kansas Press.

Rahula, W. (1974). *What the Buddha taught.* New York: Grove-Weidenfeld.

Reynolds, P. (1971). *A primer in theory construction.* Indianapolis, IN: Bobbs-Merrill.

Riezler, K. (1960). The social psychology of fear. In M. Stein, A. Vidich, & D. White (Eds.), *Identity and anxiety* (pp. 144–156). Glencoe, IL: Free Press.

Roccas, S., & Brewer, M. B. (2002). Social identity complexity. *Personality and Social Psychology Review, 6*, 88–106.

Rogers, E. (1999). Georg Simmel's concept of the stranger and intercultural communication research. *Communication Theory, 9*, 58–74.

Rogers, E., & Kincaid, D. L. (1981). *Communication networks.* New York: Free Press.

Rosenberg, M. (1979). *Conceiving the self.* New York: Basic Books.

Sampson, E. (1993). *Celebrating the other.* Boulder, CO: Westview.

Schlenker, B., & Leary, M. (1982). Social anxiety and social presentation. *Psychological Bulletin, 92*, 641–669.

Schneiderman, L. (1960). Repression, anxiety and the self. In M. Stein, A. Vidich, & D. White

(Eds.), *Identity and anxiety* (pp. 157–165). Glencoe, IL: Free Press.

Selznick, P. (1992). *The moral commonwealth.* Berkeley: University of California Press.

Simard, L., Taylor, D., & Giles, H. (1976). Attributional processes and interpersonal accommodation in a bilingual setting. *Language and Speech, 19,* 374–387.

Simmel, G. (1908/1950). The stranger. In K. Wolff (Ed. & Trans.), *The sociology of Georg Simmel* (pp. 402–408). New York: Free Press.

Smiley, M. (1992). *Moral responsibility and the boundaries of community.* Chicago: University of Chicago Press.

Smock, C. (1955). The influence of psychological stress on the intolerance of ambiguity. *Journal of Abnormal and Social Psychology, 50,* 177–182.

Sodetani, L., & Gudykunst, W. B. (1987). The effects of surprising events on intercultural relationships. *Communication Research Reports, 4*(2), 1–6.

Solomon, S., Greenberg, J., & Pyszczynski, T. (1991). A terror management theory of social behavior. In M. Zanna (Ed.), *Advances in experimental social psychology* (Vol. 23, pp. 93–159). New York: Academic Press.

Sorrentino, R., Hodson, G., & Huber, G. (2001). Uncertainty orientation and the social mind. In J. Forgas, K. Williams, & L. Wheeler (Eds.), *The social mind* (pp. 199–227). Cambridge, UK: Cambridge University Press.

Sorrentino, R., & Roney, C. (1999). *The uncertain mind: Individual differences in facing the unknown.* London: Psychology Press.

Sorrentino, R., & Short, J. (1986). Uncertainty orientation, motivation, and cognition. In R. Sorrentino & E. T. Higgins (Eds.), *Handbook of motivation and cognition* (Vol. 1, pp. 379–403). New York: Guilford.

Staub, E. (1989). *The roots of evil.* New York: Cambridge University Press.

Stephan, W., & Finlay, K. (1999). The role of empathy in improving intergroup relations. *Journal of Social Issues, 55,* 729–743.

Stephan, W., & Stephan, C. (1985). Intergroup anxiety. *Journal of Social Issues, 41*(3), 157–166.

Stephan, W., & Stephan, C. (1989). Antecedent to intergroup anxiety in Asian-Americans and Hispanic-Americans. *International Journal of Intercultural Relations, 13,* 203–219.

Stephan, W., & Stephan, C. (1992). Reducing intercultural anxiety through intercultural contact. *International Journal of Intercultural Relations, 16,* 89–106.

Stevens, L., & Fiske, S. (1995). Motivation and cognition in social life: A social survival perspective. *Social Cognition, 13,* 189–214.

Sunnafrank, M., & Miller, G. (1981). The role of initial conversation in determining attraction to similar and dissimilar strangers. *Human Communication Research, 8,* 16–25.

Suzuki, S. (1970). *Sen mind, beginner's mind.* New York: Weatherhill.

Tajfel, H. (1978). Social categorization, social identity, and social comparisons. In H. Tajfel (Ed.), *Differentiation between groups* (pp. 61– 76). London: Academic Press.

Tajfel, H. (1981). *Human categories and social groups.* Cambridge, UK: Cambridge University Press.

Taylor, C. (1992). The politics of recognition. In A. Gutmann (Ed.), *Multiculturalism and "the politics of recognition"* (pp. 25–74). Princeton, NJ: Princeton University Press.

Tesser, A. (1980). When individual dispositions and social pressures conflict: A catastrophe. *Human Relations, 33,* 393–407.

Tominaga, J., Gudykunst, W. B., & Ota, H. (2003, May). *Perceptions of effective communication in the United States and Japan.* Paper presented at the International Communication Association convention, San Diego.

Tracey, K. (2002). *Everyday talk: Building and reflecting identities.* New York: Guilford.

Triandis, H. C. (1977). *Interpersonal behavior.* Monterey, CA: Brooks/Cole.

Triandis, H. C. (1995). *Individualism & collectivism.* Boulder, CO: Westview.

Triandis, H. C., McCusker, C., & Hui, C. H. (1990). Multimethod probes of individualism and collectivism. *Journal of Personality and Social Psychology, 59,* 1006–1020.

Tuan, Y.-F. (1979). *Landscapes of fear.* New York: Pantheon.

Turner, J. C., Hogg, M., Oakes, P., Reicher, S., & Wetherell, M. (1987). *Rediscovering the social group.* London: Blackwell.

Turner, J. H. (1988). *A theory of social interaction.* Palo Alto, CA: Stanford University Press.

Turner, R. H. (1987). Articulating self and social structure. In K. Yardley & T. Honess (Eds.), *Self and society* (pp. 119–132). Chichester, UK: Wiley.

Van Lear, C. A. (1991). Testing a cyclical model of communicative openness in relationship development. *Communication Monographs, 58,* 337–361.

Walbott, H., & Scherer, K. (1986). How universal and specific is emotional experience: Evidence from 27 countries on five continents. *Social Science Information, 25,* 763–796.

Watts, A. (1951). *The wisdom of insecurity.* New York: Pantheon.

Weick, K. (1979). *The social psychology of organizing* (2nd ed.). Reading, MA: Addison-Wesley.

Wilder, D. (1993). The role of anxiety in facilitating stereotypic judgment of outgroup behavior. In D. Mackie & D. Hamilton (Eds.), *Affect, cognition, and stereotyping* (pp. 87–109). New York: Academic Press.

Wilder, D., & Allen, V. (1978). Group membership and preference for information about others. *Personality and Social Psychology Bulletin, 4,* 106–110.

Wilder, D., & Shapiro, P. (1989). Effects of anxiety on impression formation in a group context. *Journal of Experimental Social Psychology, 25,* 481–499.

Witte, K. (1993). A theory of cognition and negative affect: Extending Gudykunst and Hammer's theory of uncertainty and anxiety. *International Journal of Intercultural Relations, 17,* 197–216.

Worchel, S., & Coutant, D. (1997). The tangled web of loyalty. In D. Bar-Tal & E. Staub (Eds.), *Patriotism in the life of individuals and nations* (pp. 190–210). Chicago: Nelson-Hall.

Word, C., Zanna, M., & Cooper, J. (1974). The nonverbal mediation of self-fulfilling prophecies. *Journal of Experimental Social Psychology, 10,* 109–120.

14

Association and Dissociation

A Contextual Theory of Interethnic Communication

YOUNG YUN KIM

Any jackass can kick a barn door down, but it takes a carpenter to build one.

Sam Rayburn (1882–1961)

THE PROBLEM

The 20th-century United States was a century of a gradual ideological shift. The relatively simple civic consensus in the vision of *E Pluribus Unum* has been increasingly challenged by one that upholds ethnic identity side by side, if not in place of, the larger identity of American citizenry. Accompanying this change has been the unfortunate us-against-them posturing of identity politics that dominated daily media reports. Higher education has figured prominently in the nation's struggle toward racial and ethnic equality and integration. Yet, efforts for a greater diversity of the faculty, student body, and curriculum also have met unintended consequences of ethnic

hypersensitivity, self-segregation, and cries of reverse discrimination.

Classical Liberalism and Its Discontent

The continuing discord surrounding issues of ethnicity can be traced to the dilemma inherent in *classical liberalism,* the founding political philosophy in the Enlightenment tradition. Enshrined in the Declaration of Independence, the Constitution, and the Bill of Rights, ideals of classical liberalism constitute the core of the traditional American ethos (Rorty, 1998). Central to this ideology is *individualism,* "the social priority of the individual vis-à-vis the State, the established Church, social classes . . . or other social groups" (Abercrombie, 1980, p. 56)—an ideology that celebrates individual achievement, self-reliance, and personal responsibility. Individualism recognizes and values the fact that "we are all different," and questions the validity and morality of categorical thought. An important correlate of individualism, thus, is *universalism*, a view of human nature presupposing social categories such as ethnicity that is embodied in such cultural values as equal rights afforded to all individuals as the requisite of a free and democratic society.

The liberal themes of individualism and universalism are further linked to the theme of *procedural equality*, that is, equal rights and equal opportunities afforded to all individuals in the form of human rights—the basic requisite of a free and democratic society. Enshrined in the Declaration of Independence, the Constitution, the Bill of Rights, and democratic and capitalistic institutions, these and related liberal principles constitute the core of the American cultural ethos, projecting a vision of American society that seeks to transcend a monolithic tribal ancestral and territorial condition. Essayist Henry Grunwald (1976) captures this liberal tradition in a bicentennial essay:

> The U.S. was not born in a tribal conflict, like so many other nations, but in a conflict over principles. Those principles were thought to be universal, which was part of the reason for the unprecedented policy of throwing the new country open to all comers. (p. 35)

Assimilationism as a perspective on interethnic relations directly reflects the classical liberal ethos of individualism, universalism, and procedural equality. It seeks to transcend a tribal, ancestral, and territorial condition. Even though each person is unique, all humans are regarded as being endowed with the same set of fundamental rights and responsibilities. Prejudice directed against a particular social group, ethnic or otherwise, is wrong not only because it is irrational but also because its focus

on social categories contravenes the intellectual or moral prescription to value the unique qualities of the individual. Assimilationism advocates the primacy of *individual identity,* and its universal expression, *American identity,* that is equated with *human identity.* Reflecting this view is the universalistic ideal of a color-blind society: What is ultimately desirable is the relationship between individuals in which everyone is treated as an individual, a fellow American citizen, and a fellow human being. Assimilationism calls for the *conversion* of alien or indigenous minority cultures into a mainstream cultural tradition and the accompanying fusion of diverse elements.

The traditional assimilationist ideals, however, have been challenged by advocates of *pluralism*. Pluralism has been a response to the inevitable gap between the ideals of classical liberalism that underpins assimilationism and the reality of everyday life not measuring up to the ideals. The seed of the contradiction is the awareness that the ideals of individualism, universalism, and procedural equality are not always applied to those of traditionally nondominant group backgrounds. Pluralism challenges the status quo of Anglo-European conformity (Gordon, 1981) and the ideological underpinnings of the primacy of individual identity with contrary claims *of group identity.* Underlying this group-based construction of personhood and society is the worldview of *relativism*, which de-emphasizes universalities while highlighting group difference and insisting on the *status equality* of all groups. At least to some pluralists, then, the very notion of assimilative conversion is seen as an unjust imposition of the dominant culture on minority groups, rather than an expression of the universal and transcendental ideal of individualism.

The full spectrum of the American ideological landscape includes the marginal voices of *separatism*, often characterized as *extremism*. Whereas most assimilationists and integrationists commonly adhere to the societal goal of interethnic integration (while disagreeing on specific visions as to how to achieve this goal), extremist messages frequently express a preference for *maximum ingroup-outgroup separation*. In some cases, the claim of equal and distinct identity tends to manifest itself in tendencies of extreme *collective self-glorification* and of *denigration of other groups,* and even violence. Some of the readily identifiable separatist messages come from those identified with "extreme Right" or "extreme Left" groups. Although not always explicit, separatist views can be easily inferred from the inflammatory rhetorical devices employed to condemn or scapegoat an outgroup or to position the *ingroup as perpetual victims.*

The Focus

Amid the contentious polemics of ethnic identity, one can easily overlook the fact that the traditional ideal of transcending ethnic categories continues to be the core organizing principle for "middle America." Straddling the pole of traditional assimilationism and the counter-pole of pluralism, the majority of Americans struggle to reconcile heated ideological polemics (Kim, 1999). Theirs is an ideological position commonly referred to as *integrationism,* which emphasizes the need to accommodate the ideals of pluralism into those of assimilationism. Integrationist voices search for some kind of *reconciliation,* a position that seeks mutual tolerance, accommodation, and balance, as well as ambivalence and contradiction.

This assessment is consistent with Wolfe's (1998) characterization of "the new middle-class morality" (p. 309). Based on 200 in-depth interviews conducted in the Boston, Atlanta, Tulsa, and San Diego metropolitan areas, Wolfe finds "little support for the notion that middle-class Americans are engaged in bitter cultural conflict with one another" (p. 278). Instead, they are "struggling to find ways in which their core beliefs can be reconciled with experiences that seem to contradict them" (p. 281), while insisting on a set of values "capacious enough to be inclusive but

demanding enough to uphold standards of personal responsibility" (p. 322). Wolfe's conclusion is supported by findings from the author's own study (Kim, Kim, Duty, & Yoshitake, 2002; Kim, McClure, Ogawa, & Kim, 2003; Kim, Ogawa, Rainwater, & Kim, 2003) among undergraduate and graduate university students, as well as nonstudent adults in central Oklahoma. Results of this study show a generally positive feeling toward one's own ethnic background and toward one's American identity, a high level of willingness to socialize with people of differing ethnicities, and a moderate ideology of integrationism located in the middle of the assimilationism-pluralism continuum.

The reality of interethnic relations in middle America—not the acrimonious and sensationalized "culture war" media image—is the main interest being served by this theory. This reality is found every day in neighborhoods, workplaces, schools, and college campuses as the mainstay of the American social fabric. *With this general aim, the author's attention is trained on the interethnic behavior of individual communicators in order to develop a systematic way of understanding the various ways interethnic communication plays out at the grassroots level.* Issues of ethnicity and interethnic relations have been part and parcel, and a logical extension, of this author's research on the cross-cultural adaptation process of individuals in an unfamiliar cultural or subcultural environment (see Chapter 17 in this volume). Given the overlapping and adjacent two conceptual domains, cross-cultural adaptation and interethnic communication, the author's research on the former has generated empirical insights into intra- and interethnic communication patterns, setting the groundwork for the present theory. As well, this work is a natural outgrowth of the author's personal transformation over the past three decades—from a newcomer to American society striving for successful adaptation, to an insider who has come to care deeply about the national struggle to move forward toward "a more perfect union."

An Interdisciplinary Integration

Even a casual reading of the literature dealing with issues of ethnicity, race, and interethnic relations leaves no doubt that the field is vast and varied. Reflecting the potency of interethnic issues is the substantial amount of attention that has been received by social scientists since the beginning of the 20th century (e.g., Simmel, 1908/1950; Schuetz, 1944). Even though the field today offers an extensive and rich body of theoretical and empirical insights, such insights are largely focused on a limited number of variables within a single theme and examine the interrelationships between/among variables within a single level of analysis (e.g., the individual level).

The majority of theoretical interests in this body of literature involve an *individual-level analysis of psychological factors and their interrelationships*. Among the most frequently investigated psychological factors are: (1) cognitive factors such as ethnic or interethnic perception, racial beliefs, knowledge/ignorance, stereotyping, and attribution errors (e.g., Detweiler, 1986); (2) affective-motivational-attitudinal factors such as attitudes toward specific ethnic groups, tolerance, prejudice, ethnocentrism, and racism (e.g., Bonilla-Silva & Forman, 2000); (3) various facets of ethnic identity, including the level of ethnic commitment, sense of security or insecurity, and positive or negative feelings toward the ethnic group (e.g., Jacobs, 1992); (4) verbal and non-verbal behavior in interethnic encounters (e.g., Greenberg, Kirkland, & Pyszczynski, 1988); and (5) interethnic friendship and romantic relationship (e.g., Mack et al., 1997).

Beyond the studies focusing on individual-level psychological factors are the studies investigating *interpersonal and organizational factors* and their influence on one or more psychological factors. Among the most salient such factors are goal interdependence (e.g., Johnson, Johnson, & Maruyama, 1984),

cooperative/competitive relationship (e.g., Worchel, 1986), and status/power differential (e.g., Sachdev & Bourhis, 1987) as key relational characteristics influencing the psychological orientations of individual communicators (such as positive or negative attitudes, liking, and attraction). Other studies have focused on *macro-level intergroup phenomena* such as intergroup coalitions (e.g., Chesler, 1988; Tchen, 1990), the nature of dominant or non-dominant group status in society (e.g., Martin, 2000), racism in mass media (Corea, 1990), and the "distortion" of communication brought about by the dominance of one language over another (Tsuda, 1986).

Attempts have been made to provide a connecting link that would enable social scientists to relate person to person, person to groups, and groups to the wider social order and offer a more broadly based, multiple-level understanding of interethnic relations. Amir's (1969) "contact hypothesis," for example, links the degree of cooperative interethnic contact to conflict reduction and positive attitude development over time. Cook (1978) elaborates on Amir's theory, specifying a number of situational contingencies (e.g., characteristics of the contact situation such as equal status within the situation, opportunities to disconfirm prevailing outgroup stereotypes) on the general hypothesis that association between members of different ethnic groups will lead to an increase in liking and respect for outgroup members. Among other major integrative efforts are social identity theory of intergroup relations (Tajfel, 1974; Tajfel & Turner, 1986) and communication accommodation theory (Gallois, Giles, Jones, Cargile, & Ota, 1995).

The present theory echoes and builds on many of the existing integrative efforts. Focusing on the interethnic behavior of a single communicator, the present theory integrates and consolidates many of the existing theoretical ideas, concepts, and research findings into a set of new, more inclusive constructs.

Interethnic Communication: A Definition

The concept, ethnicity, has been approached as a group-level phenomenon in anthropological and sociological studies. Cultural anthropologists conceive ethnicity as a kind of temporal continuity or common tradition linking its members to a common future (Nash, 1989), reflected in the *communal life patterns* associated with language, behavior, norms, beliefs, myths, and values, as well as the forms and practices of social institutions. In sociological research, the complex conceptual entity of ethnicity has been operationalized in terms of a *social category* defined by membership that is differentiated from other groups by a set of objective characteristics, qualities, or conditions such as national origin, language, religion, race, and culture. This is the way, for instance, sociologists such as Glazer and Moynihan (1975) investigated the phenomenon of "ethnic stratification" in the United States.

Psychological studies, on the other hand, have approached ethnicity in terms of "the subjective orientation of an individual toward his or her ethnic origins" (Alba, 1990, p. 25). Terms such as *ethnic identity, ethnolinguistic identity,* or *ethnic identification* are, then, interchangeably used to replace ethnicity per se in most social psychological studies of intergroup behavior. Sherif's (1966) realistic conflict theory, for example, postulates that intergroup behavior occurs "whenever individuals belonging to one group interact, collectively or individually, with another group or its members in terms of their group identification" (p. 12). For De Vos (1990b), ethnic identity is rooted in "the emotionally profound 'self'-awareness of parentage and a concomitant mythology of discrete origin" (p. 14). It provides "a sense of common origin, as well as common beliefs and values, or common values" and serves as the basis of "self-defining in-groups" (De Vos, 1990a, p. 204).

All three approaches to ethnicity—anthropological, sociological, and psychological—are incorporated in the present theory. Taking the individual communicator's point of view, the author regards a communication event to be an interethnic one whenever the communicator perceives himself or herself to be different from the other interactant(s) in terms of ethnicity, ethnic group membership, and/or ingroup identification.

CONCEPTUAL GROUNDING

From a general systems perspective (e.g., Bertalanffy, 1955/1975; Ford & Lerner, 1992), each interethnic communication event is conceived as an open system that consists of subsystems (or elements) that are functionally interdependent. This systemic conception is consistent with a number of methodological perspectives commonly known as contextualism, pragmatism, or ecological psychology (e.g., Bateson, 1972; Givón, 1989; Ruesch & Bateson, 1951/1968; Watzlawick, Beavin, & Jackson, 1967). In particular, the present open-systems conception of interethnic communication highlights the interface of multilayered contextual forces surrounding a particular interethnic behavior. The behavior and the context are viewed as coconstituting the basic interethnic communication system, operating simultaneously in a dynamic interplay. Interethnic communication is, thus, treated not as a specific analytic unit (or variable), but as the entirety of an event in which the behavior and the context are taken together into a theoretical "fusion" (Fielding & Fielding, 1986), emphasizing the unitary nature of psychological and social processes. As Cronen, Chen, and Pearce (1988) put it, "all communication practices point beyond themselves to (and derive their meaning from) sets of contexts" (p. 67). In Bateson's (1972) words, "without context, there is no communication" (p. 402). In Givón's (1989) metaphor, "A picture is not fully specified unless its frame is also specified" (p. 2).

A Matrix of Interethnic Communication

From this open-systems perspective, the present theory examines interethnic communication in its simplest and most general form: a single person communicating. As such, the communicator's behavior or activity (or a series of behaviors or activities) constitutes the "stuff" of the communication event or the "what" and "how" of the messages sent and received. At the same time, the conditions that "surround" the communication behavior comprise the context, or "covert factors" (Von Raffler-Engel, 1988), that shape, as well as are shaped by, the behavior. Silently present in the context of this single-person interethnic communication system, of course, is one or more persons with whom the focal communicator interacts. Temporality, also, is built into this communication system, even though it is treated as "frozen" for the sake of analysis—rather like a motion picture is stopped so that it can be studied one frame at a time.

Figure 14.1 depicts this basic interethnic communication system. Organized as a hierarchical arrangement constructed of a progression of multiple levels of context, the model serves as a transactional matrix represented as a set of circles. Each level acts as a meta-level context for the sublevel(s) embedded in it. A communicator is himself or herself the innermost micro-level context, which is nested in an immediate social context, referred to here as the situation. The situation, in turn, is nested in a larger environmental context. The first layer of the context, the communicator, is the densest locus of structure that guides, and is guided by, the communicator's encoding and decoding activities. At this level, we are interested in what is traditionally called the mind, which organizes and processes incoming verbal and nonverbal information into forms of meaningful messages. The next contextual layer, the situation, is created when the communicator interfaces with one or more persons, either face to face or through various mediating channels from point-to-point

channels such as a computer, fax, telephone, and letter, to more public mass media channels including radio, television, and newspapers. Beyond the situational level is the larger social milieu, the environment. The environmental context includes many sublevels—from the micro-level suborganizational (e.g., an academic department or a neighborhood) and organizational (e.g., a university or a town) social entities to larger sociocultural milieus (e.g., a region, a nation, and an international relationship involving two or more nations).

Together, the behavior and the three layers of the context coconstitute a communication event in which all components operate in a reciprocal relationship of "stimulus and response" rather than a one-directional cause and effect. In varying degrees of salience and significance, all contextual forces operate in a given communication event as arising through and being sustained and altered by behavior, and vice versa. The three levels of context (and the many sublevels thereof) are sets of "gradation, continuum and non-discreteness" (Givón, 1989, p. 5). Because one level acts as the meta-level and/or the sublevel in this approach, this conceptual scheme is to be viewed as one of "mapping" or a "rigorous metaphor" (Bateson, 1972, p. 404), or one that serves as a simplified but holistic approximation of the dynamics of interethnic communication from the perspective of a single communicator.

Assumptions

The above conceptualization is summarized below in three assumptions. These assumptions serve as the foundational ideas, based on which interethnic communication is described and explained in the present theory.

Assumption 1. Interethnic communication occurs whenever a communicator sees himself or herself and the other involved party in light of the respective ethnicity and/or ethnic identity.

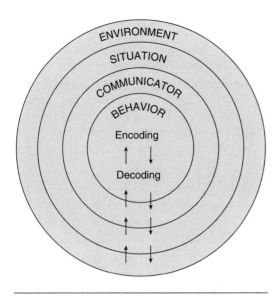

Figure 14.1   A Contextual Model of
Interethnic Communication

Assumption 2. Interethnic communication is an open system in which its components are functionally interdependent.

Assumption 3. Interethnic communication by a single communicator consists of the behavior (or action) and three layers of the context—the communicator, the situation, and the environment.

THE BEHAVIOR

The behavior, the focus of this theory, consists of various actions and reactions of a communicator involved in interethnic interactions. Communication behavior is defined broadly to include not only overtly observable (external) actions and reactions, but also covert (internal) actions and reactions. Communication behavior always involves intrapersonal behavior internal to the communicator. In the present system's perspective, all the external, observable behaviors are referred to as activities of verbal and nonverbal message *encoding*. The term *decoding* is employed to represent all the "private symbolization" (Ruben, 1975) activities that accompany encoding activities.

Elements of Dissociative Behavior

A widely investigated aspect of decoding is the *categorization* of information about or from outgroup members. Social identity theory posits that such group identification serves as both cognitive and motivational underpinnings of interethnic behavior. Group identification arises, first of all, from basic cognitive processes of social categorization. Although almost all sources of variation among human beings can be conceived of as continuous dimensions, there is a strong tendency to simplify our cognitive representations of the social world by dividing persons into discrete social categories; that is, to perceive outgroup members as "undifferentiated items in a unified social category" and not as individuals (Turner, 1982, p. 28). Once such categories have been defined and labeled, processes of *stereotyping* and *category accentuations* are set into motion. Distinction is made between ingroups ("us") and outgroups ("them"), leading to the tendency to *accentuate differences* or *de-accentuate similarities* (Oddou & Mendenhal, 1984) as well as a tendency toward *depersonalization* or *de-individuation* (Tajfel, 1970). Such categorical cognitive behavior constrains interethnic communication because it creates self-fulfilling prophecies prompting us to see behavior that confirms our expectations even when it is absent (Hamilton, Sherman, & Ruvolo, 1990).

In addition, inaccurate attribution (message interpretation) has been identified as a conspicuous feature of dissociative decoding behavior (Jaspars & Hewstone, 1982). This notion comes from attribution theorists such as Heider (1958) who proposed that the behavior of a person could be causally linked to the actor's personality, to the environment, or to a combination of both. Subsequent research has shown a tendency for people to underestimate the importance of situational causes in making inferences about others' negative behavior, an effect labeled the fundamental attribution error by L. Ross (1977).

The fundamental attribution error becomes what Pettigrew (1979) calls the *ultimate attribution error* when it involves a positive bias toward one's group and a negative bias toward outgroup members. Relatedly, Hewstone (1988) explains intergroup misattribution using the concept, *vicarious personalism.* Defining vicarious personalism as "one group's perception that the other group's actions are aimed specifically at them," Hewstone argues that this kind of attributional error or bias with respect to an outgroup is likely to encourage a hostile view of the outgroup and negative expectations for outgroup members' behaviors. Similarly, Hopper (1986) employs the term *Shibboleth schema,* based on a biblical tale, to illustrate the tendency of prejudicial listening—a tendency to interpret dialectic differences as being defective and an object of hostility and discrimination. Volkan (1992) adds yet another concept, *projection,* a tendency that leads to ego-defensive reactions such as feelings of inferiority or superiority, avoidance, suspicion, and paranoia.

The above elements of dissociative decoding behavior are theoretically linked to a number of overt encoding behaviors. Among the most salient dissociative verbal behaviors is *prejudiced talk* (e.g., Herbst, 1997; Van Dijk, 1987), with varying degrees of emotional intensity and explicitness, from the subtle expressions such as "you people" to more blatant uses of *ethnophaulism* (Ehrlich, 1973) or derogatory and dehumanizing ethnic labels and ethnic jokes, commonly known today as *hate speech* (e.g., Kirkland, Greenberg, & Pyszczynski, 1987). Similar observations have been made regarding a wide range of nonverbal expressions of *communicative distance* (Lukens, 1979), from tense voice tone, physical distance, avoidance of eye contact, and frozen facial expressions, to the more explicit nonverbal expressions and actions of anger, hatred, and aggression such as spitting, cross burning, flag burning, and rioting, to extreme acts of violence.

Elements of Associative Behavior

The above-described concepts indicating interethnic dissociation are counterbalanced by concepts characterizing associative decoding, such as cognitive *differentiation* (Brewer & Miller, 1988), *multiple categorization* (e.g., Crisp, Hewstone, & Rubin, 2001), *decategorization* (Billig, 1987), *recategorization* (Brewer & Gaertner, 2001), and *wide categorization* (Detweiler, 1986). Langer (1989) employs a more global term, *mindfulness,* to describe the pattern of perception and thought that seeks a finer cognitive discrimination and more creative ways of interpreting messages about and from outgroup members. Also useful to understanding associative encoding behavior is the notion of *message complexity* (Applegate & Sypher, 1988), which generally requires speakers to recognize another person's perspectives and is reflected in *person-centered messages* that contain high-quality responsiveness and concern for relational cohesion. Such behavioral characteristics are consistent with the meaning of *convergent behavior* in communication accommodation theory (Gallois et al., 1995). In addition, Kim (1991) places cognitive, affective, and operational *adaptation* of one's own behavior so as to enhance synchrony (Kim, 1992)—a quality of relational cohesion and mutuality.

The Association-Dissociation Continuum: Axioms

By and large, researchers employing the above-described concepts have focused either on associative behavior or on dissociative behavior. Given that the two groups of concepts represent the semantic opposites of each other, they are integrated into a single continuum in the present theory. Behaviors close to the associative end of this continuum facilitate the communication process by increasing the likelihood of understanding, cooperation, and the "coming together" of the involved parties into some kind of an at least temporary cooperative

Table 14.1   Existing Concepts Related to the Two Themes of Associative-Dissociative Interethnic Behavior

Themes	Associative Behavior	Dissociative Behavior
Individuation-Categorization	Differentiation	Stereotyping
	Decategorization	Deindividuation
	Recategorization	Category accentuation
	Wide categorization	Narrow categorization
	Mindfulness	Mindlessness
	Person-centered message	Depersonalization
		Projection
Consonance-Dissonance	Accentuate similarities	Accentuate differences
	Convergence	Divergence
	Adaptation	Communicative distance
	Synchronization	Vicarious personalism
		Shibboleth schema
		Prejudiced talk
		Ethnophaulism
		Hate speech

relationship. Comparatively, behaviors at the dissociative end tend to contribute to misunderstanding, competition, and an at least temporary "coming apart" of the relationship. As such, associative and dissociative behaviors are not two mutually exclusive categories, but vary in the degree of opposite relational functions.

Emerging from the many different terms described above are two main themes corresponding to the associative-dissociative continuum: (1) individuation-categorization and (2) consonance-dissonance. These two themes are employed as inclusive concepts in which other similar terms of greater specificity and overlapping meanings are consolidated. The first theme, *individuation-categorization*, refers to the degree to which the communicator acts or reacts relying on information about the particular interacting partner(s) involved in a particular event (individuation) versus relying on information about the ethnicity or ethnic identity of the interacting partner(s) (categorization). The second theme is *consonance-dissonance*, which the communicator uses to make adjustments in his or her habitual encoding and decoding behavior so as to facilitate relational cohesion (consonance) or engage in acts that impede or disrupt such cohesion (dissonance).

Table 14.1 lists the specific concepts that have been incorporated into each theme. Theoretical linkages between the themes and the associative or dissociative relational function in interethnic communication are theorized in three axioms (statements this author claims to be true). These axioms, in turn, serve as the foundational ideas for developing theorems (predictive statements) in each of the following sections.

Axiom 1. Individuating and congruent behaviors serve associative relational functions.

Axiom 2. Categorical and incongruent behaviors serve dissociative relational functions.

Axiom 3. Association and dissociation constitute two opposite ends of a continuum of relational functions in interethnic communication.

THE COMMUNICATOR

The first layer of the context is the communicator, who serves as the most immediate context for specific encoding and decoding behaviors. Many of the existing psychological concepts are examined below and are integrated into two broad bipolar themes of the communicator's identity orientation: (1) inclusivity (or exclusivity) and (2) security (or insecurity). These identity themes correspond to the routinized ways, or "personal schema" (Horowitz, 1991), with which individuals respond to external stimuli. As such, they are regarded here as the more or less enduring core elements of personhood that influence and are influenced by a communicator's associative or dissociative interethnic behavior.

Identity Inclusivity (Exclusivity)

Identity is a focal phenomenon in social psychological studies examining prejudicial talk (e.g., Gumperz & Cook-Gumperz, 1982), language attitudes (e.g., J. Ross, 1979), maintenance of minority languages (e.g., Lambert, 1979), and convergent behavior (Gallois et al., 1995). Social identity theory (Tajfel, 1974; Tajfel & Turner, 1986) has contributed significantly to these studies by pointing out that identification with a social group involves two key ingredients: first, that membership in the social group is an important, emotionally significant aspect of the individual's self-concept, and second, that collective interests are of concern to the individual, above and beyond their implications for personal self-interest. In effect, social identities are deemed extensions of the self; social identity entails "a shift towards the perception of self as an interchangeable exemplar of some social category and away from the perception of self as a unique person" (Turner, Hogg, Oakes, Reicher, & Wetherell, 1987, p. 50). The theory further argues that individuals identify with a group such that a positive self-identity is maintained, and that this motivational tendency is enacted in such interrelated forms as *ingroup bias, ethnic commitment, ingroup loyalty,* and *outgroup discrimination.* All of these identity-related psychological attributes have been found to facilitate dissociative decoding behaviors such as biased attribution, psychological distance, and linguistic divergence (e.g., Giles & Johnson, 1986).

In contrast, more inclusive identity orientation lends itself to more associative interethnic behaviors, as argued in a number of theories. In her theory of cross-cultural adaptation, this author (Kim, 2001) has proposed a model of *intercultural identity* development, emphasizing the adaptive and dynamic nature of identity (see Chapter 17 in this volume). The model explains that, through extensive, intensive, and prolonged experiences of adapting to a new culture, an individual's original cultural identity gradually undergoes a transformation in the direction of individuation and universalization. In this process, the individual's identity becomes increasingly inclusive, with a greater capacity to make deliberate choices of action in specific situations rather than their simply being dictated by the prevailing norms of the culture of childhood. Among other existing concepts that are linked to associative interethnic behavior are *identity integration* (e.g., Phinney, 1993), *multicultural identity* (e.g., Adler, 1982), and *double-swing* (Yoshikawa, 1986). Each of these concepts is grounded in the premise that an individual's identity can be *achieved* over time, as much as it is ascribed by birth or by society. Unlike the identity of exclusivity, then, these concepts of inclusive identity orientation suggest a level of intellectual and emotional openness and flexibility—the personal qualities that engender associative interethnic behavior.

Identity Security (Insecurity)

The degree to which a communicator feels secure or insecure in his or her identity, including ethnic identity, adds to the present aim of understanding associative and dissociative interethnic behavior. As Worchel (1979) observes, "Cooperation could be induced by having each side set aside its weapons or reduce its potential to threaten or harm the other. The less the two parties fear each other, the greater should be the likelihood that they will cooperate" (p. 266).

One's overall identity security reflects the "*ego-strength*" (Lazarus, 1966) with which to react to a stressful situation with composure and clear and rational thinking. Identity security, as such, is a kind of inner resource that allows for qualities of flexibility and relaxedness in one's behavior, that is, the ability to "bend" and empathize with others without losing the ability to maintain one's integrity, and to be creative and effective in responding to impending problems.

Identity security or insecurity serves to integrate some of the more specific terms, including *risk-taking* (e.g., Fiske & Maddi, 1961), *self-confidence* (e.g., Van den Broucke, de Soete, & Bohrer, 1989), *self-esteem* (e.g., Padilla, Wagatsuma, & Lindholm, 1985), and *hardiness* (Walton, 1990). Closely related to the strength of one's sense of identity security are one's general attitudes toward and evaluations of oneself and others. Positive identity orientation (Kim, 2001) is defined as an affirmative and optimistic outlook or general self-efficacy and serves as a source of motivation to perform a more practical adaptive role than pessimism with respect to ethnic difference. Individuals with a more positive identity orientation are more likely to reach out to individuals of differing ethnic backgrounds. As Worchel (1986) proposes, positivity is likely to help alleviate unwarranted fear and perceived threat. When directed inwardly, positivity is linked to "metamotivation" (Maslow, 1969, p. 35), a kind of self-trust that tends not to cripple oneself with irrational feelings of inferiority or worthlessness. In most social psychological studies of intergroup relations, identity security-insecurity has been examined narrowly in terms of the insecurity members of nondominant ethnic groups feel about their group's relative status in the symbolic sense of the group's importance, worth, and respectability, or in the practical sense of its social power and control. Specific concepts utilized in investigating identity security-insecurity in these studies include *status anxiety* (De Vos,

1990a, 1990b), *perceived threat* (Giles & Johnson, 1986), *collective self-esteem* (e.g., Crocker & Luthanen, 1990), *marginality* (Taft, 1977), and *identity salience* or *psychological distinctiveness* (e.g., Bourhis, Giles, Leyens, & Tajfel, 1979).

These and related concepts have been linked to various forms of dissociative behavior, including stereotyping (e.g., Francis, 1976), divergent language behavior (e.g., Giles, Bourhis, & Taylor, 1977), hostility and aggression (e.g., Berkowitz, 1962), and outgroup discrimination (e.g., Brewer & Miller, 1988). The present theoretical linkage of identity security-insecurity and associative-dissociative behavior is supported by Kleg (1993), who reports that, compared with members of ethnic minorities, many European Americans do not consider ethnicity to be an important source of personal strength and self-esteem. Similar observations are made by Brown, McNatt, and Cooper (2003), who find that ethnic minority group members (Jewish) show a stronger ingroup preference for romantic partners than ethnic majority group members, and by David, Morrison, Johnson, and Ross (2002), who report that whites identify with both black and white fashion models, whereas blacks tend to identify more strongly with black models.

Theorems

The above concepts describe some of the more prominent aspects of the communicator's identity orientation—inclusivity-exclusivity, security-insecurity, and positivity-negativity. Together, these three themes offer a psychological profile of the communicator that helps in understanding his or her associative-dissociative interethnic behavior. The generalizable pattern of mutual influence between the communicator factors and the interethnic behavior is specified in the following theorems.

Theorem 1. The more inclusive (exclusive) the communicator's identity orientation, the more associative (dissociative) his or her interethnic communication behavior.

Theorem 2. The more secure (insecure) the communicator's identity orientation, the more associative (dissociative) his or her interethnic communication behavior.

THE SITUATION

Next to the communicator is the situation of the interethnic encounter itself, when the communicator interacts with one or more people. The interaction can occur face-to-face or indirectly via some form of mediating channel from electronic mailing, letter, fax, and telephone, to various mass mediated situations such as when the communicator discusses an issue in a television program or writes about an ethnic issue in newspapers. In the present theory, *the situation is defined as the conditions of the immediate social milieu in which a person is engaged in interethnic communication.* Although each social situation presents the communicator with a unique set of constraints as well as possibilities, three key factors—ethnic proximity/distance, shared/separate goal structure, and personal network integration—are identified in the present theory as being more or less consistently relevant to understanding the nature of the communicator's interethnic behavior.

Ethnic Proximity (Distance)

Individuals associated with a given ethnic group often vary in their ethnic characteristics. Ethnicity as a group phenomenon manifests itself in individuals in two aspects. The first aspect is material/physical, that is, a set of *extrinsic ethnic markers* related to physical features (e.g., skin color, physique, hair, facial features) and material artifacts (e.g., food, dress, decorative objects, and religious practices), as well as certain noticeable behaviors such as unique gestures and paralinguistic

patterns (e.g., distinct accents, tempos of utterance, intonations, and pitch levels). Often, however, some of the obvious but superficial differences in extrinsic ethnic markers block the communicator from noticing less conspicuous secondary aspects of ethnicity, *intrinsic ethnic markers,* which include internalized beliefs, value orientations, and norms closely associated with a particular ethnic group.

Extrinsically and intrinsically, each interethnic communication event presents a level of ethnic proximity (or distance) between the involved parties. Ethnic proximity (or distance) is, thus, a relational concept comparing a given communicator's ethnicity with that of the other(s) involved. Interethnic behavior is likely to be more associative when a communicator sees in the other(s) a higher degree of similarities in extrinsic ethnic markers and/or a higher degree of compatibility in intrinsic ethnic markers. A significant amount of differences and incompatibility, on the other hand, is likely to accentuate category salience and the accompanying psychological distance, inhibiting the communicator's motivation to engage in the communication encounter and seek a cooperative relationship. Some research evidence is available to link ethnic dissimilarities to anxiety (Stephan & Stephan, 1985), miscommunication (Gumperz, 1978), and lack of attributional confidence (Gudykunst, 1995).

Shared (Separate) Goal Structure

An additional factor of the situational context closely linked to associative-dissociative behavior is the extent to which the communicator's identity is shared by, or is separate from, the identity of the other party/parties involved in interethnic communication. A shared identity—such as "our company," "our football team," "our neighborhood," or "our country"—accompanies a set of mutual goal structures, or common interests, promoting associative behaviors and development of a cooperative relationship between the involved parties. In contrast, a communicator who sees in the other interactant(s) little or no mutuality in interests or goals is likely to be less motivated to engage in associative behavior. Sometimes interethnic coalitions may be formed to pursue a common goal; but only temporarily, until it is met (Chesler, 1988).

A significant amount of social psychological research has been conducted to better understand the role of a shared-separate goal structure. Brewer and Miller (1988) theorize that associative behaviors (such as individuated decoding rather than stereotypical categorization) are more likely when the interaction is structured to promote an *interpersonal and cooperative orientation* compared to a *task-oriented and competitive one.* Cooperative work teams are often composed and structured in such a way that roles or functions within the team are correlated with subgroup category identities (such as ethnic categories). Brewer (1996) posits that *crisscrossing identities* by drawing one or two individuals from a particular identity category into a team diminishes categorical distinctions between individuals of differing subgroup identities. Relatedly, Gaertner, Dovidio, Anastasio, Bachman, and Rust (1993) espouse *the common ingroup identity* model as a means to reduce intergroup bias in contact situations. Based on a series of experimental studies, Gaertner and associates have found that conditions that enhance the salience of the team identity and reduce the salience of subcategories tend to diminish or eliminate ingroup bias in evaluation of fellow team members. To the extent that participants perceive the combined team as a single entity, rather than an aggregate of two separate groups, evaluations of former outgroup members become more positive. Likewise, Brewer and Schneider (1990) demonstrate that, when the group members are made aware of their shared membership in a *superordinate organization,* cooperative choices are significantly increased.

Personal Network Integration

The degree to which a communicator's relational network is ethnically integrated is the third situational factor identified in the present theory as having a significant relevance to interethnic behavior. Personal network—also referred to by network analysts in similar terms as "interpersonal network," "egocentric network," and "personal community"—is largely a product of voluntary association and a function of mutual interest and willingness of all persons involved. As such, a communicator whose personal network is ethnically mixed is likely to be more associative in interethnic behavior in general. Conversely, an individual whose interethnic behavior is generally associative is likely to form a more heterogeneous network of relationships (Kim, 1986; Yum, 1988).

Integration of heterogeneous relational ties in one's personal network presupposes interethnic contact, the environmental condition postulated in the "contact hypothesis" (Amir, 1969), as providing opportunities for reducing conflict and promoting positive attitudes. Mere contact, however, is unlikely to have a direct linkage to an individual's associative or dissociative interethnic behavior, as suggested in the not-so-straightforward picture of research findings (Brewer & Miller, 1984). Whereas Hallinan and Smith (1985), for example, find that opportunities for contact increase the likelihood of the development of interracial friendships in children, others have shown that intergroup contact is just as likely to heighten conflict as it is to reduce it. Worchel (1979), likewise, reports that, in some cases, integrated apartment buildings lead to a decrease in favorable racial attitudes. The environment-behavior relationship becomes even more ambiguous when one takes into account the fact that, even under a similar condition of interaction potential, individuals make different decisions regarding interethnic association-dissociation. Some may choose "self-segregation," while others may go out of their way to find an ethnically different roommate or an apartment in an ethnically mixed neighborhood.

Accordingly, this author identifies the degree of ethnic integration in a communicator's personal relational network as a more relevant, more reliable, and thus more useful alternative to understanding associative-dissociative interethnic behavior at the individual level. As Rogers and Kincaid (1981) observe, "The uniqueness of an individual's personal network is responsible for the uniqueness of his meaning" (p. 45). A personal network consists of "nodes," that is, other persons with whom the focal person at the center of a network ("Ego") has relations. Because relationship formation is largely voluntary, an ethnically integrated personal network reflects Ego's associative interethnic behaviors. The degree of ethnic integration in personal networks has been typically assessed in terms of the size or proportion of outgroup ties relative to ingroup ties. Once the overall ethnic composition of Ego's personal network is identified, one can examine the strength of heterogeneous relationships. The term "tie strength" (Granovetter, 1973) is employed to indicate two interrelated relational characteristics: (1) intimacy manifested in some form of mutual affective engagement as in friendship or other close relationships such as romantic relationships; and (2) centrality or the importance (or value) and potential social influence of a given relationship to Ego relative to others in the network (Kim, 2001).

Taken together, a large size/proportion and strength of relational ties with individuals of differing ethnic backgrounds is likely to reflect, as well as facilitate, Ego's associative interethnic behavior. This theoretical relationship is supported by a sizable pool of research findings. Parks, Stan, and Eggert (1983) have found that interethnic romantic involvement increases as a function of network involvement. In the case of American Indians (Kim, Lujan, & Dixon, 1998) and of members of an ethnically mixed community in Oklahoma (Kim et al., 2002;

Kim, McClure, et al., 2003; Kim, Ogawa, et al., 2003), those individuals who report higher levels of network heterogeneity and more friends and intimate friends of dissimilar ethnic backgrounds tend to be significantly more inclusive and secure in identity orientation and more integrative in their general ideological beliefs about interethnic relations. The same relationship between outgroup tie strength and associative interethnic behavior has been observed among immigrants who, through intermarriage, develop intimate ties with host nationals through their spouses' relational networks (e.g., Alba, 1990; Friedrich, 1985).

Theorems

The three situational factors—ethnic proximity-distance, shared-separate goal structure, and heterogeneous-homogeneous personal network structure—collectively offer a profile of the situational context in which the communicator's interethnic behavior is likely to be associative or dissociative. The specific pattern of the situation-behavior interface is identified in the following three theorems.

Theorem 3. The greater the ethnic proximity (distance) between the communicator and the other(s) involved in interethnic communication, the more associative (dissociative) the communicator's interethnic behavior.

Theorem 4. The greater the shared (separate) goal structure between the communicator and the other(s) involved in interethnic communication, the more associative (dissociative) the communicator's interethnic behavior.

Theorem 5. The more (less) ethnically integrated the communicator's personal network structure, the more associative (dissociative) the communicator's interethnic behavior.

THE ENVIRONMENT

Surrounding the situational level is the larger social milieu, or the communication environment. As previously noted, the environment is comprised of multiple sublevels of social entities ranging from a small work unit (e.g., academic departments within a university), a larger organization (e.g., a university), a neighborhood, and a local community, to even larger social entities such as a society (e.g., the U.S.) and its relationship to another country and to the world. Directly or indirectly, and no matter how strongly or weakly, certain conditions of each environmental layer potentially influence, and are influenced by, the associative-dissociative interethnic behavior of the individual communicator. The present theory identifies three themes of the environment: (1) institutional equity (inequity), (2) ingroup strength, and (3) environmental stress. Each of these inclusive themes is identified in this theory as a significant environmental factor of relevance to understanding the associative-dissociative interethnic behavior of individual communicators.

Institutional Equity (Inequity)

Whether an organization or a government, or any other level constituting the environment of an interethnic communication event, there are laws or policies that serve as organizing principles for the daily operations and practices of individuals within a given social system. The institutionalized organizing principles shape the normative beliefs and practices throughout a social system, guiding and reinforcing the judgments and behaviors of individuals within that system. Of special interest to the present theory is the degree to which such institutionalized principles are equitable for people across all ethnicities.

The question of institutional equity addresses issues of fairness and justice. Through the activities of social comparison, the lack of institutional equity along ethnic lines is bound to create resentment and anger in the minds of members of the adversely affected ethnic groups (Turner, 1975). To the

extent that inequity exists, subordinate ethnic group members' actions express their comparative feelings of dissatisfaction, or what has been referred to as "*fraternalistic relative deprivation*" (Walker & Pettigrew, 1984). Rigid socioeconomic stratification along ethnic lines, in particular, has been emphasized in social identity theory, which places particular emphasis on structural conflicts of interest between social groups as a powerful factor encouraging dissociative behaviors by increasing "category salience" in intergroup interaction (Tajfel, 1974; Tajfel & Turner, 1979).

Crucial to understanding many of the contemporary incidents of institutional inequity is the history of subjugation of one ethnic group by another. Many historical accounts have been written on the topic of colonization and the subsequent influences on interethnic discrimination and mistrust. In the case of West Indies immigrants living in England, for instance, the "imperial mythology" and the hegemonic tendencies of whites against nonwhite immigrants have been observed to be prevalent today (Rex, 1976; Richmond, 1986; Stone, 1985). Changes in institutional inequity in a given society accompany changes in the laws or other judicial actions. Societies such as the United States, Canada, and other Western European democracies have undergone a significant transformation toward an increasing equity among their majority and minority groups. There has been a series of legal actions, such as the U.S. Supreme Court's 1954 ruling against racially segregated public schools. Many of these formal barriers persist, as demonstrated by the continuing patterns of intense racial discrimination in housing. Yet enough progress has been made in some institutions, notably in education and employment, to introduce a second-generation set of less formal obstacles to institutional equity (Pettigrew & Martin, 1989). The contemporary institutional inequity is reflected in patterns of the *socioeconomic stratification* and *systemic status differential* along ethnic lines (e.g., Hechter, 1975; Wolpe, 1986).

Institutional inequity has been linked to dissociative interethnic behavior in studies that investigated within organizations in terms of objectively recognized *systemic status differential* along ethnic lines—the convergence of ethnic category and functional roles within the organization reflecting the historical interethnic power inequality in the society at large. Institutional inequity has been further linked to the subjective experiences of and responses to racism. Duncan (2003), for example, has analyzed the responses to racism and "racial signifiers" in the discourses of black South Africans prior to and after 1994, the year that marked the end of formal Apartheid and legislated racism in South Africa. Duncan reports that, in the discourses produced by the group of black high school students in 1999, the notions of race and racial difference were accepted and utilized in a much less critical manner than in the discourse produced by the group of black adults prior to 1994.

Relative Ingroup Strength

The literature suggests a linkage between the collective strength of the communicator's ethnic group and his or her associative or dissociative interethnic communication behaviors. The overall strength of an ethnic group is closely tied to the objective properties and positions of political and economic resources associated with that group, bringing status and prestige to members of that group. Strong ingroup status, thus, serves as a kind of social advantage in interethnic communication that helps to draw interest, if not acceptance, from outgroup members. A stronger ethnic group is also likely to encourage the maintenance of ethnicity and ethnic identity in the individual and discourage assimilation into the society at large. Conversely, individuals are likely to be less motivated to act associatively toward others whose ethnic groups confer little power to affect the status quo.

A number of existing theories describing the evolution of ethnic groups further suggest the linkage between the relative ingroup strength and dissociative interethnic behavior of an individual communicator. Clarke and Obler (1976), for example, argue that as an ethnic group grows from its initial, economic adjustment stage to the later stages of community building, it shows an increasing collective strength with which to manipulate its ethnic identity for *political self-assertion* for the benefit of the group's interests. Breton (1964, 1991) and Keyes (1981), among others, have articulated similar views on the developmental stages of ethnic groups and their increased *political mobilization*. A crucial force in this process is a strong communication system including ethnic media and community organizations such as churches and social clubs. As Marwell, Oliver, and Prahl (1988) observe in their theory of the "*critical mass*," the potential for organizing a group depends on the social ties in the group through which collective actions are made possible.

The theoretical relationship between relative ingroup strength and interethnic behavior is supported by the observations of Vaid-Raizada (1981) and of Brewer (1984), among others, that interethnic relationships tend to be more acrimonious in larger groups with several equal-size ethnic subgroups. In addition, Blau and Schwartz (1984) and Hoffman (1985) have argued that as the size of an ingroup increases, the likelihood of contact with outgroup members decreases and the ingroup members become more likely to interact with other ingroup members. These observations suggest that communities where ethnic minorities constitute only a small proportion of the overall population are likely to engage in more associative interethnic behaviors. Such is, indeed, the conclusion drawn from a study of Greek and Italian ethnic groups in Australia by Gallois and Pittam (1991). In this study, adolescents in the well-organized Greek community are found to place more emphasis on their ethnic identity and maintaining their heritage than their Italian counterparts, whose community is less cohesive. The study also reveals that Greek-Australian adolescents place less emphasis on adapting to the dominant Australian culture at large. Likewise, a study by Yang and Sachdev (1994) of ethnic Chinese communities in London and Taiwan indicates that greater ingroup strength is correlated with greater ingroup language use and maintenance. Similar results were reported by Cenoz and Valencia (1993) in their study of second language acquisition in the Basque Country in Spain, and by Florack and Piontkowski (1997) in a study among the Dutch and the Germans in the European Union (see also Kim, Kim, et al., 2002, Kim, McClure, et al., 2003, and Kim, Ogawa, et al., 2003, for similar findings).

Environmental Stress

The third environmental factor pertinent to understanding an individual's interethnic behavior is the level of overall environmental stress, defined in the present theory in terms of the tension stemming from such nonethnic factors as limited resources and economic hard times—conditions that are likely to intensify competition throughout a given social system, be it a society at large, a region, a town, or a small organization. Interethnic tension is also likely to increase at the individual level when the environment is under duress due to events that are linked to a particular ethnic group, as was witnessed in the increased violent or otherwise dissociative acts directed against individuals of Middle-Eastern origins following the horrendous acts of terrorism committed against the United States on September 11, 2001.

Environmental stress has been widely recognized as a factor that intensifies intergroup dissociation or conflict. Volkan (1992), for example, argues that intergroup conflicts are likely to increase when the society undergoes certain challenging circumstances caused by economic hardship, shortage of resources,

or involvement in an international crisis. Olzak (1987) explains that environmental stress tends to intensify competitive intergroup relations. Others have argued that, under stressful circumstances, more than the usual level of dissociative interethnic behaviors are enacted (e.g., Stone, 1985). Sherif's (1966) realistic conflict theory offers an additional explanation, postulating that the actual or perceived competition for scarce resources leads to bias against outgroups in the absence of existing common or complementary goals. Building on this theory, Esses, Jackson, and Armstrong (1998) proposed the instrumental model of group conflict, highlighting the role of the perception of intergroup competition and zero-sum beliefs (if one group gains, the other loses) that are accompanied by anxiety and fear. The theory states that "the combination of resource stress and the salience of a potentially competitive outgroup leads to perceived group competition for resources. The perceived competition leads to attempts to remove the source of competition, using a variety of strategies" (p. 702).

Theorems

Theorems 6 through 8 formalize the interrelationship between each of the above-identified three environmental conditions and the associative-dissociative interethnic behavior of the communicator. Together, these conditions—institutional equity, ingroup strength, and environmental stress—provide a profile of the environment that is theorized to facilitate or hinder the associative (or dissociative) behaviors of an individual communicator. It is argued that the three conditions influence an individual's interethnic associative-dissociative behavior, regardless of the particular environment being investigated, from the macrosocietal environment to the environment of an organization or a neighborhood.

Theorem 6. The greater the institutional equity (inequity) across ethnic groups in the environment, the more associative (dissociative) the communicator's interethnic behavior.

Theorem 7. The greater the relative strength (weakness) of the communicator's ethnic ingroup in the environment, the more associative (dissociative) the communicator's interethnic behavior.

Theorem 8. The greater the competition-intensifying environmental stress, the more dissociative the communicator's interethnic behavior.

DISCUSSION

Against the backdrop of the traditional melting-pot vision and the ongoing ideological polemics in the United States, the author has sought to develop a contextual theory of interethnic communication. Focusing on the behaviors of individual communicators, the present theory describes how various elements of interethnic behavior serve an associative or dissociative function in interethnic relationship, and explains how the associative or dissociative behavior influences, and is influenced by, the internal and external contextual forces. Each of the concepts is an inclusive one that consolidates and represents some of the relevant concepts that have been employed in the literature (see Table 14.2).

A Synthesis

Grounded in an open-systems perspective, the theory begins with a focus on a single communicator. From this vantage point, three basic assumptions are made describing the dynamic interface of the communicator's behavior and three layers of the communication context—the communicator, the situation, and the environment. Communication is assumed to be interethnic whenever the communicator acts and reacts taking at least partly into account the objective and subjective difference in ethnicity and ethnic identity. Figure 14.1 reflects the dynamic behavior-context interface in interethnic communication from the perspective of the

communicator. In so doing, various pertinent concepts, models, and research findings across social science disciplines have been integrated into a single theoretical framework. These foundational ideas render the present theory a distinct character, differentiating it from other existing theories of intergroup behavior and interethnic relations.

The theory describes various elements of interethnic behavior in terms of two main bipolar themes: individuation-categorization and consonance-dissonance. These themes are identified as inclusive concepts within which various associative and dissociative elements of interethnic behavior prominent in the literature are consolidated. Table 14.1 lists some of the existing social scientific concepts that are incorporated into and represented by two themes, association and dissociation. Theoretical claims are then made linking individuated and consonant behaviors to interethnic association (Axiom 1), and categorical and dissonant behaviors to interethnic dissociation (Axiom 2). The theory conceives associative and dissociative elements of interethnic behavior not as mutually exclusive categories, but as a bipolar continuum (Axiom 3). Next, the theory identifies eight contextual factors that are postulated in Theorems 1–8 to be in a reciprocal functional relationship with the communicator's associative or dissociative interethnic behavior. Theorems 1 and 2 present a profile of the communicator who is likely to be associative in interethnic behavior as someone with an inclusive and secure identity orientation. Theorems 3 through 5 address three situational factors and predict that when the communication situation created by the communicator and the other involved interactant(s) share a great deal of ethnic proximity (similarity and compatibility) and all involved parties share a goal structure, and when the communicator's personal network is ethnically integrated, then the communicator's interethnic behavior is likely to be more associative. Theorems 6 through 8 argue that

Table 14.2   Contextual Factors and Related Concepts

The Communicator	The Situation	The Environment
Identity Inclusivity (Exclusivity)	**Ethnic Proximity (Distance)**	**Institutional Equity (Inequity)**
Intercultural identity	Similarity in extrinsic ethnic markers	(Fraternalistic relative deprivation)
Multicultural identity	Compatibility of intrinsic ethnic markers	(Economic stratification)
Double-swing	(Difference in extrinsic ethnic markers)	(Systemic status differential)
Achieved identity	(Incompatibility in intrinsic ethnic markers)	(Internal colonialism)
(Ingroup bias)		
(Ethnic commitment)		
(Ingroup loyalty)		
(Outgroup discrimination)		
Identity Security (Insecurity)	**Shared (Separate) Goal Structure**	**Relative Ingroup Strength**
Ego strength	Interpersonal orientation	Political self-assertion
Risk taking	Cooperative orientation	Political mobilization
Hardiness	Superordinate organization	Collective action
Self-efficacy	(Task orientation)	Critical mass
Positivity	(Competitive orientation)	
(Status anxiety)		
(Perceived threat)		
(Marginality)		
(Psychological distinctiveness)		
	Personal Network Integration	**Environmental Stress**
	Size/proportion of outgroup ties	Economic hardship
	Intimacy of outgroup ties	Shortage of resources
	Centrality of outgroup ties	Ethnicity-linked conflicts

the communicator's interethnic behavior is likely to be more associative when the environment offers him or her a system of law, rules, policies, and practices that are fair and equitable; when the communicator's own ethnic group is relatively weak in power and status (compared to an outgroup); and when the environment is relatively calm and prosperous.

From Theory to Case Studies

Even as the theory identifies generic and generalizable regularities in interethnic communication, it also serves as an intellectual guide for case studies designed for understanding specific interethnic communication events. It does so by offering an analytic framework with which to survey the entire "field" of behavior-context interface in a given interethnic communication event. The elements of associative and dissociative behavior (Table 14.1), the key contextual factors identified (Table 14.2), and the interactive relationship between them and the behavior (Theorems 1–8) help us direct our attention to the particularities of behavioral and contextual forces operating in a given interethnic communication event. In this sense, the theory can be used in the way one selects a piece for a given position in a jigsaw puzzle: by looking at all identifiable and meaningful patterns holistically.

Once all of the constituent dimensions and factors are identified, we may zero in on those factors that are most salient and significant to understanding and explaining that event. The model allows for each event to present a unique circumstance in which some factors may be of greater relevance and play a more prominent role than others. Even a single factor may be so powerful as to overshadow every other force operating in a given encounter. Such would be the case when two individuals respond to an identical set of situational and environmental conditions in vastly different manners, or commitment to a shared goal (a situational factor) is so strong that interactants are able to overcome many of the adversarial environmental factors and manage to engage in associative behaviors and activities. Likewise, the model further allows comparisons of the way interethnic communication plays out across cultures. Born out of the experiential milieu of the United States, the contextual factors identified in the present theory are most directly relevant to understanding and explaining the interethnic communication activities between and among U.S. Americans of differing ethnic backgrounds. The same factors, however, may be employed to assess the relevance and applicability of the present theory beyond the United States. In traditional tribal societies, for example, interethnic association and dissociation may be primarily a function of ethnic proximity (a situational factor) and relative ingroup strength (an environmental factor), while personal network integration (a situational factor) may not be as relevant as it is in the United States and other more ethnically diverse places in Western democracies.

This author has sought to maintain neutrality in value judgments with respect to interethnic association and dissociation. In the provisional form of predication in the theorems, "The greater A, the greater (or lesser) B," generalizations are made without predetermined judgment as to whether associative behavior is necessarily or invariably more desirable than dissociative behavior. Questions need to be raised about the long-term role of associative or dissociative communication behavior. While we generally prefer associative behaviors to dissociative behaviors, we must recognize that dissociative behaviors are desirable and even necessary for "forcing" a change in the existing rules of interethnic communication and bringing about a more equitable long-term relationship between individuals and groups. The "problem" of dissociative interethnic communication may be little more than a function of a particular ideological viewpoint, a lack of tolerance for ambiguity, or short-sightedness (Ruben, 1978). As much as dissociative behavior can serve as a destabilizing force in human systems, it may serve as a crucial force for a defense against their stagnation, detachment, and entropy, offering an opportunity for new learning and growth of the parties involved. At least in the United States, interethnic conflict experiences clearly have brought the society to new stages of self-awareness and a broadened democracy despite the many temporary stresses that such experiences have wrought (Himes, 1974).

With issues such as these to be more fully explored, the theory in its present form is proposed as a work in progress. For now, it offers an integrative framework for investigating interethnic communication in light of the interweavings of behavioral and contextual contingencies. Interested researchers may test specific patterns of such interweavings identified in the theorems. Ethnographic researchers or practitioners (e.g., trainers, consultants, and interested nonprofessionals) may apply the overall theoretical framework for in-depth case studies to examine and describe particularities that arise in specific interethnic communication events.

Implications for Social Action

The systemic and dynamic conception of interethnic communication articulated in the present theory suggests that change in the status quo in interethnic relations can be initiated at any level. If we desire change, we may begin by looking inwardly and reflecting on the extent of inclusiveness and security in our own sense of who we are and how we relate to others vis-à-vis ethnicity. By practicing associative behaviors at the individual level, we may work to improve the quality of interethnic relations in organizations and communities around us. We may further anticipate that, by creating a situation around us in which all involved parties see the mutuality of their respective interests and aspirations, we can engender a strong sense of community and active interpersonal associations that transcend ethnic categories. Most of all, the theory speaks to the real possibility that a single communicator can make a difference for all others involved in an interethnic communication event. When sufficiently multiplied by many others, a communicator's behavior can ultimately resonate broadly to help shape the quality of interethnic relations at large in a given society.

Exactly how the nature of American interethnic relations and the underlying ideological forces will unfold in the future remains to be seen. Debates will doubtless continue, privately and publicly, as Americans struggle with competing visions of what it means to be Americans. Free and earnest debates, indeed, are essential for American society to guard itself against stagnation, disintegration, and entropy. The very fact that interethnic issues continue to engage American people's passion is itself an affirmation, and a hallmark, of classical liberalism—a tradition that has underpinned the stability of U.S. democracy. As historian and author David Halberstam (2003) puts it, "You can love your country, believe in it, argue with it . . . even though America is imperfect, it is also more perfectible than other nations." For concerned Americans, then, the theory speaks to the importance of engaging ourselves thoughtfully in each interethnic event. It affirms and upholds the simple idea that what we do every day with others of dissimilar ethnic backgrounds matters and that, in the end, it is each of us who can aid, or hinder, the success of the great American experiment—to strive for a society of "One, Out of Many."

REFERENCES

Abercrombie, N. (1980). *Class, structure and knowledge.* Oxford, UK: Basil Blackwell.

Adler, P. (1982). Beyond cultural identity: Reflections on cultural and multicultural man. In L. Samovar & R. Porter (Eds.), *Intercultural communication: A reader* (3rd ed., pp. 389–408). Belmont, CA: Wadsworth.

Alba, R. D. (1990). *Ethnic identity.* New Haven, CT: Yale University Press.

Amir, Y. (1969). Contact hypothesis in ethnic relations. *Psychological Bulletin, 7*(5), 319–342.

Applegate, L., & Sypher, H. (1988). A constructivist theory of communication and culture. In Y. Y. Kim & W. B. Gudykunst (Eds.), *Theories in intercultural communication* (pp. 41–65). Newbury Park, CA: Sage.

Bateson, G. (1972). *Steps to an ecology of mind.* New York: Ballantine.

Berkowitz, L. (1962). *Aggression: A social psychological analysis.* New York: McGraw-Hill.

Bertalanffy, L. (1975). General system theory. In B. D. Ruben & J. Y. Kim (Eds.), *General systems theory and human communication* (pp. 6–32). Rochelle Park, NJ: Hayden Book. (Original work published 1955)

Billig, M. (1987). *Arguing and thinking: A rhetorical approach to social psychology.* New York: Cambridge University Press.

Blau, P., & Schwartz, B. (1984). *Cross-cutting social circles.* New York: Academic Press.

Bonilla-Silva, E., & Forman, T. (2000, January). "I am not a racist but . . .": Mapping white college students' racial ideology in the USA. *Discourse & Society, 11*(1), 50–85.

Bourhis, R., Giles, H., Leyens, J., & Tajfel, H. (1979). Psychological distinctiveness: Language divergence in Belgium. In H. Giles & R. St. Clair (Eds.), *Language and social psychology* (pp. 158–185). Oxford, UK: Blackwell.

Breton, R. (1964). Institutional completeness of ethnic communities and the personal relations of immigrants. *American Journal of Sociology, 70*(2), 193–205.

Breton, R. (1991). *The governance of ethnic communities: Political structures and processes in Canada.* Westport, CT: Greenwood.

Brewer, M. (1984). Beyond the contact hypothesis: Theoretical perspectives on desegregation. In N. Miller & M. Brewer (Eds.), *Groups in contact: The psychology of desegregation* (pp. 281–302). New York: Academic Press.

Brewer, M. (1996). Managing diversity: The role of social identities. In S. E. Jackson & M. N. Ruderman (Eds.), *Diversity in work teams: Research paradigms for a changing workplace* (pp. 47–68). Washington, DC: American Psychological Association.

Brewer, M., & Gaertner, S. (2001). Toward reduction of prejudice. In R. Brown & S. Gaertner (Eds.), *Intergroup processes.* Oxford, UK: Blackwell.

Brewer, M., & Miller, N. (1984). Beyond the contact hypothesis: Theoretical perspectives on desegregation. In N. Miller & M. Brewer (Eds.), *Groups in contact: The psychology of desegregation* (pp. 281–302). New York: Academic Press.

Brewer, M., & Miller, N. (1988). Contact and cooperation: When do they work? In P. Katz & D. Taylor (Eds.), *Eliminating racism* (pp. 315–326). Newbury Park, CA: Sage.

Brewer, M., & Schneider, S. (1990). Social identity and social dilemmas: A double-edged sword. In D. Abrams & M. Hogg (Eds.), *Social identity theory: Constructive and critical advances* (pp. 169–184). London: Harvester-Wheatsheaf.

Brown, L., McNatt, P., & Cooper, G. (2003). Ingroup romantic preferences among Jewish and non-Jewish white undergraduates. *International Journal of Intercultural Relations, 27*(3), 335–354.

Cenoz, J., & Valencia, J. F. (1993). Ethnolinguistic vitality, social networks and motivation in second language acquisition: Some data from the Basque Country. *Language, Culture and Curriculum, 6,* 113–127.

Chesler, M. (1988). Creating and maintaining interracial coalitions. In B. Brewer & R. Hunt (Eds.), *Impacts of racism on white Americans* (pp. 217–244). Newbury Park, CA: Sage.

Clarke, S., & Obler, J. (1976). Ethnic conflict, community-building, and the emergence of ethnic political traditions in the United States. In S. Clarke & J. Obler (Eds.), *Urban ethnic conflicts: A comparative perspective* (pp. 1–34). Chapel Hill: University of North Carolina Press.

Cook, S. W. (1978). Interpersonal and attitudinal outcomes in cooperating interracial groups. *Journal of Research and Development in Education, 12,* 97–113.

Corea, A. (1990). Racism in the American way of media. In J. Downing, A. Mohammadi, & A. Sreberny-Mohammadi (Eds.), *Questioning the media: A critical introduction* (pp. 255–266). Newbury Park, CA: Sage.

Crisp, R., Hewstone, M., & Rubin, M. (2001). Does multiple categorization reduce intergroup bias? *Personality and Social Psychology Bulletin, 27,* 76–89.

Crocker, J., & Luthanen, R. (1990). Collective self-esteem and ingroup bias. *Journal of Personality and Social Psychology, 58,* 60–67.

Cronen, V., Chen, V., & Pearce, W. (1988). Coordinated management of meaning: A critical theory. In Y. Y. Kim & W. B. Gudykunst (Eds.), *Theories in intercultural communication* (pp. 66–98). Newbury Park, CA: Sage.

David, P., Morrison, G., Johnson, M., & Ross, F. (2002, June). Body image, race, and fashion models. *Communication Research, 29*(3), 270–294.

Detweiler, R. (1986). Categorization, attribution and intergroup communication. In W. B. Gudykunst (Ed.), *Inter-group communication* (pp. 62–73). London: Edward Arnold.

De Vos, G. A. (1990a). Conflict and accommodation in ethnic interaction. In G. A. De Vos & M. Suirez-Orozco (Eds.), *Status inequality: The self in culture* (pp. 204–245). Newbury Park, CA: Sage.

De Vos, G. A. (1990b). Self in society: A multilevel, psychocultural analysis. In G. A. De Vos & M. Suarez-Orozco (Eds.), *Status inequality: The self in culture* (pp. 17–74). Newbury Park, CA: Sage.

Duncan, N. (2003). "Race" talk: Discourses on "race" and racial difference. *International Journal of Intercultural Relations, 27*(2), 135–156.

Ehrlich, H. (1973). *The social psychology of prejudice.* New York: John Wiley.

Esses, V., Jackson, L., & Armstrong, T. (1998). Intergroup competition and attitudes toward immigrants and immigration. *Journal of Social Issues, 54*(4), 699–724.

Fielding, N. G., & Fielding, J. L. (1986). *Linking data.* Newbury Park, CA: Sage.

Fiske, D., & Maddi, S. (Eds.). (1961). *Functions of varied experience.* Homewood, IL: Dorsey.

Florack, A., & Piontkowski, U. (1997). Identification and perceived vitality: The Dutch and the Germans in the European Union. *Journal of Multilingual and Multicultural Development, 18,* 349–363.

Ford, D. H., & Lerner, R. M. (1992). *Developmental systems theory: An integrative approach.* Newbury Park, CA: Sage.

Francis, E. (1976). *Interethnic relations.* New York: Elsevier.

Friedrich, O. (1985, July 8). The changing faces of America. *Time,* pp. 26–33.

Gaertner, S., Dovidio, J., Anastasio, P., Bachman, B., & Rust, M. (1993). The common ingroup identity model: Recategorization and the reduction of intergroup bias. In W. Stroebe & M. Hewstone (Eds.), *European review of social psychology* (Vol. 4, pp. 1–26). Chichester, UK: Wiley.

Gallois, C., Giles, H., Jones, E., Cargile, A., & Ota, H. (1995). Accommodating intercultural encounters: Elaborations and extensions. In R. L. Wiseman (Ed.), *Intercultural communication theory* (pp. 115–147). Thousand Oaks, CA: Sage.

Gallois, C., & Pittam, J. (1991, May). *Ethnolinguistic vitality in multicultural monolingual Australia: Perceptions of Vietnamese and Anglo-Australians.* Paper presented at the annual conference of the International Communication Association, Chicago.

Giles, H., Bourhis, R., & Taylor, D. (1977). Towards a theory of language in ethnic group relations. In H. Giles (Ed.), *Language, ethnicity and intergroup relations* (pp. 307–348). London: Academic Press.

Giles, H., & Johnson, P. (1986). Perceived threat, ethnic commitment, and interethnic language behavior. In Y. Y. Kim (Ed.), *Interethnic communication* (pp. 91–116). Newbury Park, CA: Sage.

Givón, T. (1989). *Mind, code and context.* Hillsdale, NJ: Lawrence Erlbaum.

Glazer, N., & Moynihan, D. (1975). *Ethnicity: Theory and experience.* Cambridge, MA: Harvard University Press.

Gordon, M. (1981). Models of pluralism: The new American dilemma. *Annals of the American Academy of Political and Social Science, 454,* 178–188.

Granovetter, M. (1973). The strength of weak ties. *American Journal of Sociology, 78,* 1360–1380.

Greenberg, J., Kirkland, S., & Pyszczynski, T. (1988). Some theoretical notions and preliminary research concerning derogatory ethnic labels. In G. Smitherman-Donaldson & T. A. van Dijk (Eds.), *Discourse and discrimination* (pp. 74–92). Detroit, MI: Wayne State University Press.

Grunwald, H. (1976, July 5). Loving America. *Time,* pp. 35–36.

Gudykunst, W. B. (1995). Uncertainty/anxiety management (AUM) theory: Current status. In R. Wiseman (Ed.), *Intercultural communication theory* (pp. 8–58). Thousand Oaks, CA: Sage.

Gumperz, J. (1978). The conversational analysis of interethnic communication. In E. Ross (Ed.), *Interethnic communication* (pp. 13–31). Athens: University of Georgia Press.

Gumperz, J., & Cook-Gumperz, J. (1982). Introduction: Language and the communication of social identity. In J. Gumperz (Ed.), *Language and social identity* (pp. 1–21). New York: Cambridge University Press.

Halberstam, D. (Speaker). (2003, December 29). *Interview: David Halberstam on collection of essays about America* (Electronic transcript of an interview conducted by Bob Edwards, host of Morning Edition, National Public Radio). Retrieved December 31, 2003, from http://www.npr.org/transcripts/index.html

Hallinan, M., & Smith, S. (1985). The effects of classroom racial composition on students' interracial friendliness. *Social Psychology Quarterly, 48,* 3–16.

Hamilton, D., Sherman, S., & Ruvolo, C. (1990). Stereotype-based expectancies: Effects on information processing and social behavior. *Journal of Social Issues, 46*(2), 35–59.

Hechter, M. (1975). *Internal colonialist: The Celtic fringe in British national development, 1536–1966.* Berkeley: University of California Press.

Heider, F. (1958). *The psychology of interpersonal relations.* New York: John Wiley.

Herbst, P. (1997). *The color of words: An encyclopedic dictionary of ethnic bias in the United States.* Yarmouth, ME: Intercultural Press.

Hewstone, M. (1988). Attributional bases of intergroup conflict. In W. Strobe, A. Kruglanski, D. Bar-Tal, & M. Hewstone (Eds.), *The social psychology of intergroup conflict.* New York: Springer.

Himes, J. (1974). *Racial and ethnic relations.* Dubuque, IA: William C. Brown.

Hoffman, E. (1985). The effect of race-relation composition on the frequency of organizational communication. *Social Psychology Quarterly, 48,* 17–26.

Hopper, R. (1986). Speech evaluation of intergroup dialect differences: The shibboleth schema. In W. B. Gudykunst (Ed.), *Intergroup communication* (pp. 127–136). London: Edward Arnold.

Horowitz, M. (1991). Person schemas. In M. Horowitz (Ed.), *Person schemas and maladaptive interpersonal patterns* (pp. 13–31). Chicago: University of Chicago Press.

Jacobs, J. (1992). Identity development of biracial children. In M. Root (Ed.), *Racially mixed people in America* (pp. 190–206). Newbury Park, CA: Sage.

Jaspars, J., & Hewstone, M. (1982). Cross-cultural interaction, social attribution and intergroup relations. In S. Bochner (Ed.), *Cultures in contact* (pp. 127–156). Elmsford, NY: Pergamon.

Johnson, D., Johnson, R., & Maruyama, G. (1984). Goal interdependence and interpersonal attraction in heterogeneous classrooms: A meta-analysis. In N. Miller & M. Brewer (Eds.), *Groups in contact* (pp. 187–212). Orlando, FL: Academic Press.

Keyes, C. (1981). The dialectic of ethnic change. In C. Keyes (Ed.), *Ethnic change* (pp. 3–30). Seattle: University of Washington Press.

Kim, Y. Y. (1986). Understanding the social context of inter-group communication: A personal network theory. In W. B. Gudykunst (Ed.), *Intergroup communication* (pp. 86–95). London: Edward Arnold.

Kim, Y. Y. (1991). Intercultural communication competence. In S. Ting-Toomey & F. Korzenny (Eds.), *Cross-cultural interpersonal communication* (pp. 259–275). Newbury Park, CA: Sage.

Kim, Y. Y. (1992). Synchrony and intercultural communication. In D. Crookall & K. Arai (Eds.), *Global interdependence: Simulation and gaming perspectives* (pp. 99–105). New York: Springer.

Kim, Y. Y. (1999). *Unum* and *Pluribus:* Ideological underpinnings of interethnic communication in the United States. *International Journal of Intercultural Relations, 23*(4), 591–611.

Kim, Y. Y. (2001). *Becoming intercultural: An integrative theory of communication and cross-cultural adaptation.* Thousand Oaks, CA: Sage.

Kim, Y. Y., Kim, Y. S., Duty, D. M., & Yoshitake, M. (2002, November). *Interethnic communication among college students: An examination of contextual and behavioral factors.* Paper presented at the annual conference of the National Communication Association, New Orleans.

Kim, Y. Y., Lujan, P., & Dixon, L. (1998). "I can walk both ways": Identity integration of American Indians in Oklahoma. *Human Communication Research, 25*(2), 252–274.

Kim, Y. Y., McClure, R. R., Ogawa, N., & Kim, Y. S. (2003, May). *Patterns of interethnic communication: A quantitative-qualitative examination of behavioral and contextual factors among adult Americans.* Paper presented at the annual conference of the International Communication Association, San Diego, CA.

Kim, Y. Y., Ogawa, N., Rainwater, R. R., & Kim, Y. S. (2003, November). *Interethnic communication among adult Americans: An examination of behavioral and contextual factors.* Paper presented at the annual conference of the National Communication Association, Miami, FL.

Kirkland, S., Greenberg, J., & Pyszczynski, T. (1987). Further evidence of the dexterous effects of overheard DELs: Derogation beyond the target. *Personality and Social Psychological Bulletin, 13,* 126–227.

Kleg, M. (1993). *Hate, prejudice, and racism.* Albany: State University of New York Press.

Lambert, W. (1979). Language as a factor in intergroup relations. In H. Giles & R. St. Clair (Eds.), *Language and social psychology* (pp. 186–192). Baltimore, MD: University Park Press.

Langer, E. (1989). *Mindfulness.* Reading, MA: Addison-Wesley.

Lazarus, R. (1966). *Psychological stress and the coping process.* St. Louis, MO: McGraw-Hill.

Lukens, J. (1979). Interethnic conflict and communicative distance. In H. Giles & B. Saint Jacques (Eds.), *Language and ethnic relations* (pp. 143–158). Elmsford, NY: Pergamon.

Mack, D., Tucker, T., Archuleta, R., DeGroot, G., Hernandez, A., & Oh, S. (1997, October). Interethnic relations on campus: Can't we all get along? *Journal of Multicultural Counseling & Development, 25*(4), 256–268.

Martin, J. (2000). Understanding whiteness in the United States. In L. Samovar & R. Porter (Eds.), *Intercultural communication: A reader* (pp. 43–51). Belmont, CA: Wadsworth.

Marwell, G., Oliver, P., & Prahl, R. (1988, November). Social networks and collective action: A theory of the critical mass III. *American Journal of Sociology, 94*(3), 502–534.

Maslow, A. (1969). A theory of metamotivation: The biological rooting of the value-life. In H. Chiang & A. H. Maslow (Eds.), *The healthy personality* (pp. 35–56). New York: Van Nostrand Reinhold.

Nash, M. (1989). *The cauldron of ethnicity in the modern world.* Chicago: University of Chicago Press.

Oddou, G., & Mendenhall, M. (1984). Person perception in cross-cultural settings. *International Journal of Intercultural Relations, 8,* 77–96.

Olzak, S. (1987). Causes of ethnic conflict and protest in urban America, 1877–1889. *Social Science Research, 16,* 185–210.

Padilla, A., Wagatsuma, Y., & Lindholm, K. (1985). Acculturation and personality as predictors of stress in Japanese and Japanese-Americans. *Journal of Social Psychology, 125*(3), 295–305.

Parks, M. R., Stan, C. M., & Eggert, L. L. (1983). Romantic involvement and social network involvement. *Social Psychology Quarterly, 46,* 116–131.

Pettigrew, T. (1979). The ultimate attribution error: Extending Allport's cognitive analysis of prejudice. *Personality and Social Psychology Bulletin, 5,* 461–476.

Pettigrew, T., & Martin, J. (1989). Organizational inclusion of minority groups: A social psychological analysis. In J. Van Oudenhoven & T. Willemsen (Eds.), *Ethnic minorities: Social psychological perspectives* (pp. 169–200). Berwyn, PA: Swets North America.

Phinney, J. (1993). Multiple group identities: Differentiation, conflict, and integration. In J. Kroger (Ed.), *Discussions on ego identity* (pp. 47–73). Hillsdale, NJ: Lawrence Erlbaum.

Rex, J. (1976). Racial conflict in the city: The experiences of Birmingham, England from 1952–1975. In S. Clarke & J. Obler (Eds.), *Urban ethnic conflict: A comparative perspective* (pp. 132–163). Chapel Hill: University of North Carolina Press.

Richmond, A. (1986). Racial conflict in Britain. *Contemporary Sociology, 9*(2), 184–187.

Rogers, E., & Kincaid, L. (1981). *Communication networks: A new paradigm for research.* New York: Free Press.

Rorty, R. (1998). *Achieving our country: Leftist thought in twentieth-century America.* Cambridge, MA: Harvard University Press.

Ross, J. (1979). Language and the mobilization of ethnic identity. In H. Giles & B. Saint-Jacques (Eds.), *Language and ethnic relations* (pp. 1–13). Elmsford, NY: Pergamon.

Ross, L. (1977). The intuitive psychologist and his shortcomings: Distortions in the attribution process. In L. Berkowitz (Ed.), *Advances in experimental social psychology* (Vol. 10, pp. 174–220). New York: Academic Press.

Ruben, B. D. (1975). Intrapersonal, interpersonal, and mass communication processes in individual and multi-person systems. In B. D. Ruben & J. Y. Kim (Eds.), *General systems theory and human communication* (pp. 164–190). Rochelle Park, NJ: Hayden Book Co.

Ruben, B. D. (1978). Communication and conflict: A system-theoretic perspective. *Quarterly Journal of Speech, 64,* 211–232.

Ruesch, J., & Bateson, G. (1968). *Communication: The social matrix of psychiatry*. New York: Norton. (Original work published 1951)

Sachdev, I., & Bourhis, R. (1987). Status differentials and inter-group behavior. *European Journal of Social Psychology, 17,* 277–293.

Schuetz, A. (1944). The stranger. *American Journal of Sociology, 49,* 499–507.

Sherif, M. (1966). *In a common predicament.* Boston: Houghton Mifflin.

Simmel, G. (1950). The stranger. In G. Simmel, *The sociology of Georg Simmel* (K. H. Wolff, Ed. & Trans.). Glencoe, IL: Free Press. (Original work published 1908)

Stephan, C., & Stephan, W. (2003). Cognition and affect in cross-cultural relations. In W. B. Gudykunst (Ed.), *Cross-cultural and intercultural communication* (pp. 111–126). Thousand Oaks, CA: Sage.

Stephan, W., & Stephan, C. (1985). Intergroup anxiety. *Journal of Social Issues, 41*(3), 157–175.

Stone, J. (1985). *Racial conflict in contemporary society.* Cambridge, MA: Harvard University Press.

Taft, R. (1977). Coping with unfamiliar culture. In N. Warren (Ed.), *Studies in cross-cultural psychology* (Vol. 1, pp. 121–153). New York: Academic Press.

Tajfel, H. (1970). Experiments in intergroup discrimination. *Scientific American, 223*(2), 96–102.

Tajfel, H. (1974). Social identity and intergroup behavior. *Social Science Information, 13,* 65–93.

Tajfel, H., & Turner, J. (1979). An integrative theory of intergroup conflict. In W. Austin & S. Worchel (Eds.), *The social psychology of intergroup relations* (pp. 33–47). Monterey, CA: Brooks/Cole.

Tajfel, H., & Turner, J. (1986). The social identity theory of intergroup behavior. In S. Worchel & W. Austin (Eds.), *Psychology of intergroup relations* (2nd ed., pp. 7–17). Chicago; Nelson-Hall.

Tchen, J. K. W. (1990). The Chinatown-Harlem Initiative: Building multicultural understanding in New York City. In J. Brecher & T. Costello (Eds.), *Building bridges: The emerging grassroots coalition of labor and community* (pp. 186–192). New York: Monthly Review Press.

Tsuda, Y. (1986). *Language inequality and distortion in intercultural communication.* Philadelphia: John Benjamin.

Turner, J. (1975). Social comparison and social identity: Some prospects for intergroup behavior. *European Journal of Social Psychology, 5,* 5–34.

Turner, J. (1982). Towards a cognitive redefinition of the social group. In H. Tajfel (Ed.), *Social identity and intergroup relations* (pp. 15–40). Cambridge, UK: Cambridge University Press.

Turner, J., Hogg, M., Oakes, P., Reicher, S., & Wetherell, M. (1987). *Rediscovering the social group: A self-categorization theory.* Oxford, UK: Basil Blackwell.

Vaid-Raizada, V. (1981, August). Interracial attitudes and values in a university setting. *Dissertation Abstracts International, 42*(2-A), 829–830.

Van den Broucke, S., de Soete, G., & Bohrer, A. (1989). Free-response self-description as a predictor of success and failure in adolescent exchange students. *International Journal of Intercultural Relations, 13,* 73–91.

Van Dijk, T. (1987). *Communicating racism: Ethnic prejudice in thought and talk.* Newbury Park, CA: Sage.

Volkan, V. (1992, December). Ethnonationalistic rituals: An introduction. *Mind & Human Interaction, 4*(1), 3–19.

Von Raffler-Engel, W. (1988). The impact of covert factors in cross-cultural communication. In F. Poyatos (Ed.), *Cross-cultural perspectives in nonverbal communication* (pp. 71–104). Lewiston, NY: C. J. Hogrefe.

Walker, I., & Pettigrew, T. (1984). Relative deprivation theory: An overview and conceptual critique. British *Journal of Social Psychology, 23,* 301–310.

Walton, S. (1990). Stress management training for overseas effectiveness. *International Journal of Intercultural Relations, 14*(4), 507–527.

Watzlawick, P., Beavin, J., & Jackson, D. (1967). *The pragmatics of human communication.* New York: Norton.

Wolfe, A. (1998). *One nation, after all.* New York: Viking.

Wolpe, H. (1986). Class concepts, class struggle and racism. In J. Rex & D. Mason (Eds.), *Theories of race and ethnic relations* (pp. 110–130). New York: Cambridge University Press.

Worchel, S. (1979). Cooperation and the reduction of intergroup conflict: Some determining factors. In W. Austin & S. Worchel (Eds.), *The social psychology of intergroup relations* (pp. 262–273). Monterey, CA: Brooks/Cole.

Worchel, S. (1986). The role of cooperation in reducing intergroup conflict. In S. Worchel & W. Austin (Eds.), *Psychology of intergroup relations* (2nd ed., pp. 288–304). Chicago: Nelson-Hall.

Yang, H., & Sachdev, I. (1994, July). *Chinese communities in London and Taiwan: Vitality and language use.* Paper presented at the 5th International Conference on Language and Social Psychology, Brisbane, Australia.

Yoshikawa, M. (1986). Cross-cultural adaptation and perceptual development. In Y. Y. Kim (Ed.), *Cross-cultural adaptation: Current research* (pp. 140–148). Newbury Park, CA: Sage.

Yum, J. O. (1988). Network theory in intercultural communication. In Y. Y. Kim & W. B. Gudykunst (Eds.), *Theories in intercultural communication* (pp. 239–258). Newbury Park, CA: Sage.

15

Effective Intercultural Workgroup Communication Theory

JOHN G. OETZEL

Several workplace and demographic trends have created an impetus for the study of intercultural workgroups. First, demographic changes have increased the likelihood that individuals will work in diverse cultural groups on a daily basis. In the United States, for example, the projected population in 2005 includes 69.3% non-Hispanic whites, 13.3% Hispanics, 12.3% African Americans, 4.3% Asian or Pacific Islanders, and 0.8% Native Americans (U.S. Census, 2000). Judy and D'Amico (1997) projected that more than half of the new entrants into the workforce will be members of historically underrepresented groups by 2020. Second, globalization has resulted in increased interaction of people from different national cultural backgrounds. Interactions that illustrate globalization include international joint ventures (Barkema & Vermeulen, 1997), global business teams (Hofner Saphiere, 1996), and

multinational companies (Gomez-Mejia & Palich, 1997). In fact, some of these teams operate completely in a virtual environment through electronic communication (Jarvenpaa & Leidner, 1999). Third, some organizations are employing self-managed teams to reduce the number of layers in the hierarchy, thus increasing the number of workgroups (Barker, 1999). Even organizations that do not utilize self-managed teams place a premium on teamwork skills (e.g., Landrum & Harrold, 2003).

As a result of these trends, many researchers have explored how group member composition (culturally homogeneous vs. culturally diverse) influences group processes and outcomes (e.g., McLeod, Lobel, & Cox, 1996; Watson, Kumar, & Michaelsen, 1993). Some of the major conclusions reached by this line of research include (a) culturally diverse groups have more group process difficulty (e.g., more tension and conflict) than culturally homogeneous groups, (b) cultural diversity can benefit group performance because of the infusion of different ideas and approaches to solving problems, and (c) benefits occur only if diversity is managed properly. However, theoretical explanations of why cultural diversity affected small-group processes and outcomes were limited 10 years ago (Sessa & Jackson, 1995).

It was this limitation that led me to propose the effective decision-making theory (Oetzel, 1995). The basic premise of the theory (which I will elaborate on later in this chapter) is that culture (e.g., individualism and collectivism) and cultural diversity (i.e., heterogeneous vs. homogeneous group composition) influence the communication processes that occur in a workgroup. Subsequently, the communication processes will impact the outcomes of the groups (e.g., decision-making quality and satisfaction). In the past decade, research on intercultural workgroups has burgeoned, resulting in a more complex understanding of how culture and cultural diversity impact group communication process and performance. Some of this research includes my own studies to test and elaborate my theory. Thus, the purpose of this chapter is to update my original theory, which I now call the effective intercultural workgroup communication theory. To accomplish this purpose, I organize this chapter around the following sections: (a) scope and history of the theory; (b) metatheoretical and theoretical assumptions of the theory; (c) propositions of the theory (including the evidence supporting these propositions); and (d) application of the theory.

SCOPE AND HISTORY OF THE EFFECTIVE INTERCULTURAL WORKGROUP COMMUNICATION THEORY

Every theory has boundaries to what phenomena are explained. Further, this theory has a historical foundation that can be difficult to trace. Thus, this section identifies the scope or boundaries of the theory and presents the germination of the theory.

Scope

There are two key boundary aspects of this theory. The first is that the theory applies to workgroups and not necessarily to social support or social groups. A workgroup has some sort of problem-solving or decision-making task. The original theory focused exclusively on decision-making groups, but I have expanded this scope to workgroups in general. In addition, the group's task needs to be complex because a simple task is better handled by individuals than groups. Further, a simple task does not require interaction among group members to be completed well. A task is complex if it has multiple solutions, high information requirement, and high evaluation demands (Hirokawa, 1990). These criteria result in a need for interaction among members in order for the group to be effective. Examples of groups that fit this scope include the following: (a) work teams manufacturing computer chips; (b) an ad hoc group (e.g., a task force) identifying ways to decrease health care costs for state government; and (c) a group of students conducting a research project that applies communication theory to a social problem.

The second scope condition is that the groups are culturally diverse. A *culture* is a population of people who have similar attitudes, values, beliefs, and share a system of knowledge through unstated assumptions (Triandis, 1995). *Cultural diversity* "means the representation, in one social system, of people with distinctly different group affiliations of cultural significance" (Cox, 1994, p. 6). Cultural diversity can be indexed by national culture, ethnicity, language, gender, job position, age, or disability. Terms that are synonymous with cultural diversity include multicultural, intercultural, and culturally heterogeneous; these terms are used interchangeably in this chapter. A term that I use differently is cross-cultural, which compares/contrasts two or more different cultures. Thus, a cross-cultural group, for example, refers to a comparison of a group of Mexicans with a group of Brazilians, while an intercultural or multicultural group is composed of both Mexicans and Brazilians. The theory does make reference to homogeneous groups, but only relative to culturally diverse groups.

History

Personal Interests. The history of this theory includes the research that I used to form the foundation, but also my own personal interests and experiences that lead me to research these phenomena. I grew up in Ohio in the late 1960s and through the 1970s. It was a time when civil rights and advances in race relations were common topics and fresh in people's minds. Despite the popular notions of a "melting pot" and a "colorblind society," I noticed that there were inequities in how people were treated based on skin color (in my community that meant black and white). I also noticed that blacks and whites did not interact together very much except in certain school settings such as sports.

When I was 13, I moved to Albuquerque, New Mexico. It was the first time I had seen (except on TV) Hispanics (the reference for people of Spanish, Mexican, Central American, Cuban, etc., descent in New Mexico) and Native Americans. It was also the first time in my life that I was a numerical minority based on skin color (although I would later learn that my ethnic group still had political and economic majority status). My high school was composed of a majority Hispanic population with smaller Anglo (as whites or European Americans are referred to in New Mexico), Native American, and African American populations. I found it exhilarating. I loved interacting and making friends with people from different cultural backgrounds. I recall that

culturally different people in New Mexico interacted with each other more than what I experienced in Ohio. There were still "race disputes," but they seemed to be infrequent. I later learned that there were still segregated communities in Albuquerque, that some high schools were largely homogeneous, and that race relations were not ideal (much animosity was below the surface). Regardless, the seeds of interest in diversity and groups were planted in me.

After I graduated from the University of New Mexico, I went to the University of Iowa for my graduate degrees. At Iowa, I studied small-group interaction (among other topics) with Randy Hirokawa. I was fortunate to work with one of the leaders of research in small-group communication, and we conducted a few studies using his vigilant interaction theory (Hirokawa, 1985, 1988; Hirokawa & Rost, 1992). The primary assumption of vigilant interaction theory is that the way members talk about the problems and consequences associated with a decision affects how they think about problems and consequences, which, in turn, influences the quality of final decisions. The theory assumes that the quality of the group's final decision is the result of prior subdecisions made during the group's interaction. The subdecisions are based on four characteristics: (a) analysis of the problematic situation, (b) establishment of goals and criteria, (c) evaluation of the positive qualities of available choices, and (d) evaluation of the negative qualities of available choices.

I appreciated vigilant interaction theory and Hirokawa's research for their strong empirical backing and the application to "real-world" groups. However, I also had concerns about the theory in that it did not include relational aspects such as group member satisfaction. I was not able to articulate my concerns very well until I took a class in intercultural communication with Stella Ting-Toomey at California State University, Fullerton. I was living in Los Angeles and working at a community college. I needed to complete a couple of courses for my degree at Iowa and was interested in intercultural communication. I also taught in a culturally diverse college and wanted to improve my own teaching. During that class, I was introduced to intercultural theories and was finally able to articulate my criticism of the vigilant interaction theory. It was in that class that I began to develop my effective decision-making theory and blend my diversity and workgroup interests.

This brief story of my experiences and interests can be summarized by the following concerns as I wrote that original piece and now as I write this updated theory. First, I have an interest in why cultural diversity matters. How do cultural values and self-conceptions impact communication in workgroups? Second, I have a great interest in social justice and inclusion. I believe that great inequities exist in society and that social change is needed to include more people in mainstream society than in our current society (I focus mainly on the U.S. for this point). Related to these interests are questions such as, "How do certain values and practices privilege certain cultural groups over others?" and, "How can we address such privilege?" Finally, my interest in workgroups comes from the fact that work sites (and school settings) are places where different cultural groups meet and interact daily. I believe that people maintain relatively segregated personal lives. My underlying assumption is that if we can change how people work together (i.e., if we can get them to interact positively and in ways that support one another and work productively), we can improve the quality of race relations. It certainly is an idealized goal and one that may never be realized, but it provides the reader with a sense of "where I am coming from."

Research Foundation. The first foundational element in my theory is the work on cultural individualism-collectivism (I-C) and self-construals in the intercultural literature (e.g., Gudykunst et al., 1996; Hofstede, 2001; Markus & Kitayama,

1991; Triandis, 1995). Cultural I-C is the most popular concept for explaining variability in behavior across cultures (Triandis, 1995). *Individualism* is a social pattern that consists of loosely linked individuals who view themselves as independent of collectives and who give priority to their personal goals over the goals of others (Triandis, 1995). *Collectivism* is a social pattern consisting of closely linked individuals who see themselves as part of one or more collectives (family, coworkers, tribe, nation) and are willing to give priority to the goals of these collectives over their own personal goals (Triandis, 1995). While cultural I-C can be used to explain and organize a wide variety of behaviors in a number of different cultures, researchers have shown that a reliance on only cultural I-C to explain communication behavior is limited and can lead to erroneous predictions (Gudykunst et al., 1996; Kim et al., 1996).

Gudykunst and his colleagues (1996) explained that cultural I-C has a direct influence on behavior because culture socializes individuals in terms of individualistic and collectivistic tendencies. They noted, however, that the I-C tendencies also influence individual-level factors and that these factors mediate the influence of cultural I-C on communication behavior. A key individual-level factor is self-construal or how individuals conceive of themselves (Markus & Kitayama, 1991). Self-construal consists of two components—independent and interdependent. The independent construal of self is the view that an individual is a unique entity with a unique repertoire of feelings and thoughts, while the interdependent construal of self is the belief that the individual is connected to other members of the individual's group (Markus & Kitayama, 1991). Gudykunst et al. (1996) argued that independent self-construals predominate in individualistic cultures, while interdependent self-construals predominate in collectivistic cultures because of cultural socialization. Researchers have found that self-construal mediates the influence of cultural I-C on communication behavior such as communication styles (Gudykunst et al., 1996), conversational constraints (Kim et al., 1996), and conflict behavior (Oetzel et al., 2001).

The second key foundation to my theory is models of group effectiveness (e.g., Hackman, 1990; Hirokawa & Rost, 1992; Larson & LaFasto, 1989), which include Hirokawa's vigilant interaction theory. My interest is to describe what makes a group effective. This interest is shared by a number of other group scholars. For example, Larson and LaFasto (1989) studied 32 teams from a cross-section of organizations that included executive management teams, marketing teams, cardiac surgery teams, military teams, and football teams. They discovered, through extensive interviewing, eight characteristics common to effective teams. Effective teams have (a) a clear, elevating goal; (b) a results-driven structure; (c) competent team members; (d) unified commitment; (e) a collaborative climate; (f) standards of excellence; (g) external support and recognition; and (h) principled leadership. Larson and LaFasto's model (and vigilant interaction theory) emphasizes task communication (compared to relational communication) and it does not include cultural diversity.

Several models of group effectiveness for culturally diverse groups have been proposed (Hofner Saphiere, 1996; Maznevski, 1994; Maznevski & Peterson, 1997). For example, Maznevski (1994) developed a model to explain performance in decision-making groups characterized by diverse composition. She explained that diversity in decision-making groups provides several advantages and disadvantages. The advantages include a variety of knowledge, skills, and roles to draw upon. This variety is important because diverse members have the ability to see problems in different ways and, as a result, a diverse group is more creative in problem solving than a homogeneous group. The disadvantages are process difficulty (or loss), such as power struggles, that

result from different values among group members. Maznevski argued that the key for diverse groups to be effective is integration. Integration is "the combining of elements into a unified result" (Maznevski, 1994, p. 537), and the key to integration is effective communication. Maznevski posited that culturally diverse groups are more likely to make effective decisions when they share social reality, display the ability to decenter (perspective-taking), have confidence and motivation to communicate, have the ability to negotiate and endorse norms of communication, and have the ability to attribute difficulties appropriately. The strengths of Maznevski's model are that it recognizes that cultural diversity affects the communication processes in groups and that effective communication processes are important for effective decision making. The model's limitations are that it does not specify how and why culture and cultural diversity affect group process, and it focuses on a limited definition of group effectiveness (i.e., only task effectiveness).

My concern with both mainstream and cultural diversity models of group effectiveness is that they privilege one particular view of how groups should work. That is, they emphasize work outcomes over relational outcomes. Group scholars historically recognized that there are two important, interrelated, dimensions to task-oriented groups: (1) a task dimension and (2) a social or relational dimension (Bales, 1950). The task dimension refers to the productivity of the group (e.g., the quality of the decision), while the relational dimension refers to the cohesiveness of the group members (e.g., the quality of the relationships). Hackman (1990) identified an additional dimension of group effectiveness for a total of three: (a) the degree to which the group's productive output meets the standards of quality or quantity (i.e., task dimension), (b) the degree to which the group's processes enable the group to work together interdependently in the future (i.e., relational dimension), and (c) the degree to which the group experience contributes to the well-being of team members (a personal dimension).

Thus, the effectiveness of a group can be measured along three dimensions: (a) *task* effectiveness, (b) *relational* effectiveness, and (c) *personal* effectiveness. It is likely that different individuals will prefer one dimension over another because of differing values. In a study to test this assumption, my coauthor and I empirically tested whether certain individuals prefer a particular dimension of group effectiveness over another (Oetzel & Bolton-Oetzel, 1997). Specifically, we explored the impact of self-construal on dimensions of group effectiveness. We found that independent and interdependent self-construals were associated positively with both task and relational effectiveness. However, task effectiveness was explained better by independent, rather than interdependent, self-construals, while relational effectiveness was explained better by interdependent, rather than independent, self-construals. Personal effectiveness was associated positively with both independent and interdependent self-construals with neither variable being a better predictor. Given these findings, I argue that a culturally appropriate model of group effectiveness must consider both task and relational effectiveness to avoid privileging one cultural perspective over another.

ASSUMPTIONS

Metatheoretical Assumptions

Metatheoretical assumptions are the "fundamental assumptions about the nature of the world, methods of producing knowledge, and values" (Deetz, 2001, p. 3). These assumptions help to place a theory in relation to other theories and research. In addition, identifying these assumptions provides the opportunity to discuss the assumptions of the theory and the implications of such assumptions.

Deetz (2001) utilized two dimensions to characterize metatheoretical assumptions: (a) elite/a priori–local emergent; and (b) consensus–dissensus. The combination of these two dimensions yields four discourses: (a) normative (elite and consensus); (b) interpretive (local and consensus); (c) critical (elite and dissensus); and (d) dialogic (local and dissensus). Based on these discourses and dimensions as Deetz described them, I characterize my theory as predominantly normative, but with some critical discourse. Both the normative and critical approaches emphasize the elite/a priori pole of the first dimension (How do research concepts arise?). My research on this topic has been heavily theory driven and privileges the language of the research community over the local community. My theory focuses on progress, empowerment, and increased well-being through the discovery of common patterns of interactions across a variety of intercultural workgroups.

The second dimension (the presentation of unity or difference in the prevailing discourse) is where the normative and critical discourses differ. Deetz (2001) described the main goal of the consensus pole as to "display a discovered order with a high degree of fidelity" (p. 14). In contrast, the dissensus pole emphasizes conflict and struggle as the natural state and views the "lens" as the dominant metaphor (as compared to the mirror). My research blends both of these perspectives. I seek to identify a set of "law-like" statements to explain what happens in intercultural workgroups—a normative approach. I believe that there are observable and identifiable patterns of interaction that occur in these types of groups and that using the language of the research community is useful to characterize what is occurring and, more important, improve the quality of interaction in these groups. However, I am also suspicious of current research and conceptualizations of intercultural workgroups. For example, I have already stated that I believe inequities exist in society and that one of my goals is to change these inequities. When I formulated my theory, I thought about which positions privilege certain groups and thus reinforce inequity. This concern is why I critiqued previous models of group effectiveness and argued for a culturally appropriate model. Furthermore, when testing my theory (Oetzel, 1998a, 1998b), I chose to use two sets of culturally homogeneous groups (Japanese and European American) to compare to heterogeneous groups. Cox (1990) noted that when researchers compare a diverse group to only one type of homogeneous group (always European American in prior research studies), the researcher privileges the homogeneous group's interaction pattern by letting it be the standard of comparison. Thus, European American group communication becomes the norm to which all other groups are compared.

The combination of these discourses for me is consistent with Miller's (2000) description of post-positivism. I view my theory and research as a social construction of intercultural workgroups. The construction is one that seeks patterns in the world, but from a social justice and somewhat suspicious lens. Miller explained that "a social constructionist ontology is consistent with a post-positivist position that emphasizes both the patterned nature of the social construction process and the regular and predictable effects that reified social constructions have on organizational members" (p. 60). Like Miller's rejection of the positivist position on objectivity, I do not see my scholarship as value-free or objective (i.e., a complete separation of investigator and the subject of investigation). I recognize that my theory and perspective are one particular lens for viewing this phenomenon and one that has inherent assumptions guiding that lens. I hope that by specifying those assumptions it is easier to see what the theory does not tell us or limits us from seeing, as well as showing what it does focus on.

Theoretical Assumptions

The metatheoretical assumptions provide a "big picture" or fundamental grounding of my theory. The theoretical assumptions are specific to the theory at hand and provide the concrete foundation for the propositions. Since the focus of this book is on culture and communication, I discuss my assumptions about the relationship between these two concepts before describing the specific assumptions for the theory.

I assume that culture and communication are related in a recursive manner. That is, culture influences communication and communication influences culture. Triandis (1995) noted that, "Culture emerges in interaction. As people interact, some of their ways of thinking, feeling, and behavior are transmitted to each other and become automatic ways of reacting to specific situations" (p. 4). In this sense, communication and culture are intertwined, but they are not the same thing. Communicative interaction provides evidence of cultural values and beliefs at work. Culture is more stable, and thus more difficult to change, than communication because values, beliefs, and behaviors are created over time. Finally, I believe it is possible to take a snapshot of culture at a particular time (albeit an arbitrary snapshot) to determine a baseline for how culture impacts communication. I do not think you can identify a snapshot of communication that then impacts culture. Communication must be repeated before impacting culture.

The specific theoretical assumptions for the effective intercultural workgroup communication theory are as follows:

1. *Intercultural workgroups can be thought of as a system with inputs, processes, and outcomes operating in a particular context.* A system is a set of component parts that have interdependent relationships (Ellis & Fisher, 1994). The component parts of a workgroup are the individual members. Every group operates in

a particular context, such as an organization, classroom, or community. Systems theory is a popular metaphor (Morgan, 1997) for research on small groups and serves as a guiding metaphor for this theory as well.

2. *The context of the group frames the relationships among inputs, processes, and outputs.* The context is the environment the group operates in and consists of the physical surroundings, the organizational structure, the cultural situation, and the required work. Each of these factors constrains and guides the interactions among group members. For example, the country where interactions take place may dictate what language is spoken and how decisions should be reached. The physical surroundings may influence the means by which members communicate (e.g., a physically dispersed team needs to rely on such technologies as the telephone or electronic mail for daily interactions).

3. *The inputs, reflected by members' cultural values and self-conceptions and the diversity among group members, influence the communication processes of a group.* One of the basic assumptions of the theory is that culture influences communication behavior (as opposed to the other way around). The key cultural inputs for this theory are cultural I-C and individuals' self-conceptions. These factors influence individual members' behavior, but also the collective behavior of the group.

4. *Communication processes impact the outcomes of the group.* A number of research studies have demonstrated that the quality of interaction impacts the quality of group outcomes (e.g., Hackman, 1990; Hirokawa & Rost, 1992). However, research studies on culturally diverse groups often omit communication processes and examine the impact of inputs directly on outputs (e.g., McLeod et al., 1996). This type of study is what Lawrence (1997) and Pelled, Eisenhardt, and Xin (1999)

referred to as "black box" studies. The inputs go into a "black box" and outputs miraculously emerge. In reality, communication processes are the medium through which cultural diversity affects group outcomes (Lawrence, 1997; Oetzel, 1995; Pelled et al., 1999).

5. *The processes and outcomes serve as feedback for context and input.* A critical assumption of systems theory is that processes and outcomes are fed back into the inputs. For example, outcomes of a group reinforce individual decisions and satisfaction and may influence future work effort in the group. Further, if a culturally diverse workgroup has a high-quality process, it may improve the quality of intergroup relations that members have with outside people (e.g., by encouraging them to see members of other cultural groups in a positive light). This feedback rarely has a direct impact on culturally diverse workgroups and context, however; rather, it is a slow and incremental process. Historical contexts do not change overnight and certainly not as the result of one positive workgroup experience. In addition, individuals' cultural values and conceptions do not change because of a few negative interactions.

6. *Intercultural workgroups need to be evaluated in terms of both task and relational effectiveness.* This assumption was established in the section on research foundations. As a reminder, cultural values and self-conceptions influence the concern for task and relational effectiveness (Hofstede 2001; Oetzel & Bolton-Oetzel, 1997). Specifically, the more people have independent self-conceptions, the more they are concerned with task effectiveness. Further, the more people have interdependent self-conceptions, the more they are concerned with relational effectiveness. Thus, a culturally appropriate model needs to emphasize both measures of effectiveness. Indicators of task effectiveness include such outcomes as quality decisions, productivity, quality solutions, and a

lack of withholding effort (i.e., shirking work or social loafing). Indicators of relational effectiveness include such outcomes as cohesion and satisfaction.

7. *Participation, consensus decision making, cooperative conflict, and respectful communication are culturally appropriate communication behaviors in that they relate to both task and relational effectiveness.* In this chapter and elsewhere (Oetzel, 1995, 2001) I argue that the communication processes studied in culturally diverse groups should relate positively with both task and relational outcomes. In the original theory, I identified three communication processes that meet this criterion: (a) equal distribution of turns (i.e., all group members participate in the discussion at relatively equal levels—they take the same number of turns), (b) consensus decision-making styles (i.e., all members participate in, and agree with, the decision), and (c) cooperative conflict styles (i.e., conflict is managed by integrating all parties' interests—a win-win approach). Prior research has found that these communication processes relate positively to such outcomes as quality decision making and satisfaction (Deutsch, 1969; Kume, 1985; Nemeth, 1992). In a recent study (Oetzel, 2001), I also found respectful communication (i.e., demonstrating that other members are valued and important) was associated positively with satisfaction and negatively with shirking work in culturally diverse workgroups.

PROPOSITIONS AND EVIDENCE

Given the assumptions presented in the prior section, I now discuss the specific propositions of the theory and the evidence supporting these propositions. I first point out changes between the first and current versions of the theory. I then provide a model that reflects the concepts in the effective intercultural workgroup communication theory and reveal the specific propositions of the theory.

Changes in the Current Version

The original theory contained 14 propositions that focused on group-level communication behavior and decision making. Propositions 1 through 7 examined the influence of input on process. Specifically, they made the connections between the following concepts: (a) self-construals and task/relational effectiveness (P1); (b) group composition (i.e., homogeneous vs. heterogeneous) and distribution of turns (P2); (c) self-construals and decision-making style (P3); (d) group composition and commitment (P4); (e) self-construals and frequency of conflict (P5); (f) self-construals and cooperative conflict (P6); and (g) self-construals and conflict styles (P7). Propositions 8 through 14 focused on the effect of process on outcomes. Specifically, they posited the relationships between the following concepts and effective decisions (concepts listed first were proposed to be more effective than those listed last): (a) cooperative versus competitive conflict (P8); (b) personal versus social identities (P9); (c) equal versus unequal distribution of turns (P10); (d) commitment versus lack of commitment to the group (P11); (e) commitment versus lack of commitment to the decision (P12); (f) consensus versus majority decision rules (P13); and (g) addressing versus not addressing the functional requisites of the vigilant interaction theory (P14).

During the past decade, I have attempted to refine and update my theory. I noticed several factors that were missing from the original version or that needed expansion. The first change was to expand the focus to workgroups in general and not just decision-making groups. Second, the original theory briefly introduced contextual factors that influence communication processes in culturally diverse workgroups. Specifically, Proposition 9 discussed the importance of emphasizing personal identities over social identities for effective decision making. In this updated version, I expand the coverage of contextual factors (even though I dropped the personal/social identity issue). Third, I added an additional input variable, face concerns, that relates to culture and communication. *Face* represents an individual's claimed sense of positive image in the context of social interaction and consists of three types of concerns (Ting-Toomey & Kurogi, 1998). *Self-face* is the concern for one's own image, *other-face* is the concern for another's image, and *mutual-face* is concern for both parties' images and/or the "image" of the relationship (Ting-Toomey & Kurogi, 1998). Finally, I added propositions at the individual level in addition to those at the group level (though only for the influence of inputs on process).

There are also two deletions from the original theory. First, I omitted commitment (Propositions 4, 11, and 12). Upon reflection, I decided that commitment was not a communicative process and thus was inappropriate for the theory. Second, I deleted the last proposition regarding functional requisites. This proposition came directly from the vigilant interaction theory and thus should be left to others to explore and contemplate. With these changes, I now present the updated version of the theory.

Theoretical Propositions

The purpose of the theory is to explain how culture and cultural diversity affect group communication processes and how group communication processes affect both task and relational outcomes (Oetzel, 1995). Figure 15.1 displays a model for this theory. I organize this section by introducing the propositions about the influence of input on process and then discuss the propositions of process on output. Each proposition is introduced and followed with supporting evidence.

Group Inputs Influence Group Process. The theory includes three broad inputs: contextual factors, group composition, and cultural/individual factors. For a number of these propositions, I refer to effective communication. In the seventh theoretical assumption, I explain that equal participation/turn taking, respectful communication, consensus decision making, and cooperative conflict behavior were culturally appropriate because of their positive relationships with both task and relational effectiveness. In the propositions, I substitute "effective communication" for this collection of behaviors.

> *Proposition 1:* The more negative contextual factors that a culturally diverse group faces, the less likely the group will experience effective communication.

There are four contextual elements that I consider in this theory: (a) a history of unresolved conflict among cultural/ethnic groups (e.g., the conflict between Israelis and Palestinians), (b) ingroup/outgroup balance (i.e., the number of group members from each cultural group), (c) cooperative versus competitive tasks (i.e., does the task require collaboration among members or encourage members to work for their own interests, such as a mixed-motive task? [McGrath, 1984]), and (d) status differences among members (e.g., boss and employee). Essentially, each of these four factors is a condition that helps or hinders the creation of a common ingroup identity in a culturally diverse group (see Gaertner, Dovidio, & Bachman, 1996). The common ingroup identity model is based on the contact hypothesis (Allport, 1954), which argues that certain conditions enable group members to create alliances and work toward common goals. A history of unresolved conflict, imbalance in the number of group members from each cultural group, competitive tasks, and inequality of status among group members (i.e., negative contextual factors) tend to result in members' emphasizing differences among

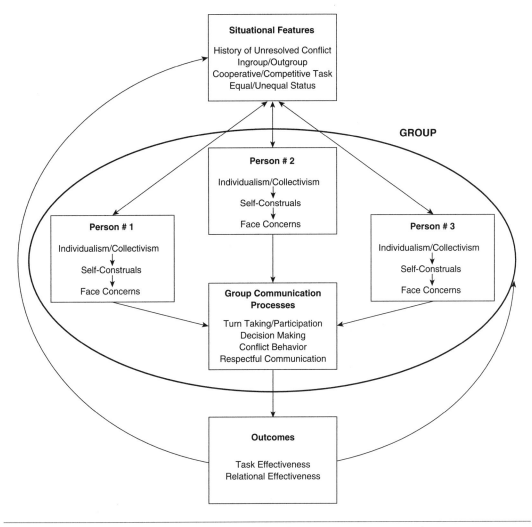

Figure 15.1 Model of the Effective Intercultural Workgroup Communication Theory

themselves and viewing those differences as negative (Gaertner et al., 1996). In such situations, group members are prone to focus on protecting their own (or the ingroup's) identity at the expense of working for group goals. Thus, they are apt to be suspicious of others and less likely to use effective communication. In contrast, a history of successfully resolving conflicts, balance in the number of group members from each cultural group, cooperative tasks, and equality among group members tend to result in members' sharing a common ingroup identity where cultural differences are

respected. In such situations, group members are more likely to have trust and work together on the group's task.

Proposition 2: The more culturally heterogeneous a group, the less likely it will experience effective communication.

A consistent finding about group composition is that culturally heterogeneous groups have less effective interaction processes (or greater process difficulty) than culturally homogeneous groups (Cady & Valentine,

1999; Oetzel, 1998a; Watson & Kumar, 1992; Watson et al., 1993). I review two studies to illustrate some of these specific findings. I studied homogeneous and heterogeneous groups working on a hypothetical decision-making task about a student allegedly caught cheating on a test (Oetzel, 1998a). There were two sets of homogeneous groups (Japanese and European American), while the heterogeneous groups were composed of two Japanese and two European Americans. I found that the heterogeneous groups utilized consensus decisions less and had less equal turn taking than homogeneous groups. Second, Watson and his colleagues (1993) compared the processes of ethnically homogeneous and heterogeneous student groups working on four business case studies over the course of a semester. The homogeneous groups were composed of European Americans, whereas the heterogeneous groups were predominantly composed of an African American, a European American, a Latin American, and a foreign national from an Asian, African, Middle Eastern, or Latin American country. Group process was measured with 23 items from Watson and Michaelsen's (1988) Group Style Description, which allowed group members to self-report the (in)effectiveness of group process in their group. Homogeneous groups were found to have more effective processes than heterogeneous groups during initial meetings. The more effective processes included fewer power struggles, cooperative interaction, and equal participation. Over a period of 12 weeks, the heterogeneous groups made adjustments and achieved processes at the level of homogeneous groups.

I need to offer one caveat about this proposition. While heterogeneity leads to less effective communication, it is important not to assume that a group is heterogeneous just because the group members come from different cultural/ethnic groups. People who come from a similar organizational or occupational culture (e.g., graduates of U.S. business schools) are likely to have a great deal of commonality even if they come from different national cultures. In a recent study, I explored the relationship between member self construal and communication processes (equal participation, cooperation, and respect) in groups of varying levels of diversity (in terms of age, gender, and ethnicity) (Oetzel, 2001). Each of the 36 groups was composed of three to six undergraduate students engaged in three group tasks relevant to a course in which the students were enrolled. I found that self-construals of group members explained the communication processes used by the group better than the composition of the group. In fact, heterogeneity did not explain differences in communication processes among culturally diverse groups. One difference from other studies is that this study took place in a culturally diverse area (Los Angeles), and the group members may have learned how to adapt their communication to fit with other cultural groups. Many other studies (e.g., Watson et al., 1993) took place in locations of the United States that are not as diverse as California.

The key conclusion of this caveat is that heterogeneity needs to be measured and not assumed. My study of culturally homogeneous and heterogeneous groups provides support for this conclusion (Oetzel, 1998a). I compared the communication patterns of these groups and found that groups composed of members with varying levels of independent or interdependent self-construals were more likely to have unequal participation than groups composed of members with similar levels of independent or interdependent self-construals.

Proposition 3: The more individualistic (or independent) a culturally diverse group, the more likely the group will utilize dominating conflict strategies.

Proposition 4: The more collectivistic (or interdependent) a culturally diverse group, the more likely the group will utilize collaborating conflict strategies.

The influence of cultural I-C and self-construals on conflict behavior is well established. Three studies help to illustrate this point. First, Cox, Lobel, and McLeod (1991) studied the effects of I-C on the cooperative and competitive choices made by individuals during a Prisoner's Dilemma game. They assigned 136 U.S. undergraduate and graduate students to one of 16 all-Anglo or 17 culturally diverse groups (with one member each from Asian American, Hispanic American, African American, and Anglo American ethnic groups). They found that all of the groups in the study produced more competitive than cooperative responses, but that groups composed of members from a collectivistic tradition (Asian American, Hispanic American, and African American) displayed more cooperative choices overall than groups composed of members with an individualistic cultural tradition.

A second study utilizing I-C also examined conflict and cooperation. Thomas (1999) studied the influence of collectivism on evaluations of conflict and cooperation in culturally diverse groups. Seventy-seven undergraduates representing 14 nationalities at a New Zealand university were randomly assigned to 24 three- or four-person groups and were required to complete five business case studies. The participants registered their opinions about a variety of processes, including conflict, cooperation and citizenship (i.e., helping others), and satisfaction with the group and the process. Thomas found that an individual's degree of collectivism was positively related to member evaluations of cooperation and citizenship.

Third, my study of culturally diverse and homogeneous groups also utilized self-construals to investigate conflict behavior (Oetzel, 1998a, 1998b). I found that (a) groups

composed of members with high independent self-construals were more likely to use competitive tactics and less likely to use cooperative tactics than groups composed of members with low independent self-construals; and (b) because of their cultural background and self-construals, European Americans initiated more conflicts and used more competitive conflict tactics than did Japanese in both homogenous and heterogeneous groups.

Finally, I want to note that Propositions 3 and 4 apply to both the group and individual levels. Previous studies (Bond & Shiu, 1997; Cox et al., 1991; Oetzel, 1998a, 2001) have found that the collective attributes of the individuals become a part of the group's personality or group syntality. These studies demonstrate that a group norm reflective of the summative cultural values of the individual members (as opposed to being dominated by one individual) can be established in culturally diverse groups. This summative norm likely occurs in the absence of negative contextual features (Proposition 1), but in their absence it is reasonable for Propositions 3 and 4 to be relevant for both individuals of culturally diverse groups and the groups as a whole.

Proposition 5: The more individualistic (or independent) individuals in a culturally diverse group, the more likely they will take turns.

Proposition 6: The more collectivist (or interdependent) a culturally diverse group, the more likely the group will have equal participation.

Cultural I-C and self-construals also influence turn taking/participation. I (Oetzel, 1998b) found that independent self-construal was associated positively with the number of turns individuals took in both culturally homogeneous and heterogeneous groups. Further, I found that members of individualistic cultures (i.e., European Americans) took more turns than members of collectivistic cultures (i.e., Japanese) in culturally heterogeneous groups. My study of 36 study groups found that the higher the groups' average interdependence, the more likely the groups had equal participation among members (Oetzel, 2001).

In the original theory, I proposed that groups with members who have interdependent self-construals would be more likely to reach consensus than groups with members who had independent self-construals. In subsequent studies (Oetzel, 1998a, 1998b, 2001) I did not find any support for this proposition and thus I have removed decision-making styles from the aforementioned propositions on self-construal/cultural I-C. Similarly, I did not find in my 2001 study that respectful communication related to self-construals; it is therefore also not in these propositions.

> *Proposition 7:* The more members of a culturally diverse group have other- or mutual-face concerns, the more likely the group will have effective communication.

There are a number of studies that examine face concerns and conflict behavior in a variety of interpersonal situations (e.g., Lindsley & Braithwaite, 1996; Oetzel et al., 2001; Tsai & Levenson, 1997). These studies consistently demonstrate that self-face concern is related positively to dominating conflict styles, while other- and mutual-face concerns are associated positively with collaborating conflict styles.

I have found only one study, however, that examines face concerns in culturally diverse workgroups (although Earley & Randel, 1997, theorized about the importance of face). My coauthors and I (Oetzel, Torres, & Sanchez, 2002) tested the effects of self-construals and face concerns on effective communication processes (including collaboration, participation, and respect). Employees ($N = 562$) belonging to established work teams at a large, electronics manufacturing company in the

southwestern United States completed self-report questionnaires about their team's processes. We found that the more individuals had other- and mutual-face concerns, the higher their rating of the group's communication process. Further, face concerns accounted for 43% of the total variance explained in communication process. Self-face concerns were not significantly related to communication process.

Group Processes Influence Outcomes. The second set of propositions focuses on the influence of group communication process on group outcomes. Again, effective communication refers to equal participation, consensus decision making, cooperative conflict, and respectful communication.

> *Proposition 8:* The more a culturally diverse group utilizes effective communication processes, the more likely the group will achieve task effectiveness.

> *Proposition 9:* The more a culturally diverse group utilizes effective communication processes, the more likely the group will achieve relational effectiveness.

There are a number of studies and theoretical models that examine the impact of communication on task outcomes (Chatman, Polzer, Barsade, & Neale, 1998; Hofner Saphiere, 1996; Maznevski, 1994; Maznevski & Peterson, 1997; Pelled et al., 1999; Watson, Johnson, Kumar, & Critelli, 1998). I review two of these studies to illustrate support for the eighth proposition. First, Watson et al. (1998) conducted a 4-month study to understand the effect of cultural diversity on group process on problem-solving tasks. The Group Style Instrument (Watson & Michaelsen, 1988) was administered to 387 student participants in homogeneous and heterogeneous groups. Performance was measured by the grade received on a case study. Analysis of the Group Style Instrument revealed two dimensions of behaviors: team orientation and individual orientation. Team orientation consists of communicative behaviors such as coordination, consensus decision making, and support. Individual orientation consists of avoiding conflict, power struggles, and dominating discussion. The authors found that individual orientation was associated negatively with performance, whereas team orientation was associated positively with performance.

Second, Chatman et al. (1998) studied the effects of demographic composition and cultural emphasis on work processes and outcomes. They utilized an organizational simulation for 258 MBA (Master of Business Administration) students to study the frequency of communication, conflict among members, idea quality, and productivity. They found that organizations emphasizing collectivism engaged in communication more frequently and had fewer incidents of conflict than organizations emphasizing individualism. Further, increased diversity was related to decreased interaction, but also to increased productivity. The authors speculate that this negative relationship between interaction and productivity may be due to two factors: (a) the tasks could be completed better by individuals than in groups; or (b) the frequency of interaction may be due to social and not task issues. However, the content of the interactions was not measured so the latter speculation could not be confirmed.

There are three studies that examine both relational and task outcomes in culturally diverse groups (but no studies that examine relational effectiveness separately) and thus provide support for both the eighth and ninth propositions. Tjosvold, Sasaki, and Moy (1998) examined several components of interactions between 29 Japanese workers in two Hong Kong organizations: cooperative goals, open discussion of differing positions, work relationships, productivity, and commitment to

their organizations. The participants in the study were interviewed about critical incidents that influenced their willingness to stay with and work hard for their current company. The participants were asked to describe the setting, what occurred, and the consequences of one critical incident that influenced them positively and one that had a negative influence. Utilizing a structural equation model, the authors determined cooperative goals positively, and competitive goals negatively, lead to open discussion, open discussion results in productive work, and productive work results in commitment from the workers.

My study of 36 culturally diverse and culturally homogeneous student groups measured the communication variables of equal participation, cooperation, and respectful communication and the outcome variables of performance, satisfaction, and withholding effort (or social loafing) (Oetzel, 2001). I found that the more group members engaged in equal participation, cooperation, and respectful communication, the more satisfied the group members were and the less likely they were to withhold effort. Withholding effort harms the performance of the group in an indirect manner because the available resources of the group are not being used to their full potential. However, the communication processes did not directly relate to performance measures. Thus, the communication processes are associated positively with relational effectiveness, but only indirectly associated with task effectiveness.

In the third study, my coauthors and I examined the effects of group communication process, self-construals, and face concerns on group performance (Oetzel et al., 2002). The study involved 562 employees belonging to established work teams at a large electronics manufacturing company. We found that group communication process accounted for 87% of the total variance explained in group performance.

PRACTICAL APPLICATIONS

I have a bias that communication theory should be applied to help people improve the quality of their relationships. In the case of the effective intercultural workgroup communication theory, the focus is on improving group effectiveness and indirectly improving intergroup relations (i.e., enhancing the effectiveness of workgroup interactions may have indirect and positive effects on intergroup relations in the future). The emphasis on general group effectiveness makes this theory applicable to a wide variety of settings, including for-profit and not-for-profit businesses, health care teams, and educational institutions. In this section, I discuss the practical implications of this theory for managers of diverse groups, educators who use student groups, and members of culturally diverse groups.

The first critical application of the theory is identifying the importance of a culturally appropriate definition of group effectiveness (i.e., both task and relational effectiveness). The majority of studies on group effectiveness examine the impact of communication on task outcomes such as productivity and performance. The amount of focus on task effectiveness reflects the Western and business bias for the "bottom line." However, the focus on task effectiveness privileges individualistic cultural values and independent self-construals, and thus individuals with these perspectives are more likely to be comfortable with and benefit from the task focus. In contrast, my theory emphasizes both task and relationships at an equal level. These goals are not independent, and several communication behaviors relate to both goals.

Given that communication processes are critical elements in achieving group effectiveness, it becomes imperative to provide training on relevant communication skills for group members. I suspect that everyone reading this chapter can recall a time when a manager or teacher placed you in a group to accomplish a

key goal but did not provide any indication of how to interact with one another on how to accomplish the goals. The professor (or manager) simply told you to do the work without providing the resources needed to work effectively. Many people believe that good communication skills are "common sense." Contrary to expectations, the problem with common sense is that it is not all that common. Thus, leaders of culturally diverse groups need to focus on skill training in participation, cooperation, consensus decision making, and respectful communication. For example, team members can be taught how to encourage participation from reticent members. In addition, group members can be taught how to use dialogue for collaboration and consensus building.

In the same vein, leaders and members of culturally diverse groups need to monitor the communication process and provide feedback on what is (or is not) working. In many settings, group members expect the leaders to provide the monitoring. However, individual group members can also take on the burden of assessing the quality of group interaction. Wheelan (1999) provided a useful set of checklists, assessments, and suggestions for both leaders and members of groups. The suggestions include concrete scenarios for what members and leaders can do or say when problems arise in a group interaction. Wheelan designed the guidelines for workgroups in general, but many of the ideas are applicable to culturally diverse groups as well.

My theory also has implications for understanding from where the communication processes are generated and how to address relevant factors. Specifically, we know that context, cultural I-C, self-construals, and face concerns have an influence on group processes. Knowledge of these factors can be used to help determine the composition of the group or to train members about the importance of understanding cultural values and history. The type of task, balance of cultural groups, and status of group members are three factors that are well suited to a priori design. Many organizations advocate the use of teamwork and place individuals in teams, but reward individual performance. For example, organizational structures are often set up to reward individual performance in groups such as giving individual bonuses or promotions (or in the classroom when teachers provide individual grades on a group project). These reward structures encourage competitive, rather than collaborative, behavior in group members, especially when there are limited resources. In addition, leaders can pay attention to the balance of cultural group members in the groups. One individual who is culturally different from the other members may feel discomfort working in that group. This discomfort may have a negative impact on the communication processes in the group. The caveat in this design is that the leader cannot rely on physical demographics to design the group, as physical difference does not equal cultural difference. Instead, leaders can utilize measures of self-construal (Gudykunst et al., 1996), for example, to identify where group members may differ from one another. Finally, the status of group members (based on organizational position) is relatively easy to control, and attempts can be made to minimize status differences among group members. In sum, there are a number of other factors that are relevant for composing effective teams (e.g., making sure the task competencies are present in the groups), but leaders also need to pay attention to the organizational structure factors that encourage competitive or cooperative behavior and the balance of cultural group members.

The remaining contextual and input factors are better suited to awareness and training than design. It is possible to design a group so there are no members who have a history of unresolved conflict or who have similar cultural values. However, this level of control can actually reinforce problematic interaction. For example, if we keep individuals with conflict apart, there is no opportunity for growth and improvement. Instead, training should focus on the aforementioned communication skills, as well as on how cultural values and history impact communication. The critical aspect is to create an awareness of how these factors matter and then give the skills to address problematic interaction when and if it occurs. The ability to manage difficult interaction provides the opportunity for group members to improve intergroup relations, if only on a local level (i.e., their workgroup or organization).

Finally, leaders of culturally diverse groups need to give the teams sufficient time to develop. This statement is true for all teams but especially relevant for culturally diverse teams, given the tendency for heterogeneous groups to have more process difficulty than homogeneous groups. Culturally diverse teams need time for members to adjust to the views and interaction patterns of other members. Given sufficient time, culturally diverse groups appear to be able to "catch up and pass" the process and performance of culturally homogeneous groups (Watson et al., 1993).

FUTURE DIRECTIONS AND CONCLUSIONS

While I have been working on this theory for the past decade, I do not view it as a complete theory. There are a couple of areas of the theory that need to be developed. Unfortunately, previous research lends very little insight into these processes and thus these aspects are left for future scholarship.

The first area for future research is the complex relationship between contextual factors and cultural factors. It is clear that both of these types of factors influence group communication. What is not clear, however, is the level of interaction between these factors. Do both factors matter all of the time, or does one matter at some times but not others? For example, some scholars have argued that there are strong situations that preclude the influence of culture (Faure &

Rubin, 1993). Strong situations are ones in which the role expectations and task demands provide a clear indication of what behavior is relevant. In these situations, the contextual factors are the predominant influences on communication behavior, and culture is not an issue. However, in weak situations where there are no clear behavioral expectations, culture has a strong influence on behavior. In contrast, other scholars (e.g., Ting-Toomey & Oetzel, 2001) argue that culture frames the way individuals perceive situations. For example, Triandis (1995) explained that individuals from collectivistic cultures make a strong distinction between ingroup and outgroup members, whereas members of individualistic cultures do not. Thus, cultural values shape whether an individual perceives other workgroup members as ingroup or outgroup. Future research is needed to determine the interaction of contextual and cultural factors on communication in culturally diverse groups.

A second, often overlooked factor is the constitutive (or creative) role of communication in the creation of group cultures. We know very little about the creation of norms in culturally diverse groups. A few studies have found that culturally diverse groups develop their own norms over time (Millhous, 1999; Watson et al., 1993). We do not know, however, what these norms are or how they are negotiated. Do norms develop in a way that privileges the mainstream cultural group or are norms created equally by members of all cultural groups? The answer to this question can be illuminating for understanding how culturally diverse groups utilize the diversity in their groups. It is easy to imagine groups that utilize communication to create an open and supportive atmosphere, while other groups create a suspicious and closed atmosphere. Understanding this constitutive process will help us understand whether and how improved communication in culturally diverse groups improves intergroup relations. However, we do not know much about how this process occurs.

In summary, I have outlined the scope and history, the assumptions and propositions, and the applications of the effective intercultural workgroup communication theory. Research and practice with culturally diverse groups is critical. The implications of cultural diversity are far reaching, and our ability to learn to accept and interact with each other will have a large impact on the nature and extent of conflict in the future. This theory has a small part in that equation, and I hope that it is useful for practitioners and researchers.

REFERENCES

Allport, G. W. (1954). *The nature of prejudice.* Cambridge, MA: Addison-Wesley.
Bales, R. F. (1950). *Interaction process analysis: A method for the study of small groups.* Reading, MA: Addison-Wesley.
Barkema, H. G., & Vermeulen, F. (1997). What differences in the cultural backgrounds of partners are detrimental for international joint ventures. *Journal of International Business Studies, 28,* 845–864.
Barker, J. R. (1999). *The discipline of teamwork: Participation and concertive control.* Thousand Oaks, CA: Sage.
Bond, M. H., & Shiu, W. Y. (1997). The relationship between a group's personality resources and two dimensions of its group process. *Small Group Research, 28,* 194–217.
Cady, S. H., & Valentine, J. (1999). Team innovation and perceptions of consideration: What difference does it make? *Small Group Research, 30,* 730–750.
Chatman, J. A., Polzer, J. T., Barsade, S. G., & Neale, M. A. (1998). Being different yet feeling similar: The influence of demographic composition and organizational culture on work processes and outcomes. *Administrative Science Quarterly, 43,* 749–780.
Cox, T. H. (1990). Problems with research by organizational scholars on issues of race and ethnicity. *Journal of Applied Behavioral Science, 26,* 5–23.
Cox, T. H. (1994). *Cultural diversity in organizations: Theory, research, and practice.* San Francisco: Berrett-Kohler.
Cox, T. H., Lobel, S. A., & McLeod, P. L. (1991). Effects of ethnic group cultural differences on cooperative and competitive behavior on a

group task. *Academy of Management Journal, 34,* 827–847.

Deetz, S. (2001). Conceptual foundations. In F. M. Jablin & L. L. Putnam (Eds.), *The new handbook of organizational communication: Advances in theory, research, and methods* (pp. 3–46). Thousand Oaks, CA: Sage.

Deutsch, M. (1969). Conflicts: Productive and destructive. *Journal of Social Issues, 25,* 7–41.

Earley, P. C., & Randel, A. E. (1997). Self and other: Face and work group dynamics. In C. S. Granrose & S. Oskamp (Eds.), *Cross-cultural work groups* (pp. 113–133). Thousand Oaks, CA: Sage.

Ellis, D. G., & Fisher, B. A. (1994). *Small group decision making: Communication and group processes* (4th ed.). New York: McGraw-Hill.

Faure, G. O., & Rubin, J. Z. (1993). Lessons for theory and research. In G. O. Faure & J. Z. Rubin (Eds.), *Culture and negotiation* (pp. 209–231). Newbury Park, CA: Sage.

Gaertner, S. L., Dovidio, J. F., & Bachman, B. A. (1996). Revisiting the contact hypothesis: The induction of a common ingroup identity. *International Journal of Intercultural Relations, 20,* 271–290.

Gomez-Mejia, L. R., & Palich, L. E. (1997). Cultural diversity and the performance of multinational firms. *Journal of International Business Studies, 28,* 308–331.

Gudykunst, W. B., Matsumoto, Y., Ting-Toomey, S., Nishida, T., Kim, K. S., & Heyman, S. (1996). The influence of cultural individualism-collectivism, self construals, and individual values on communication styles across cultures. *Human Communication Research, 22,* 510–543.

Hackman, J. R. (1990). *Groups that work and those that don't.* San Francisco: Jossey-Bass.

Hirokawa, R. Y. (1985). Discussion procedures and decision-making performance: A test of the functional perspective. *Human Communication Research, 12,* 203–224.

Hirokawa, R. Y. (1988). Group communication and decision-making performance: A continued test of the functional perspective. *Human Communication Research, 14,* 487–515.

Hirokawa, R. Y. (1990). The role of communication in effective group decision-making: A task contingency perspective. *Small Group Behavior, 21,* 190–204.

Hirokawa, R. Y., & Rost, K. M. (1992). Effective group decision-making in organizations: Field test of the vigilant interaction theory. *Management Communication Quarterly, 5,* 67–288.

Hofner Saphiere, D. M. (1996). Productive behaviors of global business teams. *International Journal of Intercultural Relations, 20,* 227–259.

Hofstede, G. (2001). *Culture's consequences: Comparing values, behaviors, institutions, and organizations across nations* (2nd ed.). Thousand Oaks, CA: Sage.

Jarvenpaa, S. L., & Leidner, D. E. (1999). Communication and trust in global virtual teams. *Organization Science, 10,* 791–815.

Judy, R. W., & D'Amico, C. (1997). *Workforce 2020: Work and workers for the 21st century.* Indianapolis, IN: Hudson Institute.

Kim, M. S., Hunter, J. E., Miyahara, A., Horvath, A., Bresnahan, M., & Yoon, H. (1996). Individual-vs. cultural-level dimensions of individualism and collectivism: Effects on preferred conversational styles. *Communication Monographs, 63,* 28–49.

Kume, T. (1985). Managerial attitudes toward decision-making: North America and Japan. In W. Gudykunst, L. Stewart, & S. Ting-Toomey (Eds.), *Communication, culture, and organizational processes* (pp. 231–251). Beverly Hills, CA: Sage.

Landrum, R. E., & Harrold, R. (2003). What employers want from psychology graduates. *Teaching of Psychology, 30,* 131–133.

Larson, C. E., & LaFasto, F. M. J. (1989). *Teamwork: What must go right/what can go wrong.* Newbury Park, CA: Sage.

Lawrence, B. S. (1997). The black box of organizational demography. *Organization Science, 8,* 1–22.

Lindsley, S. L., & Braithwaite, C. A. (1996). "You should 'wear a mask'": Facework norms in cultural and intercultural conflict in maquiladoras. *International Journal of Intercultural Relations, 20,* 199–225.

Markus, H. R., & Kitayama, S. (1991). Culture and self: Implication for cognition, emotion, and motivation. *Psychological Review, 98,* 224–253.

Maznevski, M. L. (1994). Understanding our differences: Performance in decision-making groups with diverse members. *Human Relations, 47,* 531–552.

Maznevski, M. L., & Peterson, M. F. (1997). Societal values, social interpretation, and multinational teams. In C. S. Granrose & S. Oskamp (Eds.), *Cross-cultural work groups* (pp. 61–89). Thousand Oaks, CA: Sage.

McGrath, J. E. (1984). *Groups: Interaction and performance.* Englewood Cliffs, NJ: Prentice Hall.

McLeod, P. L., Lobel, S. A., & Cox, T. H. (1996). Ethnic diversity and creativity in small groups. *Small Group Research, 27,* 248–264.

Miller, K. I. (2000). Common ground from the post-positivist perspective: From "straw person" argument to collaborative coexistence. In S. R. Corman & M. S. Poole (Eds.), *Perspectives on organizational communication: Finding common ground* (pp. 46–67). Albany, NY: Guilford.

Millhous, L. (1999). The experience of culture in multicultural groups: Case studies of Russian-American collaboration in business. *Small Group Research, 30,* 280–308.

Morgan, G. (1997). *Images of organization* (2nd ed.). Thousand Oaks, CA: Sage.

Nemeth, C. J. (1992). Minority dissent as a stimulant to group performance. In S. Worchel, W. Wood, & J. A. Simpson (Eds.), *Group process and productivity* (pp. 95–111). Newbury Park, CA: Sage.

Oetzel, J. G. (1995). Intercultural small groups: An effective decision-making theory. In R. L. Wiseman (Ed.), *Intercultural communication theories* (pp. 247–270). Thousand Oaks, CA: Sage.

Oetzel, J. G. (1998a). Culturally homogeneous and heterogeneous groups: Explaining communication processes through individualism-collectivism and self-construal. *International Journal of Intercultural Relations, 22,* 135–161.

Oetzel, J. G. (1998b). Explaining individual communication processes in homogeneous and heterogeneous groups through individualism-collectivism and self-construal. *Human Communication Research, 25,* 202–224.

Oetzel, J. G. (2001). Self-construals, communication processes, and group outcomes in homogeneous and heterogeneous groups. *Small Group Research, 32,* 19–54.

Oetzel, J. G., & Bolton-Oetzel, K. D. (1997). Exploring the relationship between self-construal and dimensions of group effectiveness. *Management Communication Quarterly, 10,* 289–315.

Oetzel, J. G., Ting-Toomey, S., Masumoto, T., Yokochi, Y., Pan, X., Takai, J., & Wilcox, R. (2001). Face and facework in conflict: A cross-cultural comparison of China, Germany, Japan, and the United States. *Communication Monographs, 68,* 235–258.

Oetzel, J. G., Torres, A. B., & Sanchez, C. (2002, November). *Antecedents and outcomes of conflict in culturally diverse work teams.* Paper presented at the annual meeting of the National Communication Association, New Orleans.

Pelled, L. H., Eisenhardt, K. M., & Xin, K. R. (1999). Exploring the black box: An analysis of work group diversity, conflict, and performance. *Administrative Science Quarterly, 44,* 1–28.

Sessa, V. I., & Jackson, S. E. (1995). Diversity in decision-making teams: All differences are not created equal. In M. M. Chemers, S. Oskamp, & M. A. Costanzo (Eds.), *Diversity in organizations: New perspectives for a changing workplace* (pp. 133–156). Thousand Oaks, CA: Sage.

Thomas, D. C. (1999). Cultural diversity and work group effectiveness: An experimental study. *Journal of Cross-Cultural Psychology, 30,* 242–263.

Ting-Toomey, S., & Kurogi, A. (1998). Facework competence in intercultural conflict: An updated face-negotiation theory. *International Journal of Intercultural Relations, 22,* 187–225.

Ting-Toomey, S., & Oetzel, J. G. (2001). *Managing intercultural conflict effectively.* Thousand Oaks, CA: Sage.

Tjosvold, D., Sasaki, S., & Moy, J. W. (1998). Developing commitment in Japanese organizations in Hong Kong: Interdependence, interaction, relationship, and productivity. *Small Group Research, 29,* 560–582.

Triandis, H. C. (1995). *Individualism and collectivism.* Boulder, CO: Westview.

Tsai, J. L., & Levenson, R. W. (1997). Cultural influences on emotional responding: Chinese American and European American dating couples during interpersonal conflict. *Journal of Cross-Cultural Psychology, 28,* 600–625.

U.S. Census. (2000). *Projections of the resident population by race, Hispanic origin, and nativity: Middle series 2001 to 2005.* Retrieved on August 27, 2003 from http://www.census.gov/population/projections/nation/summary/np-t5-b.pdf.

Watson, W. E., Johnson, L., Kumar, K., & Critelli, J. (1998). Process gain and process loss: Comparing interpersonal processes and performance of culturally diverse and non-diverse teams across time. *International Journal of Intercultural Relations, 22,* 409–430.

Watson, W. E., & Kumar, K. (1992). Differences in decision making risk taking: A comparison of culturally diverse and culturally homogeneous task groups. *International Journal of Intercultural Relations, 16,* 53–65.

Watson, W. E., Kumar, K., & Michaelsen, L. K. (1993). Cultural diversity's impact on interaction process and performance: Comparing homogeneous and diverse task groups. *Academy of Management Journal, 36,* 590–602.

Watson, W. E., & Michaelsen, L. K. (1988). Group interaction behaviors that affect group performance on an intellective task. *Group & Organizational Studies, 13,* 495–516.

Wheelan, S. A. (1999). *Creating effective teams: A guide for members and leaders.* Thousand Oaks, CA: Sage.

PART VII

Theories Focusing on Adjustment and Acculturation

16

Adapting to a New Culture

An Integrative Communication Theory

YOUNG YUN KIM

When the skies grow dark, the stars begin to shine.

Charles Austin Beard (1874–1948)

Millions of people change homes each year, crossing cultural boundaries. Immigrants and refugees resettle in search of a new life, side by side with temporary sojourners finding employment overseas as artists, musicians, writers, accountants, teachers, and construction workers. Diplomats and other governmental agency employees, business managers, Peace Corps volunteers, researchers, professors, students, military personnel, and missionaries likewise carry out their work overseas for varying lengths of time. Individuals such as these are contemporary pioneers venturing into an unfamiliar cultural terrain where many of the business-as-usual ways of doing things lose their relevance. Even relatively short-term sojourners must be at least minimally concerned with building a healthy functional relationship with the host environment in ways similar to the native population. As they confront their predicaments as strangers and engage in new learning for an improved "goodness-of-fit," they begin to undergo a gradual process of personal transformation beyond their original cultural perimeters and toward a more inclusive and less categorical self-conception and self—other orientation. This description-in-a-nutshell points to the cross-cultural adaptation phenomenon being theorized in this chapter.

BACKGROUND

Cross-cultural adaptation has been investigated extensively across social science disciplines since the 1930s in the United States, a nation that has dealt with a large and continuous influx of immigrants (e.g., Spicer, 1968;

Stonequist, 1937). More recently, significant research attention has been given to adaptation-related phenomena throughout Northern and Western European countries, Canada, Australia, New Zealand, and Israel, among others (e.g., Berry, 1980; Jasinskaja-Lahti, Liebkind, Horenczyk, & Schmitz, 2003; Ward & Kennedy, 1993).

Approaches to Cross-Cultural Adaptation: Richness and Fragmentation

Although the field has benefited from an extensive amount of information and insights, it suffers from disconnectedness, making it difficult for individual investigators to gain a clear and cohesive picture of the body of knowledge accumulated over the decades. Couched in various terms such as culture shock, acculturation, adjustment, assimilation, integration, and adaptation, the field is fractionated by differing perspectives and foci. Researchers typically isolate segments of the adaptation phenomenon specific to disciplinary and individual interests, which has resulted in the dichotomous distinction drawn between macro- and micro-level processes and between short- and long-term adaptation. A fuller, and thus more realistic, understanding of cross-cultural adaptation has been frustrated, in part, by the narrowly based linear-causal reasoning that conceives cross-cultural adaptation as either a "dependent" variable or an "independent" variable of something. This one-directional cause-and-effect notion has produced many different and often inconsistent definitions, models, indices, and scales (for a review, see Ady, 1995; Ward & Kennedy, 1999.)

Further complicating the adaptation inquiry is the ideological shift in the United States since the 1960s when the "new ethnicity" movement began, prompted by the civil rights movement (Gordon, 1981). The traditional social scientific conceptions of cross-cultural adaptation as a desirable goal for individual settlers and immigrant groups, as well as for the cohesion of a given host society over time (Gordon, 1973), were challenged by more pluralistic conceptions. Berry's (1980, 1990) model, for example, identifies four different "acculturation modes," relying on two key questions concerning the subjective identity orientation: Are cultural identity and customs of value to be retained? and, Are positive relations with the larger society of value and to be sought? By combining the response types (yes, no) to these two questions, Berry and associates identify four modes of psychological acculturation: "integration" (yes, yes), "assimilation" (no, yes), "separation" (yes, no), and "marginality" (no, no). A modified version of this model is offered in an interactive model proposed by Bourhis, Moiese, Perreault, and Senecal (1997), replacing "marginality" with "anomie" and adding "individualism." What distinguishes pluralistic models such as these from traditional models is the implicit assumption that adaptation is a matter of conscious choice individuals make for themselves, and not a matter of necessity.

The trend toward pluralistic conceptions of cross-cultural adaptation has been further spurred by recent works by "critical" or "postmodern" scholars (e.g., Hedge, 1998; Young, 1996). These scholars have questioned the legitimacy of the traditional normative-representational social scientific theories for their inherent "flaw" of not stressing cultural diversity, not highlighting the predicaments in which immigrant groups and ethnic minorities find themselves as "victims" of "systematic cultural oppression," and thereby serving to reproduce the status quo of the dominant cultural ideology of assimilationism and its "melting pot" vision of society. Based on interviews with a small group of Asian Indian immigrant women in the United States, for example, Hedge (1998) approaches the experiences of these women from the perspective of critical-feminist scholarship and emphasizes the challenges they face by employing such terms as "displacement" and "struggle" in having to deal with the contradictions between their internal identity and external "world in which hegemonic structures systematically marginalize certain types of difference" (p. 36; for a more extensive discussion of ideological divergence, see Kim, 2001, 2002.)

In Search of a Big Picture

Against this vast and fragmented backdrop of the field, the main driving force behind this author's work has been a search for a "big picture," a broadly based general theory that can help cross-pollinate various probes of limited conceptual domains with one another to gain a systemic insight into what happens when someone crosses cultural boundaries. Such a theory would offer an integrated system of description and explanation in which common themes addressed in the existing approaches, concepts, and models can be identified with their interrelationships clarified and many of the existing divisions in the field bridged. With this aim, the author has sought to address in her theory the following five key missing links in the cross-cultural adaptation literature:

1. In investigating cross-cultural adaptation of individuals, little attention has been given to macro-level factors such as the cultural and institutional patterns of the host environment and the ethnic community within it, or to micro-level factors such as the background and psychological characteristics of the individual. Both macro- and micro-level factors need to be taken into account for a fuller understanding of the cross-cultural adaptation process.

2. The two traditionally separate areas of investigation of long-term and short-term adaptation need to be integrated. These two areas have common conceptual issues that inform each other.

3. The problematic nature of cross-cultural adaptation must be viewed in the context of new learning and psychological growth. Both of these aspects of adaptation, taken together, provide a more balanced and complete interpretation of the experiences of individuals in an unfamiliar environment.

4. Different sets of factors have been identified as constituting and/or explaining (influencing) the cross-cultural adaptation process of individuals. Efforts must be made to sort and consolidate these factors so as to achieve a greater coherence in describing and explaining differing levels or rates of adaptive change in individuals.

5. The divergent ideological premises of assimilationism and pluralism need to be recognized and incorporated into a pragmatic conception of cross-cultural adaptation as a condition of the host environment as well as of the individual adapting to that environment.

A Trajectory of Theorizing and Researching

The author began a scientific investigation of cross-cultural adaptation more than two and half decades ago. As a graduate student from South Korea, she was drawn to this field prompted partly by a keen personal interest in understanding the adaptive struggles and successes that she and those around her were experiencing. The doctoral research began to address these issues through a survey among Korean immigrants in the Chicago area (Kim, 1976, 1977a, 1977b, 1978b). The author has since conducted studies among other immigrant and refugee groups in the United States, including Japanese Americans (Kim, 1978a), Mexican Americans (Kim, 1978a), and Southeast Asian refugees from Vietnam, Cambodia, and Laos (Kim, 1980, 1989, 1990). The research subjects and contexts have been extended to American Indians living in a predominantly Anglo milieu (Kim, Lujan, & Dixon, 1998a, 1998b). The author also has worked with a number of doctoral students investigating the adaptation patterns of Malaysian students in the United States (Tamam, 1993), Western and non-Western international university students in Japan (Maruyama, 1998; Maruyama & Kim, 1997), Turkish employees of an American military organization in Germany (Braun, 2002; Kim & Braun, 2002), and Korean expatriates in the United States and American expatriates in South Korea (Kim, 2003; Kim & Kim, 2004).

While the basic research issues stated above have remained the same throughout these studies, the author's methodological perspective has undergone a change—from the initial linear-causal approach exemplified in the path model developed through the doctoral research (Kim, 1976, 1977a), to a more interactive and integrative general systems perspective with a special emphasis on an open systems perspective (Bertalanffy, 1956; Jantsch, 1980) incorporated into her subsequent work. The systems approach is predicated on a set of assumptions, based on which cross-cultural adaptation is conceived of as a case of "organized complexity" and the unfolding of the natural human tendency to struggle for an internal equilibrium in the face of often adversarial environmental conditions. Focusing on the communication activities linking the individual (the "figure") and the environment (the "ground"), this open-systems perspective lends itself to a consolidation of previously separate theoretical foci such as the person, the group, and the society, and has enabled the author to find a way to integrate the existing approaches into a broadly based general theory in which communication occupies the central place.

The initial groundwork for development of a comprehensive, integrative theory was laid in 1979 in an article titled, "Toward an Interactive Theory of Communication-Acculturation" (Kim, 1979), followed by a full theory presentation in *Communication and Cross-Cultural Adaptation: An Integrative Theory* (Kim, 1988). This theory has since been further elaborated and refined in *Becoming Intercultural: An Integrative Theory of Communication and*

Cross-Cultural Adaptation (Kim, 2001), and is briefly described below.

ORGANIZING PRINCIPLES

The author's theory is rooted in a number of open-systems premises with respect to the basic nature of cross-cultural adaptation and of the scientific approach to theorizing about the phenomenon. Taken together, these premises render the present theory a distinct character, differentiating it from other existing theories that address issues related to cross-cultural adaptation.

Adaptation as a Natural and Universal Phenomenon

The author intends this theory to serve not as an advocacy of any particular ideological position, but as an accurate representation and abstraction of regularities found in the reality of individuals adapting to a new and unfamiliar culture, wherever that may be taking place. This theoretical aim hinges on the open-systems principle that adaptation manifests the natural human instinct to struggle for an internal equilibrium in the face of adversarial environmental conditions. Cross-cultural adaptation is a case of "a common process of environmental adaptation" (Anderson, 1994, p. 293), as it entails the totality of a complex, dynamic, and evolutionary process an individual undergoes. This conception elevates the ontological status of adaptation to the level of a pan-human universal phenomenon—a basic human tendency that accompanies the internal struggle of individuals to regain control over their life chances in the face of environmental challenges.

Adaptation as an All-Encompassing Phenomenon

The author regards cross-cultural adaptation not as a specific analytic unit (or variable), but as the entirety of the evolutionary process an individual undergoes vis-à-vis a new and unfamiliar environment. This process "moves" with a structure of multidimensional and multifaceted forces operating simultaneously and interactively. Some of these forces are external to the individual, setting limits on the adaptive behavior of the stranger; other forces are internally located within the individual's predispositions and behaviors. Cross-cultural adaptation is, therefore, to be understood in terms of a dynamic interplay of the person and the environment. This conception counters the reductionist strategies of explanation commonly employed in the existing theoretical models, and instead emphasizes the unitary nature of psychological and social processes and the reciprocal functional person-environment interdependence. In this view, the micro-psychological and macro-social factors are taken together into a theoretical fusion or "vertical integration" (Berkowitz, 1982; Fielding & Fielding, 1986). This systemic approach is consistent with the perspective taken in philosophical pragmatism (Givón, 1989; Joas, 1993) and with such methodological schools as "contextualism," "ecological psychology," and "evolutionary social psychology" reflected in the works of Bateson (1972), Ruesch and Bateson (1951/1968), Watzlawick, Beavin, and Jackson (1967), and Buss and Kenrick (1998).

Adaptation as a Communication-Based Phenomenon

By placing adaptation at the intersection of the person and the environment, the present approach views cross-cultural adaptation as a process that occurs in and through communication activities. Underscored in this view is that communication is the necessary vehicle without which adaptation cannot take place, and that cross-cultural adaptation occurs as long as the individual remains in interaction with the host environment. The only situation in which

adaptation cannot take place would be under the condition of complete insularity from the host environment. This interactive communication-based conception echoes the view of Ruesch and Bateson (1951/1968), who regard "all actions and events [having] communicative aspects, as soon as they are perceived by a human being. . . . Where the relatedness of entities is considered, we deal with problems of communication" (pp. 5–6). It allows the author to move beyond the linear-causal assumption underlying most existing models in which cross-cultural adaptation is treated as an independent or dependent variable.

Theory as a System of Description and Explanation

Consistent with the systems-theoretic view of the fundamental goal of science as "pattern recognizing" (Monge, 1990), the present theory is designed to identify the patterns that are commonly present within a clearly defined set of individual cases and to translate these patterns into a set of generalizable and interrelated statements. Given that adaptation is something natural and universal to all living systems, and given that communication activities serve as the very vehicle for adaptation, the author's main concern is not whether individuals adapt, but how and why they adapt when they relocate in a new and unfamiliar environment. In addressing this basic question, the author has sought to achieve a balance between the two distinct goals for social science: understanding and prediction (Dubin, 1978, pp. 9–10). Understanding is to be achieved via a thorough and accurate system of description and explanation of how cross-cultural adaptation plays out in reality, what key elements constitute the phenomenon, and how these elements interact and evolve together over time. The degree to which such understanding is provided by the present theory is assessed in terms of its descriptive power. At the same time, the present theory allows prediction of adaptive changes in individuals over time, and of the role that each identified element plays in influencing the change.

Theorizing at the Interface of Deduction and Induction

The author's theorizing process has taken a back-and-forth movement between deductive and inductive processes—between the conceptual realm of logical development of ideas from a set of basic open-systems assumptions about human adaptation and empirical substantiation of the ideas based on proofs available in social science literature. Following Blalock (1989) and Dubin (1978), the present theory has been developed without being restricted by empirical evidence. At the same time, it is firmly grounded in and strengthened by the extensive research evidence that has been made available across disciplines. Also utilized in the theorizing process are anecdotal stories and testimonials of immigrants and sojourners available in nontechnical sources such as reports, biographies, letters, diaries, dialogues, commentaries, and a host of other materials in magazines, newspapers, fiction and nonfiction books, radio programs, and television programs. Although these individual stories do not lend themselves to the prerequisites of scientific data, they serve as a vital source of insights into the "lived experiences" of cross-cultural adaptation. The practical and participatory experiences expressed in these stories offer credible, sensitive, and close-up witness to what is actually occurring in reality (see Kim, 2001).

Focal Concepts and Boundary Conditions

The author has strived to achieve maximum generality of this theory by employing concepts of higher-order abstraction and, thus, of greater integrative power and parsimony. Among the various general concepts employed

in the present theory are the two central terms *adaptation* and *stranger*. These two terms are chosen for their broad generality and as a "master concept" or "superordinate category" (White, 1976, p. 18) that helps define the domain of the theory.

The term cross-cultural adaptation *is defined in this theory as the entirety of the phenomenon of individuals who, upon relocating to an unfamiliar sociocultural environment, strive to establish and maintain a relatively stable, reciprocal, and functional relationship with the environment.* At the core of this definition is the goal of achieving an overall person-environment "fit" (Mechanic, 1974; Moos, 1976) between their internal conditions and the conditions of the new environment. Adaptation, thus, is an activity that is "almost always a compromise, a vector in the internal structure of culture and the external pressure of environment" (Sahlins, 1964, p. 136). Placed at the intersection of the person and the environment, adaptation is essentially an interactive communication process and embraces other similar but narrower terms, from *assimilation* (the acceptance of mainstream cultural elements of the host society by the individual) and *acculturation* (the process commonly defined as the acquisition of some, but not all, aspects of the host cultural elements), to *coping* and *adjustment* (both of which are often used to refer to the psychological responses to cross-cultural challenges), as well as to *integration* (often defined as social participation in the host society).

The concept "stranger" incorporates in it all individuals who enter and resettle in a new cultural or subcultural environment. Initially employed by Simmel (1908/1950), this concept has served as one of the most ubiquitous and heuristic concepts for analyzing the social processes involving individuals who confront an unfamiliar milieu. The notion of strangers integrates other more specific terms such as immigrants, refugees, and sojourners, who resettle for various lengths of time, as well as members of ethnic groups who cross subcultural boundaries within a society. All of these individuals are included in the present definition of stranger, as they commonly share the experience of beginning their adaptation experience as cultural "outsiders" and of moving in the direction of cultural "insiders" over time (see Gudykunst & Kim, 2003, for a more detailed examination of this concept).

As such, the present theoretical domain is broadly defined, limited only by three boundary conditions: (1) the strangers must have had a primary socialization in one culture (or subculture) and have moved into a different and unfamiliar culture (or subculture); (2) the strangers are at least minimally dependent on the host environment for meeting their personal and social needs; and (3) the strangers are engaged in continuous, firsthand communication experiences with that environment. These boundary conditions offer a domain that is broad and general without being delimited by either the specific reasons for or the lengths of contact with the new environment (e.g., long-term or short-term exchange students, business employees, immigrants, and refugees). Included in this domain is the adaptive experience of anyone who faces significant changes in domestic sociocultural environment, either through a voluntary relocation (e.g., American Indians leaving a tribal reservation to find employment in a predominantly Anglo urban environment) or through the demographic changes in the surrounding environment through incoming and outgoing population movements (e.g., a significant increase in Asians and Hispanics in Los Angeles). Also included in the present domain are the situations of reentry into one's original culture. Generally, the process of readapting to one's original culture is less demanding of new cultural/language learning than the process of adapting to a foreign culture. Yet, to the extent that the returnee has been changed by the sojourn experience, and to the extent that the original cultural milieu has

changed during the sojourn, he or she must, once again, go through the cross-cultural adaptation process upon returning home.

Based on the two focal terms, adaptation and stranger, and the related boundary conditions described above, the theory addresses two central questions: (1) What is the essential nature of the adaptation process individual settlers undergo over time? and (2) Why are some settlers more successful than others in attaining a level of psychosocial fitness in the host environment? The first question is addressed in the form of a process model—a theoretical representation of the process of personal evolution toward increased functional fitness and psychological health, and a gradual emergence of intercultural identity. The second question is addressed by a structural model in which key dimensions of factors that facilitate or impede the adaptation process are identified and their interrelationships articulated.

THE PROCESS OF CROSS-CULTURAL ADAPTATION

All of us are born into this world knowing little of what we need to know to function acceptably in a given culture. Nor are we born prepared to engage in the various activities out of which our sense of reality and self is constructed. Instead, we learn to relate to our social environment and its culture; that is, the universe of information and operative linguistic and nonlinguistic communication rituals that gives coherence, continuity, and distinction to a communal way of life. The familiar culture is the "home world," which is associated closely with the family or significant others. The unwritten task of every culture is to organize, integrate, and maintain the home world of the individual, primarily in the formative years of childhood. Through continuous interaction with the various aspects of the cultural environment, our internal systems undergo a progression of changes as we integrate culturally acceptable concepts, attitudes, and actions. We thus become fit to live in the company of others around us who share a similar image of reality and self.

This process is commonly called *enculturation*. The continuous enculturation process occurs in and through communication, the pillar of all human learning. We learn to speak, listen, read, interpret, and understand verbal and nonverbal messages in such a fashion that the messages will be recognized and responded to by the individuals with whom we interact. Once acquired, communicative abilities serve us as an instrumental, interpretive, and expressive means of coming to terms with our environment. Crucial features of this communication-enculturation process are the relational bonding between individuals, the forming of groups, and a cultural identity.

Entering a New Culture

In many ways, entering a new culture is like starting an enculturation process all over again. Only this time, strangers are faced with situations that deviate from the familiar and internalized original cultural script. They become more aware of the previously taken-for-granted habits of mind because, as Boulding (1956/1977) notes, the human nervous system is structured in such a way that "the patterns that govern behavior and perception come into consciousness only when there is a deviation from the familiar" (p. 13). Now, strangers discover that they lack a level of understanding of the new communication system of the host society, and must learn and acquire many of its symbols and patterns of activities. They may be forced to suspend or even abandon their identification with the cultural patterns that have symbolized who they are and what they are. The situation generates "crises" in which their mental and behavioral habits are brought into awareness and called into question.

Such inner conflicts, in turn, make strangers susceptible to external influence and compel

them to learn the new cultural system. This activity of new learning is the essence of *acculturation* (Shibutani & Kwan, 1965), the acquisition of the host cultural practices in wide-ranging areas. But new learning and adaptive change is not random (Wheatley, 1999, p. 84). Consciously or unconsciously, an individual stranger's need to maintain himself or herself influences the selection of new information. At least in early stages of cross-cultural adaptation, predisposition and self-interest influence the specific nature of acculturation as each individual tends to be more ready or willing to embrace those host cultural elements that serve his or her own needs. The selectivity in acculturation reflects the ego-protective and ego-centric psychological principle and is demonstrated in Bognar's (2001) finding of uneven development in gender role change between male and female immigrants, and in Chang's (2001) finding among Asian immigrants in Singapore of relatively higher levels of acculturation in workplace-related and public norms and values compared to private realms and home life.

Acculturation is not a process in which new cultural elements are simply added to prior internal conditions. As new learning occurs, deculturation or unlearning of some of the old cultural elements has to occur, at least in the sense that new responses are adopted in situations that previously would have evoked old ones. "No construction without destruction," in the words of Burke (1974). The cost of acquiring something new is inevitably the "losing" of something old in much the same way as "being someone requires the forfeiture of being someone else" (Thayer, 1975, p. 240). The act of acquiring something new is the "suspending" and, over a prolonged period, "losing" some of the old habits. As the interplay of acculturation and deculturation continues, strangers may undergo an internal transformation—from changes in superficial areas such as overt role behavior to more profound changes in fundamental values. They are susceptible to conformity pressure from

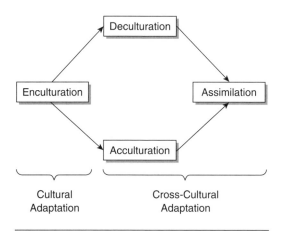

Cultural Adaptation — Cross-Cultural Adaptation

Figure 16.1 Relationships Among Key Terms Associated With Cross-Cultural Adaptation

SOURCE: Kim, 2001, p. 53.

the host environment, often in the form of simple and routine cultural assumptions and expectations extended to them. To the extent that there are discrepancies between the demands of the host environment and their internal capacity to meet those demands, and as long as there are pressures to conform, they are compelled to learn and make changes in their customary habits.

The ultimate theoretical directionality of adaptive change is toward *assimilation,* a state of the maximum possible convergence of strangers' internal and external conditions to those of the natives. For most settlers, assimilation remains a lifetime goal rather than an obtainable goal and often requires the efforts of multiple generations. Whether by choice or by circumstance, individual settlers also vary in the overall adaptation level achieved during any given period, falling at different points on a continuum ranging from minimal acculturation and deculturation to maximum acculturation and deculturation.

The Stress-Adaptation-Growth Dynamic

Each experience of adaptive change inevitably accompanies stress in the individual

psyche—a kind of identity conflict rooted in resistance to change: the desire to retain old customs in keeping with the original identity, on the one hand, and the desire to change behavior in seeking harmony with the new milieu, on the other. This conflict is essentially between the need for acculturation and the resistance to deculturation—the push of the new culture and the pull of the old. The internal turmoil created by such conflicting forces produces a state of disequilibrium, manifested in emotional "lows" of uncertainty, confusion, and anxiety. *Stress,* a broad concept variously measured by researchers in terms of "difficulties" or "culture shock" people experience (e.g., Ward, Bochner, & Furnham, 2001), is a manifestation of the generic process that occurs whenever an individual's internal capabilities are not adequate to the demands of the environment. It is an expression of the instinctive human desire to restore homeostasis, that is, to hold constant a variety of variables in internal structure to achieve an integrated whole.

The natural tendency of an open system is to resist change and to perpetuate the state of maladaptation and work against its own adaptive change. This tendency manifests itself in various forms of psychological resistance. Some people may attempt to avoid or minimize the anticipated or actual "pain" of disequilibrium by selective attention, denial, avoidance, and withdrawal, as well as by compulsively altruistic behavior, cynicism, and hostility toward the host environment (Lazarus, 1966, p. 262). Others may seek to regress to an earlier state of existence in the original culture, a state in which there is no feeling of isolation, no feeling of separation. Although stress is universal, few have an easy time accepting it. Yet, no open system can stabilize itself forever. If that were so, nothing would come of evolution. The state of misfit and a heightened awareness in the state of stress serve as the very forces that propel individuals to overcome the predicament and partake in the act of *adaptation* through the active development of new habits. This is possible as they engage in forward-looking moves, striving to meet the challenge by acting on and responding to the environment (Piaget, 1963). Out of these activities, some aspects of the environment may be incorporated into an individual's internal structure, gradually increasing its overall fitness to the external realities.

What follows the dynamic stress-adaptation disequilibrium is a subtle *growth*. Periods of stress pass as strangers work out new ways of handling problems, owing to the creative forces of self-reflexivity of human mentation. Stress, adaptation, and growth thus highlight the core of the changes individuals undergo over time. Together these forces constitute a three-pronged stress-adaptation-growth dynamic of psychological movement in the forward and upward direction of increased chances of success in meeting the demands of the host environment. Stress, in this regard, is intrinsic to complex open systems and essential in the adaptation process—one that allows for self-(re)organization and self-renewal. The *stress-adaptation-growth dynamic* does not play out in a smooth, steady, and linear progression, but in a dialectic, cyclic, and continual "draw-back-to-leap" pattern. Each stressful experience is responded to with a "draw back," which, in turn, activates adaptive energy to help individuals reorganize themselves and "leap forward." As growth of some units always occurs at the expense of others, the adaptation process follows a pattern that juxtaposes integration and disintegration, progression and regression, novelty and confirmation, and creativity and depression (Kirschner, 1994). This explanation of the adaptation process echoes Dubos's (1965) view of human adaptation as "a dialectic between permanence and change" (p. 2). It also converges with Hall's (1976) conception

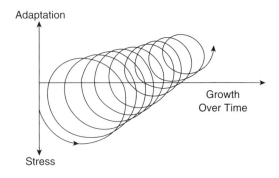

Figure 16.2   The Stress-Adaptation-Growth Dynamic

SOURCE: Kim, 2001, p. 59.

of "identity-separation-growth" syndrome and with Jourard's (1974) account of "integration-disintegration-reintegration."

The stress-adaptation-growth process continues as long as there are new environmental challenges, with the overall forward and upward movement in the direction of greater adaptation and growth. In this process, large and sudden changes are more likely to occur during the initial phase of exposure to a new culture. Such drastic changes are themselves indicative of the severity of difficulties and disruptions, as has been demonstrated in many culture shock studies (Ward et al., 2004). Over a prolonged period of undergoing internal change, the fluctuations of stress and adaptation are likely to become less intense or severe, leading to an overall "calming" of our internal condition, as depicted in Figure 16.2. In Jantsch's (1980) words,

> The higher the resistance against structural change, the more powerful the fluctuations which ultimately break through—the richer and more varied also the unfolding of self-organization dynamic at the platform of a resilient structure. The more splendid the unfolding of mind, as we may also put it. (p. 255)

THE STRUCTURE OF
CROSS-CULTURAL ADAPTATION

Building on the above description and explanation of the cross-cultural adaptation process, the theory now moves to address the second theoretical aim, that is, identifying the structure of interlocking adaptive changes and thus helping to explain the differential rates (or speeds) at which this process plays out across different individuals.

Once again, the metatheoretical perspective of open systems helps to locate relevant explanatory factors within the communicative interface of the stranger and the environment. In this communication framework, strangers' communication activities are conceptualized, following Ruben (1975), in two basic, interdependent dimensions: (1) personal communication, or "private symbolization" and all the internal mental activities that occur in individuals that dispose and prepare them to act and react in certain ways in actual social situations; and (2) social communication, or "public symbolization" that underlies "intersubjectivization" and occurs whenever two or more individuals interact with one another, knowingly or not.

Personal Communication:
Host Communication Competence

The successful adaptation of strangers is realized only when their personal communication systems sufficiently overlap with those of the natives. The capacity of strangers to receive and process information (decoding) appropriately and effectively and to design and execute mental plans in initiating or responding to messages (encoding) is labeled in the present theory as *host communication competence*. By definition, host communication competence facilitates the cross-cultural adaptation process in a most direct and significant way. It serves as an instrumental,

interpretive, and expressive means of coming to terms with the host environment. It enables strangers to understand the way things are carried out in the host society and the way they themselves need to think, feel, and act in that environment.

The key elements that generally constitute the concept of communication competence, including the present conceptualization of host communication competence, are grouped into three commonly recognized categories: (1) cognitive, (2) affective, and (3) operational. *Cognitive competence* includes such internal capabilities as the knowledge of the host culture and language, including the history, institutions, worldviews, beliefs, mores, norms, and rules of interpersonal conduct, among others. Language/culture learning is accompanied by a development of "cognitive complexity," that is, the structural refinement in an individual's internal information processing ability. Along with cognitive competence, *affective competence* facilitates cross-cultural adaptation by providing a motivational capacity to deal with various challenges of living in the host environment, the openness to new learning, and the willingness to participate in the natives' aesthetic and emotional sensibilities in their experiences of beauty, fun, joy, as well as despair, anger, and the like. Relatedly, affective competence is further reflected in one's willingness to make necessary changes in one's original cultural habits so as to incorporate some of the new habits in one's repertoire.

Among the recent studies addressing some of the affective components of host communication competence is Gong's (2003) study of international students in the United States, in which strong motivation ("learning goal orientation") is found to be positively associated with measures of both academic and social adaptation. In a study of ethnic repatriates in Finland, Israel, and Germany, Jasinskaja-Lahti et al. (2003) observe that those expatriates objecting to acculturation in the host society perceived more discrimination or reported more stress than other immigrants. This finding suggests a functional relationship between adaptive motivation and psychological health vis-à-vis the host environment.

Closely linked with the cognitive and affective components of host communication competence is *operational competence* (Taft, 1977), otherwise referred to as "behavioral competence" or "enactment tendencies" (Buck, 1984). This competence facilitates strangers' enacting, or expressing, their cognitive and affective experiences outwardly. As they try to come up with a mental plan for action, therefore, they must base the decision on their current knowledge and cognitive capacity to process information about the host culture as well as their motivational and attitudinal capacity to meaningfully appreciate and join in the natives' emotional and aesthetic experiences. The strangers' operational competence, thus, enables them to choose a "right" combination of verbal and nonverbal behaviors so as to achieve a smooth and harmonious interface with the host milieu.

Host Social Communication

Host communication competence is directly and reciprocally linked to participation in the interpersonal and mass communication activities of the host environment. A stranger's host social communication experiences are constrained by his or her host communication competence. At the same time, every host social communication event offers the stranger an opportunity for cultural learning.

Host interpersonal communication, in particular, helps strangers to secure vital information and insight into the mind-sets and behaviors of the local people, thereby providing strangers with points of reference for a check and validation of their own behaviors. Most strangers in a new culture must begin to form a new set of relationships as they find themselves without an adequate support system when they are confronted with highly uncertain and stressful situations. Participation in either or both of the host and ethnic social communication activities is an expression of the fundamental human need to belong (Baumeister & Leary, 1995). The crucial importance of host interpersonal communication activities in facilitating cross-cultural adaptation has been acknowledged and demonstrated widely and repeatedly across the social sciences.

Host mass communication facilitates the adaptation of strangers by exposing strangers to the larger environment. Serving this function are various mediated forms of communication such as radio and television programs, magazine and newspaper articles, movies, museum exhibits, theater performances, Internet Web sites, audiotapes, videotapes, and posters. While the interpersonal channel of communication offers opportunities for more personalized and, thus, meaningful involvement with members of the host culture, mass communication channels help strangers participate in vicarious learning through "para-social interactions" with the host environment at large beyond the ordinary reaches of their daily life (Horton & Wohl, 1979, p. 32). Compared to interpersonal communication activities, mediated communication activities may be governed by a lesser sense of mutual obligation and effort. Whereas host mass communication renders less opportunity for feedback than do interpersonal situations where a quick exchange of information is maximal, it serves as an important source of cultural and language learning, particularly during early phases of the adaptation process when strangers have less direct access to and less likelihood to succeed in communicating with the natives face-to-face.

Ethnic Social Communication

In many societies and communities today, strangers' interpersonal and mass communication activities involve their co-ethnics or co-nationals and home cultural experiences as well. Whether we speak of American military posts in West Germany, Puerto Rican barrios in New York City, Chinatown in Tokyo, or a Japanese student association in a Canadian university, ethnic communities provide strangers with access to their original cultural experiences. Many aliens have organized some form of mutual-aid or self-help organizations that render assistance to those who need material, informational, emotional, and other forms of social support. In the case of many larger ethnic communities, mass media (including newspapers, radio stations, and television programs that are made accessible via the Internet or in prerecorded audio- and videotapes and computer disks) perform various informational, educational, entertainment, and social services.

These ethnic interpersonal and mass communication systems serve adaptation-facilitating functions during the initial phase of strangers' adaptation process. Because many strangers initially lack host communication competence and do not have access to resources to become self-reliant, they tend to seek and depend heavily on ethnic sources of informational, material, and emotional help and thereby compensate for the lack of support they are capable of obtaining from host nationals. Due to the relatively stress-free communication experience in dealing with their own ethnic individuals and media, ethnic communication experiences may offer temporary refuge and a support system. In the case of relatively short-term residents, such as American military personnel stationed overseas, their daily duties confine their social communication activities almost exclusively to other Americans at the military base.

Beyond the initial phase, however, ethnic social communication serves the function of original cultural identity maintenance (Boekestijn, 1988) and is negatively associated with adaptation into the host culture. Whether by choice or by circumstance, strangers' heavy and prolonged reliance on co-ethnics sustains their original cultural identity and limits their opportunities to participate in the social communication activities of the host society. Implied in this observation is that strangers cannot remain exclusively ethnic in their communication activities and, at the same time, become highly adapted to the host environment. Among the extensive empirical evidence supporting this observation is Cui's (1998) finding from a study of Chinese graduate students enrolled in various academic programs in an American university indicating that ethnic communication has negative relationships with host communication competence and host interpersonal communication activities. Another recent study, by Nesdale and Mak (2003), reports that immigrants' level of ethnic identification is positively associated with "ethnic self-esteem," but not with either "personal self-esteem" or "psychological health."

Environment

To the extent that strangers participate in host social (interpersonal, mass) communication activities, the host society exerts influence on their adaptation process. The nature of such influence, in turn, is shaped by the various characteristics of the host society. For many, their social environment includes fellow co-ethnics as well. Given the mixed nature of the environment in which many strangers find themselves, three environmental conditions are identified in the present theory as affecting the individual stranger's adaptation process: (1) host receptivity; (2) host conformity pressure; and (3) ethnic group strength.

The term *host receptivity* incorporates the meaning of other similar terms such as "interaction potential" (Blau & Schwartz, 1984; Hallinan & Smith, 1985) or "acquaintance potential" (Cook, 1962), and refers to the degree to which a given environment is structurally and psychologically accessible and open to strangers. Different locations in a given society may offer different levels of receptivity toward different groups of strangers. For example, Canadian visitors arriving in a small town in the United States are likely to find a largely receptive host environment. On the other hand, the same small town may show less receptivity toward visitors from a lesser-known and vastly different culture such as Turkey or Kenya.

Along with receptivity, *host conformity pressure* varies as well across societies and communities. Host conformity pressure refers to the extent to which the environment challenges strangers to act in accordance with the normative patterns of the host culture and its communication system. In particular, the conformity pressure of a host environment is often reflected in the expectations the natives routinely have about how strangers should think and act, thereby exerting a pressure on the strangers to adapt to the host cultural milieu. Different host environments show different levels of tolerance to strangers and their ethnic/cultural characteristics. For example, heterogeneous and open host environments such as the United States generally tend to hold a more pluralistic political ideology concerning cultural/ethnic differences and exert less pressure on strangers to change their habitual ways. Within the United States, ethnically heterogeneous metropolitan areas such as Los Angeles, Miami, and New York City tend to demand less that strangers conform to the dominant Anglo-white cultural practices than do small, ethnically homogeneous rural towns. Even within a city, certain neighborhoods may be more homogeneous and expect more conformity from strangers.

The degree to which a given host environment exerts receptivity and conformity pressure on a stranger is closely influenced by the overall *ethnic group strength*, that is, a given stranger's ethnic group's capacity to influence the surrounding host environment at large. An insight into ethnic group strength has been provided by sociologists Clarke and Obler

(1976), who describe ethnic communities developing from the stages of initial economic adjustment and community building, to the subsequent stage of aggressive self-assertion and promotion of identity. Additional insights are offered in Breton's (1964) model of "institutional completeness" and the social psychological concept of "ethnolinguistic vitality" (Giles, Bourhis, & Taylor, 1977). These and related theoretical descriptions point to an observation that a strong ethnic group offers its members a strong informational, emotional, and material support system within the larger environment, facilitating the cross-cultural adaptation of strangers during the initial phase. In the long run, however, a strong ethnic community is likely to exert a stronger social pressure to conform to its own cultural practices and to maintain the strangers' ethnic group identity and discourages their participation in host social communication activities that are necessary for successful adaptation to the host society at large.

Supporting this theoretical observation is Braun's (Braun, 2002; Kim & Braun, 2002) finding that Turkish workers in an American military organization in Germany perceive the Americans to be more receptive toward them than the Germans they encounter. This difference between the two host environments is found to be linked to the extent to which the Turkish workers have formed American and German interpersonal relationships with Americans, as well as to the degree of psychological health they profess in relating to the two groups. Likewise, Maruyama's study (Maruyama, 1998; Maruyama & Kim, 1997) of international university students in Japan reports that students from other Asian countries (e.g., China, Korea, and India) report lower levels of perceived host receptivity among Japanese people they encounter than their American and Western European counterparts, affecting the two groups' psychological health differentially (see also Kim, 2003; Kim & Kim, 2004).

Predisposition

Along with the above-described host and ethnic environmental conditions, the process of cross-cultural adaptation is affected by the internal conditions of the strangers themselves prior to resettlement in the host society. To the extent that strangers differ in their backgrounds, such differences help set the perimeters for their own subsequent adaptive changes.

Strangers come to their new environment with differing levels of *preparedness;* that is, the mental, emotional, and motivational readiness to deal with the new cultural environment, including the understanding of the host language and culture. Affecting their preparedness is a wide range of formal and informal learning activities they have had prior to moving to the host society. Included in such activities are the schooling and training in, and the media exposure to, the host language and culture, and the direct and indirect experiences in dealing with members of the host society, as well as their prior cross-cultural adaptation experiences in general. In addition, strangers' preparedness is often influenced by the level of positive expectations toward the host society and of their willingness to participate in it voluntarily. Voluntary, long-term immigrants, for example, are more likely to enter the host environment with a greater readiness for making adaptive changes in themselves compared to temporary sojourners who unwillingly relocate for reasons imposed on them.

Strangers also differ in cultural, racial, and linguistic backgrounds. The term *ethnic proximity* (or ethnic distance) is employed in the theory as a relational concept comparing a given individual stranger's ethnicity and the predominant ethnicity of the host environment. Not all individuals from a given culture share similar extrinsic ethnic markers. Jewish immigrants in Israel, for example, differ significantly among themselves, from dark-skinned Ethiopian immigrants to light-skinned Russian immigrants (Abbink, 1984). What is commonly known in the United States as the "Hispanic community" is, in fact, a loose federation of individuals of widely varying racial, national, linguistic, religious, and cultural backgrounds. Given the substantial intraethnic variations, the present theory deals with extrinsic ethnic markers as a set of individual-level ethnicity-related characteristics bearing on the cross-cultural adaptation process.

The theory identifies two facets of ethnic proximity: (1) the degree of similarity (or difference) in "extrinsic ethnic markers" such as ethnic-group–related physical and facial features and material artifacts such as food, dress, decorative objects, and religious practices, as well as certain noticeable behaviors such as unique gestures and paralinguistic patterns reflected in distinct accents, tempos of utterance, intonations, and pitch levels; and (2) compatibility (or incompatibility) of "intrinsic ethnic markers" such as internalized beliefs, value orientations, and norms closely associated with a particular ethnic group (Nash, 1989). Low ethnic proximity that a given stranger brings to the host environment serves as a kind of handicap in his or her adaptive effort. Conversely, a stranger with many ethnic characteristics that are close to those of the native population is likely to enjoy a smoother transition.

An extensive amount of direct and indirect empirical evidence has been made available to support the theoretical relationship that links the salience of a stranger's ethnic markers and the difficulty he or she experiences in cross-cultural adaptation. In reviewing literature on the adaptation of Hispanic adolescents in the United States, Montalvo (1991) reports a number of studies that link darker skin color to greater "phenotyping" and thus greater adaptive stress. Other studies examining the interpersonal relationship patterns of international students report that European students interact with Americans more extensively than do students from Asia (Selltiz, Christ, Havel, & Cook, 1963). Similar results are presented in a study of international students in England (Furnham & Bochner, 1982), and in a comparative study of Asian Americans and Hispanic Americans (Stephan & Stephan, 1989) and of Malaysian and Singaporean students in New Zealand and in Singapore (Ward & Kennedy, 1993).

With respect to the adaptation-facilitating or impeding function of intrinsic ethnic markers, David Mura (1991), a third-generation Japanese-American, writes in his book, *Turning Japanese: Memoirs of a Sansei*, about the discomfort he experienced when sojourning in Japan despite his Japanese physical appearance. Research findings also support the link between the cultural compatibility of strangers and their integration in host social communication networks. Various forms of psychological distress (e.g., depression, escapism, neurosis, and psychosis) have been witnessed among those whose native culture radically departs from that of the host community (e.g., David, 1969; Krau, 1991; Searle & Ward, 1990). Studies of Southeast Asian refugee groups (e.g., Goza, 1987; Kim, 1980, 1989, 1990; Ryan, 1987) have shown that Vietnamese and Laotian refugees are adapting economically to the American environment more quickly than Cambodians and Hmongs. Such differential adaptation is attributable, at least in part, to the cultural and economic background of the first two groups, which is more comparable to that of the American society.

Personality. Along with ethnic backgrounds, strangers enter a host environment with a set of more or less enduring personality traits. They begin and continue to face the challenge of the new environment within the context of their personality, which serves as the basis upon which they pursue and internalize new experiences with varying degrees of success. Of particular interest to the present theory are those personality resources that would help facilitate strangers' adaptation by enabling them to endure stressful events and to maximize new learning, both of which are essential to their intercultural transformation. The present theory identifies three such personality resources: openness, strength, and positivity.

Openness is such a personality construct. In the systems perspective, openness is defined as an internal posture that is receptive to new information (Gendlin, 1962). Openness minimizes resistance and maximizes a willingness to attend to new and changed circumstances, and enables strangers to perceive and interpret various events and situations in the new environment as they occur with less rigid, ethnocentric judgments. As Wheatley (1999) notes, "Openness to the environment over time spawns a stronger personal system. . . . Because it [the system] partners *with* the environment, the system develops increasing autonomy from the environment and also develops new capacities that make it increasingly resourceful" (p. 84). As a theoretical concept, openness is employed in the present theory as varying in degrees among strangers. It is a broad term that incorporates other similar but more specific concepts such as "open-mindedness," "intercultural sensitivity," "empathy," and, "tolerance for ambiguity" (e.g., Ali, Van der Zee, & Sanders, 2003; Matsumoto et al., 2003; Van der Zee & Van Oudenhoven, 2000).

Coupled with openness, the *strength* of personality allows individuals to face new challenges and remain supple, effervescent, and confident (Lifton, 1993). As the inner quality that absorbs "shocks" from the environment and bounces back without being seriously damaged by them, high levels of personality strength are reflected in the tendencies of a range of more specific, interrelated personality attributes such as "resilience," "risk taking," "hardiness," "persistence," "patience," "elasticity," "resourcefulness," and "emotion regulation" (e.g., Matsumoto et al., 2003). Also important to the adaptation process is the personality attribute of *positivity,* or the proclivity for optimism and affirmative orientation in strangers' basic outlook on life, as well as a fundamental "self-trust" in the face of adverse circumstances. It is a dimension of personality that enables strangers continually to seek to acquire new cultural knowledge, and to cultivate greater intellectual, emotional/aesthetic, and behavioral compatibility with the natives.

The three broad concepts—openness, strength, and positivity—help define strangers' overall personal predisposition to "push" themselves in their adaptation process. Strangers with greater openness and strength are less likely to succumb and more likely to take on the challenging situations. Together, they serve as an inner resource for working toward developing host communication competence, so as to facilitate their own intercultural growth. A serious lack of openness and strength, on the other hand, would weaken their adaptive capacity and would serve as self-imposed psychological barriers against their own adaptation.

Intercultural Transformation

As strangers experience a progression of internal change, they undergo a set of identifiable changes in their habitual patterns of cognitive, affective, and behavioral responses. Through deculturation and acculturation, some of the "old" cultural habits are replaced by new cultural habits. Strangers acquire increasing proficiency in self-expression and in fulfilling their various social needs. The present theory identifies three interrelated aspects of strangers' intercultural transformation as the key outcomes of cross-cultural adaptation. These outcomes, in turn, facilitate the further development of their host communication competence and participation in host interpersonal and mass communication activities.

The first aspect is an increased *functional fitness*. Through repeated activities resulting in new cultural learning and self-organizing and reorganizing, strangers in time achieve an increasing "synchrony" (Hall, 1976; Kim, 1992) between their internal responses and the external

demands in the host environment. Successfully adapted strangers have accomplished a desired level of proficiency in communicating and developing a satisfactory relationship with the host environment—particularly with those individuals and situations that are of direct relevance to their daily activities. The development of strangers' functional fitness in the host society has been documented extensively. Studies of both sojourners and immigrants have shown an increase over time in various subjective indicators of functional fitness such as life satisfaction, positive feelings toward one's life in the host environment, sense of belonging, and greater congruence in subjective meaning systems (e.g., Szalay & Inn, 1987), as well as such objective socioeconomic indicators as occupational and income status (e.g., Kim et al., 1998a).

Closely associated with the increased functional fitness is increased *psychological health* vis-à-vis their host environment. Extensive data in support of this increasing trend in strangers' psychological well-being are documented in culture shock studies and similarly in the studies of mental health/illnesses among immigrants and refugees in the United States (e.g., David, 1969; Dyal & Dyal, 1981; Huhr & Kim, 1988; Kino, 1973). The development of functional fitness and psychological health in strangers further accompanies an emergent *intercultural identity*. Adversarial cross-cultural experiences bring about the experiences of what Zaharna (1989) calls "self-shock," a "shake-up" of strangers' sense of connection to their original cultural group and an accompanying growth beyond the perimeters of the original culture. The psychological movement of strangers into new dimensions produces "boundary-ambiguity syndromes" (Hall, 1976, p. 227), in which the original cultural identity begins to lose its distinctiveness and rigidity while an expanded and more flexible definition of self emerges (Adler, 1976; Kim, 1995; Kim & Ruben, 1988). The process is far from smooth, as has been shown in the upward-downward-forward-backward movement of the stress-adaptation-growth dynamic. Intense stress can reverse the process at any time, and strangers may, indeed, regress toward reaffirming and reidentifying with their ethnic origins, having found the alienation and malaise involved in maintaining a new identity too much of a strain (De Vos & Suarez-Orozco, 1990, p. 254).

As such, the emergence of an intercultural identity is a continuous search for authenticity in self and others across group boundaries. An important element of intercultural identity development is an emerging self–other orientation that is increasingly individualized. *Individualization* allows strangers to practice life that comes with diminishing grips of conventional categories. Individualization of one's self–other orientation involves a clearer self-definition and definition of the other that reflects a capacity to see the connectedness of oneself to humanity without being restricted by categories of social grouping. The resulting selfhood is one that generates a heightened self-awareness and self-identity. With this capacity, one can see oneself and others on the basis of unique individual qualities rather than categorical stereotypes, reflecting a mental outlook that exhibits greater cognitive differentiation and particularization (cf. Boekestijn, 1988; Hansel, 1993).

Accompanying the individualization of self–other orientation is *universalization*—a parallel development of a synergistic cognition "of a new consciousness, born out of an awareness of the relative nature of values and of the universal aspect of human nature" (Yoshikawa, 1978, p. 220). As people advance in their intercultural transformation process, they are better able to see the oneness and unity of humanity and locate the points of consent and complementarity beyond the points of difference and contention. As such, they are on the way to overcoming cultural parochialism and forming a wider circle of identification. Universalization frees one's mind from the exclusive parochial viewpoint, so as to attain a perspective of a larger, more inclusive whole. A universalistic outlook underlies a mind-set that integrates, rather than separates, all the perspectives represented in a communication transaction.

Research findings offer some evidence for the present theoretical claim of the emergence of an intercultural identity and its main features of individualization and universalization of self-other orientation. Amerikaner (1978) observes, in a study of military cadets, seminarians, and college fraternity members, that subjects with a high degree of personality integration (measured by the ability "to deal effectively with everyday tensions and anxieties") exhibit greater cognitive differentiation and integration, less categorical and simplistic self-identity, and greater openness to new social experiences. The author's study (Kim et al., 1998a, 1998b) has found that Native Americans in Oklahoma who are highly integrated into the predominantly Anglo-American milieu reveal a self–other orientation that transcends ethnic categories. A more recent study by Milstein (2003) indicates that the sojourn experience in Japan among exchange students from the United States and a number of other countries has resulted in increased levels of "self-efficacy." The study also shows that the increase in self-efficacy is linked positively to the self-reported level of challenge the students experience as well as to the self-reported success of the sojourn.

The Structural Model and Theorems

The six dimensions of factors identified above help explain the fact that not everyone is equally successful in making cross-cultural transitions. The dimension of personal communication or the cognitive, affective, and operational components of host communication competence (Dimension 1) serves as the very engine that pushes individual strangers along the adaptation process. Inseparably linked with host communication competence are the activities of host social communication (Dimension 2), through which strangers participate in the interpersonal and mass communication activities of the host environment. The dimension of ethnic social communication (Dimension 3) provides distinct, subcultural experiences of interpersonal and mass communication with fellow co-ethnics. Interacting with personal and social (host, ethnic) communication are the conditions of the host environment (Dimension 4), including the degree of receptivity and conformity pressure of the local population as well as the strength of the stranger's ethnic group. The stranger's predisposition (Dimension 5), consisting of preparedness for the new environment; proximity (or distance) of the stranger's ethnicity to that of the natives; and the adaptive personality attributes of openness, strength, and positivity, influences the subsequent development in the stranger's personal and social communication activities.

Each of these factors directly or indirectly facilitates or impedes the adaptation process of an individual. Like a locomotive engine, the workings of each unit operating in this process affect, and are affected by, the workings of all other units. Out of this dynamic interface among the dimensions and factors arise the fluctuating experiences of stress, adaptation, and growth—an emerging development accompanying an increasing level of congruence and ease with respect to the host environment, the original culture, and, indeed, the ongoing transformation itself. Together, all of the factors directly contribute to explaining and predicting differential rates or levels of intercultural transformation with a given time period, manifested in increased functional fitness, psychological health, and the emergence of an intercultural identity orientation (Dimension 6). The level of intercultural transformation, in turn, helps to explain and predict the levels of all other dimensions that constitute the overall structure of cross-cultural adaptation represented in Figure 16.3.

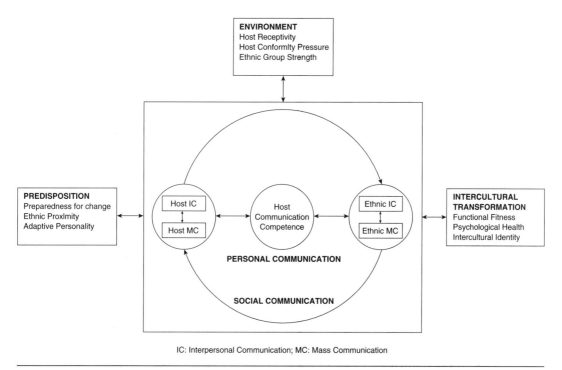

Figure 16.3   Factors Influencing Cross-Cultural Adaptation: A Structural Model
SOURCE: Kim, 2001, p. 87.

The six dimensions of factors identified above constitute an interactive and functional model in which all the linkages indicate mutual stimulations (and not unidirectional causations). These linkages emphasize reciprocal functional relationships between factors internal to a stranger and the new environment, as well as the changes the stranger undergoes over time. Unlike many existing models in which time length is included as an "independent" variable, time is a given background against which the present model identifies those dimensions of factors that contribute a facilitative or impeding function to the overall adaptation process.

Time, by Itself, Does Not Play Such a Role

The interlocking relationships identified in the structural model are formally specified in 21 theorems. The nature of each theoretical linkage in the model is specified as a theorem, that is, a generalizable and predictive statement of a functional relationship, such as: "The greater the host communication competence, the greater the participation in host social (interpersonal, mass) communication" (Theorem 1); "The greater the host interpersonal and mass communication, the greater the intercultural transformation" (Theorem 4); and, "The greater the host receptivity and host conformity pressure, the greater the host communication competence" (Theorem 8) (see Kim, 2001, pp. 91–92, for a complete list of the 21 theorems).

DISCUSSION

Building on the open-systems principle pointing to the natural drive of human beings to adapt whenever new environmental challenges threaten their internal equilibrium, the theory illuminates the process of adapting to a new cultural environment. This dynamic process acts as the prime mover of the journey of intercultural transformation, in which individuals achieve increasing levels of functional fitness, psychological health, and intercultural identity development. This cross-cultural adaptation process is influenced by a multitude of factors identified in the structural model, including the factors of the environment and of the predisposition of a stranger influencing and being influenced by the host communication competence, interpersonal communication activities, and mass communication activities of an individual stranger within and outside his or her ethnic community.

The concepts employed in the theory are sufficiently generic and abstract to accommodate other more narrowly defined concepts. The term *stranger* incorporates existing terms such as *immigrants*, *refugees*, and *sojourners*. The term *adaptation* broadly incorporates more specific terms such as *assimilation*, *acculturation*, *integration*, and *adjustment*. In addition, the theory consolidates two previously separate areas—studies of long-term and of short-term adaptation. Conceptualizing adaptation as a continuous developmental process of internal transformation, the present theory considers the distinction between long-term and short-term theoretically irrelevant.

Employing the dynamic of stress, adaptation, and growth, the process model depicts a dialectic of the two opposite psychological forces at work: resistance to change, which produces stress; and the embrace of change through self-adjustments. As such, the model juxtaposes and reconciles into a single frame the two differing perspectives: (1) the view held by many investigators of the culture-shock phenomenon that emphasizes the problematic nature of cross-cultural adaptation experiences; and (2) the contrary view that emphasizes the aspect of cross-cultural learning and growth. These two approaches are joined in the present theory in which both stressful and growth-promoting functions are identified and linked together as two competing but complementary psychological forces intrinsic to the adaptation process.

The multidimensional and multifaceted structure model reflects the open-systems perspective on human communication that emphasizes the principal features of the inseparable and interactive relationship between an individual and the environment. This holistic perspective on adaptation serves to integrate sociological and anthropological factors and psychological factors in explaining the cross-cultural adaptation of individual strangers. It brings together the macro-level analyses that have long investigated the issues of ethnic community, interethnic relations, social integration, and ethnicity into the micro-level analyses that typically have been taken in social psychology and communication for exclusively intrapersonal issues such as culture shock reactions, psychological adjustment, attitude toward the host society, and culture learning.

In addition, the present structural model bridges the division between the two opposing ideological views, assimilationism and pluralism. It does so by taking the systems-theoretic premise that cross-cultural adaptation (and, indeed, all other aspects of human adaptation) is something that occurs naturally and inevitably through communication, as strangers achieve new learning (acculturation) while some of the original cultural habits subside into the background and lose their relevance to their everyday life activities (deculturation). The assumption that adaptation is a natural and inevitable phenomenon by no means denies the fact that the ideological climate of the host environment is consequential to individual strangers' adaptation processes. To the contrary, the structural model incorporates such ideological influence in two ways. On the individual level, a given stranger's personal ideological position has to be a part of the affective-motivational component of his or her host communication competence. Strangers with an assimilative orientation are more likely to be determined to partake in the host social communication processes than those with a pluralist orientation. On the macro level of the environment, the assimilative or pluralistic ideological climate is clearly a defining element of its receptivity and conformity pressure toward strangers.

In the end, the goodness of a theory is to be determined when the logical system of ideas corresponds to the empirical reality. In the present theory, the reality is the experiences and accompanying changes in individuals who, at this very moment and at all corners of the world, are forging new lives away from their familiar ground. There is no denying that cross-cultural adaptation occurs. The present theory affirms this reality. Once the undeniable reality of cross-cultural adaptation is understood, the real choice left for us is the degree of change that we are willing to undergo. By accelerating our efforts to cultivate host communication competence and engage ourselves actively in host social communication processes, we can maximize our own adaptation. By refusing to do so, we can minimize it. As we keep our sight on the goal of successful adaptation in the host society, we will experience a gradual transformation—a subtle and largely unconscious change that leads to an increasingly intercultural personhood. Of significance in this growth process is the development of a perceptual and emotional maturity and a deepened understanding of human conditions. Despite, and because of, the many unpredictable vicissitudes of the new life, we are challenged to step into a domain that reaches beyond the original cultural perimeters. Along with increased functional fitness and psychological health, an increasingly intercultural identity and selfhood emerges from extensive experiences of stress and adaptation. In this process, we are likely to see a blurring of lines between "us" and "them." Our old identity is never completely replaced by a new one. Instead, our identity is transformed into something that will always contain the old and the new side by side to form a perspective that allows more openness and acceptance of differences in people, an understanding of "both-and," and a capacity to participate in the depth of aesthetic and emotional experience of others. Our true strength will no longer be found in rigidly insisting on who we were in the past and who we are at the moment, but in affirming our capacity for change and in embracing what we may yet become.

REFERENCES

Abbink, J. (1984). The changing identity of Ethiopian immigrants (Falashas) in Israel. *Anthropological Quarterly, 57*(4), 139–153.

Adler, P. (1976). Beyond cultural identity: Reflections on cultural and multicultural man. In L. Samovar & R. Porter (Eds.), *Intercultural communication: A reader* (pp. 389–408). Belmont, CA: Wadsworth.

Ady, J. C. (1995). Toward a differential demand model of sojourner adjustment. In R. Wiseman (Ed.), *Intercultural communication theory* (pp. 92–114). Thousand Oaks, CA: Sage.

Ali, A., Van der Zee, K., & Sanders, G. (2003). Determinants of intercultural adjustment among expatriate spouses. *International Journal of Intercultural Relations, 27*(5), 563–580.

Amerikaner, M. (1978). *Personality integration and the theory of open systems: A cross-subcultural approach.* Unpublished doctoral dissertation, University of Florida, Gainesville.

Anderson, L. (1994). A new look at an old construct: Cross-cultural adaptation. *International Journal of Intercultural Relations, 18*, 293–328.

Bateson, G. (1972). *Steps to an ecology of mind: Collected essays in anthropology, psychiatry, evolution, and epistemology.* New York: Ballantine. (Original work published 1951)

Baumeister, R. F., & Leary, M. R. (1995). The need to belong: Desire for interpersonal attachments as a fundamental human motivation. *Psychological Bulletin, 117*, 497–529.

Berkowitz, S. (1982). *An introduction to structural analysis: The network approach to social research.* Toronto: Butterworth.

Berry, J. W. (1980). Marginality, stress and ethnic identification in an acculturated aboriginal community. *Journal of Cross-Cultural Psychology, 1*, 239–252.

Berry, J. W. (1990). Psychology of acculturation: Understanding individuals moving between cultures. In R. Brislin (Ed.), *Applied cross-cultural psychology* (pp. 232–253). Newbury Park, CA: Sage.

Bertalanffy, L. (1956). *Robots, men, and minds.* New York: Braziller.

Blalock, H. M., Jr. (1989). *Power and conflict: Toward a general theory.* Newbury Park, CA: Sage.

Blau, P., & Schwartz, B. (1984). *Cross-cutting social circles.* New York: Academic Press.

Boekestijn, C. (1988). Intercultural migration and the development of personal identity. *International Journal of Intercultural Relations, 12*(2), 83–105.

Bognar, N. (2001, April). *Cross-cultural adjustment and gender-related norms: A study of Eastern Europeans in the United States.* Paper presented at the 2nd Biennial Congress of the International Academy for Intercultural Research, Oxford, MS.

Boulding, K. (1977). *The images: Knowledge in life and society.* Ann Arbor: University of Michigan Press. (Original work published 1956)

Bourhis, R., Moiese, L., Perreault, S., & Senecal, S. (1997). Towards an interactive acculturation model: A social psychological approach. *International Journal of Psychology, 32*, 369–386.

Braun, V. (2002, May). *Intercultural communication and psychological health of Turkish workers in an American workplace in Germany.* Unpublished doctoral dissertation, University of Oklahoma, Norman.

Breton, R. (1964). Institutional completeness of ethnic communities and the personal relations of immigrants. *American Journal of Sociology, 70*(2), 193–205.

Buck, R. (1984). *The communication of emotion.* New York: Guilford.

Burke, K. (1974). Communication and the human condition. *Communication 1* (pp. 135–152). United Kingdom: Gordon and Breach Science Publishers.

Buss, D. M., & Kenrick, D. T. (1998). Evolutionary social psychology. In D. T. Gilbert, S. T. Fiske, & G. Lindzey (Eds.), *Handbook of social psychology, Vol. 2* (4th ed., pp. 982–1026). New York: Oxford University Press.

Chang, W. C. (2001, April). *A model of situation-specific multiculturalism of Asian immigrants in Singapore.* Paper presented at the 2nd Biennial Congress of the International Academy for Intercultural Research, Oxford, MS.

Clarke, S., & Obler, J. (1976). Ethnic conflict, community-building, and the emergence of ethnic political traditions in the United States. In S. Clarke & J. Obler (Eds.), *Urban ethnic conflicts: A comparative perspective* (pp. 1–34). Chapel Hill: University of North Carolina Press.

Cook, W. (1962). The systematic analysis of socially significant events: A strategy for social research. *Journal of Social Issues, 18*(2), 66–88.

Cui, G. (1998). Cross-cultural adaptation and ethnic communication: Two structural equation models. *Howard Journal of Communication, 9,* 69–85.

David, H. (1969). Involuntary international migration: Adaptation of refugees. In E. Brody (Ed.), *Behavior in new environments: Adaptation of migrant populations* (pp. 73–95). Beverly Hills, CA: Sage.

De Vos, G. A., & Suarez-Orozco, M. M. (1990). *Status inequality: The self in culture.* Newbury Park, CA: Sage.

Dubin, R. (1978). *Theory building* (Rev. ed.). New York: Free Press.

Dubos, R. (1965). *Man adapting.* New Haven, CT: Yale University Press.

Dyal, J., & Dyal, R. (1981). Acculturation, stress and coping. *International Journal of Intercultural Relations, 5*(4), 301–328.

Fielding, N., & Fielding, J. (1986). *Linking data.* Newbury Park, CA: Sage.

Furnham, A., & Bochner, S. (1982). Social difficulty in a foreign culture: An empirical analysis of culture shock. In S. Bochner (Ed.), *Cultures in contact: Studies in cross-cultural interaction* (pp. 161–198). Elmsford, NY: Pergamon.

Gendlin, E. (1962). *Experiencing and the creation of meaning.* New York: Free Press.

Giles, H., Bourhis, R., & Taylor, D. (1977). Toward a theory of second language acquisition. *Journal of Multilingual and Multicultural Development, 3,* 17–40.

Givón, T. (1989). *Mind, code and context: Essays in pragmatics.* Hillsdale, NJ: Lawrence Erlbaum.

Gong, Y. (2003). Goal orientations and cross-cultural adjustment: An exploratory study. *International Journal of Intercultural Relations, 27*(3), 297–305.

Gordon, M. (1973). Assimilation in America: Theory and reality. In P. Rose (Ed.), *The study of society* (pp. 350–365). New York: Random House.

Gordon, M. (1981). Models of pluralism: The new American dilemma. *Annals of the American Academy of Political and Social Science, 454,* 178–188.

Goza, F. (1987). Adjustment and adaptation among Southeast Asian refugees in the United States. *Dissertation Abstracts International, 48*(02), 486B. (University Microfilms No. AAC87–08086).

Gudykunst, W. B., & Kim, Y. Y. (2003). *Communicating with strangers: An approach to intercultural communication* (4th ed.). New York: McGraw-Hill.

Hall, E. (1976). *Beyond culture.* Garden City, NY: Anchor.

Hallinan, M., & Smith, S. (1985). The effects of classroom racial composition on students' interracial friendliness. *Social Psychology Quarterly, 48,* 3–16.

Hansel, B. (1993). *An investigation of the re-entry adjustment of Indians who studied in the U.S.A.* (Occasional Papers in Intercultural Learning No. 17). New York: AFS Center for the Study of Intercultural Learning.

Hedge, R. S. (1998). Swinging the trapeze: The negotiation of identity among Asian Indian immigrant women in the United States. In D. V. Tanno & A. Gonzalez (Eds.), *Communication and identity across cultures* (pp. 34–55). Thousand Oaks, CA: Sage.

Horton, D., & Wohl, R. (1979). Mass communication and para-social interaction. In G. Gumpert & R. Cathcart (Eds.), *Inter/Media: Interpersonal communication in a media world* (pp. 32–55). New York: Oxford University Press.

Hurh, W., & Kim, K. (1988). *Uprooting and adjustment: A sociological study of Korean immigrants' mental health.* Final report submitted to National Institute of Mental

Health, U.S. Department of Health and Human Services (Grant No. 1 R01 MH40312–01/5 MH40312–02). Macomb: Western Illinois University.

Jantsch, E. (1980). *The self-organizing universe: Scientific and human implications of the emerging paradigm of evolution.* Elmsford, NY: Pergamon.

Jasinskaja-Lahti, I., Liebkind, K., Horenczyk, G., & Schmitz, P. (2003). The interactive nature of acculturation: Perceived discrimination, acculturation attitudes and stress among ethnic repatriates in Finland, Israel and Germany. *International Journal of Intercultural Relations, 27*(1), 79–97.

Joas, H. (1993). *Pragmatism and social theory.* Chicago: University of Chicago Press.

Jourard, S. (1974). Growing awareness and the awareness of growth. In B. Patton & K. Griffin (Eds.), *Interpersonal communication* (pp. 456–465). New York: Harper & Row.

Kim, Y. S. (2003, May). *Host communication competence and psychological health: A study of cross-cultural adaptation of Korean expatriate employees in the United States.* Paper presented at the annual conference of the International Communication Association, San Diego.

Kim, Y. Y. (1976). *Communication patterns of foreign immigrants in the process of acculturation: A survey among the Korean population in Chicago.* Unpublished doctoral dissertation, Northwestern University.

Kim, Y. Y. (1977a). Communication patterns of foreign immigrants in the process of acculturation. *Human Communication Research, 4*(1), 66–77.

Kim, Y. Y. (1977b). Inter-ethnic and intra-ethnic communication: A study of Korean immigrants in Chicago. In N. C. Jain (Ed.), *International and Intercultural Communication Annual* (Vol. 4, pp. 53–68). Falls Church, VA: Speech Communication Association.

Kim, Y. Y. (1978a, November). *Acculturation and patterns of interpersonal communication relationships: A study of Japanese, Mexican, and Korean communities in the Chicago area.* Paper presented at the Speech Communication Association Conference, Minneapolis, MN.

Kim, Y. Y. (1978b). A communication approach to acculturation processes: Korean immigrants in Chicago. *International Journal of Intercultural Relations, 2*(2), 197–224.

Kim, Y. Y. (1979). Toward an interactive theory of communication-acculturation. In B. Ruben (Ed.), *Communication yearbook 3* (pp. 435–453). New Brunswick, NJ: Transaction Books.

Kim, Y. Y. (1980). *Research project report on Indochinese refugees in Illinois. Vol. 1: Introduction, summary and recommendations. Vol. 2: Methods and procedures. Vol. 3: Population characteristics and service needs. Vol. 4: Psychological, social and cultural adjustment of Indochinese refugees. Vol. 5: Survey of agencies serving Indochinese refugees.* (Based on a grant from the Department of Health, Education and Welfare, Region V, P: 95–549). Chicago: Travelers Aid Society.

Kim, Y. Y. (1988). *Communication and cross-cultural adaptation: An integrative theory.* Clevendon, UK: Multilingual Matters.

Kim, Y. Y. (1989). Personal, social, and economic adaptation: The case of 1975–1979 arrivals in Illinois. In D. Haines (Ed.), *Refugees as immigrants: Survey research on Cambodians, Laotians, and Vietnamese in America.* Totowa, NJ: Rowman & Littlefield.

Kim, Y. Y. (1990). Communication and adaptation of Asian Pacific refugees in the United States. *Journal of Pacific Rim Communication, 1,* 191–207.

Kim, Y. Y. (1992). Synchrony and intercultural communication. In D. Crookall & K. Arai (Eds.), *Global interdependent: Simulation and gaming perspectives* (pp. 99–105). New York: Springer.

Kim, Y. Y. (1995). Identity development: From cultural to intercultural. In H. Mokros (Ed.), *Information and behavior: Vol. 6. Interaction and identity* (pp. 347–369). New Brunswick, NJ: Transaction Books.

Kim, Y. Y. (2001). *Becoming intercultural: An integrative theory of communication and cross-cultural adaptation.* Thousand Oaks, CA: Sage.

Kim, Y. Y. (2002). Unum vs. pluribus: Ideology and differing academic conceptions of ethnic identity. In W. B. Gudykunst (Ed.), *Communication yearbook 26* (pp. 298–325). Mahwah, NJ: Lawrence Erlbaum.

Kim, Y. Y., & Braun, V. (2002, July). *Host communication competence and psychological health: A study of Turkish workers' adaptation to an American-German host environment.* Paper presented at the annual conference of the International Communication Association, Seoul, South Korea.

Kim, Y. Y., & Kim, Y. S. (2004). Patterns of communication and adaptation: A comparative study of Korean expatriates in the United States and American expatriates in Korea. *Asian Communication Research, 1.*

Kim, Y. Y., Lujan, P., & Dixon, L. (1998a). "I can walk both ways": Identity integration of American Indians in Oklahoma. *Human Communication Research, 25*(2), 252–274.

Kim, Y. Y., Lujan, P., & Dixon, L. (1998b). Patterns of communication and interethnic integration: A study of American Indians in Oklahoma. *Canadian Journal of Native Education, 22*(1), 120–137.

Kim, Y. Y., & Ruben, B. (1988). Intercultural transformation: A systems theory. In Y. Kim & W. B. Gudykunst (Eds.), *International and intercultural communication annual 12. Theories in intercultural communication* (pp. 299–321). Newbury Park, CA: Sage.

Kino, F. (1973). Aliens' paranoid reaction. In C. Zwingmann & M. Pfister-Ammende (Eds.), *Uprooting and after* (pp. 60–66). New York: Springer.

Kirschner, G. (1994). Equilibrium processes: Creativity and depression. *Mind and Human Interaction, 5*(4), 165–171.

Krau, E. (1991). *The contradictory immigrant problem: A sociopsychological analysis.* New York: Peter Lang.

Lazarus, R. (1966). *Psychological stress and the coping process.* St. Louis: McGraw-Hill.

Lifton, R. (1993). *The protean self: Human resilience in an age of fragmentation.* New York: Basic Books.

Maruyama, M. (1998). *Cross-cultural adaptation and host environment: A study of international students in Japan.* Unpublished doctoral dissertation, University of Oklahoma, Norman.

Maruyama, M., & Kim, Y. Y. (1997). *Cross cultural adaptation of international students in Japan: An exploratory study.* Paper presented

at the annual conference of the International Communication Association, Montreal.

Matsumoto, D., ReRoux, J. A., Iwanoto, M., Choi, J. W., Rogers, D., Tatani, H., & Uchida, H. (2003). The robustness of the Intercultural Adjustment Potential Scale (ICAPS): The search for a universal psychological engine of adjustment. *International Journal of Intercultural Relations, 27*(5), 543–562.

Mechanic, D. (1974). Social structure and personal adaptation: Some neglected dimensions. In G. Coelho, D. Hamburg, & J. Adams (Eds.), *Coping and adaptation* (pp. 32–44). New York: Basic Books.

Milstein, T. J. (2003, May). *Transformation abroad: Communication self-efficacy via sojourning.* Paper presented at the annual conference of the International Communication Association, San Diego.

Monge, P. R. (1990). Theoretical and analytical issues in studying organizational processes. *Organization Science, 1,* 406–430.

Montalvo, F. (1991). Phenotyping, acculturation, and biracial assimilation of Mexican Americans. In M. Sotomayor (Ed.), *Empowering Hispanic families: A critical issue for the '90s* (pp. 97–119). Milwaukee, WI: Family Service America.

Moos, R. (Ed.). (1976). *Human adaptation: Coping with life crises.* Lexington, MA: D. C. Heath.

Mura, D. (1991). *Turning Japanese: Memoirs of a sansei.* New York: Atlantic Monthly Press.

Nash, M. (1989). *The cauldron of ethnicity in the modern world.* Chicago: University of Chicago Press.

Nesdale, D., & Mak, A. S. (2003). Ethnic identification, self-esteem and immigrant psychological health. *International Journal of Intercultural Relations, 27*(1), 23–40.

Piaget, J. (1963). *The origins of intelligence in children.* New York: Norton.

Ruben, B. D. (1975). Intrapersonal, interpersonal, and mass communication processes in individual and multi-person systems. In B. Ruben & J. Kim (Eds.), *General systems theory and human communication* (pp. 120–144). Rochelle Park, NJ: Hayden.

Ruesch, J., & Bateson, G. (1951/1968). *Communication: The social matrix of psychiatry.* New York: Norton.

Ryan, C. (1987). Indochinese refugees in the U.S.: Background characteristics, initial adjustment patterns, and the role of policy. *Dissertation Abstracts International, 48*(04), 1025B. (University Microfilms No. AAC87–15554)

Sahlins, M. (1964). Culture and environment: The study of cultural ecology. In S. Tax (Ed.), *Horizons of anthropology* (pp. 132–147). Chicago: Aldine.

Searle, W., & Ward, C. (1990). The prediction of psychological and sociocultural adjustment during cross-cultural transitions. *International Journal of Intercultural Relations, 14,* 449–464.

Selltiz, C., Christ, J. R., Havel, J., & Cook, S. W. (1963). *Attitudes and social relations of foreign students in the United States.* Minneapolis: University of Minnesota Press.

Shibutani, T., & Kwan, K. M. (1965). *Ethnic stratification: A comparative approach.* New York: Macmillan.

Simmel, G. (1950). The stranger. In K. Wolff (Ed. and Trans.), *The sociology of Georg Simmel.* New York: Free Press. (Original work published 1908)

Spicer, E. (1968). Acculturation. In D. Sills (Ed.), *International encyclopedia of the social sciences* (pp. 21–27). New York: Macmillan.

Stephan, W., & Stephan, C. (1989). Antecedents of intergroup anxiety in Asian Americans and Hispanic Americans. *International Journal of Intercultural Relations, 13,* 203–219.

Stonequist, E. (1937). *The marginal man.* New York: Scribner's.

Szalay, L., & Inn, A. (1987). Cross-cultural adaptation and diversity: Hispanic Americans. In Y. Y. Kim & W. B. Gudykunst (Eds.), *Cross-cultural adaptation: Current approaches* (pp. 212–232). Newbury Park, CA: Sage.

Taft, R. (1977). Coping with unfamiliar cultures. In N. Warren (Ed.), *Studies in cross-cultural psychology* (Vol. 1, pp. 121–153). London: Academic Press.

Tamam, E. (1993, December). *The influence of ambiguity tolerance, open-mindedness, and empathy on sojourners' psychological adaptation and perceived intercultural communication effectiveness.* Unpublished doctoral dissertation, University of Oklahoma, Norman.

Thayer, L. (1975). Knowledge, order, and communication. In B. Ruben & J. Kim (Eds.), *General systems theory and human communication* (pp. 237–245). Rochelle Park, NJ: Hayden.

Van der Zee, K. I., & Van Oudenhoven, J. P. (2000). Psychometric qualities of the Multicultural Personality Questionnaire: A multidimensional instrument of multicultural effectiveness. *European Journal of Personality, 14,* 291–309.

Ward, C., Bochner, S., & Furnham, A. (2001). *The psychology of culture shock* (2nd ed.). Philadelphia: Routledge.

Ward, C., & Kennedy, A. (1993). Where's the culture in cross-cultural transition? Comparative studies of sojourner adjustment. *Journal of Cross-Cultural Psychology, 24,* 221–249.

Ward, C. & Kennedy, A. (1999). The measurement of sociocultural adaptation. *International Journal of Intercultural Relations, 23,* 659–677.

Watzlawick, P., Beavin, J., & Jackson, D. (1967). *Pragmatics of human communication.* New York: Norton.

Wheatley, M. J. (1999). *Leadership and the new science: Discovering order in a chaotic world.* San Francisco: Berrett-Kohler.

White, R. (1976). Strategies of adaptation: An attempt at systematic description. In R. Moos (Ed.), *Human adaptation: Coping with life crises* (pp. 17–32). Lexington, MA: D. C. Heath.

Yoshikawa, M. (1978). Some Japanese and American cultural characteristics. In M. Prosser (Ed.), *The cultural dialogue: An introduction to intercultural communication* (pp. 220–239). Boston: Houghton Mifflin.

Young, R. (1996). *Intercultural communication: Pragmatics, genealogy, deconstruction.* Philadelphia: Multilingual Matters.

Zaharna, R. (1989). Self-shock: The double-binding challenges of identity. *International Journal of Intercultural Relations, 13*(4), 501–525.

17

Cultural Schema Theory

HIROKO NISHIDA

Communication between people from different cultures has been investigated in various research areas: for example, (a) the study of psychological reactions to unfamiliar environments such as culture shock (Adler, 1987; Bock, 1970; Bochner, 1982; Cleveland, Mangone, & Adams, 1960; Furnham & Bochner, 1986; Oberg, 1960), U-curve and W-curve (Church, 1982; Gullahorn & Gullahorn, 1963; Klineberg & Hull, 1979; Lysgaard, 1955; Nash, 1991; Torbiorn, 1982), and uncertainty reduction (Berger, 1992; Berger & Calabrese, 1975; Gudykunst, 1983, 1988, 1991, 1993; Sudweeks, Gudykunst, Ting-Toomey, & Nishida, 1990); (b) cross-cultural adjustment or adaptation (Brislin, 1981; Furnham, 1988, 1992; Kim & Ruben, 1992; Nishida, 1992; Taft, 1966; Yoshikawa, 1988) and immigrants' acculturation (Brower, 1980; Kim, 1978, 1982, 1987; Padilla, 1980; Taft, 1988; Yum, 1982); (c) intercultural communication competence (Chen & Starosta, 1996; Dinges, 1983; Hammer, Nishida, & Wiseman, 1996; McCroskey, 1984; Nishida, 1985; Wiseman, Hammer, & Nishida, 1989; Wiseman & Koester, 1993); (d) values and value orientations (Caudill & Scarr, 1962; Hofstede, 1980, 1991; Kluckhohn & Strodtbeck, 1961; Nishida, 1979; Rokeach, 1973; Schwartz, 1992, 1994); and (e) verbal and nonverbal interactions (Barnlund, 1975; Burgoon, 1985;

Author's Note: An earlier version of this chapter appeared in Nishida (1999).

Giles, 1978; Giles, Mulac, Bradac, & Johnson, 1987; Hall, 1959; Mehrabian, 1972; Morris, Collett, Marsh, & Oshaughnessy, 1979; O'Keefe & Delia, 1985; Philipsen, 1992; Watzlawick, Beavin, & Jackson, 1967).

Although we have gained considerable knowledge through these studies, there are few intercultural communication theories underlining them. Without some form of theorizing, research in intercultural communication will not take on specific foci or directions. As Berger (1991) notes,

> It is not enough for researchers to demonstrate that they can use certain methodological tools, even when they are used to study current, highly visible social issues. It is the capacity to sustain theoretically driven, programmatic research that produces significant insights about communication phenomena in the long run. (p. 110)

In this chapter, cultural schema theory is examined in order to explicate the phenomena of intercultural communication, especially of cross-cultural adaptation. The following questions will be discussed: (a) What are cultural schemas? and (b) What axioms can be generated when cultural schema theory is applied to cross-cultural adaptation?

WHAT ARE CULTURAL SCHEMAS?

When a person enters a familiar situation in his or her own culture, a stock of knowledge of appropriate behavior and an appropriate role he or she should play in the situation is retrieved. In other words, every interactant's social world is usually constituted within a framework of familiar and pre-acquainted knowledge about various situations. This familiar and pre-acquainted knowledge is called cultural schemas (or schemata). The concept of schemas is not new, but existed even in the 19th century: German philosopher Immanuel Kant developed the idea that each person's experiences are gathered together in

memory, forming higher order concepts (Kant, 1963). We can find the concept early in the 20th century, too: Piaget's work in the 1920s investigated schemas in infants, and Bartlett's research in the 1930s tested memory for schemas (Matlin, 1989). Furthermore, in the past 25 years the concept of schemas has been used and defined by quite a number of scholars (Cohen, Kiss, & Le Voi, 1993; Mandler, 1984; Rumelhart, 1980; Schank & Abelson, 1977; Taylor & Crocker, 1981; Thorndyke, 1984; and Turner, 1994, among others): Cohen et al. (1993), for example, explain schemas as "packets of information stored in memory representing general knowledge about objects, situations, events, or actions" (p. 28). Moreover, in Taylor and Crocker's (1981) words, a schema is

> a cognitive structure that consists in part of a representation of some defined stimulus domain. The schema contains general knowledge about that domain, including specification of the relationships among its attributes, as well as specific examples or instances of the stimulus domain. . . . The schema provides hypotheses about incoming stimuli, which include plans for interpreting and gathering schema-related information. (p. 91)

Schemas, then, are generalized collections of knowledge of past experiences that are organized into related knowledge groups and are used to guide our behaviors in familiar situations.

During the period from the late 1970s to the 1990s, researchers obtained massive evidence showing that people's behaviors are deeply related to what they store in their brains. Hudson (1990), for example, clearly demonstrated how schemas are stored in long-term memory and how they are used in the real world: Contrasting preschool children's memories of a specific event, attending one session of a creative movement workshop, with their memories of repeated workshop sessions, Hudson found that the children's memories of details were better for the workshop immediately preceding the test trial if only one workshop had been attended rather than four workshops. When four workshops had been attended, the children tended to recall the entire sequence of events during the workshop better than when only one workshop had been attended. Details from workshops 1, 2, and 3, however, were wrongly remembered as having occurred during workshop 4. In short, with repeated encounters of the workshop, some general knowledge of relationships between activities during the workshop (i.e., a "workshop" schema) was built up, but once the schema was formed, memory of specific details declined. Moreover, Hudson and Nelson (1983) found that even young children could repair not-quite-consistent stories with their schematic knowledge of their world. When misordered acts were reported (e.g., a not-quite-right story about a birthday party), children tended to repair them in schematically correct order.

Through these studies we learn that our behaviors rely heavily on past experiences or knowledge stored in our brain (i.e., schemas). Experiences or knowledge, however, are not a unitary dimension. Some experiences are unique to an individual; they are idiosyncratic. Any person is exposed to individualized environments and has personal experiences or knowledge. Our cultural environment provides ubiquitous experiences, however, ones to which every member of the culture is exposed. Through the former kinds of experiences we acquire personal schemas, as indicated in the workshop study by Hudson. The knowledge children obtained was unique to them (i.e., children who did not participate in the workshop do not have the "workshop" schema). On the contrary, through the latter kinds of experiences, we gain cultural schemas as found in the Hudson and Nelson study. The "birthday party" schema that children in the United States obtain through their experiences differs in many ways from the one Japanese children acquire in Japan. Besides cultural schemas and personal schemas, there are universal schemas that are shared among people in the world, such as arithmetic rules (i.e., "$3 + 1 = 4$" or "$4 - 1 = 3$") or works of worldwide celebrity, though people who did not have the chance to go to school may not share them.

Thus, we have three kinds of schemas: personal schemas, cultural schemas, and universal schemas. This chapter focuses its attention on cultural schemas, and therefore personal schemas and universal schemas are excluded from the discussion.

Cultural Schemas for Social Interactions

Cultural schemas for social interactions are cognitive structures that contain knowledge for face-to-face interactions in one's cultural environment. An existing literature (Abelson, 1981; Chi, 1981; Fiske & Taylor, 1984; Hudson & Nelson, 1983; Hudson & Shapiro, 1991; Mandler, 1984; Minsky, 1977; Schank & Abelson, 1977; Taylor & Crocker, 1981; Turner, 1994) indicates the formation of cultural schemas for social interactions as follows: When we interact with the members of the same culture in certain situations for a number of times, or talk about certain information with them for a number of times, cultural schemas are generated and stored in our brain. As we encounter more of these similar situations or as we talk more often about the information, the cultural schemas become more organized, abstract, and compact. Thus, people develop cultural schemas by their direct experiences and also by talking about cultural-schema–related information. When cultural schemas become tightly organized, the information they contain becomes more usable. They start to be accessed and used as efficient units of information among the members of the culture. As the cultural schemas become more abstract, organized, and compact, our communication becomes much easier through such thus-refined cultural schemas. Cultural schemas, therefore, can be defined as follows:

> Cultural schemas are generalized collections of the knowledge that we store in memory through experiences in our own culture. Cultural schemas contain general information about familiar situations and behavioral rules as well as information about ourselves and people around us. Cultural schemas also contain knowledge about facts we have been taught in school or strategies for problem solving, and emotional or affective experiences that are often found in our culture. These cultural schemas are linked together into related systems constructing a complex cognitive structure that underlies our behavior.

Cognitive Activity of Cultural Schemas

Underlying the cognitive activity of cultural schemas is a complex pattern of neural connections at the physiological level. The basic unit within this pattern is the neuron, on which intercellular connections (i.e., synapses) form. Neurons interact with subsets of other neurons through regular synaptic associations. A given neural pattern should have a one-to-one correspondence with some aspect of behavior. Individual neurons, however, can form multiple synapses with other neurons. So, within a specific subset of neurons, the pattern, complexity, and sheer quantity of connections are tremendous (see, e.g., Abel et al., 1995; Groeger, 1997; Haberlandt, 1999; Johnson, Munakata, & Gilmore, 2002; Rosser, 1994; and Rugg, 1997). Certain patterns of connections may be more cognitively or biologically efficient than other patterns. Experiences serve to stabilize or confirm this pattern of synaptic contacts. By the use that the environment triggers, a stable pattern survives while unconfirmed synapses, those not triggered and used, are eliminated. Thus, it is an essential fact that humans modify their nervous systems in response to their experiences.

In other words, it can be said that the brain's architecture is plastic and can be changed by experience (Diamond, 1990; Dudai, 1989; Nottebohm, 1985; Rosenzweig, 1984; Squire, 1987). In this way, neural circuits are constructed and stored in our brain.

Neurons interact and communicate at synaptic sites and form complex systems of interconnections, or circuits. Therefore, the more synaptic material (i.e., experience) that exists, the greater the patterns of neural interconnectivity are possible (Abel et al., 1995; Green, 1987; Rosser, 1994; Turner & Greenough, 1985). Activated connections, those that have occurred in response to experience, become easier to make than inactivated ones. Frequently activated connections become strengthened and increasingly efficacious in communication. Experience triggers a pattern of connections, and repeated experience functions to solidify the pattern. In other words, repeated experience constructs neural circuits, and in this process new synapses are created and strengthened in response to the experience. Thus, when humans acquire and retain information from the surrounding environment, neural circuits are generated and, as a result of this process, information-processing experience is stored in long-term memory. No cognitive function is feasible without the support of memory, whether it is learning, problem solving, perception, reasoning, or comprehension. In turn, each of these functions exerts an impact on memory. Executing mental tasks changes memory representation and makes the system more adaptive to environmental demands (Anderson, 1990; Conway, 1996; Craik & Lockhart, 1972; Crowder, 1993; Diamond, 1990; Dudai, 1989). These studies in the fields of cognitive psychology, neuropsychology, and physiology indicate that "memory representation" or neural circuits that are created in the brain as a result of information processing can be assumed as schemas. "Schemas," as a concept, provide a framework that guides information processing in the brain by predicting what is to be expected and looked for, and by filling in gaps in the currently available information (Conway, 1991; Johnson-Laird, 1983).

Thus, it can be said that experience is the impetus for construction of cultural schemas, strengthening some connections and weakening others. As people have more experience with different instances, they generalize about the commonalities among them. Developing cultural schemas become more tightly organized, so that the information they contain is not only more complex, but also more usable among the members of the culture.

Types of Cultural Schemas

Cultural schemas for social interactions are classified into several types. Taylor and Crocker (1981), for example, point out the following five schemas: (a) Person schemas, which are knowledge about different types of people, including their personality traits; (b) self schemas, which contain knowledge about themselves; (c) role schemas, which represent knowledge about social roles; (d) event schemas or scripts, which are information about the appropriate sequence of events in common situations; and (e) content-free schemas, which are information about processing rules. Following Taylor and Crocker's classification, Augoustinos and Walker (1995) claim that person, self, role, and event schemas are primary types of social interaction schemas.

Meanwhile, through experiments on artificial intelligence (AI), Turner (1994) found the following three schemas play important roles when "a schema-based reasoner" (i.e., AI) solves problems: (a) procedural schemas, which contain information about steps to take or hierarchical plans; (b) contextual schemas, which are information about the situation or appropriate setting of behavioral parameters; and (c) strategic schemas, which are knowledge about problem-solving strategies. Procedural schemas in Turner's classification are similar to Taylor

and Crocker's fourth type of schema, event schemas or scripts, and strategic schemas are similar to their fifth type, content-free schemas.

Furthermore, Chi (1981) classified knowledge into the following three types: procedural, declarative, and strategic. According to Chi, procedural knowledge is about procedural information in situations, and declarative knowledge is our knowledge about facts and concepts. Chi names procedural and declarative knowledge "content knowledge," which is characterized by domain-specific functions (e.g., their situationally dependent functions). Chi further explains that the strategic knowledge is information about strategies used in various domains (i.e., it is situationally independent), and it can be acquired only after content knowledge thoroughly develops. Here again, Chi's classification overlaps with Taylor and Crocker's and with Turner's: Chi's procedural knowledge is similar to Taylor and Crocker's event schemas or scripts and to Turner's procedural schemas; and strategic knowledge is similar to Taylor and Crocker's content-free schemas and to Turner's strategic schemas.

Through the above examination of schemas and other related literature, the following schemas can be extracted as primary types for generating human behavior for social interactions:

1. Fact-and-concept schemas: These are pieces of general information about facts, such as "Tokyo is the capital of Japan," and concepts such as "Bicycles are those vehicles that have two wheels, a seat, and handlebars" (Barsalow & Sewell, 1985; Chi, 1981; Hampton, 1982; Rosch & Mervis, 1975; Rumelhart & Ortony, 1977).

2. Person schemas: These are knowledge about different types of people, which includes their personality traits; for example, "John is neurotic," "Taro is shy," or "Mary is easy-going." Since we have some representation of what it is to be "neurotic," "shy," or "easy-going" (i.e., person schemas), we tend

to classify people in terms of their dominant personality traits (Augoustinos & Walker, 1995; Cantor & Mischel, 1979; Shaw & Pittenger, 1977; Taylor & Crocker, 1981).

3. Self schemas: These contain people's knowledge about themselves (i.e., how they see themselves and how others see them). Markus (1977), for example, describes self schemas as "cognitive generalizations about the self, derived from past experience, that organize and guide the processing of self-related information contained in the individual's social experiences" (p. 64). Thus, self schemas are components of the self-concept that are central to self-identity and self-definition (Markus, 1977, 1980; Markus & Wurf, 1987; Taylor & Crocker, 1981).

4. Role schemas: These are knowledge about social roles that denote sets of behaviors that are expected of people in particular social positions. These refer to achieved and ascribed roles (Augoustinos & Walker, 1995; Pichert & Anderson, 1977; Taylor & Crocker, 1981). Research on ascribed roles has been prolific, especially in the areas of gender and social stereotypes (Andersen & Klatzky, 1987; Markus, Crane, Bernstein, & Siladi, 1982; Ruble & Stangor, 1986; Taylor, Fiske, Etcoff, & Ruderman, 1978). According to Fiske and Taylor (1991), role schemas are used more often than person schemas because role schemas are apparently richer in detail than person schemas are, so they are more informative.

5. Context schemas: These contain information about the situations and appropriate settings of behavioral parameters. According to Turner (1994), the information contained in context schemas includes predictions about appropriate actions to take in order to achieve goals in the context (i.e., to activate procedure schemas), and suggestions for reasonable problem-solving strategies (i.e., to activate strategy schemas). In other words, context schemas are activated before other schemas are activated.

6. Procedure schemas[1]: These are knowledge about the appropriate sequence of events in common situations. They include specific steps to take and behavioral rules for the events. The application of procedure schemas causes people to take certain actions (Bower, Black, & Turner, 1979; Schank & Abelson, 1977; Taylor & Crocker, 1981). Turner (1994) claims that procedure schemas are distinct systems and are derived from past planning or past action sequences that worked, or from "experience" embodied in societal or other conventions.

7. Strategy schemas: These are knowledge about problem-solving strategies (Chi, 1981; Chi, Feltovich, & Glaser, 1981; Ericsson & Charness, 1994; Larkin, 1985; Taylor & Crocker, 1981; Turner, 1994). There is some evidence that, in humans, one factor impacting the choice of strategy is the person's expertise. For example, according to Patel, Evans, and Chawla (1987), doctors who are experts in a given type of problem tend to use a strategy called predictive reasoning, which is basically the same as hypothetic-deductive reasoning, but less-experienced clinicians, or those solving a problem outside their area of expertise, tend to use another strategy. One factor to associate with strategy schemas, then, is the experience level of the person with respect to the kind of problem under consideration. Another factor that should be included is that problem-solving constraints are context-independent. Rather than redundantly storing strategy schemas about these constraints with each context schema they affect, the information is instead recorded with strategies useful for coping with them (Turner, 1994). For example, a constraint on time may be seen in many different contexts, including an emergency situation in a hospital or a situation of being late for an appointment.

In addition to these seven schemas, recently there has been increasing interest in the affective dimension in schema research. Shaver, Schwartz, Kirson, and O'Conor (1987), for example, asked subjects to classify 135 affective words and to describe typical emotional states, and then cluster-analyzed the obtained data. Through the analysis, they found that emotions are schematically stored in long-term memory. Other studies also indicate that emotion schemas are socially constructed concepts, just as any other schemas (Christianson & Safer, 1996; Harre, 1986; Lazarus, 1991; Manstead, 1991; Wagenaar & Groeneweg, 1990). These studies suggest that emotion schemas play important roles in human social interactions, and therefore they should be included:

8. Emotion schemas: These contain information about affect and evaluation stored in long-term memory that is accessed when other schemas are activated. Emotion schemas are constructed through social interactions throughout one's life.

I will call these eight cultural schemas "primary social interaction schemas" (PSI schemas) in a culture hereafter.

How Do Cultural Schemas Function?

How, then, do these schemas actually function when people interact with each other in their culture? Through experiments on artificial intelligence (AI), Turner (1994) suggests a process to generate "behavior" (in his study, the behavior of AI called MEDIC): (a) When individuals are in a specific situation, they try to recognize whether they know the situation by retrieving one or more context schemas from memory that may represent the current situation; (b) when an appropriate context schema, which represents similar interaction situations, is found, the context schema subsequently suggests a goal to pursue (through an attention-focusing function of the context schema); (c) when a goal is selected, the context schema looks for a strategy usually useful in situations of this sort; (d) the context schema then suggests a procedure schema with which to achieve the goal, using the selected strategy schema (i.e., the procedure schema is retrieved for taking specific actions; in other

words, the procedure schema specifies steps to take, hierarchical plans, or behavioral rules); and (e) the application of the procedure schema causes an individual to take some action, such as asking questions of the other interactant, which further causes the individual to specify the current context more clearly; in other words, to find a context schema that is more specific for the situation. When the more specific context schema is applied, the schema further finds appropriate strategy and procedure schemas to apply to the new context. The more specific the current context schema is, the better the chance that more-specific strategy and procedure schemas will be suggested.

In the above discussion, Turner explained only the functions and relations among context, strategy, and procedure schemas. This is because the relations between these three and the other schemas have not been thoroughly investigated. Anderson (1983), however, demonstrated relationships between declarative and procedural memory using a computer model called ACT*, which stands for Adaptive Control of Thought; the asterisk indicates that this version is a modification of the original ACT model. Declarative memory in Anderson's study is knowledge about facts, things, and events stored in long-term memory. Procedural knowledge, on the other hand, is knowledge about how to perform cognitive activities. ACT* simulates the development of skill and expertise by starting with declarative representations relevant to the goals of a task (Anderson, 1983, 1987). For example, in simulating the development of typing skill, ACT* might begin by memorizing the locations of the keys for the letters and other characters (i.e., ACT* acquires the fact-and-concept schema about a computer keyboard). Other forms of declarative knowledge would specify how to spell a particular word, giving the sequence of letters that must be used (fact-and-concept schemas). To type a given word, the novice, as simulated by ACT*, would depend on very general rules (procedure schemas) or strategies (strategy schemas) for solving problems (e.g., take a step that moves one toward the goal). Such a strategy might direct the system to find the key for the first letter and strike it, and then find the key for the second letter. ACT* would in essence hunt and peck its way to achieving the goal. With sufficient practice, memory for where to move the fingers to find a particular letter would be converted from a declarative representation to a procedural representation. Just as typists learn to move their fingers automatically about the keyboard, ACT* simulates the gain in expertise in terms of the development of and reliance on production memory.

Tulving (1985) and Zola-Morgan and Squire (1990) claim that the distinction between declarative and procedural knowledge can be exemplified as "knowing the traditions and rules of baseball" and "being able to play baseball" (i.e., knowing what and how vs. being able to act). Their claim seems to indicate that declarative memory in Anderson's study represents schemas stored in long-term memory.

Thus, through experiments on AI, we come to understand how information stored in long-term memory (i.e., schemas) is transformed into behavioral actions. Because these computer models aim at the construction of comprehensive models of cognition in order to produce rather general theoretical orientations having wide applicability, they use a relatively small set of components (Newell, 1989); relationships among various types of schemas have therefore not yet been thoroughly examined.

WHAT AXIOMS CAN BE GENERATED WHEN CULTURAL SCHEMA THEORY IS APPLIED TO CROSS-CULTURAL ADAPTATION?

The Definition of Concepts

The term *adaptation* has been used along with other similar terms such as *acculturation* (Kim, 1982; Padilla, 1980; Snyder, 1976; Spiro,

1955) and *assimilation* (Gordon, 1964; Johnston, 1965). According to Teske and Nelson (1974), acculturation is a dynamic process that may involve either groups or individuals in direct contact situations between cultures. The changes that take place can occur in one or both cultural groups, and changes in values may be involved. Furthermore, they claim that acculturation does not require a change in the reference group, internal change, or acceptance by the outside group or culture. Thus, acculturation is potentially a bidirectional process and does not require changes in values within the acculturating group. Assimilation, to the contrary, is a unidirectional process toward the dominant host culture and requires value changes within the assimilating group. Adaptation, however, refers to "the process of change over time that takes place within individuals who have completed their primary socialization process in one culture and then come into continuous, prolonged first-hand contact with a new and unfamiliar culture" (Kim, 1988, pp. 37–38). The term *cross-cultural adaptation,* therefore, is used here to refer to the complex process through which an individual acquires an increasing level of the communication skills of the host culture and of relational development with host nationals. In other words, cross-cultural adaptation can be viewed as the transformation of one's own PSI schemas into those of the host culture and as the acquisition of new PSI schemas in the host-culture environment.

Besides the definition of adaptation, we must specify who adapts to a new (i.e., different and unfamiliar) environment. A number of different groups of people may be subject to cross-cultural adaptation: immigrants, refugees, business people, diplomats, foreign workers, students, and voluntary workers. Among these, business people, diplomats, foreign workers, students, and voluntary workers may be classified as sojourners since they differ from immigrants and refugees in two aspects: (a) Their motives are more specific and goal-oriented, and (b) their length of stay in a new culture is shorter than that of immigrants and refugees (Furnham, 1988). Furthermore, Furnham claims that sojourners usually spend a few years in a new culture while intending to return to their home countries. Therefore, it is the purpose of this section to apply cultural schema theory to sojourners' cross-cultural adaptation, and to formulate axioms in this research domain.

Before going farther, it should be stated that the goal of theory is to provide an explanation of the phenomenon being studied, and therefore some theoretical statements (axioms and theorems) can be generated. According to Blalock (1969), axioms are propositions that involve variables that are taken to be directly linked causally; axioms should therefore be statements that imply direct causal links among variables. Thus, axioms are commonly associated with covering laws theory and causal relationships. Bailey (1970), however, argues that assuming axiomatic theories must express causal relationships will result in either distorted theories or the absence of theories about noncausal relationships. He maintains that axioms may describe causal, correlational, or teleological relationships. In this section, following Bailey, axioms will express causal, correlational, or teleological relationships.

Once axioms are formulated, theorems are deduced from the axioms (Blalock, 1969). Although axioms are not directly testable, they articulate the basic assumptions of the theory. While their validity is assumed, they are also indirectly supported by theorems that are susceptible to empirical verification (theorems are not presented here).

In this section, cultural schema theory is applied to sojourners' cross-cultural adaptation in the following functional domains of cultural schemas: development, internal organization, schema-driven versus data-driven function, and modification.

The Development of Cultural Schemas

When people interact with members of the same culture in certain situations, or they talk about certain information for a number of times, cultural schemas are generated and stored in their long-term memories. The more they engage in similar situations or exchange similar information, the more organized, abstract, and compact the cultural schemas become. As individuals behave in ways that affirm these cultural schemas, the schemas are strengthened as others respond accordingly in a cyclical fashion (Abelson, 1981; Barsalow & Sewell, 1985; Hudson & Shapiro, 1991; Schank & Abelson, 1977; Turner, 1994). Thus, research on schema development implies:

Axiom 1: The more often a person repeats a schema-based behavior in his or her culture, the more likely the cultural schema will be stored in the person's memory.

One of the characteristics of cultural schemas, according to Chase and Ericsson (1982), is to guide the encoding of information into meaningful chunks. In other words, the performance of people who have well-organized cultural schemas is linked to their ability to perceive and think in terms of meaningful chunks. A study by Spilich, Vesonder, Chiesi, and Voss (1979) is an excellent demonstration. Although their study deals with personal schema, the result can be applied to cultural schema. The subjects in their study were divided into high- and low-knowledge groups on the basis of a 45-item test of baseball knowledge. A baseball text was then presented to them, and they wrote down as much as they could recall from the passage. The high-knowledge subjects recalled more statements about actions that were important to the outcome of the game, and they were also likely to recall the events in the correct order. In contrast, those with less knowledge about baseball were more likely to recall details that were peripheral to the game.

This study suggests that the background information (i.e., schemas) provides a meaningful context for the acquisition of new information. This suggests the following axioms:

Axiom 2: Sojourners' failure to recognize the actions and behaviors that are relevant to meaningful interactions in the host culture are mainly due to their lack of the PSI schemas of the culture.

Axiom 3: The acquisition of the PSI schemas of the host culture is a necessary condition for sojourners' cross-cultural adaptation to the culture.

The Internal Organization of Cultural Schemas

According to cultural schema theory, any given behavior can be subdivided into several schemas, forming a "hierarchy" (Brewer, Dull & Lui, 1981; Cantor & Mischel, 1979). For example, human behavior in a specific situation in a culture can be subdivided into such cultural schemas as context, role, strategy, and procedure, and these schemas are further subdivided into subschemas. Near the top of the hierarchy are very general schemas. These in turn organize more specific schemas that can achieve increasingly more specific goals. For example, one function of context schemas is to provide a person with information about an appropriate role and appropriate actions to take in a particular context. In other words, context schemas contain links to role schemas and procedure schemas that are often used to achieve goals in the specific situations. This further indicates that retrieving information from memory involves working through various levels of the network of schemas, that is, the activation of schemas spreads from one schema to related schemas. For example, when "being at a dentist's office" (a context schema) is selected, the role and procedure schemas that are appropriate in the context are activated. The patient (a role schema) takes a seat in the dentist's chair (a procedure schema), opens his or her mouth for the dental examination (a procedure schema), and the dentist (a role schema) conducts the examination, using dental tools, a mirror, and lights

(a procedure schema). The patient would be very surprised if the dentist were to bring a menu and asked the patient what he or she wanted to eat. Thus, when a person retrieves a schema from his or her memory, it has a chunk of related knowledge about the current problem, eliminating the need to search for each piece of that knowledge separately (Turner, 1994). An additional benefit is that knowledge that might not otherwise have been retrieved may be retrieved as part of a chunk.

Moreover, because every part of the system is related to every other part, a change in a particular part (e.g., a selection of a specific strategy schema) causes a change in all the other parts and finally in the total system (i.e., in behavior). Research on the internal organization of schemas, therefore, suggests the following axioms:

Axiom 4: Fact-and-concept, person, self, role, context, procedure, strategy, and emotion schemas (the PSI schemas of one's own culture) are interrelated with each other, forming a network of cultural schemas to generate behaviors that are appropriate in the culture. Experience in the host culture causes a change in one cultural schema. This further causes changes in all the other cultural schemas and finally in the total system (i.e., in behavior).

Axiom 5: The acquisition of information about interrelationships among the PSI schemas of the host culture is a necessary condition for sojourners' cross-cultural adaptation.

Schema-Driven Versus Data-Driven Functions

One of the most important assumptions of cultural schema theory is that cultural schemas are built up through many encounters with similar events or information in one's own culture. Once a cultural schema is developed, information tends to be processed through the schema. This kind of cognitive processing is referred to as top-down or schema-driven processes. If people are influenced by the nature of the information itself, however, their cultural schemas are not applied; that is, if people are influenced by all the original individual experiences in their raw forms, this kind of processing is called bottom-up or data-driven processes (Brewer, 1988; Fiske & Neuberg, 1990; Fiske & Taylor, 1984; Forgas, 1985). Through research on person prototypes (i.e., person schemas), Forgas (1985) found that the more culturally salient and consensual the stimulus, the more likely schematic processing was to be activated, whereas information with low cultural salience was more likely to be data driven. Other findings (Fiske & Taylor, 1984; Bower et al., 1979), however, indicate that ambiguous information can be either data driven or schema driven; that is, ambiguous information directs a search for the relevant data to complete the stimulus more fully (i.e., data-driven), or it can be filled in with "default options" or "best guesses" of the schema that is activated (i.e., schema driven). Bower et al. (1979), however, argue that people have a tendency to reorganize what they have heard or seen to fit their schema-based expectations; that is, they claim that humans tend to use schema-driven processing more often than data-driven processing. This is because schema-based processing consumes less time and effort than data-based processing (Fiske & Neuberg, 1990).

Regarding data-driven and schema-driven processing, Fiske and Neuberg's (1990) findings indicate that schema-based processing is used when the data are unambiguous and relatively unimportant to the person, whereas data-driven processing is used when the data are less clear or are of considerable importance to the person. What is important here is that data-driven processing is individuating and piecemeal processing and therefore requires attention and effort, whereas schema-based processing is effortless and sometimes unconscious. Fiske and Neuberg emphasize that most person impressions are initially schema-based. If, however, one is motivated to pay

detailed attention to the target person, then information about the person is processed in a piecemeal fashion. This aspect is also suggested by Taylor and Altman (1987), who insist that as relationships develop, communication moves from relatively shallow, nonintimate levels to deeper, more personal ones (i.e., to individuating piecemeal processing).

To conclude, although people use cultural schemas initially and fairly automatically, people can abandon them when information contradicts the schemas, especially if they are sufficiently motivated. Thus, people do not blindly use cultural schemas if they do not apply; if motivated, people pay attention to the data and modify their cognitive structures accordingly (i.e., they employ data-based processing). Through these discussions, the following axioms are suggested in this domain of research:

> *Axiom 6:* People use both schema-driven and data-driven processing to perceive new information, depending on the situation and their motivations.

> *Axiom 7:* If one has well-organized cultural schemas, schematically salient information is more likely to be processed through the schemas, whereas ambiguous information will either direct a search for the relevant data to complete the stimulus more fully, or it will be filled in with default options of the schemas.

> *Axiom 8:* Sojourners who lack the PSI schemas of the host culture are more likely to employ data-driven processing, which requires effort and attention.

Sojourners may encounter truly novel circumstances in the host culture; that is, they may have a problem that they have never before encountered. This indicates that they should make use of their native-culture schemas as much as possible in order to solve the problem (Fiske & Neuberg, 1990; Turner, 1994). In some situations, however, there may be no native-culture schemas that they can employ. In these kinds of situations, they may have to collect data in order to generate new PSI schemas in the host culture. In these situations people tend to experience cognitive uncertainty and anxiety. This domain of research suggests the following axiom:

Axiom 9: In the host culture, sojourners encounter truly novel situations where they experience cognitive uncertainty and anxiety because of their lack of the PSI schemas in the situations.

Cultural-Schema Modification

In cultural schema theory, an environmental change from one's native culture to the host culture elicits a change in a context schema, and this further changes other PSI schemas of one's native culture. In other words, when people encounter unfamiliar situations in the host culture where they lack appropriate host-culture schemas, they are subject to stress because of the disintegration of the context and other PSI schemas that they acquired in their native culture. What they usually do is direct their attention selectively through their native-culture schemas, trying to provide integration of information. This is an example of home-ostasis or self-regulation (Cannon, 1968). Yet because people are subject not only to self-regulation or homeostasis, but also to self-direction to a changing environment, they may change or elaborate their internal structures as a condition of survival (i.e., they may change or elaborate their native-culture schemas in order to acquire host-culture schemas).

These aspects have been explained by Rumelhart and Norman (1978) as tuning, accretion, and restructuring. Tuning refers to slight adjustments in native-cultural schemas that are made on a temporary basis to meet a transient problem. The schemas metaphorically stretch and shape themselves for a moment to accommodate to the novel situation. For example, an American who is visiting Australia would tune his or her native-culture schema for the wolf or the rabbit in order to understand a Tasmanian wolf or a rabbit bandicoot. His or her perception and memory of these animals would depend on simply fine-tuning native-culture schemas. Accretion refers to a gradual and permanent modification of a native-culture schema. Each time a native-culture schema accommodates to a novel object, event, or situation in the host culture, it registers the results. Slowly, the shape and complexity of the schema modify themselves to the requirements of the environment. A good example of this process is the situation in which sojourners who have stayed in the host culture for a prolonged period of time cannot distinguish their native-culture schemas from those acquired in the host culture because of their prolonged exposure to the host-culture environment. Finally, restructuring is an abrupt and massive change in existing native-culture schemas. According to Rumelhart and Norman, restructuring may come about spontaneously after enough exposure to discrepant experiences, through conscious reflection on one's experience, or through active efforts to reorganize what one knows. Thus, the following axiom is included:

Axiom 10: In the host culture, sojourners experience the stages of self-regulation and self-direction. In the stage of self-regulation, they try to resolve ambiguities and to establish integration of information using their native-culture schemas by gradually modifying them. In the stage of self-direction, on the other hand, they actively try to reorganize their native-culture schemas or to generate host-culture schemas in order to adapt to the host-culture environment.

CONCLUSION

We now know that human memory selects, abstracts, integrates, and normalizes information. Inconsistent information may be forgotten, while consistent information may be generated at later recall. All these various phenomena can be conveniently summarized by cultural schema theory. The application of cultural schema theory to sojourners' cross-cultural adaptation may be a necessary step for us to document and analyze the phenomena accurately.

The purpose of this chapter was to examine cultural schema theory in order to explicate the phenomena of intercultural communication, especially of sojourners' cross-cultural adaptation. Eight primary types of cultural schemas, which are central to human social interactions in one's own culture, were investigated, and these schemas' functions for processing information were examined. Furthermore, when applied to sojourners' cross-cultural adaptation, cultural schema theory suggested 10 axioms in the following functional domains of cultural schemas: development, internal organization, schema-driven versus data-driven function, and modification.

In future studies, theorems must be generated and tested in the field in order to verify the axioms formulated here. When this is done, the theory can be used for the design and implementation of cross-cultural training programs to facilitate individuals' adaptation to the host-culture environment.

NOTE

1. Turner (1994) calls procedure schemas procedural schemas. However, I will call them procedure schemas to emphasize the contrast with the other PSI schemas.

REFERENCES

Abel, T., Alberini, C., Ghirardi, M., Huang, Y., Nguyen, P., & Kandel, E. (1995). Steps toward a molecular definition of memory consolidation. In D. L. Schacter (Ed.), *Memory distortion: How minds, brains, and societies reconstruct the past* (pp. 298–325). Cambridge, MA: Harvard University Press.

Abelson, R. P. (1981). Psychological status of the script concept. *American Psychologist, 36,* 715–729.

Adler, P. S. (1987). Culture shock and the cross-cultural learning experience. In L. F. Luce & E. C. Smith (Eds.), *Toward internationalism* (pp. 24–35). Cambridge, MA: Newbury. (Original work published 1972)

Andersen, S. M., & Klatzky, R. L. (1987). Traits and social stereotypes: Levels of categorization in person perception. *Journal of Personality and Social Psychology, 53,* 235–246.

Anderson, J. R. (1983). *The architecture of cognition.* Cambridge, MA: Harvard University Press.

Anderson, J. R. (1987). Methodologies for studying human knowledge. *Behavioral and Brain Sciences, 10,* 465–505.

Anderson, J. R. (1990). *Cognitive psychology and its implications* (3rd ed.). New York: Freeman.

Augoustinos, M., & Walker, I. (1995). *Social cognition: An integrated introduction.* London: Sage.

Bailey, K. D. (1970). Evaluating axiomatic theories. In E. F. Borgatta (Ed.), *Sociological methodology* (pp. 48–71). San Francisco: Jossey-Bass.

Barnlund, D. (1975). *Public and private self in Japan and the United States.* Tokyo: Simul.

Barsalow, L. W., & Sewell, D. R. (1985). Contrasting the representation of scripts and categories. *Journal of Memory and Language, 24,* 646–665.

Berger, C. R. (1991). Chautauqua: Why are there so few communication theories: Communication theories and other curios. *Communication Monographs, 58,* 101–113.

Berger, C. R. (1992). Communicating under uncertainty. In W. B. Gudykunst & Y. Y. Kim (Eds.), *Readings on communicating with strangers: An approach to intercultural communication* (pp. 5–16). New York: McGraw-Hill.

Berger, C. R., & Calabrese, R. J. (1975). Some explorations in initial interaction and beyond: Toward a developmental theory of interpersonal communication. *Human Communication Research, 1,* 99–112.

Blalock, H. H. (1969). *Theory construction: From verbal to mathematical formulations.* Englewood Cliffs, NJ: Prentice Hall.

Bochner, S. (1982). The social psychology of cross-cultural relations. In S. Bochner (Ed.), *Cultures in contact: Studies in cross-cultural interaction.* Oxford, UK: Pergamon.

Bock, P. (Ed.). (1970). *Culture shock: A reader in modern anthropology.* New York: Knopf.

Bower, G. H., Black, J. B., & Turner, T. J. (1979). Scripts in memory for texts. *Cognitive Psychology, 11,* 177–220.

Brewer, M. B. (1988). A dual process model of impression formation. In T. K. Srull & R. S. Wyer, Jr. (Eds.), *Advances in social cognition* (Vol. 1, pp. 1–36)). Hillsdale, NJ: Lawrence Erlbaum.

Brewer, M. B., Dull, V., & Lui, L. (1981). Perceptions of the elderly: Stereotypes as prototypes. *Journal of Personality and Social Psychology, 41,* 656–670.

Brislin, R. W. (1981). *Cross-cultural encounters.* Elmsford, NY: Pergamon.

Brower, I. C. (1980). Counseling Vietnamese. *Personal Guidance Journal, 58*(10), 646–652.

Burgoon, J. (1985). Nonverbal signals. In M. Knapp & G. Miller (Eds.), *Handbook of interpersonal communication.* Beverly Hills, CA: Sage.

Cannon, W. B. (1968). Self-regulation of the body. In W. Buckley (Ed.), *Modern systems research for the behavioral scientist: A sourcebook* (pp. 256–258). Chicago: Aldine.

Cantor, N., & Mischel, W. (1979). Prototypes in person perception. In L. Berkowitz (Ed.), *Advances in experimental social psychology* (Vol. 12). New York: Academic Press.

Caudill, W., & Scarr, H. A. (1962). Japanese value orientations and culture change. *Ethnology, 1,* 53–91.

Chase, W. G., & Ericsson, K. A. (1982). Skill and working memory. In G. H. Bower (Ed.), *The psychology of learning and motivation* (pp. 1–58). New York: Academic Press.

Chen, G., & Starosta, W. (1996). Intercultural communication competence: A synthesis. In B. Burleson (Ed.), *Communication yearbook 19* (pp. 353–383). Thousand Oaks, CA: Sage.

Chi, M. T. H. (1981). Knowledge development and memory performance. In M. P. Friedman, J. P. Das, & N. O'Conner (Eds.), *Intelligence and learning* (pp. 221–229). New York: Plenum.

Chi, M. T. H., Feltovich, P. J., & Glaser, R. (1981). Categorization and representation of physics problems by experts and novices. *Cognitive Science, 5,* 121–152.

Christianson, S. A., & Safer, M. A. (1996). Emotional events and emotions in autobiographical memories. In D. C. Rubin (Ed.), *Remembering our past* (pp. 218–243). New York: Cambridge University Press.

Church, A. T. (1982). Sojourner adjustment. *Psychological Bulletin, 91,* 540–572.

Cleveland, H., Mangone, G. J., & Adams, J. G. (1960). *The overseas Americans.* New York: McGraw-Hill.

Cohen, G., Kiss, G., & Le Voi, M. (1993). *Memory: Current issues* (2nd ed.). Philadelphia: Open University Press.

Conway, M. A. (1991). In defense of everyday memory. *American Psychologist, 46,* 19–26.

Conway, M. A. (1996). Autobiographical knowledge and autobiographical memories. In D. C. Rubin (Ed.), *Remembering our past* (pp. 67–93). New York: Cambridge University Press.

Craik, F. I. M., & Lockhart, R. S. (1972). Levels of processing: A framework for memory research. *Journal of Verbal Learning and Verbal Behavior, 11,* 671–684.

Crowder, R. (1993). Short-term memory: Where do we stand? *Memory & Cognition, 21,* 142–145.

Diamond, M. C. (1990). How the brain grows in response to experience. In R. E. Ornstein (Ed.), *The healing brain: A scientific reader.* New York: Guilford.

Dinges, N. (1983). Intercultural competence. In D. Landis & R. Brislin (Eds.), *Handbook of intercultural training: Vol. 1. Issues in theory and design* (pp. 176–202). Elmsford, NY: Pergamon.

Dudai, Y. (1989). *The neurobiology of memory: Concepts, findings and trends.* New York: Oxford University Press.

Ericsson, K. A., & Charness, N. (1994). Expert performance. *American Psychologist, 49,* 725–747.

Fiske, S. T., & Neuberg, S. L. (1990). A continuum of impression formation, from category-based to individuating processes: Influences of information and motivation on attention and interpretation. In M. P. Zanna (Ed.), *Advances in experimental social psychology* (Vol. 23, pp. 1–74). New York: Academic Press.

Fiske, S. T., & Taylor, S. E. (1984). *Social cognition.* Reading, MA: Addison-Wesley.

Fiske, S. T., & Taylor, S. E. (1991). *Social cognition* (2nd ed.). New York: McGraw-Hill.

Forgas, J. P. (1985). Person prototypes and cultural salience: The role of cognitive and cultural factors in impression formation. *British Journal of Social Psychology, 24,* 3–17.

Furnham, A. (1988). The adjustment of sojourners. In Y. Y. Kim & W. B. Gudykunst (Eds.), *Cross-cultural adaptation* (pp. 42–61). Newbury Park, CA: Sage.

Furnham, A. (1992). The adjustment of sojourners. In W. B. Gudykunst & Y. Y. Kim (Eds.), *Readings on communicating with strangers* (pp. 336–345). New York: McGraw-Hill.

Furnham, A., & Bochner, S. (1986). *Culture shock: Psychological reactions to unfamiliar environments.* London: Routledge.

Giles, H. (1978). Linguistic differentiation between ethnic groups. In H. Tajfel (Ed.), *Differentiation between social groups* (pp. 361–393). London: Academic Press.

Giles, H., Mulac, A., Bradac, J. J., & Johnson, P. (1987). Speech accommodation. In M. McLaughlin (Ed.), *Communication yearbook 10* (pp. 13–48). Newbury Park, CA: Sage.

Gordon, M. (1964). *Assimilation in American life.* New York: Oxford University Press.

Green, S. (1987). *Physiological psychology.* New York: Routledge & Kegan Paul.

Groeger, J. A. (1997). *Memory and remembering: Everyday memory in context.* London, UK: Longman.

Gudykunst, W. B. (1983). Uncertainty reduction and predictability of behavior in low- and high-context cultures. *Communication Quarterly, 31,* 236–251.

Gudykunst, W. B. (1988). Uncertainty and anxiety. In Y. Y. Kim & W. B. Gudykunst (Eds.), *Theories in intercultural communication* (pp. 123–156). Newbury Park, CA: Sage.

Gudykunst, W. B. (1991). *Bridging differences: Effective intergroup communication.* Newbury Park, CA: Sage.

Gudykunst, W. B. (1993). Toward a theory of effective interpersonal and intergroup communication: An anxiety/uncertainty management (AUM) perspective. In R. L. Wiseman & J. Koester (Eds.), *Intercultural communication competence* (pp. 33–71). Newbury Park, CA: Sage.

Gullahorn, J. T., & Gullahorn, J. E. (1963). An extension of the U-curve hypothesis. *Journal of Social Issues, 19*(3), 33–47.

Haberlandt, K. (1999). *Human memory: Exploration and application.* Needham Heights, MA: Allyn & Bacon.

Hall, E. T. (1959). *The silent language.* Garden City, NY: Anchor.

Hammer, M. R., Nishida, H., & Wiseman, R. L. (1996). The influence of situational prototypes on dimensions of intercultural communication competence. *Journal of Cross-Cultural Psychology, 27*(3), 267–282.

Hampton, J. A. (1982). An investigation of the nature of abstract concepts. *Memory & Cognition, 9,* 149–156.

Harre, R. (Ed.) (1986). *The social construction of emotions.* New York: Basil Blackwell.

Hofstede, G. (1980). *Culture's consequences: International differences in work-related values.* Beverly Hills, CA: Sage.

Hofstede, G. (1991). *Cultures and organizations: Software of the mind.* London: McGraw-Hill.

Hudson, J. A. (1990). The emergence of autobiographical memory in mother-child conversation. In R. Fivush & J. A. Hudson (Eds.), *Knowing and remembering in young children* (pp. 166–196). New York: Cambridge University Press.

Hudson, J. A., & Nelson, K. (1983). Effect of script structure on children's story recall. *Developmental Psychology, 19,* 625–635.

Hudson, J. A., & Shapiro, L. R. (1991). From knowing to telling: The development of children's scripts, stories, and personal narratives. In A. McCabe & C. Peterson (Eds.), *Developing narrative structure* (pp. 89–136). Hillsdale, NJ: Lawrence Erlbaum.

Johnson, M. H., Munakata, Y., & Gilmore, R. O. (Eds.). (2002). *Brain development and cognition: A reader* (2nd ed.). Oxford, UK: Blackwell.

Johnson-Laird, P. N. (1983). *Mental models.* Cambridge, MA: Harvard University Press.

Johnston, R. (1965). *Immigrant assimilation.* Perth, Western Australia: Paterson Brokensha.

Kant, I. (1963). *Critique of pure reason* (2nd ed.) (N. K. Smith, Trans.). London: Macmillan. (Original work published 1787)

Kim, Y. Y. (1978). A communication approach to acculturation processes: Korean immigrants in Chicago. *International Journal of Intercultural Relations, 2*(2), 197–224.

Kim, Y. Y. (1982). Communication and acculturation. In L. A. Samovar & R. E. Porter (Eds.), *Intercultural communication: A reader* (3rd ed., pp. 359–368). Belmont, CA: Wadsworth.

Kim, Y. Y. (1987). Facilitating immigrant adaptation: The role of communication and interpersonal ties. In T. C. Albrecht & M. B. Adelman (Eds.), *Communicating social support: Process in context* (pp. 192–211). Newbury Park, CA: Sage.

Kim, Y. Y. (1988). *Communication and cross-cultural adaptation.* Clevendon, UK: Multilingual Matters.

Kim, Y. Y., & Ruben, B. (1992). Intercultural transformation. In W. B. Gudykunst & Y. Y. Kim (Eds.), *Readings on communicating with strangers: An approach to intercultural communication.* New York: McGraw-Hill.

Klineberg, O., & Hull, W. F., IV. (1979). *At a foreign university: An international study of adaptation and coping.* New York: Macmillan.

Kluckhohn, F. R., & Strodtbeck, F. L. (1961). *Variations in value orientations.* Evanston, IL: Row, Peterson.

Larkin, J. H. (1985). Understanding, problem representations, and skill in physics. In S. F. Chipman, J. W. Segal, & R. Glaser (Eds.), *Thinking and learning skills* (Vol. 2, pp. 141–159). Hillsdale, NJ: Lawrence Erlbaum.

Lazarus, R. S. (1991). Progress on a cognitive-motivational-relational theory of emotion. *American Psychologist, 46,* 819–834.

Lysgaard, S. (1955). Adjustment in a foreign society: Norwegian Fulbright grantees visiting the United States. *International Social Science Bulletin, 7*(1), 45–51.

Mandler, J. M. (1984). *Stories, scripts, and scenes: Aspects of schema theory.* Hillsdale, NJ: Lawrence Erlbaum.

Manstead, A. S. R. (1991). Emotion in social life. *Cognition and Emotion, 5,* 353–362.

Markus, H. (1977). Self-schemata and processing information about the self. *Journal of Personality and Social Psychology, 35,* 63–78.

Markus, H. (1980). The self in thought and memory. In D. M. Wegner & R. R. Vallacher (Eds.), *The self in social psychology.* New York: Oxford University Press.

Markus, H., Crane, M., Bernstein, S., & Siladi, M. (1982). Self-schemas and gender. *Journal of Personality and Social Psychology, 42,* 38–50.

Markus, H., & Wurf, E. (1987). The dynamic self-concept: A social psychological perspective. *Annual Review of Psychology, 38,* 299–337.

Matlin, M. W. (1989). *Cognition.* Chicago: Holt, Rinehart & Winston.

McCroskey, J. E. (1984). Communication competence: The elusive construct. In R. N. Bostrom (Ed.), *Competence in communication* (pp. 259–268). Beverly Hills, CA: Sage.

Mehrabian, A. (1972). *Nonverbal communication.* Chicago: Aldine.

Minsky, M. L. (1977). Frame-system theory. In P. N. Johnson-Laird & P. C. Wason (Eds.), *Thinking: Readings in cognitive science* (pp. 355–376). Cambridge, UK: Cambridge University Press.

Morris, D., Collett, P., Marsh, P., & Oshaughnessy, M. (1979). *Gestures: Their origins and distribution.* London: Jonathan Cape.

Nash, D. (1991). The course of sojourner adaptation: A new test of the U-curve hypothesis. *Human Organization, 50,* 283–286.

Newell, A. (1989). *Unified theories of cognition.* Cambridge, MA: Harvard University Press.

Nishida, H. (1979). *Variations in value orientations and cultural change in Japan and the U.S.A.: An intercultural perspective.* Unpublished doctoral dissertation, University of Minnesota, Minneapolis.

Nishida, H. (1985). Japanese intercultural communication competence and cross-cultural adjustment. *International Journal of Intercultural Relations, 9,* 247–269.

Nishida, H. (1992). *Gokai no kouzou: America-jin to hataraku toki no chishiki to gijutu no reporto* [The structure of misunderstanding: A report on knowledge and skills for working with Americans in the U.S.A.]. Tokyo: Diamond-Sha.

Nishida, H. (1999). A cognitive approach to intercultural communication based on schema theory. *International Journal of Intercultural Relations, 23,* 753–777.

Nottebohm, F. (1985). Neuronal replacement in adulthood. *Annals of the New York Academy of Science, 457,* 143–161.

Oberg, K. (1960). Cultural shock: Adjustment to new cultural environments. *Practical Anthropology, 7,* 177–182.

O'Keefe, B. J., & Delia, J. G. (1985). Psychological and interactional dimensions of communicative development. In H. Giles & R. St. Clair (Eds.), *Recent advances in language, communication and social psychology* (pp. 41–85). London: Lawrence Erlbaum.

Padilla, A. M. (Ed.). (1980). *Acculturation: Theory, models and some new findings.* Boulder, CO: Westview.

Patel, V. L., Evans, D. A., & Chawla, A. (1987). Predictive versus diagnostic reasoning in the application of biomedical knowledge. *Proceedings of the Ninth Annual Conference of the Cognitive Science Society* (pp. 221–233). Seattle, WA: Cognitive Science Society.

Philipsen, G. (1992). Speech and the communal function in four cultures. In W. B. Gudykunst & Y. Y. Kim (Eds.), *Readings on communicating with strangers: An approach to intercultural communication* (pp. 235–244). New York: McGraw-Hill.

Pichert, J. W., & Anderson, R. C. (1977). Taking different perspectives on a story. *Journal of Educational Psychology, 69,* 309–315.

Rokeach, M. (1973). *The nature of human values.* New York: Free Press.

Rosch, E. H., & Mervis, C. B. (1975). Family resemblances: Studies in the internal structure of categories. *Cognitive Psychology, 7,* 573–605.

Rosenzweig, M. R. (1984). Experience, memory and the brain. *American Psychologist, 39,* 365–376.

Rosser, R. (1994). *Cognitive development: Psychological and biological perspectives.* Boston, MA: Allyn & Bacon.

Ruble, D. N., & Stangor, C. (1986). Stalking the elusive schema: Insights from developmental and social-psychological analyses of gender schemas. *Social Cognition, 4,* 227–261.

Rugg, M. D. (Ed.) (1997). *Cognitive neuroscience.* Hove, East Sussex, UK: Psychology Press.

Rumelhart, D. E. (1980). Schemata: The building blocks of cognition. In R. J. Spiro, B. C. Bruce, & W. F. Brewer (Eds.), *Theoretical issues in reading comprehension* (pp. 33–58). Hillsdale, NJ: Lawrence Erlbaum.

Rumelhart, D. E., & Norman, D. A. (1978). Accretion, tuning, and restructuring: Three models of learning. In J. W. Cotton & R. Klatzky (Eds.), *Semantic factors in cognition* (pp. 37–53). Hillsdale, NJ: Lawrence Erlbaum.

Rumelhart, D. E., & Ortony, A. (1977). The representation of knowledge in memory. In R. C. Anderson, R. J. Spiro, & W. E. Montague (Eds.), *Schooling and the acquisition of knowledge* (pp. 99–135). Hillsdale, NJ: Lawrence Erlbaum.

Schank, R. C., & Abelson, R. P. (1977). *Script, plans, goals and understanding: An inquiry into human knowledge structures.* Hillsdale, NJ: Lawrence Erlbaum.

Schwartz, S. H. (1992). Universals in the content and structure of values: Theoretical advances and empirical tests in 20 countries. In M. Zanna (Ed.), *Advances in experimental social psychology* (Vol. 25, pp. 1–66). New York: Academic Press.

Schwartz, S. H. (1994). Beyond individualism and collectivism: New cultural dimensions of values. In U. Kim, H. C. Triandis, C. Kagitçibasi, S.-C. Choi, & G. Yoon (Eds.), *Individualism and collectivism: Theory, method, and applications* (pp. 85–122). Newbury Park, CA: Sage.

Shaver, P., Schwartz, J., Kirson, D., & O'Conor, C. (1987). Emotion knowledge: Further exploration of a prototype approach. *Journal of Personality and Social Psychology, 52,* 1061–1086.

Shaw, R., & Pittenger, J. (1977). Perceiving the face of change in changing faces: Implications for a theory of object perception. In R. Shaw & J. Bransford (Eds.), *Perceiving, acting and knowing: Toward an ecological psychology* (pp. 103–132). Hillsdale, NJ: Lawrence Erlbaum.

Snyder, P. Z. (1976). Neighborhood gatekeepers in the process of urban adaptation: Cross-ethnic commonalities. *Urban Anthropology, 5*(1), 35–52.

Spilich, G. J., Vesonder, G. T., Chiesi, H. L., & Voss, J. F. (1979). Text processing of domain-related information for individuals with high and low domain knowledge. *Journal of Verbal Learning and Verbal Behavior, 18,* 275–290.

Spiro, M. E. (1955). The acculturation of American ethnic groups. *American Anthropologist, 57,* 1240–1252.

Squire, L. R. (1987). *Memory and brain.* New York: Oxford University Press.

Sudweeks, S., Gudykunst, W. B., Ting-Toomey, S., & Nishida, T. (1990). Developmental themes in Japanese-North American relationships. *International Journal of Intercultural Relations, 14,* 207–233.

Taft, R. (1966). *From stranger to citizen.* London: Tavistock.

Taft, R. (1988). The psychological adaptation of Soviet immigrants in Australia. In Y. Y. Kim &

W. B. Gudykunst (Eds.), *Cross-cultural adaptation: Current approaches* (pp. 150–167). Newbury Park, CA: Sage.

Taylor, D. A., & Altman, I. (1987). Communication in interpersonal relationships: Social penetration theory. In M. E. Roloff & G. R. Miller (Eds.), *Interpersonal processes: New directions in communication research* (pp. 257–277). Newbury Park, CA: Sage.

Taylor, S. E., & Crocker, J. (1981). Schematic bases of social information processing. In E. T. Higgins, C. P. Herman, & M. P. Zanna (Eds.), *Social cognition: The Ontario Symposium* (Vol. 1, pp. 89–134). Hillsdale, NJ: Lawrence Erlbaum.

Taylor, S. E., Fiske, S., Etcoff, N. L., & Ruderman, A. J. (1978). Categorical and contextual bases of person memory and stereotyping. *Journal of Personality and Social Psychology, 36,* 778–793.

Teske, R. H. C., & Nelson, B. H. (1974). Acculturation and assimilation: A clarification. *American Anthropologist, 1,* 351–367.

Thorndyke, O. W. (1984). Applications of schema theory in cognitive research. In J. R. Anderson & S. M. Kosslyn (Eds.), *Tutorials in learning and memory* (pp. 167–192). San Francisco: Freeman.

Torbiorn, I. (1982). *Living abroad: Personal adjustment and personnel policy in the overseas setting.* Chichester, UK: Wiley.

Tulving, E. (1985). How many memory systems are there? *American Psychologist, 40,* 385–398.

Turner, A. M., & Greenough, W. T. (1985). Differential rearing effects on rat visual cortex synapses. *Brain Research, 329,* 195–203.

Turner, R. M. (1994). *Adaptive reasoning for real-world problems: A schema-based approach.* Hillsdale, NJ: Lawrence Erlbaum.

Wagenaar, W. A., & Groeneweg, J. (1990). The memory of concentration camp survivors. *Applied Cognitive Psychology, 4,* 77–87.

Watzlawick, P., Beavin, J. H., & Jackson, D. (1967). *Pragmatics of human communication.* New York: Norton.

Wiseman, R. L., Hammer, R. R., & Nishida, H. (1989). Predictors of intercultural communication competence. *International Journal of Intercultural Relations, 13,* 349–370.

Wiseman, R. L., & Koester, J. (Eds.). (1993). *Intercultural communication competence.* Newbury Park, CA: Sage.

Yoshikawa, M. J. (1988). Cross-cultural adaptation and perceptual development. In Y. Y. Kim & W. B. Gudykunst (Eds.), *Cross-cultural adaptation: Current approaches* (pp. 140–148). Newbury Park, CA: Sage.

Yum, J. O. (1982). Communication patterns and information acquisition among Korean immigrants, Hawaii. *Human Communication Research, 8*(2), 154–169.

Zola-Morgan, S., & Squire, L. R. (1990). Neurophysiological investigations of memory and amnesia: Findings from humans and non-human primates. In A. Diamond (Ed.), *The development and neural bases of higher cognitive functions* (pp. 434–456). New York: New York Academy of Sciences Press.

18

An Anxiety/Uncertainty Management (AUM) Theory of Strangers' Intercultural Adjustment

WILLIAM B. GUDYKUNST

I became interested in intercultural adjustment when I served as an Intercultural Relations Specialist with the U.S. Navy in Yokosuka, Japan. My duties involved conducting a 3-day intercultural adjustment training program for naval personnel and their families, and consulting on intercultural relation problems between Japanese and naval personnel. The training program was designed to assist the participants in adapting to living and working in Japan. Because of my experiences as an Intercultural Relations Specialist, I decided to pursue a Ph.D. in intercultural communication.

When I completed my graduate work, there was no theory of sojourners' intercultural adjustment (Note: Kim's, 1977, theory of communication acculturation of immigrants appeared about this time). I decided that one way of beginning to theorize would be to adapt an existing theory. I selected uncertainty reduction theory (URT; e.g., Berger & Calabrese, 1975) as a starting point for several reasons. First, URT intuitively made sense to me. Second, URT focuses on uncertainty (e.g., the inability to predict others' behavior), which can be linked directly to intercultural adjustment. Third, I could see direct

Author's Note: I want to thank Mitch Hammer for his collaboration on the first version of the AUM theory of intercultural adjustment. I also want to acknowledge that the theory would not be possible without Georg Simmel's writing on the stranger, Chuck Berger's work on uncertainty, Walter Stephan and Cookie Stephan's work on intergroup anxiety, and Ellen Langer's work on mindfulness.

applications of URT to improving sojourners' ability to adapt to new cultures.

Mitch Hammer and I developed the first anxiety/uncertainty management (AUM) theory of intercultural adjustment (Gudykunst & Hammer, 1988b; Note: this version of the theory was not labeled AUM; see Witte, 1993, for an alternative conceptualization of this theory). This theory used uncertainty and anxiety *reduction* to explain intercultural adjustment. The Gudykunst (1988) version of AUM theory included axioms that address both effective communication and intercultural adjustment (this version also was not labeled AUM). The second version of the theory that focused on intercultural adjustment (Gudykunst, 1998) was a straightforward extension of the 1995 version of the AUM theory of effective communication (Gudykunst, 1995). My purpose in presenting that version of the adjustment theory was to use it to demonstrate how the theory could be used to design intercultural adjustment training programs.

My purpose in this chapter is to present an updated version of the AUM theory of intercultural adjustment. This version of the theory draws on the AUM theory of effective communication (presented in Chapter 13 in this volume), as well as research on intercultural adjustment (see Ward, 2001, and Ward et al., 2001, for recent reviews). There is redundancy between this theory and the AUM theory of effective communication because they are parts of the same theoretical research program (Laktos, 1970). The perspectives and the outcomes, however, are different. The theory presented here also incorporates factors not included in the effective communication theory (e.g., social support, self construals, host attitudes toward strangers).

ASSUMPTIONS

There is a difference between the adjustment of "sojourners" and the assimilation or acculturation of immigrants or refugees. "Sojourners"

are visitors who travel to another culture to reside for a period of time (e.g., a few months to several years), but do *not* intend to reside permanently in the host culture. Immigrants or refugees are people who travel to another culture with the purpose of permanently residing in that culture. The different goals often lead to differences in the ways sojourners and immigrants adapt to living in host cultures (e.g., "sojourners" generally do not change their cultural identities, while immigrants may). The present theory is limited to "sojourners'" short-term adjustment to host cultures.

The metatheoretical assumptions on which this theory is based are the same as those in the AUM theory of effective communication, so I will not restate them here (see Chapter 13 in this volume). I, therefore, begin with the theoretical assumptions.

Theoretical Assumptions

I begin with the primary concept I use to explain "sojourners'" adjustment, the stranger. Following this, I present my assumptions about uncertainty, anxiety, intercultural adjustment, and being mindful. These assumptions are similar to those of the effective communication theory, but they are also different because of the different perspectives involved.

Strangers. All sojourners are strangers in the cultures they are visiting. Simmel (1908/1950) views strangers as possessing the contradictory qualities of being both near and far at the same time: "the unity of nearness and remoteness in every human relation is organized, in the phenomenon of the stranger, in a way which may be most briefly formulated by saying that in the relationship to him [or her], distance means that he [or she], who is also far, is actually near" (p. 402). Strangers represent both the idea of nearness in that they are physically close and the idea of remoteness in that they have different values and ways of doing things.

Schuetz (1944) takes a broader view of the concept of the stranger than Simmel. He views a stranger as "an adult individual . . . who tries to be permanently accepted or at least partially tolerated by the group which he [or she] approaches" (p. 499). Schuetz argues that strangers do not understand the social world inhabited by the members of the host culture they approach. Parrillo (1980) succinctly summarizes Schuetz's perspective:

> Because this is a shared world, it is an intersubjective one. For the native, then, every social situation is a coming together not only of roles and identities, but also of shared realities—the intersubjective structure of consciousness. What is taken for granted by the native is problematic for the stranger. In a familiar world, people live through the day by responding to daily routine without questioning or reflection. To strangers, however, every situation is new and is therefore experienced as a crisis. (p. 3)

One of the defining characteristics of this view is that strangers often perceive their interactions in host cultures as a series of crises.

Herman and Schield (1961) point out that "the immediate psychological result of being in a new situation is lack of security. Ignorance of the potentialities inherent in the situation, of the means to reach a goal, and of the probable outcomes of an intended action causes insecurity" (p. 165). Attempts to deal with the ambiguity of new situations involve a pattern of information-seeking (managing uncertainty) and tension reduction (managing anxiety) (Ball-Rokeach, 1973). Managing uncertainty and anxiety, therefore, are central processes affecting strangers' adjustment to new cultures.

Since the stranger-ingroup relationship is a figure-ground phenomenon, it is necessary to take one perspective in stating axioms. In constructing the theory of intercultural adaptation, I use the perspective of strangers approaching host cultures. My use of "we" or "our" throughout the remainder of this chapter, therefore, assumes that "we" are strangers trying to adjust in host cultures. I use "we" and "our" to make the theory easier to apply than if I used "strangers." I use strangers rather than "sojourners" throughout the remainder of the chapter.

Uncertainty. Marris (1996) argues that "uncertainty is created by our own preconceptions . . . because events only appear uncertain in some context of purposes, and expectations of orderliness" (p. 16). He goes on to point out that "what constitutes uncertainty depends on what we want to be able to predict, what we can predict, and what we might be able to do about it" (p. 16). When we are strangers in host cultures, one of our major concerns is predicting host nationals' behavior.

Uncertainty is a cognitive phenomenon; it affects the way we think about host nationals. Predictive uncertainty involves our inability to predict host nationals' attitudes, feelings, beliefs, values, and behavior (Berger & Calabrese, 1975) (Note: I adapt researchers' terminology to fit strangers' interaction with host nationals throughout the chapter. These changes do not distort the findings of their research.). We need to be able, for example, to predict which of several alternative behaviors host nationals will employ in specific situations (Note: I focus on behavior in the axioms of the theory, but the axioms also apply to host nationals' feelings, beliefs, attitudes, values, etc.). Explanatory uncertainty involves the uncertainty we have about explaining host nationals' behavior, attitudes, feelings, thoughts, and beliefs (e.g., making causal attributions). We experience more uncertainty when we communicate with members of host cultures than when we communicate with members of our native cultures (e.g., Gudykunst, 1985a; Lee & Boster, 1991).

We do not always want to minimize our uncertainty. Weick (1979), for example, contends that equivocality can lead to creativity. We also may not be able to minimize our uncertainty because "ambiguous modes of expression are rooted in the very nature of language and thought" (Levine, 1985, p. 20), or host nationals transmit equivocal messages (e.g., Bavelas et al., 1990). When communicating with host nationals, we may be ambiguous on purpose. To illustrate, Levine contends that ambiguity allows us to protect ourselves through "opaqueness." Eisenberg (1984) also believes that ambiguity has benefits in some situations (e.g., it allows us to maintain power over host nationals).

We have minimum and maximum thresholds for uncertainty that are different across cultures and individuals (this idea was first introduced in Gudykunst, 1991). Our maximum thresholds are the highest amount of uncertainty we can have and still think we can predict host nationals' behavior sufficiently to feel comfortable interacting with them. Our minimum thresholds are the lowest amount of uncertainty we can have and not feel bored or overconfident about our predictions of host nationals' behavior.

If our uncertainty is above our maximum thresholds or below our minimum thresholds, we cannot interact effectively with host nationals or adjust to host cultures. When uncertainty is above our maximum thresholds, host nationals' behavior is seen as unpredictable and we do not have confidence in our predictions of or explanations for their behavior. When our uncertainty is below our minimum thresholds, we are overconfident and we are likely to misinterpret host nationals' messages because we do not consider the possibility that our interpretations of their messages are wrong. Where our minimum and maximum thresholds are located is a function of the general acceptance of uncertainty in our cultures (e.g., Hofstede's, 2001, uncertainty avoidance dimension of cultural variability) and our tolerance for ambiguity (e.g., Budner, 1962) and certainty-uncertainty orientation

(e.g., Sorrentino & Short, 1986) (Note: these ideas are discussed in detail below).

Adjusting to host cultures (see below) requires that our uncertainty be between our minimum and maximum thresholds (Gudykunst, 1995). When our uncertainty is between the two thresholds, we have sufficient confidence in our ability to predict host nationals' behavior that we feel comfortable, but our confidence is not sufficiently high that we become overconfident. Since we are not overconfident, we can recognize cues indicating potential misunderstandings when they occur, especially if we are mindful (see below).

Anxiety. Anxiety is the affective (emotional) equivalent of uncertainty. We experience some degree of anxiety any time we communicate with host nationals. Anxiety is a "generalized or unspecified sense of disequilibrium" (Turner, 1988, p. 61). It stems from feeling uneasy, tense, worried, or apprehensive about what might happen when we interact with host nationals (Note: the focus here is on state anxiety, not trait anxiety; see Britt et al., 1996, for a discussion of trait intergroup anxiety). Anxiety is based on the anticipation of negative consequences from our interactions with host nationals (Stephan & Stephan, 1985).

We have minimum and maximum thresholds for anxiety (Gudykunst, 1991). Our maximum thresholds are the highest amount of anxiety we can have and feel comfortable interacting with host nationals. If our anxiety is above our maximum thresholds, we are so uneasy that we do not want to communicate with host nationals. When our anxiety is above our maximum thresholds, the source of our anxiety may be unknown or "vague—but it is more powerful for its vagueness. As there is no definite threat or danger upon which we could act, it paralyzes action" (Riezler, 1960, p. 147; Turner, 1988, calls this "diffuse" anxiety). Of course, there also may be a specific source (e.g., we feel that our identities are threatened) that brings our anxiety above our maximum thresholds. No matter how our anxiety gets above our maximum thresholds, our attention focuses exclusively on the anxiety and not on our ability to adjust when it is. When anxiety is above our maximum thresholds, we tend to process information about host nationals in a simplistic fashion (Wilder & Shapiro, 1989).

Our minimum thresholds are the lowest amount of anxiety we can have and care about our interactions with host nationals. If our anxiety is below our minimum thresholds, there is not enough adrenaline running through our system to motivate us to communicate effectively with host nationals. Tuan (1979), for example, points out that our curiosity is primed by our anxiety. When our anxiety is below our minimum thresholds, we do not care what happens in our interactions with host nationals (e.g., we do not have any curiosity).

To be motivated to adjust to host cultures, our anxiety has to be below our maximum thresholds and above our minimum thresholds. Some anxiety, but not too much, can be "transformed into a type of useful highly-adaptive social response, which leaves the self protected from the impact of its own emotions and its own imperatives while it promotes the highest vigilance, albeit uncritical, toward the behavior of others" (Schneiderman, 1960, pp. 161–162). The argument being made here is consistent with Janis' (1958, 1971, 1985) theory of anticipatory fear. He argues that moderate levels of fear lead to adaptive processes, but low and high levels do not. My position also is compatible with Csikszentmihalyi's (1990) argument that there is an optimal level of anxiety that facilitates experiencing "flow," or having optimal experiences. The argument is comparable with research suggesting there is a curvilinear relationship between anxiety and performance as well (e.g., Halvari & Gjesme, 1995; Pickersgill & Owen, 1992).

The anxiety we experience when we communicate with host nationals usually is based on negative expectations. Stephan and Stephan (1985) argue that we fear four types of negative consequences when interacting with host nationals: we fear negative consequences for our self-concepts, we fear negative behavioral consequences, we fear negative evaluations by host nationals, and we fear negative evaluations by our co-nationals in the host culture.

One of the behavioral consequences of anxiety is avoidance (Stephan & Stephan, 1985). We avoid host nationals because it allows us to manage our anxiety (e.g., spending our time in the co-national enclave in the host culture). Schlenker and Leary (1982), however, argue that avoiding interaction has negative consequences (e.g., we do not develop the skills necessary to manage anxiety in the host culture). When we are experiencing anxiety and cannot avoid host nationals, we tend to terminate interactions as soon as we can. Cognitively, anxiety leads to biases in how we process information. The more anxious we are, the more likely we will focus on host nationals' behaviors we expect to see, such as those based on our negative stereotypes, and the more likely we are to confirm these expectations and not recognize behavior that is inconsistent with our expectations (Stephan & Stephan, 1985).

The amount of anxiety we experience in stranger-host interactions is partly a function of the degree to which we feel in control (Fiske & Morling, 1996). The less powerful we feel in a situation, the more anxious we are. Strangers tend to feel like they have little power in host cultures and, therefore, they tend to experience high levels of anxiety. Schlenker and Leary (1982) also point out that our anxiety leads us to feel uncomfortable interacting with host nationals and reinforces our views of ourselves that we are not competent to interact with host nationals. Devine et al. (1996) contend that strangers' uncomfortableness leads to nervous behavior that may be perceived as prejudice by host nationals.

When our anxiety or uncertainty is too high or too low, we cannot adjust to host cultures. In the 1995 version of the AUM theory of effective communication, I suggested that our minimum and maximum thresholds are catastrophe points. That is, there are drastic changes in our adjustment to host cultures when anxiety and uncertainty drop below our maximum thresholds and rise above our minimum thresholds. This position is based on the assumption of catastrophe theory (e.g., Tesser, 1980) that there are sudden, discontinuous changes in one variable (e.g., adjustment) when other variables (e.g., anxiety, uncertainty) reach a catastrophe point. In other words, anxiety and uncertainty are not related to intercultural adjustment above our maximum thresholds or below our minimum thresholds, but anxiety and uncertainty are related to intercultural adjustment between the two thresholds.

Intercultural Adjustment. There are many ways to conceptualize intercultural adjustment (see Ady, 1995, for a review; only examples are presented here). One way is to think of adjustment as successfully coping with "culture shock." Oberg (1960) views culture shock as involving strain, feelings of deprivation, feeling rejected by host nationals, and feeling impotent in the host culture. Bock (1970) sees culture shock as an emotional reaction to being unable to predict host nationals' behavior. While most views of culture shock are negative, David (1971) argues that coping with culture shock provides the foundation for personal growth. This view of adjustment often is associated with the U- and W-curves that are used to describe the stages that strangers go through during the process of adjustment to host cultures and reentry into their native cultures (e.g., Gullahorn & Gullahorn, 1963; there is little research supporting the curve explanations). There is extensive research focusing on the stress and coping that sojourners experience in host cultures (see Ward, 2001, for a review).

Another way that intercultural adjustment can be viewed is through our general satisfaction with living in the host culture (e.g., Church, 1982; Lysgaard, 1955; Ruben & Kealey, 1979; Sewell & Davidson, 1961). In this view, we have adjusted to the host culture if we are emotionally stable, have feelings of well-being, or we are satisfied with our stay in the host culture. We can feel adjusted even when our behavior in the host culture is not effective or appropriate to the host culture. It also is possible for strangers to develop ways of coping in the host culture that do not involve much social interaction with host nationals.

Still another way to conceive of intercultural adjustment is to view it as behaving in ways that are socially appropriate and interpersonally effective in the host culture (Furnham & Bochner, 1982; Grove & Torbiorn, 1985; Torbiorn, 1982). In this view, strangers have adjusted when they have learned to interact effectively with host nationals and their behavior is appropriate to the host culture. This conceptualization of adjustment is related closely to a communication competence view of adjustment (e.g., Spitzberg & Cupach, 1984). In their model of competence, Spitzberg and Cupach view adjustment "as an end state of having developed competence in interactions generally" (p. 35). It is important to recognize, however, that there are cultural differences in perceptions of effectiveness (Tominaga et al., 2003).

In both the culture shock and satisfaction views of adjustment, adjustment involves strangers' coping with their reactions to the new cultures (e.g., managing the stress associated with culture shock, finding ways to feel satisfied in the host culture). In the appropriate and effective view of adjustment, strangers' adjustment involves some degree of coordination with the host culture (adapting communication and behaving appropriately to the host culture).

Ward and her colleagues (e.g., Searle & Ward, 1990; Ward & Kennedy, 1992) differentiate between psychological and sociocultural adjustment. Psychological adjustment focuses on "feelings of well-being or satisfaction" during intercultural transitions, and sociocultural adjustment "refers to the ability to 'fit in' or execute effective interactions in a new cultural milieu" (Ward, 2001, p. 414). Ward argues that these two forms of adjustment "are conceptually related, but empirically distinct" (p. 414). She contends that psychological and sociocultural adjustment exhibit different patterns over time and are predicted by different variables. Ward (2001) points out that psychological adjustment fluctuates over the sojourn and is predicted by variables such as social support, personality, and life changes. Sociocultural adjustment, in contrast, tends to be predicted by "contact variables" such as cultural similarity and the quantity/quality of contact with host nationals.

I view intercultural adjustment as a process involving feeling comfortable in the host culture, as well as communicating effectively and engaging in socially appropriate behavior with host nationals (Note: I am *not* suggesting that we engage in behavior that is appropriate in the host culture that violates our ethical principles). If we communicate with host nationals the way we communicate with members of our own cultures, we will not be effective and our behavior may not be appropriate. We, therefore, will not be able to adjust successfully to living in the host culture. Interacting effectively with host nationals and adapting our behavior so that it is socially appropriate in the host culture requires that we consciously (i.e., mindfully) manage our anxiety and uncertainty.

Mindfulness. Most of the time when we communicate we are not highly aware of our behavior. In other words, we communicate mindlessly or automatically (Langer, 1989). When we are consciously aware of our communication behavior, we become mindful to some extent. Mindfulness involves "(1) creation of new categories; (2) openness to new information; and (3) awareness of more than one perspective" (Langer, 1989, p. 62). Langer (1989) argues that "categorizing is a fundamental and natural human activity. . . . Any attempt to eliminate bias by attempting to eliminate the perception of differences is doomed to failure" (p. 154). Being mindful involves making more, not fewer, distinctions. When we are mindless, for example, we tend to use broad categories to predict host nationals' behavior (e.g., their ethnicities, genders, or roles). When we are mindful, we can create new categories that are more specific (e.g., we can subdivide the broad categories into more specific categories). The more subcategories we use, the more personalized the information we use to make predictions about host nationals' behavior.

Mindfulness also involves being open to new information (Langer, 1989). When we are mindfully open to new information, we see aspects of our own and host nationals' behavior that we do not see when we are mindless. Being open to new information involves focusing on the process of communication that is taking place, not the outcomes of our interactions. When we focus on the outcomes, we miss subtle cues in our interactions with host nationals and this often leads to misunderstandings. When strangers are mindful of their behavior, they tend to focus on the outcomes of, not the processes involved in, their interactions with host nationals.

To be mindful, we must recognize that host nationals use different perspectives to understand or explain our interactions with them than we do (Langer, 1989). When we are mindless, we tend to assume host nationals interpret our messages the way we intended. When we are mindful, in contrast, we can recognize that host nationals interpret our messages differently than we do. Being mindful allows us to see the choices we have regarding how to communicate when interacting with host nationals (Langer, 1989, 1997; also see Bellah et al., 1991).

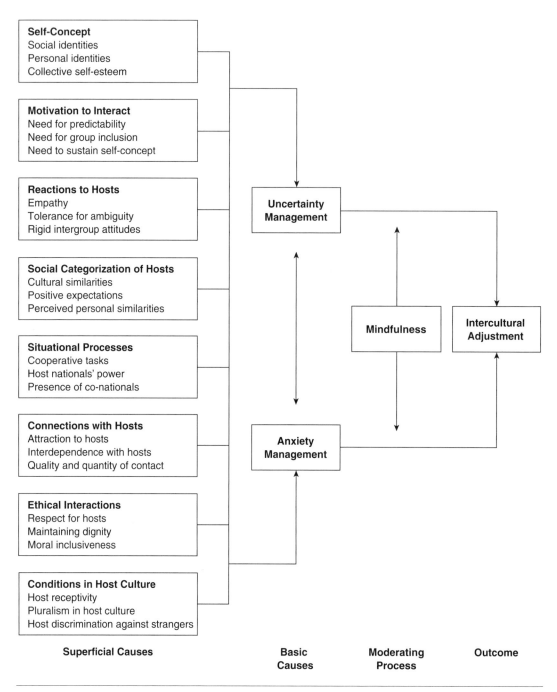

Figure 18.1 A Representation of the AUM Theory of Adjustment

Theory Construction

Two types of theoretical statements are used in the theory: axioms and theorems. Axioms are "propositions that involve variables that are taken to be directly linked causally; axioms should therefore be statements that imply direct causal links among variables" (Blalock, 1969, p. 18, italics omitted). Some axioms do not apply in all situations. Boundary conditions specify when the axioms hold. The axioms can be combined to derive theorems. When combined, the axioms and theorems form a "causal process" theory (Reynolds, 1971) that explains intercultural adjustment.

There are a large number of axioms (47) in this working version of the theory, but they are not excessive. Reynolds (1971) points out that "in dealing with logical systems that are completely abstract . . . a common criteria is to select the smallest number of axioms from which all other statements can be derived, reflecting a preference for simplicity and elegance. There is reason to think that this is inappropriate for a substantive theory, particularly when it makes it more difficult to understand the theory" (p. 95). Since one of my concerns is applying the theory, I have included a sufficient number of statements to make anxiety/uncertainty management processes clear to those who want to use it to help them adjust to host cultures.

Lieberson (1985) suggests that we need to isolate the "basic causes" of the phenomenon under investigation. In generating the axioms for the theory, I assume that managing anxiety and uncertainty are "basic causes" influencing our intercultural adjustment. Other variables (which are organized using the categories of self-concepts; motivation; reactions to host nationals; social categorization; situational processes; connections with host nationals; ethical interactions; conditions in host culture), therefore, are treated as "superficial causes" of intercultural adjustment. The influence of these "superficial causes" on intercultural adjustment is mediated through anxiety and uncertainty. Gao and Gudykunst's (1990) study supports this assumption. Being mindful allows us to engage in anxiety and uncertainty management.

There are at least three ways that I deviate from the traditional social science construction of causal process theories. First, I include ethical concerns in the theory. Johannesen (2001)

argues that moral issues are inherent in the communication process, and that "ethical concerns have been central to communication theory and practice at least since Plato" (p. 202). In the 1998 version, I included two axioms dealing with ethical issues in the "connections with strangers" section. In this version, I add an additional axiom and discuss ethical concerns in a separate section to emphasize their importance. Second, I include mindfulness in the theory. I argue that sometimes our communication is "determined" by our personalities or the context (i.e., when we are mindless) and sometimes our communication is based on "free will" (i.e., when we are mindful). Third, this theory is designed to be applied and most theories are not.

A schematic summary of AUM theory is presented in Figure 18.1 (Note: not all of the superficial causes are listed in the figure). The figure involves only one person (i.e., the stranger). Host nationals would be a mirror image of the stranger.

THE AUM THEORY OF INTERCULTURAL ADJUSTMENT

It is necessary to use some sort of schema to organize the axioms. To maintain consistency, I generally follow the organizational schema (i.e., the categories at the left of Figure 18.1) in this version that I used in the 1998 version. I begin by looking at how our self-concepts influence our anxiety and uncertainty management.

Self-Concepts

Our self-concepts are our views of ourselves. Turner et al. (1987) argue that we place ourselves in categories with others whom we see as similar to ourselves on some dimension and different from others on that dimension. Grieve and Hogg (1999) argue that we "apply social categorizations to [ourselves] and others to clarify [our] perception of the social world and [our] place in it and thus render it more meaningful and predictable—identification reduces subjective uncertainty" (p. 926). Social categorizations lead us to define ourselves in terms of our social identities. Cultural identities are the major generative mechanisms for our interactions with host nationals, but we also use other social identities (e.g., based on occupation, ethnicity) and our personal identities to guide our interactions with host nationals. Our social and personal identities influence our behavior in virtually all of our interactions. In any particular situation, however, one identity tends to predominate in guiding our behavior (Turner, 1987).

Bochner and Perks (1971) report that host nationals view strangers (sojourners) in cultural terms (e.g., hosts categorize strangers based on their cultures). The identity that predominates for strangers' interactions with host nationals, especially at the beginning of sojourns, therefore, tends to be strangers' cultural identities (e.g., U.S. Americans' identities as "Americans"). In the long-term adaptation of immigrants or refugees, strangers' cultural identities may change from being based on their native cultures to being based on the host culture (e.g., if immigrants assimilate into the host culture). This, however, usually does not occur with strangers who plan to reside in the host culture for a period of time and then return home. There are, nevertheless, some strangers who "go native" and identify with the host culture. Strangers who "go native" are the exception, not the rule. Ward and her colleagues (Ward & Kennedy, 1994; Ward & Rana-Deuba, 1999) report that strangers' cultural identities are associated with psychological adjustment, and strangers' identifications with the host culture are associated with sociocultural adjustment.

The strength of our cultural identities facilitates our ability to manage our anxiety and uncertainty. This claim, however, has to be qualified. The strength of our cultural identities reduces uncertainty only when we perceive host nationals to be typical members of their cultures (Gudykunst & Hammer, 1988b). When we perceive host nationals to be atypical members of their culture, we do not treat them based on their culture (e.g., we see them as "exceptions to the rule"). In this case, our communication is guided by our personal identities, and we use information about the individual host nationals with whom we are interacting to manage our uncertainty.

How secure we feel in our cultural identities has to be taken into consideration. Strangers with insecure cultural identities are biased toward their cultures more than strangers with secure cultural identities (Jackson & Smith, 1999). The stronger strangers' cultural identities, the greater the anxiety they experience interacting with host nationals (e.g., Dyal & Dyal, 1981; Padilla, 1980). Ward and Kennedy's (1993a, 1993b, 1993c) research also suggests that the strength of our cultural identities generally inhibits our sociocultural adaptation (but not always; see Ward, 1999). These studies, however, do not take into consideration how secure strangers are in their cultural identities. Identity security is critical to managing anxiety and uncertainty.

Our self-esteem, the positive or negative feelings we have about ourselves (e.g., Rosenberg, 1979), also influences our anxiety/uncertainty management with host nationals. Our self-esteem affects the way we process information about host nationals and the amount of anxiety we experience. Burns (1985), for example, argues that low self-esteem leads us to distort our cognitive processing of information about ourselves and host nationals. When our self-esteem is high, in contrast, we are able to look for objective information about ourselves and host nationals, even in stressful situations.

Low self-esteem leads us to be anxious about interacting with host nationals. The greater our self-esteem, the better we are able to manage our anxiety about interacting with host nationals (e.g., Becker, 1971;

Cozzarelli & Karafa, 1998; Epstein, 1976). Strangers' self-esteem changes during their stay. Heine and Lehman (1997) report that Canadian English teachers' self-esteem decreased over 7 months in Japan, but Japanese students' self-esteem increased over 7 months in Canada. They suggest the differences are a function of strangers' becoming similar to host nationals (e.g., individual self-esteem is emphasized more in Canada than Japan).

The collective self-esteem associated with our cultural identities also affects our anxiety/uncertainty management with host nationals. Collective self-esteem is the degree to which we evaluate our social groups (e.g., our cultures) positively (Luhtanen & Crocker, 1992). Extending research on individual self-esteem, the greater the collective self-esteem about our cultural identities, the more we should be able to look for objective information about host nationals and the less anxious we should be about interacting with them. Kosmitzki (1996) reports that Germans and U.S. Americans living abroad have more positive cultural identities than Germans and U.S. Americans who have never traveled abroad.

Another aspect of our self-concepts that influences our intercultural adjustment is our self construals. Markus and Kitayama (1991) differentiate between the independent self construal (e.g., viewing ourselves as separate and distinct from others) and the interdependent self construal (e.g., viewing ourselves as interconnected with other ingroup members). We use both self construals, but we tend to activate one more than the other. Members of individualistic cultures (e.g., cultures that value individuals over groups; Triandis, 1995) tend to emphasize the independent self construal, while members of collectivistic cultures (e.g., cultures that emphasize ingroups over individual members) emphasize the interdependent self construal.

It is not the specific self construal that influences our adjustment to host cultures, but the fit of the self construal guiding our behavior with the one used by host nationals. Ward and Chang's (1997) "cultural fit" hypothesis suggests that adjustment is facilitated when strangers' personalities are similar to the prototypical personalities used in the host culture. Strangers traveling to individualistic cultures adjust better if they emphasize their independent self construals in host cultures, rather than their interdependent self construals (e.g., Cross, 1995; Oguri & Gudykunst, 2002; Yamaguchi & Wiseman, 2003). Similarly, strangers traveling to collectivistic cultures should adjust better if they emphasize their interdependent self construals in host cultures, rather than their independent self construals. Emphasizing the prototypical self construal used in host cultures should lead to low levels of anxiety and to accuracy in predicting host nationals' behavior because emphasizing the prototypical self construal helps us to understand host nationals' perspectives.

Social identity theory posits that we strive to have the most positive self-images we can (e.g., cultural identities; Tajfel, 1978). When our cultural identities are threatened, we attempt to raise our esteem. Threats to our cultural identities may come from co-nationals in the host culture or from host nationals, but both types of threats to our cultural identities lead to discrimination against host nationals (Worchel & Coutant, 1997). Threats to our cultural identities, therefore, lead to anxiety and uncertainty about interacting with host nationals.

To summarize, our self-concepts influence our anxiety/uncertainty management. Six axioms regarding self-concepts, therefore, are included in the theory:

Axiom 1: An increase in the degree to which our cultural identities guide our interaction with host nationals will produce a decrease in our anxiety and increase in our confidence in predicting their behavior. *Boundary Conditions:* This axiom holds only when we are secure in our cultural identities, when host nationals are perceived to be typical members of their culture, when our anxiety and uncertainty are between our minimum and maximum thresholds, and we are not mindful.

Axiom 2: An increase in degree to which our personal identities guide our interactions with host nationals will produce a decrease in our anxiety and an increase in our ability to predict their behavior accurately. *Boundary Conditions:* This axiom holds only when we are secure in our personal identities, when our anxiety and uncertainty are between our minimum and maximum thresholds, and we are not mindful.

Axiom 3: An increase in our self-esteem when interacting with host nationals will produce a decrease in our anxiety and an increase in our ability to predict their behavior accurately. *Boundary Conditions:* This axiom holds only when our anxiety and uncertainty are between our minimum and maximum thresholds, and we are not mindful.

Axiom 4: An increase in our collective self-esteem associated with our cultural identities when interacting with host nationals will produce a decrease in our anxiety and an increase in our ability to predict their behavior accurately. *Boundary Conditions:* This axiom holds only when our anxiety and uncertainty are between our minimum and maximum thresholds, and we are not mindful.

Axiom 5: An increase in the extent to which we emphasize the prototypical self construal used in host cultures will produce a decrease in our anxiety and an increase in our ability to predict host nationals' behavior accurately. *Boundary Conditions:* This axiom holds only when our anxiety and uncertainty are between our minimum and maximum thresholds, and we are not mindful.

Axiom 6: An increase in threats to our cultural identities when interacting with host nationals will produce an increase in our anxiety and a decrease in our confidence in our predictions of their behavior. *Boundary Condition:* This holds only when we are not mindful.

Our self-concepts influence our motivation to communicate with host nationals. When we are motivated to communicate with host nationals, we try to manage our anxiety and uncertainty about interacting with host nationals.

Motivation to Interact With Host Nationals

Turner (1988) suggests that when our needs are met, we are motivated to interact with host nationals. Needs are "fundamental states of being that create feelings of deprivation" that mobilize us "to eliminate this sense of deprivation" if they are not satisfied (p. 59). Four needs are critical to AUM: (1) our need for a sense of predictability, (2) our need for a sense of group inclusion, (3) our need to avoid diffuse anxiety, and (4) our need to sustain our self-conceptions.

We need to see that "for the purposes of a given interaction, [host nationals] are 'reliable' and their responses 'predictable'" (Turner, 1988, p. 56). When we categorize host nationals, our stereotypes are activated. Our stereotypes of host nationals provide predictions for their behavior. If host nationals conform to our stereotypes, we see their behavior as predictable. If host nationals do not conform to our stereotypes, we see their behavior as unpredictable, if we are using only group-based information to predict their behavior. If we see host nationals' behavior as reliable and predictable, it helps confirm our self-concepts and helps us to feel included.

Our need for group inclusion results from *not* feeling involved in the host culture (Turner, 1988). When we do not feel included, we experience anxiety and uncertainty. The need for inclusion is related directly to how we see our social identities, especially our cultural identities in the host culture. Our social identities are derived from a tension between our need to be seen as similar to and fit in with others and our need to be seen as unique (Brewer, 1991; also see Brewer & Roccas, 2001). The need to be seen as similar allows us to identify with different groups and involves the general process of inclusion. Belonging to groups is an important motive for our behavior because it removes ambiguity about ourselves and others (e.g., host nationals) and helps us plan our actions (Stevens & Fiske, 1995; also see Baumeister & Leary, 1995). The need to be seen as unique is expressed in the general process of differentiation. If our attempts to communicate with host nationals are not successful, our need for group inclusion is unsatisfied. This leads to anxiety about ourselves and our standing in the host culture (Turner, 1988).

Our anxiety and uncertainty are interrelated. Demerath's (1993) knowledge-based affect theory, for example, suggests that increases in uncertainty leads to negative affect (e.g., fear, anxiety). Turner's (1988) theory of motivation links lack of predictability (e.g., uncertainty) to anxiety. Increases in anxiety, however, also lead to increases in uncertainty (e.g., Hammer et al., 1998; Hubbert et al., 1999).

Closely related to our need for inclusion is our need for self-concept confirmation. When our self-concepts are confirmed, we feel secure in our identities. When we feel secure in our identities, we feel confident in our interactions with host nationals. The more secure we are in our cultural identities, the better able we are to manage our anxiety and the more confident we are in predicting host nationals' behaviors. As our anxiety increases, our need for group inclusion and our need to sustain our self-concepts increases (Turner, 1988).

If our needs are not met, we are not motivated to communicate with host nationals. If our needs are met, in contrast, we tend to be motivated to manage our anxiety and uncertainty. Four axioms regarding our motivation to communicate with host nationals, therefore, are included in the theory:

Axiom 7: An increase in our need for group inclusion when interacting with host nationals will produce an increase in our anxiety. *Boundary Condition:* This axiom holds only when we are not mindful.

Axiom 8: An increase in our need to sustain our self-conceptions when interacting with host nationals will produce an increase in our anxiety. *Boundary Condition:* This axiom holds only when we are not mindful.

Axiom 9: An increase in the degree to which host nationals confirm our self-conceptions will produce a decrease in our anxiety. *Boundary Conditions:* This axiom holds only when our anxiety and uncertainty are between our minimum and maximum thresholds, and when we are not mindful.

Axiom 10: An increase in our confidence in our ability to predict host nationals' behavior will produce a decrease in our anxiety; a decrease in our anxiety will produce an increase in our confidence in predicting host nationals' behavior. *Boundary Conditions:* This axiom holds only when our anxiety and uncertainty are between our minimum and maximum thresholds, and we are not mindful.

When our needs are met, we are motivated to interact with host nationals. When we interact with host nationals, how we react to them cognitively, affectively, and behaviorally influences our ability to manage our anxiety and uncertainty.

Reactions to Host Nationals

Cognitively complex strangers form impressions of host nationals that are more extensive, more differentiated, and represent the behavioral variability of host nationals more than cognitively simple strangers (O'Keefe & Sypher, 1981). There is a negative association between cognitive complexity and perceived uncertainty (Downey et al., 1977). The more we are able to process information complexly, the more we search for alternative explanations for host nationals' behavior. Being able to isolate alternative explanations for host nationals' behavior facilitates accurately predicting their behavior. Strangers' cognitive complexity vis-à-vis host nationals increases as a function of time in the host culture (Coelho, 1958).

When our attitudes toward host nationals are rigid and divisive (e.g., ethnocentrism, prejudice, racism, authoritarianism, sexism, ageism, dogmatism, social dominance orientation, closed-mindedness, etc.), we tend to be intolerant of host nationals' viewpoints. Holding rigid attitudes leads us to need non-specific closure when we are interacting with host nationals (Kruglanski, 1989). If we have rigid attitudes, we prefer any form of closure to ambiguity because closure provides "assured knowledge that affords predictability and a base for action" (Kruglanski, 1989, p. 14). Rigid attitudes toward host nationals are associated negatively with intercultural adjustment (e.g., Basu & Ames, 1970; Mischel, 1965).

Rigid attitudes create negative expectations for our interactions with host nationals. The more ethnocentric and prejudiced we are, the more anxiety we experience interacting with host nationals (Stephan & Stephan, 1985, 1989, 1992). When we have rigid attitudes and have negative expectations, we do not look for new information about the host nationals with whom we interact. The more rigid our attitudes, therefore, the lower our ability to predict host nationals' behavior accurately.

Our uncertainty orientation influences whether we try to manage our uncertainty with host nationals (Huber & Sorrentino, 1996). Uncertainty-oriented strangers tend to be more accurate in their recall of past interactions with host nationals (either positive or negative) and are less likely "to think in terms of categories and stereotypes" than certainty oriented strangers (p. 607). More generally, uncertainty-oriented strangers try to deal with their uncertainty about host nationals (e.g., resolve or manage it) more than certainty oriented strangers. Certainty-oriented strangers tend "to maintain the certainty or clarity associated with their existing cognitions, rather than striving to resolve uncertainty" (pp. 592–593). Uncertainty-oriented strangers, therefore, should make more accurate predictions about host nationals' behavior than certainty-oriented strangers.

Our tolerance for ambiguity affects the type of information we gather about host nationals. Lack of tolerance for ambiguity involves perceiving ambiguous situations as threatening and undesirable (Budner, 1962). If we have a low tolerance for ambiguity, we tend to base our judgments of host nationals on our first impressions, which are formed prematurely, before all information is available (Smock, 1955). If we have a high tolerance for ambiguity, in contrast, we tend to seek out "objective" information about the situation and the host nationals with whom we interact (Pilisuk, 1963). If we have a high tolerance for ambiguity, we also tend to be open to new information about ourselves and host nationals. The greater our tolerance for ambiguity, the more effective we are in completing task assignments in host cultures (Ruben & Kealey, 1979) and the better adjusted they are (Cort & King, 1979).

Empathy also facilitates anxiety and uncertainty management. Bell (1987) points out that "cognitively, the empathic [stranger] takes the perspective of [host nationals], and in so doing strives to see the world from the [host nationals'] point of view. Affectively, the empathic [stranger] experiences the emotion of [host nationals]; he or she *feels* the [host nationals'] experiences" (p. 204). An increase in our empathy is associated with a decrease in the anxiety we experience in host cultures (Stephan & Stephan, 1992). Stephan and Finlay (1999), however, point out that "empathy that is not accompanied by respect for [host nationals] is clearly problematic" (e.g., it can lead to condescension) (p. 727). Since we are trying to understand host nationals' perspectives when we empathize, the greater our ability to empathize, the more accurate our predictions should be.

To interact effectively with host nationals and adjust to the host culture requires that we be able to adapt our behavior. Duran (1983) argues that adaptability involves: "(1) The requirement of both cognitive (ability to perceive) and behavioral (ability to adapt) skills; (2) Adaptation not only of behaviors but also interaction goals; (3) The ability to adapt to the requirements posed by different communication contexts; and (4) The assumption that perceptions of communicative competence reside in the dyad" (p. 320). The more we are able to adapt our behavior, the more confident we are in our ability to deal with new situations. The more we are able to adapt our behavior, the more we are able to adapt the way we think about host nationals. Increases in adaptability, therefore, lead to lower levels of anxiety and increases in our confidence in predicting host nationals' behavior.

Adapting our behavior involves developing the social skills necessary to interact with host nationals. Furnham and Bochner (1982) report that strangers generally are unskilled when they enter host cultures. Ward and her colleagues (e.g., Searle & Ward, 1990; Ward & Kennedy, 1999) observe that developing social skills helps strangers meet the social demands to interact with host nationals. Scott and Scott (1991) note that developing culture-specific skills is associated positively with adjustment. Oguri and Gudykunst (2002) report that one important social skill that strangers need to develop is the ability to use the prototypical communication styles that predominate in the host culture.

Hall (1976) differentiates between low-context (e.g., most of the information necessary to determine meaning is in the message itself) and high-context (e.g., most of the information needed to determine meaning is in the context or internalized in the person) communication styles. Gudykunst and Ting-Toomey (1988) argue that low-context communication styles are emphasized in individualistic cultures, while high-context communication styles are emphasized in collectivistic cultures (especially for ingroup interaction). Oguri and Gudykunst's (2002) research suggests that

Asian international students' adjustment to the U.S. culture is facilitated by using the low-context communication styles that predominate in the United States.

The way we think about host nationals, our affective responses to strangers, and the ways we behave toward them affect our ability to manage our anxiety and uncertainty. Six axioms regarding how we react to strangers, therefore, are included in the theory:

Axiom 11: An increase in our ability to process information complexly about host nationals will produce a decrease in our anxiety and an increase in our ability to predict their behavior accurately. *Boundary Conditions:* This axiom holds only when our anxiety and uncertainty are between our minimum and maximum thresholds, and we are not mindful.

Axiom 12: An increase in the rigidity of our attitudes toward host nationals will produce an increase in our anxiety and a decrease in our ability to predict their behavior accurately. *Boundary Conditions:* This axiom holds only when our anxiety and uncertainty are between our minimum and maximum thresholds, and we are not mindful.

Axiom 13: An increase in our uncertainty orientation will produce an increase in our ability to predict host nationals' behavior accurately. *Boundary Conditions:* This axiom holds only when our uncertainty is between our minimum and maximum thresholds, and we are not mindful.

Axiom 14: An increase in our tolerance for ambiguity will produce a decrease in our anxiety. *Boundary Conditions:* This axiom holds only when our anxiety and uncertainty are between our minimum and maximum thresholds, and we are not mindful.

Axiom 15: An increase in our ability to empathize with host nationals will produce a decrease in our anxiety and an increase in our ability to predict their behavior accurately. *Boundary Conditions:* This axiom holds only when we respect host nationals, when our anxiety and uncertainty are between our minimum and maximum thresholds, and when we are not mindful.

Axiom 16: An increase in our ability to adapt our behavior to host nationals will produce a decrease in our anxiety and an increase in our confidence in predicting their behavior. *Boundary Conditions:* This axiom holds only when our anxiety and uncertainty are between our minimum and maximum thresholds, and when we are not mindful.

The way we react to host nationals affects our ability to manage our anxiety and uncertainty. There are, however, many different ways we can react to host nationals. Our reactions are dependent, in part, on how we categorize host nationals.

Social Categorizations of Host Nationals

Social categorizations refer to the way we order our social environments by grouping people into categories that make sense to us (Tajfel, 1978, 1981). Social categorization results in the activation of our cultural identities and engaging in intergroup behavior with host nationals. This leads to anxiety and uncertainty.

The ways that we socially categorize host nationals is influenced by our knowledge of the host culture. Knowledge of the host culture is necessary to predict host nationals' behavior.

Knowledge of another person's culture—its language, dominant values, beliefs, and prevailing ideology—often permits predictions of the person's probable response to certain messages. . . . Upon first encountering a . . . [host national], cultural information provides the only grounds for communicative predictions. This fact explains the uneasiness and perceived lack of control most people experience when thrust into an alien culture: they not only lack information about the individuals with whom they must communicate, they are bereft of information

concerning shared cultural norms and values. (Miller & Sunnafrank, 1982, pp. 226–227)

Inaccurate knowledge of the host culture has negative consequences for adjustment (Bochner, 1972; Hull, 1978). Ward and Searle (1991) report that culture-specific knowledge is associated with sociocultural adjustment. The more knowledge strangers have about the host culture, the less anxiety and uncertainty they experience (Hammer et al., 1998).

We tend to view our own culture as more differentiated than the host culture (Linville et al., 1989). The more familiar we are with the host culture, however, the greater our perceived differentiation of host nationals. The more knowledge we have about the host culture and the more variability we perceive in the host culture, the less our tendency to treat host nationals negatively (Johnston & Hewstone, 1990).

When we categorize host nationals, we form expectations for their behavior. Expectations involve our anticipations and predictions about how host nationals interact with us. Negative expectations (e.g., based on ethnocentrism, negative stereotypes, prejudice) lead to uncertainty and anxiety about interacting with host nationals (Hubbert et al., 1999; for a related idea, see Torbiorn's [1988] discussion of culture barriers). Positive expectations (e.g., based on positive stereotypes), in contrast, help us manage uncertainty and anxiety about host nationals. Positive expectations lead us to behave in a positive manner toward host nationals (see Hamilton et al., 1990) and to find satisfaction in the host culture (Hawes & Kealey, 1980). The more positive our expectations for host nationals' behavior, the less our anxiety and the greater our confidence in predicting their behavior (Gudykunst & Shapiro, 1996; Hubbert et al., 1999). Positive expectations alone, however, do not necessarily lead to accurate predictions of host nationals' behavior. To make accurate predictions, we need to have accurate information regarding the host culture and the individual host nationals with whom we are communicating.

When our experiences in host cultures are more positive than we expected, we tend to have positive experiences during our sojourns. Black and Gregersen (1990), for example, report that when U.S. American managers in Japan have experiences that are more positive than their expectations, the managers are satisfied with their lives in Japan and do not return home early. Similar results emerge from studies of international students (e.g., Martin et al., 1995; Rogers & Ward, 1993). Weissman and Furnham (1987) also observe that discrepancies between expectations and experiences are associated with problems in psychological adjustment.

Mindfully managing our reactions when our negative stereotypes are activated is necessary to control our prejudiced responses to host nationals (Devine, 1989). Devine points out that "nonprejudiced responses are . . . a function of intentional controlled processes and require a conscious decision to behave in a nonprejudiced fashion. In addition, new responses must be learned and well practiced before they can serve as competitive responses to the automatically activated stereotype-congruent response" (p. 15). When we are mindful that our negative expectations are activated, we can manage our reactions to host nationals cognitively. Being mindful of negative expectations for host nationals' behavior, therefore, allows us to manage our anxiety and increase our ability to predict host nationals' behavior accurately.

We tend to base our categorizations of host nationals on their skin color, dress, accents, and so forth (Clark & Marshall, 1981). The cues we use, however, are not always accurate ways to categorize host nationals (e.g., an inaccurate categorization occurs when we put host nationals in a category in which they do not place themselves in the specific interaction). Our predictions of host nationals'

behavior may not be accurate because the group memberships we use to categorize host nationals may not be affecting their behavior in the situation. We might categorize host nationals based on one group membership (e.g., gender) and assume that the social identity based on this category is influencing their behavior. Host nationals, however, may be basing their behavior on a different social identity (e.g., social class, role) or a personal identity. To make accurate predictions, we must understand which identity is guiding host nationals' behavior in particular situations.

Babiker et al. (1980) argue that the similarities between strangers' native cultures and the host culture in which they reside facilitate their intercultural adjustment. Furnham and Bochner (1982) report that the greater the cultural distance between strangers' cultures and the host culture, the more social difficulties strangers have in the host culture. Similarly, Ward and her colleagues observe that the greater the similarity between strangers' cultures and the host culture, the less difficulty strangers have in the host culture (e.g., Ward & Kennedy, 1999). Stephan and Stephan (1992) also note that the greater the cultural similarities strangers perceive between their cultures and the host culture, the less anxiety strangers experience. More generally, cultural similarity is associated positively with strangers' adjustment (e.g., David, 1971; Hull, 1978; Morris, 1960; Taft, 1966; Torbiorn, 1982). Perceived cultural similarity should influence strangers' anxiety and confidence in predicting host nationals' behavior, while actual similarity should influence the accuracy of strangers' predictions of host nationals' behavior.

Cultural similarity is not the only form of similarity that influences our interactions with host nationals. Perceiving personal similarities between ourselves and host nationals influences whether we approach them or form relationships with them (see Berscheid, 1985). Perceived similarity is related to managing uncertainty (e.g., Gudykunst, Chua, & Gray,

1987; Hubbert et al., 1999) and anxiety (e.g., Hubbert et al., 1999; Stephan & Stephan, 1985). The greater the perceived differences between our groups and host nationals' groups, the more intense the negative affect (e.g., anxiety) we have about interacting with them (Dijker, 1987).

The way we categorize host nationals affects the amount of anxiety and uncertainty we experience when interacting with them. The way we categorize host nationals also influences the accuracy of our predictions about their behavior. Seven axioms regarding social categorizations, therefore, are included in the theory:

Axiom 17: An increase in our knowledge of the host culture (e.g., understanding of similarities and differences between our culture and the host culture) will produce a decrease in our anxiety and an increase in our ability to predict host nationals' behavior accurately. *Boundary Conditions:* This axiom holds only when our anxiety and uncertainty are between our minimum and maximum thresholds, and we are not mindful.

Axiom 18: An increase in the similarities we perceive between our native culture and the host culture will produce a decrease in our anxiety and an increase in our confidence in predicting host nationals' behavior; an increase in the actual similarity between our native cultures and the host culture will produce an increase in our ability to predict host nationals' behavior accurately. *Boundary Conditions:* This axiom holds only when our anxiety and uncertainty are between our minimum and maximum thresholds, and we are not mindful.

Axiom 19: An increase in the personal similarities we perceive between ourselves and host nationals will produce a decrease in our anxiety and an increase in our ability to predict their behavior accurately. *Boundary Conditions:* This axiom holds only when our anxiety and uncertainty are between our minimum and maximum thresholds, and we are not mindful.

Axiom 20: An increase in our ability to categorize host nationals in the same categories they categorize themselves will produce an increase in our ability to predict their behavior accurately. *Boundary Conditions:* This axiom holds only when our anxiety and uncertainty are between our minimum and maximum thresholds, and we are not mindful.

Axiom 21: An increase in the variability we perceive in host nationals will produce a decrease in our anxiety and an increase in our ability to predict their behavior accurately. *Boundary Conditions:* This axiom holds only when our anxiety and uncertainty are between our minimum and maximum thresholds, and we are not mindful.

Axiom 22: An increase in our positive expectations for host nationals' behavior will produce a decrease in our anxiety and an increase in our confidence in predicting their behavior. *Boundary Conditions:* This axiom holds only when our anxiety and uncertainty are between our minimum and maximum thresholds, and we are not mindful.

Axiom 23: An increase in our ability to suspend our negative expectations for host nationals' behavior when they are activated will produce a decrease in our anxiety and an increase in our ability to predict their behavior accurately. *Boundary Conditions:* This axiom holds only when we are mindful of the process of communication, and our anxiety and uncertainty are between our minimum and maximum thresholds.

The way we categorize host nationals affects the amount of anxiety and uncertainty we experience interacting with them. The amount of anxiety and uncertainty we experience, however, is mediated by the situations in which we are interacting with host nationals.

Situational Processes

One of the major ways that situations influence our behavior is in the scripts we activate in different situations. A script is "a coherent sequence of events expected by the individual, involving him [or her] either as a participant or an observer" (Abelson, 1976, p. 33). Scripts provide guides for the conversations we have in different situations, and help us manage the uncertainty we have about how to behave in various situations (Berger & Bradac, 1982).

Although we know thousands of scripts, most of us do not know the scripts that are used in host cultures. When we do not have scripts for interactions with host nationals, we do not feel in control interacting with them and we experience anxiety (Britt et al., 1996). Our anxiety is a function of the host nationals with whom we are interacting and the situation in which the interaction occurs (Britt et al., 1996). Some scripts, however, may be useful in interacting with host nationals. Activating an information seeking script, for example, reduces our anxiety about interacting with host nationals (Leary et al., 1988). The critical issue is whether our information gathering strategies are appropriate in the host culture.

The conditions under which we have contact with host nationals influence our anxiety and uncertainty. Argyle (1991), for example, argues that cooperation leads to positive feelings toward the people with whom we cooperate. When we work on cooperative goals with host nationals, we do not experience high levels of anxiety and have confidence in our ability to predict host nationals' behavior. Also, we experience less anxiety when there are other strangers present in the situation than we are alone because there is security in numbers. Communicating with other strangers facilitates short-term adaptation (see Kim, 2001).

The situation also influences the power (e.g., the ability to influence others; French & Raven, 1959) strangers and host nationals have. Lack of power leads to anxiety and attempts to cope with the anxiety (Fiske et al., 1996). Strangers generally have less power than host nationals. Strangers also tend to be more aware of power differences between themselves and host nationals than host nationals (e.g., Gurin et al., 1999). The more power host nationals have over strangers, the more anxiety strangers have about interacting with host nationals.

The situations in which we interact with host nationals affect the amount of anxiety and uncertainty we experience interacting with them. Three axioms regarding situational influences on anxiety and uncertainty management, therefore, are included in the theory:

Axiom 24: An increase in the cooperative structure of the goals on which we work with host nationals will produce a decrease in our anxiety and an increase in our confidence in predicting their behavior. *Boundary Conditions:* This axiom holds only when our anxiety and uncertainty are between our minimum and maximum thresholds, and we are not mindful.

Axiom 25: An increase in the percentage of strangers present in a situation will produce a decrease in our anxiety. *Boundary Conditions:* This axiom holds only when our anxiety and uncertainty are between our minimum and maximum thresholds, and we are not mindful.

Axiom 26: An increase in the power we perceive that host nationals have over us will produce an increase in our anxiety. *Boundary Condition:* This axiom holds only when we are not mindful.

The situations in which we interact with host nationals affect the nature of the contact we have with them. The nature of the contact we have with host nationals, in turn, affects whether we form connections with them.

Connections to Host Nationals

Attraction, or liking, is one of the major factors contributing to the development of relationships with host nationals. If we are not attracted to host nationals, we will not want to form connections with them. We tend to be attracted to host nationals we perceive to be similar to us. This is especially true before we interact with host nationals (Sunnafrank & Miller, 1981). When we have a chance to interact with host nationals we perceive to be dissimilar to us, however, we often become attracted to them. Attraction to host nationals reduces our uncertainty (Berger & Calabrese, 1975; Gudykunst, Chua, & Gray, 1987; Hammer et al., 1998) and anxiety (Hammer et al., 1998; Stephan & Stephan, 1985).

Stephan and Stephan (1985, 1989, 1992) argue that the quality of our contact with host nationals affects the amount of anxiety we experience interacting with them. Hammer et al. (1998) also report that the more favorable our contact with host nationals, the less anxiety we experience. Islam and Hewstone (1993) contend that the quantity of contact we have also affects the amount of anxiety we experience. Lack of interaction with host nationals is associated with strangers' experiencing high levels of anxiety (Gullahorn & Gullahorn, 1966).

The quantity and quality of contact we have with host nationals also affects the amount of uncertainty we experience. URT, for example, suggests that the more verbal communication in which we engage with host nationals, the less uncertainty we have about their behavior (Berger & Calabrese, 1975). URT also suggests that the greater the intimacy of our communication with others (e.g., nonsuperficial contact), the less uncertainty we have about them. Extending URT implies that the more contact we have with host nationals and the greater the quality of the contact (e.g., favorable contact), the more information we are able to collect about host nationals, and the less uncertainty we have. Hammer et al. (1998) report that the more favorable our contact with host nationals, the less uncertainty we have about predicting their behavior.

Our contact with host nationals is linked with our ability to adjust to the host culture. Numerous studies suggest that the greater the contact strangers have with host nationals, the better their adjustment to the host culture

(e.g., Gullahorn & Gullahorn, 1966; Lysgaard, 1955; Noels et al., 1996; Pruitt, 1978; Selltiz et al., 1963; Sewell & Davidson, 1961; Shah, 1991; Takai, 1991). Lack of contact with host nationals, in contrast, impedes strangers' adjustment and is associated with psychological distress in the host culture (e.g., Pruitt, 1978; Stone Feinstein & Ward, 1990). Closely related to lack of contact, strangers' detachment from or avoidance of host nationals as ways to cope with stress is associated with psychological problems in the host culture (e.g., Chataway & Berry, 1989).

Our interdependence with host nationals affects how we communicate with them. When we are interdependent with host nationals, for example, we do not experience high levels of anxiety about interacting with them. When we are interdependent, we also tend to have confidence in our ability to predict their behavior. Fiske and Morling (1996) argue that "interdependence usually motivates accuracy in impression formation" (p. 324). Interdependence, therefore, should lead to accuracy in predicting host nationals' behavior.

The intimacy of our relationships with host nationals also affects how we interact with them. As our relationships with host nationals become more intimate (e.g., move from initial interactions to close friend), interaction becomes more personalized, more synchronized, and there is less difficulty (Gudykunst, Nishida, & Chua, 1987). Developing friendships with host nationals and satisfaction with these relationships facilitate strangers' adjustment to the host culture (e.g., Furnham & Li, 1993; Kleinberg & Hull, 1979; Sano, 1990; Searle & Ward, 1990; Selltiz et al., 1963). Strangers, however, often are not interested in developing relationships with host nationals and focus only on their task in the host culture (e.g., Selby & Wood, 1966). The greater the intimacy of the relationships strangers form with host nationals, the less the anxiety and uncertainty they experience (Hammer et al., 1998).

Our relationships with host nationals are embedded in social networks. Communication with members of host nationals' social networks (e.g., their family and friends) helps us reduce uncertainty about them (Parks & Adelman, 1983). Not sharing social networks with host nationals (e.g., living in stranger-enclaves) is associated negatively with adjustment to the host culture (e.g., Gullahorn & Gullahorn, 1966; Herman & Schield, 1961). Bochner and his colleagues (e.g., Bochner et al., 1979; Bochner et al., 1977; Furnham & Bochner, 1982) report that learning about the host culture is facilitated by developing social networks with host nationals. Strangers tend to develop increasingly strong ties with host nationals as a function of the length of their stay in the host culture (Okazaki-Luff, 1991).

The amount of uncertainty we experience when we communicate with host nationals is influenced by the degree to which we share communication networks with host nationals (e.g., Gudykunst, Chua, & Gray, 1987). Shared networks also help us manage anxiety about interacting with host nationals (e.g., Dyal & Dyal, 1981). The more we share social networks with host nationals with whom we are interacting, the more we can manage our uncertainty and anxiety about host nationals.

One of the functions of shared social networks is providing social support for strangers. Strangers' social support can come from a number of sources, including strangers' families, friends, and acquaintances, as well as from sources like clerks in stores, hairdressers, and others. Bochner et al. (1977) argue that strangers prefer host nationals for informational support (e.g., language problems, academic problems) and prefer co-nationals for emotional support. Social support from strangers' family members is linked to low levels of stress and to psychological well-being in the host culture (e.g., Naidoo, 1985; Stone Feinstein & Ward, 1990). Strangers' co-nationals can be an important source of social support and facilitate adjustment (e.g., Ward &

Kennedy, 1993c; Ying & Liese, 1991). Emphasizing interaction with co-nationals and not interacting with host nationals, however, impedes strangers' adjustment (e.g., Pruitt, 1978; Richardson, 1974). Strangers' adjustment to the host culture tends to be facilitated when they receive social support from both co-nationals and host nationals (e.g., Furnham & Alibhai, 1985; Ward & Rana-Deuba, 2000). Social support is related to the anxiety strangers experience in the host culture.

The nature of the connections we have with host nationals affects the amount of anxiety and uncertainty we experience interacting with them. Six axioms dealing with the nature of our connections with host nationals, therefore, are included in the theory:

Axiom 27: An increase in our attraction to host nationals will produce a decrease in our anxiety and an increase in our confidence in predicting their behavior. *Boundary Conditions:* This axiom holds only when our anxiety and uncertainty are between our minimum and maximum thresholds, and we are not mindful.

Axiom 28: An increase in the quantity and quality of our contact with host nationals will produce a decrease in our anxiety and an increase in our ability to predict their behavior accurately. *Boundary Conditions:* This axiom holds only when our anxiety and uncertainty are between our minimum and maximum thresholds, and we are not mindful.

Axiom 29: An increase in our interdependence with host nationals will produce a decrease in our anxiety and an increase in our ability to predict their behavior accurately. *Boundary Conditions:* This axiom holds only when our anxiety and uncertainty are between our minimum and maximum thresholds, and we are not mindful.

Axiom 30: An increase in the intimacy of our relationships with host nationals will produce a decrease in our anxiety and an increase in our ability to predict their behavior accurately. *Boundary Conditions:* This axiom applies only to broad trends across stages of relationship development, when our anxiety and uncertainty are between our minimum and maximum thresholds, and we are not mindful.

Axiom 31: An increase in the networks we share with host nationals will produce a decrease in our anxiety and an increase in our ability to predict their behavior accurately. *Boundary Conditions:* This axiom holds only when our anxiety and uncertainty are between our minimum and maximum thresholds, and we are not mindful.

Axiom 32: An increase in the amount of social support we receive in the host culture will produce a decrease in our anxiety. *Boundary Conditions:* This axiom holds only when social support is not limited to co-nationals, when our anxiety is between our minimum and maximum thresholds, and we are not mindful.

The nature of our connections with host nationals does not directly affect our intercultural adjustment. Their influence is mediated through our ability to manage our anxiety and accurately predict host nationals' behavior. Our ability to manage our anxiety also is influenced by whether we interact ethically with host nationals.

Ethical Interactions With Host Nationals

Strangers often evaluate host nationals' behavior negatively. This causes problems in strangers' interactions with host nationals, as well as in strangers' adjustment to the host culture. To overcome these problems it is necessary to have ethical interactions with host nationals. Pritchard (1991) argues that the "overridingness of morality" requires that our "conduct be limited to what is morally acceptable" (p. 226). Being ethical involves treating host nationals with dignity, respecting host nationals, and being morally inclusive toward host nationals.

Dignity involves a minimal level of self-respect, or feeling worthy, honored, and respected as a person (Pritchard, 1991). Being ethical or moral requires that we maintain our own and host nationals' sense of dignity in our interactions with them. Since behavior in early stages of interaction tends to be reciprocated (Gouldner, 1960), if we treat host nationals with dignity, they will probably treat us with dignity. This should lead to low levels of anxiety about interacting with host nationals.

Respecting host nationals also is necessary to behave in a moral fashion (Gutmann, 1992). We need to interact with host nationals on the basis of a "presumption of equal worth" (Taylor, 1992, p. 72). When we respect host nationals, we unconsciously assume that host nationals respect us. This leads to low levels of anxiety about interacting with host nationals.

When we respect host nationals, we treat them in a morally inclusive fashion. Optow (1990) points out that "moral exclusion occurs when individuals or groups are perceived as outside the boundary in which moral values, rules, and considerations of fairness apply. Those who are morally excluded are perceived as nonentities, expendable, or undeserving" (p. 1, italics omitted). If host nationals are perceived as nonentities (or as "gooks"), "harming them appears acceptable, appropriate, or just" (p. 1). When we are morally inclusive, we assume that considerations of fair play apply to host nationals and we are willing to make sacrifices to help them.

Moral exclusion emerges from blaming host nationals and distancing ourselves psychologically from them (Optow, 1990). It, therefore, leads to high levels of anxiety about interacting with host nationals. We have high levels of anxiety because we do not expect those we treat morally exclusively to apply the rules of fair play to us. When we are morally inclusive toward host nationals, in contrast, we expect host nationals to apply the rules of fair play to us. When we expect to be treated fairly, we are not highly anxious about communicating with host nationals.

Treating host nationals in an ethical fashion affects the anxiety we experience interacting with them. Three axioms regarding ethical treatment of host nationals, therefore, are included in the theory:

Axiom 33: An increase in our ability to maintain our own and host nationals' dignity in our interactions with them will produce a decrease in our anxiety. *Boundary Conditions:* This axiom holds only when our anxiety is between our minimum and maximum thresholds, and we are not mindful.

Axiom 34: An increase in our respect for host nationals will produce a decrease in our anxiety. *Boundary Conditions:* This axiom holds only when our anxiety is between our minimum and maximum thresholds, and we are not mindful.

Axiom 35: An increase in our moral inclusiveness toward host nationals will produce a decrease in our anxiety. *Boundary Conditions:* This axiom holds only when our anxiety is between our minimum and maximum thresholds, and we are not mindful.

For most of us, maintaining our own and host nationals' dignity, respecting host nationals, and being morally inclusive toward host nationals requires that we be mindful. This is especially true when our anxiety is above our maximum thresholds.

Anxiety, Uncertainty, Mindfulness, and Intercultural Adjustment

To interact effectively with host nationals, we must be able to understand their perspectives. This requires mindfulness. As indicated earlier, Langer (1989) argues that mindfulness involves creating new categories, being open to new information, and recognizing hosts' perspectives. Interacting effectively with host nationals requires that we develop mindful ways of learning about host nationals and the host culture. Langer (1997) contends this

involves "(1) openness to novelty; (2) alertness to distinctions; (3) sensitivity to different contexts; (4) implicit, if not explicit, awareness of multiple perspectives; and (5) orientation in the present" (p. 23). These processes are all interrelated and lead us to be "receptive to changes in an ongoing situation" (p. 23).

Strangers tend to be more mindful in intergroup interactions than host nationals. Strangers pay attention to how their interactions with host nationals are going and are aware of alternative ways the interactions may develop (Frable et al., 1990). Often strangers' mindfulness is a defensive strategy because they are unsure how host nationals will respond to them (Frable et al., 1990). The extent that strangers' mindfulness leads to effective interactions depends on strangers' biases and objectivity (Devine et al., 1996). It can be argued that strangers are "generally mistrusting and suspicious" of host nationals' "intentions and motives" (Devine et al., 1996, p. 445). Strangers' responses to host nationals also are affected by strangers' "attributional ambiguity" (e.g., strangers may attribute host nationals' behavior to host nationals' personal qualities or host nationals' stereotypes of strangers' groups; Crocker et al., 1991).

If we interpret host nationals' messages from our own perspectives, as we do when we communicate mindlessly, we tend to interact ineffectively. The more we are able to learn how to describe host nationals' behavior and the less evaluative we are, the more positive host nationals will perceive our intentions to be. Describing host nationals' behavior helps us understand how host nationals interpret messages because we do not automatically assume that host nationals interpret messages the same way we do, and we can try to understand host nationals' interpretations. Our ability to differentiate host nationals' interpretations of messages from our interpretations of messages leads to predicting host nationals' behavior accurately.

Fluency in the host language facilitates interaction with host nationals (Gullahorn & Gullahorn, 1966) and sociocultural adaptation (Ward & Kennedy, 1993c). Host language competence is associated positively with psychological adjustment to the host culture (Gullahorn & Gullahorn, 1966; Morris, 1960), and effective interactions with host nationals (Nishida, 1985). Strangers who are perceived as competent in the host languages are liked more by host nationals than strangers who are not perceived as competent in the language (Kim, 1991). Takai (1991), however, reports that fluency in Japanese is associated negatively with international students' satisfaction with living in Japan. He suggests that this is due to international students' perceiving that Japanese reject them when they speak Japanese. This may be a function of Japanese not expecting strangers to speak their language. The effect of competence in the hosts' language may be limited to host cultures where host nationals expect strangers to speak their language.

Understanding host nationals' languages or dialects also facilitates managing our anxiety and uncertainty, in large part, because it helps us understand host nationals' perspectives. Host language competence, for example, increases our ability to cope with uncertainty in cultures where the language is spoken (Naiman et al., 1978). Knowledge of the host language also helps us manage our anxiety (Stephan & Stephan, 1985). The more competent strangers are in the host language, the less their anxiety and uncertainty interacting with host nationals (Hammer et al., 1998).

Experiencing anxiety when we interact with host nationals leads us to engage in social categorizations (e.g., Greenland & Brown, 1999). The anxiety we experience interacting with host nationals affects our ability to process information about host nationals and the host culture. When anxiety is high (e.g., above our maximum thresholds), we tend to process information about host nationals in a

simplistic fashion (Wilder & Shapiro, 1989). High levels of anxiety generate arousal, which leads to self-focused attention that distracts us from what is happening and decreases our ability to make differentiations regarding host nationals (Wilder, 1993). This line of reasoning suggests that we are not able to gather new or accurate information about host nationals when our anxiety is high and, therefore, we are not able to make accurate predictions or explanations of host nationals' behavior.

If our anxiety and uncertainty are above our maximum thresholds, we must first mindfully manage our anxiety (e.g., bring it below our maximum threshold) before we can predict host nationals' behavior accurately (e.g., manage our uncertainty). Managing our anxiety requires controlling our bodily symptoms (e.g., shortness of breath) and controlling our worrying thoughts (Kennerley, 1990). Once we mindfully manage our bodily symptoms (e.g., by physically or mentally breaking from the situation, taking deep breaths), we can mindfully manage the worrying thoughts that cause the anxiety (e.g., all-or-nothing thinking; see Burns, 1989, for a discussion of cognitive distortions that can cause anxiety and how to manage them). Managing the worrying thoughts is important because if we do not manage them they will interfere with our ability to process information complexly about host nationals (Fiske & Morling, 1996).

Managing anxiety involves coping with our emotions. Lazarus (1991) argues that coping involves changing the person-environment fit. He differentiates between "problem-focused" coping and "emotion-focused" or "cognitive" coping. Problem-focused coping involves changing the environment causing the stress. This strategy generally does not work for strangers in new cultural environments because strangers cannot change host cultures. Emotion-focused or cognitive coping, in contrast, involves "thinking rather than acting to change the person-environment relationship" (p. 112). This type of coping changes the ways that strangers view the things causing them stress. Emotion-focused coping allows "short-circuiting" strangers' emotional reactions. Burns' (1989) "daily mod log" is useful in helping strangers accomplish this (the log involves describing stressors, giving the usual interpretation, looking at the distorted thought process involved, and reinterpreting the stressors).

Ward et al. (1998) report that using emotion-focused coping mechanisms for dealing with stress such as positive reinterpretations or cognitive appraisals of stressful events is associated with lowering perceived stress, but problem-focused coping mechanisms such as active coping or planning is not. Cross (1995), however, observes that problem-focused coping with academic problems is associated with lowering stress for Asian international students.

We cannot interact effectively with host nationals or adjust to the host culture if our anxiety and uncertainty are too high or too low. The optimal level of anxiety and uncertainty that facilitates effective interaction and adjustment is somewhere between our minimum and maximum thresholds. For uncertainty, our optimal level is when we think that host nationals' behavior is predictable, but we also recognize that we may not be able to explain their behavior accurately. Mindfulness, however, may still be necessary to make accurate predictions of host nationals' behavior. For anxiety, our optimal level is when we feel comfortable interacting with host nationals, but we still have sufficient anxiety that we are not complacent in our interactions with them. Reducing anxiety and uncertainty about host nationals leads to strangers' being satisfied with their stay in the host culture (Gao & Gudykunst, 1990; Hammer et al., 1998).

When our anxiety and uncertainty are not at optimal levels, we can manage them mindfully to bring them between our minimum and maximum thresholds. When our anxiety and

uncertainty are at optimal levels, we can interact effectively and adjust to the host culture only if we are mindful. We do not, however, want to be overly vigilant (Langer, 1997). If we engage in "soft vigilance," in contrast, we will be open to new information and aware of host nationals' perspectives.

When our anxiety and our uncertainty are between our minimum and maximum thresholds, we can communicate effectively with strangers when we are mindful. Four axioms summarize the relationships among anxiety, uncertainty, mindfulness, and effective communication:

Axiom 36: An increase in our ability to describe host nationals' behavior will produce an increase in our ability to predict their behavior accurately. *Boundary Conditions:* This axiom holds only when we are mindful of the process of communication and we are not overly vigilant, and our anxiety and uncertainty are between our minimum and maximum thresholds.

Axiom 37: An increase in our knowledge of host nationals' languages and/or dialects will produce a decrease in our anxiety and an increase in our ability to predict their behavior accurately. *Boundary Conditions:* This axiom holds only when our anxiety and uncertainty are between our minimum and maximum thresholds, when host nationals expect strangers to speak their language, and we are not mindful.

Axiom 38: An increase in our mindfulness of processes occurring in our interactions with host nationals will produce an increase in our ability to manage our anxiety and an increase in our ability to manage our uncertainty. *Boundary Condition:* This axiom holds only when we are not overly vigilant.

Axiom 39: An increase in our ability to manage our anxiety about interacting with host nationals *and* an increase in the accuracy of our predictions and explanations regarding host nationals' behavior will produce an increase in the effectiveness of our interactions with them and our ability to adapt to the host culture. *Boundary Conditions:* This axiom holds only when we are mindful of the processes occurring in our interactions with host nationals and we are not overly vigilant, and our anxiety and uncertainty are between our minimum and maximum thresholds.

These four axioms are critical for effective interaction and intercultural adjustment; they focus on the basic causes of intercultural adjustment. The preceding axioms (1–35) provide ways that we can manage our anxiety and uncertainty (e.g., they focus on the superficial causes of intercultural adjustment).

Conditions in the Host Culture

Host cultures vary in the degree to which they are receptive to strangers. Host receptivity involves the host nationals' "openness toward strangers and willingness to accommodate strangers with opportunities to participate in the local social communication process" (Kim, 2001, p. 148). Host receptivity toward strangers is associated with host nationals' having positive attitudes toward strangers. Gudykunst (1983) argues that host attitudes toward strangers can be positive, ambivalent, or negative. These attitudes, in combination with strangers' goals vis-à-vis the host culture (i.e., to visit, to reside, to join), affect the stranger-host relationship. The type of stranger-host relationship that is formed influences how host nationals deal with strangers.

Since the focus here is on strangers who reside in the host culture and do not want to become members, only host attitudes toward strangers needs to be considered. Gudykunst (1985b) contends that the more negative host attitudes toward strangers, the more concerned host nationals are with strangers' behavior. The more negative host nationals' attitudes toward strangers, the greater the anxiety strangers experience (Dyal & Dyal,

1981; Hammer et al., 1998). The more host nationals are receptive to strangers, the more strangers feel comfortable in the host culture and the less anxiety strangers experience interacting with host nationals. The more strangers perceive that host nationals are ethnocentric, the less their work adjustment in multinational firms (Florkowski & Fogel, 1999).

Host cultures also vary in the degree to which they put pressure on strangers to conform to the host culture's patterns of behavior (Kim, 2001). Kim (2001) argues that conformity pressure is related to the assimilative or pluralistic ideology that predominates in the host culture (Note: Gudykunst [1985b] also argues that the strangers' goals vis-à-vis the host culture also affect conformity pressure, but here the focus is only on strangers who want to reside, not to join or just visit). Small cultural differences in assimilative societies produce high levels of stress for strangers, while large cultural differences in pluralistic societies produce low levels of stress (Berry, 1975).

Strangers often perceive that they are discriminated against in host cultures. Discrimination against strangers can vary from minor (e.g., host nationals do not sit next to strangers on public transportation) to major (e.g., host nationals ostracize strangers). Perceived discrimination toward strangers by host nationals may, in part, be a function of host nationals' ingroup bias (e.g., Tajfel, 1978). Wibulswadi (1989), for example, reports that northern Thais perceive U.S. Americans more negatively than other Thais, Chinese, or Hmong in Northern Thailand. Perceived discrimination is associated with strangers' experiencing stress in the host culture (e.g., Vega et al., 1991) and problems in psychological adjustment (e.g., Ward & Chang, 1994, cited in Ward, 2001).

The conditions in the host culture influence strangers' anxiety. Three axioms regarding conditions in the host culture, therefore, are included:

Axiom 40: An increase in the host nationals' receptivity toward strangers will produce a decrease in the anxiety strangers experience. *Boundary Condition:* This axiom holds only when we are not mindful.

Axiom 41: An increase in the pluralistic tendencies in the host culture will produce a decrease in the anxiety strangers experience. *Boundary Condition:* This axiom holds only when we are not mindful.

Axiom 42: An increase in host nationals' discrimination toward strangers will produce an increase in the anxiety strangers experience. *Boundary Condition:* This axiom holds only when we are not mindful.

These conditions generally do not change during strangers' stay in host cultures. The condition, however, may vary in different locations in host cultures (e.g., host receptivity to strangers may be higher in southern California than in Iowa), and vary from rural to urban areas (e.g., urban areas are more pluralistic; Laumann, 1993).

Cross-Cultural Variability in Strangers' Adjustment

In the 1998 version of the adjustment theory, I included one cross-cultural axiom for each axiom in the main part of the theory. I now believe this was unnecessary and a mistake. In terms of adjustment, what is critical is explaining how cultural differences affect strangers' adjustment. My goal here is to explain how cultural variability in host cultures influences the anxiety and uncertainty strangers experience when interacting with host nationals.

To begin, there are differences in the nature of stranger-host national relationships across cultures. Triandis (1995) points out that members of collectivistic cultures (e.g., cultures that emphasize the ingroup over individuals) emphasize ingroup membership more and draw a sharper distinction between ingroups

and outgroups than members of individualistic cultures (e.g., cultures that emphasize individual members over their ingroups). It is more difficult for members of a culture to become ingroup members in collectivistic cultures than in individualistic cultures (Triandis, 1995). Strangers from individualistic cultures, therefore, have a difficult time becoming ingroup members in collectivistic cultures.

The type of information that strangers use to manage their uncertainty is influenced by cultural individualism-collectivism. Gudykunst and Nishida (1986), for example, report that members of individualistic cultures focus on person-based information (e.g., values, attitudes, beliefs) to manage uncertainty, and members of collectivistic cultures focus on group-based information (e.g., group memberships, age, status) to manage uncertainty. Similarly, Gelfand et al. (2000) observe that individuating information is used to make social predictions in individualistic cultures more than in collectivistic cultures, and relational information is used to make social predictions in collectivistic cultures more than in individualistic cultures.

Norenzayan et al. (2002) point out that members of collectivistic cultures use situation-based information to make social inferences more than members of individualistic cultures when situational information is salient. Members of collectivistic cultures also tend to use high-context communication more than members of individualistic cultures, especially with ingroup members (Hall, 1976). Understanding high-context communication requires being able to interpret the context or situation. Strangers from individualistic cultures generally do not have the cultural knowledge necessary to interpret high-context messages accurately. These cultural differences suggest the following axiom:

Axiom 43: An increase in cultural collectivism in host cultures will produce an increase in strangers' anxiety and a decrease in strangers' ability to predict host nationals' behavior accurately. *Boundary Condition:* This axiom holds only when we are not mindful.

The focus on person-based information leads members of individualistic cultures to look for personal similarities with host nationals. Person-based information, however, generally is not useful in predicting the behavior of host nationals in collectivistic cultures (the exception is when strangers form close friendships with host nationals).

Cultural individualism-collectivism is not the only dimension of cultural variability that affects strangers' ability to adjust to host cultures. Hofstede (2001) argues that xenophobia is higher in cultures high in uncertainty avoidance (e.g., cultures where uncertainty is viewed as dangerous) than in cultures low in uncertainty avoidance (e.g., cultures where uncertainty is viewed as interesting). Tolerance for diversity, on the other hand, is higher in cultures low in uncertainty avoidance than in cultures high in uncertainty avoidance. Hofstede (2001) claims that members of high uncertainty avoidance cultures reject members of other races as neighbors, think immigrants should be sent back to their native cultures, are suspicious of foreign managers, and are not prepared to travel abroad. Members of low uncertainty avoidance cultures, in contrast, accept members of other races as neighbors, tolerate immigrants, accept foreign managers, and are prepared to travel abroad.

High uncertainty avoidance cultures develop clear norms and rules and require extensive ritualistic behavior in order to help members of the culture manage their anxiety and uncertainty (Hofstede, 2001). Strangers generally are not familiar with the norms and rules and have not learned the ritualistic behavior necessary to interact in high uncertainty avoidance cultures. This line of reasoning suggests the following axiom:

> *Axiom 44:* An increase in the cultural uncertainty avoidance of host cultures will produce an increase in strangers' anxiety and a decrease

in strangers' ability to predict host nationals' behavior accurately. *Boundary Condition:* This axiom holds only when we are not mindful.

This axiom can be combined with the previous axiom to predict the influence of cultural variability on strangers' adjustment. To illustrate, strangers should have the most difficulty adjusting to collectivistic cultures that are high in uncertainty avoidance, and the least difficulty adjusting to cultures that are individualistic and low in uncertainty avoidance.

Specific types of stranger-host national relationships are influenced by other dimensions of cultural variability. The effect of the gender composition of the stranger-host national relationship on strangers' adjustment is affected by cultural variability in masculinity-femininity. Hofstede (2001) points out that members of masculine cultures (e.g., cultures with highly differentiated gender roles) are socialized with members of the same sex and have little contact with members of the opposite sex. Members of feminine cultures (e.g., cultures with little gender role differentiation), in contrast, are socialized with members of the same and opposite sex. Members of masculine cultures, therefore, draw a sharper distinction between same- and opposite-sex relationships than members of feminine cultures. Since they will expect to interact equally with same- and opposite-sex host nationals, female strangers from feminine cultures should have more difficulty adjusting in masculine cultures than female strangers from masculine cultures have in feminine cultures.

The effect of the status/power of strangers and host nationals on strangers' adjustment is affected by cultural variability in power distance. Hofstede (2001) points out that members of high power distance cultures view power as being distributed unequally in society. Members of low power distance cultures, on the other hand, view power as distributed equally in society. Members of high power distance cultures, therefore, draw a sharper distinction between low- and high-status communicators than members of low power distance cultures. Because they will expect to be viewed as equals, low-status strangers from low power distance cultures should have more difficulty adjusting to high power distance cultures than low-status strangers from high power distance cultures will have in low power distance cultures.

Hofstede (2001) links generational attitudes to cultural uncertainty avoidance. He points out that favorable attitudes toward younger people and favorable attitudes toward older people are both correlated positively with uncertainty avoidance at the cultural level. Hofstede argues that older people in high uncertainty avoidance cultures are "more likely to disapprove of the behavior of young people and to wait longer before leaving the responsibility in the hands of juniors" than older people in low uncertainty avoidance cultures (pp. 158–159). This leads to a larger generation gap in high uncertainty avoidance cultures than in low uncertainty avoidance cultures. Because they expect a small generation gap, younger strangers from low uncertainty avoidance cultures should have greater difficulty adjusting in high uncertainty avoidance cultures than younger strangers from high uncertainty avoidance cultures have in low uncertainty avoidance cultures. The reasoning outlined here suggests three axioms:

Axiom 45: An increase in the cultural masculinity of host cultures will produce an increase in female strangers' anxiety when interacting with male host nationals and a decrease in female strangers' ability to predict male host nationals' behavior accurately. *Boundary Condition:* This axiom holds only when we are not mindful.

Axiom 46: An increase in the cultural distance of host cultures will produce an increase in low-status strangers' anxiety when interacting with high-status host nationals and a decrease in low-status strangers' ability to

predict high-status host nationals' behavior accurately. *Boundary Condition:* This axiom holds only when we are not mindful.

Axiom 47: An increase in the cultural uncertainty avoidance of host cultures will produce an increase in younger strangers' anxiety when interacting with older host nationals and a decrease in younger strangers' ability to predict older host nationals' behavior accurately. *Boundary Condition:* This axiom holds only when we are not mindful.

These three axioms should be additive. That is, younger, low-status, female strangers from cultures that are feminine, as well as low in power distance and low in uncertainty avoidance should have the most difficulty adjusting in cultures that are masculine, as well as high in power distance and high in uncertainty avoidance.

Theorems

Theorems can be generated by logically combining the axioms, but space does not allow them to be presented here. If axioms 7 and 8 are combined, for example, the theorem that "there is a positive association between our need for group inclusion and sustaining our self-conceptions" can be generated. This theorem is consistent with Turner's (1988) theory of motivation. Some theorems generated will be consistent with previous research and some will form hypotheses for future research. To illustrate, combination of axioms 19 and 27 yields the similarity-attraction hypothesis (i.e., "the more similarities we perceive between ourselves and strangers, the more we are attracted to them"), which has received extensive empirical support (e.g., Byrne, 1971). Combination of axioms 11 and 12 yields the theorem that "the rigidity of our attitudes is related negatively to our ability to process information complexly," a hypothesis for future research.

Not all axioms should be combined to form theorems. The conditions in the host culture axioms (40–42) and the cross-cultural axioms (43–47), for example, should not be combined with the axioms in the main part of the theory (axioms 1–39). This would involve the ecological fallacy or the reverse ecological fallacy. Also, some combinations of axioms will involve the fallacy of the excluded middle and should not be generated. If A → C and B → C, for example, it can be deduced that A and B are related. The fallacy of the excluded middle involves not recognizing that there may be another variable mediating the relationships between the two variables (e.g., A → D → B).

APPLYING THE THEORY

There are two basic applications for the AUM theory of intercultural adjustment. The first is using the theory to help strangers adjust to host cultures. The theory provides concrete suggestions to help strangers adjust in new cultural environments. The theory suggests, for example, that strangers must manage their anxiety and uncertainty to adjust to the host culture. Managing anxiety and uncertainty requires that strangers be mindful about the processes occurring in their interactions with host nationals.

When strangers are mindful, they can consciously choose to think or behave differently than they do when they are not mindful to manage their anxiety and uncertainty. Strangers, for example, can chose to learn about the host culture, learn the host language, or form social networks and develop friendships with host nationals in order to decrease their anxiety and increase the accuracy of their predictions of host nationals' behavior.

The second application of the theory involves using it to design intercultural adjustment training programs. The major goals of an adjustment training program based upon AUM theory would be (1) to help trainees understand how their ability to manage their uncertainty and anxiety influence their ability

to adapt to new cultures, (2) to help trainees successfully manage their anxiety in new cultural environments, and (3) to help trainees successfully manage their uncertainty in new cultural environments.

The theory suggests that the first goal must be addressed prior to addressing the second and third. If trainees do not understand that their uncertainty and anxiety are related directly to their ability to adapt to new cultural environments, they will not be open to sessions focusing on managing uncertainty and anxiety. While the goals focus on uncertainty and anxiety, I do *not* mean to imply that the training focus exclusively on uncertainty and anxiety. Other factors (e.g., developing cultural knowledge, being mindful) must be incorporated in order to meet the second and third goals.

For trainees to understand how their uncertainty and anxiety influence their abilities to adapt to new cultural environments, they must see this through their own experience. In other words, the first goal requires experiential learning. I, therefore, would begin with a culture general simulation such as BAFA BAFA. After running the simulation, I would debrief it focusing on how uncertainty and anxiety influences trainees' ability to interact effectively with host nationals and to adjust to the new culture (see Gudykunst, 1998).

In the next session, I would emphasize the importance of being mindful if trainees are going to be able to make accurate predictions (manage uncertainty) and manage their anxiety. There are many ways this could be accomplished. Since the preceding session was exclusively experiential, I would probably use didactic techniques in this session (in order to mix training techniques). This might involve a short lecture on being mindful, and the use of critical incidents to help the trainees understand the importance of creating new categories (or looking for individuating information about individuals from other cultures), being open to new information, and being aware of alternative perspectives (the three characteristics of mindfulness; Langer, 1989).

The third session would be devoted to managing anxiety. Managing anxiety is addressed prior to managing uncertainty because accurate predictions cannot be made when anxiety is high. There are many ways this session could be organized (e.g., there are many factors that influence the amount of anxiety individuals experience, in AUM theory). One critical issue that must be addressed, however, is helping trainees learn specific techniques for managing their anxiety (e.g., breaking from the situation, deep breathing, meditation). Other influences on managing anxiety (e.g., rigid attitudes toward host nationals; negative expectations, including negative stereotypes; ability to tolerate ambiguity) could be illustrated through the use of critical incidents.

The fourth session would focus on managing uncertainty. The goal of this session is to help trainees learn how to make accurate predictions about host nationals' behavior. To accomplish this, cultural similarities and differences must be addressed. Trainees need a framework within which they can interpret the behavior of members of the host culture. I, therefore, would introduce major dimensions of cultural variability (e.g., individualism-collectivism, uncertainty avoidance; Hofstede, 2001) trainees can use to interpret host nationals' behavior initially (i.e., before they have much culture-specific knowledge). In addition to cultural differences, other influences on managing uncertainty need to be addressed (again, there are many from which to choose). The importance of positive expectations, for example, could be introduced through the use of critical incidents.

The fifth session would focus on giving trainees an opportunity to apply what they have learned in interactions with host nationals. Ideally, host nationals would be available for this session. If no host nationals are available, the objective can be accomplished by culture-specific role-playing. AUM theory suggests several important issues to be addressed in this session. To illustrate, AUM theory suggests that the ability to be mindful when negative expectations are activated is critical to effective communication. Role plays could be designed where trainees' negative expectations are activated to provide them an opportunity to practice being mindful.

The sixth session of the training program would be devoted to presenting survival skills trainees will need when they arrive in the new culture (e.g., using local transportation, finding a place to live). The final session should be a wrap-up session. In this session, trainees are asked to summarize what they have learned in the sessions (this is based upon the experiential learning assumption that adults remember the conclusions they draw for themselves better than the conclusions they are told by others). Also during this session trainees might be asked to develop a plan for continuing their learning about the new culture after they arrive in the culture.

CONCLUSION

In presenting the theory here, I have dropped a large number of axioms from the 1998 theory (e.g., axioms regarding shame, informality of situations, gathering appropriate information, self-monitoring; as well as most previous axioms dealing with cross-cultural variability in specific variables) and I added several axioms dealing with intergroup processes (e.g., axioms focusing on power, threatened identities, collective self-esteem) and how cross-cultural variability influences anxiety and uncertainty in stranger-host national interactions. The axioms I dropped are ones that I currently do not think are critical to managing anxiety and uncertainty and intercultural adjustment.

Some readers may argue that the theory is too complicated with 47 axioms. This version of the theory has only about one half the number of axioms in the 1998 version. It is, nevertheless, important to keep in mind that the goals of theories must be balanced with the number of theoretical statements when theories are constructed. Since one of the goals of the AUM theory of adjustment is to improve strangers' ability to adjust in new cultural environments, the axioms cannot be highly abstract. Increasing the abstractness of the axioms could make the theory simpler, but it would decrease its applicability. The present form of the theory allows direct application.

REFERENCES

Abelson, R. (1976). Script processing in attitude formation and decision making. In J. Carroll & J. Payne (Eds.), *Cognition and social behavior* (pp. 33–45). Hillsdale, NJ: Lawrence Erlbaum.

Ady, J. (1995). Toward a differential demand model of sojourner adjustment. In R. Wiseman (Ed.), *Intercultural communication theory* (pp. 92–114). Thousand Oaks, CA: Sage.

Argyle, M. (1991). *Cooperation.* London: Routledge.

Babiker, I., Cox, J., & Miller, P. (1980). The measurement of cultural distance and its relationship to medical consultations, symptomology, and examination performance of overseas students at Edinburgh University. *Social Psychiatry, 15,* 109–116.

Ball-Rokeach, S. (1973). From pervasive ambiguity to definition of the situation. *Sociometry, 36,* 378–389.

Basu, A., & Ames, R. (1970). Cross-cultural contact and attitude formation. *Sociology and Social Research, 55,* 5–16.

Baumeister, R., & Leary, M. (1995). The need to belong: Desire for interpersonal attachments as a fundamental human motive. *Psychological Bulletin, 117,* 497–529.

Bavelas, J., Black, A., Chovil, N., & Mullett, J. (1990). *Equivocal communication.* Newbury Park, CA: Sage.

Becker, E. (1971). *The birth and death of meaning.* New York: Harper & Row.

Bell, R. (1987). Social involvement. In J. McCroskey & J. Daly (Eds.), *Personality and interpersonal communication* (pp. 195–242). Newbury Park, CA: Sage.

Bellah, R., Madsen, R., Sullivan, W., Swidler, A., & Tipton, S. (1991). *The good society.* New York: Basic Books.

Berger, C. R., & Bradac, J. (1982). *Language and social knowledge.* London: Edward Arnold.

Berger, C. R., & Calabrese, R. (1975). Some explorations in initial interactions and beyond: Toward a developmental theory of interpersonal communication. *Human Communication Research, 1,* 99–112.

Berry, J. W. (1975). Ecology, cultural adaptation, and psychological differentiation. In R. Brislin, S. Bochner, & W. Lonner (Eds.), *Cross-cultural perspectives on learning* (pp. 207–228). Beverly Hills, CA: Sage.

Berscheid, E. (1985). Interpersonal attraction. In G. Lindzey & E. Aronson (Eds.), *The handbook of social psychology* (3rd ed., Vol. 2, pp. 413–484). New York: Random House.

Black, J., & Gregerson, H. (1990). Expectations, satisfaction, and intention to leave of American expatriate adjustment in Pacific Rim overseas assignments. *International Journal of Intercultural Relations, 14,* 485–506.

Blalock, H. (1969). *Theory construction.* Englewood Cliffs, NJ: Prentice Hall.

Bochner, S. (1972). Problems in culture learning. In S. Bochner & P. Wicks (Eds.), *Overseas students in Australia* (pp. 65–81). Sydney: University of New South Wales Press.

Bochner, S., Lin, A., & McLeod, B. (1979). Cross-cultural contact and the development of an international perspective. *Journal of Social Psychology, 107,* 29–41.

Bochner, S., McLeod, B., & Lin, A. (1977). Friendship patterns of overseas students. *International Journal of Psychology, 12,* 277–297.

Bochner, S., & Perks, R. (1971). National role evocation as a function of cross-national interaction. *Journal of Cross-Cultural Psychology, 2,* 157–164.

Bock, P. (Ed.). (1970). *Culture shock.* New York: Knopf.

Brewer, M. B. (1991). The social self. *Personality and Social Psychology Bulletin, 17,* 475–485.

Brewer, M. B., & Roccas, S. (2001). Individual values, social identity, and optimal distinctiveness. In C. Sedikides & M. B. Brewer (Eds.),

Individual self, relational self, collective self (pp. 219–237). Philadelphia: Psychology Press.

Britt, T., Boniecki, K., Vescio, T., Biernot, M., & Brown, L. (1996). Intergroup anxiety: A person × situation approach. *Personality and Social Psychology Bulletin, 22,* 1177–1188.

Budner, S. (1962). Intolerance of ambiguity as a personality variable. *Journal of Personality, 30,* 29–50.

Burns, D. (1985). *Intimate connections.* New York: Signet.

Burns, D. (1989). *The feeling good handbook.* New York: William Morrow.

Byrne, D. (1971). *The attraction paradigm.* New York: Academic Press.

Chataway, C., & Berry, J. (1989). Acculturation experiences, appraisal, coping, and adaptation. *Canadian Journal of Behavioral Science, 21,* 295–301.

Church, A. (1982). Sojourner adjustment. *Psychological Bulletin, 91,* 540–572.

Clark, H., & Marshall, C. (1981). Definite reference and mutual knowledge. In A. Joshi, B. Webber, & I. Sag (Eds.), *Elements of discourse understanding* (pp. 10–63). Cambridge, UK: Cambridge University Press.

Coelho, G. (1958). *Changing images of America: A study of Indian students' perceptions.* New York: Free Press.

Cort, D., & King, M. (1979). Some correlates of culture shock among American tourists in Africa. *International Journal of Intercultural Relations, 3,* 211–225.

Cozzarelli, C., & Karafa, J. (1998). Cultural estrangement and terror management theory. *Personality and Social Psychology Bulletin, 24,* 253–267.

Crocker, J., Voekl, K., Testa, M., & Major, B. (1991). Social stigma: The affective consequences of attributional ambiguity. *Journal of Personality and Social Psychology, 60,* 218–228.

Cross, S. (1995). Self construals, coping, and stress in cross-cultural adaptation. *Journal of Cross-Cultural Psychology, 26,* 673–697.

Csikszentmihalyi, M. (1990). *Flow: The psychology of optimal experience.* New York: Harper & Row.

David, K. (1971). Culture shock and the development of self awareness. *Journal of Contemporary Psychotherapy, 4,* 44–48.

Demerath, L. (1993). Knowledge-based affect. *Social Psychology Quarterly, 56,* 136–147.

Devine, P. (1989). Stereotypes and prejudice: Their automatic and controlled components. *Journal of Personality and Social Psychology, 56,* 5–18.

Devine, P., Evett, S., & Vasquez-Suson, K. (1996). Exploring the interpersonal dynamics of intergroup contact. In R. Sorrentino & E. T. Higgins (Eds.), *Handbook of motivation and cognition* (Vol. 3, pp. 423–464). New York: Guilford.

Dijker, A. (1987). Emotional reactions to ethnic minorities. *European Journal of Social Psychology, 17,* 305–325.

Downey, H., Hellriegel, D., & Slocum, J. (1977). Individual characteristics as sources of perceived uncertainty variability. *Human Relations, 30,* 161–174.

Duran, R. (1983). Communicative adaptability. *Communication Quarterly, 31,* 230–236.

Dyal, J., & Dyal, R. (1981). Acculturation, stress, and coping. *International Journal of Intercultural Relations, 5,* 301–328.

Eisenberg, E. (1984). Ambiguity as a strategy in organizational communication. *Communication Monographs, 51,* 227–242.

Epstein, S. (1976). Anxiety arousal and the self-concept. In I. Sarason & C. Spielberger (Eds.), *Stress and anxiety* (Vol. 3, pp. 185–224). New York: John Wiley.

Fiske, S., & Morling, B. (1996). Stereotyping as a function of personal control motives and capacity constraints: The odd couple of power and anxiety. In R. Sorrentino & E. T. Higgins (Eds.), *Handbook of motivation and cognition* (Vol. 3, pp. 322–346). New York: Guilford.

Fiske, S., Morling, B., & Stevens, L. (1996). Controlling self and others: A theory of anxiety, mental control, and social control. *Personality and Social Psychology Bulletin, 22,* 115–123.

Florkowski, G., & Fogel, D. (1999). Expatriates adjustment and commitment. *International Journal of Human Resource Management, 10,* 783–807.

Frable, D., Blackstone, T., & Sherbaum, C. (1990). Marginal and mindful. *Journal of Personality and Social Psychology, 59,* 140–149.

French, J., & Raven, B. (1959). The basis of social power. In D. Cartwright (Ed.), *Studies in social* power (pp. 150–167). Ann Arbor, MI: Institute for Social Research.

Furnham, A., & Alibhai, N. (1985). The friendship networks of foreign students. *International Journal of Psychology, 20,* 709–722.

Furnham, A., & Bochner, S. (1982). Social difficulty in a foreign culture. In S. Bochner (Ed.), *Cultures in contact* (pp. 161–198). Oxford, UK: Pergamon.

Furnham, A., & Li, Y. (1993). The psychological adjustment of the Chinese community in Britain. *British Journal of Psychiatry, 162,* 109–113.

Gao, G., & Gudykunst, W. B. (1990). Uncertainty, anxiety, and adaptation. *International Journal of Intercultural Relations, 14,* 301–317.

Gelfand, M., Spurlock, D., Smilzek, J., & Shao, L. (2000). Culture and social prediction. *Journal of Cross-Cultural Psychology, 31,* 498–516.

Gouldner, A. (1960). The norm of reciprocity. *American Sociological Review, 25,* 161–179.

Greenland, K., & Brown, R. (1999). Categorization and intergroup anxiety in contact between British and Japanese nationals. *European Journal of Social Psychology, 29,* 503–521.

Grieve, P., & Hogg, M. (1999). Subjective uncertainty and intergroup discrimination in the minimal group situation. *Personality and Social Psychology Bulletin, 25,* 926–940.

Grove, C., & Torbiorn, I. (1985). A new conceptualization of intercultural adjustment and the goals of training. *International Journal of Intercultural Relations, 9,* 205–233.

Gudykunst, W. B. (1983). Toward a typology of stranger-host relationships. *International Journal of Intercultural Relations, 7,* 401–415.

Gudykunst, W. B. (1985a). A model of uncertainty reduction in intercultural encounters. *Journal of Language and Social Psychology, 4,* 79–98.

Gudykunst, W. B. (1985b). Normative power and conflict potential in intergroup relations. In W. B. Gudykunst, L. Stewart, & S. Ting-Toomey (Eds.), *Communication, culture, and organizational processes* (pp. 155–176). Beverly Hills, CA: Sage.

Gudykunst, W. B. (1988). Uncertainty and anxiety. In Y. Y Kim & W. B. Gudykunst (Eds.), *Theories in intercultural communication* (pp. 123–156). Newbury Park, CA: Sage.

Gudykunst, W. B. (1991). *Bridging differences: Effective intergroup communication.* Newbury Park, CA: Sage.

Gudykunst, W. B. (1993). Toward a theory of effective interpersonal and intergroup communication: An anxiety/uncertainty management perspective. In R. L. Wiseman & J. Koester (Eds.), *Intercultural communication competence* (pp. 33–71). Newbury Park, CA: Sage.

Gudykunst, W. B. (1995). Anxiety/uncertainty management (AUM) theory: Current status. In R. L. Wiseman (Ed.), *Intercultural communication theory* (pp. 8–58). Thousand Oaks, CA: Sage.

Gudykunst, W. B. (1998). Applying anxiety/uncertainty management (AUM) theory to intercultural adjustment training. *International Journal of Intercultural Relations, 22,* 227–250.

Gudykunst, W. B., Chua, E., & Gray, A. (1987). Cultural dissimilarities and uncertainty reduction processes. In M. McLaughlin (Ed.), *Communication yearbook 10* (pp. 456–469). Newbury Park, CA: Sage.

Gudykunst, W. B., & Hammer, M. R. (1988a). The influence of social identity and intimacy of interethnic relationships on uncertainty reduction processes. *Human Communication Research, 14,* 569–601.

Gudykunst, W. B., & Hammer, M. R. (1988b). Strangers and hosts. In Y. Y. Kim & W. B. Gudykunst (Eds.), *Cross-cultural adaptation* (pp. 106–139). Newbury Park, CA: Sage.

Gudykunst, W. B., & Nishida, T. (1986). Attributional confidence in low- and high-context cultures. *Human Communication Research, 12,* 525–549.

Gudykunst, W. B., Nishida, T., & Chua, E. (1987). Perceptions of social penetration in Japanese-North American dyads. *International Journal of Intercultural Relations, 11,* 171–189.

Gudykunst, W. B., & Shapiro, R. (1996). Communication in everyday interpersonal and intergroup encounters. *International Journal of Intercultural Relations, 20,* 19–45.

Gudykunst, W. B., & Ting-Toomey, S. (with Chua, E.). (1988). *Culture and interpersonal communication.* Newbury Park, CA: Sage.

Gullahorn, J. E., & Gullahorn, J. T. (1966). American students abroad. *The Annals, 368,* 43–59.

Gullahorn, J. T., & Gullahorn, J. E. (1963). An extension of the U-curve hypothesis. *Journal of Social Issues, 19*(3), 33–47.

Gurin, P., Peng, T., Lopez, G., & Nagda, B. (1999). Context, identity, and intergroup relations. In D. Prentice & D. Miller (Eds.), *Cultural divides* (pp. 133–170). New York: Russell Sage.

Gutmann, A. (1992). Introduction. In A. Gutmann (Ed.), *Multiculturalism and "the politics of recognition"* (pp. 3–24). Princeton, NJ: Princeton University Press.

Hall, E. T. (1976). *Beyond culture.* Garden City, NY: Doubleday.

Halvari, H., & Gjesme, T. (1995). Trait and state anxiety before and after performance. *Perceptual Motor Skills, 81,* 1059–1074.

Hamilton, D., Sherman, S., & Ruvolo, C. (1990). Stereotyped-based expectancies. *Journal of Social Issues, 46*(2), 35–60.

Hammer, M. R., Wiseman, R. L., Rasmussen, J., & Bruschke, J. (1998). A test of uncertainty/anxiety management theory: The intercultural adaptation context. *Communication Quarterly, 46,* 309–326.

Hawes, F., & Kealey, D. (1980). *Canadians in development.* Ottawa: Canadian International Development Agency.

Heine, S., & Lehman, D. (1997, August). *Acculturation and self-esteem change.* Paper presented at the Asian Association of Social Psychology conference, Kyoto, Japan.

Herman, S., & Schield, E. (1961). The stranger group in cross-cultural interaction. *Sociometry, 24,* 165–176.

Hofstede, G. (2001). *Culture's consequences* (2nd ed.). Thousand Oaks, CA: Sage.

Hubbert, K. N., Gudykunst, W. B., & Guerrero, S. L. (1999). Intergroup communication over time. *International Journal of Intercultural Relations, 23,* 13–46.

Huber, G., & Sorentino, R. (1996). Uncertainty in interpersonal and intergroup relations. In R. Sorrentino & E. T. Higgins (Eds.), *Handbook of motivation and cognition* (Vol. 3, pp. 591–619). New York: Guilford.

Hull, W. F. (1978). *Foreign students in the United States of America.* New York: Praeger.

Islam, M. R., & Hewstone, M. (1993). Dimensions of contact as predictors of intergroup anxiety, perceived out-group variability, and out-group attitudes. *Personality and Social Psychology Bulletin, 19,* 700–710.

Jackson, J., & Smith, E. (1999). Conceptualizing social identity. *Personality and Social Psychology Bulletin, 25,* 120–135.

Janis, I. (1958). *Psychological stress.* New York: John Wiley.

Janis, I. (1971). *Stress and frustration.* New York: Harcourt, Brace, Jovanovich.

Janis, I. (1985). Stress inoculation in health care. In A. Monat & R. Lazarus (Eds.), *Stress and coping* (pp. 330–355). New York: Columbia University Press.

Johannesen, R. L. (2001). Communication ethics. In W. B. Gudykunst (Ed.), *Communication yearbook 25* (pp. 201–235). Mahwah, NJ: Lawrence Erlbaum.

Johnston, L., & Hewstone, M. (1990). Intergroup contact. In D. Abrams & M. Hogg (Eds.), *Social identity theory* (pp. 185–210). New York: Springer.

Kennerley, H. (1990). *Managing anxiety.* New York: Oxford University Press.

Kim, H. K. (1991). Influence of language and similarity on initial intercultural attraction. In S. Ting-Toomey & F. Korzenny (Eds.), *Cross-cultural interpersonal communication* (pp. 213–229). Newbury Park, CA: Sage.

Kim, Y. Y. (1977). Communication patterns of foreign immigrants in the process of acculturation. *Human Communication Research, 4,* 66–77.

Kim, Y. Y. (2001). *Becoming intercultural: An integrative theory of communication and cross-cultural adaptation.* Thousand Oaks, CA: Sage.

Kleinberg, O., & Hull, W. (1979). *At a foreign university.* New York: Praeger.

Kosmitzki, C. (1996). The reaffirmation of cultural identity in cross-cultural encounters. *Personality and Social Psychology Bulletin, 22,* 238–248.

Kruglanski, A. (1989). *Lay epistemics and human knowledge.* New York: Plenum.

Laktos, I. (1970). Falsification and the methodology of scientific research programs. In I. Laktos & A. Musgrave (Eds.), *Criticism and the growth of knowledge* (pp. 91–196). Cambridge, UK: Cambridge University Press.

Langer, E. (1989). *Mindfulness.* Reading, MA: Addison-Wesley.

Langer, E. (1997). *The power of mindful learning*. Reading, MA: Addison-Wesley.

Laumann, E. (1993). *Bonds of pluralism*. New York: John Wiley.

Lazarus, R. (1991). *Emotion and adaptation*. New York: Oxford University Press.

Leary, M., Kowalski, R., & Bergen, D. (1988). Interpersonal information acquisition and confidence in first encounters. *Personality and Social Psychology Bulletin, 14*, 68–77.

Lee, H. O., & Boster, F. (1991). Social information for uncertainty-reduction during initial interaction. In S. Ting-Toomey & F. Korzenny (Eds.), *Cross-cultural interpersonal communication* (pp. 189–212). Newbury Park, CA: Sage.

Levine, D. (1985). *The flight from ambiguity*. Chicago: University of Chicago Press.

Lieberson, S. (1985). *Making it count: The improvement of social research and theory*. Berkeley: University of California Press.

Linville, P., Fischer, G., & Salovey, P. (1989). Perceived distribution of the characteristics of ingroup and outgroup members. *Journal of Personality and Social Psychology, 57*, 165–188.

Luhtanen, R., & Crocker, J. (1992). A collective self-esteem scale. *Personality and Social Psychology Bulletin, 18*, 302–318.

Lysgaard, S. (1955). Adjustment in a foreign society. *International Social Science Bulletin, 7*, 45–51.

Markus, H., & Kitayama, S. (1991). Culture and the self. *Psychological Review, 98*, 224–253.

Marris, P. (1996). *The politics of uncertainty*. New York: Routledge.

Martin, J., Bradford, L., & Rohrlich, B. (1995). Comparing predeparture expectations and post sojourn reports. *International Journal of Intercultural Relations, 19*, 87–110.

Miller, G. R., & Sunnafrank, M. (1982). All is for one but one is not for all. In F. Dance (Ed.), *Human communication theory* (pp. 220–242). New York: Harper & Row.

Mischel, W. (1965). Predicting the success of Peace Corps volunteers in Nigeria. *Journal of Personality and Social Psychology, 1*, 510–517.

Morris, R. (1960). *The two-way mirror*. Minneapolis: University of Minnesota Press.

Naidoo, J. (1985). A cultural perspective on the adjustment of South Asian women in Canada. In I. Lagunes & Y. Poortinga (Eds.), *From a different perspective* (pp. 76–92). Lisse, The Netherlands: Swets & Zeitlinger.

Naiman, N., Frohlich, M., Stern, H., & Todesco, A. (1978). *The good language learner*. Toronto: Ontario Institute for Studies in Education.

Nishida, H. (1985). Japanese intercultural communication competence and cross-cultural adjustment. *International Journal of Intercultural Relations, 9*, 247–269.

Noels, K., Pon, G., & Clément, R. (1996). Language, identity, and adjustment. *Journal of Language and Social Psychology, 15*, 246–264.

Norenzayan, A., Choi, I., & Nisbett, R. (2002). Cultural similarities and differences in social inference. *Personality and Social Psychology Bulletin, 28*, 109–120.

Oberg, K. (1960). Culture shock and the problems of adjustment to new cultural environments. *Practical Anthropology, 7*, 170–170.

Oguri, M., & Gudykunst, W. B. (2002). The influence of self construals and communication styles on sojourners' psychological and sociocultural adjustment. *International Journal of Intercultural Relations, 26*, 577–593.

Okazaki-Luff, K. (1991). On the adjustment of Japanese sojourners. *International Journal of Intercultural Relations, 15*, 85–102.

O'Keefe, D., & Sypher, H. (1981). Cognitive complexity measures and the relationship of cognitive complexity to communication. *Human Communication Research, 8*, 72–92.

Optow, S. (1990). Moral exclusion and injustice: An introduction. *Journal of Social Issues, 46*(1), 1–20.

Padilla, A. (1980). The role of cultural awareness and ethnic loyalty in acculturation. In A. Padilla (Ed.), *Acculturation: Theory, models, and some new findings* (pp. 47–84). Boulder, CO: Westview.

Parks, M., & Adelman, M. (1983). Communication networks and the development of romantic relationships. *Human Communication Research, 10*, 55–80.

Parrillo, V. (1980). *Strangers to these shores*. Boston: Houghton Mifflin.

Pickersgill, M., & Owen, A. (1972). Mood-states, recall and subjective comprehensibility of medical information in non-patient volunteers.

Personality and Individual Differences, 13, 1299–1305.

Pilisuk, M. (1963). Anxiety, self acceptance and open-mindedness. *Journal of Clinical Psychology, 19,* 386–391.

Pritchard, M. (1991). *On becoming responsible.* Lawrence: University of Kansas Press.

Pruitt, F. (1978). The adaptation of African students to American society. *International Journal of Intercultural Relations, 21,* 90–118.

Riezler, K. (1960). The social psychology of fear. In M. Stein, A. Vidich, & D. White (Eds.), *Identity and anxiety* (pp. 144–156). Glencoe, IL: Free Press.

Reynolds, P. (1971). *A primer in theory construction.* Indianapolis, IN: Bobbs-Merrill.

Richardson, A. (1974). *British immigrants and Australia.* Canberra: Australian National University Press.

Rogers, J., & Ward, C. (1993). Expectation-experience discrepancies and psychological adjustment during cross-cultural reentry. *International Journal of Intercultural Relations, 17,* 185–196.

Rosenberg, M. (1979). *Conceiving the self.* New York: Basic Books.

Ruben, B., & Kealey, D. (1979). Behavioral assessment of communication competency and the prediction of cross-cultural adaptation. *International Journal of Intercultural Relations, 3,* 15–47.

Sano, H. (1990). Research on social difficulties in cross-cultural adjustment. *Japanese Journal of Behavioral Therapy, 16,* 37–44.

Schlenker, B., & Leary, M. (1982). Social anxiety and social presentation. *Psychological Bulletin, 92,* 641–669.

Schneiderman, L. (1960). Repression, anxiety and the self. In M. Stein, A. Vidich, & D. White (Eds.), *Identity and anxiety* (pp. 157–165). Glencoe, IL: Free Press.

Schuetz, A. (1944). The stranger. *American Journal of Sociology, 49,* 599–607.

Scott, W., & Scott, R. (1991). Adaptation of native and immigrant Australians. *Australian Psychologist, 26,* 43–48.

Searle, W., & Ward, C. (1990). The prediction of psychological and sociocultural adjustment during cross-cultural transitions. *International Journal of Intercultural Relations, 14,* 449–464.

Selby, H., & Wood, C. (1966). Foreign students at a high pressure university. *Sociology of Education, 39,* 139–154.

Selltiz, C., Christ, J., Havel, J., & Cook, S. (1963). *Attitudes and social relations of foreign students in the United States.* Minneapolis: University of Minnesota Press.

Sewell, W., & Davidson, O. (1961). *Scandinavian students on an American campus.* Minneapolis: University of Minnesota Press.

Shah, H. (1991). Communication and cross-cultural adaptation patterns of Asian Indians. *International Journal of Intercultural Relations, 15,* 311–321.

Simmel, G. (1950). The stranger. In K. Wolff (Ed. & Trans.), *The sociology of Georg Simmel* (pp. 402–408). New York: Free Press. (Original work published 1908)

Smock, C. (1955). The influence of psychological stress on the intolerance of ambiguity. *Journal of Abnormal and Social Psychology, 50,* 177–182.

Sorrentino, R., & Short, J. (1986). Uncertainty orientation, motivation, and cognition. In R. Sorrentino & E. T. Higgins (Eds.), *Handbook of motivation and cognition* (Vol. 1, pp. 379–403). New York: Guilford.

Spitzberg, B., & Cupach, W. (1984). *Interpersonal communication competence.* Beverly Hills, CA: Sage.

Stephan, W., & Finlay, K. (1999). The role of empathy in improving intergroup relations. *Journal of Social Issues, 55,* 729–743.

Stephan, W., & Stephan, C. (1985). Intergroup anxiety. *Journal of Social Issues, 41*(3), 157–166.

Stephan, W., & Stephan, C. (1989). Antecedents to intergroup anxiety in Asian-Americans and Hispanic-Americans. *International Journal of Intercultural Relations, 13,* 203–219.

Stephan, W., & Stephan, C. (1992). Reducing intercultural anxiety through intercultural contact. *International Journal of Intercultural Relations, 16,* 89–106.

Stevens, L., & Fiske, K. (1995). Motivation and cognition in social life: A social survival perspective. *Social Cognition, 13,* 189–214.

Stone Feinstein, F., & Ward, C. (1990). Loneliness and psychological adjustment of sojourners. In D. Keats, D. Munro, & L. Mann (Eds.), *Heterogeneity in cross-cultural psychology* (pp. 537–547). Lisse, The Netherlands: Swets & Zeitlinger.

Sunnafrank, M., & Miller, G. (1981). The role of initial conversation in determining attraction to similar and dissimilar strangers. *Human Communication Research, 8,* 16–25.

Takai, J. (1991). Host contact and cross-cultural adjustment in international students in Japan. *Research in Higher Education—Daigaku Ronshu, 20,* 195–228.

Taft, R. (1966). *From stranger to citizen.* London: Tavistock.

Tajfel, H. (1978). Social categorization, social identity, and social comparisons. In H. Tajfel (Ed.), *Differentiation between groups* (pp. 61–76). London: Academic Press.

Tajfel, H. (1981). *Human categories and social groups.* Cambridge, UK: Cambridge University Press.

Taylor, C. (1992). The politics of recognition. In A. Gutmann (Ed.), *Multiculturalism and "the politics of recognition"* (pp. 25–74). Princeton, NJ: Princeton University Press.

Tesser, A. (1980). When individual dispositions and social pressures conflict: A catastrophe. *Human Relations, 33,* 393–407.

Tominaga, J., Gudykunst, W. B., & Ota, H. (2003, May). *Perceptions of effective communication in the United States and Japan.* Paper presented at the International Communication Association convention, San Diego.

Torbiorn, I. (1982). *Living abroad.* New York: John Wiley.

Torbiorn, I. (1988). Culture barriers as a social psychological construct. In Y. Y. Kim & W. B. Gudykunst (Eds.), *Cross-cultural adaptation* (pp. 168–190). Newbury Park, CA: Sage.

Triandis, H. C. (1995). *Individualism & collectivism.* Boulder, CO: Westview.

Tuan, Y.-F. (1979). *Landscapes of fear.* New York: Pantheon.

Turner, J. C., Hogg, M., Oakes, P., Reicher, S., & Wetherell, M. (1987). *Rediscovering the social group.* London: Blackwell.

Turner, J. H. (1988). *A theory of social interaction.* Palo Alto, CA: Stanford University Press.

Turner, R. H. (1987). Articulating self and social structure. In K. Yardley & T. Honess (Eds.), *Self and society* (pp. 119–132). Chichester, UK: Wiley.

Vega, W., Khoury, E., Zimmerman, R., Gil, A., & Warheit, G. (1991). Cultural conflicts and problem behaviors of Latino adolescents in home and school environments. *Journal of Community Psychology, 23,* 167–179.

Ward, C. (1999). Models and measurements of acculturation. In W. Lonner, D. Dinnel, D. Forgays, & S. Hayes (Eds.), *Merging past, present and future in cross-cultural psychology* (pp. 221–230). Lisse, The Netherlands: Swets & Zeitlinger.

Ward, C. (2001). The A, B, Cs of acculturation. In D. Matsumoto (Ed.), *The handbook of culture and psychology* (pp. 411–445). New York: Oxford University Press.

Ward, C., Bochner, S., & Furnham, A. (2001). *The psychology of culture shock.* London: Routledge.

Ward, C., & Chang, W. (1994). [Adaptation of American sojourners in Singapore]. Unpublished raw data (cited by Ward, 2001).

Ward, C., & Chang, W. (1997). "Cultural fit": A new perspective on personality and sojourner adjustment. *International Journal of Intercultural Relations, 21,* 525–533.

Ward, C., & Kennedy, A. (1992). Locus of control, mood disturbance and social difficulty during cross-cultural transitions. *International Journal of Intercultural Relations, 16,* 175–194.

Ward, C., & Kennedy, A. (1993a). Acculturation and cross-cultural adaptation of British residents in Hong Kong. *Journal of Social Psychology, 133,* 395–397.

Ward, C., & Kennedy, A. (1993b). Psychological and socio-cultural adjustment during cross-cultural transitions. *International Journal of Psychology, 28,* 129–147.

Ward, C., & Kennedy, A. (1993c). Where's the culture in cross-cultural transition? *Journal of Cross-Cultural Psychology, 24,* 221–249.

Ward, C., & Kennedy, A. (1994). Acculturation strategies, psychological adjustment, and sociocultural competence in cross-cultural transitions. *International Journal of Intercultural Relations, 18,* 329–343.

Ward, C., & Kennedy, A. (1999). The measurement of sociocultural adaptation. *International Journal of Intercultural Relations, 23,* 1–19.

Ward, C., Leong, C.-H., & Kennedy, A. (1998, April). *Self construals, stress, coping and adjustment during cross-cultural transition.* Paper presented at the Society of Australian Social Psychologists conference, Christchurch, New Zealand.

Ward, C., & Rana-Deuba, A. (1999). Acculturation and adaptation revisited. *Journal of Cross-Cultural Psychology, 30,* 372–392.

Ward, C., & Rana-Deuba, A. (2000). Home and host culture influence on sojourner adjustment. *International Journal of Intercultural Relations, 24,* 291–306.

Ward, C., & Searle, W. (1991). The impact of value discrepancies and cultural identity on psychological and socio-cultural adjustment of sojourners. *International Journal of Intercultural Relations, 15,* 209–225.

Weick, K. (1979). *The social psychology of organizing* (2nd ed.). Reading, MA: Addison-Wesley.

Weissman, D., & Furnham, A. (1987). The expectations and experiences of a sojourning temporary resident abroad. *Human Relations, 40,* 313–326.

Wibulswadi, P. (1989). The perception of group self-image and other group images among the Thai, Chinese, Thai Hmong hill-tribes and Americans in the Province of Chiang Mai. In D. Keats, D. Munro, & L. Mann (Eds.), *Heterogeneity in cross-cultural psychology* (pp. 204–209). Lisse, The Netherlands: Swets & Zeitlinger.

Wilder, D. (1993). The role of anxiety in facilitating stereotypic judgment of outgroup behavior. In D. Mackie & D. Hamilton (Eds.), *Affect, cognition, and stereotyping* (pp. 87–109). New York: Academic Press.

Wilder, D., & Shapiro, P. (1989). Effects of anxiety on impression formation in a group context. *Journal of Experimental Social Psychology, 25,* 481–499.

Witte, K. (1993). A theory of cognition and negative affect: Extending Gudykunst and Hammer's theory of uncertainty and anxiety. *International Journal of Intercultural Relations, 17,* 197–216.

Worchel, S., & Coutant, D. (1997). The tangled web of loyalty. In D. Bar-Tal & E. Staub (Eds.), *Patriotism in the life of individuals and nations* (pp. 190–210). Chicago: Nelson-Hall.

Yamaguchi, Y., & Wiseman, R. (2003). Locus of control, self construals, intercultural communication effectiveness, and the psychological health of international students in the United States. *Journal of Intercultural Communication Research, 32,* 227–246.

Ying, Y.-W., & Liese, L. (1991). Emotional well-being of Taiwan students in the U.S. *International Journal of Intercultural Relations, 15,* 345–366.

Index

Abbink, J., 389
Abe, H., 97
Abelson, R. P., 95, 96, 403, 409, 437
Abercrombie, N., 324
Abrams, D., 259
Abrams, J., 206
Accommodation, accommodation
    theory. *See* Communication
    accommodation theory (CAT)
Acculturation:
    and adjustment acculturation
        theories, 6
    defined, 380, 382, 408
    interactive acculturation model, 22–23
    networks and, *20, 21, 27nn. 19*
    See also Anxiety/uncertainty
        management (AUM) theory, of
        strangers' intercultural
        adjustment; Cultural schema
        theory; Integrative
        communication theory
Acitelli, L. K., 206
ACT* (Adaptive Control of Thoughts)
    computer model, 407–408
Adaptation, defined, 408
Adaptations in interactions, 5–6
    See also Co-cultural theory, in diverse
        contexts; Communication
        accommodation theory (CAT);
        Expectancy violations theory;
        Interaction adaptation theory
Adaptive Control of Thoughts (ACT*)
    computer model, 407–408
Adelman, M., 439
Adjustment, defined, 380
Adjustment and acculturation theories, 6
    See also Anxiety/uncertainty
        management (AUM) theory, of
        strangers' intercultural
        adjustment; Cultural schema
        theory; Integrative
        communication theory
Adler, P., 332, 391
Ady, J. C., *27n. 21,* 376
African Americans:
    co-cultural communication, 174,
        182–183, 188, 195–196
    communication and identity
        relationship, 261
    cultural identity negotiation, 268
    ethnic identity, 215, 216, 240, 265–266
    powerlessness, identity freezing, 200
    racial, ethnic identity formation, 224
African culture, self in, 258
Agency levels affecting intercultural
    relationships, 244–245, 247, 250

Aggressive accommodation
    communication style, 16, 177*table,*
    180*table,* 181
Aggressive assimilation communication
    style, 16, 176*table,* 180, 180*table*
Aggressive conflict style, 85
Aggressive separation communication
    style, 16, 177*table,* 180*table,* 181
Aging, adaptive communication
    models, 124
Alba, R., 215, 327, 336
Albert, E. M., 63
Alberts, J. K., 199, 200, 206, 265
Alexander, A., 45
Alfifi, W., 77, 212, 213
Ali, A., 390
Allen, B. J., 182
Allport, G. W., 51, 360
Amerikaner, M., 392
Ames, R., 432
Amir, Y., 326, 335
Anastasio, P., 335
Andersen, P., 77, 212, 213
Anderson, L., 378
Anderson, R., 52
Anonymity, of on-line communication,
    271–272
Antipositivism, 5*table*
Anxiety/uncertainty management
    (AUM) theory, of effective
    communication, 12–13, 27n. 14
    anxiety, 12, 287–289
    anxiety management, 23–24,
        27n. 26, 292*fig.*
    application of theory, 313
    avoidance, 288–289
    collective self-esteem, 294
    connections to strangers, 301–303
    cultural variability, 307–311
    effective communication, 305–306
    empathy, 297
    ethical issues, 303–304
    ingroup *vs.* outgroup differences,
        307–308
    minimum/maximum thresholds,
        287–288
    motivation to interact, 295–296
    reaction to strangers, 296–298
    research regarding, 311–313
    situational processes, 300–301
    social categorizations, 298–300
    strangers, 285, 288–289
    trust, 288
catastrophe theory, 289
causal process theories, 290–291
conclusions regarding, 313–314

cross-cultural variability, 283, 307–311
    cultural anxiety factors, 307
    diversity tolerance, 308
    effective communication, 310
    gender composition factor, 308
    generational attitudes, 309
    individualism *vs.* collectivism,
        307–311
    information management, 309–310
    power distance, 308–309
    stranger-ingroup relationships, 307
    theorems regarding, 311
    uncertainty avoidance, 310
cultural communication, 283
determinism, 284
effective communication, 12–13, 23–24,
    282, 289, 292*fig.,* 304–307
    mindfulness, 289–290
    research regarding, 311–313
epistemological assumptions, 284
ethical issues, 291, 292*fig.,* 303–304
human identity behavior, 283–284
human nature assumptions, 284–285
individual communication, 283
intercultural communication, 282, 285
intergroup communication, 12, 282,
    283–284, 293
    anxiety, 287, 289
    mindfulness, 304
    social categorization, 298, 329
    strangers, 285
interpersonal communication, 282,
    283–284, 293
    strangers, 285
metatheoretical assumptions, 12,
    284–285
mindfulness concept, 12–13, 24, 282,
    284, 289–290, 292*fig.*
    application of theory, 313
    effective communication,
        289–290
    negotiating meanings with
        strangers, 290, 304–305
    openness to new information, 290
    research regarding, 313
motivation to interact, 292*fig.,*
    295–296
ontological assumptions, 284
personal identity behavior,
    283–284, 293
scope of theory, 283–284
self-concepts, 292*fig.*
    collective self-esteem, 293–294
    personal identities, 293
    social identities, 293
similarity concept, 282

459

situational processes, 292*fig.*, 300–301
  cooperative tasks, 301
  ingroup power, 301
social categorizations
  group similarities/differences, 299
  positive expectations, 298–299
social identity behavior, 283–284, 293
social identity theory, 282, 294
strangers, 12, 23–24, 285
  ambiguity tolerance, 296–297,
    304–305
  anxiety management, 285, 288–289
  application of theory, 313
  attraction to, 301
  bystander behavior, 303–304
  connections with, 292*fig.*, 301–303
  dignity maintenance, 303, 304
  effective communication,
    289, 306, 307
  ethical issues, 303–304
  interdependence with, 302
  intimacy with, 302–303
  language competence, 305, 306
  mindfulness, 290, 304, 306
  moral inclusiveness, 303, 304
  motivation to interact, 295–296
  quantity, quality of contact with, 302
  reactions to, 292*fig.*, 296–298
  rigid attitudes, 296
  social categorization of, 292*fig.*,
    298–300, 305
  social identities, 293, 294
  social networks, 302, 303
  trust, 288
  uncertainty/unpredictability, 285–286
superficial causes concept, 291, 292*fig.*
theoretical research program,
  explained, 282
theory, research supporting, 311–313
theory application, 313
theory background, 282–283
theory construction, 290–291, 292*fig.*
uncertainty concept, 12, 285–287
uncertainty management, 23–24,
  27*n.* 26, 292*fig.*, 304–307
  ambiguity, 286–287
  application of theory, 313
  connections to strangers, 301–303
  cultural variability, 307–311
  effective communication, 305–306
  empathy, 297
  ethical issues, 303–304
  ingroup *vs.* outgroup differences,
    307–308
  minimum/maximum thresholds,
    285–286
  reactions to strangers, 296–298
  research regarding, 311–313
  situational processes, 300–301
  social categorizations, 298–300
  social identities, 293
  strangers, 285–286
uncertainty reduction theory (URT),
  282–283, 302
voluntarism, 284
Anxiety/uncertainty management
  (AUM) theory, of strangers'
  intercultural adjustment, 427–430
  anxiety, 422–424, 426*fig.*, 441–444
    avoidance behavior consequence
      of, 423
    diffuse anxiety, 422
    fear of negative consequences, 423
    minimum/maximum thresholds
      of, 422–423
    motivation to adjust, 423

negative information processing, 423
  powerlessness feeling, 423
anxiety management, 420
  attraction to host nationals,
    437–438, 439
  behavior (of host) expectations,
    434–435, 436
  cooperative goals with hosts, 437
  cultural identities, 428, 429–430
  cultural similarities, 435, 436
  empathy factor, 432, 433–444
  ethical interactions, 440–441
  host receptivity, 444, 445
  identity security, 428
  interdependence with host, 438, 439
  intimacy of relationship,
    438, 439–440
  knowledge of host culture, 434, 436
  language fluency, 443
  mindfullness of, 442–443
  percentage of strangers present, 437
  personal similarities, 435–436
  power distribution, 437
  quantity and quality of contact,
    438, 439
  scripts as conversation guides, 437
  self-construals, 429, 430
  self-esteem/collective self-esteem,
    428–429, 430
  social categorizations, 442
  social networks, 439, 440
  by stranger/sojourner, 421
assumptions
  anxiety, 422–424
  intercultural adjustment, 424–425
  mindfulness, 425
  strangers, 420–421
  theoretical assumptions, 420–425,
    426*fig.*
  uncertainty, 421–422
causal process theories, 426–427
conclusions regarding, 449–450
cross-cultural variability
  cultural uncertainty avoidance
    variable, 447
  individualism-collectivism variable,
    445–446
  masculinity-femininity variable,
    446, 447
  power distance variable, 446–447
  ritualistic behavior, 446
  tolerance for diversity, 446
effective communication, 420
ethical issues, 426*fig.*, 427, 440–441
intercultural adjustment, 420,
  424–425, 426*fig.*, 441–444
  anxiety, uncertainty threshold
    limits, 424
  communication competence, 424
  culture shock coping, 424
  ethical interactions, 440–441
  identity security, 428
  individualism-collectivism
    variability, 445–446
  interdependence with host, 438, 439
  intimacy of relationship, 438,
    439–440
  psychological *vs.* sociocultural
    adjustment, 424–425
  satisfaction of living in host
    culture, 424
  self-concepts, 426*fig.*, 427–430
  self-construals, 429, 430
  self-esteem/collective self-esteem,
    428–429
  social networks, 439, 440

intercultural adjustment, host nationals
  adaptability of behavior
    (stranger's), 432–433, 434
  ambiguity tolerance, 432, 433
  attitudes toward strangers, 420
  attraction to host nationals,
    437–438, 439
  avoid diffuse anxiety, 430–431
  behavior (of host) expectations,
    434–435, 436
  certainty *vs.* uncertainty oriented
    strangers, 432
  conditions in, 444–445
  conformity pressure, pluralistic
    ideology, 444, 445
  connections to, 426*fig.*, 437–440
  cooperative goals with hosts, 437
  cultural similarities, 435, 436
  discrimination toward strangers,
    444, 445
  ethical interactions with, 426*fig.*,
    427, 440–441
  host receptivity, 444, 445
  information management, 445
  knowledge of host culture, 434, 436
  low- *vs.* high-context
    communication style, 433
  motivation to interact with,
    426*fig.*, 430–431
  percentage of strangers present, 437
  personal similarities, 435–436
  power distribution, 437
  quantity and quality of contact,
    438, 439
  reaction to, 426*fig.*, 431–434
  rigid attitudes toward, 432, 433
  scripts as conversation guides,
    436–437
  self-concept confirmation, 430–431
  sense of group inclusion, 430–431
  sense of predictability, 430–431
  social categorizations of, 426*fig.*,
    427–248, 434–436
  social skills development, 433
mindfulness, 426*fig.*, 441–444
  of anxiety, uncertainty
    management, 442–443
  communication behavior
    awareness, 425
  of hosts' perspectives, 425
  of interaction processes, 443
  language fluency, 442, 443
  learning host behavior, culture,
    440–441, 443
  open to new information, 425
  perception of differences, 425
  social categorizations, 442
practical applications, 448–449
self-construals, 420
situational processes, 426*fig.*, 436–437
social support, 420
strangers/sojourners
  ambiguity of new situation, 421
  near *vs.* far quality, 420–421
  vs. immigrants, 420
theorems, 447–448
theory construction, 426–427
uncertainty, 421–422, 426*fig.*, 441–444
  ambiguity, benefits of, 422
  minimum/maximum thresholds
    of, 422
  predicting host behavior, 421, 433
uncertainty management, 420
  attraction to host nationals,
    437–438, 439
  cognitive complexity, 431

cultural identities, 428, 429–430
cultural individualism-
    collectivism, 445
empathy factor, 432, 433–434
identity security, 428
intimacy of relationship, 438, 439
knowledge of host culture, 434, 436
language fluency, 443
mindfulness of, 442–443
personal similarities, 435–436
quantity and quality of contact,
    438, 439
self-construals, 429, 430
self-esteem/collective self-esteem,
    428–429, 430
by stranger/sojourner, 421
tolerance for diversity, 446
uncertainty reduction theory (URT),
    419–420
Apache culture, 286
Applegate, J., 3, 6, 26n. 5, 184
Applegate, L., 330
Appropriateness:
    effective communication, 19, 264
    of social communication, 98, 99–102
Approval-seeking strategies, 99
Archuleta, R., 326
Ardener, S., 16
Argyle, M., 103, 300, 437
Arkin, R. M., 99
Armstrong, T., 340
Asante, M. K., 178, 258
Asian Americans:
    cross-cultural adaptation, 377
    ethnic identity, 267
    ethnic markers, 389
    racial, ethnic identity formation, 224
Asian culture, self in, 258
Assertive accommodation
    communication style, 16, 177table,
    180–181, 180table, 182
Assertive assimilation communication style,
    16, 176table, 179, 180table, 182
Assertive separation communication
    style, 16, 177table, 180table, 181
Assimilation:
    defined, 380, 408
    deviance and alienation, 24
    identity negotiation theory goal, 223,
        224, 224fig.
    in interethnic relations, 324
Association and dissociation, 13–14
    assumptions, 328–329
    the behavior, 329–331
        association-dissociation continuum,
            axioms, 330–331
        associative behavior,
            elements of, 330
        attribution error, 329–330
        categorization of information, 329
        consonance-dissonance, 330,
            330table
        dissociative behavior,
            elements of, 329–330
        encoding and decoding, 329
        individuation-categorization, 330,
            330table
    case studies, 341–342
    the communicator, 331–332, 341table
        identity inclusivity (exclusivity), 332
        identity security (insecurity), 332–333
        psychological attributes, 332
        social identity theory, 332
        theorems, 333–334
    conceptual grounding, 327–328
    the environment, 336–337, 341table

critical mass, 338
environmental stress, 339
fraternalistic relative deprivation,
    336–337
institutional equity (inequity),
    337–338
political mobilization, 338
political self-assertion, 338
relative ingroup strength, 338–339
socioeconomic stratification, 337
systemic status differential,
    337–338
theorems, 339–340
interethnic communication
    assumptions, 328–329
    contextual element of, 327, 329fig.
    defined, 327
    matrix, 328, 329fig.
the problem
    assimilationism-pluralism
        continuum, 324, 325
    association and dissociation
        focus, 325
    classical liberalism, 323–325
    individual vs. group identity, 323–324
    integrationism, 325
    interdisciplinary integration, 326
    interethnic communication,
        defined, 327
    interethnic identity, 323
    macro-level intergroup
        phenomena, 326
    procedural equality, 324
    psychological factors, 326
    relativistic world view, 324
    separatism, extremism, 324–325
    status equality of all groups, 324
    universalism, 324
the situation, 341table
    common ingroup identity, 335
    contact hypothesis, 335
    crisscrossing identities, 335
    ethnic proximity (distance), 334
    extrinsic ethnic markers, 334
    interpersonal and cooperative
        orientation, 335
    intrinsic ethnic markers, 334
    personal network integration,
        335–336
    shared (separate) goal structure,
        334–335
    superordinate organization, 335
    task-oriented and competitive
        orientation, 335
    theorems, 336
    tie strength, 335
    social action implications, 343
    synthesis, 340–341
Attkinson, D., 224
Attribution theory, 123–124, 136,
    141–142
Augoustinos, M., 405, 406
Autonomy-connection theme, identity
    negotiation theory, 218, 219,
    219table, 220–221, 225
Avoiding conflict style, 10, 80, 85

Babiker, I., 435
Bachman, B, 335, 360, 361
Bachman, J. G., 265
Bales, R. F., 355
Ball-Rokeach, S., 421
Banton, M., 260
Barber, B. R., 48
Barge, J. K., 37
Barkema, H. G., 351

Barker, J. R., 351
Barnes, S. B., 271
Barnett, G. A., 11–12
Barraclough, R., 308, 312
Barsade, S. G., 364, 365
Basu, A., 432
Bateson, G., 327, 328, 379
Bator, R., 266
Baumeister, R. F., 386, 432
Bavelas, J., 422
Baxter, L. A., 60, 204, 220
Beard, Charles Austin, 375
Beauvais, F., 264
Beavin, J., 327, 379, 402
Bell, R., 432
Benet-Martinez, V., 6
Bennett, J., 216, 223
Bennett, J. M., 110
Bennett, M., 223
Bennett, S., 224
Benson, T., 37
Bergen, D., 437
Berger, C. R., 12, 26, 96, 257, 281,
    286, 300, 301, 302, 314, 401, 402,
    419, 421, 437, 438
Berger, J., 282
Berger, P. L., 36, 48
BerGudy, 421
Berkowitz, L., 333
Berkowitz, S., 379
Bernstein, B., 212
Berry, J., 223, 224fig.
Berry, J. W., 107, 376, 444
Berscheid, E., 435
Bertalanffy, L., 327, 378
Bewes, T., 259
Bicultural identity, 223–224, 224fig.
Bieike, D. R., 104
Biernot, M., 422, 437
Billig, M., 330
Bilmes, J., 63, 64
Bitzer, L. F., 51
Bixler, N., 55
Black, A., 422
Black, J. B., 411, 434
Blackfeet Indians speech community
    research, 56–57, 62
Blackstone, T., 441
Blake, R. R., 80
Blalock, H. M., Jr., 380, 409, 426
Blau, P., 338, 387
Blum-Kulka, S., 96, 97, 99
Bochner, S., 222, 383, 390, 401, 420,
    424, 428, 433, 434, 435, 439
Body talk concept, 270
Boekestijn, C., 387, 392
Bognar, N., 382
Bohrer, A., 333
Bolton-Oetzel, K. D., 356, 358
Bond, M., 8, 9, 81, 103, 312
Bond, M. H., 105, 107, 281, 307, 308,
    312, 363
Bond, R. N., 269
Boniecki, K., 422, 437
Bonilla-Silva, E., 326
Borker, R., 213
Bornman, E., 240
Boski, P., 223
Boster, F., 421
Boulding, K., 382
Boundaries:
    boundary-ambiguity syndromes, 391
    See also Identity negotiation theory
Boundary crossing, intercultural,
    216–223
Bourhis, R., 22–23, 326, 333, 376, 388

Bourhis, R. Y., 183
Bower, G. H., 411
Bradac, J. J., 14, 187, 300, 402, 437
Bradford, L., 245, 435
Braithwaite, C., 59, 364
Branham, R. J., 51
Braun, V., 378, 388
Breckler, S. J., 107
Bresnahan, M., 100, 101, 106, 107,
	108, 109, 110, 111, 354, 355
Bresnahan, M. J., 108
Breton, R., 338
Brewer, M., 220, 330, 333, 335, 338
Brewer, M. B., 108, 110, 430
Bridging Differences (Gudykunst), 282
Britt, T., 422, 437
Broski, P., 224fig.
Brown, K., 333, 422, 437
Brown, P., 77, 79, 81, 96, 97, 98, 99, 198
Brown, R., 65
Brown, W. J., 108, 110, 111
Bruschke, J., 24, 434, 438
Buck, R., 386
Budner, S., 422, 432
Bullis, C., 182
Burgoon, J. K., 8, 27n. 12, 401, 461
Burke, K., 382
Burke, P. J., 197, 198, 262, 265, 269
Burks, D. M., 187
Burrell, G., 4
Bush, R., 229
Buss, D. M., 379
Buzzannell, P. M., 182
Byrne, D., 447

Cady, S. H., 361
Cahn, D., 228
Cai, D., 108
Cai, D. A., 83
Calabrese, R., 12, 282, 286, 301, 302,
	314, 401, 419, 421, 438
Canary, D. J., 97, 99
Cappella, J. N., 96, 99
Carbaugh, D., 51, 56, 58, 59, 62, 63, 262
Cargile, A., 14, 26, 326, 330
Carlson, R. E., 187
Carson-Stern, E., 183, 187
Cartledge, P., 259
Carver, C. S., 269
Catastrophe theory, 289
Causal process theories, 290–291
Cenoz, J., 339
Chaffee, J., 188
Chang, W. C., 382, 429, 444
Chatman, J. A., 364, 365
Chau, 438
Chayko, M., 272
Chen, G. M., 83, 241
Chen, V., 4, 6–7, 94, 187, 327
Chesler, M., 326, 335
Cheung, Y. W., 264, 265
Chi, M. T. H., 403, 405, 406
Childers, P. G., 96
Chinese culture:
	communication expectancies, 152
	communication valence, 157–158
	communication violations, interpersonal
		relationship factor, 159
	non-verbal cues, 159
Chiu, C. Y., 6
Choi, J. W., 390
Choi, S. C., 25, 112, 309
Chovil, N., 422
Christ, J. R., 389, 438
Chua, E., 302, 311–312, 435, 438, 439
Chung, L. C., 224, 225, 227

Cissna, K. N., 52, 227
Civil Rights Health (CRH) Project,
	184–185
Clark, H., 435
Clarke, L. H., 270
Clarke, S., 338, 388
Classic liberalism, 323–325
Classism focus:
	cultural identification, 243, 245–246,
		252, 254
Clune, M. K., 52
CMC (computer mediated
	communication), 271
CMM. See Coordinated management of
	meaning (CMM), role of culture in
Co-cultural theory, in diverse contexts:
	abilities to enact practices, 16, 178
	accommodation goals, 16, 178, 223
	African Americans, 174, 182–183, 188
	aggressive accommodation
		communication style, 16,
		177table, 180table, 181
	aggressive assimilation
		communication style, 16,
		176table, 180, 180table
	aggressive separation communication
		style, 16, 177table, 180table, 181
	assertive accommodation
		communication style, 16,
		177table, 180–181, 180table, 182
	assertive assimilation communication
		style, 16, 176table, 179,
		180table, 182
	assertive separation communication
		style, 16, 177table, 180table, 181
	assimilation goals, 16, 175, 223
	Civil Rights Health Project, 184–185
	classism status, 174, 175, 183
	co-cultural factors, 175, 178, 186–187
	co-cultural identity, complications of,
		187–189
	co-cultural practices, 175,
		176–177table, 180table, 185–186
	Co-Cultural Theory Scales, 186
	communication accommodation
		theory, 187
	communication approach, 16,
		179–181, 180table, 184–185, 186
	conclusions regarding, 189
	defiant discourse behavior, 185–186
	disabled people, 174, 183
	dominant communication structures,
		174, 185–186
	dominant group members, 16, 173–174
	feminist sociology, 182, 185
	field of experience factors, 16, 178
	first generation college student
		research, 188
	future research directions, 185–189
	gays/lesbians/bisexuals, 174, 175,
		183, 187
	Israeli community theater research, 183
	marginalization, 16, 173–174, 175
	muted group theory, 16, 174, 185, 187
	narrative paradigm, 187
	Native Hawaiian research, 185
	nonassertive accommodation
		communication style, 16,
		176table, 180, 180table
	nonassertive assimilation
		communication style,
		16, 176table, 179, 180table, 182
	nonassertive separation
		communication style,
		16, 177table, 180table, 181
	organization research, 182–183

people of color, 174, 175, 182
perceived costs and rewards, 16, 178
phenomenology, 185, 187
practical applications, 183–184
preferred outcome, 175, 178,
	180table, 184, 186
rap therapy, 184
research literature regarding, 181–183
rhetorical sensitivity theory, 187
separation goals, 16, 178, 223
situational context factors, 16, 178
social hierarchies, 16, 174
standpoint theory, 16, 174,
	182–183, 185, 187
theoretical connections/
	intersections, 187
theory overview, 173–175
underrepresented group members,
	16, 174
women, 174, 175, 182–183
Co-Cultural Theory Scales (C-CTS), 186
Cocroft, B., 83
Coelho, G., 431
Cognitive differentiation, 330
Cohen, B., 4
Cole, M., 74, 79
Coleman, J., 63
Collective self-esteem, of identity
	security-insecurity, 333
	anxiety/uncertainty management,
		293–294, 429–429, 430
	low- vs. high-context communication
		style, 433
	person- vs. group-based
		information, 445
	self-construal, 429
Collectivism dimension, of cultural
	variability:
	in African cultures, 258
	approval seeking behavior, 99
	in Asian cultures, 258
	autonomy-connection issue, 221
	communication accommodation
		theory, 132, 134
	communication expectancies, 151–152
	communication violations, interpersonal
		relationship factor, 159
	conversational constraints,
		10, 26n. 11, 102–103
	cultural-level assumptions, 82–84,
		83fig., 84fig.
	cultural-level propositions, 84–85
	effective communication, 310–311
	ethnic value content, 216
	expectancy valence, 153
	expectancy violations, 11, 154
	face content domains, 81–82
	face orientation, 10, 74–75
	face-threatening process, 77
	facework interaction strategies, 77–80
	information management, 309–310
	ingroup vs. outgroup conflict, 87–88,
		307–308
	ingroup vs. outgroup emotion
		expression, 153
	intercultural workgroup communication,
		354–355, 362–363
	multicultural identity, 108–110
	positional family systems, 213
	process orientation, 226
	self-construals, 85–86
		independent and interdependent,
			354–355, 363
		intracultural variability, 107–108,
			111–112, 113n. 2
		social vs. individual identity, 212

strangers' linguistic convergence, 297
truthtelling, 165
value contents, 215
Collier, M. J., 17, 27n. 17, 81, 94, 196,
    197, 198, 199, 200, 206, 222, 236,
    240, 241, 255, 258, 261, 262, 263,
    266, 267, 461
Collins, R. L., 264
Communal identity layer, CTI, 19, 262,
    263, 264, 266–267, 271
Communication accommodation theory
    (CAT), 257
  accent mobility, 14
  accommodation, reception of,
      128–130, 141–143
  accommodative orientation, 15, 137
  accommodative orientation,
      maintenance strategy, 123
  accommodative strategies, 137–138,
      140–141
  addressee focus, 14
  attribution theory, 123–124, 136,
      141–142
  attuning strategies, 134, 140
  behavior tactics evaluation, 15, 141–143
  communicative predicament model of
      aging, 124
  convergence strategy, 14, 123, 124,
      125–126
    evaluation of, 128–130, 129table
  divergence/maintenance strategy, 124,
      125–126
    evaluation of, 128–130, 129table
  ELIT (ethnolinguistic identity theory),
      14, 132
  ethnic intergroup communication, 124
  ethnolinguistic identity theory, 14
  future intentions, 15, 141–143
  goals and addressee focus, 15
  historical perspective on, 124–125,
      124table
  impression management, 130
  individualism/collectivism variable,
      132, 134
  ingroup vs. outgroup concept, 132, 134
  initial orientations, 15, 133fig.,
      135fig., 138–139
  intercultural communication, 123,
      124, 132, 134
  interethnic relationships, 326
  intergender communication,
      124, 130, 141
  intergenerational communication,
      14, 124, 130, 132, 136, 309
  intergroup communication theory,
      135–136, 135fig.
  intergroup communication theory,
      propositions, 138–143
  intergroup factors, 2, 15, 123, 124,
      127–128, 132, 133fig., 135–136,
      135fig., 143–144nn. 1
  interpersonal variables, 133fig., 134,
      135, 135fig., 138–139
  intrapersonal factors, 2, 15, 123,
      127–128, 143–144nn. 1
  labeling and attributions, 15
  linguistic strategies, 14
  macro contextual factors, 14
  nonaccommodation strategies, 141, 142
  objective vs. subjective linguistic
      accommodation, 137
  over-accommodation strategies, 141, 142
  perceived relationships between
      groups, 15
  personal vs. social identities, 136–137
  power factors, 14

psychological accommodation, 132,
    133fig., 135fig., 139–140
  from SAT to, 130, 131table
  second-language acquisition, 124
  self-presentation, 130
  social identity theory, 123, 127–128,
      132, 136
  social norms or rules, 138
  sociohistorical context of, 15, 132,
      133fig., 135, 135fig., 136
  sociolinguistic strategies, 15, 128,
      132, 136
  sociopsychological states, 15, 123,
      127, 132, 133fig., 135fig.
  See also Speech accommodation
      theory (SAT)
Communication incorporating culture:
    constructivist theory, 6
  coordinated management of
      meaning, 6–7
  cultural communication, 7
  See also Coordinated management of
      meaning (CMM), role of culture
      in; Speech codes theory
Communication management effects
    model of successful aging, 124
Communication theory of identity
    (CTI), 27n. 17
  affective, cognitive, behavioral,
      spiritual focus, 19, 263
  African American research focus, 261,
      265–266, 268
  appropriate, effective communication,
      19, 264
  coding, symbols, labels, 19, 263, 265
  communal identity layer, 19, 262,
      263, 264, 266–267, 271
  communication and identity, 261–262
  conclusions regarding, 273–274
  content and relationship focus, 19, 263
  cultural contracts theory, 267–268
  cultural identity, negotiation of,
      267–268
  development of, 261–262
  dialectical theory, 19
  enactment identity layer, 19, 261, 262,
      263, 264, 266–267, 269, 270, 271
  endurance, changes, 19, 263, 266
  ethnic labeling and ethnicity, 261,
      264–266
  expectation and motivation source,
      19, 264
  groups and networks, identities from,
      19, 264, 271–272
  health/illness identity, CTI applied to,
      269–271
  hierarchically ordered meanings, 19, 264
  identity as relational and discursive,
      260, 264, 266–267
  identity from role behaviors, 19
  identity from social categorization,
      19, 259–260, 262
  identity from social role behaviors,
      19, 260, 262
  identity gaps, 268–269
  identity negotiation, 3, 266–267,
      297nn. 2
  identity negotiation, cultural, 267–268
  identity theory, 259, 260–261,
      262, 274n. 2
  individual, social, communal
      properties, 19, 263, 266
  interdisciplinary nature of
      communication, 257–259
  interpenetration among identity
      layers, 268–269

Jewish identity, 266–267
  meanings ascribed to self by others, 19
  Mexican American research focus,
      261, 266
  modernism, postmodernism influence
      on, 259, 262, 266–267, 271–272
  personal identity layer, 19, 262, 263,
      264, 266–267, 269, 270
  propositions of CTI, 263–264
  reality interpretation, 19
  relational identity layer, 19, 262, 263,
      264, 266–268, 269, 270, 271–272
  self in African cultures, 258
  self in Asian cultures, 258
  self in Greek cultures, 258–259
  semantic properties, 19
  social identity theory, 259–260, 262
  subjective vs. ascribed meanings,
      19, 263
  symbolic meaning, 262, 263, 264,
      265, 267, 268
  technology, CTI applied to, 271–273
Communicative conduct, 56–57
  constituting meanings of, 62
  distinctive codes of, 56–57, 58–59, 61
  intelligibility, prudence and morality
      of, 63–64
  multiple speech codes, 59–61
  persons linked in social relations, 61
  social codes, 63–64, 66
  terms, rules, premises of, 62–63
Communicative predicament model of
    aging, 124
Computer mediated communication
    (CMC), 271
Conflict face-negotiation theory (FNT), 9
  aggressive conflict style, 85
  autonomy face content domain, 81
  avoiding conflict style, 10, 80, 85
  avoiding facework interaction
      strategy, 78, 84
  betrayal issue, 88
  collectivistic cultures, 9–10, 73, 74–75
  communal norm, 87
  competence face content domain, 81
  compromising conflict style, 80, 85
  conflict as face-negotiation process, 9
  conflict communication styles, 74,
      80–81
  content conflict goals, 72
  cultural-level assumptions, 82–84,
      83fig., 84fig.
  cultural-level propositions, 84–85
  cultural value dimensions, 73, 74–76
  culture, shared identity and
      community, 71–72
  dominating/competing conflict styles,
      10, 80
  dominating facework interaction
      strategy, 78, 84–85
  emotional conflict style, 81, 85
  equity norm, 87
  face concept, defined, 73
  face concerns and intercultural
      conflicts, 72–73
  face content domains, 74, 81–82
  face movements, face moves' patterns,
      74, 76–77, 77fig.
  face movements, research, 89–90
  face orientations, 73, 74–76
  face-threatening process (FTP), 76
  facework, defined, 73
  facework emotions research, 88–89
  facework interaction strategies,
      74, 77–80
  facework situational research, 89

forgiveness issue, 88
high-premium conflicts, 87
identity conflict goals, 72–73
inclusion face content domain, 81
individual-level assumptions, 85–86
individual-level propositions, 86
individualistic cultures, 9–10, 10, 73, 74–75
ingroups, 87, 132, 134
integrating/collaborative conflict style, 80, 85
integrating facework interaction strategy, 78, 84
intercultural conflict, 72
intercultural conflict, face concerns and, 72–73
lien (moral) face content domain, 82
low to moderate conflict, 87
mien-tzu (social image) face content domain, 82
moral face content domain, 81–82
mutual-face conflict style, 83, 83*fig.*, 84*fig.*
mutual-face dimension, 74, 76–77, 77*fig.*
mutual-face maintenance concerns, 84
obliging conflict style, 10, 80, 85
orientation of face, 74
other-face conflict style, 83, 83*fig.*, 84*fig.*
other-face dimension, 74, 76–77, 77*fig.*
other-face maintenance concerns, 84
outgroups, 87, 132, 134
passive-aggressive conflict style, 81
positive dispositional facework account, 80
power distance cultures, 10, 73, 75–76
preventive facework strategy, 79
relational and situational assumptions, 86–87
relational and situational propositions, 87–88
relational conflict goals, 72
relational conflict resolution mode, 10
reliability face content domain, 81
respect issue, 88
restorative facework strategy, 79–80
self-construal cultural variability dimension, 85–86
self-face conflict style, 83, 83*fig.*, 84*fig.*
self-face dimension, 74, 76–77, 77*fig.*
self-face maintenance concerns, 84
situational facework account, 80
social self-worth, 9
status face content domain, 81
substantive conflict resolution modes, 10
theory, defined, 71
theory assumptions, 73–74
third-party consultation conflict style, 81
trust issue, 88
See also Identity management theory (IMT)
Confucianism, 258
Consistency-change theme, identity negotiation theory, 218, 219, 219*table*, 221–222, 225
Constructivist theory, on intercultural communication:
complex message behavior, 6
culture defines logic of communication, 6
person centered communication, 6
personal construct theory and, 6
Contarello, A., 103
Content intercultural conflict goals, 72

Context communication, of cultural variability, 8, 26*n. 10*
See also Association and dissociation
Contextual age concept, 270
Convergence model of communication, 11–12, 27*n. 13*
Convergence strategy, of communication accommodation theory, 14, 123, 124, 125–126
evaluation of, 128–130, 129*table*
Conversational constraints theory (CCT), 8, 10–11, 26*n. 11*, 102–103
See also Culture-based conversational constraints theory (CCT)
Cook, S. W., 326, 389, 438
Cook, W., 387
Cook-Gumperz, J., 332
Cooley, C. H., 260, 269
Cooper, G., 333
Cooperrider, D., 52
Coordinated management of meaning (CMM), role of culture in:
appreciative inquiry, 51
Central and North America case example, 37–38, 39, 41, 42*table*, 47, 48
CMM, making better social worlds, 49–51
CMM as interpretive theory, 37, 39–43, 41*table*, 42*table*
CMM as practical theory, 37, 45–48, 47*fig.*, 48*fig.*
CMM's critical edge, 37, 43–45, 44*fig.*
coevolving structures and actions, 7
coherence and mystery, 50
communication as performance *vs.* reference, 39
communication study history, 2, 35–37, 53*nn. 1*
conjoint action of multiple persons, 43
contextual and prefigurative forces, 41–42
contextual reconstruction, 51
coordination, 50
daisy communication model, 46–47, 47*fig.*, 50
deontic logic philosophical concept, 40, 42, 43, 47, 48
diversity, 7
family violence application, 46
fighting *vs.* communication, 48–49
goals of, 6
hierarchy of embedded contexts, 39–40, 41–42, 42*table*, 43, 46
idiosyncratic and social communication, 6–7
imperfection of communication, 7
LUUTT communication model, 47–48, 48*fig.*
management of meaning, 50
moral orders, 7
New Religious Right *vs.* secular humanists, American politics, 45
Palestinian *intifada* example, 44–45
pluralism, effects of, 36
poyphonic characteristic, 7
research activity of social practice, 7
"rules" focus, 7
serpentine model, 43–44, 44*fig.*, 46, 50
speech codes concept, 39
study what works, 52
terrorism, two moralities of, 38–39
transformative communication skills, 52
value commitments, 50–51

World Trade Center bombing case example, 38–39, 40–41, 41*table*, 43–44, 44*fig.*, 46–47, 47*fig.*, 50, 51
zone of proximal development, concept, 49–50
Coping:
with culture shock, 424
defined, 380
Corea, A., 326
Cort, D., 432
Coupland, J., 14
Coupland, N., 14, 110
Coutant, D., 429
Coutu, L. M., 4, 6, 60, 65, 461
Covarrubias, P., 4, 6, 59, 60, 65, 461
Cox, J., 435
Cox, T. H., 351, 352, 357, 358, 363
Cozarelli, C., 429
Crawley, R., 268
CRH (Civil Rights Health) Project, 184–185
Crisp, R., 330
Critelli, J., 362, 364
Crocker, J., 333, 402, 403, 405, 406, 429, 441
Cronen, V., 4, 6–7, 37, 39, 45, 94, 327
Cross, S., 429, 443
Cross, W., Jr., 223, 224
Cross-cultural adaptation, 21–22
defined, 380
See also Integrative communication theory
Cross-cultural variability in communication, 5, 26*n. 7*
conversational constraints theory, 8, 10–11
expectancy violation theory, 8, 11
face-negotiation theory, 7, 9–10
Hofstede's dimensions of, 8–9
individualism-collectivism dimension, 8, 10
low-high context communication, 8, 26*n. 10*
low-high power distance dimension, 9
low-high uncertainty avoidance dimension, 9
masculinity-femininity dimension, 9, 10–11
See also Anxiety/uncertainty management (AUM) theory, of effective communication; Anxiety/uncertainty management (AUM) theory, of strangers' intercultural adjustment; Conflict face-negotiation theory; Culture-based conversational constraints theory
CTI. *See* Communication theory of identity
Cui, G., 387
Cultural boundaries. *See* Identity negotiation theory
Cultural convergence theory, 11–12, 27*n. 13*
Cultural identity:
defined, 197, 214
identity management theory, 17, 195–196, 197, 199
salience, 215, 333
value content, 214–215
See also Communication theory of identity (CTI); Identity management theory (IMT); Identity negotiation theory; Theorizing cultural identification

Cultural schema theory, 24–25
  acculturation, 401
    defined, 408
  adaptation, defined, 408
  assimilation, defined, 408
  conclusions regarding, 412–413
  cross-cultural adaptation, 401, 402, 408
  cultural schemas
    cognitive activity of, 404–405
    context schemas, 406, 407–408, 412
    declarative memory, 407–408
    development of, 409–410
    emotion schemas, 406–407
    fact-and-concept schemas, 405
    function of, 407–408
    hierarchy organization of, 410
    homeostasis, self-regulation, 412
    modification of, 412
    person schemas, 405–406, 409, 410
    primary social interaction (PSI)
        schemas, 405–407, 411–412
    primary social interaction
        schemas, 410
    procedural knowledge, 407–408
    procedural schemas, 406, 407–408,
        410, 413n. 1
    role schemas, 406, 410
    schema- vs. data-driven functions,
        410–412
    self schemas, 406
    for social interactions, 403–404
    strategy schemas, 406, 407–408
  cultural schemas, defined, 402–403
  intercultural communication
      competence, 401, 402
  personal schemas, 402
  psychological reactions, 401
  uncertainty reduction, 401
  universal schemas, 402
  values and value orientations, 401
  verbal and nonverbal interactions, 401
Cultural variability, Hofstede's
    dimensions of, 8–9, 27n. 10
Culture, defined, 71–72
Culture-based conversational constraints
    theory (CCT):
  appropriateness constraint, 97–98,
      99–102
  communicative strategy selection
      differences, 10
  concern for avoiding negative evaluation,
      99, 100–101, 100fig., 102, 107
  concern for clarity, 10, 27n. 11, 96,
      98, 100fig., 101, 102, 103, 107
  concern for effectiveness, 97–98,
      99–102, 100fig., 113n. 1
  concern for nonimposition, 98–99,
      100fig., 101, 102, 103
  concern for other's feelings, 97, 99,
      100fig., 101, 102, 107
  conflict management strategies, 103
  constraints, explained, 93
  cultural contexts, 104–105
  cultural variability in perceived
      importance of, 102–103, 112
  culture and individual-level analyses
      of, 105–106
  implicit theories of requesting, 101–102
  individualism vs. collectivism
      contexts, 10, 103–105, 106, 112
  interpersonal communication, goals
      approach to, 95–97, 111
    global constraint goals, 96
    practical goals, 96
  interpersonal communication, norms-
      based explanations of, 94–95

intracultural variability, 106–108,
    109table, 113n. 2
  limitations regarding, 112–113
  multicultural identity, 108–110
  practical implications of, 110–111
  relational vs. clarity constraints, 10,
      27n. 11
  relationship- vs. task-orientation, 103
  research regarding, 112–113
  self-concepts mediating role, 104–105
  self-construals, 105, 106, 108–110
  self-construals, intracultural
      variability, 107–108, 109table,
      111–112, 113n. 2
  self-construals, multicultural identity,
      108–110
  selfways, sociocultural participation, 105
  social-related constraints, 10
  summary regarding, 111–112
  task-oriented constraints, 10
Cupach, W., 17–18, 26, 27n.16, 79,
    195–197, 199, 201, 203–204, 206,
    207n. 1, 208, 228, 424, 461
Cushman, D., 7
Cutler, M., 262, 266, 267

Daisy communication model, of
    coordinated management of
    meaning, 46–47, 47fig., 50
D'Amico, C., 351
Dasen, P. R., 107
David, H., 390, 391
David, K., 435
David, P., 333
Davis, D., 264
de Soete, G., 333
De Vos, G. A., 327, 333, 392
DeCarlo, A., 183
Decategorization, 330
Deemer, H. N., 270
Deetz, S., 187, 356
Deference politeness, conversational
    constraint, 98–99
DeGroot, G., 326
Delia, J., 6
Demerath, L., 431
Deontic logic philosophical concept,
    coordinated management of
    meaning, 40, 42, 43, 47, 48
Determinism, 5table
Detweiler, R., 326, 330
Deutchberger, P., 198
Deutsch, M., 359
Devine, P., 435, 441
DiBenedetto, T., 175
Dijker, A., 436
Dillard, J. P., 97
Disabled people:
  co-cultural communication, 174, 183
  identity management, 196
Dissociation. See Association and
    dissociation
Divergence/maintenance strategy, of
    communication accommodation
    theory, 124, 125–126
  evaluation of, 128–130, 129table
Dixon, L., 336, 377, 391
Dixon, L. D., 183, 185, 186, 187
Doi, T., 25
Domenici, K., 50, 229
Douglas, W., 98
Dovidio, J., 335, 360, 361
Downey, H., 431
Dubin, R., 27n. 15, 379, 380
Dubos, R., 384
Duck, S., 204

Dugan, S., 74
Duncan, N., 338
Dunne, J., 235
Duran, R., 432
Duster, T., 188
Duty, D. M., 325, 336, 339
Dyal, J., 391, 428, 439, 444
Dyal, R., 391, 428, 439, 444

Eadie, W. F., 187
Earley, P. C., 81, 364
Ebesu Hubbard, A. S., 462
Edwards, A., 183, 187
Edwards, J., 216
Effective communication and
    decisions, 6, 13
  intercultural conversations, 99–102,
      113n. 1
  See also Anxiety/uncertainty
      management (AUM) theory, of
      effective communication;
      Association and dissociation;
      Intercultural workgroup
      communication theory
Effective decision making theory, 13
Eggert, L. I., 336
Ego-strength of identity security, 333
Ego-Task Analysis Scale, 107
Ehrlich, H., 330
Eisenberg, E., 422
Eisenhardt, K. M., 358, 364
EIT (ethnolinguistic identity theory),
    14, 132
Eliasoph, N., 57
ELIT (ethnolinguistic identity theory),
    14, 132
Ellingsworth, H. W., 14, 15–16
Ellis, D. G., 357
Emmons, R. A., 95
Emotional conflict style, 81, 85
Enactment identity layer, CTI, 19,
    261, 262, 263, 264, 266–267,
    269, 270, 271
Enculturation, defined, 381–382
Endres, D., 55
Enker, M., 63
Enmeshment, identity management
    theory, 18, 204, 206–207
Enos, R. L., 35
Environmental stress, 339
Epiritu, Y., 224
Epistemology, 5table
Epstein, S., 429
Erland, E., 55
Esses, V., 340
Ethical issues:
  in anxiety/uncertainty management,
      291, 292fig., 303–304
Ethnic identity. See Identity negotiation
    theory
Ethnolinguistic identity theory (ELIT),
    14, 132
Ethnophaulism, 330
European Americans:
  anxiety/uncertainty management, 312
  cultural identity negotiation, 268
  ethnic identity, 265, 266
  ethnic markers, 389–390
  racial, ethnic identity
      formation, 224
Evett, S., 441
EVT. See Expectancy violations theory
Expectancy violations theory (EVT), 8, 11
  behavior and violation valence,
      155–158, 161
  behavioral disconfirmation, 154

communication expectancies,
149–150, 151–154
communicator factors, of predictive
expectancies, 151
communicator valence, 154–155, 161
context factors, of predictive
expectancies, 151
cross-cultural variability in
communication, 8, 27n. 12,
151–154
expectancy violations, 154
expectancy violations, benefits of, 150
individualistic vs. collectivistic
cultures, 11
limitations regarding, 161
power distance factors, 11
predictive expectations, 151, 153
prescriptive expectations, 151, 153
relationship factors, of predictive
expectancies, 151
social norms, 11
summary regarding, 160–161, 166
uncertainty avoidance, 11
valence continuum, 153
violations
effects of, 158–161
interpersonal relationship factor,
159, 161
positive vs. negative, 159
proximic violations, 159–160
reciprocity vs. compensation
response to, 158–159, 161
uncertainty, 160
See also Interaction adaptation theory
Extrinsic ethnic markers, 334, 389–390

Face:
defined, 73
face content domains, 74, 81–82
face movements, face moves' patterns,
74, 76–77, 77fig.
face movements, research, 89–90
face orientations, 73, 74–76
face-threatening process (FTP), 76
intercultural conflicts and, 72–73
intercultural workgroup
communications, 360
lien (moral) face content domain, 82
mien-tzu (social image) face content
domain, 82
mutual-face conflict style, 83, 83fig.,
84fig.
mutual-face dimension, 74, 76–77, 77fig.
mutual-face maintenance, 84
orientation of face, 74
other-face conflict style, 83, 83fig., 84fig.
other-face dimension, 74, 76–77, 77fig.
other-face maintenance, 84
positive dispositional facework
account, 80
self-face conflict style, 83, 83fig., 84fig.
self-face dimension, 74, 76–77, 77fig.
self-face maintenance, 84
See also Face-negotiation theory (FNT);
Facework; Facework, identity
management theory; Identity
management theory (IMT)
Face-negotiation theory (FNT), Conflict
face-negotiation theory (FNT)
communication expectancies, 151–152
See also Face; Facework; Facework,
identity management theory;
Identity management theory (IMT)
Facework:
avoiding facework interaction
strategy, 78, 84
competence face content domain, 81

conflict as face-negotiation process, 9
defined, 73
dominating facework interaction
strategy, 78, 84–85
facework emotions research, 88–89
facework interaction strategies, 74,
77–80
facework situational research, 89
integrating facework interaction
strategy, 78, 84
preventive facework strategy, 79
restorative facework strategy, 79–80
situational facework account, 80
See also Face; Face-negotiation theory
(FNT); Facework, identity
management theory; Identity
management theory (IMT)
Facework, identity management theory,
17, 18, 196, 198–199
face challenge, 198
face dialectic, 200
face threat, 199, 204
facework strategies, 201–203tables, 206
fellowship face vs. autonomy face, 18
Faulkner, S. L., 262, 266, 267
Femininity dimension, of cultural
variability. See Masculinity-femininity
dimension, of cultural variability
Feminist sociology, 182, 185
Fielding, J., 379
Fielding, J. L., 327
Fielding, N., 379
Fielding, N. G., 327
Fink, E. L., 83
Finlay, K., 432
First, A., 183
Fiscek, M., 282
Fischer, G., 434
Fisher, B. A., 357
Fiske, A., 74, 301, 302, 403, 409
Fiske, D., 333
Fiske, K., 431
Fiske, S., 423, 437, 438, 442
Fitch, K., 59, 60
Fitzpatrick, M. A., 213
Florack, A., 339
Flores, L. A., 241, 245
Folger, J., 229
Fong, M., 59
Ford, D. H., 327
Ford-Ahmed, T., 174, 175
Forman, T., 326
Foss, K. A., 52
Foss, S. K., 52
Fox, S., 183
Frable, D., 441
Francis, E., 333
Frankenburg, R., 248
Franklyn-Stokes, A., 14
Fraternalistic relative deprivation, of
institutional inequity, 337
French, J., 437
Friedman, T. L., 44, 48
Friedrich, O., 336
Furnham, A., 222, 383, 390, 401, 409,
420, 424, 433, 435, 438, 439

Gaertner, S., 330, 335, 360, 361
Galanter, E., 95, 96
Gallois, C., 14, 26, 297, 326, 330, 332,
338, 462
Gannon, M. J., 76
Gao, G., 24, 81, 83, 281, 308, 312,
427, 443
Garcia, W. R., 76
Gardner, W., 110
Garfinkel, H., 63

Gates, D., 182, 183, 187
Gays/lesbians/bisexuals:
co-cultural communication, 174, 175,
183, 187
Geertz, C., 63, 237
Gender socialization, 211, 213–214
Gendlin, E., 390
Generational factors:
anxiety/uncertainty management, 309
intergenerational communication, 14,
124, 130, 132, 136
Gergen, K. J., 52, 259, 272
Ghua, E., 281
Giesler, R. B., 269
Giles, H., 14, 26, 110, 183, 187,
206, 297, 326, 330, 332, 333,
388, 402, 462
Gilman, A., 65
Givón, T., 327, 328, 379
Glazer, N., 327
Goffman, E., 17, 76, 77, 96, 196, 198,
260, 269, 298
Gold, R. S., 264
Golden, D., 262, 266, 267
Goldsmith, D., 59
Gomez-Mejia, L. R., 351
Gong, Y., 385
Gonzalez, A., 26n. 9
Gordon, M., 223, 324, 376
Gould, S. J., 264
Gouldner, A., 440
Goza, F., 390
Gozalez, A., 187
Granovetter, M., 336
Gray, A., 302, 435, 438, 439
Greek culture, self in, 258–259
Greenberg, J., 326, 330
Greene, J. O., 97, 99
Greenwald, A. G., 107
Greer, C. M., 183
Greer-Williams, N., 182, 187
Gregerson, H., 434
Grice, H. P., 96, 97, 98
Grieve, P., 286, 293, 427
Griffin, E., 56, 64
Groscurth, C. R., 188
Grunwald, H., 324
Gudykunst, W. B., 3, 4, 5table, 8, 9,
11, 12, 13, 23–24, 26 nn. 4, 7, 8,
27nn. 24, 26, 74, 85, 105, 108,
110, 111, 199, 220, 235, 257,
282, 283, 285–287, 289, 293,
298, 299, 301, 302, 307–313,
334, 354, 355, 367, 381, 401,
420, 422, 424, 427, 428, 429,
431, 433, 434, 435, 436, 438,
439, 443, 444, 445, 459
Guerrero, L., 77, 212, 213, 312, 434
Guerrero, S., 281, 290, 295, 431, 436
Gugler, B., 96
Gullahorn, J. E., 439, 442
Gullahorn, J. T., 439, 442
Gumperz, J. J., 102, 332, 334
Gurin, P., 437
Guthrie, G. M., 97
Gutmann, A., 440

Hackman, J. R., 355, 358
Halberstam, D., 343
Hall, B., 63
Hall, E., 384, 391
Hall, E. T., 8, 26n. 1, 27n. 10, 72, 78,
433, 448
Hallinan, M., 335, 387
Hamill, J., 284
Hamilton, D., 329, 434
Hamilton, J. C., 270

Hammer, M., 12, 23, 24, 281, 282, 283, 293, 311, 312, 401, 419, 420, 428, 431, 434, 438, 442, 443, 444
Hanna, M. S., 179
Hansel, B., 392
Hantz, A. M., 179
Hardiness, of identity security, 333
Harrison, E., 57
Harrold, R., 351
Hart, H., 63
Hart, R. P., 187
Harter, L. M., 183, 187
Harvey, D., 259
Haslett, B., 212
Haspel, K., 248
Hate speech, 330
Havel, J., 389, 438
Hawaiian culture:
  bicultural identity, 110
  co-cultural communication theory, 185
  conflict management strategies, 103
  conversational constraints, importance of, 102–103
  corporate mentality, 187
  effectiveness of communication, 100
Hawes, F., 434
HCI (human-computer interaction), 272–273
Health/illness identity formation, 269–271
Hecht, M. L., 19, 27n. 17, 27n. 17, 198, 199, 200, 202, 206, 215, 224, 240, 258, 261, 262, 263, 265, 266, 267, 268, 269, 462
Hechter, M., 337
Hedge, R. S., 376
Hegde, R. S., 235, 240, 241, 255
Heider, F., 329
Hein, S., 429
Hellriegel, D., 431
Helms, J., 224, 225fig.
Henwood, K., 14
Herbst, P., 330
Herman, S., 421, 439
Hermandez, A., 326
Herring, S., 175
Heuman, A., 182, 183, 187
Heuristic communication, 3, 7
Hewstone, M., 329, 330, 434
Heyman, S., 85, 108, 110, 111, 354, 355, 367
Hierarchy of embedded contexts, coordinated management of meaning, 39–40, 41–42, 42table, 43, 46
Higgins, E. T., 95, 96, 269
Himes, J., 342
Hirokawa, R. Y., 13, 352, 353, 355, 358
Hispanic Americans, ethnic markers, 389–390
Hocker, J., 72
Hoffman, E., 338
Hofner Saphiere, D. M., 351, 355, 364
Hofstede, G., 8–9, 74, 75, 76, 108, 212, 213, 215, 287, 308, 309, 310, 354, 358, 401, 422, 446, 447
Hofstede's dimensions of cultural variability, 8–9, 27n. 10
Hogg, M. A., 197, 259, 283–284, 286, 292, 293, 332, 427
Holtgraves, T., 97, 99
Hong, Y. Y., 6
Hopper, J., 64
Hopper, R., 330
Hopson, M., 183, 187, 188
Horenczyk, G., 376, 385
Horowitz, M., 332

Horton, D., 386
Horvath, A., 106, 107, 108, 109, 110, 111, 354, 355
Houston, M., 187
Hu, H. C., 82
Hubbert, K., 281, 290, 295, 298, 299, 312, 431, 434, 436
Huber, G., 432
Hudson, J. A., 402, 403
Huhr, W., 391
Hull, W. F., 434, 435
Human-computer interaction (HCI), 272–273
Hunter, J. E., 106, 107, 108, 109, 110, 111, 354, 355
Huntington, S. P., 57
Huspek, M., 60, 63
Husserd, E, 174
Hymes, D., 56, 60, 62, 63, 64, 65

IAT. *See* Interaction adaptation theory
Identity freezing, 199, 201–203tables, 201table, 204, 207, 208n. 2
Identity intercultural conflict goals, 72–73
Identity management theory (IMT):
  autonomy face *vs.* fellowship face, 18
  competence, defined, 196
  competence face *vs.* autonomy face, 18
  cultural identity, 17, 195–196, 197, 199
  cultural identity, defined, 197
  disabled persons identity, 196
  dominant culture factor, 196, 200
  enmeshment identity management phase, 18, 204, 206–207
  face challenge, 198
  face concept, 198
  face dialectic, 200
  face threat, 199, 204
  facework, 17, 18, 196, 198–199
  facework strategies, 201–203tables, 206
  fellowship face *vs.* autonomy face, 18
  identity freezing problematic, 199, 201–203tables, 201table, 204, 207, 208n. 2
  identity negotiation theory, 195
  intensity factor, 17, 198
  intercultural communication competence, 18, 195–196, 198
  interethnic identity management, 196, 199–200, 206
  interpersonal communication competence, 18, 195–196, 198
  intracultural communication, 18, 196, 198
  Japanese culture studies, 199
  metatheoretical and theoretical assumptions, 196–199
  mutual negative face support, 201–203tables, 202, 203, 206
  mutual positive face support, 201–203tables, 202, 203, 206, 207
  nonsupport problematic, 200, 204, 208n. 1
  other negative face support, 203, 203table
  other positive face support, 201–202tables, 202
  positive negative face dialectic, 198, 199, 200, 203, 203table, 204, 207
  propositions, re: face problematics and dialectics, 199–203, 201–203tables
  propositions, re: identity management phases, 203–207

relational identity, 17, 196, 197, 198, 199, 203, 205–206, 207
relationship worldview concept, 205
renegotiation of identity, 18, 205–206
research evidence related to phases, 206–207
salience factor, 17, 197–198, 205, 333
scope factor, 17, 197
self-other face dialectic, 202, 203, 203table, 204, 206, 207
self positive face support, 201–202tables, 202
self-presentation, 17, 197, 198
similar identity identification, 18
stereotyping, 18, 200, 202, 204, 207
symbolic interactionism, 196, 204–205, 207
theoretical scope, 196
trial identity management phase, 203–204, 207
Identity negotiation theory, 257
  acculturation, 221, 223
  assimilation goal, 223, 224, 224fig.
  autonomy-connection theme, 218, 219, 219table, 220–221, 225
  bicultural identity, 223–224, 224fig.
  coherent sense of self, 18
  communication resourcefulness, 18
  consistency-change theme, 218, 219, 219table, 221–222, 225
  content focus, 217
  core assumptions, 217
  core theoretical assumptions, 217–223, 219table
  cultural contracts theory, 267–268
  cultural identity conceptualization, 214–215
  cultural variability, 18, 218
  enculturation, 221
  ethnic-cultural identity typology, 211, 223–224, 224fig.
  ethnic identity, defined, 215
  ethnic identity conceptualization, 215–216
  family socialization, interaction patterns, 211, 212–213
  feeling of being affirmatively valued, 229–230
  feeling of being respected, 229
  feeling of being understood, 228–229
  gender socialization, interaction patterns, 211, 213–214
  identity, defined, 212
  identity boundary regulation, 18, 216, 220
  identity knowledge component, 226
  identity negotiation competence, outcomes, 218, 226, 228–230
  identity negotiation process, criteria, 227–228
  identity negotiation skills component, 227
  identity satisfaction, 228–229
  identity validation/rejection, 227
  immersion-emersion stage of racial/ethnic identity development, 224
  inclusion-differentiation dialectic, 18–19, 217, 218, 219table, 220, 225
  ingroup/outgroup membership, 216–223
  intercultural boundary-crossing, 216–223
  intercultural communication competence, defined, 18
  intercultural identity negotiation competence, 225–230

internalization-commitment stage of racial/ethnic identity development, 224–225
Japanese intercultural communication, 199
marginal identity, 224, 224*fig.*
mindfulness component, 226–227
negotiation process, defined, 217
personal identity, 212, 217
personal *vs.* positional family system, 212–213
personality trait and ability factors, 222–223
pre-encounter stage of racial/ethnic identity development, 224
predictability-unpredictability theme, 218, 219, 219*table,* 220, 225
racial/ethnic identity development model, 224–225, 225*fig.*
relational boundaries, 18
salience, 215, 216, 217, 219, 223, 226, 227, 333
security/vulnerability theme, 18–19, 217, 218, 219–220, 219*table,* 225
self-identification, 18–19
situational norms and rules, 222, 224
social identity, defined, 212
stress-adaptation-growth experience, 216
symbolic communication, 218, 219, 222
trust, 217, 220
value content, 214–215
Identity salience, of identity security-insecurity, 333
Identity theories, 6, 260–261
See also Communication theory of identity; Cultural schema theory; Identity management theory; Identity negotiation theory
Idiographic methodology, 5*table*
Iizuka, Y., 103
Illness identity formation, 269–271
Imahori, T. T., 2, 17–18, 25, 26, 27*n. 16,* 195–197, 199–204, 206, 207, 207*nn. 1,* 228, 462
Impression management goals, 99
IMT. *See* Identity management theory
Inclusion-differentiation dialectic, identity negotiation theory, 18–19, 217, 218, 219*table,* 220, 225
Indermuhle, K., 96
Individualism dimension, of cultural variability:
in African cultures, 258
approval seeking behavior, 99
autonomy-connection issue, 221
communication accommodation theory, 132, 134
communication expectancies, 151–152
communication violations, interpersonal relationship factor, 159
conversational constraints, 10, 26*n. 11,* 102–103
cultural-level assumptions, 82–84, 83*fig.,* 84*fig.*
cultural-level propositions, 84–85
effective communication, 310–311
ethnic value content, 216
expectancy valence, 153
expectancy violations, 11, 154
face content domains, 81–82
face orientation, 10, 74–75
face-threatening process, 77
facework interaction strategies, 77–80
in Greek culture, 258–259

independent and interdependent self-construals, 106, 354–355
information management, 309–310
ingroup *vs.* outgroup anxiety/uncertainty management, 307–308
ingroup *vs.* outgroup concept, 87–88, 153
intercultural workgroup communication, 354–355, 362–363
low- *vs.* high-context communication style, 433
multicultural identity, 108–110
outcome orientation, 226
person- *vs.* group-based information, 445
self-construal, 85–86, 429
self-construals, intracultural variability, 107–108, 112, 363
social *vs.* individual identity, 212
truthtelling, 165
value contents, 215
Individualization of self-other orientation, 392
Ingroups, 87–88, 132, 134, 153
anxiety/uncertainty management collective self-esteem, 293–294
mindfullness, 304–305
situational processes, 300–301
social categorization of strangers, 298–300
strangers ingroup relationships, 285
strangers' linguistic convergence, 297
uncertainty *vs.* certainty orientated people, 296
insecure social identities, 293
intercultural workgroup communication, 360
Jewish identity, 257
relative ingroup strength, 338
separatism, extremism, 325
social categorizations, 329
Inn, A., 391
Integrated theory of interethnic communication, 13–14
Integrating/collaborative conflict style, 80, 85
Integrative communication theory, 13–14
adjustment, 380
background regarding, 375–378
as communication-based phenomenon, 379
coping, 380
cross-cultural adaptation, 383*fig.,* 394
acculturation, 380, 382–383, 394
as all-encompassing phenomenon, 378–379
assimilation, 377, 380, 383, 394, 395
defined, 380
cross-cultural adaptation, approaches to, 376–377
open systems perspective, 378, 379, 385, 395
pluralistic conceptions, 376–377, 395
psychological acculturation, 376, 377, 395
cross-cultural adaptation, process of, 381–384
deculturation, unlearning old, 382, 383, 395
enculturation, defined, 381–382
entering a new culture, 382
psychological resistance, 383
stress-adaptation-growth dynamic, 383–384, 384*fig.,* 393, 394

cross-cultural adaptation, structure of, 385–394, 393*fig.*
affective competence, 385–386
boundary-ambiguity syndromes, 391
cognitive competence, 385
elite group strength, 388
environment, 377, 387–388
ethnic group strength, 388
ethnic proximity, 389, 393
ethnic social communication, 386–387, 393
extrinsic and intrinsic ethnic markers, 389–390
functional fitness, 391
host communication competence, 385–386, 392
host interpersonal communication, 386, 392–393
host mass communication, 386, 392–393
host receptivity, 387–388
host social communication, 386, 392
individualization of self-other orientation, 392
intercultural identity orientation, 391, 393
intercultural transformation, 391–392
openness personality trait, 390, 393
operational competence, 386
personal communication, 385–386, 393
personality traits, 390
phenotyping, 389–390
positive personality trait, 390–391, 393
predisposition, 389–391, 393
preparedness, 389, 393
psychological health, 391
strength personality trait, 390, 393
structural model and theorems, 392–394, 393*fig.*
time, 394
universalization of self-other orientation, 392
discussion regarding, 394–396
focal concepts and boundary conditions, 380–381
integration, 380
long and short term, 377
as natural and universal phenomenon, 378
person and environment interplay, 378–379
pluralism, 377
stranger, defined, 380–381, 394
theoretical domain, 381
theorizing and researching, 377–378
theorizing as deduction and induction interface, 380
theory as system of description and explanation, 379–380
Interaction adaptation theory (IAT):
accommodation boundaries, 162
actual communication behavior, 163
adaptation, limitations on, 162
applications, 165–166
approach *vs.* avoidance principle, 161–162
classroom adaptation patterns, 165–166
dating partner research, 163–164
desires, 163, 165, 166
entrainment and synchrony principle, 161
expectation violations, 150
expectations, 163, 165, 166
grouping *vs.* single behaviors, 162

human adaptation principle, 161
interaction position, 163, 164
key concepts, 162–164
matching and reciprocity principle, 162, 164–165, 166
pre-interactional factors, 162
principles of, 161–162
reciprocity and compensation principle, 162, 164–165
required behavioral level, 163, 166
rhythmic patterns, 164
social contact standards, 162, 164
social skill variable, 164
summary regarding, 166
tests, 164–165
truthtelling, 165
Interactions adaptations. *See* Co-cultural theory, in diverse contexts; Communication accommodation theory (CAT); Expectancy violations theory; Interaction adaptation theory; Interaction adaptation theory (IAT)
Interactive acculturation model, 22–23
Intercultural communication:
communication theories, 26*n*. 2, 26*n*. 6
constructivist theory, 4, 26*n*. 5
coordinated management of meaning theory, 4
culture in communication theories, 3–4
logical consistency, 4–5
metatheoretical assumptions, 4
subjectivist *vs.* objectivist approaches to, 4, 5*table*, 6, 26*n*. 9
theories, historic perspective on, 3–6, 26*nn*. 1–8
vs. intergroup communication, 4
See also Anxiety/uncertainty management (AUM) theory, of effective communication; Anxiety/uncertainty management (AUM) theory, of strangers' intercultural adjustment; Association and dissociation; Co-cultural theory, in diverse contexts; Communication accommodation theory (CAT); Communication theory of identity; Coordinated management of meaning (CMM), role of culture in; Cultural schema theory; Culture-based conversational constraints theory; Expectancy violations theory; Face-negotiation theory (FNT); Identity management theory; Identity negotiation theory; Integrative communication theory; Interaction adaptation theory; Intercultural workgroup communication theory; Speech codes theory; Theorizing cultural identification
Intercultural communication competence, 18, 195–196, 198
See also Identity management theory (IMT)
Intercultural conflict, defined, 72
Intercultural workgroup communication theory, 363, 364
collaborating conflict strategies, 363
communication behaviors, 359
conflict styles, types, 359
contextual factors, 358, 360–361
critical discourse, 356
cross-cultural group, defined, 353

cultural diversity, defined, 352–353
cultural diversity factor, 352, 354
culture, defined, 352
culture and communication relationship, 357
decision-making quality, 352, 354, 355, 359, 364
effective communication, 364
equal participation feature, 363–364
face factors, 360, 364
future directions, 367–368
globalization trends, 351
group composition factor, 359, 361–362
group effectiveness model, 355–356
group inputs influence group process, 360–364, 361*fig.*
group member satisfaction, 353–354
group processes influence outcomes, 364–365
history of, 353–356
individualism-collectivism factors, 352, 354–355, 362–363
intercultural workgroup communication system, 357–258
metatheoretical assumptions, 356–357
mutual-face, 360, 364
normative discourse, 356
other-face, 360, 364
personal effectiveness, 356
practical applications, 366–367
privilege focus, 354, 357
process affecting outcomes, 359
propositions and evidence, 359–365
relational effectiveness, 356, 364–365
research literature regarding, 354–356
satisfaction, 352
scope of, 352–353
self-construal factor, 354–355, 356, 359, 364
self-face, 360
social justice and inclusion focus, 354
taking turns feature, 363–364
task effectiveness, 356, 364–365
theoretical assumptions, 357–359
vigilant interaction theory, 353–354, 355, 360
work *vs.* relational outcomes, 355–356
workgroup evaluation, 358–359
workgroup inputs, 358
workgroup outputs, 358
workgroups boundary, 352, 354
workplace demographics, 351
Interethnic communication, 13–14, 327
See also Association and dissociation; Integrative communication theory; Intercultural communication; Interethnic identity management
Interethnic identity management, 196, 199–200, 206
Intergender communication. *See* Communication accommodation theory (CAT)
Intergenerational communication. *See* Communication accommodation theory (CAT)
Intergenerational contact model, of communication, 124
Intergroup communication. *See* Anxiety/uncertainty management (AUM) theory, of effective communication; Communication accommodation theory (CAT)

International and Intercultural Communication Annual, 3, 3, 26*nn*. 2
Interpersonal communication variables. *See* Communication accommodation theory (CAT)
Intracultural variability of conversational constraints, 106–108, 109*table*, 112, 113*n*. 2
Intrapersonal communication variables. *See* Communication accommodation theory (CAT)
Intrinsic ethnic markers, 334, 389–390
Invisible illness concept, 270
Israel/Palestine cultural identification case study, 237, 242, 243, 244–245, 249–250, 251, 253
Israeli culture:
community theater research, 183
expectancy violations, 157
gay men and media consumption study, 187
Iwanoto, M., 390
Iwawaki, S., 87

Jack, D. C., 269
Jackson, D., 327, 379, 402
Jackson, J., 428
Jackson, J. A., 260
Jackson, L., 340
Jackson, R., 216, 224
Jackson, R. L., 215, 241, 261, 262, 265, 266, 267, 268
Jackson, S. E., 352
Jacobs, C. S., 95
Jacobs, J., 326
Jahn, J., 258
James-Hughes, J., 268
Janata, J. W., 270
Jandt, F. E., 254
Janis, I., 423
Jantsch, E., 378, 384
Japanese Americans:
cross-cultural adaptation, 377, 392
Japanese culture:
attributional confidence, 312
communication effectiveness, 310–311, 312
communication expectancies, 152
communication violations, interpersonal relationship factor, 159
conflict management technique, 103
conversational constraints, importance of, 102–103
expectancy valence, 153
expectancy violations, 157
ingroup *vs.* outgroup emotion expression, 153
intercultural communication, 199
non-verbal cues, 159
salience of cultural identity, 197
Jarvenpaa, S. LO., 351
Jasinskaja-Lahti, I., 376, 385
Jaspars, J., 329
Jeffries, T., 188
Jewish Americans ethnic identity, 266–267
Jiang, W., 96, 113
Joas, H., 379
Johnson, D., 326
Johnson, D. A., 175
Johnson, J. N., 261
Johnson, K. E., 268
Johnson, L., 362, 364
Johnson, L. D., 265
Johnson, M., 333
Johnson, P., 14, 187, 332, 333, 402

Johnson, R., 326
Johnston, L., 434
Jones, E., 14, 26, 326, 330
Jourard, S., 384
Judy, R. W., 351
Jung, E., 268, 269, 462

Kagitçibasi, C., 104, 112
Kalbermatten, U., 96
Kama, A., 183, 187
Kant, I., 402
Karafa, J., 429
Katriel, T., 59, 61, 63, 81
Kealey, D., 432, 434
Kellermann, K., 93, 94, 95, 96, 97, 98
Kellner, D., 259
Kelly, G. A., 6
Kendall, K., 60
Kendrick, D. T., 379
Kennedy, A., 376, 390, 424, 428, 433,
    435, 439, 442, 443
Keyes, C., 338
Kiesler, S., 272
Kilmann, R. H., 80
Kim, H. S., 83
Kim, K., 108, 110, 111, 391
Kim, K. S., 85, 354, 355, 367
Kim, M. S., 10, 27n. 11, 93, 94, 97, 98,
    100, 101, 102, 105, 106, 107, 108,
    112, 113, 310, 354, 355, 462
Kim, U., 223, 224fig.
Kim, Y. S., 325, 336, 339, 378, 388
Kim, Y. Y., 8, 11, 13–14, 20, 21–22,
    25, 26n. 2, 27n. 11, 221, 285, 325,
    330, 332, 333, 335, 336, 339, 377,
    378, 380, 381, 383fig., 384fig.,
    388, 391, 393fig., 394, 401, 408,
    419, 437, 442, 444, 463
Kincaid, D. L., 11–12, 27n. 30
Kincaid, L., 336
King, M., 432
Kino, F., 391
Kintsch, W., 96
Kirkland, S., 326, 330
Kirschner, G., 384
Kitayama, S., 82, 85, 104, 105, 106,
    107, 222, 290, 306, 354, 429
Kleg, M., 333
Klein, R., 269
Klingle, R. S., 108
Knee, C. R., 206
Koerner, A., 213
Koester, J., 26n. 3, 111, 401
Kolko, B. E., 272
Korean Americans, cross-cultural
    adaptation, 377
Korean culture:
    ambiguous communication, 286
    collectivistic culture of, 103
    communication expectancies, 152
    conflict management strategies, 103
    conversational constraints,
        importance of, 102–103
    effectiveness of communication, 101
    implicit theories of requesting, 101–102
    norms-based communication
        behavior, 94
    relationship- vs. task-orientation, 103
    social appropriateness of
        communication, 100–101
    social-relation constraints, 103
    truthtelling, 165
Kosmitzki, C., 429
Kowalski, R., 437
Krahn, L. E., 270
Kramarae, C., 16, 174

Krau, E., 390
Krieger, J. L., 463
Kruglanski, A., 432
Kulis, S., 266
Kumar, K., 351, 362, 364, 367, 368
Kume, T., 5958
Kundrat, A. L., 270
Kurogi, A., 8, 9, 10, 71, 73, 74, 81, 360
Kwan, K.-L., 224
Kwan, K. M., 382

LaFasto, F. M. J., 355
Laing, D., 229
Lakoff, R. T., 97
Laktos, I., 420
Lambert, W., 332
Landrum, R. E., 351
Lang, P., 46
Langer, E., 12, 23, 24, 226, 281, 282,
    284, 290, 304, 306, 313, 330, 419,
    425, 441, 443
Lanigan, R.L., 174, 195, 196
Lapinski, M. K., 108, 186
Lara, E., 83
Larkey, L. K., 200, 202, 261, 265
Larson, C. E., 355
Latino/a Americans:
    cultural identification, 237
    racial, ethnic identity formation, 224
Lawrence, B. S., 358
Lazarus, R., 333, 383
Leary, M. R., 386, 423, 432, 437
Lee, C., 108
Lee, C. M., 8, 9, 26n. 7, 463
Lee, H. O., 421
Lee, W., 236, 240, 241, 255
Leech, G. N., 98
Lehman, D., 429
Leidner, D. E., 351
Leighter, J., 55
Leong, C.-H., 443
Lerner, R. M., 327
Leung, K., 74, 87, 106, 107, 108, 109,
    307, 308, 312
Lev-Aladgem, S., 183
Levenson, R. W., 364
Levine, D., 286, 289, 422
Levine, R. M., 270
Levine, T. R., 108
Levinson, S., 77, 81, 96, 97, 98,
    99, 198
Lewin, Kurt, 281
Leyens, J., 333
Li, H., 270, 438
Liberalism, 323–325
Lichterman, P., 57
Lieberson, S., 12, 24, 427
Liebkind, K., 376, 385
Lifton, R., 390
Lim, T. S., 81
Lin, S. L., 83
Lindholm, K., 333
Lindsey, A. E., 97, 99
Lindsley, S., 268
Lindsley, S. L., 364
Linville, P., 434
Littlejohn, S. W., 45, 50, 229
Lobel, S. A., 351, 358, 363
Locke, D., 214
Longshore, D., 264
Lopez, G., 437
Luhtanen, R., 429
Lujan, P., 336, 377, 391
Lukens, J., 330
Lustig, M. W., 99
Luthanen, R., 333

Mack, D., 326
Maddi, S., 333
Major, B., 441
Mak, A. S., 387
Malaysian Americans:
    cross-cultural adaptation, 377
    ethnic markers, 389–390
Maltz, D., 213
Marginality, of identity
    security-insecurity, 333
Marginalized populations. See Co-cultural
    theory, in diverse contexts
MarkPark, H. S., 108
Markus, H. R., 82, 85, 104, 105, 106,
    107, 222, 262, 307, 354, 429
Marris, P., 421
Marshall, C., 435
Marsiglia, F. F., 266, 267
Martin, J., 265, 326, 330, 337, 435
Martin, J. N., 26n. 9, 202, 241, 245
Maruyama, G., 326, 378, 388
Marwell, G., 338
Masculinity-femininity dimension, of
    cultural variability:
    anxiety/uncertainty management, 308,
        309, 446
    communication expectancies, 151–152
    conversational constraints, 10–11
Maslow, A., 333
Masumoto, T., 78, 355, 364
Mathieson, C. M., 270
Matsumoto, D., 390
Matsumoto, Y., 85, 108, 110, 111, 354,
    355, 367
Matveev, A. V., 97
Maxim of manner, clarity of
    communication, 98
Maznevski, M. L., 355, 364
McCall, G. J., 197
McCann, C. D., 95, 96
McClanahan, A., 183, 187
McClelland, D. C., 95
McClure, R. R., 325, 336, 339
McDermott, S., 24, 27n. 28
McGaughey, D., 270
McGrath, J. E., 360
McGuire, M., 24, 27n. 28
McKinnon, D., 266
McLeod, P. L., 351, 358, 363
McNamara, R. S., 60
McNamee, S., 52
McNatt, P., 333
McNulty, S. E., 269
Mead, G. H., 212, 260, 269
Meares, M., 83
Mechanic, D., 380
Meltzer, B. N., 260
Mendenhall, M., 329
Merrigan, G., 196
Metts, S., 79, 198, 208
Mexican Americans:
    communication and identity
        relationship, 261
    cross-cultural adaptation, 377
    ethnic identity, 266
    gender socialization, 213–214
Meyer, C. R., 262, 266, 267
Mezirow, J., 52
Michaelsen, L. K., 351, 362, 364, 367, 368
Miike, Y., 25
Miller, G. A., 95, 96
Miller, K. I., 357
Miller, L., 64
Miller, L. C., 95, 96
Miller, N., 220, 330, 333, 335
Miller, P., 435

Millhous, L., 368
Milstein, T. J., 392
Mindfulness, 226–227
    See also Anxiety/uncertainty
        management (AUM) theory, of
        effective communication;
        Anxiety/uncertainty management
        (AUM) theory, of strangers'
        intercultural adjustment
Mischel, W., 432
Miura, S. Y., 183, 187
Miyahara, A., 102, 103, 105, 106, 107,
    108, 109, 110, 111, 354, 355
Miyahira, K., 59
Model of Multiculturalism, 124
Moise, L., 22–23, 376
Montagu, A., 264
Montalvo, F., 389
Montgomery, B. M., 197, 204, 220
Moon, D., 246, 265
Moore, S., 202
Moos, R., 380
*Moral Conflict: When Social Worlds
    Collide* (Pearce & Littlejohn), 45
Morgan, G., 4, 358
Morisaki, S., 310
Morling, B., 423, 437, 438, 442
Morris, M., 6, 435
Morrison, G., 333
Mouton, J. S., 80
Moy, J. W., 365
Moynihan, D., 327
Mulac, A., 14, 187, 402
Mullally, P. R., 105, 107
Mullett, J., 422
Multiple categorization, 330
Mura, D., 390
Muted group theory, 16, 174,
    185, 187
Mutual negative face support,
    201–203*tables*, 202, 203, 206
Mutual positive face support,
    201–203*tables*, 202, 203, 206, 207
Myers, K., 83
Myers, M., 242, 243, 245, 251, 252,
    254, 255

"Nacirema" speech community
    research, 59
Nagda, B., 437
Nakayama, T. K., 26*n. 9*, 236, 240,
    241, 245, 255
Nash, M., 327, 389
Nass, C., 272
Native Americans:
    cross-cultural adaptation, 377, 392
    cultural identification, 237–238
    ethnic identity, 215
Neale, M. A., 364, 365
Nelson, K., 403
Nelson, P. E., 97
Nemeth, C. J., 359
Nesdale, D., 387
Networks:
    acculturation and, 20, 21, 27*nn. 19*
    anxiety/uncertainty management, 302,
        303, 439, 440
    identities from, 19, 264, 271–272
    intracultural *vs.* intercultural
        networks, 20–21
    outgroup communication
        competence, 20
    social networks, 302, 303
Newton, L., 270
Niedenthal, P. M., 104
Niles, T. A., 262, 266, 267
Nishida, H., 25, 442, 463

Nishida, T., 3, 4, 5*table*, 24–25, 26*n. 4*,
    83, 85, 108, 110, 111, 281, 302,
    308, 309, 310, 311–312, 354, 355,
    367, 401, 438, 445, 463
Nominalism, 5*table*
Nomothetic methodology, 5*table*
Nonassertive accommodation
    communication style, 16, 176*table*,
    180, 180*table*
Nonassertive assimilation
    communication style, 16, 176*table*,
    179, 180*table*, 182
Nonassertive separation communication
    style, 16, 177*table*, 180*table*, 181
Nonsupport problematic, of identity
    management theory, 200, 204,
    208*n. 1*
Nussbaum, J., 270
Nwosu, P. O., 268

Oakes, P. J., 197, 283–284, 292, 332, 427
Oberg, K., 424
Objectivist approach, to intercultural
    communication, 4, 5*table*, 6, 26*n. 9*
Obler, J., 338, 388
Obliging conflict style, 10, 80, 85
O'Conner, M. K., 270
O'Connor, J., 206
Oddou, G., 329
Oetzel, J., 11, 13, 72, 75, 78, 83, 84,
    85, 87, 89, 90*n. 1*, 226, 352, 355,
    356, 357, 358, 359, 360, 362, 363,
    364, 365, 368, 464
Ogawa, N., 310, 325, 336, 339, 464
Ogay, T., 14, 464
Oguri, M., 429, 433
Oh, S., 326
O'Keefe, D., 431
Olebe, M., 111
Oliver, P., 338
Olzak, S., 339
O'Malley, P., 265
Onken, S. J., 270, 271
Online communication, 271–272
Ontology, 5*table*
Onwumechilik, S. N., 268
Optow, S., 440
Orbe, M. P., 14, 16, 173–175, 177*table*,
    178–179, 182–187, 216, 223, 464
Orr, Ya'acov "Mendy," 44
Ota, H., 14, 26, 310, 311, 312, 326,
    330, 424
Other-face conflict style, 83, 83*fig.*, 84*fig.*
Other negative face support, 203, 203*table*
Other positive face support,
    201–202*tables*, 202
Outgroups, 87–88, 132, 134, 153
    anxiety/uncertainty management, 287
    situational processes, 300–301
    social categorization of strangers,
        298–300
    strangers, uncertainty, 286
    attribution error, 330
    communication competence, 20
    ethnic identity, 265
    intercultural workgroup
        communication, 360
    Jewish identity, 257
    separatism, extremism, 325
    social categorizations, 329
Oyserman, D., 108

Padilla, A., 333, 401, 408, 428
Palestine/Israel cultural identification
    case study, 237, 242, 243,
    244–245, 249–250, 251, 253
Palestinian *intifada* case example, 44–45

Palich, L. E., 351
Pan, X., 355, 364
Pannu, R., 224
Parillo, V., 421
Park, H. S., 108
Parker, P., 182
Parks, M. R., 43, 336
Parnham, T., 224
Passive-aggressive conflict style, 81
Payne, Y., 223
Pearce, B., 464
Pearce, K. A., 37, 47, 50, 262
Pearce, W., 327
Pearce, W. B., 4, 6–7, 37, 39, 45, 47,
    51, 53, 94
Pelled, E. H., 358, 364
Peng, T., 437
Pennington, D. L., 188
People of color:
    co-cultural communication,
        174, 175, 182
    perceived threat, of identity
        security-insecurity, 333
Performative communication, 7
Perks, R., 428, 439
Perreault, S., 22–23, 376
Perry, R., 281
Personal construct theory, 6
Personal family system, 212–213
Personal identity layer, CTI,
    19, 262, 263, 264, 266–267,
    269, 270
Peterson, M. F., 74, 355, 364
Petras, J. W., 260
Petronio, S., 269
Pettigrew, T., 330, 337
Phenotyping, 389–390
Philipsen, G., 4, 6, 7, 39, 51, 55, 56–65,
    240, 402, 464
Phillips-Gott, P. C., 182
Phinney, J., 222, 332
Phinney, J. S., 264
Piaget, J., 384*fig.*, 402
Pilisuk, M., 432
Piontkowski, U., 339
Pittam, J., 338
Political mobilization, of ingroup
    strength, 338
Political self-assertion, of ingroup
    strength, 338
Polzer, J. T., 364, 365
Popper, Karl, 281
Positional family system, 212–213
Positive face, 99
Positive identity orientation, 333
Positive-negative face dialectic, of
    identity management theory,
    198, 199, 200, 203, 203*table*,
    204, 207
Positivism, 5*table*
Power distance dimension, of cultural
    variability, 9
    anxiety/uncertainty management,
        308–309, 446–447
    communication expectancies,
        151–152, 152
    expectancy violation, 11
    face-negotiation, 9–10, 73, 75–76
    generational attitudes, 309
    personal family system, 212
    positional family systems, 213
    See also Conflict face-negotiation
        theory (FNT)
Powers, W., 269
Practical wisdom concept, 235–236, 237
Prahl, R., 338
Pratt, S., 62

Predictability-unpredictability theme, identity negotiation theory, 218, 219, 219*table,* 220, 225
Prejudiced talk, 330
Pribram, K. H., 95, 96
Pritchard, M., 440
Procedural equality, in human rights, 324
Psychological accommodation, 132, 133*fig.,* 135*fig.,* 139–140
Psychological distinctiveness, in identity security-insecurity, 333
Puerto Rico, ambiguity in culture, 286
Putnam, L., 80
Putnam, L. L., 96, 99
Pyszczynski, T., 326, 330

Racism focus:
   in cultural identification, 243, 247–248, 252, 253–254
Rahim, M. A., 80
Rainwater, R. R., 336, 339
Raja, N. S., 108
Rama-Deuba, A., 428
Randel, A. E., 364
Rap therapy, 184
Rasmussen, J., 24, 431, 434, 438, 442, 443, 444
Raven, B., 437
Rayburn, Sam, 323
Read, S. J., 95, 96
Realism, *Stable*
Recategorization, 330
Reeves, B., 272
Reicher, S. D., 197, 283–284, 292, 332, 427
Reitzes, D. C., 262
Relational identity, identity management theory, 17, 196, 197, 198, 199, 203, 205–206, 207
Relational identity layer, CTI, 19, 262, 263, 264, 266–268, 269, 270, 271–272
Relational intercultural conflict goals, 72
ReRoux, J. A., 390
Rex, J., 337
Reynolds, P., 12
Ribeau, S., 27*n. 17,* 198, 199, 200, 206, 215, 224, 240, 258, 261, 262, 263, 265, 266, 267, 268
Richman, J. A., 63
Richmond, A., 337
Riezler, K., 422
Risk-taking in identity security, 333
Roberts, G., 174, 175
Roccas, S., 430
Rogers, D., 390
Rogers, E., 11, 285, 336
Rogers, J., 435
Rogers, S, 206
Rohrlich, B., 435
Rokeach, M., 95, 401
Rorty, R., 323
Rosaldo, M., 61, 62, 65
Ross, F., 333
Ross, J., 332
Ross, L., 329
Rost, K. M., 13, 353, 355, 358
Rosteck, T., 59
Rothman, J., 72, 228
Rowe, W., 224
Ruben, B., 21, 391, 401, 432
Ruben, B. D., 342, 385
Rubin, M., 330, 368
Ruesch, J., 327, 379
Ruiz, A., 224
Rust, M., 335

Ruud, G., 60
Ruvolo, C., 329, 434
Ryan, C., 390

Sachdev, I., 326, 339
Sacks, H., 237
Sahlins, M., 380
Salience:
   in identity management theory, 17, 197–198, 205, 333
   in identity negotiation theory, 215, 216, 217, 219, 223, 226, 227, 333
Sanchez, C., 364, 365
Sanders, F. L., 173, 182
Sanders, G., 390
Sanders, R., 7
Sasaki, S., 365
SAT. *See* Speech accommodation theory
Schaefer, R., 215
Schank, R. C., 95, 96, 409
Scheier, M. F., 269
Schield, E., 421, 439
Schlenker, B. R., 77, 260, 270, 288, 423
Schmidt, K., 281, 308, 311, 312
Schmitz, P., 376, 385
Schneider, S., 335
Schneiderman, L., 423
Schuetz, A., 326, 421
Schwartz, B., 338, 387
Schwartz, S., 63, 401
Scollon, R., 98
Scollon, S., 98
Scott, R., 433
Scott, W., 433
Searle, W., 390, 424, 433, 434, 438
Security/vulnerability theme, identity negotiation theory, 18–19, 217, 218, 219–220, 219*table,* 225
Sedano, M. V., 200, 261
Sedikides, C., 108
Self:
   in African cultures, 258
   in Asian cultures, 258
   in Greek culture, 258–259
Self-confidence, of identity security, 333
Self-construals:
   conflict face-negotiation, 85–86
   culture-based conversational constraints theory, 105, 106, 108–110
   face and, 364
   group effectiveness, 356
   independent and interdependent, 106, 354–355, 356
   intercultural workgroup communication, 354–355
   intracultural variability, 107–108, 109*table,* 111–112, 113*n.* 2
   multicultural identity, 108–110
Self-esteem, identity security, 333
Self-other face dialectic, 202, 203, 203*table,* 204, 206, 207
Self positive face support, 201–202*tables,* 202
Selfways, sociocultural participation, 105
Selltiz, C., 389, 438
Senecal, S., 22–23, 376
Sentis, K., 262
Sequeira, D., 60
Serpentine model, of coordinated management of meaning, 43–44, 44*fig.,* 46, 50
Sessa, V. L., 352
Sewell, E. H., 183
Shapiro, P., 281, 302, 304, 312, 403, 423, 434, 442

Shared identity:
   affirmation, 7
   creation of, 7
Sharkey, W. F., 107, 108
Sherbaum, C., 441
Sherif, M., 327, 339
Sherman, S., 329, 434
Shibboleth schema (prejudicial listening), 330
Shibutani, T., 382
Shimanoff, S., 204
Shin, C. L., 241
Shin, H. C., 103
Shiu, W. Y., 363
Short, J., 422
Sieburg, E., 227
Simmel, G., 12, 281, 285, 326, 380, 419, 420
Simmons, J. L., 197
Simpson, K., 268
Singelis, T. M., 107, 108, 110, 111
SIT (social identity theory of intergroup relations), 123, 127–128, 132
Slaten, E., 270, 271
Slocum, J., 431
Smith, D. E., 16, 174
Smith, D. H., 108
Smith, E., 428
Smith, L., 223
Smith, L. R., 21
Smith, M. B., 104
Smith, P., 14
Smith, P. B., 74, 105
Smith, S., 335, 387
Smock, C., 432
Social appropriateness, 98
Social identity theory of intergroup relations (SIT), 123, 127–128, 132
   collective interests, importance of, 332
   communication theory of identity (CTI) and, 259–260
   inclusion-differentiation identity negotiation factor, 220
   individual self-concept, 332, 429
   interethnic relationships, 326
   positive self-images, 429
   social categorization, 329
   social identities, 294
   socioeconomic ethnic stratification, 337
Socioeconomic stratification, 337
Sociohistorical context, of communication accommodation theory, 15, 132, 133*fig.,* 135, 135*fig.,* 136
Sociolinguistic strategies, of communication accommodation theory, 15, 128, 132, 136
Sociopsychological states, of communication accommodation theory, 15, 123, 127, 132, 133*fig.,* 135*fig.*
Sodetani, L., 281, 287, 312
Sodowsky, G., 224
Solovey, P., 434
Sorentino, R., 432
Sorrentino, R., 422
South Africa:
   cultural identification case study, 237, 240, 242, 243, 248–249, 250–251
Spano, S., 50
Speech accommodation theory (SAT), 14, 122–123, 140–141
   accommodative strategies, 126–127, 140–141
   affective function, 126
   attribution process, errors in, 129–130

attribution theory, 123–124, 136
CAT theory from, 130, 131*table*
cognitive function, 125–126
cognitive organization, 126
communicational efficiency goal, 126
convergence and divergence/maintenance
    structure, 125, 126, 127
convergence and divergence/
    maintenance structure,
    evaluations of, 128–130, 129*table*
facilitate comprehension function,
    125–126
historical perspective on, 124–125,
    124*table*
identity maintenance, 126
internal *vs.* external attribution,
    128–130, 129*table*
interpersonal and intergroup
    accommodation, 2, 127–128,
    143–144*nn. 1*
linguistic *vs.* psychological
    accommodation, 126
objective *vs.* subjective
    accommodation dimension, 127
reception of accommodation,
    128–130
self-handicapping function, 126
similarity-attraction theory, 123
social and situational norms, 129
sociolinguistic strategies, 128
sociopsychological processes,
    15, 123, 127
speech complimentarity, 127
types of accommodation, 126–127
Speech codes theory, 39
    Blackfeet Native Americans speech
        community research, 56–57, 62
    characteristics of, 56–57
    communal conversation, 7, 56
    communicative conduct, 56–66
    concept of codes in, 57
    conclusion regarding, 66
    cultural codes negotiation, 7
    culture, defined, 58
    culture as deterministic, 65–66
    deterministic *vs.* contingent resources,
        57, 65–66
    elements of, 61–62
    heuristic communication, 3, 7
    individualism *vs.* community balance, 7
    limitations of, 64–66
    "Nacirema" speech community
        research, 59
    performative communication, 7
    power in a discourse, 64–65
    psychology, sociology, rhetoric
        elements of, 61–62
    responses to criticism of, 64–66
    shared identity, creation/affirmation, 7
    situated resources, 57
    social codes, behavior conforming to,
        63–64
    speech codes, defined, 7, 57
    "Teamsterville" speech community
        research, 59, 65
    terms, rules, premises of, 62–63
    See also Communicative conduct
Spellers, R. E., 16, 173, 182, 186, 266, 464
Spencer-Oatey, H., 96, 113
Spitzberg, B. H., 97, 99, 195,
    196, 228, 424
Sprague, J., 60
Sproull, L., 272
Stam, H. J., 270
Stan, C., 336
Stanback, H., 186

Standpoint theory:
    co-cultural communication, 16, 174,
        182–183, 185, 187
Starosta, W. J., 241
Status anxiety, of identity
    security-insecurity, 333
Stephan, C., 23, 281, 282, 287, 288,
    289, 296, 297, 299, 301, 334, 390,
    419, 422, 423, 432, 435, 438, 442
Stephan, W., 23, 282, 287, 288, 289,
    296, 297, 299, 301, 334, 390, 419,
    422, 423, 432, 435, 438, 442
Stephen, T., 204, 205
Stereotyping, in identity management
    theory, 18, 200, 202, 204, 207
Stets, J. E., 197, 198
Steuer, J., 272
Stevens, L., 431, 437
Stewart, J., 56, 64, 235
Stone, J., 337, 339
Stonequist, E., 376
Strangers:
    defined, 380–381
    See also Anxiety/uncertainty
        management (AUM) theory, of
        effective communication;
        Anxiety/uncertainty management
        (AUM) theory, of strangers'
        intercultural adjustment
Strauman, T., 269
Strauss, S., 268
Street, R. L., 96, 99
Stryker, S., 197
Suarez-Orozco, M. M., 392
Subjectivist approach, to intercultural
    communication, 4, *Stable, 6, 26n. 9*
Subjugating ascriptions, 245–249,
    251–252, 253
Sue, D., 224
Sue, D. W., 224
Swann, W., 269
Swidler, A., 57, 63
Symbols:
    communication theory of identity, 19,
        262, 263, 264, 265, 267, 268
    symbolic communication, identity
        negotiation theory, 218, 219, 222
    symbolic interactionism, identity
        management theory, 196,
        204–205, 207
Sypher, H., 3, 6, 26n. 5, 330, 431
Systemic status differential, along ethnic
    lines, 337–338
Szalay, L., 391

Taft, R., 333, 386, 401, 435
Tajfel, H., 197, 281, 283, 294, 298,
    314, 326, 329, 332, 333, 337, 429,
    434, 444
Takai, J., 78, 355, 364, 438, 442
Tamam, E., 378
Tannen, D., 102, 213
Tanno, D., 26n. 9
Tanno, D. V., 254
Tatani, H., 390
Taylor, C., 440
Taylor, D., 333, 388, 411
Taylor, S. E., 402, 403, 405, 406, 411
Tchen, J. K. W., 326
"Teamsterville" speech community
    research, 59, 65
Technology, communication theory of
    identity applied to, 271–273
Testa, M., 441
Tewksbury, R., 270
Tezuka, C., 25

Tharp, T., 223, 226
Thayer, L., 382
Theorizing cultural identification:
    African American examples, 240
    agency levels affecting intercultural
        relationships, 244–245, 247, 250
    both/and concept, 237, 243
    classism focus, 243, 245–246, 252, 254
    communication ethnography/
        philosophy, 239–240
    contextual forces intersecting cultural
        identifications, 249–253
    cultural competencies focus, 237–238
    cultural conduct labels, 239
    culture, conceptualization of, 236–237
    ethics, 236
    expanding view of culture, 241–242
    individual *vs.* group membership, 251
    interracial relationship case study,
        243–244, 247–248
    Latino/a examples, 237
    Native American examples, 237–238
    Palestine/Israel region case study, 237,
        242, 243, 244–245, 249–250,
        251, 253
    patriarchy, 245–246, 252
    personal *vs.* political focus, 237–241
    positionality issue, 242
    practical wisdom, 235–236, 237
    privilege and hierarchy focus, 243
    racism focus, 243, 247–248, 252,
        253–254
    scholar/practitioner/instructor/
        interlocutor goals, 236–237
    sexism focus, 243, 252
    social change, 236
    social justice focus, 236, 241
    South Africa case study, 237, 240,
        242, 243, 248–249, 250–251
    subjugating ascriptions, 245–249,
        251–252, 253
    teaching, relevance of, 237
    theoretical/metatheoretical
        perspectives, integration, 242
    theorizing as intimate engagement, 241
    unequal privilege issue, 240, 251–252
    United States, 237
    whiteness ideology, 245–247, 254
    women, domestic abuse case study,
        242–243, 243, 245–246, 251–252
Third-party consultation conflict style, 81
Thomas, D. C., 363
Thomas, K. W., 80
Thomas, M., 17, 196, 197, 198, 222, 239
Thomas, S. B., 264
Thompson, J., 243, 247, 254
Ting-Toomey, S., 7–8, 8, 9–10, 13, 18–19,
    25, 27n. 12, 71–75, 78, 79, 81–85,
    87–89, 98, 99, 105, 108, 110, 111,
    195, 199, 215, 217, 219, 220, 221,
    222, 224, 225, 226, 227, 228, 229,
    257, 267, 274n. 3, 353, 354, 355,
    360, 364, 367, 368, 401, 433, 465
Tjosvold, D., 365
Todd-Mancillas, W., 185, 186
Tominaga, J., 281, 310, 311, 424
Torbiorn, I., 434, 435
Torres, A. B., 364, 365
Toulmin, S., 35
Tracy, K., 198
Triandis, H. C., 8, 74, 75, 87, 102, 112,
    212, 222, 281, 289, 307, 308, 310,
    352, 354, 357, 368, 429, 445
Trimble, J. E., 264
Trost, M., 266
Trubisky, P., 83

Tsi, J. L., 364
Tsuda, Y., 326
Tuan, Y.-F., 423
Tucker, T., 326
Turkle, S., 271, 272
Turner, J., 63, 326, 329, 332, 337
Turner, J. C., 197, 259, 283–284, 287, 292, 293, 295, 427
Turner, J. H., 217, 219, 422, 430, 432, 447
Turner, R. H., 428
Turner, R. M., 405, 406, 409, 411, 413n. 1
Turner, T. J., 411

Uchida, H., 390
Uncertainty avoidance dimension, of cultural variability, 9
   communication expectancies, 11, 151–152, 154
   See also Anxiety/uncertainty management (AUM) theory, of effective communication; Anxiety/uncertainty management (AUM) theory, of strangers' intercultural adjustment
Uncertainty management theory, 199
   See also Anxiety/uncertainty management (AUM) theory, of effective communication; Anxiety/uncertainty management (AUM) theory, of strangers' intercultural adjustment
United States culture:
   anxiety/uncertainty management, 312
   communication effectiveness, 312
   communication expectancies, 152
   communication violations, 159
   conflict management strategies, 103
   conversational constraints, 102–103
   effectiveness of communication, 101, 310
   expectancy violations, 156–158
   gender socialization in, 213
   implicit theories of requesting, 101–102
   ingroup *vs.* outgroup emotion expression, 153
   non-verbal cues, 159
   norms-based communication behavior, 94
   relationship- *vs.* task-orientation, 103
   social appropriateness of communication, 100–101
   truthtelling, 165
Universalization of self-other orientation, 392
U.S. Census, 351

Vaid-Raizada,V., 338
Valencia, J. F., 339
Valentine, J., 361
Van den Broucke, S., 333
Van der Zee, K. I, 390
van Dijk, T., 96, 330
Van Oudenhoven, J. P., 390
Vasquez-Suson, K., 441
Vermeuen, F., 351
Verschueren, J., 103
Vescio, T., 422, 437
Vicarious personalism, 330
Voeld, K., 441
Volkan, V., 330, 339
Voluntarism, *Stable*
von Cranach, M., 96
Von Raffler-Engle, W., 328
Vygotsky, L. S., 49

Wagatsuma, Y., 333
Walker, H., 4
Walker, I., 405, 406
Walker, L., 337
Wallace, J. M., Jr., 265
Walton, S., 333
Wang, G., 308, 312
Wanniski, J., 38
Ward, C., 222, 376, 383, 384, 390, 420, 424, 425, 428, 429, 433, 434, 435, 438, 439, 442, 443, 444
Warren, J. R., 465
Warren, R. C., 264
Waters, K., 272
Waters, M., 215
Watson, W. E., 351, 362, 364, 367, 368
Watzlawick, P., 327, 379, 402
Weary, G., 99
Wei-ming, T., 258
Weick, K., 421
Weinreich, P., 214
Weinstein, E. A., 198
Weissman, D., 435
Wetherell, M. S., 197, 292, 332, 427
Wheatley, M. J., 382, 390
Wheelan, S. A., 366
White, C. L., 265
White, R., 380
Whiteness ideology, in cultural identification, 245–247, 245–249, 254
   identity negotiation contracts, 268
Whitney, D., 52
Wide categorization, 330
Wieder, L., 62, 63
Wiemann, J. M., 110
Wiggins, E. C., 107

Wilcox, R., 355, 364
Wilder, D., 423, 442
Wilensky, R., 93, 95, 96, 98
Williams, D. R., 264
Wilmot, W., 72
Wilson, C. E., 80
Wilson, G. L., 179
Wilson, S. R., 96, 98, 99, 100, 103
Winchatz, M. R., 59, 60, 62
Wiseman, R. L., 3, 24, 26n. 3, 97, 196, 401, 429, 431, 434, 438, 442, 443, 444
Witte, K., 27n. 25, 282, 420
Witteborn, S., 265
Wohl, R., 386
Wolfe, A., 325
Wolpe, H., 337
Women:
   co-cultural communication, 174, 175, 182–183
   cultural identification case study, 242–243, 243, 245–246, 251–252
   inauthentic selves enactment, 269
Wood, J., 213
Wood, J. T., 197, 204
Woodyard, J. L., 258
Worchel, S., 326, 332, 333, 335, 429
Workplace gender nonaccommodation cycle model, 124
Wurf, E., 104

Xin, K. R., 358, 364

Yamaguchi, Y., 429
Yang, H., 339
Yang, J. N., 99
Yang, S.-M., 307, 312
Yang, Z., 83
Yankelovich, D., 49
Yee-Jung, K., 85
Yep, G., 235, 240, 241, 255
Yinger, M., 215, 224
Yokochi, Y., 78, 355, 364
Yoon, G., 112, 354, 355
Yoon, H. J., 106, 107, 108, 109, 110, 111
Yoon, K., 103
Yoshikawa, M., 222, 332, 392, 401
Yoshitake, M., 325, 336, 339
Young, R., 376
Yuego, G., 108
Yum, J. O., 20–21, 25, 258, 335, 401

Zaharna, R., 391
Zeiker, K., 235
Zenicki, N., 97

About the Editor

William B. Gudykunst is Professor of Human Communication Studies and Asian American Studies at California State University, Fullerton. He became interested in intercultural communication while working as an Intercultural Relations Specialist with the U.S. Navy in Yokosuka, Japan. His work focuses on developing a theory of interpersonal and intergroup communication (anxiety/uncertainty management theory) that can be applied to improving the quality of interpersonal and intergroup communication and helping sojourners adjust to new cultural environments. He also has a special interest in explaining similarities and differences in communication between Japan and the United States.

He is the author of *Asian American Ethnicity and Communication,* and *Bridging Differences* (in its fourth edition), as well as the coauthor of *Culture and Interpersonal Communication* (with Stella Ting-Toomey),

Communicating With Strangers (in its fourth edition, with Young Yun Kim), *Bridging Japanese/North American Differences* (with Tsukasa Nishida), and *Ibunkakan Komyunikeishon Myumon: Nichibei Kanno Sougorikai Notameri* (Introduction to Intercultural Communication: Developing Mutual Understanding Between Japanese and North Americans, with Tsukasa Nishida), among others. He also has edited or coedited numerous books, including *Communication in Japan and the United States, Intergroup Communication,* and *Handbook of International and Intercultural Communication* (second edition, with Bella Mody), among others. He served as editor of the *International and Intercultural Communication Annual* (Volumes 7–9, 1983–1985) and *Communication Yearbook 24–26* (2000–2002). He is a Fellow of the International Communication Association.

About the Contributors

Judee Burgoon is Professor of Communication, Professor of Family Studies and Human Development, and Director of Human Communication Research for the Center for the Management of Information at the University of Arizona. She has authored or coauthored seven books and monographs and nearly 200 articles, chapters, and reviews related to nonverbal, group, and computer-mediated communication. Her current research on communication via new technologies and on deception detection has been funded by the Department of Defense and Department of Homeland Security, among other agencies. An elected Fellow of the International Communication Association, she is the recipient of its Aubrey Fisher Mentorship Award, and the National Communication Association's Distinguished Scholar Award.

Mary Jane Collier is a Professor in the Department of Human Communication Studies at the University of Denver. Her work appears in national and international journals. She was editor of Volumes 23–25 of the *International and Intercultural Communication Annual*. She has been a visiting scholar at the University of Cape Town and the University of London. Her current research involves integrating interpretive and critical theoretical perspectives to the study of the negotiation of interrelated cultural identifications, contextual structures, and intercultural relationships.

Lisa M. Coutu is a Senior Lecturer in the Department of Communication at the University of Washington. She studies culture and communication from an ethnographic perspective, and is particularly interested in how groups of people with differing perspectives discuss controversial topics, especially war.

Patricia Covarrubias is an Assistant Professor of Communication Studies at the University of Montana. Her research interests are cultural communication, communication in small groups, language and culture, and ethnographic research methods.

William R. Cupach received his Ph.D. in Communication Arts and Sciences from the University of Southern California. Currently he is a Professor of Communication at Illinois State University. His research pertains to problematic interactions in interpersonal relationships, including such contexts as embarrassing predicaments, relational transgressions, interpersonal conflict, and obsessive relational pursuit. In addition to numerous monographs and journal articles, he has coauthored or coedited eight books. His most recent book, with Brian Spitzberg, is *The Dark Side of Relationship Pursuit: From Attraction to Obsession and Stalking* (2004). He previously served as Associate Editor for the *Journal of Social and Personal Relationships* and is Past President of the International Association for Relationship Research.

Cynthia Gallois is Director of the Centre for Social Research in Communication and Professor of Psychology at the University of

Queensland in Brisbane, Australia. She is a Fellow of the Academy of the Social Sciences in Australia. Her research interests focus on intergroup communication in intercultural, health, and organizational contexts, and especially on the process of communication accommodation.

Howard Giles is a Professor of Communication (with affiliated positions in Psychology and Linguistics) at the University of California, Santa Barbara. His research explores different areas of applied intergroup communication research and theory, with a longstanding focus on intergenerational communication, and more recently, police-citizen relations. He is the Executive Director of the new interdisciplinary research Center on Police Practices and Community at UCSB.

Michael L. Hecht is a Professor of Communication Arts at Penn State University. He has published widely on issues related to culture and identity, including two books (*African American Communication, Communicating Prejudice*) and numerous articles on this topic. His communication theory of identity grew out of these studies, and he has applied this interest to examine cultural factors in adolescent substance abuse. His National Institute of Drug Abuse–funded drug resistance strategies project has developed a successful, multicultural school-based intervention for middle and high school students. His recent book, *Adolescent Relationships and Drug Use,* summarizes some of this work.

Amy S. Ebesu Hubbard is an Associate Professor of Speech at the University of Hawaii at Manoa. She received her B.A. degree in marketing and her M.A. in speech at the University of Hawaii, and her Ph.D. degree in communication from the University of Arizona. Her research interests include the study of nonverbal communication, conflict, deception, and relational messages. Her most recent work examines the association between nonverbal

immediacy and learning using interaction adaptation theory.

Tadasu Todd Imahori is a Professor of Communication Studies in the Department of Foreign Languages and Studies at Seinan Gakuin University in Fukuoka, Japan. He also has taught at Illinois State University and San Francisco State University. In addition to research on identity management, he also has conducted cross-cultural studies on face and facework. His writings have appeared in *International Journal of Intercultural Relations, Journal of Cross-Cultural Psychology, Western Journal of Communication,* and *International and Intercultural Communication Annual.* He has held leadership positions in the International and Intercultural Communication Division of the National Communication Association.

Eura Jung is an Assistant Professor of Communication at Mississippi State University. He received his MA from the University of New Mexico and his Ph.D. from Penn State University. He is interested in intercultural communication, intergroup relations, identity issues in communication and their relationship with psychological problems. Currently, he is working on his dissertation on Korean Americans' identity gaps in interethnic interactions and levels of depression.

Min-Sun Kim is a Professor in the Department of Speech at the University of Hawaii at Manoa. Her research has focused on the role of cognition in conversational styles among people of different cultural orientations. She has written on requesting styles, re-requesting styles, communication motivation, conflict management, deception, health behavior in various cultural conflicts, and the influence of the self on many other communication behaviors. Her most recent work is in the area of cultural relativity of communication theories. She received her B.A. degree from Ewha Women's University in Korea, her M.A. degree from the University of Maryland, and her Ph.D. from Michigan State University. In 2002, she was elected the Vice Chair (and eventually, Chair) of the Intercultural and Development Communication Division of the International Communication Association, and she also was elected President of the Korean American Communication Association.

Young Yun Kim is a Professor of Communication at the University of Oklahoma. Her research is aimed primarily at explaining the role of communication in the cross-cultural adaptation process. She has conducted research in the United States among Asians, Hispanics, American Indians, and European Americans. She has published more than 60 journal articles and book chapters, and has authored or edited 11 books, including *Interethnic Communication* (1986), *Communication and Cross-Cultural Adaptation* (1988), *Becoming Intercultural: An Integrative Theory of Communication and Cross-Cultural Adaptation* (2001), and *Communicating with Strangers* (4th ed., 2003, with W. Gudykunst). She is a Fellow of the International Communication Association.

Janice L. Krieger is a doctoral candidate in Communication Arts and Sciences at Penn State University. Her research focuses on the intersections among culture, identity, and health throughout the life span. She completed an internship at the National Cancer Institute and currently works with the northern Appalachian Cancer Network to create culturally appropriate cancer interventions for medically underserved, rural populations.

Carmen M. Lee is a doctoral student in the Department of Communication at the University of California, Santa Barbara. Her research interests focus on intercultural and interpersonal communication. Her intercultural interests focus on intercultural attraction and her interpersonal interests focus on communicative abuse in relationships. She has presented papers at national and international conferences and has published in *Human Communication Research, International Journal of Intercultural Relations,* and the *Journal of Family Communication.*

Hiroko Nishida is a Professor of Intercultural Communication at the University of Shizuoka, Japan. She received her Ph.D. from the University of Minnesota. She is currently engaged in research on cognitive and affective similarities and differences among Japanese and local employees who are working for Japanese subsidiaries in China, Malaysia, the Philippines, and the United States. The research, which is based on cultural schema theory, has been funded by the Ministry of Education in Japan for 7 years. Her research has been published in such journals as the *Journal of Cross-Cultural Psychology* and *International Journal of Intercultural Relations.* She has published *Ningen no Koudou Genri ni Motozuita Ibunkakan Komyunikeishon* (Intercultural Communication Research Based on Cultural Schema Theory) and *Mareisia, Firipin, Shinshutu, Nikkei, Kigyou niokeru Ibunkakan Komyunikeishon Masatsu* (Intercultural Communication Gaps among Japanese, Malaysians, and Filipinos Who Are Working for Japanese Subsidiaries), among others. She is Vice President of the Association of International Behavioral Studies in Japan.

Tsukasa Nishida is a Professor of Intercultural Communication at Nihon University, Mishima, Japan. He currently is interested in conducting research on uncertainty reduction processes among North Americans and East Asian nationalities. He is the author of *Ibunka no Ningen Koudo no Bunseki* (Intercultural Communication Behavior), *Bridging Japanese/North American Differences* (with William Gudykunst), and *Ibunkakan Komyunikeishon Nyumon* (Introduction to Intercultural Communication, with William Gudykunst), among other works.

John G. Oetzel is an Associate Professor in the Department of Communication and

Journalism at the University of New Mexico. His research interests focus on the impact of culture on conflict communication in work groups, organizations, and health settings. His work has appeared in such journals as *Human Communication Research, Communication Monographs,* and the *International Journal of Intercultural Relations.* He is coauthor (with Stella Ting-Toomey) of *Managing Intercultural Conflict Effectively,* and coeditor (with Stella Ting-Toomey) of the forthcoming *Handbook of Conflict Communication: Integrating Theory, Research, and Practice* (Sage).

Naoto Ogawa is a doctoral student in the Department of Communication at the University of Oklahoma. His research interests include understanding similarities and differences in communication in a variety of situations across cultures that can facilitate mutual understanding of people living in different cultures. He has presented papers at national and international communication conferences and has published in *Intercultural Communication Studies* and the *Japanese Journal of Social Psychology.*

Tania Ogay is an Assistant Professor of International Education at the University of Geneva, Switzerland. Her research explores the dynamics of intercultural communication and, in particular, how interactants make sense of and use the concept of "cultural difference." A privileged context for her research is the intercultural training and practice of teachers.

Mark P. Orbe is an Associate Professor of Communication and Diversity at Western Michigan University, where he also has a joint appointment in the Center for Women's Studies. His research focuses on the inextricable relationship between culture and communication across various contexts.

Barnett Pearce is a Professor in the doctoral program of the School of Human and Organization Development at the Fielding Graduate Institute. He received his graduate degrees from Ohio University and has worked at the University of North Dakota, the University of Kentucky, the University of Massachusetts at Amherst, and Loyola University Chicago, serving as Department Chair at the latter two institutions. He lives near the community tennis courts in northern California. Improving the quality of communication has been his driving professional commitment, first taking the form of developing a conceptual understanding of communication known as "the coordinated management of meaning" (or CMM), and more recently integrating scholarship with training and facilitating communication, particularly in public meetings about public issues. He has published eight books, including *Moral Conflict: When Social Worlds Collide* (1997, with Stephen Littlejohn), *Interpersonal Communication: Making Social Worlds* (1994), and *Communication and the Human Condition* (1989).

Gerry Philipsen is a Professor of Communication at the University of Washington. His research interests are cultural communication, communication codes, communication in small groups, and racialized interactions in the contemporary United States. He is a former chair of the Department of Speech Communication at the University of Washington.

Regina E. Spellers is an Assistant Professor of Communication at Western Michigan University. Her research focuses on intercultural and organizational communication issues emphasizing workplace diversity and black body politics. She has published in journals such as *The Journal of Substance Use and Misuse;* edited volumes such as *Readings in Cultural Contexts;* and such magazines as *Black Executive* and *Boardroom Monitor.*

Stella Ting-Toomey is a Professor of Human Communication Studies at California State University, Fullerton. She is the author or editor of 14 books, most recently *Understanding Intercultural Communication* (2005; with Leeva

Chung), *Communicating Across Cultures* (1999), *Communicating Effectively With the Chinese* (coauthored, 1998), and *Managing Intercultural Conflict Effectively* (coauthored, 2002). Her research interests focus on testing face-negotiation theory and identity negotiation theory. She has held major leadership roles in international communication associations and has served on numerous editorial boards.

Jennifer R. Warren is a doctoral candidate in Communication Arts and Sciences at Penn State University. Her interests include culture, identity, and technology. Her master's thesis focused on African American women's identity management and interpersonal communication online, in addition to their interaction with the computer.